W9-BVP-025

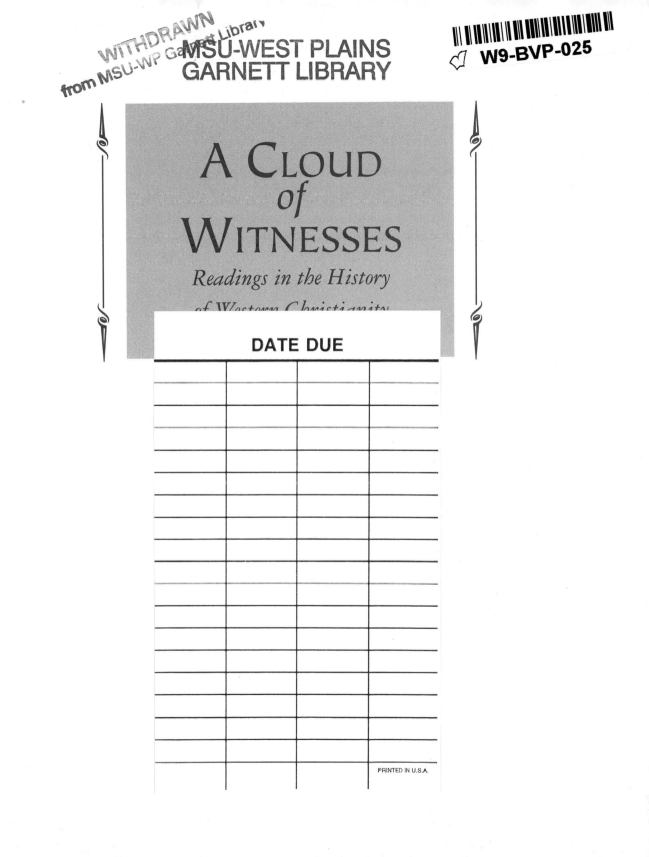

A Cloud
of
Witnesses

*Readings in the History
of Western Christianity*

DATE DUE

PRINTED IN U.S.A.

Therefore, since we are surrounded by so great a cloud of witnesses, let us also lay aside every weight and sin which clings so closely, and let us run with perseverance the race that is set before us, looking to Jesus the pioneer and perfecter of our faith, who for the joy that was set before him endured the cross, despising the shame, and is seated at the right hand of the throne of God.

Letter to the Hebrews, 12:1–2

A Cloud of WITNESSES

of

Readings in the History of Western Christianity

Joel F. Harrington

Vanderbilt University

HOUGHTON MIFFLIN COMPANY   BOSTON   NEW YORK

For Beth

Editor in Chief: Jean L. Woy
Associate Editor: Katherine Meisenheimer
Associate Project Editor: Jane Lee
Editorial Assistant: Martha Rogers
Associate Production/Design Coordinator: Lisa Jelly
Senior Manufacturing Coordinator: Florence Cadran
Senior Marketing Manager: Sandra McGuire

Credits

Cover Image: Bayerische Staatsbibliothek, Munich, Germany
Cover Design: Leonard Massiglia/LMA Communications

Text credits on p. 537

Printed in the U.S.A.

Library of Congress Catalog Card Number: 00-104958

ISBN: 0-395-96883-6

123456789-CRS-04 03 02 01 00

Contents

CHAPTER 6
The Confessional Age   289

CHAPTER 7
North American Christianity to 1860   335

CHAPTER 8
Nineteenth-Century Europe   376

CHAPTER 9
The Twentieth Century   430

CHAPTER 10
Western Christianity
and Contemporary Society   491

Appendices

Thematic Contents

Learning and Philosophy

Liturgy and Worship

Personal Piety

Preaching and Conversion Work

Violence

Women Leaders

Preface

To explore a religious tradition as rich and ancient as that of western Christianity is an exhilarating yet daunting project. *A Cloud of Witnesses* is intended as an aid and a comfort to the general reader who is just beginning that long journey of discovery. This book is not a history of Christianity in the usual sense; it is not an account of various events written from the perspective of a single historian. Instead, it is a collection of original documents—letters, pamphlets, journal entries, sermons, and more—written by men and women who have lived and created that history themselves. These writers, most of them professed Christians, come from a myriad of diverse cultures and time periods—from the cities and temples of the ancient Roman empire to the monasteries and convents of the Middle Ages to the American pulpits and universities of today. The overriding goal of this anthology is to let these authors speak for themselves as much as possible. In that sense, this is not a history but a collection of voices—or in the phrase from the New Testament Letter to the Hebrews, "a cloud of witnesses"—brought together to speak in a complex yet direct way to the contemporary student of western Christianity.

The intended audience for the book is a diverse one. Most obviously, this anthology is ideal for use in historical surveys of western Christianity, whether taught in smaller chronological segments (e.g., "Christianity to 1300") or as a one-semester overview of the last 2000 years (such as my own "History of Christian Traditions"). Because western civilization surveys (particularly for the period before 1700) also deal extensively with religious ideas and practices, *A Cloud of Witnesses* could also be a very useful reader for instructors of these courses. Instructors of comparative religion courses (e.g., "World Religions") will similarly

find much useful material here, from the thorough contextualizing of ancient Christianity among other ancient religions to the readings in the final chapters on such subjects as ecumenism and religious pluralism. Finally, the book's balanced presentation of the necessary historical background to the sources makes it a unique introductory tool suitable for divinity students or reading groups of any denomination, as well as for any interested general reader.

My criteria for selecting the documents themselves (from among thousands of potential readings) were based mostly on the book's central objectives of breadth and diversity. While theologians and church leaders are obviously important, I have gone to great lengths to include works by as many lesser-known Christian authors—particularly women—as possible. Because the anthology is intended to convey as much of the Christian experience as possible, I have sought documents that illustrate popular practices as well as learned doctrine, of violent conflict as well as consensus and common tradition. I have also avoided reproducing excerpts from highly accessible books, such as the Bible, and from longer well-known works, which instructors may wish to assign in their entirety, such as Augustine's *City of God* or Luther's *Three Treatises*.

This brings us to the book's organization. To help the reader find his or her bearings amid two millennia of history, the book's ten chapters are arranged in chronological order. Each chapter is introduced by a general overview of the period and its issues, accompanied by a timeline for reference. Within the chapter itself, the sources are sorted under four to six thematic Key Terms: "bishop," for example, or "revivalism," or "bioethics." Some of these Key Terms are accompanied by only one reading, others by as many as four or five. The purpose of this arrangement is to provide the reader with a crucial historical roadmap—beyond mere chronology—for navigating in a vast and potentially overwhelming landscape of names and events. In this volume, the Key Terms function as signposts to direct the reader's attention to certain themes that were critically important to the development of western Christianity within each chronological period. (Although some Key Terms could arguably appear in several chapers, each is used only once, in the chapter that covers the time period in which that Key Term bore some special significance for Christianity's development.) By paying heed to these signposts, students will gain not merely a knowledge of what happened when, but a deeper understanding of some of the important ideas, issues, events, and practices that shaped Christian history. An internal reference sysem (e.g., 2B1 = Chapter 2, Key Term B, Document 1) provides further connections, both in the guide to Thematic Contents and throughout the text. Readers who are particularly intrigued by any of the authors or topics they encounter here may also refer to the bibliography of primary and secondary books at the end of each chapter. These works have all been chosen, like the excerpts themselves, with the beginning student in mind.

* * *

Compiling a work of this scope single-handedly has often struck me as an act of the utmost hubris. Fortunately, I have been aided and comforted every step of the way, most crucially by my wife, Beth Monin Harrington. It's customary to recognize contributions of the author's spouse at the end of acknowledgments, but in this case it would be unconscionable of me to put her in any but the first place. If not for her careful, professional editing of the entire manuscript, the text would have been unreadable for all but the most indulgent of readers. If not for assistance in other ways too numerous to mention, I never could have finished the book by the agreed publication deadline. If not for her constant love and encouragement, I wonder whether I would have finished it at all. By all rights she is my co-editor, but her own modesty prevents me from acknowledging that role anywhere but on this page. It is

a feeble token of my own respect and appreciation for her painstaking and indispensable work, but it will have to do.

I have also benefited considerably from the advice of a generous cohort of friends and colleagues. As always, the most invaluable support has come from my gifted and selfless colleagues in the History Department at Vanderbilt University, particularly Bill Caferro, David Carlton, Joyce Chaplin, Paul Conkin, Dennis Dickerson, Matt Ramsey, and Margo Todd. I am also grateful to other members of the Vanderbilt academic community who have generously shared their expertise on various issues, especially Bob Drews and Tom McGinn of the Classics Department, as well as Dale Johnson, A.J. Levine, and Gene TeSelle of the Divinity School. Lisa Pruitt, now at Middle Tennessee State University, saved me many hours by typing the entire first draft of the manuscript, providing several insightful comments along the way. Jim Turrell came up with an apt title for the book. Jill Bepler (Herzog August Bibliothek, Wolfenbüttel) and Heiko Droste (Universität Hamburg) helped me clear up some murky translation questions; Susan Thorne (Duke University) supplied some invaluable help on missionary societies; and Brian Bornstein (Louisiana State University) supplied more than one helpful suggestion. The staff at Houghton Mifflin—Jean Woy, Jane Lee, Sandra McGuire, and especially Katherine Meisenheimer—have been exemplars of patient and constructive guidance. I am especially grateful to them for the excellent readers they selected for the manuscript, for these experts' countless suggestions have improved the book at every level. I would thus like to conclude by acknowledging Kenneth C. Barnes (University of Central Arkansas), Jodi Bilinkoff (University of North Carolina-Greensboro), Carlos Eire (Yale University), R. Guy Erwin (Yale University), James E. Kirby (Southern Methodist University), Bernard Lightman (York University), Philip Soergel (Arizona State University), Thomas Tentler (University of Michigan), Maureen A. Tilley (University of Dayton), and Merry Wiesner-Hanks (University of Wisconsin-Milwaukee).

A Note on Scriptural References

For the reader's convenience, I have provided the precise citations for all scriptural references throughout the book. I have not, however, attempted to standardize the English versions used by various authors and translators; identical biblical passages may thus read differently in different documents. The following abbreviations have been employed for the canonical and apocryphal books of the Old and New Testaments (* = New Testament):

Acts	Acts*	*Jn*	John*	*2 Pet*	2 Peter*
Amos	Amos	*1 Jn*	1 John*	*Phil*	Philippians*
1 Chr	1 Chronicles	*2 Jn*	2 John*	*Phlm*	Philemon*
2 Chr	2 Chronicles	*3 Jn*	3 John*	*Prov*	Proverbs
Col	Colossians	*Job*	Job	*Ps*	Psalms
1 Cor	1 Corinthians*	*Joel*	Joel	*Rev*	Revelation
2 Cor	2 Corinthians	*Jonah*	Jonah		(a.k.a. Apoca-
Dan	Daniel	*Josh*	Joshua		lypse)*
Deut	Deuteronomy	*Jude*	Jude*	*Rom*	Romans*
Eccl	Ecclesiastes	*Judg*	Judges	*Ruth*	Ruth
Eph	Ephesians*	*1 Kgs*	1 Kings	*1 Sam*	1 Samuel
Esth	Esther	*2 Kgs*	2 Kings	*2 Sam*	2 Samuel
Ex	Exodus	*Lam*	Lamentations	*Sir*	Sirach (a.k.a.
Ezek	Ezekiel	*Lev*	Leviticus		Ecclesiasticus)
Ezra	Ezra	*Lk*	Luke*	*Song*	Song of Songs
2 Ezra	2 Ezra	*1 Mac*	1 Maccabees	*1 Thes*	1 Thessalonians*
Gal	Galatians*	*2 Mac*	2 Maccabees	*2 Thes*	2 Thessalonians*
Gen	Genesis	*Mal*	Malachi	*1 Tim*	1 Timothy*
Hab	Habakkuk	*Micah*	Micah	*2 Tim*	2 Timothy*
Hag	Haggai	*Mk*	Mark*	*Tit*	Titus*
Heb	Hebrews*	*Mt*	Matthew*	*Tob*	Tobit
Hos	Hosea	*Nah*	Nahum	*Wis*	Wisdom of
Isa	Isaiah	*Neh*	Nehemiah		Solomon
Jas	James*	*Num*	Numbers	*Zech*	Zechariah
Jdt	Judith	*Obad*	Obadiah	*Zeph*	Zephaniah
Jer	Jeremiah	*1 Pet*	1 Peter*		

CHAPTER 1

The Ancient Church in Religious Context

THE CATACOMB OF CALLISTUS, on the southern outskirts of ancient Rome. Before Constantine's erection of a basilica on the alleged site of St. Peter's grave in the fourth century, bishops of Rome were buried in this underground vault, which also served as a place of worship for early Christians. *(Scala/Art Resource, New York)*

During the early years of the first century C.E., the life, teachings, death, and reported resurrection of Jesus of Nazareth inspired a loosely organized and extremely apocalyptic religious movement among a small number of Jesus' fellow Palestinian Jews. Within two generations, this localized phenomenon had developed into a network of Christian communities, based in cities throughout the Roman Empire. A century later, the growth of this "superstition" had become widespread enough that it was considered dangerous by many Roman intellectuals and emperors, and repeated attempts were made to exterminate it, both by persuasion and by force. Yet another century later, the Christian religion had not only survived several brutal persecutions, but had even been embraced by a Roman emperor, Constantine, who in 313 lifted the long-standing ban on the practice of Christianity. Less than seventy years after that, the Roman emperor Theodosius (r. 379–395) finally proclaimed Christianity the new state religion of the empire.

Despite its eventual triumph, Christianity faced many daunting obstacles along the road to becoming the officially sanctioned religion of the largest state in the ancient world. As successive generations of believers struggled to define their movement's distinctive claims and identity, the unity and very future of a common, or "catholic," church were far from certain. First, Christians had to define the relationship of their movement to its parent religion, Judaism. For example, was Christianity a kind of Judaism or a movement of its own, and could non-Jews become Christians? Next they needed to determine to what degree they would allow the surrounding Gentile cultures to influence Christian beliefs and practices. Christians also had to survive the powerful and sometimes lethal attacks on their religion launched by the Roman state and other enemies. And finally, the diverse Christian communities had to come to agreement on a host of potentially divisive theological and organizational issues in order to avoid the schisms that destroyed many other developing religions. All of this, moreover, had to be accomplished among diverse and relatively isolated congregations, admittedly aided by the excellent roads and common languages of the Roman Empire, but still without benefit of any modern communication technology or strong organizational structure.

The first challenge, defining the continuing relevance of Jewish beliefs and practices, was no simple matter. Many of the earliest Christians were themselves Jews and considered their religion to be simply a new sect of Judaism. And even as Christianity became a predominantly Gentile religion, its roots in Judaism ran deep. Jesus' followers continued to recognize the same all-powerful God, the same history of his relationship to his "chosen people," the same written tradition (i.e., the Hebrew Bible, later known as the Christian Old Testament), and the same demand for the exclusive devotion of adherents. In addition,

Christianity's pronounced apocalypticism—or expectation of an imminent final judgment—as well as its faith in a Messiah (Hebrew "anointed one") grew out of beliefs held by certain sects of Judaism.

On the other hand, however, Jesus and his disciples also deviated from Jewish tradition in several notable ways. Most Jews, for instance, did not accept Jesus' claim that faith was more important than strict observance of ancient rituals and Mosaic Law, the cornerstone of Judaism. In addition, most Jews—with the exception of members of certain apocalyptic sects—did not share the early Christians' belief in the importance of the afterlife or their conviction that the end of the world was very close at hand. Most decisively, the majority of Jews rejected Jesus' claim that he was the prophesied Messiah or Christ (Greek *Christos*). Meanwhile, most early Christians, in keeping with Jesus' own acceptance of Gentile followers, decisively broke with the ethnic exclusiveness of Judaism and permitted non-Jews to join their gatherings. This practice eventually diluted the strong Jewish influence seen in early Christian teachings, organization, and acts of worship. All of these differences gradually wore away at the common thread that had bound Christianity to Judaism, and by the end of the first century the breach between the two religions was irreparable.

At the same time that Christianity was struggling to determine its relationship to Judaism, it also had to define and defend itself amid the welter of diverse religious and political forces in the Roman Empire. Many of the religious beliefs and practices of the emerging Christian faith already had counterparts in the ancient world. Ritual sacrifice, for example, constituted a central act of piety in all religious traditions of the time. Holy shrines and especially temples also played key roles in all ancient worship. Early Christians used both of these elements in their own tradition to some degree, most notably in their ritual commemoration of Jesus' crucifixion, which they regarded as the supreme sacrifice. But they showed an even more pronounced affinity for a third common element of many ancient religions, namely prophecy, or the ability of certain blessed individuals to speak for a deity. Also known as divination, this rare spiritual gift was greatly treasured in all ancient religions, and prophets appeared in many forms, from the professional oracles who worked at temples or shrines giving advice about the future to the many nonaffiliated individuals of diverse backgrounds who regularly interpreted dreams, cast horoscopes, read palms, or even performed miraculous healing. Greek and Roman rhetorical traditions also influenced the oral and written teachings of Christian preachers and missionaries whose work made possible the proliferation of Jesus' message throughout the Roman Empire. Moreover, by the second and third centuries, many Christian writers would come to admire certain of the philosophical traditions of the Greco-Roman world and to incorporate them into their interpretations of Christianity.

One key distinction, however, did separate Christians (like Jews) from other ancient worshippers, namely, their exclusiveness. Despite its openness to new converts, Christianity, like Judaism, recognized only one true god and demanded unwavering loyalty from his worshippers. Most ancient religions, by contrast, did not require their followers' exclusive devotion or even a core belief. As long as believers participated faithfully in all the prescribed public rituals, they were free to believe in and worship as many other deities as they pleased. Accordingly, ancient people—particularly in urban areas—held a wide variety of personal beliefs and often mixed ideas and practices from several diverse religious traditions. Some individuals believed in an afterlife (Greek *Hades*; Latin *Inferni*; Hebrew *Sheol*); many clearly did not. Even those who did varied widely in the degree to which they believed that reward or punishment awaited departed souls in "the other place." The same is true of attitudes towards the various Greek and Roman gods. For some individuals, these were tangible super-humans; for others they were merely allegorical figures. Though few people would openly deny the existence of the gods, many philosophers did assert that the Olympians were indifferent to human affairs. Orthodoxy ("right teaching" or "right belief"), a cornerstone of Christianity, was consequently an alien concept to the leaders of most ancient religions—unimportant as well as largely unenforceable.

Despite these key differences, it is possible that early Christians might have enjoyed the religious toleration granted by the Roman state to Judaism and many other minority sects had it not been for two factors in particular. The first was the new religion's ambivalent attitude towards secular authority. Although both Jesus and St. Paul preached compliance to the Roman state, they also taught that the faithful should abstain from two important duties that were expected of all Roman citizens, namely, serving in the army and worshipping the emperor as a god. Because of the Christian refusal to do these things, many Roman officials deemed the faith seditious. The second reason the Roman government categorized the new faith as an "illicit cult" was its transregional appeal. Most ancient religions drew their members only from a certain ethnic group or geographical region. Early Christianity, however, was at its core a faith of converts, or proselytes (literally, "one who comes to a place") and accepted adherents from any culture or geographical area. This created a growing network of Roman subjects who claimed to owe their highest allegiance not to the emperor but to an all-powerful god—a situation that seemed to threaten the Roman government's position as the only universal, or empirewide, authority. Rome was in fact extremely tolerant toward indigenous, nonproselytizing religions, including Judaism, as long as they posed no threat to its political power. But an empirewide, convert-seeking cult—not to mention one that opposed war and emperor worship—was clearly another matter.

The final challenge facing early Christianity, preventing schism, was an inevitable problem for such a highly decentralized movement based largely on orally transmitted beliefs. For modern readers, accustomed to assuming that there was some sort of monolithic Christian unity up until the Protestant Reformation, the wide-ranging diversity of ancient Christian congregations is astonishing. The key issues dividing them, however—the gifts of the Holy Spirit, the use of philosophy by Christians, and liturgical conformity—are familiar points of contention that have continued to trouble Christians ever since. We cannot know what the future of Christianity would have been had such early dissident groups as the Gnostics and Montanists survived. We do know, however, that in joining together to suppress these sects, the majority of Christian bishops not only established the importance of doctrinal unity, they also took the first steps toward creating the very bureaucratic processes and hierarchical leadership structure that would be used to determine official Christian doctrine for centuries to come.

Seen in the context of other ancient religions, then, Christianity appears unique but not isolated and without strong affinities. Indeed certain elements of early Christianity set it apart from other religions—and in opposition to the Roman government. And yet many of the beliefs and practices of Judaism and other non-Christian faiths—as well as certain aspects of Greco-Roman culture—were to exert an important influence on the development of Christian traditions during the new religion's crucial formative period.

	Politics	Literature	Individuals	Other
1st cent. B.C.E.	37 B.C.E. Herodian dynasty in Palestine 31 B.C.E. Augustus emperor 6 B.C.E. Judaea under Roman occupation			
1st cent. C.E.	14–37 Tiberius emperor 70 Destruction of Jerusalem 81–96 Domitian emperor	c. 50–66 Apostolic letters of Paul c. 70 Gospel of Mark c. 90 *Didache* 93 Josephus, *Antiquities*	d. c. 30 C.E. John the Baptist c. 4–c. 30 C.E. Jesus of Nazareth c. 20 B.C.E.–50 C.E. Philo of Alexandria d. c. 65 St. Peter 5–c. 67 St. Paul 61–114 Pliny the Younger 56–120 Tacitus	64 Fire in Rome; Nero's persecution of the Christians 80 Roman colosseum dedicated
2nd cent. C.E.	98–117 Trajan emperor 117–138 Hadrian emperor 132–135 Jewish Bar-Kochba revolt 161–180 Marcus Aurelius emperor	c. 120–140 apocryphal gospels c. 130 Hermas, *Shepherd* c. 150 Gospel of Thomas 155 Justin Martyr, *Apology* c. 197 Tertullian, *Apology*	d. c. 115 Ignatius of Antioch c. 69–c. 155 Polycarp d. 160 Marcion c. 130–200 Irenaeus c. 150–c. 214 Clement of Alexandria	166 Great plague in Roman Empire 177 Martyrdoms at Lyon
3rd cent. C.E.	193–235 Severi emperors 235–284 Civil chaos in Rome; 19 emperors 284–305 Diocletian emperor 293 Tetrarchy & decentralization of empire	c. 245 Origen, *Contra Celsum* c. 274 Porphyry, *Against the Christians*	d. c. 203 SS. Perpetua & Felicita 185–254 Origen 205–270 Plotinus c. 210–270 Gregory Thaumaturgus c. 250–355 Anthony of Egypt	242 Mani preaches in Persia 249–251 Persecutions under Decius
4th cent. C.E.	306/312–337 Constantine emperor			301–311 Last & worst persecutions under Diocletian 312 Donatist schism in Africa 313 Edict of Milan 313 Edict of Toleration

A. Cult Worship

For almost all ancient people, the primary human bond with the divine (*religio*) was something to be expressed publicly and communally rather than privately. In other words, the key measure of an individual's devotion or piety (Latin *pietas*) was his or her conscientiousness in performing certain prescribed duties toward family (living and dead), the king or city-state, and of course the gods. Personal beliefs were not entirely irrelevant in this respect but ranked in importance far beneath the public display of reverence for traditional authorities. The main way to demonstrate such reverence was by observing the proper rituals of worship (Greek *orthopraxis*, "right practice") either at home altars or public temples. In this context, the Latin word *cultus* ("cultivation" or "worship") had none of the sinister associations now associated with the term "cult." Most simply it referred to any act of ritual animal sacrifice or votive offering that was intended to cultivate, or obtain, the protection of some god. By the time of Jesus, however, the word *cultus* had taken on a second, broader meaning and was also used to describe religions that required dominant or even exclusive devotion to one deity. In this second sense, the word *cultus* might be contrasted with the term *pietas*, which referred to the more widely accepted practice of worshipping a variety of different gods. Thus, for people of the ancient Mediterranean world, Judaism, as well as various pagan religions that called for devotion to a single or dominant god, were all considered to be cults. Likewise, Christianity was thought of by people of the time as a cult—albeit an illegal one—that was devoted to the worship of its man-god Christos.

During the first few generations following the death and reported resurrection of Jesus, Christian congregations began to engage in many of the rituals and traditions typical of all cult worship. Most of these—such as purifying immersion in water ("baptism") and a communal feast of thanksgiving ("Eucharist") —were also practiced by members of other ancient faiths, particularly among some sects of Christianity's parent Judaism. Initially, the many different Christian communities enacted these sacred rituals in a variety of ways. Over time, however, the diverse observances of widely scattered groups developed more formalistic unity, gradually yielding an increasingly distinctive Christian "liturgy," or "public service." Church councils, beginning with the one held in Nicaea in 325, furthered this process of standardization but never entirely eliminated minor local variations in prayers and rites. The result was not only an increasingly ritualized celebration of the Lord's Day, later known as the mass, but also numerous other communal celebrations as well as the emergence of church liturgies for almost every individual rite of passage.

1. LETTER OF EMPEROR TIBERIUS ON THE IMPERIAL CULT (c. 15 C.E.)

The imperial cult of Rome grew out of traditions of civic piety as well as the expanding empire's dealings with eastern peoples accustomed to deification of rulers. Both Julius Caesar and Augustus embraced the practice and permitted temples to be dedicated to "honor" them in Rome, thus skirting the Senate's prohibition of worshipping a living person. Some of their successors, most notably Caligula and Nero, went even further in promoting their own treatment as gods. Most of the early emperors, however, treated the practice with reserve; Vespasian (r. 69–79 C.E.) even joked on his deathbed, "I think I am becoming a god." Nonetheless, the promotion of an imperial cult had become a tradition by the time of Jesus, as can be deduced from the routine tone of a letter from the emperor Tiberius (r. 14–37 C.E.) to a group of subjects from the Spartan city of Gytheon who wished to establish an imperial cult. It remained against official Senate policy for a living emperor to be worshipped as a god, but it was permitted for admiring citizens and subjects to pay tribute to his unique divine spirit (*numen* or *genius*), usually through festive dances and games. Tiberius refers his petitioners to the established cult regulations for worship of himself and certain members of his family and provides a few additional instructions as well. Though participation in the imperial cult remained technically voluntary until the mid third century, it was part of traditional piety among many Romans as well as assimilated foreigners of the empire. In fact, the position of high priest of a local cult was considered among the highest of civic honors.

Tiberius Caesar Augustus, son of the god Augustus, pontifex maximus, holding tribunician power for the sixteenth time, to the magistrates and city of Gytheon, greetings. The envoy Decimus Tyrannius Nicanor whom you sent to me and my mother delivered your letter to me, in which were enclosed regulations you established for due worship of my father and the honoring of myself. In reply, I express my approval of your actions, for I suppose it is appropriate both to all men in common and to your city in particular to keep exceptional those honors suitable to the gods for the magnitude of the benefactions of my father toward all the world. I myself, however, am satisfied with the more modest and mortal. My mother [Julia Augusta] will respond to you when she learns from you what decision you have made about honors for her.

[This is followed by an excerpt from the *lex sacra,* or cult regulations:]

He [the priest?] should place an image of the god Augustus Caesar the father on the first [chair?], one of Julia Augusta on the second

from the right, and one of Tiberius Caesar Augustus on the third, the city providing him with them. Let a table [for sacrifices] be set by him in the middle of the theater and an incense burner be placed there, and let the representatives and all magistrates offer sacrifice—but not until the musical performances enter—on behalf of our rulers' salvation. Let him conduct the festival on the first day in honor of the god Augustus the Savior and Liberator, son of the god Caesar; the second, of the emperor Tiberius Caesar Augustus, father of the fatherland; the third, of Julia Augusta, Good Fortune of our province and city; the fourth, of [her grandson] Germanicus Caesar, who shares a temple with Victory; the fifth, of [her grandson] Drusus Caesar, who shares a temple with Aphrodite; the sixth, of Titus Quinctius Flamininus;[1] and let him see to the good order of competitors.

After the competition, in the first Assembly, let him supply the city with the accounts for all the costs of the musical performances and administration of the sacred monies. If he is found to have diverted funds or proved to have falsified accounts, he may no longer hold any office

---

[1]Roman conqueror of Macedonia in 197 B.C.E.

and his property shall be confiscated; and, if his possessions are ever confiscated, that money shall be set aside as sacred and used by the annual magistrates to provide amenities. Any citizen of Gytheon who wishes may prosecute for such sacred monies, without personal liability.

After the celebration of the days for the gods and rulers, the market supervisor shall introduce the musical portions of the theatrical competition, for two days, one in memory of Gaius Julius Eurycles, [ruler and] benefactor of the nation and of our city in many matters; the other day, in honor of Gaius Julius Laco,[2] patron of the watchfulness and safety of our nation and city. Let him put on the competitions beginning with the day of the goddess, on those days in which he may be able to do so; but when he leaves office, let him turn over to his successor supervisor, by written public record, all the sacrificial victims for the competitions, and the city shall get a receipt from the recipient. When the supervisor is putting on the theatrical competitions, he should direct the parade to proceed from the temple of Asclepius and Hygieia[3] with the youths and all the young men and other citizens participating in the parade wearing wreaths of bay and clad in white. The priestesses, maidens, and wives shall move in procession with them in their sacred garments. When the procession reaches the imperial cult temple, let the magistrates make sacrifice of a bull for the well-being of the rulers and gods, and the eternal continuation of their rule; and, when they have made sacrifice, let them require the Table Companies and the officials to offer incense in the public square. If they do not carry out the procession, or sacrifice, or if, having done so, they do not require the Table Companies and officials to offer incense in the public square, they shall be fined 2,000 drachmae,[4] payable to the gods. Any citizen of Gytheon who wishes may bring accusation against them.

In the presidency of Chairon and his priesthood of the god Augustus [i.e., 14–19 C.E.], the magistrates under Terentius Viada shall present three painted portraits of the god Augustus, Julia Augusta, and Tiberius Caesar Augustus, and the stage for the chorus in the theater and four actors' entrances and stools for the orchestra. They shall set up a stone column, engraving on it the cult regulations, and deposit a copy of the cult regulations also in the municipal archives, so that the regulations, in a public place and in the open and visible to all, may make continually manifest to all men the gratitude of the Gythean people toward the rulers.

---

[2]Son and successor to Eurycles, c. 14 C.E.
[3]God and goddess of health.

[4]Roughly $50,000 in current terms. Later this refusal by Christians could be grounds for execution.

---

2. Apuleius
METAMORPHOSES (c. 150 C.E.)

Most religions of the ancient world were limited in their influence to a particular political or geographic region (such as a city or province) or to a single ethnic group. One major departure from this tradition was the so-called mystery cult. Though some of these groups, such as the cult of Mithras, limited their membership to men, most were universal in every sense, accepting men and women of all social classes and establishing cells in cities throughout the empire. The second major distinction between mystery cults and other religions was that such groups required a gradual process of initiation into the secret knowledge or *gnosis* of the cult. Usually, as in the cult of Mithras, members subscribed to a central myth of death and rebirth, which had its origins in even more ancient fertility cults. In some mystery cults, members engaged in extended rites of frenzied ecstasy. The most infamous of these was the springtime rite of the cult of Dionysius, or Bacchus, in which semipossessed women known as *maenads* tore apart and consumed live animals. Some political authorities understandably considered the mystery cults dangerous, not just for excesses such as those of the *maenads* (rare by the time of Jesus), but also for their potential to undermine civic and royal cults. The Senate of Rome suppressed the cult of Dionysius at times, as well as the even more popular cult of Isis.

One of the best accounts we have of the inner workings of such secretive cults is the *Metamorphoses* of Lucius Apuleius Africanus (c. 123–185 C.E.). This fictional work follows the spiritual odyssey of one Lucius who, having dabbled in magic and accidentally turned himself into an ass, is finally restored to human form after becoming a convert to the cult of Isis. The author was a highly educated North African, and, although he later identified himself as a Neo-Platonist, he spent a portion of his adult life as a convert to the religion of Isis. (In fact, Apuleius's tale of the protagonist Lucius's conversion may also be read as a semiautobiographical account of his own turning from a profligate youth by embracing the cult of Isis.) Like members of other mystery cults, the followers of Isis commemorated a cycle of death and resurrection (that of the goddess's husband Osiris) and were required to undergo an elaborate process of initiation. In this excerpt, Apuleius effectively conveys the sensual appeal of the cult's colorful processions (here to mark the beginning of the spring sailing season) as well as the more emotional appeal of the maternal tenderness associated with the goddess, who was often portrayed nursing her son Horus. After restoring the repentant Lucius to human form, Isis—much like the later Christian figure of the Virgin Mary—lovingly forgives and embraces the new convert, who in turn finds himself emotionally overwhelmed by the experience.

And now, behold, the prelude to the grand procession came gradually into action. The persons who composed it were all finely caparisoned in various ways, each according to his own taste and inclination. This man, being girded with a belt, represented a soldier; another was equipped as a hunter, with a short scarf, a hunting-knife, and javelin. Another, wearing gilded sandals, a silken garment, and precious female ornaments, and with false hair on his head, personated a woman by his appearance and his gait. Another, with his boots, his shield, his helmet, and his sword, appeared as though he had come straight from the school of the gladiators. There was one who played the part of a magistrate, with the fasces [i.e., bundles of rods, signifying authority] and the purple robe; another that of a philosopher, with his cloak, his staff, his wooden-clogged shoes, and his goatish beard; two persons, with dissimilar reeds, represented, the one a fowler with bird-lime, and the other a fisherman with his hook. I also saw a tame she-bear, wearing the dress of a woman, and carried in a chair; an ape, too, with a plaited straw hat on its head, and clothed with a Phrygian garment of saffron color, carrying in its hand a golden cup, and representing the shepherd Ganymede; likewise an ass, on which wings were glued, and which walked near a feeble old man; so that you would certainly have said that the one was Bellerophon, and the other Pegasus;[5] but still you would have enjoyed your laugh at both.

---

[5]Pegasus was a famed winged horse in Greek mythology; Bellerophon was the human rider who finally broke him.

Amid this merry masquerade of the swarming people, the procession proper of the guardian goddess now advanced. Females, splendidly arrayed in white garments, expressing their joy by various gestures, and adorned with [green wreaths], scattered flowers on the ground from their bosoms, along the path of the sacred procession. Others, again, with mirrors placed on their backs, showed all who followed to the Goddess, with their faces towards her as if they were coming to meet her. Others carrying ivory combs, imitated the combing and bedecking of her regal hair, with the motion of their arms, and the twisting of their fingers. There were others, too, who sprinkled the streets with drops of genial balsam, and other kinds of perfume. In addition to all this, there was a great multitude of men and women, who propitiated the goddess, offspring of the celestial stars, by bearing lamps, torches, waxtapers, and others of artificial light. Next came musicians, playing sweetly on pipes and flutes. A graceful choir of chosen youths, in snow-white garments, followed them, repeating a beautiful song, which an excellent poet had composed under the favor of the Muses, the words of which explained the first origin of the votive procession. Pipers also, consecrated to the great Serapis,[6] played an air appropriate to the worship of the god, on pipes with transverse mouth-pieces, and tubes held obliquely towards their right ears.

There were, also, a number of persons, whose office it was to give notice that room should be left for the sacred procession to pass. Then came a multitude of those who had been initiated into the sacred rites of the goddess, consisting of men and women of all classes and ages, resplendent with the pure whiteness of their linen garments. The women had their anointed hair enveloped in a transparent covering; but the men had shaven and shining pates;

earthly stars were these of extreme sanctity, who kept up a shrill and incessant tinkling on brazen, silver, and even gold sistra [i.e., rattles]. But the chief ministers of the sacred rituals, clothed in garments of white linen, drawn close over the breast, and hanging down to their feet, carried the insignia of the mighty goddess, exposed to full view. The first held aloft a brilliant lamp, not by any means resembling those lamps of ours which illumine banquets at night; but it was of gold, of a boat-like form, and emitted a flame of considerable magnitude, from an aperture in the middle. The second was arrayed in a similar manner, but carried in both of his hands models of altars, to which the auxiliary providence of the supreme goddess gave the appropriate name of *auxilia* [aids]. The third bore a palm tree, the leaves of which were beautifully wrought in gold, as also the caduceus of Mercury.[7] The fourth displayed the symbol of Equity, a left hand, fashioned with the palm extended; which seems more adapted to administering Equity than the right, from its natural inertness, and its being endowed with no craft and no subtlety. The same person also carried a golden vessel, which was rounded in the shape of a female breast, and from which he poured forth milk on the ground. The fifth bore a golden corn-fan, made with thickest branches of gold; while another carried an amphora.

In the next place, appeared the gods who deigned to walk with the feet of men.[8] Here, dreadful to view, was the messenger of the gods above, and of those of the realms beneath, standing erect, with a face partly black, and partly of a golden hue,[9] bearing in his left hand a caduceus, and shaking in his right a green branch of palm; close upon whose footsteps

---

[6]An Egyptian deity closely associated with Isis and often portrayed as a kindly Zeus. His already popular cult was encouraged at Rome by the emperor Antoninus Pius in 146 C.E.

[7]The staff of Mercury, given to him by Apollo in exchange for his lyre; an emblem of power, with two serpents forming semicircles at its end.

[8]I.e., people dressed up as gods walking in the procession as their representatives.

[9]Gold was the color representing the gods of the upper-world, black the gods of the underworld. The messenger god in this instance is the dog-faced Egyptian god Anubis.

followed a cow, in an erect position; this cow being the prolific resemblance of the all-parent goddess, and seated on the shoulders of one of the blessed devotees of this divinity, who acted gesticulating as he walked. Another carried a chest, containing the secret utensil of this stupendous mystery. Another bore in his beatified bosom a venerable effigy of his supreme Divinity, bearing no resemblance to any bird or beast, wild or tame, or even to man; but worthy of all veneration for the exquisite art with which it was wrought, as also for its very originality, and an ineffable symbol of the sublime religion, the mysteries of which were ever to be kept in deep silence. It was of burnished gold, after the following manner: there was a small urn, hollowed out in a most artistic manner, with a bottom quite round, and which outside was covered with the wonderful hieroglyphics of the Egyptians. The spout of this urn was very long, not much elevated; a handle was attached to the other side, and projected from the urn with a wide sweep. On this lay an asp, uplifting its scaly, wrinkled, and swollen throat, and embraced it with its winding folds.

At last the moment was at hand, when I was to experience the blessing promised me by the most potent goddess; and the priest, attired just as she had described, approached with the means of my deliverance. In his right hand he carried the sistrum of the goddess, and a crown of roses; and by Hercules, a crown it was for me; since by the providence of the mighty goddess, after having endured so many hardships, and escaped so many dangers, I should now achieve a victory over my cruel enemy, Fortune. Still, however, though agitated by a sudden burst of joy, I did not rush forward at once, lest the tranquil order of the procession should be disturbed by the impetuosity of a quadruped; but passed through the crowd with a quiet and altogether human step, and a sidelong movement of my body, and as the people gave way, through the interference, no doubt, of the goddess, I gradually crept nearer and nearer. But the priest, as I could plainly perceive, recollecting the nocturnal oracle, and struck with wonder at the coincidence with the duty which he had been commanded to perform, instantly stood still, and extending his right hand of his own accord, presented the {wreath} to my very mouth. Trembling, and with great beating of my heart, I seized the bright rosy {wreath}, and greedily, most greedily devoured it.

Nor did the celestial promise deceive me; for immediately my unsightly and brutal figure left me. First of all, my rough hair fell off, and next my thick skin became thin; my big belly shrank in; my hoofs spread out into feet and toes; my hands were no longer feet, but ready for the duties of their elevated position. My long neck was shortened; my face and my head became round; my enormous ears were restored to their former small dimensions; my stony teeth returned to the diminutive size of those of men; and the tail, which before especially annoyed me, was nowhere to be seen. The people were astonished, and the religious adored the power of the supreme divinity, so manifested in the facility of my restoration, which resembled the visions of a dream. Extending their hands towards the heavens, they attested, with loud and unanimous voice, the favor of the goddess thus signally displayed.

As for me, I stood riveted to the spot in excessive astonishment, my mind being unable to contain a delight so sudden and so great, quite at a loss what first and in especial to say, how to make a commencement with a new voice, how most auspiciously to prepare my address, my tongue being now born again, and in what words sufficiently to express my thanks to a goddess so great. The priest, however, who through the divine admonition knew all my misfortunes from the beginning, though he himself also was in a state of utter astonishment at this remarkable miracle, at once signified his wish by nodding his head, and ordered that a linen garment should be given me, for the purpose of covering my nakedness. For, the very instant that the ass had laid aside his abominable covering, I carefully shaded myself with a natural screen, as much as it was possible for a naked person to do so, by closely compressing my thighs, and applying my hands. Upon this one of the throng of devotees promptly throwing me his upper tunic, covered me therewith; which being done, the priest with a benign countenance, and, by Hercules, astonished at my perfectly human appearance, thus addressed me:

"At last, Lucius, you have arrived at the haven of peace and the altar of mercy, after the many and various hardships you have undergone, and all the buffetings of stormy Fortune. Neither the nobility of your descent, nor your dignified position, nor even the learning in which you excel, have benefited you in the slightest degree; but falling into the slavery of pleasure, in the wantonness of buxom youth, you have reaped the inauspicious reward of your ill-fated curiosity. Nevertheless, blind Fortune, while harassing you with the worst of dangers, has conducted you, in her short-sighted malice, to this state of religious beatitude. Let her go now, and rage with all her fury, and let her seek some other object for her cruelty; for direful calamity has no power over those whose lives the majesty of our goddess has claimed for her own service. What advantage has unscrupulous Fortune derived from robbers, from the wild beasts, from the servitude, from the long toils on rugged roads, and from the fear of death to which you were daily exposed? You are now received under the guardianship of Fortune, but of a Fortune who can see, and who even illuminates the other deities with the splendor of her light. Assume henceforth a more joyous countenance, such as befits that white garment which you wear. Follow the train of the goddess your deliverer with triumphant steps. Let the irreligious see, let them see and acknowledge their error. Behold now, Lucius, rejoicing in the providence of great Isis, and freed from his former miseries, triumphs over his destiny. Nevertheless, that you may be more secure and better protected, enroll your name in this holy militia, which you will hereafter rejoice to belong to; dedicate yourself to the service of our religion, and voluntarily bend your neck to the yoke of this ministry; for when you have once begun to serve the goddess, you will then in a still higher degree enjoy the fruit of your liberty."

The worthy priest having uttered these words, while his breath heaved with inspiration, concluded his address, and I mingling with the throng of devotees, accompanied the procession; an object of curiosity to the whole city. All pointed at me with their fingers and heads, and said, "This day has the august power of the almighty goddess restored that person to human form. Happy, by Hercules! and thrice blessed he, to have merited, by the innocence and probity of his past life, such special patronage of heaven; in that, being after a manner born again, he is immediately affianced to the service of the sacred ministry. . . ."

[The procession then reaches the seashore, witnesses the dedication of a new ship to the goddess, and returns to the temple of Isis. The assembly is dismissed by the chief priest, but Lucian remains, securing lodging at the temple and daily begging the chief priest to initiate him into the cult. The priest, however, responds that he cannot comply until he receives a sign of approval from Isis herself.]

Thus did the priest express himself, nor was my compliance interrupted by feelings of impatience; but I attentively performed the daily duties of the sacred ministry, intent upon maintaining a calm demeanor and laudable silence. Nor did the salutary benevolence of the powerful goddess disappoint me, or torment me with a long delay; but she clearly admonished me by no obscure mandates in the darksome night, that the day was now arrived that had always been the object of my desire, and in which she would put me in possession of my extreme wishes. She also stated what sum of money would be requisite for the expenses of the ceremonial, and at the same time appointed for me, as the dispenser of the rites, the same Mithras,[10] her own high priest, who, she said,

---

[10] A reference to the mystery cult of Mithras, a man-god who conquered death. The central ritual performed by his followers commemorated his killing of a bull.

was united to me by a certain conjunction of the stars.

Refreshed in mind by these and other benevolent precepts of the supreme goddess, and shaking off slumber, though it was not yet clear day, I hastened at once to the dwelling of the priest, and saluted him just as he was coming out of his bedchamber. I had now determined to request more earnestly than ever initiation into the sacred rites, as being a thing that was due to me. He, however, the instant that he saw me, was the first to speak: "O my Lucius, how happy and blessed are you, whom the august divinity has thus greatly honored by her propitious will! And why," said he, "do you now stand idle, or make any delay? The day you so earnestly prayed for has now arrived, in which you will be initiated into the most holy mysteries by these hands of mine, in obedience to the divine mandates of the many-titled goddess."

And the old man, taking me by the right hand, led me immediately to the doors of the vast temple; and having performed the office of opening them in the accustomed solemn way, and celebrated the morning sacrifice, he drew forth from the secret recesses of the shrine certain books, written in unknown characters, partly representing in compendious form the words expressive of their meaning by figures of animals of every kind, and partly fortified against the inquisitive perusal of the profane, by characters wreathed like knots, and twisting round in shape of a wheel, and with extremities twining one with another, like the tendrils of vine. From these books he informed me what was necessary to be provided by me for the purpose of initiation.

Immediately, therefore, I diligently set about purchasing and procuring requisites, and even on a more liberal scale than I was ordered to do, partly at my own expense, and partly through my friends. And when, now the time, as the priest said, required it, he led me to the nearest bath, accompanied by a crowd of devotees; and after I had taken the customary bath, he himself washed and sprinkled me with the purest water, having first implored the pardon

of the gods. Then, again, he brought me back to the temple, and there placed me at the very feet of the goddess,[11] two-thirds of the day having now elapsed; and giving certain secret instructions, which are too holy to be uttered, he distinctly ordered, before all who were present, that I should abstain from luxurious food for the ten succeeding days, and that I should eat the flesh of no animal, and should abstain from wine.

These ten days having been duly passed by me in reverential abstinence, the day now arrived for pledging myself to the sacred ministry, and the sun descending, was ushering in the evening. Then, behold, there was a concourse of the people flocking from every side, every one honoring me with various gifts, according to the ancient custom of these sacred rites. After this, the priest, all the profane being removed to a distance, taking hold of me by the hand, brought me into the inner recesses of the sanctuary itself, clothed in a new linen garment. Perhaps, curious reader, you may be eager to know what was then said and done? I would tell you, were it lawful for me to tell you; you should know it, if it were lawful for you to hear. But both the ears that heard these things, and the tongue that told them, would reap the evil results of their rashness. Still, however, kept in suspense as you probably are with religious longing, I will not torment you with long-protracted anxiety. Hear, therefore, but believe what is the truth. I approached the confines of death, and having trod on the threshold of Proserpine,[12] I returned therefrom, being borne through all the elements. At midnight I saw the sun shining with its brilliant light; and I approached the presence of the gods beneath, and the gods of heaven, and stood near, and worshipped them. Behold, I have related to you things of which, though heard of

---

[11]I.e., the statue of Isis.

[12]Roman goddess who ruled with her husband Pluto over the underworld. Lucius is experiencing a spiritual death and rebirth.

by you, you must necessarily remain ignorant. I will therefore only relate that which may be enunciated to the understanding of the uninitiated without crime.

The morning came, and, the solemnities being performed, I came forth consecrated by being dressed in twelve stoles, an [outfit] no doubt of the most religious character, but of which I am not forbidden by any obligation to speak, because it was seen by many who were present on the occasion. For, by order of the priest, I ascended a wooden pulpit, which was in the very middle of the sacred dwelling, and placed before the image of the goddess, full in view, in a garment which was of linen, but elegantly colored. A precious scarf also descended from my shoulders behind my back down to my ankles, and to whatever part of me you directed your view, you would have seen something to arrest your attention in the animals which were painted round my vestment in various colors. Here were Indian serpents, there Hyperborean griffins,[13] which the other hemisphere generates in the form of a bird wearing wings. The persons devoted to the service of the

divinity call this the Olympic stole. Then, in my right hand I carried a burning torch; while a graceful chaplet encircled my head, the shining leaves of the palm tree projecting from it like rays of light. Thus arrayed like the sun, and placed so as to resemble a statue, on a sudden, the curtains being drawn aside, I was exposed to the gaze of the multitude. After this, I celebrated the most joyful day of my initiation, as my natal day, and there was a joyous banquet and mirthful conversation. The third day was also celebrated with the like rites and ceremonies, and was accompanied by a religious breakfast, and the due termination of the ceremonial. After this, having stayed for some days in that place, I enjoyed the inexplicable pleasure of viewing the holy image, being indebted to it for a benefit which can never be sufficiently rewarded. At length, however, through the admonition of the goddess, having suppliantly given her thanks, not such as she deserved, but still to the best of my ability, I prepared myself, though very slowly, to return home.

[Whereupon Lucius tearfully thanks the goddess and her priest and carries on as a transformed man.]

---

[13]Creatures with the bodies of lions and the heads and wings of eagles, supposedly from the mythic land of Hyperborea, where inhabitants lived to ages of 1,000 years.

---

3. DAY OF ATONEMENT *(YOMA)* FROM THE MISHNAH (late-second century C.E.)

Jewish piety also relied greatly on properly performed ritual sacrifices to maintain the special relationship, or covenant, between Yahweh and his people. During most of the millennium before Jesus, all ritual sacrifices were performed in the Temple of Jerusalem by the high priest and his assistants. Following the destruction of the Temple in 70 C.E. the focus of sacrifice and worship for the dispersed Jews of the empire changed. With no Temple—and thus no corps of temple priests to pass down the elaborate instructions for performing proper ritual sacrifices—Judaism needed a new source of instruction about *orthopraxis.* Thus rabbis, or learned interpreters of the Scriptures, began to play an increasingly prominent role. Even before the Temple's destruction, these rabbis had begun to write down their teachings about Scripture and included long passages on their understanding of what Yahweh required for the proper performance of ritual sacrifice. The result was the Talmud ("study"), comprised of the Mishnah ("repetition") and the Gemara ("completion"). In this selection from the Mishnah, the Rabbi Judah the Patriarch (fl. late second century C.E.) describes in detail the correct ritual for sacrifices on the Day of Atonement (Yom Kippur). Note here too the careful attention to the procedure itself, particularly the sequence of movements and words.

[The High Priest] came to his bullock[14] and his bullock was standing between the Porch and the Altar, its head to the south and its face to the west; and he set both his hands upon it and made confession. And thus used he to say: "O God, I have committed iniquity, transgressed, and sinned before thee. I and my house. O God, forgive the iniquities and transgressions and sins which I have committed and transgressed and sinned before thee, I and my house, as it is written in the Law of thy servant Moses, *For on this day shall atonement be made for you to cleanse you; from all your sins shall ye be clean before the Lord* (Lev 16. 30)". And they answered after him, "Blessed be the name of the glory of his kingdom for ever and ever!" . . .

They brought out to him the ladle and the fire-pan and he took his two hands full [of incense] and put it in the ladle, which was large according to his largeness [of hand], or small according to his smallness [of hand]; and such [alone] was the prescribed measure of the ladle. He took the fire-pan in his right hand and the ladle in his left. He went through the Sanctuary until he came to the space between the two curtains separating the Sanctuary from the Holy of Holies.[15] And there was a cubit's space between them [about 1 1/2 feet]. [Rabbi Yose][16] says:

Only one curtain was there, for it is written, *And the veil shall divide for you between the holy place and the most holy* (Exod 26. 33). The outer curtain was looped up on the south side and the inner one on the north side. He went along between them until he reached the north side; when he reached the north he turned round to the south and went on with the curtain on his left hand until he reached the Ark. When he reached the Ark he put the fire-pan between the two bars. He heaped up the incense on the coals and the whole place became filled with smoke. He came out by the way he went in, and in the outer space he prayed a short prayer. But he did not prolong his prayer lest he put Israel in terror.

After the Ark was taken away[17] a stone remained there from the time of the early prophets, and it was called "Shetiyah." It was higher than the ground by three fingerbreadths. On this he used to put [the fire-pan].

He took the blood from him that was stirring it and entered [again] into the place where he had entered and stood [again] on the place whereon he had stood, and sprinkled [the blood] once upwards and seven times downwards, not as though he had intended to sprinkle upwards or downwards but as though he were wielding a whip. And thus used he to count: One, one and one, one and two, one and three, one and four, one and five, one and six, one and seven. He came out and put it on the golden stand in the Sanctuary. . . .

[Rabbi Yose]. The *Yoma* then describes the sacrifice of one of the pair of goats.]

---

[14]The high priest was obliged first of all to offer sacrifice on account of his own sins.

[15]A special chamber in the Temple housing the Ark of the Covenant, which the high priest alone entered once a year. The Ark of the Covenant, the most sacred religious symbol of the ancient Jews, was an ornately decorated rectangular chest containing the tablets of the Ten Commandments and other very holy items.

[16]Yose Ben Halaphta (c. 97–c. 180 C.E.), a student of the famous Rabbi Akiva. After the forced diaspora of the emperor Hadrian, he was leader of the Academy at Sapphoris in Babylon.

---

[17]The Ark was apparently captured at the beginning of the Babylonian captivity, c. 587 B.C.E.; its subsequent whereabouts are unknown.

The two he-goats of the Day of Atonement should be alike in appearance, in size, and in value, and have been bought at the same time. Yet even if they are not alike they are valid, and if one was bought one day and the other on the morrow they are valid. If one of them died before the lot was cast, a fellow may be bought for the other; but if after the lot was cast, another pair must be bought and the lots cast over them anew. And if that cast for the Lord died, he [the high priest] should say, "Let this on which the lot 'For the Lord' has fallen stand in its stead"; and if that cast for Azazel[18] died, he should say, "Let this on which the lot 'For Azazel' has fallen stand in its stead." The other is left to pasture until it suffers a blemish, when it must be sold and its value falls to the Temple fund; for the Sin-offering of the congregation may not be left to die. Rabbi Judah says: It is left to die. Moreover Rabbi Judah said: If the blood was poured away the scapegoat is left to die; if the scapegoat died the blood is poured away.

He then came to the scapegoat and laid his two hands upon it and made confession. And thus used he to say: "O God, thy people, the House of Israel, have committed iniquity, transgressed, and sinned before thee. O God, forgive, I pray, the iniquities and transgressions and sins which thy people, the House of Israel, have committed and transgressed and sinned before thee; as it is written in the Law of thy servant Moses, *For on this day shall atonement be made for you to cleanse you; from all your sins shall ye be clean before the Lord*" (Lev 16. 30). And when the priests and the people which stood in the Temple Court heard the Expressed Name[19] come forth from the mouth of the High Priest, they used to kneel and bow themselves and fall down on their faces and say, "Blessed be the name of the glory of his kingdom for ever and ever!" . . .

Then the High Priest came to read. If he was minded to read in the linen garments he could do so; otherwise he would read in his own white vestment. The minister of the synagogue used to take a scroll of the Law and give it to the chief of the synagogue, and the chief of the synagogue gave it to the Prefect,[20] and the Prefect gave it to the High Priest, and the High Priest received it standing and read it standing. And he read *After the death* . . . (Lev 16) and *Howbeit on the tenth day* . . . (Lev 23:26–32). Then he used to roll up the scroll of the Law and put it in his bosom and say, "More is written here than I have read out before you." *And on the tenth* . . . (Num 29:7–11) which is in the Book of Numbers, he recited by heart. Thereupon he pronounced eight Benedictions: for the Law, for the Temple-Service, for the Thanksgiving, for the Forgiveness of Sin, and for the Temple separately, and for the Israelites separately, and for the priests separately; and for the rest a [general] prayer.

---

[18]The identity of Azazel is ambiguous in ancient times, though in Jewish apocalyptic literature the figure is often conceived of as a fallen angel or demon. The goat offered to him in compensation for the sins of the community is sometimes referred to as a scapegoat.

[19]The tetragrammaton, or sacred name of God—YHWH—was uttered with the proper vowels only by the high priest on the Day of Atonement.
[20]Actually, "the prefect of the priests," a high dignitary set over the building and services of the Temple.

---

4. THE TEACHINGS *(DIDACHE);* OR, THE LORD'S INSTRUCTION TO THE GENTILES THROUGH THE TWELVE APOSTLES (c. 90 C.E.)

The document known as the *Didache* ("Two Ways") is an early manual of instruction for new converts to Christianity. Only rediscovered in the late nineteenth century, it contains several ethical directives as well as instructions for performing the oldest elements of Christian liturgy, i.e., baptism, fasting, the Eucharist, and the Lord's Prayer. It also dramatically illustrates the continuing strong affinity between first-century Christianity and Judaism. Some practices, such as the baptism and strict ascetic regime of the Essene sect of Jews, are adopted virtually unchanged; other customs are slightly modified. For example, the weekly Monday and Tuesday fasts observed by all devout Jews are shifted to Wednesday and Friday for Christians. All rituals are adapted to center on the life and teachings of Jesus and to emphasize the Christian faith in the imminent arrival of the apocalypse, or end of the world. In outward form, however, these earliest Christian gatherings would be hard to distinguish from the religious rites of most other Jewish sects.

Two Ways there are, one of Life and one of Death, and there is a great difference between the Two Ways.

Now, the Way of Life is this: first, love the God who made you; secondly, your neighbor as yourself [cf. Mt 22:37, 39]: do not do to another what you do not wish to be done to yourself.

The lesson of these words is as follows: bless those that curse you, and pray for your enemies; besides, fast for those that persecute you. For what thanks do you deserve when you love those that love you? Do not the heathen do as much? For your part, love those that hate you; in fact, have no enemy [Mt 7]. Abstain from gratifying the carnal (and bodily) impulses [1 Pet 2:11]. When anyone gives you a blow on the right cheek, turn to him the other as well, and be perfect [Mt 5:39, 48]; when anyone forces you to go one mile with him, go two with him; when anyone takes your cloak away, give him your coat also [ibid.]; when anyone robs you of your property, demand no return. You really cannot do it. Give to anyone that asks you, and demand no return [Lk 6:30; Mt 5:42]; the Father wants His own bounties to be shared with all. Happy the giver who complies with the commandment, for he goes unpunished. Trouble is in store for the receiver: if someone who is in need receives, he will go unpunished; but he who is not in need will have to stand trial as to why and for what purpose he received; and, if he is thrown into prison, he will be questioned about his conduct, and will

not be released from that place until he has paid the last penny. However, in this regard, there is also a word of Scriptures: Let your alms sweat in your hands until you find out to whom to give. . . .

Regarding baptism. Baptize as follows: after first explaining all these points, baptize in the name of the Father and of the Son and of the Holy Spirit, in running water. But if you have no running water, baptize in other water; and if you cannot in cold, then in warm. But if you have neither, pour water on the head three times in the name of the Father and of the Son and of the Holy Spirit. Before the baptism, let the baptizer and the candidate for baptism fast, as well as any others that are able. Require the candidate to fast one or two days previously.

Your fasts should not coincide with those of the hypocrites.[21] They fast on Mondays and Tuesdays; you should fast on Wednesdays and Fridays. And do not pray as the hypocrites do, but pray as the Lord has commanded in the Gospel: "Our Father, who art in heaven; hallowed be Thy name; Thy kingdom come; Thy will be done on earth as it is in heaven; give us this day our daily bread, and forgive us our debts as we also forgive our debtors; and lead us not into temptation, but deliver us from evil; for Thine is the power and the glory for evermore [Mt 6:9–13]. Say this prayer three times a day.

---

[21]Presumably a reference to Pharisees or perhaps to unconverted Jews in general.

Regarding the Eucharist. Give thanks as follows: First, concerning the cup: "We give Thee thanks, Our Father, for the Holy Vine of David Thy servant, which Thou hast made known to us through Jesus, Thy Servant." "To Thee be the glory for evermore." Next, concerning the broken bread: "We give Thee thanks, Our Father, for the life and knowledge which Thou hast made known to us through Jesus, Thy Servant." "To Thee be the glory for evermore." "As this broken bread was scattered over the hills and then, when gathered, became one mass, so may Thy Church be gathered from the ends of the earth into Thy Kingdom." "For Thine is the glory and the power through Jesus Christ for evermore." Let no one eat and drink of your Eucharist but those baptized in the name of the Lord; to this, too, the saying of the Lord is applicable: Do not give to dogs what is sacred [Mt 7:6].

After you have taken your fill of food, give thanks as follows: "We give Thee thanks, O Holy Father, for Thy holy name which Thou hast enshrined in our hearts, and for the knowledge and faith and immortality which Thou hast made known to us through Jesus, Thy Servant." "To Thee be the glory for evermore." "Thou, Lord Almighty, hast created all things for the sake of Thy name and hast given food and drink for men to enjoy, that they may give thanks to Thee; but to us Thou hast vouchsafed spiritual food and drink and eternal life through Jesus, Thy Servant." "Above all, we give Thee thanks because Thou art mighty." "To Thee be the glory for evermore." "Remember, O Lord, Thy Church: deliver her from all evil, perfect her in Thy love, and from the four winds assemble her, the sanctified, in Thy kingdom which Thou hast prepared for her." "For Thine is the power and the glory for evermore." "May Grace come, and this world pass away!" "Hosanna to the God of David! [Mt 21:9, 15]" "If anyone is holy, let him advance; if anyone is not, let him be converted. *Marana tha!*[22] [1 Cor 16:32]" "Amen."

. . . On the Lord's own day, assemble in common to break bread and offer thanks; but first confess your sins, so that your sacrifice may be pure. However, no one quarreling with his brother may join your meeting until they are reconciled; your sacrifice must not be defiled. For here we have the saying of the Lord: In every place and time offer me a pure sacrifice; for I am a mighty King, says the Lord; and my name spreads terror among the nations [Mal 1:11, 14].

Accordingly, elect for yourselves bishops and deacons, men who are an honor to the Lord, of gentle disposition, not attached to money, honest and well-tried; for they, too, render you the sacred service of the prophets and teachers. Do not, then, despise them; after all, they are your dignitaries together with the prophets and teachers.

Furthermore, correct one another, not in anger, but in composure, as you have it in the Gospel; and when anyone offends his neighbor, let no one speak with him—in fact, he should not even be talked about by you—until he has made amends. As regards your prayers and alms and your whole conduct, do exactly as you have it in the Gospel of Our Lord.

Watch over your life; your lamps must not go out, nor your loins be ungirded; on the contrary, be ready. You do not know the hour in which Our Lord is coming [Mt 22, 42, 44; 25:13]. Assemble in great numbers, intent upon what concerns your souls. Surely, of no use will your lifelong faith be to you if you are not perfected at the end of time. For in the last days the false prophets and corrupters will come in swarms; the sheep will turn into wolves, and love will turn into hate. When lawlessness is on the increase, men will hate and persecute and betray one another; and then the Deceiver of this world will appear, claiming to be the Son of God, and give striking exhibitions of power; the earth will be given over into his hands, and he will perpetrate outrages such as have never taken place since the world began. Then humankind will undergo the fiery test, and many will lose their faith and perish;

---

[22] Aramaic: "Lord, come."

but those who stand firm in their faith will be saved by none other than the Accursed. And then the proofs of the truth will appear; the first proof, an opening in the heavens; the next proof, the sounding of the trumpet [Mt 24:30–31]; and the third, the resurrection of the dead—not of all indeed, but in accordance with the saying: The Lord will come and all the saints with Him. Finally, the world will behold the Lord riding the clouds in the sky.

---

5. Justin Martyr
APOLOGIA (c. 150 C.E.)

Justin Martyr (d. 165 C.E.) was a Palestinian who converted to Christianity only after a long spiritual odyssey, which included a significant period of adherence to Platonic philosophy. His *apologia*, or defense, was written for a non-Christian audience, and he seeks to portray his adopted religion as a serious and truly pious option for potential converts, calling it "the only safe and worthy philosophy." Justin presents all of the established elements of the Christian liturgy and takes care to explain each in learned but nontechnical terms that an uninformed and even biased readership could understand. As a result, modern readers also gain insight into how the Christian liturgy had evolved during the approximately sixty years that had passed since the writing of the *Didache*. Of particular note are the increasingly important role of the presiding elder or priest (*presbyter*; here translated as "president") during the eucharistic offering of bread and wine as well as the by-then regular reading of the gospels—both part of a weekly gathering on the day of the Sun.

But I will explain the manner in which we who have been made new through Christ have also dedicated ourselves to God, lest by passing it over I should seem in any way to be unfair in my explanation. As many as are persuaded and believe that the things are true which are taught and said by us, and promise that they are able to live accordingly, they are taught to pray and with fasting to ask God forgiveness of their former sins, while we pray and fast with them. Thereupon they are brought by us to where there is water, and are born again in the same manner of a new birth as we, also, ourselves were born again. For in the name of God the Father and Lord of all, and of our Savior Jesus Christ, and of the Holy Spirit, they then receive the washing in the water. For Christ said: *"Except ye be born again, ye shall not enter into the kingdom of heaven"* [Jn 3:3]. But that it is impossible for those once born to enter into the wombs of their mothers is manifest to all. . . . And this washing is called enlightenment, because those who learn these things have their understandings enlightened. But, also, in the name of Jesus Christ who was crucified under Pontius Pilate, and in the name of the Holy Spirit who by the prophets foretold all things pertaining to Jesus, he who is illuminated is washed. . . .

But after we have thus washed him who is persuaded and has assented, we bring him to those who are called the brethren, to where they are gathered together, making earnest prayer in common for ourselves and for him who is enlightened, and for all others everywhere, that we may be accounted worthy, after we have learned the truth, by our works also to be found right livers and keepers of the commandments, that we may be saved with the eternal salvation. We salute each other with a kiss when we conclude our prayers. Thereupon to the president of the brethren bread and a cup of water and wine are brought, and he takes it and offers up praise and glory to the Father of the universe through the name of the Son and the Holy Spirit, and gives thanks at length that we have been accounted worthy of these things from Him; and when he has ended the prayers and thanksgiving the whole people present assent, saying "Amen." Now the word Amen in the Hebrew language signifies, So be it. Then after the president has given thanks and all the people have assented, those who are called by us deacons give to each one of those present to partake of the bread and of the wine and water for which thanks have been given, and for those not present they take away a portion.

And this food is called by us eucharist, and it is not lawful for any man to partake of it but him who believes the things taught by us to be true, and has been washed with the washing which is for the remission of sins and unto a new birth, and is so living as Christ commanded. For not as common bread and common drink do we receive these; but just as Jesus Christ our Savior, being made flesh through the word of God, had for our salvation both flesh and blood, so, also, we are taught that the food for which thanks are given by the word of prayer which is from Him, and from which by conversion our flesh and blood are nourished, is the flesh and blood of that Jesus who was made flesh. For the Apostles in the memoirs composed by them, which are called Gospels, thus delivered what was commanded them: that Jesus took bread and gave thanks and said, This do in remembrance of Me, this is My body; and that He likewise took the cup, and when He had given thanks, said, This is My blood [Mt 26:17–19; Mk 14:12–16; Lk 22:7–13], and gave only to them. And this the evil demons imitating, commanded it to be done also in the mysteries of Mithras;[23] for

that bread and a cup of water are set forth with certain explanations in the ceremonial of initiation, you either know or can learn.

But we afterward always remind one another of these things, and those among us who are wealthy help all who are in want, and we always remain together. And for all things we eat we bless the Maker of all things through His Son Jesus Christ and through the Holy Spirit. And on the day called the Day of the Sun there is a gathering in one place of us all who live in cities or in the country, and the memoirs of the Apostles or the writings of the prophets are read as long as time allows. Then, when the reader has ceased, the president gives by word of mouth his admonition and exhortation to imitate these excellent things. Afterward we all rise at once and offer prayers; and as I said, when we have ceased to pray, bread is brought and wine and water, and the president likewise offers up prayers and thanksgivings as he has the ability, and the people assent, saying "Amen." The distribution to each and the partaking of that for which thanks were given then take place; and to those not present a portion is sent by the hands of the deacons. Those who are well-to-do and willing give, every one giving what he will, according to his own judgment, and the collection is deposited with the president, and he assists orphans and widows, and those who through sickness or any other cause are in want, and those who are in bonds, and the strangers that are sojourning, and, in short, he has the care of all that are in need. Now we all hold our common meeting on the Day of the Sun, because it is the first day on which God, having changed the darkness and matter, created the world; and Jesus Christ our Savior on the same day rose from the dead. For on the day before Saturn's they crucified Him [i.e., Good Friday]; and on the day after Saturn's, which is the Day of the Sun, having appeared to his Apostles and disciples, He taught them these things which we have offered you for consideration.

---

[23]A popular mystery cult; see 1A.

B. Charisma

Christianity was far from unique in claims that *charismata*, or "divine gifts," were bestowed upon its leaders. One of the most common elements of all ancient religions was belief in the ability of certain individuals to interpret divine wishes or commands, a gift known as prophecy or divination. The people thought to be endowed with this power received their divinely inspired messages by many different means. Some interpreted the will of the divine by studying such natural phenomena as lightning, hail, or the flight of birds, while others received personal communications from a deity through more direct means, such as dreams. The messages received varied widely according to the situation, ranging from briefly stated direct advice on personal matters to lengthy generalized prophecies of the doom that awaited a city or entire kingdom if its people did not turn from their current evil ways. In almost every case, a prophecy was considered to be less of a fatalistic prediction about a certain future than an admonition to proper action (*orthopraxis*). It was believed that those who heeded the prophets' messages by propitiating the gods with elaborate rituals and better behavior could always forestall divine punishment.

The early Christian movement made extensive use of divine prophecy both during and after the life of Jesus. Some early Christians were also said to possess other *charismata*—such as the ability to heal the sick and perform various miracles—providing further evidence of divine favor and power. Though these *charismata* were also common among other ancient religions, only a very few of the mystery cults (see 1A2) combined such powers with an ambitious proselytizing mission in the manner of early Christianity. From the time of Jesus and the apostles to the eventual conversion of barbarian Europe, this dynamic fusion of preaching and charismatic acts fueled the engine of Christianity's growth. Ironically, these same claims to "special gifts" from the Holy Spirit also sparked heated conflicts that threatened to divide Christianity from within during its most formative stage. The Montanist "heresy" and schism of the second century (see 1B5) merely provides the most famous example. Charisma, in other words, was the double-edged sword by which early Christianity thrived and very nearly died.

1. Artemidorus of Daldis
THE INTERPRETATION OF DREAMS
(mid-second century C.E.)

One type of expert divination popular in the ancient world dealt with the interpretation of dreams, or oneiromancy. Unlike modern analyses, which usually seek to shed light on an individual's psychological past or present, dream interpretation in the ancient world was invariably employed as a guide to the future. Like oracular prophecy, this was an ancient practice, as can be deduced from its appearance in such documents as the Old Testament Book of Genesis, in which the Hebrew slave Joseph interprets Pharaoh's dream of the seven fat and seven lean cows [Gen 41:1–36]. By the beginning of the Christian era, some followers of Asclepius, the Greek god of healing, had attempted to formalize the inspired interpretation of dreams into a quasi-science. Believing that the key to curing many patients' illnesses lay in their dreams, Artemidorus of Daldis (fl. second century C.E.) wrote an influential book to help other physician-oneiromancers. Like oracular divination, his method combines interpretation of traditional notions of "auspicious" signs from the gods with close attention to an individual's immediate situation and needs. In discussing dreams of flying, for instance, Artemidorus states that the meaning of such dreams varies depending on the. manner in which the dreamer flew and on such real-life circumstances as whether the dreamer is rich or poor, a free man or a slave, a a law-abiding citizen or a criminal.

Sacrificing to the gods what is prescribed for each means good luck for everyone. For men sacrifice to the gods when they have received benefits or when they have escaped some evil. But to sacrifice to the gods offerings that are unholy or inappropriate foretells the wrath of the gods to whom the person has sacrificed. If a sick man dreams that other men are sacrificing, even if he sees them sacrificing to Asclepius, it is a bad sign, since the sacrificial victim is destroyed. It portends death.

To wreathe the gods with flowers and branches that are fitting and prescribed by law as sacred to these deities signifies good fortune for all men, but it will not come to pass without anxieties. This dream admonishes a slave to obey his master and to do things that are pleasing to him. To wipe off, to anoint, or to clean the statues of the gods, to sweep in front of statues and to sprinkle everything in the temple with water signifies that a man has committed a sin against those very gods. I know of a man who forswore himself after this dream by the very god whose statue he had dreamt he was cleaning. What the dream was telling him was this, that he must implore the god for forgiveness.

To destroy statues of the gods, to throw out of a house the statues that are inside, to raze a temple, or to commit any sacrilegious act in a temple is inauspicious for all men and portends great crises. For men who are in great distress also abandon their reverence towards gods.

If the gods depart of their own free will and their statues fall down, it portends death for the dreamer or for one of his family. If gods are sacrificing to other gods, it signifies that the house of the dreamer will be deserted. For the gods sacrifice to one another only when they feel there are no human beings present.

If the statues of the gods move, it signifies fears and disturbances for all but those who are imprisoned or who intend to take a trip. It signifies that the former will be released, so that they can move about easily. It moves the latter from their dwelling place and leads them out. . . .

If a man dreams that he is flying not very far above the earth and in an upright position, it means good luck for the dreamer. The greater the distance above the earth, the higher his position will be in regard to those who walk beneath him. For we always call those who are more prosperous the "higher ones." It is good if this does not happen to a man in his own country, since it signifies emigration because the person does not set his foot upon the ground. For the dream is saying to some extent that the dreamer's native land is inaccessible to him.

Flying with wings is auspicious for all men alike. The dream signifies freedom for slaves, since all birds that fly are without a master and have no one above them. It means that the poor will acquire a great deal of money. For just as money raises men up, wings raise birds up. It signifies offices for the rich and very influential. For just as the creatures of the air are above those that crawl upon the earth, rulers are above private citizens. But to dream that one is flying without wings and very far above the earth signifies danger and fear for the dreamer.

Flying around tiled roofs, houses, and blocks of houses signifies confusion of the soul and disturbances. For slaves, dreaming that one is flying up into the heavens always signifies that they will pass into more distinguished homes and frequently even that they will pass into the court of a king. I have often observed that free men, even against their will, have journeyed to Italy. For just as the sky is the home of the gods, Italy is the home of kings. But the dream indicates that those who wish to hide and conceal themselves will be discovered. For everything in the sky is clear and easily visible to everyone.

Flying with the birds signifies that one will dwell with men of foreign nationalities and with strangers. The dream is inauspicious for criminals, since it signifies punishment for wrongdoers and frequently crucifixion. Flying a course that is not very high above the earth nor, again, very low but at a height where one is able to distinguish clearly objects on the ground signifies a trip or a change of address. One can ascertain from the things that are seen on the earth the kind of events that the dreamer will encounter during his trip abroad. For example, if a man sees plains, grain-lands, cities, villages, fields, all kinds of human activity, beautiful rivers, marshes, a calm sea, harbors, or ships that are sailing with a fair wind, it foretells a good trip. On the other hand, valleys, ravines, wooded glens, rocks, wild animals, river torrents, mountains, and steep cliffs signify that only misfortunes will occur on the trip. But it is always good, after one has flown above, to fly back down and to awaken in this way. But it is best of all to fly at will [wishing to soar above] and to stop at will. For it foretells great ease and skill in one's business affairs.

It is not auspicious, however, if a man dreams that he is flying while he is being pursued by a wild animal, a man, or a demon. For it portends great fears and dangers. For in these dreams the person's fear was so great that he did not think that he would be sufficiently safe fleeing upon the earth, but he took to the skies. If a slave dreams that he is flying in the house of his master, it means good luck. For he will surpass many in the house. But if he is flying outside the house, he will leave the house as a dead man after days of health and happiness, if he has gone out through the gate-house, he will be sold. If he has gone through a window, he will leave the house by running away.

---

2. 1 ENOCH (c. 200 B.C.E.–25 C.E.)

The ancient tradition of prophecy among the Jews was especially important in the development of Christianity, which had deep roots in Judaism. Like other gods of the ancient world, Yahweh was long known to speak to his people through certain chosen individuals, sometimes in dreams but often through more direct inspiration. By the beginning of the second century B.C.E., the prophetic tradition of Ezekiel and Isaiah was joined by a new type of divination in some Jewish groups that was notably more apocalyptic in vision. The Ethiopian book of Enoch, or 1 Enoch, was not included among the canonical Hebrew scriptures of the period (later the Christian Old Testament) and is thus labeled "apocryphal." In many ways, however, it resembles certain familiar works such as the Old Testament Book of Daniel and especially the New Testament

Book of Revelation. As Enoch ascends through the cosmos and ultimately confronts the Lord himself, he learns the secrets of creation and the divine commands that must be conveyed to the godly. Even more significantly as a context for later Christianity, the book describes a conflict between forces of light and darkness, the coming of a "Son of Man" (a term Jesus was to use in reference to himself), and ultimately a final judgment where the virtuous are rewarded and the wicked punished. Not all Jews of this period accepted this prophecy as divinely inspired nor did they necessarily share its apocalyptic outlook. The influence of this type of literature on Jesus and others of his generation, however, was obviously profound.

PARABLE OF ENOCH ON THE FUTURE LOT OF THE WICKED AND THE RIGHTEOUS

I 1 The words of the blessing of Enoch, wherewith he blessed the elect and righteous, who will be living in the day of tribulation, when all the wicked and godless are to be removed.

2 And he took up his parable and said—Enoch a righteous man, whose eyes were opened by God, saw the vision of the Holy One in the heavens, which the angels showed me, and from them I heard everything, and from them I understood as I saw, but not for this generation, but for a remote one which is for to come.

3 Concerning the elect I said, and took up my parable concerning them:
The Holy Great One[24] will come forth from His dwelling,

4 And the eternal God will tread upon the earth,
(even) on Mount Sinai,
[And appear from His camp]
And appear in the strength of His might from the heaven of heavens.

5 And all shall be smitten with fear,
And the Watchers shall quake,
And great fear and trembling shall seize them unto the ends of the earth.

6 And the high mountains shall be shaken,
And the high hills shall be made low,
And shall melt like wax before the flame

7 And the earth shall be wholly rent in sunder,
And all that is upon the earth shall perish,
And there shall be a judgment upon all (men).

8 But with the righteous He will make peace,
And will protect the elect,
And mercy shall be upon them.

And they shall all belong to God
And they shall be prospered,
And they shall all be blessed.

And He will help them all,
And light shall appear unto them,
And He will make peace with them.

9 And behold! He cometh with ten thousands of His holy ones
To execute judgment upon all,
And to destroy all the ungodly:
And to convict all flesh
Of all the works of their ungodliness which they have ungodly committed,
And of all the hard things which ungodly sinners have spoken against Him. . . .

V 5 Therefore shall ye execrate your days,
And the years of your life shall perish,
And the years of your destruction shall be multiplied in eternal execration,
And ye shall find no mercy.

6 In those days ye shall make your names an eternal execration unto all the righteous,
And by you shall all who curse, curse.

---

[24]This title distinguishes God from the many "holy ones," the angels (cf. v. 9).

And all the sinners and godless shall impre-
cate by you,
And for you, the godless, there shall be a
curse.

And all the [righteous] shall rejoice,
And there shall be forgiveness of sins,
And every mercy and peace and forbearance:
There shall be salvation unto them, a goodly
light.

And for all of you sinners there shall be no
salvation,
But on you all shall abide a curse.

7 But for the elect there shall be light and
grace and peace,
And they shall inherit the earth.

8 And then there shall be bestowed upon the
elect wisdom,
And they shall all live and never again sin,
Either through ungodliness or through
pride;
But they who are wise shall be humble.

9 And they shall not again transgress,
Nor shall they sin all the days of their life,
Nor shall they die of (the divine) anger or
wrath,
But they shall complete the number of the
days of their life.

And their lives shall be increased in peace,
And the years of their joy shall be multiplied,
In eternal gladness and peace,
All the days of their life.

THE HEAD OF DAYS
AND THE SON OF MAN

XLVI   1 And there I saw One, who had a
head of days,
And His head was white like wool,
And with Him was another being whose
countenance had the appearance of a man,
And his face was full of graciousness, like
one of the holy angels.

2 And I asked the angel who went with me
and showed me all the hidden things,
concerning that Son of Man, who he was,
and whence he was, (and) why he went
with the Head of Days?

3 And he answered and said unto me:
This is the Son of Man who hath righteous-
ness,
With whom dwelleth righteousness,
And who revealeth all the treasures of that
which is hidden,

Because the Lord of Spirits[25] hath chosen
him,
And whose lot hath the pre-eminence before
the Lord of Spirits in uprightness for ever.

4 And this Son of Man whom thou hast seen
Shall raise up the kings and the mighty from
their seats,
[And the strong from their thrones]
And shall loosen the reins of the strong,
And break the teeth of the sinners;

5 [And he shall put down the kings from their
thrones and kingdoms]
Because they do not extol and praise Him,
Nor humbly acknowledge whence the kingdom was bestowed upon them.

6 And he shall put down the countenance of
the strong,
And shall fill them with shame.
And darkness shall be their dwelling,
And worms shall be their bed,

And they shall have no hope of rising from
their beds,
Because they do not extol the name of the
Lord of Spirits.

7 And these are they who judge the stars of
heaven,
[And raise their hands against the Most High],
And tread upon the earth and dwell upon it.

---

[25] An allusion to his title, "the Chosen One." The title "the
Lord of Spirits" is probably derived from the biblical title
"Lord of Hosts" (cf. Isa 6:3), reformulated in line with
Num 16:22.

And all their deeds manifest unrighteousness,
And their power rests upon their riches,
And their faith is in the gods which they
have made with their hands,
And they deny the name of the Lord of
Spirits,

8 And they persecute the houses of His congregations,
And the faithful who hang upon the name of
the Lord of Spirits.

THE FOUNT OF RIGHTEOUSNESS: THE SON OF MAN—THE STAY OF THE RIGHTEOUS: JUDGMENT OF THE KINGS AND THE MIGHTY

XLVIII 1 And in that place I saw the
fountain of righteousness,
Which was inexhaustible:
And around it were many fountains of
wisdom:

And all the thirsty drank of them,
And were filled with wisdom,
And their dwellings were with the righteous
and holy and elect.

2 And at that hour that Son of Man was named
In the presence of the Lord of Spirits,
And his name before the Head of Days.

3 Yea, before the sun and the signs were
created,
Before the stars of the heaven were made,
His name was named before the Lord of
Spirits.

4 He shall be a staff to the righteous whereon
to stay themselves and not fall,
And he shall be the light of the Gentiles,
And the hope of those who are troubled of
heart.

5 All who dwell on earth shall fall down and
worship before him,
And will praise and bless and celebrate with
song the Lord of Spirits.

6 And for this reason hath he been chosen and
hidden before Him,
Before the creation of the world and for evermore.

7 And the wisdom of the Lord of Spirits hath
revealed him to the holy and righteous;
For he hath preserved the lot of the righteous;
Because they have hated and despised this
world of unrighteousness,
And have hated all its works and ways in the
name of the Lord of Spirits:
For in his name they are saved,
And according to his good pleasure hath it
been in regard to their life.

8 In those days downcast in countenance shall
the kings of the earth have become,
And the strong who possess the land because
of the works of their hands;

For on the day of their anguish and affliction they shall not (be able to) save
themselves,

9 And I will give them over into the hands of
Mine elect:

As straw in the fire so shall they burn before
the face of the holy:
As lead in the water shall they sink before
the face of the righteous,
And no trace of them shall any more be
found.

10 And on the day of their affliction there
shall be rest on the earth,
And before them they shall fall and not rise
again:

And there shall be no one to take them with
his hands and raise them:
For they have denied the Lord of Spirits and
His Anointed.[26]
The name of the Lord of Spirits be blessed.

---

[26]I.e., "his Messiah." Cf. Ps 2:2: "against the Lord and his
anointed."

THE POWER AND WISDOM
OF THE ELECT ONE

XLIX 1 For wisdom is poured out like water,
And glory faileth not before him for ever-more.

2 For he is mighty in all the secrets of right-eousness,
And unrighteousness shall disappear as a shadow,
And have no continuance;
Because the Elect One standeth before the Lord of Spirits,

And his glory is for ever and ever,
And his might unto all generations.

3 And in him dwells the spirit of wisdom,
And the spirit which gives insight,
And the spirit of understanding and of might,
And the spirit of those who have fallen asleep in righteousness.

4 And he shall judge the secret things,
And none shall be able to utter a lying word before him;
For he is the Elect One before the Lord of Spirits according to His good pleasure.

---

3. Gregory of Nyssa
LIFE OF ST. GREGORY THAUMATURGUS
(c. 340 C.E.)

Jesus and all of his apostles were credited with many charismatic works of healing, prophecy, and other miracles. Though this aspect of Christian prose-lytizing waned in subsequent generations, it remained a crucial component of conversion efforts for centuries to come. The missionary work of Gregory of Neocaesarea (c. 210–c. 270 C.E.) was an example of Christian charisma at its most successful. Born to a wealthy pagan family in what is now north-central Turkey, Gregory converted to Christianity while studying in Beirut. Although known to historians as an influential pupil of the great scriptural scholar Origen (c. 185–c. 254 C.E.), Gregory was famous among his contemporaries as "the Wonderworker" (*Thaumaturgus*). It was not his learning but his battles with evil spirits and pagan priests that most often impressed bystanders and won converts. The admiring biography below was written roughly a century after Gregory's death. It begins as Gregory, recently returned from a period of wandering in the hillsides around his hometown of Neocaesarea, sets about trying to convert his fellow citizens to Christianity. The document's account of how Gregory drove out pagan spirits with his superior spiritual strength is intended to remind readers of similar feats performed by Jesus in the gospels, as is the story of Gregory's healing of the sick during a great plague. The cumulative effect on his reputation is also significant, since it results in the eventual conversion of most of the district and spawns dozens of popular local stories that were still being told a century later when this biography was written.

So, leaving the back-country, he turned his face toward the city [Neocaesarea] where he needed to raise a church to God. When he discovered that the whole region was under the spell of spirits'[27] deceits and that no temple to the true God had been prepared, while the city and its environs were filled with (pagan) holy altars and chapels and the population shared a common zeal in beautifying the precincts of the idols and shrines, and in seeing to it that men's idolatry might cling to them, fortified by processions, sacrifices and the defilements around altars, like a noble warrior engaged in combat with the chief of a company—and through him all the subordinates are defeated—so this great man commenced from the very leadership of the spirits themselves. How did he do this?

While he was traversing the road from the back-country to the city, nightfall overtook him along with a violent drawn-out rainstorm. He found himself in a certain shrine with his companions. Now the shrine was one of the famous ones, in which the spirits being worshipped appeared openly to the temple-wardens, when a certain prophetic oracle was activated by them. Going up into the shrine with his companions, he intimidated the spirits on the instant by calling the name of Christ. He purified the air, polluted with the stench of sacrifices, by a gesture of the Cross, in his usual fashion and spent the whole night awake in prayers and psalm-singing, so transforming into a house of prayer a building befouled by the altar's filth and the chapels. Having passed his night in this fashion, he had his journey to pursue once again, at dawn. The temple-warden, however, at dawn went about his usual care of the spirits; and they say that the spirits appeared and spoke to him, saying the shrine was barred to them because of the man who had stayed there; and the temple-warden made use of certain purifications and sacrifices thereby to get the spirits to return and live in the temple, applying every means, but his zeal was unre-

warded: the demons did not respond to his summons as had been their custom; and, roused by indignation and anger, the temple-warden then caught up with the great man, uttering the most terrible threats, saying he would bring charges before the magistrates and apply force against him and inform the emperor of the outrage and of his being a Christian, an enemy of the gods, who had dared to set foot inside the palace [i.e., the temple]; and his entrance had removed the force that worked within the shrines, and the spirits' oracular force was no longer present in those places as it had been. And when he [Gregory] put down the temple-warden's violent and boorish anger through his more elevated attitude, opposing the alliance of the true God to every threat and declaring that he so relied on the power of his champion that, by Jesus' authority, he could drive them away from wherever he wished or settle them in whatever place he wanted; and when he had promised to give proof of what he had just said, then the temple-warden was astonished and overwhelmed by the greatness of such authority and adjured him to demonstrate his power from these very deeds, by making the spirits return to the temple.

When the great man heard this, he broke off a little bit of his book, inscribed in it a certain injunction to the spirits, and gave it to the man in charge of the temple; and the writing said verbatim, "Gregory to Satan: Enter." And they say that the temple-warden took the writing and put it on the altar and applied their accustomed fumes of sacrifice and foulnesses, and beheld again the things he earlier beheld, before the spirits were dislodged from the place of idols; and after these happenings he began to think that there must be some divine force with Gregory by which he appeared the superior of the spirits; and quickly catching up with him once more before he reached the city, he asked if he could learn the secret from him, and what that God was that held the whip hand over the nature of spirits. And when the great man briefly related the secret of piety, the man in charge of the temple reacted as might be

---

[27]*Daimones*, in this case referring to pagan gods.

expected of a person uninitiated in divine matters, by supposing it was beneath his conception of god to believe that the divinity had been persuaded to appear to man in the flesh; and, when the other replied, it was not by words that faith in this had prevailed but that belief arose from the miracles of the events themselves, the temple-warden still sought from him the sight of some marvel, so as thus to be brought around to agreement with the faith through what happened.

Thereupon, it is said that the great man wrought the great miracle, the most incredible of all: for when the temple-warden asked that a stone of a good size right under their eyes, without a human hand but solely through the power of belief, by the command of Gregory, should be transferred to some other place, the great man hesitated not a moment, but immediately commanded the stone, as if it were alive, to move to that place that the temple-warden had indicated. When that happened, straightway he believed in the Word, giving up everything—clan, house, wife, children, friends, priesthood, hearth, possessions—considering it worth everything he had to join the company of the great man and share his toils, and that divine way of life [*philosophia*] and teaching. . . .

Henceforward, that great man, beginning from his triumph over the spirits, leading the temple-warden about with him like a trophy of victory over them, that awe might strike the population through report of him, advanced on the city with confidence and boldness of speech, not upon chariots and steeds and mules, not flaunting the multitude of his retinue, but rather having his miraculous deeds as a guard about him. All the inhabitants in a mob poured out from the city as if at the news of some novel spectacle, all eager to see what sort of man Gregory was, who, though a man, by his command over the beings they considered gods, as if by a king's power, moved and led the spirits about by his command wherever he wished, and banished or recalled them, to all appearance, from wherever he wanted, just like

slaves—a man who had that servant of his as if enslaved to some authority, now scornful of his previous status, having exchanged all his possessions for a new way of life with him.

In this mood, everyone welcomed him on the outskirts of the city, and, when he was among them and everyone was looking at him earnestly, he moved past the men as if they had been lifeless matter, turning to none of those whom he encountered but walking steadily into the city; and so he aroused in them all the more astonishment, appearing to viewers even to surpass report. The fact that he was first entering the great city, though it had not been any custom of his, and was not overwhelmed by such a mass assembled on his account but walked as if in a desert with his eyes only for himself and his path, turning aside to nobody among those gathered about him, all this appeared to people to be something even beyond the miracle of the stone. For that reason—although, as was earlier said, there had been very few who had received the faith before his visitation—as virtually the entire city accepted his priesthood in honor, he entered thus, on all sides pressed by the crowd of those that accompanied him. From the moment he took up his *philosophia*, he freed himself from everything else at once, as if from a burden, so to speak, though he had none of the necessities of life— no field, no location, no house, but was himself everything to himself (rather his virtue and faith was his homeland and hearth and wealth). So he was in the city, but a lodging for him to rest in there was not—neither one belonging to the church nor privately owned. The crowd around was at a loss about how he would be lodged and from whom he might seek shelter. "Why," the teacher asked them, "are you at a loss about such things as where people should rest their bodies, as if you were beyond the shelter of God? Or do you think God is a small house, if in him we live and move and exist?" . . .

While he was discussing these matters with his companions, one of the men notable through family and wealth came up, numbered among the leaders for all his power. His name was Musonius. When he saw the matter of such concern to so many, who were ready to take the man into their homes, he pushed ahead of them all and snatched the goodwill for himself: he invited the great man to stay with him and to honor his house by entering so that it might be more distinguished and of good repute in times to come, since time would transmit to others, later, the memory of such an honor. Since many others, however, turned up to beg the same favor, he thought it right to bestow it on him who asked first. The rest, he put off with words of kindness, and returned the honor they showed, and so was lodged with the man who got there first. . . .

Since, however, only a few people had heard him earlier, so great a number added themselves to the gathering before the day ended and the sun set that the number of believers appeared like the assembly of the citizen body. The next day, once again the populace was on his doorstep, along with their wives and children and the aged and those on whom the spirits or some other misfortune had laid some bodily affliction. In their midst, that man measured out what was suitable to the needs of each person in the assemblage, through the power of the Spirit—preaching, jointly examining, admonishing, teaching and healing. For he won over the greatest number to his preaching because what they saw coincided with what they heard, and the tokens of divine power shone upon him through the divine power through both. His words confirmed what they heard, the miracles of healing astonishingly confirmed what they saw. The griever was comforted, youth made wise, the aged ministered to by appropriate words. Slaves were taught to be loyal to their masters; the powerful, to be kind to the lowly; the poor, that virtue alone is wealth and the winning of it is within everyone's reach; and the man fortunate in his riches was properly admonished that he should consider himself not the master but the steward of his possessions. To women he dispensed what was profitable to them; to chil-

dren, what suited their age; to parents, what was proper. . . .

The conversion of the entire province from pagan folly to the recognition of the truth, let everyone behold with wonder who reads this, and let no one doubt, looking rather to the management whereby so great a change was wrought among those converted from lies to truth. For what happened in the first days of his ministration, something that my account passed by in its hurry to get to others of his miracles, I will now pick up and recount. There was a certain mass festival in the city conducted according to tradition in honor of one of the local spirits, and almost the whole province streamed in to it, all the countryside joining the city in the celebration. The theater filled up with visitors and the crowd that flowed in spread over all the seats, everyone eagerly looking down on the orchestra to see and hear the performance. The scene-area was filled with noise, and the magicians could not put on their show. The uproar not only prevented the crowd from enjoying the music but the magicians from having the opportunity to perform whereupon the massed voice of the populace broke forth, calling upon the spirit honored by the festival and demanding that he make room for them all. When all of them were clamoring to each other, and the sound was raised aloft to the sky, it seemed as if the whole city spoke from one mouth, which bore the prayer to the spirit. The prayer, as one can hear verbatim, ran, "Zeus, make room for us!"

When the great man heard the noise of those that called upon the spirit by name, and from whom they sought adequate space for the city, he said, through one of the persons standing around him, that more room would be given them than they had ever prayed for. This speech from him was borne out to them as a rather somber declaration; for a plague succeeded this mass holiday. Songs of lamentation were straightway mingled with the dances and turned the delights among them into grief and affliction: in the place of pipes and castanets, repeated dirges possessed the city. Once the disease struck, faster than any expectation it spread like wildfire feeding on households. And the temples were filled with people suffering from the disease who fled there in hopes of healing. Springs, fountains, wells were filled with those on fire with thirst from the pestilential fever (whose fever the water could not quench and who both before and after drinking suffered alike, once the disease seized them). Many betook themselves like deserters to the cemeteries and the survivors no longer were enough to bury all the dead. An attack of the evil was not without forewarning for the people, but when a sort of phantasm appeared in a household about to be destroyed, then inevitably destruction would result.

The cause of the disease was evident to everyone: the spirit invoked by them was evilly answering the prayers of the foolish, making a baneful space within the city by means of the sickness. So they became the supplicants of the great man and besought him to put a stop to the destruction wrought by this ill through the God he knew and preached, who, they agreed, was the one true God and ruled all things. For from that phantasm appearing before a household's destruction and producing an instant despair of life, there was for the endangered people only one means of salvation, through having the great Gregory in the house, and so through prayer to repel the disease that fell upon it. Quickly, through those people who had been the first to be saved in such a way, the report spread about to everyone else; and all

seemed idle and in vain that had been valued previously by their foolishness—oracles, ablutions and hanging about idols.

They all now looked to the great priest. Each of them claimed him for himself, to save his whole family. His reward for those he saved was the salvation of their souls. For by that sort of demonstration the holiness of the priest was made plain. There was no longer any delay in agreeing to the holy mystery among those who had, through deeds, been taught the power of the faith. In this manner did the disease prove more salutary than good health among those men, for, as weak as had been their thoughts in good health, so far as concerned the reception of the holy rites, to the same degree were they made stronger toward faith through bodily sickness. So their error about their idols was tested and discovered—they all were turned toward the name of Christ, some guided to the truth by the affliction of the disease while others opposed faith in Christ as a safeguard against the plague.

There are other miracles of the great Gregory surviving in memory to this day, which we withhold from a disbelieving audience lest people be harmed supposing the truth a lie, through the sheer magnitude of the account; so we have not added these to what we have written. To Christ who performs such wonders through his servants be the fame, the glory and the supplication, now and forever, and for ages upon ages. Amen.

---

4. Hermas
THE SHEPHERD (c. 130 C.E.)

The Shepherd of Hermas unveils both the power and the potential divisiveness of charisma among early Christians. Little is known about the author except that he was a Roman freedman, living in the second century, who had experienced certain visions, which he then wrote down. His book includes five visions, twelve commands, and ten parables, all disclosed by an angel of penance disguised as a shepherd. The angel preaches the common Christian ideals of faith, chastity, and charity, as well as some insights about the gift of prophecy itself. Most notably, the shepherd draws sharp distinctions between the qualities of true and false prophets. This preoccupation with inspired leadership suggests that there was intense competition for followers, not just between Christians and pagans but among various Christian factions as well. Perhaps it was Hermas's recognition of the authority of local church leaders in determining the legitimacy of prophets that helped persuade many of them to include his book in early editions of the Christian Bible. Of course, by the end of the third century, when the present-day Bible was officially codified, learned consensus had decided otherwise, and Hermas was excluded from the Scriptures.

He [the angel] showed me men sitting on a bench, and another man sitting on a chair. And he said to me, Seest thou them that sit on the bench? I see them, sir, quoth I. These, quoth he, are faithful, but he that sitteth on the chair is a false prophet who destroyeth the servants of God; to wit, of the double-minded, but not of the faithful. These men of two minds then come to him as to a soothsayer, and ask him what [might] befall them; and the false prophet, having in himself no power of the divine Spirit, answereth them according to their demands and according to their unholy desires, and filleth their souls even as they wish. For being himself void, he gives void answers to the void; because, whatsoever he be asked, he answereth according to the emptiness of the man. Yet he speaketh some true words also; for the devil filleth him with his spirit, [in the hope that] he may be able to break some one of the righteous. As many therefore as have put on the truth and are strong in the faith of the Lord cleave not to such spirits but keep away from them. But men who are of two minds and often repent use divination like the heathen, and bring upon themselves the greater sin by their idolatry; for he that enquireth of a false prophet about any matter is an idolater and void of the truth and foolish. For any Spirit given of God is not enquired of, but having the power of the Godhead, it speaketh all things of itself, because it is from above, from the power of the divine Spirit. But the Spirit that is enquired of and speaketh according to the desires of men is earthly and light and hath no power, and it speaketh not all except it be enquired of.

How then, sir, quoth I, shall a man know which of them is a prophet and which a false prophet? Hear, quoth he, concerning both the prophets; and as I will now tell thee, so shalt thou [distinguish between] the prophet and the false prophet. From his life prove thou the man that has the divine Spirit. First he that hath the divine Spirit which is from above is meek and peaceable and lowly, and refraineth himself from every wickedness and vain desire of this world, and he maketh himself more needy than all men, and answereth nothing to any when enquired of, and speaketh not solitarily, neither when a man would speak doth the Holy Spirit speak; but when God willeth that he should speak, then he speaketh. Whensoever therefore the man who hath the divine Spirit cometh into a synagogue of just men who have faith in the divine Spirit, and the congregation of those men make their prayer unto God, then the Angel of the prophetic spirit which besetteth him filleth the man, and the man being filled with the Holy Spirit speaketh to the multitude as the Lord willeth. Thus then shall the Spirit of the Godhead be manifest. Concerning the divine Spirit of the Lord, such is its power.

Hear now, quoth he, about the spirit that is earthly and void and hath no power, but is foolish. First the man who thinketh that he hath the Spirit exalteth himself and wisheth to have the pre-eminence, and straightway he is heady and shameless and full of talk and [at ease] among many luxuries and other deceits; and he receiveth [payment] for his prophecy, and if he receive not he prophesieth not. Can then a divine Spirit receive [pay] and prophesy? It cannot be that a prophet of God should do this, but the spirit of such prophets is earthly. And then he never at all approacheth an assembly of righteous men, but fleeth from them. And he joineth himself to the double-minded and empty, and prophesieth unto them in corners, and deceiveth them by speaking in all things emptily according to their lusts; for it is to the empty that he replieth. Because an empty vessel set with empty ones is not crushed, but they agree with one another.

5. Tertullian
ON THE SOUL (c. 210 C.E.)

About the same time that *The Shepherd* appeared, an extremely charismatic and ultimately schismatic Christian prophet by the name of Montanus emerged in Phrygia (modern Turkey). Most of the details of his life are unknown to us, largely because almost all writings associated with him were later destroyed as heretical. Like Hermas, Montanus and his chief prophetesses, Maximilla and Priscilla, claimed direct inspiration by the Holy Spirit and visions of the world's end. They also shared Hermas's belief in the importance of extreme penance and asceticism among faithful Christians. Given the paucity of further details about Montanus's teaching, it is difficult to ascertain exactly why many prominent church leaders so strongly disapproved of Montanism. Only the influential Christian writer Tertullian (c. 160–c. 220 C.E.) consistently defended the movement, and in later life he actually converted to what was by then considered among most church authorities to be a schismatic heresy. In the following excerpt from a religious tract, Tertullian extols the belief that God does not reserve spiritual gifts, such as prophecy, for great historical figures such as John the Baptist, but also bestows them on ordinary Christians. Despite Tertullian's championing of Montanism, the movement had completely disappeared by the middle of the third century—though its legacy of unorthodox visions and other "gifts" would continue to divide Christians for centuries to come.

. . . For seeing that we acknowledge spiritual *charismata,* or gifts, we too have merited the attainment of the prophetic gift, although coming after John [the Baptist]. We have now amongst us a sister whose lot it has been to be favored with [various] gifts of revelation, which she experiences in the Spirit by ecstatic vision during the sacred rites of the Lord's Day in the church; she converses with angels, and sometimes even with the Lord; she both sees and hears mysterious communications; some men's hearts she understands, and to them who are in need she distributes remedies. Whether it be in the reading of the Scriptures, or in the chanting of psalms, or in the preaching of sermons, or in the offering up of prayers, in all these religious services matter and opportunity are afforded her of seeing visions. It may possibly have happened to us, whilst this sister of ours was rapt in the Spirit, that we had discoursed in some ineffable way about the soul. After the people are dismissed at the conclusion of the sacred services, she is in the regular habit of reporting to us whatever things she may have seen in vision; for all her communications are examined with the most scrupulous care, in order that their truth may be probed. "Amongst other things," says she, "there has been shown to me a soul in bodily shape, and a spirit has been in the habit of appearing to me; not, however, a void and empty illusion, but such as would offer itself to be even grasped by the hand, soft and transparent and of an ethereal color, and in form resembling that of a human being in every respect." This was her vision, and for her witness there was God; and the apostle most assuredly foretold [1 Cor 12:1–11] that there were to be Spiritual gifts in the Church.

C. Martyr

It was not surprising that early Christians, as members of an illicit cult, were frequently the victims of mob or state violence. What was often astounding—both to their persecutors and to subsequent Christians—was the courage and serenity many of these early victims displayed in the face of such brutality. Perhaps even more than charismatic preaching or healing, the strength of these "witnesses," or "martyrs," inspired many bystanders to embrace Christianity themselves, prompting the theologian Tertullian's famous exhortation that "the blood of the martyrs is seed." Their sacrificial deaths, which they believed had been foretold in the Book of Revelation (2:13, 17:6), provided inspiration for ever-growing numbers of converts. The reading of accounts of the martyrs' lives and deaths also became a focus of Christian worship. By the third century, this practice had evolved into an even more extensive cult of the martyrs, characterized by the veneration of certain relics—objects believed to be actual bones or tissue fragments from the martyrs' bodies—and certain locations that were associated with the martyrs' deeds or deaths (see 2D). Finally, in 313, the fortitude of the early Christians was rewarded. In that year, the emperor Constantine, himself a convert to Christianity, put a stop to all imperial persecution of Christianity and promoted the faith to the status of a legal religion. Subsequent Christians would find other opportunities to die for the faith—most notably in crusades and foreign missions—but the classical age of martyrdom had finally come to an end.

1. Anonymous
THE MARTYRDOMS OF PERPETUA AND FELICITAS (third century C.E.)

During the first two centuries of its existence, Christianity remained an underground religion, more often the victim of popular discrimination than of governmental purges. Although the empire encouraged the persecution and execution of Christians and other subversives—most famously during the emperor Nero's anti-Christian rampage in the year 64—the truly tiny church was generally considered more of an annoyance than a genuine threat and was thus only sporadically persecuted. The persecutions of the third century, by contrast, were very often initiated and orchestrated by imperial forces, most notably under Septimus Severus (193–211) and Decius (249–251), who launched the first empirewide persecutions. The martyrdoms of Perpetua and Felicitas took place in North Africa in about 203, during the Severan persecution. Perpetua's account, partly told in her own words, was intended to present a more personalized and even domestic perspective of the martyr's ordeal. This story of the torture and execution of a young nursing mother from a respectable family and her pregnant servant presents in dramatic detail the contrast between the gentleness and courage of the early Christian martyrs and the cruelty of their persecutors. The document is also heavily apocalyptic, with many references to the Book of Revelation as well as "new," possibly Montanist, prophecies. In this respect, it also provides a reasonably accurate portrait of the North African church as it entered its most trying era.

A number of young catechumens[28] were arrested, Revocatus and his fellow slave Felicitas, Saturninus and Secundulus, and with them Vibia Perpetua, a newly married woman of good family and upbringing. Her mother and father were still alive and one of her two brothers was a catechumen like herself. She was about twenty-two years old and had an infant son at the breast. (Now from this point on the entire account of her ordeal is her own, according to her own ideas and in the way that she herself wrote it down.)

While we were still under arrest (she said) my father out of love for me was trying to persuade me and shake my resolution. "Father," said I, "do you see this vase here, for example, or waterport or whatever?"

"Yes, I do," said he.

And I told him: "Could it be called by any other name than what it is?"

And he said: "No."

"Well, so too I cannot be called anything other than what I am, a Christian."

At this my father was so angered by the word "Christian" that he moved towards me as though he would pluck my eyes out. But he left it at that and departed, vanquished along with his diabolical arguments.

For a few days afterwards I gave thanks to the Lord that I was separated from my father,

and I was comforted by his absence. During these few days I was baptized, and I was inspired by the Spirit not to ask for any other favor after the water but simply the perseverance of the flesh. A few days later we were lodged in the prison; and I was terrified, as I had never before been in such a dark hole. What a difficult time it was! With the crowd the heat was stifling; then there was the extortion of the soldiers; and to crown all, I was tortured with worry for my baby there.

Then Tertius and Pomponius, those blessed deacons who tried to take care of us, bribed the soldiers to allow us to go to a better part of the prison to refresh ourselves for a few hours. Everyone then left that dungeon and shifted for himself. I nursed my baby, who was faint from hunger. In my anxiety I spoke to my mother about the child, I tried to comfort my brother, and I gave the child in their charge. I was in pain because I saw them suffering out of pity for me. These were the trials I had to endure for many days. Then I got permission for my baby to stay with me in prison. At once I recovered my health, relieved as I was of my worry and anxiety over the child. My prison had suddenly become a palace, so that I wanted to be there rather than anywhere else.

Then my brother said to me: "Dear sister, you are greatly privileged; surely you might ask for a vision to discover whether you are to be condemned or freed."

Faithfully I promised that I would, for I knew that I could speak with the Lord, whose

---

[28] A probationary status before baptism, sometimes lasting years.

great blessings I had come to experience. And so I said: "I shall tell you tomorrow." Then I made my request and this was the vision I had.

I saw a ladder of tremendous height made of bronze, reaching all the way to the heavens, but it was so narrow that only one person could climb up at a time. To the sides of the ladder were attached all sorts of metal weapons: there were swords, spears, hooks, daggers, and spikes; so that if anyone tried to climb up carelessly or without paying attention, he would be mangled and his flesh would adhere to the weapons.

At the foot of the ladder lay a dragon [cf. Rev 12:3] of enormous size, and it would attack those who tried to climb up and try to terrify them from doing so. And Saturus was the first to go up, he who was later to give himself up of his own accord. He had been the builder of our strength, although he was not present when we were arrested. And he arrived at the top of the staircase and he looked back and said to me: "Perpetua, I am waiting for you. But take care; do not let the dragon bite you."

"He will not harm me," I said, "in the name of Christ Jesus."

Slowly, as though he were afraid of me, the dragon stuck his head out from underneath the ladder. Then, using it as my first step, I trod on his head and went up.

Then I saw an immense garden, and in it a gray-haired man sat in shepherd's garb; tall he was, and milking sheep. And standing around him were many thousands of people clad in white garments. He raised his head, looked at me, and said: "I am glad you have come, my child."

He called me over to him and gave me, as it were, a mouthful of the milk he was drawing; and I took it into my cupped hands and consumed it. And all those who stood around said: "Amen!" At the sound of this word I came to, with the taste of something sweet still in my mouth. I at once told this to my brother, and we realized that we would have to suffer, and that from now on we would no longer have any hope in this life.

A few days later there was a rumor that we were going to be given a hearing. My father also arrived from the city, worn with worry, and he came to see me with the idea of persuading me.

"Daughter," he said, "have pity on my gray head—have pity on me your father, if I deserve to be called your father, if I have favored you above all your brothers, if I have raised you to reach this prime of your life. Do not abandon me to be the reproach of men. Think of your brothers, think of your mother and your aunt, think of your child, who will not be able to live once you are gone. Give up your pride! You will destroy all of us! None of us will ever be able to speak freely again if anything happens to you."

This was the way my father spoke out of love for me, kissing my hands and throwing himself down before me. With tears in his eyes he no longer addressed me as his daughter but as a woman. I was sorry for my father's sake, because he alone of all my kin would be unhappy to see me suffer.

I tried to comfort him saying: "It will all happen in the prisoner's dock as God wills; for you may be sure that we are not left to ourselves but are all in his power."

And he left me in great sorrow.

One day while we were eating breakfast we were suddenly hurried off for a hearing. We arrived at the forum, and straight away the story went about the neighborhood near the forum and a huge crowd gathered. We walked up to the prisoner's dock. All the others when questioned admitted their guilt. Then, when it came my turn, my father appeared with my son, dragged me from the step, and said: "Perform the sacrifice—have pity on your baby!"

Hilarianus the governor, who had received his judicial powers as the successor of the late proconsul Minucius Timinianus, said to me: "Have pity on your father's gray head; have pity on your infant son. Offer the sacrifice for the welfare of the emperors."

"I will not," I retorted.

"Are you a Christian?" said Hilarianus.

And I said: "Yes, I am."

When my father persisted in trying to dissuade me, Hilarianus ordered him to be thrown to the ground and beaten with a rod. I felt sorry for father, just as if I myself had been beaten. I felt sorry for his pathetic old age.

Then Hilarianus passed sentence on all of us: we were condemned to the beasts, and we returned to the prison in high spirits. But my baby had got used to being nursed at the breast and to staying with me in prison. So I sent the deacon Pomponius straight away to my father to ask for the baby. But father refused to give him over. But as God willed, the baby had no further desire for the breast, nor did I suffer any inflammation; and so I was relieved of any anxiety for my child and of any discomfort in my breasts. . . .

As for Felicitas, she too enjoyed the Lord's favor in this wise. She had been pregnant when she was arrested, and was now in her eighth month. As the day of the spectacle drew near she was very distressed that her martyrdom would be postponed because of her pregnancy; for it is against the law for women with child to be executed. Thus she might have to shed her holy, innocent blood afterwards along with others who were common criminals. Her comrades in martyrdom were also saddened; for they were afraid that they would have to leave behind so fine a companion to travel alone on the same road to hope. And so, two days before the contest, they poured forth a prayer to the Lord in one torrent of common grief. And immediately after their prayer the birth pains came upon her. She suffered a good deal in her labor because of the natural difficulty of an eight months' delivery.

Hence one of the assistants of the prison guards said to her: "You suffer so much now— what will you do when you are tossed to the beasts? Little did you think of them when you refused to sacrifice."

"What I am suffering now," she replied, "I suffer by myself. But then another will be inside me who will suffer for me, just as I shall be suffering for him."

And she gave birth to a girl; and one of the sisters brought her up as her own daughter. . . .

[Here the account switches from Perpetua's voice back to the narrator's.]

The military tribune had treated them with extraordinary severity because on the information of certain very foolish people he became afraid that they would be spirited out of the prison by magical spells.

Perpetua spoke to him directly. "Why can you not even allow us to refresh ourselves properly? For we are the most distinguished of the condemned prisoners, seeing that we belong to the emperor; we are to fight on his very birthday. Would it not be to your credit if we were brought forth on the day in a healthier condition?"

The officer became disturbed and grew red. So it was that he gave the order that they were to be more humanely treated; and he allowed her brothers and other persons to visit, so that the prisoners could dine in their company. . . .

The day of their victory dawned, and they marched from the prison to the amphitheater joyfully as though they were going to heaven, with calm faces, trembling, if at all, with joy rather than fear. Perpetua went along with shining countenance and calm step, as the beloved of God, as a wife of Christ, putting down everyone's stare by her own intense gaze. With them also was Felicitas, glad that she had safely given birth so that now she could fight the beasts, going from one blood bath to another, from the midwife to the gladiator, ready to wash after childbirth in a second baptism.

They were then led up to the gates and the men were forced to put on the robes of priests of Saturn, the women the dress of the priestesses of Ceres. But the noble Perpetua strenuously resisted this to the end.

"We came to this of our own free will, that our freedom should not be violated. We agreed to pledge our lives provided that we would do no such thing. You agreed with us to do this."

Even injustice recognized justice. The military tribune agreed. They were to be brought into the arena just as they were. Perpetua then began to sing a psalm: she was already treading on the head of the Egyptian.[29] Revocatus, Saturninus, and Saturus began to warn the onlooking mob. Then when they came within sight of Hilarianus, they suggested by their motions and gestures: "You have condemned us, but God will condemn you" was what they were saying.

At this the crowds became enraged and demanded that they be scourged before a line of gladiators. And they rejoiced at this that they had obtained a share in the Lord's sufferings.

But he who said, *Ask and you shall receive* [Jn 16:24], answered their prayer by giving each one the death he had asked for. For whenever they would discuss among themselves their desire for martyrdom, Saturninus indeed insisted that he wanted to be exposed to all the different beasts, that his crown might be all the more glorious. And so at the outset of the contest he and Revocatus were matched with a leopard, and then while in the stocks they were attacked by a bear. As for Saturus, he dreaded nothing more than a bear, and he counted on being killed by one bite of the leopard. Then he was matched with a wild boar; but the gladiator who had tied him to the animal was gored by the boar and died a few days after the contest, whereas Saturus was only dragged along. Then when he was bound in the stocks awaiting the bear, the animal refused to come out of the cages, so that Saturus was called back once more unhurt.

For the young women, however, the Devil had prepared a mad heifer. This was an unusual animal, but it was chosen that their sex might be matched with that of the beast. So they were stripped naked, placed in nets and thus brought out into the arena. Even the crowd was horrified when they saw that one was a delicate young girl and the other was a woman fresh from childbirth with the milk still dripping from her breasts. And so they were brought back again and dressed in unbelted tunics.

First the heifer tossed Perpetua and she fell on her back. Then sitting up she pulled down the tunic that was ripped along the side so that it covered her thighs, thinking more of her modesty than of her pain. Next she asked for a pin to fasten her untidy hair: for it was not right that a martyr should die with her hair in disorder, lest she might seem to be mourning in her hour of triumph.[30]

Then she got up. And seeing that Felicitas had been crushed to the ground, she went over to her, gave her hand, and lifted her up. Then the two stood side by side. But the cruelty of the mob was by now appeased, and so they were called back though the Gate of Life.

There Perpetua was held up by a man named Rusticus who was at the time a catechumen and kept close to her. She awoke from a kind of sleep (so absorbed had she been in ecstasy in the Spirit) and she began to look about her. Then to the amazement of all she said: "When are we going to be thrown to that heifer or whatever it is?"

When told that this had already happened, she refused to believe it until she noticed the marks of her rough experience on her person and her dress. Then she called for her brother and spoke to him together with the catechumens and said: "You must all stand fast in the faith and love one another, and do not be weakened by what we have gone through."

. . . Shortly after he [Saturus] was thrown unconscious with the rest in the usual spot to have his throat cut. But the mob asked that their bodies be brought out into the open that their eyes might be the guilty witnesses of the sword that pierced their flesh. And so the martyrs got up and went to the spot of their own accord as the people wanted them to, and kissing one another they sealed their martyrdom

---

[29]Perpetua's opponent in a previous dream; also possibly a reference to the conflict between Moses and the Egyptian pharaoh (cf. Gen. 3:15).

[30]Disheveled hair and torn clothing were customary signs of mourning in the ancient world. This should not be interpreted as last-minute vanity on the part of Perpetua but rather as evidence of great personal dignity.

with the ritual kiss of peace. The others took the sword in silence and without moving, especially Saturus, who being the first to climb the stairway was the first to die. For once again he was waiting for Perpetua. Perpetua, however, had yet to taste more pain. She screamed as she was struck on the bone; then she took the trembling hand of the young gladiator and guided it to her throat. It was as though so great a woman, feared as she was by the unclean spirit, could not be dispatched unless she herself were willing.

---

2. Eusebius
THE ECCLESIASTICAL HISTORY (c. 310 C.E.)

In his widely respected *Ecclesiastical History*, the bishop Eusebius of Caesarea (c. 260–340) tells another story from the Severan persecution. In Egypt, then part of the Roman Empire, many Christians were also executed, including one Leonides, whose son Origen (c. 185–254) would later become a renowned theologian. Eusebius, who was writing during the subsequent (and final) great persecution of Christians under the emperor Diocletian (301–311), looks back over the years and recounts the affecting tale of the boy Origen's thirst to join his father in martyrdom and his mother's ingenious prevention of the same. Origen went on to become a great biblical scholar and eventually to lead the highly influential Catechetical School at Alexandria, but his appetite for the "martyr's crown" never waned. Ultimately, as an old man, he was indeed imprisoned and tortured for the faith during the persecution of Decius in 250. Origen died a few years later, his passion remaining an inspiration for persecuted Christians for years to come.

Now when Severus also was stirring up persecution against the churches, in every place splendid martyrdoms of the champions of piety were accomplished, but with especial frequency at Alexandria. Thither, as to some great arena, were escorted from Egypt and the whole Thebais[31] God's champions, who, through their most steadfast endurance in diverse tortures and modes of death, were wreathed with the crowns laid up with God. Among these was Leonides, known as "the father of Origen," who was beheaded, leaving his son behind him quite young. It will not be out of place to describe briefly how deliberately the boy's mind was set on the Divine Word from that early age, especially as the story about him has received exceedingly widespread notoriety.

. . . Severus was in the tenth year of his reign [203 C.E.], and Laetus was governor of Alexandria and the rest of Egypt, and Demetrius had just then received the episcopate of the communities there in succession to Julian. When, therefore, the flame of persecution was kindled to a fierce blaze, and countless numbers were being wreathed with the crowns of martyrdom, Origen's soul was possessed with such a passion for martyrdom, while he was still quite a boy, that he was all eagerness to come to close quarters with danger, and to leap forward and rush into the conflict. In fact, it were but a very little step and the end of his life was at hand, had not the divine and heavenly Providence, acting for the general good through his mother, stood in the way of his zeal. She, at all events, at first had recourse to verbal entreaties, bidding him spare a mother's feelings; then, when he learnt

---

[31]An area of Egypt in which the city of Thebes is located.

that his father had been captured and was kept in prison, and his whole being was set on the desire for martyrdom, perceiving that his purpose was more resolute than ever, she hid all his clothes, and so laid upon him the necessity of remaining at home. And since nothing else remained for him to do, and a zeal, intense beyond his years, suffered him not to be quiet, he sent his father a letter on martyrdom most strongly urging him on, in which he advises him in these very words, saying: "Take care not to change thy mind on our account." Let this be recorded as the first proof of Origen's boyish readiness of mind and genuine love of godliness.

D. Philosophy

Philosophy represented a decisive alternative to the popular mixture of traditional beliefs and practices that comprised ancient *pietas*. All self-professed "lovers of wisdom" (Greek *philo* +*sophia*) agreed that human happiness was not to be attained through cultivating beneficial relations with the gods, especially since the majority of philosophers believed that the gods (if they existed at all) were supremely indifferent to human affairs. Most of them therefore taught a kind of self-liberation from worldly pain and suffering, available to anyone willing to cast aside customs (*nomoi*) and think about humans and the cosmos in a different manner. Belief and understanding thus played a much more pivotal role among philosophers than among most practitioners of traditional religion, which emphasized proper worship. It is important to stress, however, that the "schools" of philosophy that emerged from the fourth century B.C.E. through late antiquity were not involved in the removed, theoretical contemplation that the term "philosophy" calls to mind today but in finding (and practicing) a "right" way of living. Though these schools often differed widely on the issue of what constituted such right living, all shared at least two fundamental beliefs: 1) that Nature (*physis*) could be sufficiently grasped by the intellect to provide some guidance; and 2) that the key to personal happiness was to attain self-sufficiency within the cosmic order. Of course, this still left considerable room for disagreement on the definition of "happiness" as well as the specific means to achieving it. Reason was commonly cited as the guiding principle among all philosophers. But it is important to note that each of the philosophical schools based its teachings on a series of unproveable assumptions. Although the systems of belief the philosophers derived from these assumptions were developed by the use of rational thought, the assumptions themselves were essentially ideas to be taken on faith and were thus, in that sense, similar to the beliefs upon which religions were based.

The Christian emphasis on faith and special knowledge (*gnosis*)—over and above ritual sacrifice and worship—resulted in some superficial similarities to many pagan philosophies. During the first century, though, the proper Christian *gnosis* remained firmly grounded in Jewish traditions and added only a few new core articles of belief, known collectively as the *kerygma* ("proclamation"). These were: the death and resurrection of Jesus the Messiah; the power of the Holy Spirit; baptism and the forgiveness of sins; and a blessed afterlife for the faithful. By the second century, however, the growth and dispersion of Christian congregations throughout the empire increased the need for a more clearly defined set of Christian beliefs or philosophy. Without such a defined faith, Christianity ran the risk of devolving into a host of isolated congregations with many different—and even conflicting—interpretations of Jesus' life and teachings. Some of the doctrinal issues that arose during this period, such as the definition of a Christian canon of writings (i.e., the Old and New Testaments), were accomplished by the time the emperor Constantine proclaimed Christianity a tolerated religion in 313. Others, such as the debate over the value of Greco-Roman philosophy for Christians, have yet to be resolved among Christian churches today. Most importantly, the Christian "philosophy," or *gnosis*, which emerged from these early conflicts represented a much more sophisticated formulation of doctrine and belief than the *kerygma*, thus meriting new intellectual respect, if not acceptance, among pagan philosophers of the day.

1. Marcus Aurelius
MEDITATIONS (c. 180 C.E.)

By the time of Jesus, there were numerous philosophical schools vying for converts and followers. Many shared an atomist view of the cosmos, believing that the tiniest pieces of all matter ("atoms") were constantly rearranged into different forms, both living and not. The immediate implications of this belief were that there was no eternal individual soul, no reward or punishment in an afterlife, and that in fact the gods were generally indifferent about humans altogether. Though they shared a common rejection of traditional religious teachings, the atomist schools drew radically different conclusions about "right living." Cynics such as Diogenes of Sinope (c. 400–325 B.C.E.), for instance, believed that happiness lay in complete freedom from all social constraints, including freedom from unquestioned political allegiances as well as freedom from conformity to social conventions as seemingly innocuous as bathing. Epicurians, on the other hand, believed that, given the absence of an afterlife, one must therefore seek the maximum pleasure possible in this short existence, chiefly through intellectual stimulation, but also through enjoying fine foods and the company of good friends.

Perhaps the most influential philosophical school for ancient Christians, though, was that of the Stoics. The Roman emperor Marcus Aurelius (121–180 C.E.) was a staunch advocate of Stoicism, and this excerpt from his private writings provides us with a brief glimpse of its teachings and appeal. A real-life philosopher-king, Marcus Aurelius was both highly educated in the classics and actively involved in politics and war. His "Meditations" were in fact probably composed during one of his frequent military campaigns. Like the Cynic and the Epicurean, the Stoic seeks his happiness in this life; unlike them, he looks for it in a willing submission to the order of things and in an unending attempt to make reason the master of emotion. Like the Christians he detests, Marcus Aurelius looks for peace from within and leaves the course of human and natural events to "Providence." In this way, the Stoic emperor represents a bridge between the self-reliance of most pagan philosophies and Christian reliance on divine grace. Later Christian thinkers such as John Calvin were especially appreciative of the ethics if not the metaphysics of Stoic teaching.

Begin the morning by saying to thyself, I shall meet with the busybody, the ungrateful, arrogant, deceitful, envious, unsocial. All these things happen to them by reason of their ignorance of what is good and evil. But I who have seen the nature of the good that it is beautiful and of the bad that it is ugly, and the nature of him who does wrong, that it is akin to me, not [only] of the same blood or seed, but that it participates in [the same] intelligence and [the same] portion of the divinity, I can neither be injured by any of them, for no one can fix on me what is ugly, nor can I be angry with my kinsman, nor hate him. For we are made for co-operation, like feet, like hands, like eyelids, like the rows of the upper and lower teeth. To act against one another then is contrary to nature; and it is acting against one another to be vexed and to turn away.

Whatever this is that I am, it is a little flesh and breath, and the ruling part. Throw away thy books; no longer distract thyself: it is not allowed; but as if thou wast now dying, despise the flesh, it is blood and bones and a network, a contexture of nerves, veins and arteries. See the breath also, what kind of a thing it is; air, and not always the same, but every moment sent out and again sucked in. The third then is the ruling part: consider thus: Thou art an old man; no longer let this be a slave, no longer be pulled by the strings like a puppet to unsocial movements, no longer be either dissatisfied with thy present lot, or shrink from the future.

All that is from the gods is full of providence. That which is from fortune is not separated from nature or without an interweaving and involution with the things which are ordered by Providence. From thence all things flow, and there is

besides necessity, and that which is for the advantage of the whole universe, of which thou art a part. But that is good for every part of nature which the nature of the whole brings, and what serves to maintain this nature. Now the universe is preserved, as by the changes of the elements so by the changes of things compounded of the elements. Let these principles be enough for thee; let them always be fixed opinions. But cast away the thirst after books, that thou mayest not die murmuring, but cheerfully, truly, and from thy heart thankful to the gods.

Remember how long thou hast been putting off these things, and how often thou hast received an opportunity from the gods, and yet dost not use of it. Thou must now at last perceive of what universe thou art a part, and of what administrator of the universe thy existence is an efflux, and that a limit of time is fixed for thee, which if thou dost not use for clearing away the clouds from thy mind, it will go and thou wilt go, and it will never return.

Every moment think steadily as a Roman and a man to do what thou hast in hand with perfect and simple dignity, and feeling of affection, and freedom, and justice; and to give thyself relief from all other thoughts. And thou wilt give thyself relief, if thou doest every act of thy life as if it were the last, laying aside all carelessness and passionate aversion from the commands of reason, and all hypocrisy, and self-love, and discontent with the portion which has been given thee. Thou seest how few the things are, the which if a man lays hold of, he is able to live a life which flows in quiet, and is like the existence of the gods; for the gods on their part will require nothing more from him who observes these things.

Do wrong to thyself, do wrong to thyself, my soul; but thou wilt no longer have the opportunity of honoring thyself. Every man's life is sufficient. But thine is nearly finished, though thy soul reverences not itself, but places thy felicity in the souls of others.

Do the things external which fall upon thee distract thee? Give thyself time to learn something new and good, and cease to be whirled around. But then thou must also avoid being carried about the other way. For those too are triflers who have wearied themselves in life by their activity, and yet have no object to which to direct every movement, and, in a word, all their thoughts.

Through not observing what is in the mind of another a man has seldom been seen to be unhappy; but those who do not observe the movements of their own minds must of necessity be unhappy.

This thou must always bear in mind, what is the nature of the whole, and what is my nature, and how this is related to that, and what kind of a part it is of what kind of a whole; and that there is no one who hinders thee from always doing and saying the things which are according to the nature of which thou art a part.

Theophrastus,[32] in his comparison of bad acts—such a comparison as one would make in accordance with the common notions of mankind—says, like a true philosopher, that the offenses which are committed through desire are more blamable than those which are committed through anger. For he who is excited by anger seems to turn away from reason with a certain pain and unconscious contraction; but he who offends through desire, being overpowered by pleasure, seems to be in a manner more intemperate and more womanish in his offences. Rightly then, and in a way worthy of philosophy, he said that the offense which is committed with pleasure is more blamable

than that which is committed with pain; and on the whole the one is more like a person who has been first wronged and through pain is compelled to be angry; but the other is moved by his own impulse to do wrong, being carried toward doing something by desire.

Since it is possible that thou mayest depart from life this very moment, regulate every act and thought accordingly. But to go away from among men, if there are gods, is not a thing to be afraid of, for the gods will not involve thee in evil; but if indeed they do not exist, or if they have no concern about human affairs, what is it to me to live in a universe devoid of gods or devoid of providence? But in truth they do exist, and they do care for human things, and they have put all the means in man's power to enable him not to fall into real evils. And as to the rest, if there was anything evil, they would have provided for this also, that it should be altogether in a man's power not to fall into it. Now, that which does not make a man worse, how can it make a man's life worse? But neither through ignorance, nor having the knowledge, but not the power to guard against or correct these things, is it possible that the nature of the universe has overlooked them; nor is it possible that it has made so great a mistake, either through want of power or want of skill, that good and evil should happen indiscriminately to the good and the bad. But death certainly, and life, honor and dishonor, pain and pleasure, all these things equally happen to good men and bad, being things which make us neither better nor worse. Therefore they are neither good nor evil.

How quickly all these things disappear, in the universe the bodies themselves, but in time the remembrance of them; what is the nature of all sensible things, and particularly those which attract with the bait of pleasure or terrify by pain, or are noised about by vapory fame; how worthless, and contemptible, and sordid and perishable, and dead they are—this it is the part of the intellectual faculty to observe. To observe too who these are whose opinions and voices give reputation; what death is, and the

---

[32]Philosopher (c. 370–287 B.C.E.) who was Aristotle's pupil and successor as head of the Peripatetic school of philosophy in Athens. He was best known for his minor work on the thirty types of human character.

fact that, if a man looks at it in itself, and by the abstractive power of reflection resolves into their parts all the things which present themselves to the imagination in it, he will then consider it to be nothing else than an operation of nature; and if any one is afraid of an operation of nature he is a child. This, however, is not only an operation of nature, but it is also a thing which conduces to the purposes of nature. To observe, too, how man comes near to the Deity, and by what part of him, and when this part of man is so disposed.

Nothing is more wretched than a man who traverses everything in a round, and pries into things beneath the earth, as the poet says, and seeks by conjecture what is in the minds of his neighbors, without perceiving that it is sufficient to attend to the daemon[33] within him, and to reverence it sincerely. And reverence of the daemon consists in keeping it pure from passion and thoughtlessness, and dissatisfaction with what comes from gods and men. For the things from the gods merit veneration for their excellence; and the things from men should be dear to us by reason of kinship; and sometimes even, in a manner, they move our pity by reason of men's ignorance of good and bad; this defect being not less than that which deprives us of the power of distinguishing things that are white and black.

Though thou shouldest be going to live three thousand years, and as many times ten thousand years, still remember that no man loses any other life than this which he now lives, nor lives any other than this which he now loses. The longest and shortest are thus brought to the same. For the present is the same to all, though that which perishes is not the same; and so that which is lost appears to be a mere moment. For a man cannot lose either the past or the future: for what a man has not, how can any one take this from him? These two

things then thou must bear in mind: the one, that all things from eternity are of like forms and come round in a circle, and that it makes no difference whether a man shall see the same things during a hundred years or two hundred, or an infinite time; and the second, that the longest liver and he who will die soonest lose just the same. For the present is the only thing of which a man can be deprived, if it is true that this is the only thing which he has, and that a man cannot lose a thing if he has it not.

Remember that all is opinion. For what was said by the Cynic Monimus[34] is manifest: and manifest too is the use of what was said, if a man receives what may be got out of it as far as it is true.

The soul of man does violence to itself, first of all when it becomes an abscess and, as it were, a tumor on the universe, so far as it can. For to be vexed at anything which happens is a separation of ourselves from nature, in some part of which the natures of all other things are contained. In the next place, the soul does violence to itself when it turns away from any man, or even moves towards him with the intention of injuring, such as are the souls of those who are angry. In the third place, the soul does violence to itself when it is overpowered by pleasure or by pain. Fourthly, when it plays a part, and does or says anything insincerely and untruly. Fifthly, when it allows any act of its own and any movement to be without an aim, and does anything thoughtlessly and without considering what it is, it being right that even the smallest things be done with reference to an end; and the end of rational animals is to follow the reason and the law of the most ancient city and polity.

Of the human life the time is a point, and the substance is in a flux, and the perception dull, and the composition of the whole body subject to putrefaction, and the soul of a whirl,

---

[33]Not in this sense a foreign or evil presence but a divine "spirit," with no particular personal identity. Heracleitus equaled it with the power to shape one's own destiny.

[34]Corinthian slave who feigned madness to obtain his liberty and follow the Cynic philosopher Diogenes (c. 400–c. 325 B.C.E.).

and fortune hard to divine, and fame a thing devoid of judgment. And, to say all in a word, everything which belongs to the body is a stream, and what belongs to the soul is a dream and a vapor, and life is a warfare and a stranger's sojourn, and after-fame is oblivion. What, then, is that which is able to conduct a man? One thing, and only one—philosophy. But, this consists in keeping the daemon within a man free from violence and unharmed, superior to pains and pleasures, doing nothing without a purpose, nor yet falsely and with hypocrisy, not feeling the need of another man's doing or not doing anything; and be-

sides, accepting all that happens, and all that is allotted, as coming from thence, wherever it is, from whence he himself came; and, finally, waiting for death with a cheerful mind, as being nothing else than a dissolution of the elements of which every living being is compounded. But if there is no harm to the elements themselves in each continually changing into another, why should a man have any apprehension about the change and dissolution of all the elements? For it is according to nature, and nothing is evil which is according to nature.

---

2. Philo of Alexandria
ON THE PRELIMINARY STUDIES (c. 30 C.E.)

Philo of Alexandria (c. 20 B.C.E.–50 C.E.) represents a unique type of philosophical bridge in the ancient world. In addition to his Stoic, Neo-Pythagorean, and especially Platonist leanings, Philo was a devout Jew. His numerous writings on a variety of subjects all maintained the principal objective of establishing for Jewish scriptures and teachings the same intellectual credentials enjoyed by Gentile philosophies. Like many other Hellenistic Jews, Philo sought to bridge the gap between the two parts of his personal identity. On the one hand, he considered the Hebrew Bible divinely inspired and God's covenant with his chosen people still fully intact. On the other hand, he agreed with many Gentile philosophers about the superiority of the soul to the body and the chiefly intellectual nature of true happiness. His solution to this inner conflict was to apply the techniques of Greek allegorical exegesis, or analysis, to the Bible, illustrating the compatibility of both types of belief. Thus in this excerpt from one of his many philosophical writings, the biblical story of Sarah—who, unable to bear her husband Abraham a son, offers him her servant Hagar as a concubine—becomes an allegory of the relationship between piety and philosophy. In Philo's interpretation, the figure of Sarah represents generic virtue or wisdom, and her servant Hagar symbolizes philosophy and its component liberal arts, such as rhetoric, grammar, and geometry. Significantly, though Hagar is more fertile (and thus useful to Abraham), she remains subordinate to Sarah, who also represents faith and good action, as opposed to empty philosophical words. Thus Philo does not disparage philosophy but rather relegates it to a position supporting true piety. In addition to Platonist mind-body dualism and Stoic self-control, the later Christian concept of the divine *Logos* (Word; Idea; Plan), is a key notion in Philo's thought, although Philo does not consider the *Logos* to be synonymous with an actual Messiah, as it would be among later Christian theologians. Most importantly, Philo attempts, as would the medieval theologian Thomas Aquinas, to find an acceptable relationship between philosophy and faith, extolling the usefulness of the former while never forgetting its subordination to the latter.

"Sarah the wife of Abraham was not bearing him children. Now she had an Egyptian maidservant named Hagar. And Sarah said to Abraham, 'Behold the Lord has closed me that I should not bear. Go in unto my maid that you may beget children from her'" [Gen 16:1, 2]. Sarah's name translated signifies "my sovereignty," and the wisdom in me, the self-control in me, the individual justice and each of the other virtues that belong only to me, are my sovereignty alone. That sovereignty has charge over me and rules me who have resolved to obey her, since she is by nature a queen.

This power Moses quite paradoxically represents both as barren and as exceedingly prolific, since he acknowledges that from her was produced the most populous of nations. For virtue is truly sterile in respect of all that is bad, whereas she is so prolific of the virtues as not to require the art of midwifery, for she bears before the midwife comes. Animals and plants bear the fruit proper to them only after long intervals, once or twice at most in the year, in accordance with the number established for each by nature and harmonized with the annual seasons. But virtue, knowing no such intervals, ever bears unceasingly and uninterruptedly, without time pause, not infants, to be sure, but good words, blameless plans, and praiseworthy acts.

But as wealth that one cannot use does not benefit its possessor, so it is with wisdom's fertility, if she does not bear offspring that is profitable for ourselves. Some she judges quite worthy of living with her, but others do not appear to her to have attained the maturity to submit to her commendable and moderate domesticity. To these she permits the execution of the preliminaries of marriage and affords the hope of celebrating the full marriage rite in the future.

So Sarah, the virtue ruling my soul, engendered, but did not engender for me. For in my youthfulness I was not yet able to receive her offspring, wisdom, justice, piety, because of the multitude of bastard children whom empty imaginings had borne to me. The nurture of these, the constant pains and ceaseless cares, compelled me to neglect the genuinely true citizens. It is well then to pray that virtue may not only engender (she is prolific even without our prayer), but also may engender for ourselves, so that we may share in what she sows and produces and be truly happy. For she customarily engenders for God alone, thankfully rendering the first fruits of the goods she has obtained to him who, as Moses says, opens the very virgin womb [Gen 29:31].

Thus, too, the candelabrum, the archetypal pattern of its later copy, gives light from one part only, namely that which is directed toward God. For being seventh and situated in the middle of six branches, divided two ways into triads that guard it on either side, it sends its rays upward toward the Existent, considering its light too bright for mortal sight to impinge on it [Ex 25: 37, 31].

For this reason Moses does not say that Sarah did not engender, but only that she did not engender for some particular person. For we are not yet capable of receiving the seed of virtue unless we have first mated with her handmaiden, and the handmaiden of wisdom is the general culture gained through the preliminary learning of the schools. For just as in houses there are outer entrances in front of the apartment doors, and in cities suburbs through which we are able to proceed into the interior part, so the school course precedes virtue; the former is a route that leads to the latter.

We must understand that great themes require great introductions, and the greatest of all themes is virtue, for it is concerned with the greatest of materials, the entire life of man. It is thus natural that it will employ no minor preludes, but grammar, geometry, astronomy, rhetoric, music, and all the other branches of intellectual theory. These are symbolized by Hagar, the handmaid of Sarah, as we shall show. For Sarah, we are told, said to Abraham: *"Behold the Lord has closed me that I should not bear, go in unto my maid that you may beget children from her."* We must exclude from the present discussion bodily unisons or intercourse having pleasure as its object. The union in question is a mating of mind with virtue, a mind desirous of having children by her, and if it is unable to do so immediately, it is instructed to be betrothed to her handmaid, the intermediate education. . . .

Grammar teaches us the accounts of both poets and prose writers and produces intelligence and vast knowledge. It will teach us also to despise all that our empty imaginings falsely invent, through the misadventures that heroes and demigods who are celebrated by them are said to have experienced. Music will charm away the unrhythmic by its rhythm, the disharmonic by its harmony, the out of tune and unmelodious by its melody, and thus bring concord out of discord. Geometry will implant in the soul that loves to learn the seeds of equality and proportion, and by the subtlety of its sequential speculations will produce a zeal for justice. Rhetoric, sharpening the mind for speculation and exercising and welding thought to expression, will render man truly rational, thus cultivating the peculiar and remarkable gift that nature has not bestowed on any other living creature. Dialectic, the sister and twin, as some have said, of Rhetoric, by distinguishing true arguments from false and refuting plausible sophistries, will heal that great disease of the soul, deceit.

It is profitable then to associate with these and similar disciplines and train in them in a preliminary way; for perhaps, yea perhaps, as it has happened with many, we shall through the vassals be made acquainted with the sovereign virtues. Similarly consider that the encyclical studies with the subject matter belonging to each of them are prepared as childhood nourishment for the soul, whereas the perfect and proper food for those who are truly men are the virtues. . . .

Now it belongs to the best of races, Israel, to see the best, the truly Existent, for Israel means seeing God. The kind that aims at the second place sees the second, the sense-perceptible heaven, and the harmonious order of stars within it, with their truly musical orbital motion. Third are the skeptics, who do not apply themselves to the best things in nature, whether sensible or intelligible, but are engrossed with petty quibbles and wrangling over trifles. With them swells the concubine Reuma, who "sees something," even if the most minute, for they are incapable of going in quest of the better things by which they might bring profit to their lives. As in the practice of medicine, the so-called word therapy is far removed from yielding benefit to the sick, for diseases are treated by drugs and surgery and regimen, but not by words; so too in philosophy there are those who are merely word hucksters and word hunters, who have not wish nor make it their business to cure their life brimming with infirmities, but from earliest youth to extreme old age do not blush to contend obstinately and battle over syllables, as if happiness depended on the unlimited and ineffectual overelaboration of words and expressions and not on improving one's character, the fountainhead of human life, by banishing the vices beyond its borders and establishing the virtues instead. . . .

Enticed by the love charms of the handmaids, some have spurned the mistress,[35] Philosophy, and have grown old, either in the company of poems or among geometrical figures, or among the blendings of chromatic genera, or among innumerable other things, and have been unable to soar upward to obtain the true-born wife. For

---

[35]Here Philo is still speaking of Hagar, who represents the mistress of all the arts (philosophy), but is herself still handmaiden to Sarah, representing wisdom and piety.

each art has its refinements, its powers of attraction, and some lured by these remain with them and forget their compacts with Philosophy. But he who abides by the agreements made provides all sorts of things from every source to please her. Rightly then did Holy Writ say in admiration of Abraham's fidelity that even then was Sarah his wife when, to please her, he wedded the handmaid. And indeed just as the school learning contributes to the acquisition of philosophy, so does philosophy to the attaining of wisdom. For philosophy is the pursuit of wisdom, and wisdom is the science of things divine and human and their causes. Therefore just as the encyclical culture is the bondmaid of philosophy, so is philosophy the maid of wisdom. Now philosophy teaches us the control of the belly and the parts below it, and control also of the tongue. These powers of control, it is said, are to be chosen for their own sake, but they will assume a more august aspect if pursued for the sake of honoring God and pleasing him. We must therefore keep the sovereign lady in mind, when we are about to woo her handmaids, and let us be called their husbands, but let her be our wife in actuality, and not merely in name.

---

3. GOSPEL OF THOMAS (c. 150 C.E.)

By the second century, some Christians had developed a different bridge between pagan philosophy and faith. The so-called Gnostic schism of the second century emanated from the controversial interpretation by some congregations of the essential message of Christianity. According to Gnostic leaders, the chief transformative gift of Jesus—and therefore of Christianity—was not his redemptive death but his *gnosis*, or enlightened understanding of the true nature of the universe. Among these "secret truths" was the central belief in a perennial struggle between a good god, whose realm was entirely spiritual, and a less-powerful bad god, who had created all matter. Gnostic salvation thus consisted of liberating one's spirit from the clutches of the body and material world and reclaiming one's place in the spiritual world. This enlightenment had supposedly been passed down from true followers of Jesus, such as his twin brother Judas Thomas, to the current generations. Certainly many Gnostic ideas—particularly their identification of the Old Testament Yahweh as a separate demigod in rebellion against a supreme, transcendent God—seem in retrospect patently un-Christian. The dualist interpretation of spirit and matter, however, as well as the rejection of a fully human (and therefore material) Christ do not seem quite as alien to other Christian traditions, both orthodox and heretical. Nevertheless, the Gnostic tradition was widely condemned by most Christian contemporaries, particularly for its alternate version of the gospels and its complete exclusion of the Old Testament from Holy Scripture. In fact, third- and fourth-century church leaders so effectively suppressed this early dissident tradition that all Gnostic writings were presumed destroyed until a collection of ancient works surfaced at Nag Hammadi (Egypt) in 1945. The Gospel of Thomas, which was part of this collection, recounts the life of Jesus in a fashion that is sometimes quite similar to that of the accepted biblical gospels of Matthew, Mark, and Luke, and to a lesser degree, John. Where it differs from these books, however, the Gospel of Thomas offers a fascinating example of how Jesus' life and teachings were interpreted by Gnostic Christians.

These are the secret sayings which the living Jesus spoke and which Didymos [i.e., "the twin"] Judas Thomas wrote down.[36]

(1) And he said, "Whoever finds the interpretation of these sayings will not experience death."

(2) Jesus said, "Let him who seeks continue seeking until he finds. When he finds, he will become troubled. When he becomes troubled, he will be astonished, and he will rule over the all."

(3) Jesus said, "If those who lead you say to you, 'See, the kingdom is in the sky,' then the birds of the sky will precede you. If they say to you, 'It is in the sea,' then the fish will precede you. Rather, the kingdom is inside of you, and it is outside of you. When you come to know yourselves, then you will become known, and you will realize that it is you who are the sons of the living father. But if you will not know yourselves, you dwell in poverty and it is you who are that poverty."

(4) Jesus said, "The man old in days will not hesitate to ask a small child seven days old about the place of life, and he will live. For many who are first will become last, and they will become one and the same."

(5) Jesus said, "Recognize what is in your sight, and that which is hidden from you will become plain to you. For there is nothing hidden which will not become manifest."

(6) His disciples questioned him and said to him, "Do you want us to fast? How shall we pray? Shall we give alms? What diet shall we observe?"

Jesus said, "Do not tell lies, and do not do what you hate, for all things are plain in the sight of heaven. For nothing hidden will not become manifest, and nothing covered will remain without being uncovered."

(7) Jesus said, "Blessed is the lion which becomes man when consumed by man; and cursed is the man whom the lion consumes, and the lion becomes man."

(8) And he said, "The man is like a wise fisherman who cast his net into the sea and drew it up from the sea full of small fish. Among them the wise fisherman found a fine large fish. He threw all the small fish back into the sea and chose the large fish without difficulty. Whoever has ears to hear, let him hear."

(9) Jesus said, "Now the sower went out, took a handful (of seeds), and scattered them. Some fell on the road; the birds came and gathered them up. Others fell on rock, did not take root in the soil, and did not produce ears. And others fell on thorns; they choked the seed(s) and worms ate them. And others fell on the good soil and it produced good fruit: it bore sixty per measure and a hundred and twenty per measure."

(10) Jesus said, "I have cast fire upon the world, and see, I am guarding it until it blazes."

(11) Jesus said, "This heaven will pass away, and the one above it will pass away. The dead are not alive, and the living will not die. In the days when you consumed what is dead, you made it what is alive. When you come to dwell in the light, what will you do? On the day when you were one you became two. But when you become two, what will you do?"

(12) The disciples said to Jesus, "We know that you will depart from us. Who is to be our leader?"

Jesus said to them, "Wherever you are, you are to go to James the righteous, for whose sake heaven and earth came into being."

(13) Jesus said to his disciples, "Compare me to someone and tell me whom I am like."

Simon Peter said to him, "You are like a righteous angel."

Matthew said to him, "You are like a wise philosopher."

Thomas said to him, "Master, my mouth is wholly incapable of saying whom you are like."

Jesus said, "I am not your master. Because you have drunk, you have become intoxicated from the bubbling spring which I have measured out."

And he took him and withdrew and told him three things. When Thomas returned to

---

[36]The multiple parallels to the canonical gospels have not been annotated.

his companions, they asked him, "What did Jesus say to you?"

Thomas said to them, "If I tell you one of the things which he told me, you will pick up stones and throw them at me; a fire will come out of the stones and burn you up."

(14) Jesus said to them, "If you fast, you will give rise to sin for yourselves; and if you pray, you will be condemned; and if you give alms, you will do harm to your spirits. When you go into any land and walk about in the districts, if they receive you, eat what they will set before you, and heal the sick among them. For what goes into your mouth will not defile you, but that which issues from your mouth—it is that which will defile you."

(15) Jesus said, "When you see one who was not born of woman, prostrate yourselves on your faces and worship him. That one is your father."

(16) Jesus said, "Men think, perhaps, that it is peace which I have come to cast upon the world. They do not know that it is dissension which I have come to cast upon the earth: fire, sword, and war. For there will be five in a house: three will be against two, and two against three, the father against the son, and the son against the father. And they will stand solitary."

(17) Jesus said, "I shall give you what no eye has seen and what no ear has heard and what no hand has touched and what has never occurred to the human mind."

(18) The disciples said to Jesus, "Tell us how our end will be."

Jesus said, "Have you discovered, then, the beginning, that you look for the end? For where the beginning is, there will the end be. Blessed is he who will take his place in the beginning; he will know the end and will not experience death."

(19) Jesus said, "Blessed is he who came into being before he came into being. If you become my disciples and listen to my words, these stones will minister to you. For there are five trees for you in Paradise which remain undisturbed summer and winter and whose leaves do

not fall. Whoever becomes acquainted with them will not experience death."

(20) The disciples said to Jesus, "Tell us what the kingdom of heaven is like."

He said to them, "It is like a mustard seed. It is the smallest of all seeds. But when it falls on tilled soil, it produces a great plant and becomes a shelter for birds of the sky.". . .

(28) Jesus said, "I took my place in the midst of the world, and I appeared to them in flesh. I found all of them intoxicated; I found none of them thirsty. And my soul became afflicted for the sons of men, because they are blind in their hearts and do not have sight; for empty they came into the world, and empty too they seek to leave the world. But for the moment they are intoxicated. When they shake off their wine, then they will repent."

(29) Jesus said, "If the flesh came into being because of spirit, it is a wonder. But if spirit came into being because of the body, it is a wonder of wonders. Indeed, I am amazed at how this great wealth has made its home in this poverty."

(30) Jesus said, "Where there are three gods, they are gods. Where there are two or one, I am with him.". . .

(38) Jesus said, "Many times have you desired to hear these words which I am saying to you, and you have no one else to hear them from. There will be days when you will look for me and will not find me."

(39) Jesus said, "The pharisees and the scribes have taken the keys of knowledge (gnosis) and hidden them. They themselves have not entered, nor have they allowed to enter those who wish to. You, however, be as wise as serpents and as innocent as doves.". . .

(49) Jesus said, "Blessed are the solitary and elect, for you will find the kingdom. For you are from it, and to it you will return."

(50) Jesus said, "If they say to you, 'Where did you come from?', say to them, 'We came from the light, the place where the light came into being on its own accord and established [itself] and became manifest through their image.' If they say to you, 'Is it you?', say, 'We are its

children, and we are the elect of the living father.' If they ask you, 'What is the sign of your father in you?', say to them, 'It is movement and repose.'"

(51) His disciples said to him, "When will the repose of the dead come about, and when will the new world come?"

He said to them, "What you look forward to has already come, but you do not recognize it."

(52) His disciples said to him, "Twenty-four prophets spoke in Israel, and all of them spoke in you."

He said to them, "You have omitted the one living in your presence and have spoken (only) of the dead."

(53) His disciples said to him, "Is circumcision beneficial or not?"

He said to them, "If it were beneficial, their father would beget them already circumcised from their mother. Rather, the true circumcision in spirit has become completely profitable.". . .

(68) Jesus said, "Blessed are you when you are hated and persecuted. Wherever you have been persecuted they will find no place."

(69) Jesus said, "Blessed are they who have been persecuted within themselves. It is they who have truly come to know the father. Blessed are the hungry, for the belly of him who desires will be filled."

(70) Jesus said, "That which you have will save you if you bring it forth from yourselves. That which you do not have within you [will] kill you if you do not have it within you."

(71) Jesus said, "I shall [destroy this] house, and no one will be able to build it [. . .]"

(72) [A man said] to him, "Tell my brothers to divide my father's possessions with me."

He said to him, "O man, who has made me a divider?"

He turned to his disciples and said to them, "I am not a divider, am I?"

(73) Jesus said, "The harvest is great but the laborers are few. Beseech the lord, therefore to send out laborers to the harvest."

(74) He said, "O lord, there are many around the drinking trough, but there is nothing in the cistern."

(75) Jesus said, "Many are standing at the door, but it is the solitary who will enter the bridal chamber.". . .

(80) Jesus said, "He who has recognized the world has found the body, but he who has found the body is superior to the world."

(81) Jesus said, "Let him who has grown rich be king, and let him who possesses power renounce it."

(82) Jesus said, "He who is near me is near the fire, and he who is far from me is far from the kingdom."

(83) Jesus said, "The images are manifest to man, but the light in them remains concealed in the image of the light of the father. He will become manifest, but his image will remain concealed by his light."

(84) Jesus said, "When you see your likeness, you rejoice. But when you see your images which came into being before you, and which neither die nor become manifest, how much you will have to bear!"

(85) Jesus said, "Adam came into being from a great power and a great wealth, but he did not become worthy of you. For had he been worthy, [he would] not [have experienced] death."

(86) Jesus said, "[The foxes have their holes] and the birds have their nests, but the son of man has no place to lay his head and rest."

(87) Jesus said, "Wretched is the body that is dependent upon a body and wretched is the soul that is dependent on these two."

(88) Jesus said, "The angels and the prophets will come to you and give to you those things you (already) have. And you too, give them those things which you have, and say to yourselves, 'When will they come and take what is theirs?'"

(89) Jesus said, "Why do you wash the outside of the cup? Do you not realize that he who made the inside is the same one who made the outside?"

(90) Jesus said, "Come unto me, for my yoke is easy and my lordship is mild, and you will find repose for yourselves."

(91) They said to him, "Tell us who you are so that we may believe in you."

He said to them, "You read the face of the sky and of the earth, but you have not recognized the one who is before you, and you do not know how to read this moment."

(92) Jesus said, "Seek and you will find. Yet, what you asked me about in former times and which I did not tell you then, now I do desire to tell, but you do not inquire after it."

(93) [Jesus said,] "Do not give what is holy to dogs, lest they throw them on the dung heap. Do not throw the pearls [to] swine. . . ."

(94) Jesus [said], "He who seeks will find, and [he who knocks] will be let in.". . .

(108) Jesus said, "He who will drink from my mouth will become like me. I myself shall become he, and the things that are hidden will be revealed to him."

(109) Jesus said, "The kingdom is like a man who had a [hidden] treasure in his field without knowing it. And [after] he died, he left it to his [son]. The son [did] not know (about the treasure). He inherited the field and sold [it]. And the one who bought it went plowing and [found] the treasure. He began to lend money at interest to whomever he wished."

(110) Jesus said, "Whoever finds the world and becomes rich, let him renounce the world."

(111) Jesus said, "The heavens and the earth will be rolled up in your presence. And the one who lives from the living one will not see death." Does not Jesus say, "Whoever finds himself is superior to the world"?

(112) Jesus said, "Woe to the flesh that depends on the soul; woe to the soul that depends on the flesh."

(113) His disciples said to him, "When will the kingdom come?"

[Jesus said,] "It will not come by waiting for it. It will not be a matter of saying 'here it is' or 'there it is'. Rather, the kingdom of the father is spread out upon the earth, and men do not see it."

(114) Simon Peter said to them, "Let Mary leave us, for women are not worthy of life."

Jesus said, "I myself shall lead her in order to make her male, so that she too may become a living spirit resembling you males. For every woman who will make herself male will enter the kingdom of heaven."

---

4. Clement of Alexandria
MISCELLANIES (c. 200 C.E.)

The other crisis of early Christian teaching was much less easily resolved. As Christianity entered its second century, it had begun to attract a small but ever-growing number of intellectuals trained in various philosophical schools. As these converts tried to reconcile their philosophical learning with their new religion, they developed two distinctly different approaches. The first, favored by Clement of Alexandria (c. 150–c. 214 C.E.), perceived Christian faith as an arduous process, in which true *gnosis* (not to be confused with the teachings of the condemned Gnostics) was the pinnacle of achievement and piety. Based on his long experience as an instructor of catechumens, Clement believed that a good classical education was not only compatible with the perfection of faith but was essential to it. Only with such a foundation of understanding, he argued, could an individual fully embrace the wisdom and salvation of Christ. While Clement abhorred the elitist and secretive approach of the Gnostics, he agreed at least that unformed faith was not faith at all and that willful ignorance of the Truth was as great a failing as any sin of the flesh.

The man of understanding and perspicacity is, then, a Gnostic.[37] And his business is not abstinence from what is evil (for this is a step to the highest perfection), or the doing of good out of fear. . . . Nor any more is he to do so from hope of promised recompense. . . . But only the doing of good out of love, and for the sake of its own excellence, is to be the Gnostic's choice. Now, in the person of God it is said to the Lord, *Ask of me, and I will give the heathen for thine inheritance* [Ps 2:8]; teaching him to ask a truly regal request—that is, the salvation of men without price, that we may inherit and possess the Lord. For, on the contrary, to desire knowledge about God for any practical purpose, that this may be done, or that may not be done, is not proper to the Gnostic; but the knowledge itself suffices as the reason for contemplation. For I will dare aver that it is not because he wishes to be saved that he, who devotes himself to knowledge for the sake of the divine science itself, chooses knowledge. For the exertion of the intellect through training is prolonged to a perpetual exertion. And the perpetual exertion of the intellect is the essence of an intelligent being which results from an uninterrupted process of admixture, and remains eternal contemplation, a living substance.

Could we, then, suppose any one proposing to the Gnostic whether he would choose the knowledge of God or everlasting salvation; and if these, which are entirely identical, were separable, he would without the least hesitation choose the knowledge of God, deeming that property of faith, which from love ascends to knowledge, desirable for its own sake. This, then, is the perfect man's first form of doing good, when it is done not for any advantage in what pertains to him, but because he judges it right to do good; and the energy being vigorously exerted in all things, in the very act becomes good; not, good in some things, and not good in others; but consisting in the habit of doing good, neither for glory, nor as the philosophers say, for reputation, nor for re-

ward either from men or God; but so as to pass life after the *image and likeness of the Lord* [Gen 1:26]. . . .

Such an one is no longer continent, but has reached a state of passionlessness, waiting to put on the divine image. *If thou doest alms,* it is said, *let no one know it; and if thou fastest, anoint thyself, that God alone may know* [Mt 6: 2–4, 16–18], and not a single human being. Not even he himself who shows mercy ought to know that he does show mercy; for in this way he will be sometimes merciful, sometimes not. And when he shall do good by habit, he will imitate the nature of good, and his disposition will be his nature and his practice. . . .

Knowledge *{gnosis}*, so to speak, is a perfecting of man as man, which is brought about by acquaintance with divine things; in character, life, and word harmonious and consistent with itself and the divine Word. For by it faith is made perfect, inasmuch as it is solely by it that the man of faith becomes perfect. Faith is an internal good, and without searching for God confesses His existence and glorifies Him as existent. Hence by starting with this faith, and being developed by it, through the grace of God, the knowledge respecting Him is to be acquired as far as possible. . . .

But it is not doubting, in reference to God, but believing, that is the foundation of knowledge. But Christ is both the foundation and the superstructure, by whom are both the beginning and the end. And the extreme points, the beginning and the end, I mean faith and love, are not taught. But knowledge, which is conveyed from communication through the grace of God as a deposit, is intrusted to those who show themselves worthy of it; and from it the worth of love beams forth from light to light. For it is said, "To him that hath shall be given" [cf. Mt 13:12] — to faith, knowledge; and to knowledge, love; and to love, the inheritance. . . .

Faith then is, so to speak, a compendious knowledge of the essentials; but knowledge is the sure and firm demonstration of what is received by faith, built upon faith by the Lord's teaching, conveying us on to unshaken convic-

---

[37]Again, not in the sense of the schismatic Christians led by Marcion.

tion and certainty. And, as it seems to me, the first saving change is that from heathenism to faith, as I said before; and the second, that from faith to knowledge. And this latter passing on to love, thereafter gives a mutual friendship between that which knows and that which is known. And perhaps he who has already arrived at this stage has attained equality with the angels. At any rate, after he has reached the final ascent in the flesh, he still continues to advance, as is fit, and presses on through the holy Hebdomad[38] into the Father's house, to that which is indeed the Lord's abode.

[38]Clement is incautiously reflecting Gnostic language in his reference to the Hebdomad. The Hebdomad is the abode of the Demiurge (identified by Gnostic heretics with the Jewish Yahweh); Ogdoad is the abode of Sophia (Wisdom) and the gateway to the Pleroma, or Gnostic spiritual world.

5. Tertullian
ON THE PRESCRIPTION AGAINST HERETICS (c. 200 C.E.)

Not all early church leaders shared Clement of Alexandria's admiration of pagan philosophy or emphasis on Christian learning. Tertullian (c. 160–post 220 C.E.), for one, vehemently rejected all such attempts to mix Christian and pagan "knowledge." Despite his own extensive background in Greek and Latin rhetoric, he held that there was no benefit whatsoever in philosophical study and instead saw very real dangers, such as the current seduction of the Gnostic heresy, which continued to attract new followers among overly curious Christians. No doubt Tertullian's distaste for the intellectualizing of faith helps account for his embrace of charismatic Montanist prophecies (see 1B). His position, however, has been supported by many subsequent Christians who, regardless of their attitude towards charisma, question the wisdom of mixing reasoned and revealed "truths."

For philosophy is the material of the world's wisdom, the rash interpreter of the nature and the dispensation of God. Indeed heresies are themselves instigated by philosophy. From this source came the "Aeons,"[39] and I know not what infinite "forms," and the "trinity of man" in the system of Valentinus; he was a Platonist. From the same source came Marcion's better god with his tranquillity; he came of the Stoics. Then, again, the opinion that the soul dies is held by the Epicureans; while the denial of the restoration of the body is taken from the uniform teaching of all the philosophers; also, when matter is made equal to God, then you have the teaching of Zeno; and when any doctrine is alleged touching a god of fire, then Heraclitus comes in.[40] The same subject-matter is discussed over and over again by

[39]A reference to the Gnostic Pleroma, which is divided into fifteen opposing pairs (syzygies) of aeons, or ages. The aeon of Christ brings *gnosis*.

[40]Valentinus and Marcion were leading Gnostic Christians during the second century. Zeno was the founder (c. 335–c. 263 B.C.E.) of Stoicism. Heraclitus was a Greek disciple (fl. c. 145–180 C.E.) of the Gnostic Valentinus. Tertullian purposely confounds ancient philosophical schools, such as the Stoics and Epicureans, with heretical Christian teachings.

heretics and philosophers; the same arguments are reconsidered. Whence comes evil? and why? Whence man? and how? Besides the question which Valentinus has very lately proposed—Whence comes God? No doubt from *desire* and *abortion!* . . .[41]

What indeed has Athens to do with Jerusalem? What has the Academy to do with the Church? What have heretics to do with Christians? Our instruction comes from *the porch of Solomon*[42] [Acts 3:11], who had himself taught that *the Lord should be sought in simplicity of heart* [Wis 1:1]. Away with all attempts to produce a Stoic, Platonic, and dialectic Christianity! We want no curious disputation after possessing Christ Jesus, no inquisition after receiving the gospel! When we believe, we desire no further belief. For this is our first article of faith, that there is nothing which we ought to believe besides.

----

[41] A mythological reference to the illicit desire of wisdom (Sophia) to have intercourse with Abyss (Bythos), resulting in the birth of a monstrous creature.

[42] The Academy refers to the philosophers' school at Athens, founded by Plato in 387 B.C.E. and functioning continuously until 529 C.E. Tertullian contrasts this type of "wisdom," also represented by the porch at Athens where the Stoic philosopher Zeno taught, with the porch of Solomon, i.e., divine revelation.

E. Bishop

One of the most distinctive developments of ancient Christianity was its organization into a network of congregations, or *ekklesia* ("assemblies" or "churches"), each led by a "bishop" (from the Greek *episkopos*, or "overseer"). Yet despite the frequent mention of bishops in ancient Christian sources, it is not easy to define exactly what the word meant to first-century Christians. In the most general terms, a bishop was the leader of a congregation, often chosen by election. Each of the first-century congregations, however, apparently had a unique organizational structure. Thus the role of the bishop—also sometimes called *presbyter* (Greek "elder" or "priest")—varied widely from place to place. In writings of the period, the bishop was often compared to a shepherd (Acts 20:28), but also to a teacher (or "rabbi"), a host, and an ambassador. By the second century, the role of the bishop had become much more clearly defined, and his status and power within the congregation had been greatly enhanced. This evolution occurred for three reasons. First, as each Christian congregation grew, so did the need for its bishop to act as an administrator, not only leading his congregation in celebration of the Eucharist and other rituals, but also handling correspondence on his church's behalf and representing the congregation abroad. The second factor was closely related to the first, namely, his authority as a teacher, both at home and in conjunction with other bishops. Yet even combined, these two factors would not necessarily have produced a strong episcopal hierarchy had it not been for a third and decisive element, namely, the threat of schism. Because of their key role in suppressing the minority congregations of Gnostics and other "heretics," bishops thereafter became the guardians of orthodoxy ("right teaching")—a development that greatly enhanced their power and prestige within the church.

1. St. Ignatius of Antioch
LETTER TO THE EPHESIANS (c. 115 C.E.)

Ignatius of Antioch (c. 35–c. 115 C.E.) knew the dangers of factionalism from his own episcopal experience of nearly forty years. Like another influential bishop of his time, Clement of Rome (d. c. 101 C.E.), Ignatius believed in Apostolic Succession. This doctrine held that the apostles, who were considered to have been the first bishops, had delegated to their chosen successors the responsibility and authority for maintaining Christian unity, both within and among congregations. While he professed to "give no orders," Ignatius nonetheless frequently exercised his right as bishop to instruct, particularly on the dangers of Docetism, a variant of Christianity that claimed that Christ was not truly human. He was the first writer to refer to a "catholic" (or universal) church and the first to state that the bishop of Rome (later known as the Pope) should be considered the supreme head of the church. While on his way to trial and martyrdom in Rome, Ignatius wrote seven letters which have survived: six to churches in Asia Minor (including Ephesus and the church in Smyrna, headed by Polycarp) and one to the church at Rome. His Letter to the Ephesians is a prime example of his core belief in the bishop's role as arbiter of dissent and preserver of Christian unity.

IGNATIUS, also called Theophorus,[43] sends heartiest good wishes for unalloyed joy in Jesus Christ to the Church at Ephesus in Asia;[44] a church deserving of felicitation, blessed, as she is, with greatness through the fullness of God the Father; predestined, before time was, to be—to her abiding and unchanging glory—forever united and chosen, through real suffering, by the will of the Father and Jesus Christ our God.

With joy in God I welcomed your community, which possesses its dearly beloved name because of a right disposition, enhanced by faith and love through Christ Jesus our Savior. Being imitators of God, you have, once restored to new life in the Blood of God, perfectly accomplished the task so natural to you. Indeed,

as soon as you heard that I was coming from Syria in chains for our common Name and hope—hoping I might, thanks to your prayer, obtain the favor of fighting wild beasts at Rome and through this favor be able to prove myself a disciple—you hastened to see me. In the name of God, then, I have received your numerous community in the person of Onesimus, a man of indescribable charity and your bishop here on earth. I pray you in the spirit of Jesus Christ to love him, and wish all of you to resemble him. Blessed, indeed, is He whose grace made you worthy to possess such a bishop. . . .

I give you no orders as though I were somebody. For, even though I am in chains for the sake of the Name, I am not yet perfected in Jesus Christ. Indeed, I am now but being initiated into discipleship, and I address you as my fellow disciples. Yes, I ought to be anointed by you with faith, encouragement, patient endurance, and steadfastness. However, since affection does not permit me to be silent when you are concerned, I am at once taking this opportunity to exhort you to live in harmony with

---

[43]Literally, "bearer of God," an epithet chosen by Ignatius himself.
[44]One of the earliest and most important congregations of early Christianity, founded by St. Paul. Ephesus was one of the largest cities of the Roman Empire and the capitol of the Proconsular Province of Asia (today western Turkey and Syria).

the mind of God. Surely, Jesus Christ, our inseparable life, for His part is the mind of the Father, just as the bishops, though appointed throughout the vast, wide earth, represent for their part the mind of Jesus Christ.

Hence it is proper for you to act in agreement with the mind of the bishop; and this you do. Certain it is that your presbytery,[45] which is a credit to its name, is a credit to God; for it harmonizes with the bishop as completely as the strings with a harp. This is why in the symphony of your concord and love the praises of Jesus Christ are sung. But you, the rank and file, should also form a choir, so that, joining the symphony by your concord, and by your unity taking your key note from God, you may with one voice through Jesus Christ sing a song to the Father. Thus He will both listen to you and by reason of your good life recognize in you the melodies of His Son. It profits you, therefore, to continue in your flawless unity, that you may at all times have a share in God.

For a fact, if I in a short time became so warmly attached to your bishop—an attachment not on human grounds but on spiritual— how much more do I count you happy who are as closely knit to him as the Church is to Jesus Christ, and as Jesus Christ is to the Father! As a result, the symphony of unity is perfect. Let no one deceive himself: unless a man is within the sanctuary, he has to go without *the Bread of God*. Assuredly, if the prayer of one or two has such efficacy, how much more that of the bishop of the entire Church! It follows, then: he who absents himself from the common meeting, by that very fact shows pride and becomes a sectarian; for the Scripture says: *God resists the proud* [Jas 4:6]. Let us take care, therefore, not to oppose the bishop, that we may be submissive to God.

Furthermore: the more anyone observes that a bishop is discreetly silent, the more he should stand in fear of him. Obviously, anyone whom the Master of the household puts in charge of His domestic affairs, ought to be received by us in the same spirit as He who has charged him with this duty. Plainly, then, one should look upon the bishop as upon the Lord Himself. Now, Onesimus for his part overflows with praise of the good order that, thanks to God, exists in your midst. Truth is the rule of life for all of you, and heresy has no foothold among you. The fact is, you have nothing more to learn from anyone, since you listen to Jesus Christ who speaks truthfully.

Some there are, you know, accustomed with vicious guile to go about with the Name on their lips, while they indulge in certain practices at variance with it and an insult to God. These you must shun as you would wild beasts: they are rabid dogs that bite in secret; you must beware of them, for they are hard to cure. There is only one Physician, both carnal and spiritual, born and unborn, God become man, true life in death; sprung both from Mary and from God, first subject to suffering and then incapable of it—Jesus Christ Our Lord. . . .

Make an effort, then, to come more frequently to celebrate God's Eucharist and to offer praise. For, when you meet frequently in the same place, the forces of Satan are overthrown, and his baneful influence is neutralized by the unanimity of your faith. Peace is a precious thing: it puts an end to every war waged by heavenly or earthly enemies.

Nothing of this escapes you; only persevere to the end in your faith in, and your love for, Jesus Christ. Here is the beginning and the end of life: faith is the beginning, *the end is love* [1 Tim 1:5]; and when the two blend perfectly with each other, they are God. Everything else that makes for right living is consequent upon these. No one who professes faith sins; no one who possesses love hates. *The tree is known by its fruit* [Mt 12:33; Lk 6:44]. In like manner, those who profess to belong to Christ will be known as such by their conduct. Certainly, what matters now is not mere profession of faith, but whether one is found to be actuated by it to the end.

---

[45]The congregation's leaders, or elders.

It is better to keep silence and be something than to talk and be nothing. Teaching is an excellent thing, provided the teacher practices what he teaches. Now, there is one Teacher *who spoke and it was done.* But even what He did silently is worthy of the Father. He who has made the words of Jesus really his own is able also to hear His silence. Thus he will be perfect: He will act through his speech and be understood through his silence. Nothing is hidden from the Lord; no, even our secrets reach Him. Let us, then, do all things in the conviction that He dwells in us. Thus we shall be His temples and He will be our God within us. And this is the truth, and it will be made manifest before our eyes. Let us, then, love Him as He deserves. . . .

If Jesus Christ, yielding to your prayer, grants me the favor and it is His will, I shall, in the subsequent letter which I intend to write to you, still further explain the dispensation which I have here only touched upon, regarding the New Man Jesus Christ—a dispensation founded on faith in Him and love for Him, on His Passion and Resurrection. I will do so especially if the Lord should reveal to me that you—the entire community of you!—are in the habit, through grace derived from the Name, of meeting in common, animated by one faith and in union with Jesus Christ—who *in the flesh was of the line of David* [Rom 1:3], the Son of Man and the Son of God—of meeting, I say, to show obedience with undivided mind to the bishop and the presbytery, and to break the same Bread, which is the medicine of immortality, the antidote against death, and everlasting life in Jesus Christ.

I offer my life as a ransom for you and for those whom for the Glory of God you sent to Smyrna, where, too, I am writing to you with thanks to the Lord and with love for Polycarp[46] and you. Remember me, as may Jesus Christ remember you! Pray for the Church in Syria, whence I am being led away in chains to Rome, though I am the least of the faithful there. But then, I was granted the favor of contributing to the honor of God. Farewell! May God the Father and Jesus Christ, *our common hope,* bless you!

---

[46]Bishop of Smyrna and early leader of the anti-Gnostic faction of early Christianity. Polycarp (c. 69–c.155 C.E.) was also a famous martyr for the faith.

---

2. Irenaeus
AGAINST HERESIES (c. 175 C.E.)

A few generations after Ignatius of Antioch, another influential bishop made use of a similar argument in his fight against a much greater threat to early Christian unity. From his church in Lyons, Irenaeus (c. 130–c. 200 C.E.) conducted a fervent campaign against the Gnostic Christians whose teachings he considered heretical. Like Ignatius, Irenaeus proposed apostolic tradition, and thus the authority of bishops, as a universal truth of the Christian faith. From this foundation, he then proceeded to fill five volumes with devastating criticism of the "un-apostolic" beliefs of the Gnostic leaders. Irenaeus's faith in the bishop's role as a preserver of correct belief and Christian unity is especially obvious in his account of how his mentor Polycarp unambiguously rebuked the Gnostic leader Marcion. Although Irenaeus was himself a bishop, his insistence on the importance of episcopal authority should not be seen as a crude ploy to gain more personal power. Irenaeus's focus was always the importance of unity in "the universal Church," which he saw as a body that was threatened by the disease of Gnosticism. For Irenaeus, appealing to the episcopal network for help in quashing the Gnostics was merely the most effective way of severing the heresy-infected limb and saving the rest of the body.

The tradition, therefore, of the Apostles, manifested throughout the world, is a thing which all who wish to see the facts can clearly perceive in every church; and we are able to count up those who were appointed bishops by the Apostles, and to show their successors to our own time, who neither taught nor knew anything resembling these men's ravings. For if the Apostles had known hidden mysteries [i.e., Gnostics' *gnosis*] which they used to teach the perfect, apart from and without the knowledge of the rest, they would have delivered them especially to those to whom they were also committing the churches themselves. For they desired them to be very perfect and blameless in all things, and were also leaving them as their successors, delivering over to them their own proper place of teaching; for if these should act rightly great advantage would result, but if they fell away the most disastrous calamity would occur.

But since it would be very long in such a volume as this to count up the successions [i.e., series of bishops] in all the churches, we confound all those who in any way, whether through self-pleasing or vainglory, or through blindness and evil opinion, gather together otherwise than they ought by pointing out the tradition derived from the Apostles of the greatest, most ancient, and universally known Church, founded and established by the two most glorious Apostles, Peter and Paul, and also the faith declared to men which through the succession of bishops comes down to our times.[47] For with this Church, on account of its more powerful leadership, every church, that is, the faithful, who are from everywhere, must needs agree; since in it that tradition which is

from the Apostles has always been preserved by those who are from everywhere.

The blessed Apostles having founded and established the Church, entrusted the office of the episcopate to Linus. Paul speaks of this Linus in his Epistles to Timothy. Anacletus succeeded him, and after Anacletus, in the third place from the Apostles, Clement received the episcopate. He had seen and conversed with the blessed Apostles, and their preaching was still sounding in his ears and their tradition was still before his eyes. Nor was he alone in this, for many who had been taught by the Apostles yet survived. In the times of Clement, a serious dissension having arisen among the brethren in Corinth, the Church of Rome sent a suitable letter to the Corinthians, reconciling them in peace, renewing their faith, and proclaiming the doctrine lately received from the Apostles. . . .

Evaristus succeeded Clement, and Alexander Evaristus. Then Sixtus, the sixth from the Apostles, was appointed. After him Telesephorus, who suffered martyrdom gloriously, and then Hyginus; after him Pius, and after Pius Anicetus; Soter succeeded Anicetus, and now, in the twelfth place from the Apostles, Eleutherus [r. 174–189] holds the office of bishop. In the same order and succession the tradition and the preaching of the truth which is from the Apostles have continued unto us.

But Polycarp, too, was not only instructed by the Apostles, and acquainted with many that had seen Christ, but was also appointed by Apostles in Asia bishop of the church in Smyrna, whom we, too, saw in our early youth (for he lived a long time, and died, when a very old man, a glorious and most illustrious martyr's death); he always taught the things which he had learned from the Apostles, which the Church also hands down, and which alone are true. To these things all the Asiatic churches testify, as do also those who, down to the present time, have succeeded Poly-

---

[47] I.e., the church in Rome, traditionally founded by Saints Peter and Paul.

carp, who was a much more trustworthy and certain witness of the truth than Valentinus and Marcion and the rest of the evil-minded.[48] It was he who was also in Rome in the time of Anicetus[49] and caused many to turn away from the above-mentioned heretics to the Church of God, proclaiming that he had received from the Apostles this one and only truth which has been transmitted by the Church. And there are those who heard from him that John, the disciple of the Lord, going to bathe in Ephesus, when he saw Cerinthus[50] within, ran out of the bath-house without bathing, crying: "Let us flee, lest even the bath-house fall, because Cerinthus, the enemy of the truth, is within." And Polycarp himself, when Marcion once met him and said, "Knowest thou us?" replied, "I know the first-born of Satan." Such caution did the Apostles and their disciples exercise that they might not even converse with any of those who perverted the truth; as Paul, also, said: *"A man that is a heretic after the first and second admonition, reject; knowing that he that is such subverteth and sinneth, being condemned by himself"* [Tit 3:10–11].

---

[48]Gnostic Christian leaders; see 1D3.
[49]Bishop of Rome from c.155 to c.166 C.E..

[50]Gnostic Christian (fl. c. 100 C.E.), also denounced by Polycarp and other orthodox leaders.

BIBLIOGRAPHY

Primary Sources

Anthologies and Readers

Barrett, C. K., ed., *The New Testament Background: Writings from Ancient Greece and the Roman Empire That Illuminate Christian Origins* (San Francisco, Harper SanFrancisco, 1993).

Beard, Mary, John North, Simon Price, eds., *Religions of Rome, Vol. 2: A Sourcebook* (Cambridge: Cambridge University Press, 1998).

Charlesworth, James H., ed., *Apocrypha and Pseudoepigrapha of the Old Testament*, 2 vols. (New York: Doubleday, 1983).

Ehrman, Bart D., ed., *The New Testament and Other Early Christian Writings: A Reader* (Oxford: Oxford University Press, 1997).

————, *After the New Testament: A Reader in Early Christianity* (Oxford: Oxford University Press, 1998).

Elliott, J. K., ed., *The Apocryphal Jesus: Legends of the Early Church* (Oxford: Oxford University Press, 1996).

Inwood, Brad and Lloyd Gerson, eds., *Hellenistic Philosophy: Introductory Readings*, 2nd ed. (Indianapolis: Hackett, 1998).

Kee, Howard Clark, ed., *The New Testament in Context: Sources and Documents* (Englewood Cliffs, New Jersey: Prentice-Hall, 1984).

Layton, Bentley, ed., *The Gnostic Scriptures* (New York: Doubleday, 1987).

Lewis, N., and M. Reinhold, eds., *Roman Civilization: A Sourcebook*, 2 vols. (New York: Columbia University Press, 1990).

MacMullen, Ramsay, and E. N. Lane, eds., *Paganism and Christianity, 100–425 CE: A Sourcebook* (Minneapolis: Fortress Press, 1992).

Musurillo, Herbert, ed. and trans., *Acts of the Christian Martyrs* (Oxford: Clarendon Press, 1972).

Nickelsburg, George and Michael Stone, eds., *Faith and Piety in Early Judaism: Texts and Documents* (Harrisburg, P.A.: Trinity Press International, 1991).

Robinson, James M., ed., *The Nag Hammadi Library in English* (New York: Harper & Row, 1977).

Shelton, Jo-Ann, ed., *As the Romans Did: A Sourcebook in Roman Social History*, 2nd ed. (Oxford: Oxford University Press, 1997).

Stevenson, J., ed., *A New Eusebius* (London: SPCK, 1987).

Vermes, Geza, ed., *The Complete Dead Sea Scrolls in English*, 4th ed. (New York: Penguin, 1995).

Selected Authors

Apuleius, *Apuleius' Golden Ass and Other Philosophical Writings*, trans. P. G. Walsh (Oxford: Oxford University Press, 1999).

Aristotle, *Vol. VIII: On the Soul; Parva Naturalia; On Breath*, Loeb Classical Library, 288 (Cambridge: Harvard University Press, 1997).

————, *Selections*, ed. Terence Irwin and Gail Fine (Indianapolis: Hackett, 1995).

Artemidorus, *Oneirocritica*, trans. Robert J. White (Westwood, N.J.: Noyes Press, 1975).

Book of Enoch, trans. R. H. Charles (London: SPCK, 1992).

Clement of Alexandria, *Stromateis*, trans. John Ferguson (Washington, D.C.: Catholic University of America Press, 1991).

————, *Didache*, trans. James A. Kleist (Westminster, M.D.: Newman Press, 1948).

Gregory of Nyssa, *Life of St. Gregory Thaumaturgus: Life and Works*, trans. Michael Slusser (Washington, D.C.: Catholic University of America Press, 1998).

Hippolytus, *Canons of Hipplytus*, ed. Paul Bradshaw (New York: Grove Books, 1987).

Ignatius of Antioch, *The Four Authentic Letters of Ignatius*, trans. Joseph Rius-Camps (Rome: Pontificum Institutum Orientalium Studiorum, 1980).

Irenaeus, *St. Irenaeus of Lyons: Against the Heresies*, trans. Dominic Unger (Mahwah, N.J.: Paulist Press, 1992).

————, *Irenaeus of Lyons on Baptism and Eucharist: Selected Texts*, trans. David N. Power (New York: Grove Books, 1991).

Josephus, *Antiquities*, trans. H. St. J. Thackeray and Ralph Marcus (Cambridge: Harvard University Press, 1998).

————, *The Jewish War*, trans. G. A. Williamson (New York: Penguin Classic, 1958).

Justin Martyr, *The First and Second Apologies*, trans. Leslie William Barnard (Mahwah, N.J.: Paulist Press, 1957).

Marcus Aurelius, *Meditations*, trans. Maxwell Staniforth (New York: Penguin Popular Classics, 1964).

The Classic Midrash: Tannaitic Commentaries on the Bible, trans. Reuven Hammer (Mahwah, N.J.: Paulist Press, 1997).

Origen, *Selected Writings*, trans. and ed. Rowan A. Greer (Mahwah, N.J.: Paulist Press, 1979).

Philo of Alexandria, *The Contemplative Life, Giants, and Selections*, trans. David Winston (Mahwah, N.J.: Paulist Press, 1981).

Plato, *The Portable Plato*, ed. Scott Buchanan (New York: Penguin, 1979).

————, *Great Dialogues of Plato*, ed. Eric H. Warmington and Philip G. Rouse (New York: Penguin, 1956).

Seneca, *Letters from a Stoic*, trans. Robin Campbell (New York: Penguin Classic, 1969).

Tertullian, *De Idolatria: Critical Text, Translation and Commentary*, trans. J. H. Waszink and J. C. M. van Winden (Leiden, The Netherlands: Brill, 1987).

————, *Disciplinary, Moral and Ascetical Works*, trans. Rudolph Arbesmann et al. (New York: Fathers of the Church, 1959).

See also the Loeb Classical Library series for the writings of these and other ancient Christian and pagan writers.

Secondary Works

Historical Overviews

Benko, Stephen, *Pagan Rome and the Early Christians* (Bloomington, Ind.: Indiana University Press, 1984).

Chadwick, Henry, *The Early Church* (New York: Penguin, 1990).

Ehrman, Bart D., *The New Testament: A Historical Introduction to the Early Christian Writings* (Oxford: Oxford University Press, 1996).

Ferguson, Everett, *Background of Early Christianity*, 2nd ed. (Grand Rapids, Mich.: Eerdmans, 1993).

Green, Peter, *Alexander to Actium: The Historical Evolution of the Hellenistic Age* (Berkeley and Los Angeles: University of California Press, 1991).

Koester, Helmut, *Ancient Christian Gospels: Their History and Development* (Alexandria, V.A.: Trinity Press International, 1990).

Le Glay, Marcel et al., *A History of Rome* (Cambridge: Harvard University Press, 1996).

Meeks, Wayne A., *The First Urban Christians: The Social World of the Apostle Paul* (New Haven: Yale University Press, 1983).

Ancient Judaism

Irving, J., *The Midrashic Process: Tradition and Interpretation in Rabbinic Judaism* (Cambridge: Cambridge University Press, 1995).

Flanders, Henry Jackson, Jr., et al., *People of the Covenant: An Introduction to the Hebrew Bible*, 4th ed. (Oxford: Oxford University Press, 1996).

Smallwood, Mary E., *The Jews under Roman Rule from Pompey to Diocletian* (Leiden, The Netherlands: Brill, 1976).

Solomon, Norman, *Judaism: A Very Short Introduction* (Oxford: Oxford University Press, 1997).

Strack, H. L. and G. Stemberger, *Introduction to the Talmud and Midrash* (Minneapolis: Fortress Press, 1982).

Other Ancient Cults and Religions

Beard, Mary, John North, and Simon Price, *Religions of Rome, Vol. I: A History* (Cambridge: Cambridge University Press, 1998).

Burkert, Walter, *Ancient Mystery Cults* (Cambridge: Harvard University Press, 1987).

Graf, Fritz, *Magic in the Ancient World* (Cambridge: Harvard University Press, 1997).

Graves, Robert, *The Greek Myths: Illustrated Edition* (New York: Penguin, 1981).

MacMullen, Ramsay, *Paganism in the Roman Empire* (New Haven: Yale University Press, 1981).

Martin, Luther, *Hellenistic Religions: An Introduction* (Oxford: Oxford University Press, 1987).

Witt, R. E., *Isis in the Ancient World* (Baltimore: Johns Hopkins University Press, 1997).

Ancient Philosophy

Downing, Gerald F., *Cynics and Christian Origins* (New York: Routledge, 1992).

Long, A. A., *Hellenistic Philosophy: Stoics, Epicureans, Sceptics* (Berkeley and Los Angeles: University of California Press, 1986).

Routledge History of Philosophy, Vol. I: From the Beginning to Plato, ed. C. C. W. Taylor (New York: Routledge, 1997); *Vol. II: Aristotle to Augustine,* ed. David Furley (New York: Routledge, 1997).

Williamson, Ronald, *Jews in the Hellenistic World: Philo* (Cambridge: Cambridge University Press, 1989).

Christian Liturgy

Bradshaw, Paul, *Early Christian Worship: A Basic Introduction to Ideas and Practices* (London: SPCK, 1996).

Martin, Ralph P., *Worship in the Early Church* (Grand Rapids, Mich.: Eerdmans, 1964).

Charisma and Conversion

Ferguson, Everett, *Demonology of the Early Christian World* (Lewiston, N.Y.: Edwin Mellen, 1984).

Kee, Howard C., *Miracle in the Early Christian World* (New Haven: Yale University Press, 1983).

MacMullen, Ramsay, *Christianizing the Roman Empire (A.D. 100–400)* (New Haven: Yale University Press, 1984).

Nock, A. D., *Conversion: The Old and the New in Religion from Alexander the Great to Augustine of Hippo* (Baltimore: Johns Hopkins University Press, 1998).

Martyr

Bowersock, G. W., *Martyrdom and Rome* (Cambridge: Cambridge University Press, 1995).

Salisbury, Joyce, *Perpetua's Passion: The Death and Memory of a Young Roman Woman* (New York: Routledge, 1997).

Wilken, R. L., *The Christians as the Romans Saw Them* (New Haven: Yale University Press, 1984).

Gnosticism

Chadwick, Henry, *Early Christian Thought and the Classical Tradition* (Oxford: Oxford University Press, 1966).

Pagels, Elaine, *The Gnostic Gospels* (New York: Random House, 1979; Vintage Books, 1989).

Rudolph, Kurt, *Gnosis: The Nature and History of Gnosticism* (New York: Harper & Row, 1987).

Bishop

Brown, Raymond, *Priest and Bishop* (New York: Paulist Press, 1970).

———, *The Churches the Apostles Left Behind* (New York: Paulist Press, 1984).

Kaufman, Peter, *Church, Book and Bishop: Conflict and Authority in Early Latin Christianity* (Boulder, Colo.: Westview Press, 1996).

Late Antiquity and the Early Middle Ages

THE RELIQUARY CASKET OF PEPIN OF AQUITAINE. During late antiquity and the early Middle Ages, the physical remnants of famous and especially holy Christians were increasingly credited with supernatural powers and accordingly treasured by their owners, who sometimes preserved the relics in ornate cases such as this one. *(Giraudon/Art Resource, New York)*

During the six centuries following Constantine's Edict of Toleration in 313, Christianity, like the Roman Empire itself, underwent a profound transformation. The most obvious and dramatic change was the church's gradual metamorphosis from a small minority outlawed cult to the unquestioned official religion of the empire and eventually of all its successor states in Europe. In fact, by the time of the millennium, church and state had become so thoroughly intertwined in Europe that it was often impossible to say exactly where one type of authority stopped and the other began. Kings and emperors, who were considered secular rulers, now underwent elaborate church coronations, while bishops and abbots, once powerful only within the sphere of the church, now ruled over large territories and wielded immense political power.

This massive transformation is perhaps best viewed in two historical stages. During the first period, from toleration to the decline of the western Roman Empire in the late fifth century, Christianity was gradually assimilated into the cultural and political life of the empire. As Christianity grew in "most favored religion" status with emperors from Constantine on, most of the social and intellectual elite adopted the faith as well. The political patronage wielded by this new imperial Christianity, known as Caesaro-papism in the Eastern Empire, eventually proved irresistible. Over the course of several generations, more and more members of senatorial families converted to what was by 394 the official state religion, so that by the early fifth century only a few nobles clung stubbornly to ancestral ways.

Another sign of the church's rapid growth during this first stage was the way classically educated converts to Christianity increasingly interwove the teachings of their new religion with Greek philosophy. This inevitably caused heated conflicts among believers. Bishops, as we have already seen in Chapter 1, had emerged by the end of the second century as the key organizational checks against such divisiveness. During the first two centuries after toleration, the expansion of the church and the new disagreements it brought dramatically increased the need for bishops to act as the interpreters and guardians of orthodoxy, or correct belief. Now freed from the risk of persecution, Christianity developed a new and very public method for resolving such disagreements, namely, the universal church council. The meeting and decrees of the first such gathering, the famed Council of Nicaea in 325, signaled the beginning of the church as a political institution just as surely as did the growing number of bishops who were drawn from senatorial and other leading families. Whether the dispute was over priestly and episcopal authority (as in the Donatist controversy of the fourth century), the nature of Jesus and the Trinity (as in the Arian and Nestorian disputes in the fourth and fifth centuries), or original sin and the nature of salvation (as in the debate over Pelagianism in the early fifth century), the method of resolution remained the same: a council of bishops and theologians from all over the Christian world met to discuss, decide on, and then pronounce the church's official teaching. The decrees of these councils shaped the very definition of orthodox or "catholic" Christianity and marked the emergence of a much more sophisticated theological tradition.

Two other types of individuals also particularly shaped the beliefs and practices of the post-Constantine church. The first was the ascetic. In an era without martyrs, it was the lone desert hermit or other holy man (or woman) who captured both the imagination and admiration of the average Christian. Though very few in number, such individuals dramatically defined the extreme limits of piety through their all-encompassing devotions. At the same time, they inspired somewhat less vigorous imitations of their feats—such as temporary fasting—among the rest of the faithful, a legacy that helped redefine what it meant to be a pious Christian. Even more significant was the rise of monasticism, which represented a formalized and communal version of the life of the ascetic. Beginning in the fourth century, Christians founded hundreds of monasteries and convents all over Europe, thus ensuring the perpetuation of the values and practices of asceticism in the subsequent centuries that have come to be known as the Middle Ages.

The other type of individual who was particularly influential during this first phase of tolerated Christianity was the saint. The saints—whose ranks included martyrs, bishops, ascetics, and others—were deceased Christians who had lived lives of exemplary piety and sacrifice. Ordinary Christians looked to the saints both as role models and as benevolent spiritual patrons who would plead for them before God in much the same way an earthly patron might intercede for them with an emperor or king. The reverence and gratitude that Christians felt for these holy people inspired them to venerate the saints, and often certain relics, or remnants, of the saints' earthly bodies as well. Though their role may appear passive (especially compared to those of bishops and ascetics), the saints of the fourth and fifth centuries held enormous sway in the lives and hearts of believers, providing both standards for Christian piety and an essential human connection with many intangible aspects of the faith.

The disintegration of the western half of the Roman Empire, which occurred in the fifth century, initiated a second transformational stage in Christian history. During the very same decades that Christianity had succeeded in penetrating all levels of Roman society, the northern provinces of the empire and eventually Rome itself were subjected to waves of migration and repeated military attacks by various Germanic peoples the Romans called "barbarians." By the beginning of the sixth century, barbarian kings and other potentates ruled all Roman territory west of the Balkans, signaling an increasing devolution of all political power and a fragmentation of all governmental institutions. The emperor Justinian (r. 527–565), still ruling the unified eastern part of the empire, attempted a reconsolidation but ultimately failed, as did the Frankish king Charlemagne, who conquered and ruled over a significant portion of the former western Roman Empire for a brief period in the early ninth century. Instead, from the sixth century to the eleventh century, political authority throughout Europe became more and more fragmented.

This political collapse of the western empire might have been fatal to Christian unity in the West. Instead the opposite occurred: Christianity—or rather its institutions, leaders, and practices—provided the very cultural glue that gave the increasingly diverse societies of Europe some sense of common heritage and identity. Again bishops, monks, and nuns as well as saints played pivotal roles. Bishops became less concerned with theological disputes and imperial politics and more involved with the everyday maintenance of public buildings and administration of services, such as poor relief in the cathedral cities that were their episcopal seats (the word "cathedral" comes from the Greek *cathedra,* or seat). Their prestige and political power were greatly strengthened as were their symbiotic relationships with secular rulers, who were often related to them by blood. Monks and nuns, for their part, exercised influence in a number of ways. First, they continued to provide religious models for other Christians while also often serving as missionaries to pagan peoples in northern and eastern Europe. Second, the heads of some monasteries (known as abbots) gained substantial political power, usually as a result of receiving and subsequently ruling over large tracts of land that had been donated by pious Christians. The third and by far the most celebrated legacy of medieval monasticism, though, was the meticulous preservation and copying of ancient pagan and Christian manuscripts, a labor that provided later generations with their greatest literary link to the vanished worlds of Greece and Rome. Meanwhile, the saints—and the culture of relics, shrines, and pilgrimages that surrounded them—continued to offer ordinary Christians a tangible bond with the traditions of the past. And because relics were portable, they and the stories attached to them circulated widely in Europe, providing a common cultural currency among otherwise very diverse societies. It is an indication of the depth of their meaning for Christians of the time that such cherished objects were so often purchased, traded, and even stolen during the early Middle Ages.

The Christianity that emerged over the course of this long period thus differed in many ways from the small, persecuted, otherworldly sect of earlier days. Now in a position of both spiritual and earthly power, the church had become an enormous, influential, and often very worldly institution. And it was an institution whose traditions, though still deeply rooted in the teachings of Jesus and the apostles, had been just as deeply transformed by its new relationship with the state. Paradoxically, the collapse of the western Roman Empire and its separation from the empire and church of the East had not spelled the end of Western Christianity but rather its distinctive beginning.

CHAPTER 2 CHRONOLOGY

	Politics	Literature	Individuals	Other
4th cent.	308–337 Constantine emperor 313 Edict of Milan 360–363 Julian the Apostate emperor 395 Division into eastern & western empires	325 Eusebius, *Ecclesiastical History* c. 357 Athanasius, *Life of Antony* c. 380 St. Jerome (c. 341–420) begins translation of Bible (Vulgate) c. 400 Augustine, *Confessions*	c. 250–336 Arius c. 251–356 Antony of Egypt c. 339–397 Ambrose of Milan 347–407 John of Chrysotom 354–430 Augustine of Hippo c. 350–425 Pelagius	312 ff. Donatist schism in Africa 325 Council of Nicaea 340 Old Roman Creed
5th cent.	410 Visigoths sack Rome 455 Vandals sack Rome 476 Last western emperor deposed by Odoacer		d. 452 Nestorius d. 461 Pope Leo the Great	432–461 Patrick's mission to Ireland 451 Council of Chalcedon 496 Baptism of Clovis
5th cent.	527–565 Justinian Byzantine emperor 568 Lombards invade Italy	c. 523 Boethius, *Consolation of Philosophy*	c. 480–c. 547 Benedict of Nursia c. 540–604 Pope Gregory I (the Great) c. 570–632 Mohammed	529 Benedict founds monastery at Monte Casino; composes Rule 534 Justinian code 596–604 Augustine of Canterbury's mission to England
7th cent.				664 Synod of Whitby chooses Roman over Celtic Christianity
8th cent.	732 Muslim European expansion slowed by Charles Martel at Tours	731 Bede, *Eccles. Hist. of the Engl. People*	c. 675–754 St. Boniface c. 700–780 St. Leoba 735–804 Alcuin of York	716–754 Boniface's mission to Frisia & Germany 782 Second Council of Nicaea
9th cent.	800 Charlemagne crowned by Pope Leo III in Rome 843 Treaty of Verdun divides Carolingian empire into three parts ca. 750–950 Viking and Magyar invasions 871–899 Alfred the Great king of Wessex	c. 820 Einhard, *Life of Charlemagne*		865 SS. Cyril & Methodius begin mission Slavs
10th cent.	962 Pope crowns Otto emperor			910 Beginning of monastic reform at Cluny 950–1050 Conversion of Scandinavia
11th cent.	1066 Norman invasion of England			1054 Schism between western & eastern churches

A. Asceticism

Like the gifts of prophecy and healing or the violent suffering of martyrdom, the extreme spiritual discipline—or asceticism—of a few remarkable individuals provided a clear example of personal holiness for early Christians. Already by the fourth century, stories of astounding ascetic feats among Egyptian holy men had begun to rival accounts of the martyrs in popularity among Christians. Most of these ascetics demonstrated their intense devotion to God by retreating from the comforts of society to live alone in the wilderness. Known as hermits (from the Greek *erêmia,* "desert"), they lived lives marked by constant prayer, severe physical deprivation, and, in many cases, astonishing acts of self-mortification ("grazers," for instance, survived only on grass and water). The word "asceticism" comes from the Greek *askesis,* or exercise, and the early Christian ascetics were sometimes described as spiritual athletes because of the rigorous discipline that they embraced (cf. 1 Cor 9:25). They displayed a heroism similar to that of Christians who had died for their belief as they bravely defied the devil, the contempt of others, and most of all, their own fears and human weaknesses. In fact, as the great age of martyrdom drew to a close with the imperial Edict of Toleration in 313, the ascetic life provided a new arena in which extremely pious Christians could express their commitment to the faith. The increasing number of ascetics in turn provided new spiritual models and objects of veneration for ordinary Christians of the time. By the end of the sixth century, the routines of spiritual discipline forged in solitude by the early hermits had been gradually formalized and adopted by large communities of ascetics. These communities— which ironically came to be known as monasteries (from the Greek *monachos,* "one who lives alone")—were to exert exceptional influence over the growth and development of Christianity during the next thousand years.

1. St. Athanasius
THE LIFE OF SAINT ANTONY (c. 357)

Undoubtedly the most influential book ever written on Christian asceticism was the biography of St. Antony of Egypt (c. 251–356) by Athanasius of Alexandria. An influential bishop at the Council of Nicaea, Athanasius (c. 295–373) had heard tales of the holy men in the desert since he was a boy, but only later in life decided to investigate the phenomenon in person. His encounter with the Egyptian hermit Antony, also known as St. Antony the Great, provoked an account that stunned his Christian readers. "Go and sell all that you have" (Mt 19:21) was the simple gospel message that inspired Antony—like the much later Francis of Assisi—to abandon his comfortable existence for a life of radical poverty and simplicity. As he wrestled alone in the desert with his own appetites and other diabolical temptations, Antony developed an inner strength and piety which Athanasius attributed to his literal imitation of Christ. Through fasting and numerous other hardships, Athanasius believed, Antony and the other desert fathers had truly perfected the Christian ideal of humility. Their teachings and examples were enthusiastically embraced by all of the most influential thinkers of the Western church, most notably St. Jerome and St. Augustine.

Antony was an Egyptian by birth. His parents were of good stock and well-to-do; and because they were Christians he himself was brought up a Christian. . . . Upon his parents' death he was left alone with an only sister who was very young. He was about eighteen or twenty years old at the time and took care of the house and his sister. Less than six months had passed since his parents' death when, as usual, he chanced to be on his way to church. As he was walking along, he collected his thoughts and reflected how the Apostles left everything and followed the Savior; also how the people in Acts sold what they had and laid it at the feet of the Apostles for distribution among the needy; and what great hope is laid up in Heaven for such as these [Acts 4:35; Mt 4:20, 19:21]. With these thoughts in his mind he entered the church. And it so happened that the Gospel was being read at that moment and he heard the passage in which the Lord says to the rich man: *If thou wilt be perfect, go sell all that thou hast, and give it to the poor; and come, follow me and thou shalt have treasure in Heaven* [Mt 19:21]. As though God had put him in mind of the saints and as though the reading had been directed especially to him, Antony immediately left the church and gave to the townspeople the property he had from his forebears—three hundred *arurae*,[1] very fertile and beautiful to see. He did not want it to encumber himself or his sister in any way whatever. He sold all the rest, the chattels they had, and gave the tidy sum he received to the poor, keeping back only a little for his sister.

But once again as he entered the church, he heard the Lord saying in the Gospel: *Be not solici-*

tous for the morrow [Mt 6:34]. He could not bear to wait longer, but went out and distributed those things also to the poor. His sister he placed with known and trusted virgins, giving her to the nuns to be brought up. Then he himself devoted all his time to ascetic living, intent on himself and living a life of self-denial, near his own house. For there were not yet so many monasteries in Egypt, and no monk even knew of the faraway desert. Whoever wished to concern himself with his own destiny practiced asceticism by himself not far from his own village.

Now, at that time there was in the next village an old man who had lived the ascetic life in solitude from his youth. When Antony saw him, he was *zealous for that which is good* [Gal 1:18]; and he promptly began to stay in the vicinity of the town. Then, if he heard of a zealous soul anywhere, like a wise bee he left to search him out, nor did he return home before he had seen him; and only when he had received from him, as it were, provisions for his journey to virtue, did he go back.

There, then, he spent the time of his initiation and made good his determination not to return to the house of his fathers nor to think about his relatives, but to devote all his affections and all his energy to the continued practice of the ascetic life. He did manual labor, for he had heard that *he that is lazy, neither let him eat* [Thes 3:10]. Some of his earnings he spent for bread and some he gave to the poor. He prayed constantly, having learnt that we must pray in private without cease. Again, he was so attentive at the reading of the Scripture lessons that nothing escaped him: he retained everything and so his memory served him in place of books.

Thus lived Antony and he was loved by all. He, in turn, subjected himself in all sincerity to

---

[1] In general terms, *aroura* signifies arable land, but here the reference is to an Egyptian measure of land, i.e., 100 square cubits. This makes the property of Antony's family the equivalent of 207 acres—a sizeable holding.

the pious men whom he visited and made it his endeavor to learn for his own benefit just how each was superior to him in zeal and ascetic practice. He observed the graciousness of one, the earnestness at prayer in another; studied the even temper of one and the kindheartedness of another; fixed his attention on the vigils kept by one and on the studies pursued by another; admired one for his patient endurance, another for his fasting and sleeping on the ground; watched closely this man's meekness and the forbearance shown by another; and in one and all alike he marked especially devotion to Christ and the love they had for one another.

Having thus taken his fill, he would return to his own place of asceticism. Then he assimilated in himself what he had obtained from each and devoted all his energies to realizing in himself the virtues of all. Moreover, he had no quarrels with anyone of his own age, excepting this that he would not be second to them in the better things; and this he did in such a way that no one was hurt in his feelings, but they, too, rejoiced on his account. And so all the villagers and the good men with whom he associated saw what kind of a man he was and they called him "God's Friend"; and they were fond of him as a son or as a brother.

But the Devil, the hater and envier of good, could not bear to see such resolution in a young man, but set about employing his customary tactics also against him. First he tried to make him desert the ascetic life by putting him in mind of his property, the care of his sister, the attachments of kindred, the love of money, the love of fame, the myriad pleasures of eating, and all the other amenities of life. Finally, he represented to him the austerity and all the toil that go with virtue, suggesting that the body is weak and time is long. In short, he raised up in his mind a great dust cloud of arguments, intending to make him abandon his set purpose.

The Enemy saw, however, that he was powerless in the face of Antony's determination and that it was rather he who was being bested because of the man's steadfastness and vanquished by his solid faith and routed by Antony's con-stant prayer. He then put his trust in the weapons that are *in the navel of his own belly* [Job 40:11]. Priding himself in these—for they are his choice snare against the young—he advanced to attack the young man, troubling him so by night and harassing him by day, that even those who saw Antony could perceive the struggle going on between the two. The Enemy would suggest filthy thoughts, but the other would dissipate them by his prayers; he would try to incite him to lust, but Antony, sensing shame, would gird his body with his faith, with his prayers and his fasting. The wretched Devil even dared to masquerade as a woman by night and to impersonate such in every possible way, merely in order to deceive Antony. But he filled his thoughts with Christ and reflected upon the nobility of the soul that comes from Him, and its spirituality, and thus quenched the glowing coal of temptation. And again the Enemy suggested pleasure's seductive charm. But Antony, angered, of course, and grieved, kept his thoughts upon the threat of fire and the pain of the worm. Holding these up as his shield, he came through unscathed.

The entire experience put the Enemy to shame. Indeed, he who had thought he was like to God, was here made a fool of by a stripling of a man. He who in his conceit disdained flesh and blood, was now routed by a man in the flesh. Verily, the Lord worked with this man— He who for our sakes took on flesh and gave to his body victory over the Devil. Thus all who fight in earnest can say: *Not I, but the grace of God with me* [1 Cor 15:10]. . . .

This was Antony's first victory over the Devil; rather, let me say that this singular success in Antony was the Savior's, who *condemned sin in the flesh that the justification of the law might be fulfilled in us who walk not according to the flesh, but according to the spirit* [Rom 8:3–4]. Now, Antony did not grow careless and take too much for granted with himself, merely because the demon had been brought to his knees; nor did the Enemy, worsted as he was in the conflict, cease to lie in wait for him. He kept going around again like a lion seeking a chance against him. But Antony, having learned from the Scriptures that the wiles of the Evil One are manifold, practiced asceticism in earnest, bearing in mind that even if he could not beguile his heart by pleasure of the body, he would certainly try to ensnare him by some other method; for the demon's love is sin. So he more and more mortified his body and brought it into subjection, lest having conquered on one occasion, he should be the loser on another. He resolved, therefore, to accustom himself to a more austere way of life. And many marvelled at him, but he bore the life easily. The zeal that had pervaded his soul over a long time, had effected a good frame of mind in him, with the result that even a slight inspiration received from others caused him to respond with great enthusiasm. For instance, he kept nocturnal vigil with such determination that he often spent the entire night sleepless, and this not only once, but many times to their admiration. Again, he ate but once a day, after sunset; indeed, sometimes only every other day, and frequently only every fourth day did he partake of food. His food was bread and salt; his drink, water only. Meat and wine we need not even mention, for no such thing could be found with the other ascetics either. He was content to sleep on a rush mat, though as a rule he lay down on the bare ground. He deprecated the use of oil for the skin, saying that young men should practice asceticism in real earnest and not go for the things that enervate the body; rather they should accustom it to hard work, bearing in mind the words of the Apostle: *When I am weak, then am I powerful* [2 Cor 12:10]. It was a dictum of his that the soul's energy thrives when the body's desires are feeblest.

He further held to the following truly remarkable conviction: he thought he should appraise his progress in virtue and his consequent withdrawal from the world not by any length of time spent in them, but by his attachment and devotion to them. Accordingly, he gave no thought to the passage of time, but day by day, as though he were just beginning the ascetic

life, he made greater effort toward perfection. He kept repeating to himself the words of Paul: *Forgetting the things that are behind, and reaching out to the things that are before* [Phil 3:13], remembering, too, the voice of Elias the Prophet saying: *The Lord liveth, in whose sight I stand this day* [2 Kgs 17:1; 18:15]. He observed that when he said *"this* day," he was not counting the time that was past, but as though constantly beginning anew, he worked hard each day to make of himself such as one should be to appear before God—pure of heart and ready to follow His will and none other. And he used to say to himself that the life led by the great Elias should serve the ascetic as a mirror in which always to study his own life. . . .

So he spent nearly twenty years practicing the ascetic life by himself, never going out and but seldom seen by others. After this, as there were many who longed and sought to imitate his holy life and some of his friends came and forcefully broke down the door[2] and removed it, Antony came forth as out of a shrine, as one initiated into sacred mysteries and filled with the spirit of God. It was the first time that he showed himself outside the fort to those who came to him. When they saw him, they were astonished to see that his body had kept its former appearance, that it was neither obese from want of exercise, nor emaciated from his fastings and struggles with the demons: he was the same man they had known before his retirement.

Again, the state of his soul was pure, for it was neither contracted by grief, nor dissipated by pleasure nor pervaded by jollity or dejection. He was not embarrassed when he saw the crowd, nor was he elated at seeing so many there to receive him. No, he had himself completely under control—a man guided by reason and stable in his character.

Through him the Lord cured many of those present who were afflicted with bodily ills, and freed others from impure spirits. He also gave

---

[2] Built to enforce his solitude.

Antony charm in speaking; and so he comforted many in sorrow, and others who were quarrelling he made friends. He exorted all to prefer nothing in the world to the love of Christ. And when in his discourse he exhorted them to be mindful of the good things to come and of the goodness shown us by God, *who spared not His own Son, but delivered Him up for us all* [Rom 8:32] he induced many to take up the monastic life. And so now monasteries also sprang up in the mountains and the desert was populated with monks who left their own people and registered themselves for citizenship in Heaven.

When the need arose for him to cross the canal of Arsinoë—and the occasion was a visitation of the brethren—the canal was full of crocodiles.[3] And simply praying, he went in with all his companions, and passed over unscathed. Returning to his monastery, he zealously applied himself to his holy and vigorous exercises. By ceaseless conferences he fired the zeal of those who were already monks, and incited most of the others to a love of the ascetic life; and soon, as his message drew men after him, the number of monasteries multiplied and to all he was a father and guide.

Now, one day when he had gone out, all the monks came to him and asked to hear a discourse. He spoke to them in the Egyptian tongue as follows:

"The Scriptures are really sufficient for our instruction. Yet it is well for us to encourage each other in the faith and to employ words to stimulate ourselves. Be you, therefore, like children and bring to your father what you know and tell it, while I, being your senior, share with you my knowledge and my experience.

"To begin with, let us all have the same zeal, not to give up what we have begun, not to lose heart, nor to say: 'We have spent a long time in this asceticism.' No, beginning over each day,

let us increase our zeal. The whole of man's life is very short measured by the ages to come, so that all our time is as nothing compared to eternal life. And in the world everything is sold at its worth and like value is bartered for like; but the promise of eternal life is bought for very little. For Scripture says: *The days of our life have seventy years in them; but if in the mighty they are eighty years and more, they are a labor and a burden* [Ps 89:10]. If, then, we live the full eighty years, or even a hundred, in the practice of asceticism, we shall not reign the same period of a hundred years, but instead of the hundred we shall reign for ever and ever. And though our striving is on earth, we shall not receive our inheritance on earth, but what is promised us is in Heaven. Moreover, we shall put aside our corruptible body, and receive it back incorruptible [cf. 1 Cor 15:42].

"So, children, let us not grow weary nor think that we are toiling a long time or that we are doing something great. For *the sufferings of this present time are not worthy to be compared with the glory to come that shall be revealed to us* [Rom 8:18]. Neither let us look back upon the world and think that we have renounced great things. For even the whole world is a very trifling thing compared with all of Heaven. Accordingly, if we should be lords of the whole earth and renounced the whole earth, this would again mean nothing as compared with the Kingdom of Heaven. As though a person should despise one copper drachma to gain a hundred drachmas of gold, so he who is lord of all the earth, and renounces it, really gives up but little and receives a hundredfold. If, then, even the whole earth is not equal in value to Heaven, certainly one who gives up a few acres must not boast nor be careless; for what he leaves behind is practically nothing, even though it be a home or a tidy sum of money he parts with.

"We must further bear in mind that if we do not give up these things for virtue's sake, later we must leave them behind and often, too, as Ecclesiastes reminds us [4:8, 6:2], even to persons to whom we do not wish to leave them. Then why not give them up for virtue's sake so that we may

---

[3]Arsinoë and its canal, which connected Lake Moeris and the Nile, stood in Arcadia to the west of the river some 150 miles south of Alexandria, and was also known as Crocodilopolis.

inherit a kingdom besides? Therefore, let none of us have even the desire to possess riches. For what does it avail us to possess what we cannot take with us? Why not rather possess those things which we can take along with us—prudence, justice, temperance, fortitude, understanding, charity, love of the poor, faith in Christ, meekness, hospitality? Once we possess these we shall find them going before us, preparing a welcome for us in the land of the meek.

"With these thoughts let a man persuade himself that he must not grow careless, and that all the more as he considers that he is a servant of the Lord and bound to serve his Master. Now, a servant would not dare to say, 'Since I worked yesterday, I am not working today.' Nor will he count up the time that has elapsed and rest during the days that lie ahead of him; no, day in and day out, as is written in the Gospel [Lk 17:7 ff.], he shows the same willingness in order that he may please his master and not incur any trouble. So let us also persist in the daily practice of asceticism, knowing that if we are negligent a single day, He will not forgive us for old time's sake, but will be angry at us because of our carelessness. So, too, we have heard in Ezechiel; so also Judas because of one single night destroyed the toil of an entire past. . . .

As Antony discussed these matters with them, all rejoiced. In some the love of virtue increased, in some negligence was discarded, and in others conceit was checked. All heeded his advice to despise the schemings of the Devil, and were in admiration of the grace given to Antony by the Lord for the discerning of spirits.

So, then, their solitary cells[4] in the hills were like tents filled with divine choirs—singing Psalms, studying, fasting, praying, rejoicing in the hope of the life to come, and laboring in order to give alms and preserving love and harmony among themselves. And truly it was like seeing a land apart, a land of piety and justice. For there was neither wrongdoer nor sufferer of wrong, nor was there reproof of the tax-collec-

tor;[5] but a multitude of ascetics, all with one set purpose—virtue. Thus, if one saw these solitary cells again and the fine disposition of the monks, he could but lift up his voice and say: *How fair are thy dwellings, O Jacob—thy tents, O Israel! Like shady glens and like a garden by a river, and like tents that the Lord hath pitched and cedars beside the waters!* [Num 24:5–6].

Antony himself went back as usual to his own cell and intensified his ascetic practices. Day by day he sighed as he meditated on the heavenly mansions, longing for them and seeing the short-lived existence of man. When he was about to eat and sleep and provide for the other needs of the body, shame overcame him as he thought of the spiritual nature of the soul. Often when about to partake of food with many other monks, the thought of spiritual food came upon him and he would beg to be excused and went a long way from them, thinking that he should be ashamed to be seen eating by others. He did eat, of course, by himself because his body needed it; and frequently, too, with the brethren—embarassed because of them, yet speaking freely because of the help his words gave them. He used to say that one should give all one's time to the soul rather than to the body. True, because necessity demands it, a little time should be given to the body; but on the whole we should give our first attention to the soul and look to its advantage. It must not be dragged down by the pleasures of the body, but rather the body must be made subject to the soul. This, he stated, was what the Savior said: *Be not solicitous for your life, what you shall eat, nor for your body what you shall put on. And seek not you what you shall eat or what you shall drink, and be not lifted up on high; for all these things do the nations of the world seek. But your Father knoweth that you have need of all these things.*

---

[4]Small, spartan rooms for prayer and sleep; from the Latin *cella*, "chamber."

[5]The Greek word for withdrawal into the desert (*anachoresis*) was originally applied to group flights in protest against taxation. By the Roman period, however, it had come to refer to an individual retreat made by one who had withdrawn into the caves at the desert's edge, thus giving rise to the Christian term "anchorite."

*But seek you first His kingdom and all these things
shall be added to you* [Lk 12:22, 29–31]. . . .

The fame of Antony reached even to emperors; for when Constantine Augustus and his sons Constantius Augustus and Constans Augustus heard about these things, they wrote to him as to a father and begged him to write back.[6] He, however, did not make much of the documents nor did he rejoice over the letters; but he was the same as he was before the emperor wrote to him. When the documents were brought to him, he called the monks and said: "You must not be surprised if an emperor writes to us, for he is a man; but you should rather be surprised that God has written the law for mankind and has spoken to us through His own Son." Indeed, he did not like to accept the letters, saying that he did not know what to answer to such things. But being persuaded by the monks who urged that the emperors were Christians and that they might take offense at being ignored, he had them read. And he wrote back, commending them for worshipping Christ, and giving them salutary advice not to think highly of the things of this world, but rather to bear in mind the judgment to come; and to know that Christ alone is the true and eternal King. He begged them to show themselves humane and to have a regard for justice and for the poor. And they were glad to receive his answer. So was he beloved by all, and all wished to have him as a father. . . .

The fact that he became famous everywhere and that he found universal admiration and his loss is felt even by people who have never seen him, betokens his virtue and a soul beloved of God. For Antony gained renown not for his writings, nor for worldly wisdom, nor for any art, but solely for his service of God.

And that this was something God-given no one could deny. For whence was it that this man who lived hidden in a mountain was heard of in Spain and Gaul, in Rome and in Africa, if it was not God who everywhere makes known His own, who, moreover, had told this to Antony at the very beginning? For though they do their work in secret and though they wish to remain obscure, yet the Lord shows them forth as lamps to all men, that thus again those who hear of them may realize that the commandments can lead to perfection, and may take courage on the path to virtue.

---

[6]Constantine (r. 308–337) was succeeded by his sons, whose reigns overlapped, with Constans emperor in 337–350 and Constantius in 337–361.

---

2. St. Ephraem of Edessa
LIFE OF ST. MARY THE HARLOT, NIECE OF THE HERMIT ABRAHAM (c. 370)

The life of a hermit was not limited to men, of course, and stories and sayings of the desert fathers (*abba*) were soon accompanied by tales of desert mothers (*ama*), such as Ama Sarah and Ama Syncletica (both fifth century). Mary the Harlot, an early desert ascetic, was the niece of the great hermit Abraham (fourth century), and her life story was recorded by Abraham's friend and disciple Ephraem of Edessa (d. 373). Ephraem's account combines the common ascetic themes of dramatic conversion and worldly renunciation with the equally traditional Christian theme of forgiveness of sinners. Mary's tearful repentance of her fallen life recalls the gospel stories of both Mary Magdalene and the Prodigal Son. Although Ephraem probably drew on Mary's own account of her life in writing the document, he also appears to have incorporated well-known biblical themes and quotations to further the story's didactic purpose, a common practice among writers of the period. Thus, for example, at the story's climactic moment, to which Ephraem almost certainly was not a witness, he is able to have Abraham pronounce the central message of the tale, namely, that the greatest sin Mary had committed was despair, and that even so she could be touched by divine forgiveness.

The Blessed Abraham had a brother after the flesh, and when this brother died, he left behind him an only daughter, a child of seven. Her father's friends and acquaintances, seeing her bereft of her parents, lost no time in bringing her to her uncle. The old man saw her, and had her housed in the outer room of his cell. There was a small window between the two rooms, and through this he taught her the psalter and other passages of Holy Writ, and she kept vigil with him in praising God and would sing the Psalms along with him, and tried to copy her uncle in all abstinence. Eagerly did she seize on this way of life, and made haste to practice all the powers of the soul. And the holy man ceased not to pray with tears, that her mind might not be tangled with the cares of the doings of earth: for her father in dying had left her vast wealth: but the brother being dead, and the daughter taking refuge with him, the servant of Christ gave orders that it should be shared among the poor and the orphaned. She herself would ask her uncle every day to pray God for her, that she might be caught away from evil imaginings and the diverse traps and snares of the devil.

And so she steadily followed her rule of life. Her uncle had joy to see her so swift and unhesitant in all good, in tears, in humbleness, in modesty, in quiet: and what is higher than all these, in great devotion towards God. Twenty years she lived with him in abstinence, even as an innocent lamb and an untarnished dove. But by the end of those years, the evil one began to wax violent against her, laying down his wonted snares; for let him once have her webbed in his net, and he could strike grief and anxiety into the holy man and separate some part of his mind at least from God.

Now a certain monk, but a monk in profession only, was in the habit of journeying often to visit the old man, under colour of edification. But gazing on that blessed creature through the window, he was pricked with the goads of lust: he began to long to speak with her, for wanton love had kindled his heart like a fire. For a great while he lay in ambush about her, so that a whole year went by before he had enervated her imagination by the softness of his words. But at the last she opened the window of her cell and came out to him: and forthwith he debauched and defiled her with evil and lust. But when the deed of shame was done, her heart trembled: and tearing the hair shift that clothed her, she began beating her face with her hands, and in her sorrow would have sought for death. Weighed down with anguish she could see no harbor wherein she might flee and take thought: swayed to and fro on shifting tides of imagination, she wept that she was no longer what she had been, and her speech was broken with wailing.

"From this time forward," she said, "I feel as one that has died. I have lost my days and my travail of abstinence, and my tears and prayers and vigils are brought to nothing: I have angered my God, and have destroyed myself. Sorrow upon me, with every spring of tears! I have bowed down that saint my uncle with grief most bitter: shame has gone over my soul: I am become the devil's mock. Why should such as I live on? Sorrow upon me, what have I done? Sorrow upon me, what came upon me? Sorrow upon me, what evil have I wrought? Sorrow upon me, from what have I fallen? How was my mind darkened? I know not how I fell, I know not how I was defiled, I know not what cloud darkened my heart, how I could be ignorant of what I was doing. Where shall I flee to hide? Where can I find a pit wherein to throw myself? Where was my uncle's teaching, and the counsels of Ephraem his friend [i.e., the author], that would urge me to abide in my virginity and keep my soul unsullied for the immortal Bridegroom? For your Bridegroom, they would say, is holy and jealous. Sorrow upon me, what am I to do? I dare not look at heaven, I that am dead to God and man. I shall not dare now to go near that window. How could I attempt ever to talk again with my good uncle, filthy as I am with all uncleanness? If I did, would not a flame leap from the window and burn me there to ashes? Better to go away to some other country where there is no one who could know me, for I am nought but a dead woman now, and there is no hope left to me any more." So she rose, and made her way to another city, and changing the garb of her youth, took refuge in a certain brothel. . . .

So then, it was two years before he [Abraham] discovered where she was and what she did: and he asked a singular good friend of his to go to the place and find out all he could. The friend set out, and coming again he told him all the truth, and how he himself had seen her: and at the old man's asking, he brought him a military habit, and a horse to ride. So he opened his door, and dressed himself in military garb, and set a great hat upon his head, so as to cover his face. But he also took a gold piece with him, and got up on the horse, and made all haste upon the road. Even as one desirous of spying out a country or a city will put on the garb of its inhabitants lest he be recognized, so did the blessed Abraham make use of the garb of the enemy to put him to rout. . . .

So then, arrived at the town, he stepped aside into the tavern, and with anxious eyes he sat looking about him, glancing this way and that in hopes to see her. The hours went by, and still no chance of seeing her appeared: and finally he spoke jestingly to the innkeeper. "They tell me, friend," said he, "that thou hast a very fine wench: if it were agreeable to thee, I should like well to have a look at her."

The innkeeper regarded the hoary head, the old frame bowed with its weight of years, and in no hope that this desire for a sight of her was prompted by lechery, made reply that it was indeed as he had heard, that she was an uncommon handsome lass. And indeed Mary in beauty of body was fair, wellnigh beyond aught that nature demandeth. The old man asked her name, and was told that they called her Mary. Then, with merry countenance, "Come now," said he, "bring her in and show her to me, and let me have a fine supper for her this day, for I have heard the praises of her on all hands." So they called her: but when she came in and the good old man saw her in her harlot's dress, his whole body wellnigh dissolved in grief. Yet he hid the bitterness of his soul behind a cheerful countenance, and checked by force of his manhood the starting tears, for fear that the girl might recognize him and take flight.

So as they sat and drank their wine, the great old man began to jest with her. The girl rose and put her arms about his neck, beguiling him with kisses. And as she was kissing him, she smelt the fragrance of austerity that his lean body breathed, and remembered the days when she too had lived austere: and as if a spear had pierced her soul, she gave a great moan and began to weep: and not able to endure the pain in her heart, she broke out into words, "Woe's me, that am alone unhappy!"

The innkeeper was dumbfounded. "What ails thee, Mistress Mary," said he, "to burst out all of a sudden into this sore lamenting? It is two years today that thou hast been here, and no one ever heard a sigh from thee or a sad word: indeed I know not what has come over thee."

"I had been happy," said the girl, "if three years ago I had died."

At this the good old man, afraid that she might recognize him, spoke to her genially enough, "Now, no!" said he, "here am I come to make merry, art going to begin the tale of thy sins?" . . .

So then, the good old man produced the gold piece he had brought with him and gave it to the innkeeper. "Now, friend," said he, "make us a right good supper, so that I may make merry with the lass: for I am come a very long journey for love of her." O wisdom as of God! O wise understanding of the spirit! O memorable discretion in salvation! Throughout fifty years of abstinence he had never tasted bread: and now without a falter eats meat to save a lost soul. The company of the holy angels, rejoicing over the discretion of the blessed man, were mazed at that which he ate and drank, light-hearted and nothing doubting, to deliver a soul sunken in the mire. O wisdom and understanding of the wise! O discrimination of the discerning! Come, marvel at this madness, this reversal, when an upright and wise and discreet and prudent man is made a reckless fool to snatch a soul from the jaws of the lion, and set free a captive bound and thrust away from its chains and its dark prison-house.

So, when they had feasted, the girl began to provoke him to come to her room to lie with her. "Let us go," said he. Coming in, he saw a lofty bed prepared, and straightway sat gaily down upon it. . . .

"Come close to me, Mistress Mary," said the old man. And when she was beside him he took her firmly by the hand as if to kiss her, then taking the hat from his head and his voice breaking into weeping, "Mary, my daughter," said he, "dost thou not know me? My heart, was it not I that brought thee up? What has come to thee, my child? Who was it destroyed thee? Where is that angel's garb thou didst wear, my daughter? Where is thy continence, thy tears, thy vigils, thy bed on the ground? How didst thou fall from heaven's height into this pit, my daughter? Why, when thou didst sin, didst thou not tell me? Why didst thou not come to me there and then? And indeed I would have done thy penance for thee, and my dear Ephraem too. Why didst thou act like this? Why didst thou desert me, and bring me into this intolerable sorrow? For who is without sin, save God Himself?"

This and much else he said: but all the while she stayed in his hands, motionless as a stone. Fear and shame had filled her full.

And again the old man began, weeping, "Mary, child, wilt thou not speak to me? Wilt thou not speak to me, half of my heart? Was it not because of thee, my child, that I came here? Upon me be this sin, O my daughter. It is I that shall answer for thee to God at the Day of Judgment. It is I that shall give satisfaction to God for this sin." And until midnight he sought to comfort her, with such words as these, encouraging her with many tears. Little by little she took courage, and at last she spoke to him, weeping, "I cannot," she said, "look on your face for shame. And how can I pour out a prayer to God, so foul as I am with the mud of this uncleanness?"

Then said the holy man, "Upon me be thy guilt, my daughter: at my hand shall God require this sin: do but listen to me, and come, let us go home. For look you, there is our dear Ephraem, grieving sore for thee, and forever pleading with God for thee. Be not mistrustful, daughter, of the mercy of God; let your sins be as mountains, His mercy towers above His every creature. We read that an unclean woman came to Him that was clean, and she did not soil Him, but was herself made clean by Him: she washed the Lord's feet with her tears, and dried them with her hair. If a spark can set on fire the sea, then can your sins stain His whiteness: it is no new thing to fall in the mire, but it is an evil thing to lie there fallen. Bravely return again to that place from whence thou camest. . . ."

Then she said, "If you are sure that I can do penance and that God will accept my atonement, behold I shall come as you bid me: go before and I shall follow your goodness and kiss the track of your feet, you that have so grieved for me, that you would draw me out of this cesspit." And laying her head at his feet, she wept all night, saying, "What shall I render to Thee for all this, O Lord my God?"

When dawn had come, the blessed Abraham said to her, "Rise up, daughter, and let us go home to our cell." And answering him, she said, "I have a little gold here, and some clothes, what would you have me do with them?" But the

Blessed Abraham made answer, "Leave all those things here, for they were earned from the Evil One." And they rose up and went away. And he set her upon his horse and led it, going before, even as the good shepherd when he has found his lost sheep, carries it with joy upon his shoulder: and so the blessed Abraham, with joy in his heart, journeyed along the road with his niece. And when he had come home, he set her in the inner cell which had been his own, and himself remained in the outer. And she, clad in her hair shift, did there abide in humility of soul and in tears from the heart and the eyes, disciplining herself with vigils and stern travail of abstinence, in quiet and modesty unweariedly calling upon God, bewailing her sin but with sure hope of pardon, with supplication so moving that no man, even were he without bowels of compassion, could hear her sorrowful crying and not be stirred. . . . So urgently did she pray God to pardon the thing she had done that she obtained from on high a sign that her penitence was accepted. And God the compassionate, who will have no man perish but that all should come to repentance, so accepted her atonement that after three full years He restored health to many at her prayer. For crowds flocked to her, and she would pray to God for their healing, and it was granted her.

And the Blessed Abraham, after living for another ten years in this life, and seeing her blessed penitence, and giving glory to God, rested in peace in the seventieth year of his age. For fifty years in devotion and humility of heart and love unfeigned, he had fulfilled his vow. . . .

And Mary also lived another five years, yet more devoutly ruling her life, and persevering night and day in prayer to God, with lamentation and tears, so that many a one passing that place at night and hearing the voice of her grieving would himself be turned to weeping, and add his tears to hers. But when the hour of her sleeping came, wherein she was taken up from this life, all that saw her gave glory to God, for the splendor of her face.

---

3. St. Benedict of Nursia
RULE (c. 530)

During the two centuries following the publication of the *Life of St. Antony,* two simultaneous developments affected the reception of the ascetic ideal in the West. The first was the embrace of asceticism by such remarkable individuals as St. Martin of Tours (355–397) and John Cassian (c. 360–435). The second was the growing popularity of a communal version of the ascetic life, which reached fruition in the West under the influence of St. Benedict of Nursia (c. 480–c. 547). Since the time of the earliest Christian hermits, disciples and other pious on-lookers had begun gathering around the holy men and women, seeking guidance and inspiration. Some of the desert fathers and mothers permitted the development of small encampments, or *laura,* around them. Others, most famously Simeon Stylites (c. 390–459), sought to escape such followers, in his case through life on a succession of pillars (the last one about 55 feet high), yet even here without success. Responding to similar pleas for guidance, the hermit Benedict eventually founded twelve small ascetic communities, or monasteries, in central Italy and one large community at Monte Cassino (near Naples). He set up a routine of prayer and work for these monasteries that was focused on cultivating the supreme virtue of humility, and he codified this way of life in a document known as the Rule. In Benedict's Rule, the self-discipline and deprivation of the hermit are systematized for a community of self-selected men, all of whom have sworn to obey a single "father," or abbot (from the Hebrew *abba*). Benedict's sister Scholastica later used his Rule as the foundation for a community of women she established near Monte Cassino. From that time on, the founders of nearly every monastery and convent in the West derived their communities' governing documents from Benedict's work. When we consider the profound influence of monasticism on medieval Christianity, the magnitude of Benedict's achievement becomes clear.

CHAPTER 2: WHAT THE ABBOT SHOULD BE

An abbot to be fit to rule a monastery should ever remember what he is called[7] and in his acts illustrate this high calling. For in a monastery he is considered to take the place of Christ, since he is called by His name as the apostle saith, *Ye have received the spirit of the adoption of sons, whereby we cry, Abba, Father* [Rom 8:15]. Therefore the abbot should neither teach, ordain, nor require anything against the command of our Lord (God forbid!), but in the minds of his disciples let his orders and teaching be mingled with the leaven of divine justice.

The abbot should ever be mindful that at the dread judgment of God there will be inquiry both as to his teaching and as to the obedience of his disciples. Let the abbot know that any lack of goodness, which the master of the family shall find in his flock, will be accounted the shepherd's fault. On the other hand, he shall be acquitted in so far as he shall have shown all the watchfulness of a shepherd over a restless and disobedient flock: and if as their pastor he shall have employed every care to cure their corrupt manners, he shall be declared guiltless in the Lord's judgment, and he may say with the prophet, *I have not hidden Thy justice in my heart; I have told Thy truth and Thy salvation; but they {scorned} and despised me* [Ps 40:10]. And then in the end shall death be inflicted as a meet punishment upon the sheep which have not responded to his care. When, therefore, any one

shall receive the name of abbot, he ought to rule his disciples with a twofold teaching: that is, he should first show them in deeds rather than words all that is good and holy. To such as are understanding, indeed, he may expound the Lord's behests by words; but to the hard-hearted and to the simple-minded he must manifest the divine precepts in his life. Thus, what he has taught his disciples to be contrary to God's law, let him show in his own deeds that such things are not to be done, lest preaching to others *he himself become a castaway* [1 Cor 9:27], and God say unto him thus sinning, *Why dost thou declare My justices, and take My testament in thy mouth? Thou hast hated discipline, and cast My speeches behind thee* [Ps 50:16–17]. And *Thou, who didst see the mote in thy brother's eye, hast thou not seen the beam that is in thine own* [Mt 7:3]?

Let him make no distinction of persons in the monastery. Let not one be loved more than another, save such as be found to excel in obedience or good works. Let not the free-born be put before the serf-born in religion, unless there be other reasonable cause for it. If upon due consideration the abbot shall see such cause he may place him where he pleases; otherwise let all keep their own places, because *whether bond or free we are all one in Christ* [Rom 2.11], and bear an equal burden of service under one Lord: *for with God there is no accepting of persons.* For one thing only are we preferred by Him, if we are found better than others in good works and more humble. Let the abbot therefore have equal love for all, and let all, according to their deserts, be under the same discipline.

---

[7] *Abba* = Father.

The abbot in his teaching should always observe that apostolic rule which saith, *Reprove, entreat, rebuke* [1 Tim 4:2]. That is to say, as occasions require he ought to mingle encouragement with reproofs. Let him manifest the sternness of a master and the loving affection of a father. He must reprove the undisciplined and restless severely, but he should exhort such as are obedient, quiet and patient, for their better profit. We charge him, however, to reprove and punish the stubborn and negligent. Let him not shut his eyes to the sins of offenders; but, directly they begin to show themselves and to grow, he must use every means to root them up utterly, remembering the fate of Hell, the priest of Silo. To the more virtuous and apprehensive, indeed, he may for the first or second time use words of warning; but in dealing with the stubborn, the hard-hearted, the proud and the disobedient, even at the very beginning of their sin, let him chastise them with stripes and with bodily punishment, knowing that it is written, *The fool is not corrected with words* [Prov 29:19]. And again, *Strike thy son with a rod and thou shalt deliver his soul from death* [Prov 23:14].

The abbot ought ever to bear in mind what he is and what he is called; he ought to know that to whom more is entrusted, from him more is exacted. Let him recognize how difficult and how hard a task he has undertaken, to rule souls and to make himself a servant to the humours of many. One, forsooth, must be led by gentle words, another by sharp reprehension, another by persuasion; and thus shall he so shape and adapt himself to the character and intelligence of each, that he not only suffer no loss in the flock entrusted to his care, but may even rejoice in its good growth. Above all things let him not slight nor make little of the souls committed to his care, heeding more fleeting, worldly and frivolous things; but let him remember always that he has undertaken the government of souls, of which he shall also have to give an account. And that he may not complain of the want of temporal means, let him remember that it is written, *Seek first the kingdom of God, and His justice, and all things shall be given to you* [Mt 6:33]. And again, *Nothing is wanting to such as fear Him* [Ps 34:10].

He should know that whoever undertakes the government of souls must prepare himself to account for them. And however great the number of the brethren under him may be, let him understand for certain that at the Day of Judgment he will have to give to our Lord an account of all their souls as well as of his own. In this way, by fearing the inquiry concerning his flock which the Shepherd will hold, he is solicitous on account of others' souls as well as of his own, and thus whilst reclaiming other men by his corrections, he frees himself also from all vice. . . .

CHAPTER 7: ON HUMILITY

Brethren, Holy Scripture cries out to us, saying, *Every one who exalteth himself shall be humbled, and he who humbleth himself shall be exalted* [Lk 14:11]. In this it tells us that every form of self-exaltation is a kind of pride, which the prophet declares he carefully avoided, where he says, *Lord, my heart is not exalted, neither are my eyes lifted up; neither have I walked in great things, nor in wonders above myself. And why? If I did not think humbly, but exalted my soul; as a child weaned from his mother, so wilt Thou reward my soul* [Ps 131:1–2].

Wherefore, brethren, if we would scale the summit of humility, and swiftly gain the heavenly height which is reached by our lowliness in this present life, we must set up a ladder of climbing deeds like that which Jacob saw in his dream, whereon angels were descending and ascending [cf. Gen 28:12]. Without doubt that descending and ascending is to be understood by us as signifying that we descend by exalting ourselves and ascend by humbling ourselves. But the ladder itself thus set up is our life in this world, which by humility of heart is lifted by our Lord to heaven. Our body and soul we may indeed call the sides of the ladder in which our divine vocation has set the divers steps of humility and discipline we have to ascend.

The first step of humility, then, is reached when a man, with the fear of God always before his eyes, does not allow himself to forget, but is ever mindful of all God's commandments. He remembers, moreover, that such as [scorn] God fall into hell for their sins, and that life eternal awaits such as fear Him. And warding off at each moment all sin and defect in thought and word, of eye, hand or foot, of self-will, let such a one bestir himself to prune away the lusts of the flesh.

Let him think that he is seen at all times by God from heaven; and that wheresoever he may be, all his actions are visible to the eye of God and at all times are reported by the angels. The prophet shows us this when he says that God is ever present to our thoughts: *God searcheth the hearts and reins* [Ps 7:9]. And again, *The Lord knoweth the thoughts of men that they are vain* [Ps 94:11]. He also saith, *Thou hast understood my thoughts afar off* [Ps 139:2]; and again, *The thought of man shall confess Thee* [Ps 76:10]. In order, then, that the humble brother may be careful to avoid wrong thoughts let him always say in his heart, *Then shall I be without spot before Him, if I shall keep me from my iniquity* [Ps 18:23]. . . .

We have therefore to beware of evil desires, since death stands close at the door of pleasure. It is for this reason that Scripture bids us, *Follow not thy {lusts}* [Eccl 18:30]. If, therefore, *the eyes of the Lord behold both the good and the bad* [Prov 15:3]; if He be ever looking down from heaven upon the sons of men to find one who thinks of God or seeks Him; and if day and night what we do is made known to Him—for these reasons, by the angels appointed to watch over us, we should always take heed, brethren, lest God may sometime or other see us, as the prophet says in the Psalm, *inclined to evil and become unprofitable servants.* Even though He spare us for a time, because He is loving and waits for our conversion to better ways, let us fear that He may say to us hereafter, *These things thou hast done and I held my peace* [Ps 49:21].

The second step of humility is reached when any one not loving self-will takes no heed to satisfy his own desires, but copies in his life what our Lord said, *I came not to do My own will, but the will of Him Who sent Me* [Jn 6:38]. Scripture likewise proclaims that self-will engendereth punishment, and necessity purchaseth a crown.[8]

The third step of humility is reached when a man, for the love of God, submits himself with all obedience to a superior, imitating our Lord, of whom the apostle saith, *He was made obedient even unto death* [Phil 2:8].

The fourth step of humility is reached when any one in the exercise of his obedience patiently and with a quiet mind bears all that is inflicted on him, things contrary to nature, and even at times unjust, and in suffering all these he neither wearies nor gives over the work, since the Scripture says, . . . *Thou has proved us, O Lord; Thou hast tried us, as silver is tried, with fire. Thou hast brought us into the snare; Thou hast laid tribulation upon our backs* [Ps 66:10]. And to show that we ought to be subject to a prior (or superior) it goes on, *Thou hast placed men over our heads* [Ps 66:12]. And, moreover, they fulfil the Lord's command by patience in adversity and injury, who, *when struck on one cheek, offer the other;* when one *taketh away their coat leave go their cloak also,* and who being compelled to carry a burden one mile, go two; who, with Paul the apostle, suffer false brethren, and bless those who speak ill of them [cf. Mt 5:39 ff.].

The fifth step of humility is reached when a monk manifests to his abbot, by humble confession, all the evil thoughts of his heart and his secret faults. The Scripture urges us to do this where it says, *Reveal thy way to the Lord and hope in Him* [Ps 37:5]. It also says, *Confess to the Lord, because He is good, because His mercy endureth for ever* [Ps 106:1]. And the prophet also says, *I have made known unto Thee mine offence, and mine injustices I have not hidden. I have said, I will declare openly against myself mine injustices to the Lord; and Thou hast pardoned the wickedness of my heart* [Ps 32:5].

The sixth step of humility is reached when a monk is content with all that is mean and vile;

---

[8]From the *Acts of the Martyrs.*

and in regard to everything enjoined him accounts himself a poor and worthless workman, saying with the prophet, *I have been brought to nothing, and knew it not. I have become as a beast before Thee, and I am always with Thee* [Ps 73: 22–23].

The seventh step of humility is reached when a man not only confesses with his tongue that he is most lowly and inferior to others, but in his inmost heart believes so. Such a one, humbling himself, exclaims with the prophet, *I am a worm and no man, the reproach of men and the outcast of the people* [Ps 22:6]. *I have been exalted and am humbled and confounded* [Ps 88:15]. And again, *It is good for me that Thou hast humbled me, that I may learn Thy commandments* [Ps 119:71].

The eighth step of humility is reached when a monk does nothing but what the common rule of the monastery, or the example of his seniors, enforces.

The ninth step of humility is reached when a monk restrains his tongue from talking, and, practising silence, speaks not till a question be asked him, since Scripture says, *In many words thou shalt not avoid sin* [Prov 10:19], and *a talkative man shall not be directed upon the earth* [Ps 140:11].

The tenth step of humility is attained to when one is not easily and quickly moved to laughter, for it is written, *The fool lifteth his voice in laughter* [Eccl 21:23].

The eleventh step of humility is reached when a monk, in speaking, do so quietly and without laughter, humbly, gravely and in a few words and not with a loud voice, for it is written, *A wise man is known by a few words* [Prov 10:14].

The twelfth step of humility is reached when a monk not only has humility in his heart, but even shows it also exteriorly to all who behold him. Thus, whether he be in the oratory at the "Work of God," in the monastery, or in the garden, on a journey, or in the fields, or wheresoever he be, sitting, standing or walking, always let him, with head bent and eyes fixed on the ground, bethink himself of his sins and imagine that he is arraigned before the dread judgment of God. Let him be ever saying to himself, with the publican in the Gospel, *Lord, I a sinner am not worthy to lift mine eyes to heaven* [Lk 18:13] and with the prophet, *I am bowed down and humbled on every side* [Ps 38:8].

When all these steps of humility have been mounted the monk will presently attain to that love of God which is perfect and casteth out fear. By means of this love everything which before he had observed not without fear, he shall now begin to do by habit, without any trouble and, as it were, naturally. He acts now not through fear of hell, but for the love of Christ, out of a good habit and a delight in virtue. All this our Lord will vouchsafe to work by the Holy Ghost in His servant, now cleansed from vice and sin. . . .

CHAPTER 23: OF EXCOMMUNICATION FOR OFFENCES

If any brother be found stubborn, disobedient, proud, murmuring, or in any way acting contrary to the Holy Rule, or [scorning] the orders of his seniors, let him, according to the precept of our Lord be secretly admonished by those seniors, once or twice. If he will not amend let him be publicly reproved before all. But if even then he does not correct his faults, let him, if he understand the nature of the punishment, be subject to excommunication. But if he be obstinate he is to undergo corporal punishment.

CHAPTER 24: WHAT THE MANNER OF EXCOMMUNICATION SHOULD BE

The mode of excommunication or punishment should be proportioned to the fault, and the gravity of the fault shall depend on the judgment of the abbot. If any brother be detected in small faults let him be excluded from eating at table with the rest. The punishment of one thus separated from the common table shall be of this kind: in the oratory he shall not intone either psalm or antiphon; neither shall he read any lesson until he has made satisfaction. He shall take his portion of food alone, after the brethren have had their meal, and in such quantity and at such time as the abbot shall think fit. So that if, for example, the brethren take their meal at the sixth hour let him take his at the ninth; if the brethren take theirs at the ninth, let him have his in the evening, till such time as by due satisfaction he obtain pardon.

CHAPTER 25: OF GRAVER FAULTS

Let the brother who is guilty of some graver fault be excluded both from the common table and from the oratory. None of the brethren shall talk to him or consort with him. Let him be alone at the work which is set him, let him remain in penance and sorrow, and keep before his mind that terrible sentence of the apostle where he says, *Such a one is delivered over to Satan for the destruction of the flesh, that his spirit may be saved in the day of our Lord* [1 Cor 5:5]. Let him take his food alone, in such quantity and at such time as the abbot shall think fit. Let no one bless him as he passes by, nor ask a blessing on the food that is given him. . . .

CHAPTER 28: OF THOSE WHO, BEING OFTEN CORRECTED, DO NOT AMEND

If any brother does not amend after being often corrected for any fault, and even excommunicated, let a sharper punishment be administered to him, that is, let him be corrected by stripes. And if even after this he shall not correct himself, or being puffed up by pride (which God forbid) shall attempt to defend his doings, then let the abbot act like a wise physician. If after applying the fomentations and ointments of exhortation, the medicine of the Holy Scriptures and the final cautery of excommunication and scourging, he find that his labours have had no effect, then let him try

what is more than all this, his own prayer and those of the brethren for him, that the Lord, who can do all things, may work the cure of the sick brother. If he be not healed by this means then let the abbot use the serving knife, according to that saying of the apostle, *Put away the evil one from among you* [1 Cor 5:13]; and again, *If the faithless one depart, let him depart* [1 Cor 7:15], lest one diseased sheep should infect the whole flock.

CHAPTER 29: WHETHER BRETHREN WHO LEAVE THEIR MONASTERY MUST BE RECEIVED BACK

If the brother, who through his own bad conduct leaves or is expelled from the monastery, shall desire to return, he must first promise full amendment of the fault for which he left it. He may then be received back to the lowest place, that by this his humility may be tried. If he shall again leave he may be received back till the third time, but he shall know that after this all possibility of returning will be denied to him. . . .

CHAPTER 48: OF DAILY MANUAL LABOUR

Idleness is an enemy of the soul. Because this is so the brethren ought to be occupied at specified times in manual labour, and at other fixed hours in holy reading. We therefore think that both these may be arranged for as follows: from Easter to the first of October, on coming out from Prime, let the brethren labour till about the fourth hour [about 9:30 a.m. in summer]. From the fourth till close upon the sixth hour let them employ themselves in reading. On rising from table after the sixth hour let them rest on their beds in strict silence; but if any one shall wish to read, let him do so in such a way as not to disturb any one else.

Let None be said somewhat before the time, about the middle of the eighth hour [ca. 3:30

p.m.], and after this all shall work at what they have to do till evening. If, however, the nature of the place or poverty require them to labour at gathering in the harvest, let them not grieve at that, for then are they truly monks when they live by the labour of their hands, as our Fathers and the Apostles did. Let everything, however, be done with moderation for the sake of the faint-hearted.

From the first of October till the beginning of Lent let the brethren be occupied in reading till the end of the second hour [ca. 9:30 a.m.]. At that time Tierce shall be said, after which they shall labour at the work enjoined them till None [c.a. 1:30 p.m.]. At the first signal for the Hour of None all shall cease to work, so as to be ready when the second signal is given. After their meal they shall be employed in reading or on the psalms.

On the days of Lent, from the morning till the end of the third hour, the brethren are to have time for reading, after which let them work at what is set them to do till the close of the tenth hour. During these Lenten days let each one have some book from the library which he shall read through carefully. These books are to be given out at the beginning of Lent.

It is of much import that one or two seniors be appointed to go about the monastery at such times as the brethren are free to read, in order to see that no one is slothful, given to idleness or foolish talking instead of reading, and so not only makes no profit himself but also distracts others. If any such be found (which God forbid) let him be corrected once or twice, and if he amend not let him be subjected to regular discipline of such a character that the rest may take warning. Moreover one brother shall not associate with another at unsuitable hours.

On Sunday also, all, save those who are assigned to various offices, shall have time for reading. If, however, any one be so negligent and slothful as to be unwilling or unable to read or meditate, he must have some work given him, so as not to be idle. For weak brethren, or those of delicate constitutions, some work or craft shall be found to keep them from idleness, and yet not such as to crush them by the heavy labour or to drive them away. The weakness of such brethren must be taken into consideration by the abbot....

CHAPTER 73: THAT ALL PERFECTION IS NOT CONTAINED IN THIS RULE

We have written this Rule, that, by its observance in monasteries, we may show that we have in some measure uprightness of manners or the beginning of religious life. But for such as hasten onward to the perfection of holy life there are the teachings of the Holy Fathers, the observance whereof leads a man to the heights of perfection. For what page or what passage of the divinely inspired books of the Old and the New Testament is not a most perfect rule for man's life? Or what book is there of the Holy Catholic Fathers that doth not proclaim this, that by a direct course we may come to our Creator? Also, what else are the *Collations* of the Fathers, their Institutes, their *Lives,* and the Rule of our Holy Father St. Basil[9] but examples of the virtues, of the good living and obedience of monks? But to us who are slothful, and lead bad and negligent lives, they are matter for shame and confusion.

Do thou, therefore, whosoever thou art who hasteneth forward to the heavenly country, accomplish first, by the help of Christ, this little Rule written for beginniners, and then at length shalt thou come, under God's guidance, to the lofty heights of doctrine and virtue, which we have spoken of above.

---

[9]The first two works were written by John Cassian (c. 360–435), one of the earliest and most influential importers of Egyptian monasticism to Europe. The Rule of St. Basil the Great (c. 330–374), which influenced Benedict's own formulation, continued to play a significant role in medieval monasticism and is still used by monks of Eastern churches.

B. Arianism

The Arian controversy of the early fourth century coincided precisely with one of the most important watersheds in all of Christian history: the end of persecution and the beginning of legal toleration under the Roman emperor Constantine. Because of this timing, the Arian controversy provided the church with its first opportunity to act as a legal, "catholic" (or universal) organization. The doctrinal statement that resulted from this controversy was in itself important. But the process that produced the decree—a council of bishops from all over the Mediterranean world met at Nicaea in 325 to debate the issue—was equally significant, since it became a blueprint for how Christian leaders would deal with all future theological disputes.

The controversy stemmed from the teachings of a Libyan priest named Arius (c. 250–336), who emphasized the reality of Christ's human nature and its relative separateness from his divine nature. Jesus, he argued, was indeed sinless, but he was still fully human and thus capable of sinning, and thus also (at least in that way) not identical with God the Father. Even more controversially, Arius reasoned that one should not believe—as many Christians did—that both the Son and the Father were unbegotten (or uncreated and thus eternal). Such a belief, he said, would imply the existence of two distinct gods, hence his famous dictum, "There was a time when He [the Son] was not." In other words, according to Arius, only God the Father was truly eternal and unbegotten; the Son, or *Logos* ("Word"), was created by God the Father and was thus neither coequal nor eternal.

The definitive decree of the Nicene council, which condemned the teachings of Arius, did not end theological controversies about the divine and human natures of Christ. Over a century later, for example, the Council of Chalcedon took up the issue again but could not produce a definition that satisfied all representatives, a failure that resulted in the splitting off of the Monophysite ("one [divine] nature") churches of the East. Nor did Nicaea provide sufficient mechanisms for enforcement, an oversight that allowed missionaries to convert most pagan Germanic peoples to an Arian version of Christianity. It did, however, set an important precedent for dealing with potentially schismatic issues, a precedent that would become increasingly significant as the membership of the Church expanded to include most of the Roman world.

1. THE PRELIMINARY EPISTOLARY WAR

Within a year of his first public preaching on the nature of Christ in 319, Arius was condemned and excommunicated by a council of almost 100 Libyan and Egyptian bishops. The first reading below is a letter that Arius wrote while he was in exile in Palestine, appealing for help to Eusebius of Nicomedia (d. 341), who, like Arius, had been a pupil of the theologian Lucian of Antioch

(c. 240–312). As a fellow disciple of Lucian, Eusebius both shared Arius' beliefs and was sympathetic to his plight. As a leading advisor to the emperor Constantine, he was also in a position of some political influence and thus able to protect Arius from the coalition mounted against him by Alexander of Alexandria. The second reading is a letter in which Alexander vehemently rejected what he considered to be a contrived and forced choice between belief in two gods or acceptance of the interpretation of Arius. Instead, he proposed that the Son was a nonidentical copy of the Father who had not been created by the Father but had issued forth from him—or, in the terminology that would be adopted by the council of Nicaea, that Christ was "begotten not created."

---

a. LETTER OF ARIUS TO EUSEBIUS, BISHOP OF NICOMEDIA (c. 320)

To his very dear lord, the faithful man of God, orthodox Eusebius, Arius, unjustly persecuted by Pope Alexander on account of that all-conquering truth which you also *defend as with a shield* [Ps 47:9], sends greeting in the Lord.

As Ammonius, my father, was going to Nicomedia, I thought it right and my bounden duty to greet you by him, and also to make mention of that inborn love and kindly disposition which you bear towards the brethren for the sake of God and of his Christ; I want to tell you that the bishop[10] makes great havoc of us and persecutes us severely, and is in full sail against us: he has driven us out of the city as atheists, because we do not concur in what he publicly preaches, namely, that "God has always been, and the Son has always been: Father and Son exist together: the Son has his existence unbegotten along with God, ever being begotten, without having been begotten: God does not precede the Son by thought or by an interval however small: God has always been, the Son has always been; the Son is from God himself."

Eusebius, your brother in Caesarea, Theodotus, Paulinus, Athanasius, Gregory, Aëtius, and all the bishops of the East, have been made anathema because they say that God has existence without beginning prior to his Son: except Philogonius, Hellanicus, and Macarius, who are heretical fellows, and uncatechized. One of them says that the Son is an effusion,[11] another that he is an emission, another that he is also unbegotten.

These are impieties to which we could not listen, even though the heretics should threaten us with a thousand deaths. But as for us, what do we say, and believe, and what have we taught, and what do we teach? That the Son is not unbegotten, nor in any way part of the unbegotten; nor from some lower essence (i.e. from matter); but that by his own (i.e. the Father's) will and counsel he has subsisted before time, and before ages as God *full <of grace and truth>* [Jn 1:14], only-begotten, unchangeable.

And that he was not, before he was begotten, or created, or purposed, or established. For he was not unbegotten. We are persecuted because we say, "the Son had a beginning, but God is without beginning." This is really the cause of our persecution; and, likewise, because we say that he is from nothing. And this we say, because he is neither part of God, nor of any lower essence. For this are we persecuted; the rest you know. Farewell in the Lord. As a fellow-disciple of Lucian, and as a truly pious man, as your name implies, remember our afflictions.

---

[10]Alexander of Alexandria (d. 328), one of those who later attended the Council of Nicaea and the author of excerpt 2B1b.

[11]Literally, "something belched out" (cf. Ps 44:2 of the Septuagint).

b. CIRCULAR LETTER OF ALEXANDER OF ALEXANDRIA (c. 324)

Impelled by avarice and ambition[,] knaves are constantly plotting to gain possession of the dioceses that seem greatest. Under various pretexts they trample on the religion of the Church. For they are driven mad by the devil *who works in them* [Eph 2:2], and abandon all reverence and despise the fear of God's judgment. As I suffer from them myself, I had to explain to your Reverence, that you be on your guard against such individuals, lest any of them dare enter your dioceses also, either in person (for the impostors are skilled deceivers), or by false and specious letters. By both means they can delude one who clings to faith, though it be a pure faith.

Arius then and Achillas lately made a conspiracy, in which they ... could not still remain subject to the Church, but build for themselves *dens of robbers* [Mt 21:13], in which they constantly assemble and by night and day indulge in slanders against Christ and us. They cry down all the pious apostolic doctrine and, just as the Jews do, have organized a gang to fight Christ. They deny his divinity, and declare him to be on a level with all mankind. They pick out every saying relative to his saving dispensation, and to his *humiliation* for us, and try to compound from them the proclamation of their own impiety, by abandoning the words showing his divinity *from the beginning* [cf. Jn 1:1] and his ineffable glory with the Father. They make their own the impious view of Greeks and Jews about Christ, and endeavor, as far as they possibly can, to get praised among them. They busy themselves with the parts of our doctrine that excite derision among Greeks and Jews. They daily excite disorders and persecutions against us: on the one hand they have courts assembled (i.e., to accuse us) on the petition of disorderly women whom they have deceived, on the other they discredit Christianity by the younger women who support them running around every street in an indecent fashion. But they have even dared to rend the seamless robe of Christ, which the executioners did not resolve on dividing. Because of their subterfuges we only gradually got to know of their teaching which suits their way of life and their unholy project; we drove them by a unanimous vote from the Church which reverences the Divinity of Christ.

They tried by running to and fro to reach our fellow ministers who were of one mind with us. They make a show of reverence for the fair name of peace and union, but in fact endeavor to infect some of them with their own disease by means of fair words, and ask them for all too verbose letters, which they read aloud to those that they have deceived, and confirm them as unrepentant in their error, on the ground that they have bishops to agree and be of one mind with them. They do not confess to them the wicked teaching and actions that led to their expulsion, but they either pass these over in silence or deceive by concealing them with specious words and writings. They hide their corrupting teaching with all too persuasive and tricky conversations, and carry away anyone ready to be deceived, and they do not scruple to calumniate *our* religion. And so it comes about that some people sign their letters and receive them into the Church. I think that the greatest blame rests on our fellow ministers who dare to do this: the apostolic canon does not permit it, and their conduct inflames the diabolical activity of our opponents against Christ.

[Alexander then proceeds to a long account of Arian teaching, dwelling on their misinterpretation of scripture, and on the limitation of human intelligence. He is particularly severe on the Arian assertion "there was when he was not": *"Is it not incredible to say that he who made times, ages and seasons, in which 'he was not' must be comprised, 'once was not'?"*]

---

2. THE COUNCIL OF NICAEA

Finally, in 325, the emperor Constantine was persuaded to intervene in the debate over Arianism and Christian orthodoxy, summoning an ecumenical, or world, council at Nicaea (modern Isnik in Turkey). The number of bishops in attendance has been estimated at anywhere from 228 to 318. In a letter written years later and excerpted in the first reading below, Anthanasius describes how his own anti-Arian faction carried the day. In the heated and contentious atmosphere of the council, identical scriptural passages were interpreted in radically different ways; attending bishops alternately huddled in strategy sessions and shouted down opponents in debate. In the end, the theological formulation of *homoousion*—that Jesus was "of the same essence" as God the Father and "begotten not created"—satisfied all but five of the council's participants, two of whom refused to sign and were subsequently sent into exile. The creed drawn up at Nicaea, given in the second reading below, was revised in 381 at the Council of Constantinople, where it was combined with a traditional baptismal formula to create the version known to Christians ever since as the Nicene Creed.

a. LETTER OF ATHANASIUS "TO THE AFRICANS" (369)

. . . When the assembled bishops [at the Council of Nicaea] were resolved to put down the impious phrases invented by the Arians, that the Son was from things which did not exist, and that the Son was a creature and a thing made, and that there was [a time] when he was not, and that He was of a changeable nature, and to write down the acknowledged sayings of Scripture, that the Word is from God, by nature Only-begotten, the only Power and Wisdom of the Father, *true God*, as John [says] [1 Jn 20], and, as Paul wrote, *effulgence of the Father's glory and impress of His hypostasis* [Heb 1:3]: the Eusebians,[12] drawn away by their own vain opinions, began to say to each other, "Let us agree to this, for we also are from God: for *there is one God from Whom are all things* [1 Cor 8:6], and, *The old things are passed away; behold, all things are become new, and all things are from God* [2 Cor 5:17–18]. They also took account of that passage in "The Shepherd":[13] "First of all things, believe that the God who created

and organized all things, and brought them out of non-existence into existence, is one." But the bishops, having observed their craftiness and the artifice of impiety, gave a clearer explanation of the phrase "from God," and wrote that the Son was "from the essence of God"; that the creatures might be said to be "from God," because they are not from themselves without a cause, but have a beginning of their coming into existence, but the Son alone might be regarded as proper to the Father's essence, for this properly belongs to an only-begotten and veritable son in regard to a father. And this was the occasion of the adoption of the phrase "from the essence." Again, when the bishops asked those who seemed to be a small number whether they would say that the Son was not a creature, but the only Power and Wisdom of the Father, and in all points the eternal and unvarying image of the Father, and true God, they caught the Eusebians making signals to each other,[14] to this effect: "These expressions belong

---

[12]Eusebius of Nicomedia, Eusebius of Caesarea, and other supporters of Arius.

[13]*The Shepherd* of Hermas, a second-century collection of Christian revelations, considered by some to have near canonical status (see 1B4).

[14]Lit., "nodding"; "whispering and winking" in the parallel account of Athanasius.

to us also, for we are called *God's image and glory* [1 Cor 11:7]; and of us it is said, *For we, the living, always* [2 Cor 4:11]; and there are many 'powers,' and *all the power of the Lord went forth from the land of Egypt* [Exod 12:41], and the caterpillar and the locust are called *a great power* [Jl 2:25], and, *The Lord of powers is with us, the God of Jacob is our helper* [Ps 46:7]. And we indeed are in the position of belonging properly to God, not in a commonplace way, but because He has called us brethren. And if also they even call the Son true 'God,' that does not trouble us; for since He has been made so He is true (God)."

Such were the unsound thoughts of the Arians. But here also the bishops, perceiving their craftiness, collected from the Scriptures the phrase "effulgence," and the "fountain" and "stream," and "impress" in relation to "hypostasis," and the text, *In Thy light shall we see light* [Ps 36:9], and *I and the Father are one* [Jn 10:30]. And then they inserted in their formulary a clearer and compendious phrase that the Son was "co-essential with the Father"; for all the expressions above quoted have this meaning.

b. THE CREED OF NICAEA (325)

We believe in one God, the Father All Governing, creator of all things visible and invisible;

And in one Lord Jesus Christ, the Son of God, begotten of the Father as only begotten, that is, from the essence of the Father, God from God, Light from Light, true God from true God, begotten not created, of the same essence [reality; *homoousion*] as the Father, through whom all things came into being, both in heaven and in earth; Who for us men and for our salvation came down and was incarnate, be-coming human. He suffered and the third day he rose, and ascended into the heavens. And he will come to judge both the living and the dead.

And [we believe] in the Holy Spirit.

But, those who say, Once he was not, or he was not before his generation, or he came to be out of nothing, or who assert that he, the Son of God, is of a different *hypostasis* [i.e., substance] or *ousia,* or that he is a creature, or changeable, or mutable, the Catholic and Apostolic Church anathematizes [i.e., condemns] them.

C. Original Sin

Since the earliest letters of the apostle Paul (Rom 5:12–19; Eph 2:3), Christians had preached about the sinfulness of humanity and the consequent need for redemption through Christ. It was not until the second century, however, that general references to Adam and Eve's sinfulness gave way to more precise formulations about how their disobedience of God—which came to be known as the "original sin"—had affected the rest of mankind. Most of the Greek fathers, from Justin Martyr (c.110–165) to John Chrysotom (347–407), actually denied that the guilt of the first humans could be inherited and instead believed that all of Adam and Eve's descendants merely imitated them in sinfulness, thereby generating their own guilt. In the western part of the empire, though, Christian writers from Tertullian on spoke of a more direct transmission of both guilt and sinful nature. Ambrose of Milan (c. 339–397) was an especially influential voice on this question, most obviously through the writings of his famous protégé, Augustine of Hippo. For it was Augustine who eventually coined the term *peccatum originale* ("original sin") and who provided the careful articulation of a doctrine that would shape all later Christian theology.

1. St. Augustine of Hippo
CONFESSIONS (c. 400)

Augustine (354–430) was a North African who began his career as a teacher of rhetoric in his home province of Numidia and later moved to Milan. In his *Confessions,* which is considered to be the first spiritual autobiography in the Western world, Augustine recounts his odyssey from belief in the dualism of a Gnostic-influenced sect called the Manichees to faith in the teachings of the Christian Neo-Platonists and ultimately to baptism in the established catholic church under the influence of the renowned Christian intellectual Ambrose. In his account, Augustine seeks to make sense of the experiences and questions that led him from his self-described "idolatrous" ways to his later vocation as a priest and bishop. In one of his most powerful and influential insights, Augustine decides that both his sensual desires and his intellectual yearnings spring from the same source, namely the corruptibility and imperfection of the human body, will, and intellect. Finding it impossible to believe that a good and omnipotent God would make corrupt and imperfect creatures, Augustine goes on to conclude that God created humans to be good but that Adam and Eve, using their God-given free will, turned away from their Creator, thus committing *peccatum originale,* the original, or first, sin. This sin, Augustine reasons, irreparably marred Adam and Eve's once sinless souls. Thus all subsequent humans, as their descendants, inherit at birth a corrupt and sinful nature and, under the influence of that nature, continue to commit sins throughout their lives. Therefore, one of the most important consequences of original sin is the fundamental inability of every human to achieve reconciliation with God except through the mediation of Christ. According to Augustine, sin, in all its manifestations, has become so intertwined with human nature that Christians can never escape its power on their own but are absolutely reliant on the grace of God at every turn. Although Augustine doesn't use the actual term *peccatum originale* in the following excerpt, the conversion experience he relates at the end of the passage is strongly marked by his realization of the inescapable effect of original sin on his own soul and his consequent need for divine grace.

I searched for the origin of evil, and I searched for it in an evil way, and I did not see the evil in the very method of my search. I put the whole creation in front of the eyes of my spirit, both what was visible—like earth, sea, air, stars, trees, and mortal creatures—and what was invisible—like the firmament of the heaven above and all the angels and spiritual beings there. Though even these spiritual beings I conceived of as bodies, each in its imagined place. And I thought of all your[15] creation as one great mass, distinguished

---

[15]"You," throughout the text, refers to God, always in the second person familiar, formerly rendered "thou."

in accordance with the kinds of bodies of which it was made up, some being real bodies, others the kind of bodies which I imagined instead of spirits. I thought of this mass as being of an enormous size, not the size which it actually was (which I could not know), but the size which seemed to me convenient; though I conceived of it as being finite on every side. And I thought of you, Lord, as surrounding it on every side and penetrating it, but being in all directions infinite. It was as though there were a sea, which everywhere and on all sides through immensity was just one infinite sea, but which had inside it a sponge which, though very big, was still bounded. This sponge of course would in all its parts be completely filled with the immeasurable sea.

So I thought of your creation as finite and as filled with you, who were infinite. And I said: "Here is God, and here is what God has created; and God is good and is most mightily and incomparably better than all these. Yet He, being good, created them good, and see how He surrounds them and fills them. Where, then, is evil? Where did it come from and how did it creep in here? What is its root and seed? Or does it simply not exist? In that case why do we fear and take precautions against something that does not exist? Or if there is no point in our fears, then our fears themselves are an evil which goads and tortures the heart for no good reason—and all the worse an evil if there is nothing to be afraid of and we are still afraid. Therefore, either there is evil which we fear or else the fact that we do fear is evil. Where then does evil come from, seeing that God is good and made all things good? Certainly it was the greater and supreme Good who made these lesser goods, yet still all are good, both the creator and his creation. Where then did evil come from? Or was there some evil element in the material of creation, and did God shape and form it, yet still leave in it something which He did not change into good? But why? Being omnipotent, did He lack the power to change and transform the whole so that no trace of evil should remain? Indeed why should He choose

to use such material for making anything? Would He not rather, with this same omnipotence, cause it not to exist at all? Could it exist against His will? Or, supposing it was eternal, why for so long through all the infinite spaces of time past did He allow it to exist and then so much later decide to make something out of it? Or, if He did suddenly decide on some action, would not the omnipotent prefer to act in such a way that this evil material should cease to exist, and that He alone should be, the whole, true, supreme, and infinite Good? Or, since it was not good that He who was good should frame and create something not good, then why did He not take away and reduce to nothing the material that was evil and then Himself provide good material from which to create all things? For He would not be omnipotent if He could not create something good without having to rely on material which He had not Himself created."

These were the kind of thoughts which I turned over and over in my unhappy heart, a heart overburdened with those biting cares that came from my fear of death and my failure to discover the truth. Yet the faith of your Christ, our Lord and Savior, professed in the Catholic Church, remained steadfastly fixed in my heart, even though it was on many points still unformed and swerving from the right rule of doctrine. But, nevertheless, my mind did not abandon it, but rather drank more and more deeply of it every day. . . .

I was admonished by all this to return to my own self, and, with you to guide me, I entered into the innermost part of myself, and I was able to do this because you were my helper. I entered and I saw with my soul's eye (such as it was) an unchangeable light shining above this eye of my soul and above my mind. It was not the ordinary light which is visible to all flesh, nor something of the same sort, only bigger, as though it might be our ordinary light shining much more brightly and filling everything with its greatness. No, it was not like that; it was different, entirely different from anything of the kind. Nor was it above my mind as oil floats on water or as the heaven is above the earth. It was higher than I, because it made me, and I was lower because I was made by it. He who knows truth knows that light, and he who knows that light knows eternity. Love knows it. O eternal truth and true love and beloved eternity! You are my God; to you I sigh by day and by night. And when I first knew you, you raised me up so that I could see that there was something to see and that I still lacked the ability to see it. And you beat back the weakness of my sight, blazing upon me with your rays, and I trembled in love and in dread, and I found that I was far distant from you, in a region of total unlikeness, as if I were hearing your voice from on high saying: "I am the food of grown men. Grow and you shall feed upon me. And you will not, as with the food of the body, change me into yourself, but you will be changed into me." And I learned that *You, for iniquity, chasten man and You made my soul to consume away like a spider* [Ps 39:11] And I said: "Is truth therefore nothing because it is not extended through any kind of space, whether finite or infinite?" And from far away you cried out to me: "I am that I am." And I heard, as one hears things in the heart, and there was no longer any reason at all for me to doubt. I would sooner doubt my own existence than the existence of that truth *which is clearly seen being understood by those things which are made* [Rom 1:20]. . . .

And it became clear to me that things which are subject to corruption are good. They would not be subject to corruption if they were either supremely good or not good at all; for, if they were supremely good, they would be incorruptible, and, if there was nothing good in them, there would be nothing which could be corrupted. For corruption does harm, and, unless what is good in a thing is diminished, no harm could be done. Therefore, either corruption does no harm (which is impossible), or (which is quite certain) all things which suffer corruption are deprived of something good in them. Supposing them to be deprived of all good, they will cease to exist altogether. For, if they continue to exist and can no longer be cor-

rupted, they will be better than before, because they will be permanently beyond the reach of corruption. What indeed could be more monstrous than to assert that things could become better by losing all their goodness? So if they are deprived of all good, they will cease to exist altogether. Therefore, so long as they exist, they are good. Therefore, all things that are, are good, and as to that evil, the origin of which I was seeking for, it is not a substance, since, if it were a substance, it would be good. For it would either have to be an incorruptible substance (which is the highest form of goodness) or else a corruptible substance (which, unless it had good in it, could not be corruptible). So I saw plainly and clearly that you have made all things good, nor are there any substances at all which you have not made. And because you did not make all things equal, therefore they each and all have their existence; because they are good individually, and at the same time they are altogether very good, because our God *made all things very good* [Gen 1:31].

To you, then, there is no such thing at all as evil. And the same is true not only of you but of your whole creation, since there is nothing outside it to break in and corrupt the order which you have imposed on it. But in some of its parts there are some things which are considered evil because they do not harmonize with other parts; yet with still other parts they do harmonize and are good and they are good in themselves. And all these things which do not fit in with each other do fit in with that lower part of creation which we call the earth, which has its own cloudy and windy sky which again is fitting to it. Far be it that I should say: "I wish these things did not exist," because even if these were the only things I saw, though certainly I should long for something better yet, still for these things alone I ought to praise you; for things from the earth show that you are to be praised—*dragons, and all deeps, fire, hail, snow, ice, and stormy wind, which fulfill Your Word; mountains, and all hills, fruitful trees and all cedars; beasts and all cattle, creeping things and flying fowls; kings of the earth, and all people, princes and all judges of the earth; young men and maidens, old men and young, praise Your name* [Ps 148:7–13]. And since from the heavens these *praise You, praise You, our God, in the heights, all Your angels, all Your hosts, sun and moon, all the stars and light, the heaven of heavens, and the waters that be above the heavens, praise Your name* [Ps 148:1–5]. So I no longer desired better things. I had envisaged all things in their totality, and, with a sounder judgment, I realized that, while higher things are certainly better than lower things, all things together are better than the higher things by themselves. . . .

I knew from my own experience that there is nothing strange in the fact that a sick person will find uneatable the same bread which a healthy person enjoys, or that good eyes love the light and bad eyes hate it. Your justice too displeases the wicked, and even more displeasing are vipers and reptiles, though you created them good and well fitted to the lower parts of your creation, and to these lower parts of creation the wicked themselves are well fitted and become the better fitted the more they are unlike you, although in becoming more like you they will become better fitted to the higher parts of your creation. And I asked: "What is wickedness?" and found that it is not a substance but a perversity of the will turning away from you, God, the supreme substance, toward lower things—casting away, as it were, its own insides, and swelling with desire for what is outside it. . . .

When this man of yours, Simplicianus, told me all this about Victorinus,[16] I was on fire to be like him, and this, of course, was why he had told me the story. He told me this too—that in the time of the Emperor Julian, when a law was passed forbidding Christians to teach literature

and rhetoric,[17] Victorinus had obeyed the law, preferring to give up his talking-shop rather than your Word, by which you make even the tongues of infants eloquent. In this I thought that he was not only brave but lucky, because he had got the chance of giving all his time to you. This was just what I longed for myself, but I was held back, and I was held back not by fetters put on me by someone else, but by the iron bondage of my own will. The enemy held my will and made a chain out of it and bound me with it. From a perverse will came lust, and slavery to lust became a habit, and the habit, being constantly yielded to, became a necessity. These were like links, hanging each to each (which is why I called it a chain), and they held me fast in a hard slavery. And the new will which I was beginning to have and which urged me to worship you in freedom and to enjoy you, God, the only certain joy, was not yet strong enough to overpower the old will which by its oldness had grown hard in me. So my two wills, one old, one new, one carnal, one spiritual, were in conflict, and they wasted my soul by their discord.

In this way my personal experience enabled me to understand what I had read—that *the flesh lusts against the spirit and the spirit against the flesh* [Gal 5:17]. I, no doubt, was on both sides, but I was more myself when I was on the side which I approved of for myself than when I was on the side of which I disapproved. For it was no longer really I myself who was on this second side, since there to a great extent I was rather suffering things against my will than doing them voluntarily. Yet it was my own fault that habit fought back so strongly against me; for I had come willingly where I now did not will to be. And who has any right to complain when just punishment overtakes the sinner? Nor did I have any longer the excuse which I used to think I had when I said that the reason why I had not yet forsaken the world and given myself up to your service

---

[16]Simplicianus was a Milanese priest who had trained Augustine's own "spiritual father," Ambrose of Milan. His story about the conversion of Marius Victorinus—like Augustine a Platonist professor of rhetoric—was no doubt intended to overcome Augustine's continuing wariness towards Christianity.

[17]Julian the Apostate (r. 360–363) initiated a brief restoration of pagan worship in the Roman Empire. Theodosius I (r. 379–395) later outlawed all pagan worship and recognized Christianity as the only licit religion.

was because I could not see the truth clearly. Now I could see it perfectly clearly.

But I was still tied down to earth and refused to take my place in your army. And I was just as frightened of being freed from all my hampering baggage as I ought to have been frightened of being hampered. The pack of this world was a kind of pleasant weight upon me, as happens in sleep, and the thoughts in which I meditated on you were like the efforts of someone who tries to get up but is so overcome with drowsiness that he sinks back again into sleep. Of course no one wants to sleep forever, and everyone in his senses would agree that it is better to be awake; yet all the same, when we feel a sort of lethargy in our limbs, we often put off the moment of shaking off sleep, and, even though it is time to get up, we gladly take a little longer in bed, conscious though we may be that we should not be doing so. In just the same way I was quite certain that it was better to give myself up to your charity rather than to give in to my own desires; but, though the former course was a conviction to which I gave my assent, the latter was a pleasure to which I gave my consent. For I had no answer to make to you when you called me: *Awake, you that sleep, and arise from the dead, and Christ shall give you light* [Eph 5:14]. And, while you showed me wherever I looked that what you said was true, I, convinced by the truth, could still find nothing at all to say except lazy words spoken half asleep: "A minute," "just a minute," "just a little time longer." But there was no limit to the minutes, and the little time longer went a long way. It was in vain that *I delighted in Your law according to the inner man, when another law in my members rebelled against the law of my mind, and led me captive under the law of sin which was in my members* [Rom 7:23]. For the law of sin is the strong force of habit, which drags the mind along and controls it even against its will—though deservedly, since the habit was voluntarily adopted. *Who then should deliver me thus wretched from the body of this death, but Your grace only, through Jesus Christ our Lord?* [Rom 7:24]

Now, Lord, my helper and my redeemer, I shall tell and confess to your name how it was

that you freed me from the bondage of my desire for sex, in which I was so closely fettered, and from slavery to the affairs of this world . . . .

[Augustine then tells how he and his friend Alypius[18] listened to tales of the famous hermit St. Antony recounted by a visitor from the imperial court at Trier, and how such stories had moved two fellow courtiers to renounce the world entirely.]

This was what Ponticianus[19] told us. But you, Lord, while he was speaking, were turning me around so that I could see myself; you took me from behind my own back, which was where I had put myself during the time when I did not want to be observed by myself, and you set me in front of my own face so that I could see how foul a sight I was—crooked, filthy, spotted, and ulcerous. I saw and I was horrified, and I had nowhere to go to escape from myself. If I tried to look away from myself, Ponticianus still went on with his story, and again you were setting me in front of myself, forcing me to look into my own face, so that I might see my sin and hate it. I did know it, but I pretended that I did not. I had been pushing the whole idea away from me and forgetting it.

But now the more ardent was the love I felt for those two men of whom I was hearing and of how healthfully they had been moved to give themselves up entirely to you to be cured, the more bitter was the hatred I felt for myself when I compared myself with them. Many years (at least twelve) of my own life had gone by since the time when I was nineteen and was reading Cicero's *Hortensius*[20] and had been fired

---

[18]Longtime friend and spiritual fellow traveler of Augustine, who also followed the path from Manicheanism to Platonism to Christianity. Like Augustine, he eventually become a bishop (of Thagaste, in North Africa).

[19]A fellow African as well as a member of the Imperial Reserve of Special Agents.

[20]The famous rhetorical exemplar of Cicero (106–43 B.C.E.) contained an exhortation to philosophy in terms of discipline, self-sacrifice, and transcendence—also traits of monasticism admired by later Christians such as Augustine.

with an enthusiasm for wisdom. Yet I was still putting off the moment when, despising this world's happiness, I should give all my time to the search for that of which not only the finding but merely the seeking must be preferred to the discovered treasures and kingdoms of men or to all the pleasures of the body easily and abundantly available. But I, wretched young man that I was—even more wretched at the beginning of my youth—had begged you for chastity and had said: "Make me chaste and continent, but not yet." I was afraid that you might hear me too soon and cure me too soon from the disease of a lust which I preferred to be satisfied rather than extinguished. And I had gone along evil ways, following a sacrilegious superstition [i.e., Manicheanism]—not because I was convinced by it, but simply preferring it to the other doctrines into which I never inquired in a religious spirit, but merely attacked them in a spirit of spite.

I had thought that the reason why I was putting off from day to day the time when I should despise all worldly hopes and follow you alone was because I could see no certainty toward which I could direct my course. But now the day had come when in my own eyes I was stripped naked and my conscience cried out against me: "Can you not hear me? Was it not this that you used to say, that you would not throw off the burden of vanity for a truth that was uncertain? Well, look. Now the truth is certain, and you are still weighed down by your burden. Yet these others, who have not been so worn out in the search and not been meditating the matter for ten years or more, have had the weight taken from their backs and have been given wings to fly."

So I was being gnawed at inside, and as Ponticianus went on with his story I was lost and overwhelmed in a terrible kind of shame. When the story was over and the business about which he had come had been settled he went away, and I retired into myself. Nor did I leave anything unsaid against myself. With every scourge of condemnation I lashed my soul on to follow me now that I was trying to follow

you. And my soul hung back; it refused to follow, and it could give no excuse for its refusal. All the arguments had been used already and had been shown to be false. There remained a mute shrinking; for it feared like death to be restrained from the flux of a habit by which it was melting away into death. . . .

What can be the explanation of such an absurdity? Enlighten me with your mercy, so that I may ask the question, if perhaps an answer may be found in the secret places of man's punishment and in those darkest agonies of the sons of Adam. What can be the explanation of such an absurdity? The mind gives an order to the body, and the order is obeyed immediately: the mind gives an order to itself, and there is resistance. The mind orders the hand to move, and such readiness is its execution. Yet the mind is mind, and the hand is body. The mind orders the mind to will; it is the same mind, yet it does not obey the order. The fact is that it does not will the thing entirely; consequently it does not give the order entirely. The force of the order is in the force of the will, and disobedience to the order results from insufficiency of the will. For the will orders that there should be a will—not a different will, but itself. But it is not entire in itself when it gives the order, and therefore its order is not obeyed. For if it were entire in itself, it would not give the order to will; the will would be there already. So it is not an absurdity partly to will and partly not to will; it is rather a sickness of the soul which is weighted down with habit so that it cannot rise up in its entirety, lifted aloft by truth. So the reason why there are two wills in us is because one of them is not entire, and one has what the other lacks.

Let them perish from your presence, God, as perish empty talkers and seducers of the soul, who, having observed that there are two wills in the act of deliberating, conclude from this that we have in us two minds of two different natures, one good and one evil. They themselves are truly evil, when they hold these evil opinions, and they are just as capable of becoming good if they will realize the truth and agree with the truth, so that your apostle may say to them: *You were sometimes darkness, but now light in the Lord* [Eph 5:8]. But these people, by imagining that the nature of the soul is what God is, want to be light, not in the Lord, but in themselves, and the result is that they have become an even deeper darkness, since in their appalling arrogance they have gone further away from you—from you, *the true Light that enlightens every man that comes into the world* [Jn 1:19]. Take heed what you say, and blush for shame: *draw near unto Him and be enlightened, and your faces shall not be ashamed* [Ps 34:4–5].

As to me, when I was deliberating about entering the service of the Lord my God, as I had long intended to do, it was I who willed it, and it was I who was unwilling. It was the same "I" throughout. But neither my will nor my unwillingness was whole and entire. So I fought with myself and was torn apart by myself. It was against my will that this tearing apart took place, but this was not an indication that I had another mind of a different nature; it was simply the punishment which I was suffering in my own mind. It was not I, therefore, who caused it, but *the sin dwells in me* [Rom 7:17], and, being a son of Adam, I was suffering for his sin which was more freely committed. . . .

So I was sick and in torture. I reproached myself much more bitterly than ever, and I turned and twisted my chain till I could break quite free. Only a little of it still held me, but it did still hold me. And you, Lord, in the secret places of my soul, stood above me in the severity of your mercy, redoubling the lashes of fear and shame, so that I should not give way once more and so that that small weak piece of chain which still remained should not instead of snapping grow strong again and tie me down more firmly than before. I was saying inside myself: "Now, now, let it be now!" and as I spoke the words I was already beginning to go in the direction I wanted to go. I nearly managed it, but I did not quite manage it. Yet I did not slip right back to the beginning; I was a stage above that, and I stood there to regain my breath. And I tried again and I was very nearly

there; I was almost touching it and grasping it, and then I was not there, I was not touching it, I was not grasping it; evil had more power over me than the novelty of good, and as that very moment of time in which I was to become something else drew nearer and nearer, it struck me with more and more horror. But I was not struck right back or turned aside; I was just held in suspense.

Toys and trifles, utter vanities had been my mistresses, and now they were holding me back, pulling me by the garment of my flesh and softly murmuring in my ear: "Are you getting rid of us?" and "From this moment shall we never be with you again for all eternity?" and "From this moment will you never for all eternity be allowed to do this or that?" My God, what was it, what was it that they suggested in those words "this" or "that" which I have just written? I pray you in your mercy to keep such things from the soul of your servant. How filthy, how shameful were these things they were suggesting! And now their voices were not half so loud in my ears; now they no longer came out boldly to contradict me face to face; it was more as though they were muttering behind my back; stealthily pulling at my sleeve as I was going away so that I should turn and look at them. Yet still they did hold me back as I hesitated to tear myself away and to shake them off and to take the great step in the direction where I was called. Violence of habit spoke the words: "Do you think that you can live without them?"

And now from my hidden depths my searching thought had dragged up and set before the sight of my heart the whole mass of my misery. Then a huge storm rose up within me bringing with it a huge downpour of tears. So that I might pour out all these tears and speak the words that came with them I rose up from Alypius (solitude seemed better for the business of weeping) and went further away so that I might not be embarrassed even by his presence. This was how I felt and he realized it. No doubt I had said something or other, and he could feel the weight of my tears in the sound of my voice. And so I rose to my feet, and he, in a state of utter amazement, remained in the place where we had been sitting. I flung myself down on the ground somehow under a fig tree and gave free rein to my tears; they streamed and flooded from my eyes, an *acceptable sacrifice to You* [Phil 4:18]. And I kept saying to you, not perhaps in these words, but with this sense: "*And You, O lord, how long? How long, Lord; wilt You be angry forever? Remember not our former iniquities* [Ps 79:5, 8]" For I felt that it was these which were holding me fast. And in my misery I would exclaim: "How long, how long this 'tomorrow and tomorrow'? Why not now? Why not finish this very hour with my uncleanness?"

So I spoke, weeping in the bitter contrition of my heart. Suddenly a voice reaches my ears from a nearby house. It is the voice of a boy or a girl (I don't know which) and in a kind of singsong the words are constantly repeated: "Take it and read it. Take it and read it." At once my face changed, and I began to think carefully of whether the singing of words like these came into any kind of game which children play, and I could not remember that I had ever heard anything like it before. I checked the force of my tears and rose to my feet, being quite certain that I must interpret this as a divine command to me to open the book and read the first passage which I should come upon. For I had heard this about Antony: he had happened to come in when the Gospel was being read, and as though the words read were spoken directly to himself, had received the admonition: *Go, sell all that you have, and give to the poor, and you shall have treasure in heaven, and come and follow me* [Mt 19:21]. And by such an oracle he had been immediately converted to you.

So I went eagerly back to the place where Alypius was sitting, since it was there that I had left the book of the Apostle when I rose to my feet. I snatched up the book, opened it, and read in silence the passage upon which my eyes first fell: *Not in rioting and drunkenness, not in chambering and wantonness, not in strife and envying: but put you on the Lord Jesus Christ, and make not provision for the flesh in concupiscence* [Rom 13:13–14]. I had no wish to read further; there was no need to. For immediately I had reached the end of this sentence it was as though my heart was filled with a light of confidence and all the shadows of my doubt were swept away. . . .

---

2. Pelagius
LETTER TO DEMETRIAS (c. 413)

The doctrine of original sin as it was developed by Augustine evolved largely in response to the teachings of a British monk named Pelagius (c. 350–425). In 410, Pelagius and several of his followers fled to North Africa to escape the Goths' sacking of Rome. Two years later, the growing popularity of Pelagian teachings in Augustine's own diocese led the bishop to write the first of a series of polemics against "Pelagianism." It is not clear which of the teachings that Augustine attributes to Pelagius actually originated among the monk's followers. Without doubt, however, there were some fundamental points of disagreement between the two men, most notably on the inheritance of original sin and guilt and the perfectibility of the pious individual. Because of his belief that humans were tainted by original sin from the moment of birth, Augustine was a supporter of infant baptism, a practice that had become common among Christians of the time. Pelagius firmly rejected Augustine's "fatalist" formulation of an overpowering legacy of guilt and desire for self-gratification, which condemned even unbaptized infants to eternal Hell. In his letter to a young woman named Demetrias who was in his spiritual charge, Pelagius asserts that God does not command the impossible and that the Fall of Adam and Eve did not extinguish all goodness and free will. Though Pelagius had several important followers in the East, Augustine and others persuaded Pope Innocent I (r. 401–417) to condemn the monk's writings. In 431 the Council of Ephesus excommunicated Pelagius posthumously. Subsequent councils and popes similarly endorsed Augustine's interpretation of original sin, though the writings of some later monks and theologians seem to provide evidence that a "semi-Pelagian" perspective persisted in some corners of Christendom throughout the Middle Ages.

. . . As often as I have to speak of the principles of virtue and a holy life, I am accustomed first of all to call attention to the capacity and character of human nature, and to show what it is able to accomplish; then from this to arouse the feelings of the hearer, that he may strive after different kinds of virtue, that he may permit himself to be roused to acts which perhaps he had regarded as impossible. For we are quite unable to travel the way of virtue if hope does not accompany us. For all attempts to accomplish anything cease if one is in doubt whether he will attain the goal. This order of exhortation I follow in other minor writings and in this case also. I believe it must be kept especially in mind where the good of nature needs to be set forth the more in detail as the life is to be more perfectly formed, that the spirit may not be more neglectful and slow in its striving after virtue, as it believes itself to have the less ability, and when it is ignorant of what is within it, think that it does not possess it.

One must be careful to see to it that . . . one does not think that a man is not made good because he can do evil and is not compelled to an immutable necessity of doing good through the might of nature. For if you diligently consider it and turn your mind to the subtler understanding of the matter, the better and superior position of man will appear in that from which his inferior condition was inferred. But just in this freedom in either direction, in this liberty toward either side, is placed the glory of our rational nature, therein its dignity; from this the

very good merit praise, from this their reward. For there would be for those who always remain good no virtue if they had not been able to have chosen the evil. For since God wished to present to the rational creature the gift of voluntary goodness and the power of the free will, by planting in man the possibility of turning himself toward either side, He made His special gift the ability to be what he would be in order that he, being capable of good and evil, could do either and could turn his will to either of them. . . .

We defend the advantage of nature not in the sense that we say it cannot do evil, since we declare that it is capable of good and evil; we only protect it from reproach. It should not appear as if we were driven to evil by a disease of nature, we who do neither good nor bad without our will, and to whom there is always freedom to do one of two things, since always we are able to do both. . . . Nothing else makes it difficult for us to do good than long custom of sinning which has infected us since we were children, and has gradually corrupted us for many years, so that afterward it holds us bound to it and delivered over to it, so that it almost seems as if it had the same force as nature.

If before the Law, as we are told, and long before the appearance of the Redeemer, various persons can be named who lived just and holy lives, how much more after His appearance must we believe that we are able to do the same, we who have been taught through Christ's grace, and born again to be better men;

and we who by His blood have been reconciled and purified, and by His example incited to more perfect righteousness, ought to be better than they who were before the Law, better than they who were under the law. . . .

"*Without murmurings and disputings*" [Phil 2:14]. We see masters of mean condition and low origin openly looked down upon by bits of servants; who, in respect of the smallest commands, as often as not resist them to their face. But this is not the case with persons of good birth. The more powerful the master, the more ready the servants to obey; and the more difficult their commands, the more readily are they listened to. At the command of a king all are so well prepared and so equipped in readiness to obey that they wish to be commanded; and, not only do they believe themselves good servants if they do what is commanded, but, as if they were good servants for having been commanded; so, in proportion to the rank of him who gives them their commands, they regard their service as a privilege. In our case, God Himself, that eternal Majesty, that ineffable and inestimable Sovereignty, has sent us the Holy Scriptures, as the crown of His truly adorable precepts; and, so far from recovering them at once with joy and veneration, and taking the commands of so illustrious a Sovereign for a high privilege (especially as there is no thought of advantage for Him who gives the command, but only of profit for him who obeys it), on the contrary, with hearts full of scorn and slackness, like proud and worthless servants, we shout in God's face and say, "It's

hard! It's difficult! We can't! We are but men, encompassed by the frailty of the flesh!" What blind folly! What rash profanity! We make the God of knowledge guilty of twofold ignorance: of not knowing what He has made, and of not knowing what He has commanded. As if, in forgetfulness of human frailty, which He made, He had laid upon men commandments which they could not bear; and at the same time (oh, the shame of it!) we ascribe unrighteousness to the Just one, and cruelty to the Holy One, first by complaining that He has commanded something impossible, and next by thinking that a man will be condemned by Him for things that he could not help; so that (sacrilegious it is even to hint it), God seems to have been seeking not so much our salvation as our punishment. And so the Apostle, knowing that from a God of righteousness and majesty no precept is impossible, would keep us far from the fault of murmuring; which as a rule comes to birth either when what is commanded is unfair, or not worthy of the person of him who gives the command. Why do we shuffle to no purpose, and confront Him who lays His commands upon us with the frailty of our flesh? No one knows better the measure of our strength than He who gave us our strength; and no one has a better understanding of what is within our power than He who endowed us with the very resources of our power. He has not willed to command anything impossible, for He is righteous; and He will not condemn a man for what he could not help, for He is Holy.

D. Relic Veneration

The ancient practice known as relic veneration grew out of the early Christians' desire to honor certain followers of Jesus who had died but whose virtuous and pious lives were seen as an inspiration. This group included not only Paul and the twelve apostles but also certain well-known martyrs for the faith (see 1C) as well as several ascetics (see 2A) who had dedicated their lives to God. These spiritual heroes became known as holy ones, or saints (from the Latin *sanctus*, "holy"). Sometimes the veneration of such saints took the form of naming churches or children after a holy person. At other times, a specific prayer or even an entire liturgy was written based on the life and virtues of a particular individual. Early Christians also petitioned the saints to intercede with God on their behalf. Such requests for intercession were common among early Christians, who generally thought of themselves as being in ongoing communion with their own dead, all of whom were considered part of the mystical body of Christ. By the end of the fourth century, however, the early Christians' impulse to honor and seek help from the saints had evolved into a much more concrete, material practice. Now Christians not only recognized the saints as powerful intercessors for earthly petitioners, they also believed that the saints' special powers were particularly strong—were in fact physically located—in certain holy places and objects. Such holy sites were often places where a saint was thought to have performed a miracle or to have been martyred. Holy objects were, more often than not, actual physical relics—that is, preserved body parts of individual saints. Churches were built to mark such sacred places or to house particularly precious saintly relics, and stories abounded of the miracles wrought by the saints in these holy shrines. Thus it became increasingly common for Christians not merely to pray to a saint for intercession but to appeal to that saint by venerating the actual earthly places and physical relics associated with that holy person. The growing popularity of relics gave rise to an increasingly fierce competition among Christians for possession of these objects. By the early Middle Ages, it was not at all uncommon for holy objects to be sold for exorbitant prices or stolen outright. There was also a thriving traffic in counterfeit relics that lined the pockets of charlatans and corrupt church officials alike.

1. St. Jerome
AGAINST VIGILANTIUS (406)

The ubiquitous practice of relic veneration was apparently not accepted by all Christians of late antiquity. A presbyter in Aquitaine by the name of Vigilantius thought the custom dangerous and perhaps even idolatrous. It is impossible to know how many others shared his opinion, particularly because Vigilantius had the misfortune to irritate one of the most formidable and respected Christian intellects of all time, St. Jerome (c. 341–420). Jerome was born in Dalmatia (modern Slovenia), educated in Rome, and later became active as a scholar and a monk in Gaul, northern Italy, and Syria. His greatest and best-known achievement was his careful retranslation of the entire Bible from Hebrew and Greek sources into Latin, the so-called Vulgate edition. This massive task took over thirty years of his life to complete. Jerome was also famous as a particularly fierce polemicist, turning his talents against Pelagians, Arians, and in this instance, the relatively obscure Vigilantius. In defending the "ancient" practice of relic veneration, he makes use of several time-honored polemical tools. Of particular note is his implication of guilt-by-association when he likens Vigilantius to past heretics and even the treacherous Judas. More significantly, Jerome articulates a rationale for relic veneration—calling it a respectful honoring of "temples of the Holy Spirit"—which was to become the standard justification for the practice among medieval theologians such as Thomas Aquinas. In the excerpt below, Jerome begins his argument by abusing Vigilantius as a madman.

. . . But Gaul supports a native foe, and sees seated in the Church a man who has lost his head and who ought to be put in the strait-jacket which Hippocrates[21] recommended. Among other blasphemies, he may be heard to say, "What need is there for you not only to pay such honor, not to say adoration, to the thing, whatever it may be, which you carry about in a little vessel and worship?" And again, in the same book, "Why do you kiss and adore a bit of powder wrapped up in a cloth?" And again, in the same book, "Under the cloak of religion we see what is all but a heathen ceremony introduced into the churches, while the sun is still shining, heaps of tapers [i.e., candles] are lighted, and everywhere a paltry bit of powder, wrapped up in a costly cloth, is kissed and worshipped. Great honor do men of this sort pay to the blessed martyrs, who, they think, are to be made glorious by trumpery tapers, when the Lamb who is in the midst of the throne, with all the brightness of His majesty, gives them light?"

Madman, who in the world ever adored the martyrs? who ever thought man was God? Did not Paul and Barnabas, when the people of Lycaonia thought them to be Jupiter and Mercury, and would have offered sacrifices to them, rend their clothes and declare they were men? [cf. Acts 14:11–16] Not that they were not better than Jupiter and Mercury, who were but men long ago dead, but because, under the mistaken ideas of the Gentiles, the honor due to God was being paid to them. . . .

As to the question of tapers, however, we do not, as you in vain, misrepresent us, light them in the daytime, but by their solace we would cheer the darkness of the night, and watch for the dawn, lest we should be blind like you and sleep in darkness. And if some persons, being ignorant and simple minded laymen, or, at all events, religious women—of whom we can truly say, *"I allow that they have a zeal for God, but not according to knowledge"* [Rom 10:2]—adopt the practice in honor of the martyrs, what harm is thereby done to you? Once upon a time even the Apostles pleaded that the ointment was wasted, but they were rebuked by the voice of the Lord [Mt 26:8, Mk 14:4]. Christ did not need the ointment, nor do martyrs need the light of tapers; and yet that woman poured out the ointment in honor of Christ, and her heart's devotion was accepted. All those who light these tapers have their reward according to their faith, as the Apostle says: *"Let every one abound in his own meaning"* [Rom 14:5]. Do you call men of this sort idolaters? I do not deny that all of us who believe in Christ have passed from the error of idolatry. For we are not born Christians, but become Christians by being born again. And because we formerly worshipped idols, does it follow that we ought not now to worship God lest we seem to pay like honor to him and to idols? In the one case respect was paid to idols, and therefore the ceremony is to be abhorred; in the other the martyrs are venerated, and the same ceremony is therefore to be allowed. Throughout the whole Eastern Church, even when there are no relics of the martyrs, whenever the Gospel is to be read the candles are lighted, although the dawn may be reddening the sky, not of course to scatter the darkness, but by way of evidencing our joy. And accordingly the virgins in the Gospel always have their lamps lighted [Mt 25:1]. And the Apostles are told to have their loins girded, and their lamps burning in their hands [Lk 12:35]. And of John Baptist we read, *"He was the lamp that burneth and shineth"* [Jn 5:35]; so that, under the figure of corporeal light, that light is represented of which we read

---

[21]Ancient Greek "father" of medicine (460–357 B.C.E.) and alleged author of the physician's "Hippocratic oath."

in the Psalter, *"Thy word is a lamp unto my feet, O Lord, and a light unto my paths"* [Ps 119:105].

Does the bishop of Rome do wrong when he offers sacrifices to the Lord over the venerable bones of the dead men Peter and Paul, as we should say, but according to you, over a worthless bit of dust, and judges their tombs worthy to be Christ's altars? And not only is the bishop of one city in error, but the bishops of the whole world, who, despite the tavern-keeper Vigilantius, enter the basilicas of the dead, in which "a worthless bit of dust and ashes lies wrapped up in a cloth," defiled and defiling all else. Thus, according to you, the sacred buildings are like the sepulchres of the Pharisees, whitened without, while within they have filthy remains, and are full of foul smells and uncleanliness. And then he dares to expectorate his filth upon the subject and to say: "Is it the case that the souls of the martyrs love their ashes, and hover round them, and are always present, lest haply if any one come to pray and they were absent, they could not hear?"

Oh, monster, who ought to be banished to the ends of the earth! do you laugh at the relics of the martyrs, and in company with Eunomius,[22] the father of this heresy, slander the Churches of Christ? Are you not afraid of being in such company, and of speaking against us the same things which he utters against the Church? For all his followers refuse to enter the basilicas of Apostles and martyrs, so that, forsooth, they may worship the dead Eunomius, whose books they consider are of more authority than the Gospels; and they believe that the light of truth was in him, just as other heretics maintain that the Paraclete [i.e., the Holy Spirit] came into Montanus, and say that Manichaeus himself was the Paraclete.[23] You cannot find an occasion of boasting even in supposing that you are the inventor of a new

kind of wickedness, for your heresy long ago broke out against the Church. It found, however, an opponent in Tertullian, a very learned man, who wrote a famous treatise which he called most correctly *Scorpiacum*,[24] because, as the scorpion bends itself like a bow to inflict its wound, so what was formerly called the heresy of Cain pours poison into the body of the Church; it has slept or rather been buried for a long time, but has been now awakened by Dormitantius.[25] I am surprised you do not tell us that there must upon no account be martyrdoms, inasmuch as God, who does not ask for the blood of goats and bulls, much less requires the blood of men. This is what you say, or rather, even if you do not say it, you are taken as meaning to assert it. For in maintaining that the relics of the martyrs are to be trodden under foot, you forbid the shedding of their blood as being worthy of no honor.

Respecting vigils and the frequent keeping of night-watches in the basilicas of the martyrs, I have given a brief reply in another letter which, about two years ago I wrote to the reverend presbyter Riparius.[26] You argue that they ought to be abjured, lest we seem to be often keeping Easter, and appear not to observe the customary yearly vigils. If so, then sacrifices should not be offered to Christ on the Lord's day lest we frequently keep the Easter of our Lord's Resurrection, and introduce the custom of having many Easters instead of one. We must not, however, impute to pious men the faults and errors of youths and worthless women such as are often detected at night. It is true that, even at the Easter vigils, something of the kind usually comes to light;[27] but the faults of a few form no argument against religion in general, and such persons, without keeping vigil, can go wrong either in their own houses or in those of other people. The treachery

---

[22]Bishop of Cyzicus (d. 395) who was forced to resign in 360 because of his Anomoean Arian views.

[23]Jerome further defames Vigilantius by associating him with two famous heretics: Montanus, the charismatic prophet and leader of an apocalyptic movement in the late second century (see 2A), and Manichaeus or Mani, leader of a dualist version of Christianity in the third century. Both groups were eventually declared unorthodox and heretical.

[24]I.e., antidote to the scorpion's bite.

[25]A pun on Vigilantius' name, suggesting that rather than being "vigilant," he is "dormant" or asleep.

[26]The presbyter who had first reported Vigilantius' views to Jerome in c. 404.

[27]Jerome anticipates and rejects the insinuation that the sexual promiscuity often associated with religious feasts might be a motivation for the celebration of Easter vigils or vigils to honor saints

of Judas did not annul the loyalty of the Apostles. And if others keep vigil badly, our vigils are not thereby to be stopped; nay, rather let those who sleep to gratify their lust be compelled to watch that they may preserve their chastity. For if a thing once done be good, it cannot be bad if often done; and if there is some fault to be avoided, the blame lies not in its being done often, but in its being done at all. And so we should not watch at Easter-tide, for fear that adulterers may satisfy their long pent-up desires, or that the wife may find an opportunity for sinning without having the key turned against her by her husband. The occasions which seldom recur are those which are most eagerly longed for.

2. Gregory of Tours
GLORY OF THE MARTYRS (c. 588)

Gregory of Tours (c. 539–594) was, like Vigilantius, a native of Gaul but did not share his distaste for relic veneration. Living more than 150 years later, and after the disintegration of the western Roman Empire, Gregory had quite a different perspective on saintly intercession. During his youth he became especially devoted to a local saint, St. Julian, and enthusiastically promoted pilgrimages to the latter's shrine, which was near Gregory's home in Auvergne. As an adult, he followed in the tradition of many in his family and became a bishop, ruling over the diocese of Tours from 573 until his death. He also wrote several books, including valuable chronicles of the Frankish kings as well as seven books on saintly miracles and intercession. In this selection from his *Glory of the Martyrs,* Gregory displays his pious yet also fairly rigorous approach to passing along accounts of miraculous relics. Though clearly a believer in the power of such objects, he is careful to note his own initial skepticism as well as his sources for most stories, ostensibly allowing the reader to make up his own mind. While primarily aiming to edify the faithful, he is also aware of his role as storyteller and thus includes several entertaining and probably irrelevant details. Finally, in his candor—he admits to not even knowing the name of the saints whose relics he carries—Gregory provides us with some understanding of the uncritical acceptance of the practice of relic veneration by the early Middle Ages.

... HIS CROSS AND HIS MIRACLES AT POITIERS

The cross of the Lord that was found by the empress Helena[28] at Jerusalem is venerated on Wednesday and Friday. Queen Radegund,[29] who is comparable to Helena in both merit and faith, requested relics of this cross and piously placed them in a convent at Poitiers that she founded out of her own zeal. She repeatedly sent servants to Jerusalem and throughout the entire region of the East. These servants visited the tombs of holy martyrs and confessors and brought back relics of them all. After placing them in the silver reliquary with the holy cross itself, she thereafter deserved to see many miracles.

Of these miracles I will first mention this one that the Lord deigned to reveal during the days of his suffering. On the [Good] Friday before holy Easter when [the nuns] were spending

---

[28]The discovery of the True Cross had long been associated with the emperor Constantine (d. 337), but by the end of the fourth century his mother Helena was given the credit for actually finding it.

[29]Daughter of the king of Thuringia, captured and married by King Chlothar in 531. After he had her brother killed, she left him to become a nun, founding a convent in Poitiers whose most notable patron saint was its fourth-century bishop Hilary.

the night in vigils without any light, about the third hour of the night a small light appeared before the altar in the shape of a spark. Then it was enlarged and scattered bright beams here and there. Slowly it began to rise higher, and after becoming a huge beacon it offered light for the dark night and for the congregation that was keeping vigil and praying. As the sky began to brighten it gradually faded until, upon the return of daylight to the lands, it vanished from the sight of the onlookers.

Often I heard how even the lamps that were lit in front of these relics bubbled up because of the divine power and dripped so much oil that frequently they filled a vessel underneath. But because of the foolishness of my closed mind I was never motivated to believe these stories until that power which is at present being revealed reproved my slow-witted hesitation.

For that reason I will describe what I saw with my own eyes. While visiting the tomb of St. Hilary [at Poitiers], I happened out of respect to arrange a conversation with this queen [Radegund]. I entered the convent, greeted the queen, and bowed before the venerable cross and the holy relics of the saints. Then, at the conclusion of my prayer, I stood up. To my right was a burning lamp that I saw was overflowing with frequent drips. I call God as my witness, I thought that its container was broken, because placed beneath it was a vessel into which the overflowing oil dripped. I turned to the abbess [Agnes] and said: "Is your thinking so irresponsible that you cannot provide an unbroken lamp in which the oil can be burned, but instead you use a cracked lamp from which the oil drips?" She replied: "My lord, such is not the case; it is the power of the holy cross you are watching." Then I reconsidered and remembered what I had heard earlier. I turned back to the lamp [that was now] heaving in great waves like a boiling pot, overflowing in swelling surges throughout that hour, and (I believe in order to censure my incredulity) being more and more replenished, so that in the space of one hour the container produced more than four times the oil that it held.

Stunned, I was silent, and finally I proclaimed the power of the venerable cross.

A girl named Chrodigildis was punished by the loss of her eyesight while she was living in the territory of Le Mans after the death of her father. Later, however, while the blessed queen Radegund was still alive, at the command of king Chilperic she entered the rule of the aforementioned convent. With the most blessed Radegund as a guide, she bowed before the holy reliquary and there kept vigils with the other nuns. When morning came and the others left, she remained in the same place prostrate on the ground. In a vision it seemed to her as if someone had opened her eyes. One eye was restored to health; while she was still concerned about the other, suddenly she was awakened by the sound of a door being unlocked and regained the sight of one eye. There is no doubt that this was accomplished by the power of the cross. The possessed, the lame, and also other ill people are often cured at this place. Enough on this topic.

The nails of the Lord's cross, which held the blessed limbs, are splendid and superior to all metal. They were found by the empress Helena after the discovery of the holy cross itself. With two nails she reinforced the bridle of the emperor so that whenever hostile peoples resisted the emperor, they might more easily be dispersed by this power. It is not unknown that the prophet Zachariah offered a prediction about these events; he says: "What is placed in the mouth of a horse will be holy to the Lord" [Zech 14:20].

At that time huge waves disturbed the Adriatic Sea, on which so many ships were wrecked and so many men were drowned that it was called the whirlpool of sailors. The far-sighted empress [Helena], concerned over the disasters of these miserable men, ordered one of the four nails to be thrown into the sea. She relied upon the pity of the Lord that he was able easily to calm the savage rolling of the waves. Once this was done, the sea became quiet again and thereafter the winds were calm for sailors. From then until today once sailors have piously set sail on the sanctified sea they have time for fasting, praying, and reciting psalms. . . .

THE POWER OF THE RELICS THAT WERE BROUGHT TO ME FROM ROME

Through their confession the glorious martyrs have earned the unspeakable benefits of gifts that are always salutary. To petitioners they have revealed themselves by this power that the Lord Creator shared with them. I know that this happened just as my deacon recently told me. This deacon received relics of some martyrs and confessors from pope Pelagius [II] of Rome [r. 579–590].[30] A large chorus of monks who were chanting psalms and a huge crowd of people escorted him to Ostia. After he boarded a ship the sails were unfurled and hoisted over the rigging of a mast that presented the appearance of a cross. As the wind blew, they set out on the high seas. When they were sailing to reach the port of Marseilles, they began to approach a certain place where a mountain of stone rose from the shore of the sea and, sinking a bit, stretched into the sea to the top of the water. As the wind forced them on, the ship was lifted by a mighty blast into danger. When the ship was shaken as if struck by the rock, the sailors recognized their peril and announced their death. The deacon lifted the reliquary with the holy relics. He groaned and in a loud voice began to invoke the names of the individual saints. He prayed that their power might liberate from danger those who were about to die. The ship, as I said, sailed closer and closer to the rock. Suddenly, out of respect for the holy relics, a wind blew from that spot with great force against the other wind. It crushed the waves and repulsed the opposing wind. By recalling the ship to the deep sea, the wind freed everyone from the danger of death. So they circumvented this impending danger, and

by the grace of the Lord and the protection of the saints they arrived at the port they had hoped for. For these were relics of the saints whose sacred feet had been washed by the hands of the Lord. [There were also relics] of Paul, Laurentius, Pancratius, Chrysanthus, the virgin Daria, and John and his brother, the other Paul. Rome, the capital of the world, piously celebrates their struggles and the prizes of their victories.

THE RELICS THAT MY FATHER OWNED

I will now narrate what happened with regard to the relics that my father once carried with him. At the time when Theudebert ordered the sons of Clermont to be sent off as hostages,[31] my father had been recently married. Because he wished himself to be protected by relics of saints, he asked a cleric to grant him something from these relics, so that with their protection he might be kept safe as he set out on this long journey. He put the sacred ashes in a gold medallion and carried it with him. Although he did not even know the names of the blessed men, he was accustomed to recount that he had been rescued from many dangers. He claimed that often, because of the powers of these relics, he had avoided the violence of bandits, the dangers of floods, the threats of turbulent men, and attacks from swords.

I will not be silent about what I witnessed regarding these relics. After the death of my father my mother carried these relics with her. It was the time for harvesting the crops, and huge piles of grain had been collected on the threshing floors. Just like the Limagne,[32] which is clothed with crops but stripped of its trees, so during those days when the seeds were already

---

[30]Not to be confused with the condemned heretic of the early fifth century.

[31]When Theudebert, son of the Frankish king Theodric, left his family behind at Clermont, he took some prominent locals with him (including Gregory's father) as hostages to ensure their safety.
[32]A plain in southern Auvergne, noted for its fertility and beauty.

threshed there was no place to light a fire when a frost appeared. So the threshers kindled fires for themselves from the straw. Then everyone retired to eat. And behold, the fire gradually began to be spread through the straw bit by bit. Quickly, fanned by the wind, the fire spread to the piles of grain. The fire became a huge blaze and was accompanied by the shouts of men, the wails of women, and the crying of children. This happened in our field. When my mother, who was wearing these relics around her neck, learned of this, she rushed from the meal and held the sacred relics in front of the balls of flames. In a moment the entire fire so died down that no sparks were found among the piles of burned straw and the seeds. The grain the fire had touched had suffered no harm.

Many years later I received these relics from my mother. While I was travelling from Burgundy to Clermont, a huge storm appeared in my path. The storm frequently flashed with lightning in the sky and rumbled with loud crashes of thunder. Then I took the holy relics from my pocket and raised my hand before the cloud. The cloud immediately divided into two parts and passed by on the right and the left; it threatened neither me nor anyone else. Then, as a presumptuous young man is expected to behave, I began to be inflated by the arrogance of vain glory. I silently thought that this concession had been made especially for me, rather than because of the merits of the saints. I boasted to my travelling companions and insisted that I had deserved that which God had bestowed upon my naïveté. Immediately my horse suddenly slipped beneath me and threw me to the ground. I was so seriously bruised during this accident that I could hardly get up. I understood that this accident had happened because of my pride; and it was sufficient to note that afterwards the urge of vain glory did not bother me. For if it happened that I was worthy to observe some manifestations of the powers of saints, I have proclaimed that they were due to the gift of God through the faith of the saints.

E. Barbarian Conversion

Converting nonbelievers to the faith had been a cornerstone of Christianity from its earliest days. Not long after 313, when Christianity became an officially tolerated religion in the Roman Empire, church leaders began to aspire to the establishment of a universal or "catholic" church, which for a variety of political and theological reasons would have its capital in Rome. With the political collapse of the western Roman Empire in the fifth and sixth centuries, however, the prospects for the establishment of such a worldwide church seemed to dim considerably. Church leaders faced enormous administrative problems caused by the demise of a central government and its institutions (not to mention the West's complete severance from the Eastern Empire and its church); many European peoples held no allegiance whatsoever to the Roman church. Most of the recently converted barbarians in fact subscribed to outlawed Arian teachings (see 2B), and many more remained steadfastly pagan. In response to this dire situation, a variety of Christian leaders began new and vigorous drives to convert barbarian peoples all over Europe to Catholic Christianity. But the soul of pagan Europe wasn't the only thing at stake in this campaign; in fact the very survival of the Rome-based church as a universal institution depended on its success.

Two key developments had laid the foundation for this mission, and without them the ambitious dream of a Europewide "Christendom" could never have become a reality. The first was the successful conversion of much of the British Isles to Christianity, most famously through the work of St. Patrick (c. 390–c.461) in Ireland and St. Augustine of Canterbury (d. 604) among the Anglo-Saxons at Kent. The second pivotal event was the conversion of the Frankish king Clovis around the year 500 to Roman or Catholic Christianity (as opposed to the common Arian variant). Using the monasteries of Ireland, Britain, and the Frankish kingdom as sources of missionaries, and calling upon the abbots and secular rulers in those territories for political and financial support, a succession of bishops of Rome from Gregory the Great (d. 604) onward set off a very gradual chain reaction of barbarian conversions that lasted from the seventh through the eleventh centuries. Without these Irish, British, and Frankish "base camps" of Christianity to draw on, it is doubtful that the Roman bishops would have succeeded—as they ultimately did—in bringing most of northern and central Europe into the fold of the Catholic church. Though certain individuals usually receive most of the credit for this astounding feat, the conversion of the remaining pagans in Europe was a slow and painstaking process, based on the work of many dedicated missionaries rather than the miraculous efforts of a handful of saints.

1. St. Boniface
MISCELLANEOUS DOCUMENTS

Undoubtedly the most famous of the new English missionaries to the continent was St. Boniface (c. 675–754), who was known as the "apostle to the Germans." Wynfrith, as Boniface was christened, had been a monk since childhood and had already earned renown as a scriptural scholar when he decided at age 40 to become a missionary to the pagan Germans. His first efforts were far from successful, but after a trip to Rome he returned to Frisia, in northern Germany, and began anew. For the next thirty-five years, Boniface preached, converted pagans, and established new dioceses and monasteries in what is now northern and central Germany. As following excerpts from his biography and his own letters make clear, Boniface's work relied greatly on the political backing of the Frankish kings, who ruled over significant portions of present-day France and Germany and who were longtime supporters of Catholic Christianity. Boniface, however, remained uncomfortable in the Frankish king Charles Martel's court—where many of the nobles were "pagan" Arian Christians—and clearly preferred his work "in the field." His initial approach to conversion was much more aggressive than the gradual assimilationist strategy that his friend and correspondent Bishop Daniel of Winchester advised. However, with the exception of few dramatic incidents—such as chopping down the Saxons' sacred Oak of Jupiter—Boniface gradually began to follow Daniel's advice, first working to establish the authority of Christianity and later concerning himself with transforming certain pagan customs into Christian practices. After his violent death, there was such a great cry for a biography of the martyr that the bishops of Mainz and Würzburg eventually commissioned another English missionary named Willibald (700–786) to write one. Never having known the saint, Willibald relied mainly on interviews with Boniface's associates, some of whom he mentions in the biography. The form of Willibald's document is reminiscent of many ancient martyrologies, including scenes of public confrontation between Boniface and unbelieving pagans as well as an account of the saint's courageous (and bloody) death for the faith.

a. WILLIBALD, *LIFE OF ST. BONIFACE* (c. 765)

. . . After Boniface had passed by devious ways through the densely populated territories of the Franks he came at last into the presence of the aforesaid prince[33] and was received by him with marks of reverence. He delivered to him the letters of the Bishop of Rome[34] and of the Apostolic See, and after acknowledging the prince as his lord and patron, returned with the duke's permission to the land of the Hessians in which he had previously settled.

Now many of the Hessians who at that time had acknowledged the Catholic faith were confirmed by the grace of the Holy Spirit and received the laying-on of hands. But others, not yet strong in the spirit, refused to accept the pure teachings of the Church in their entirety. Moreover, some continued secretly, others openly, to offer sacrifices to trees and springs, to inspect the entrails of victims; some practiced divination, legerdemain and incantations; some turned their attention to auguries, auspices and other sacrificial rites; whilst others, of a more reasonable character, forsook all the profane practices of heathenism and committed none of these crimes. With the counsel and advice of the latter persons, Boniface in their presence attempted to cut down, at a place called Gaesmere,[35] a certain oak

of extraordinary size called by the pagans of olden times the Oak of Jupiter. Taking his courage in his hands (for a great crowd of pagans stood by watching and bitterly cursing in their hearts the enemy of the gods), he cut the first notch. But when he had made a superficial cut, suddenly the oak's vast bulk, shaken by a mighty blast of wind from above, crashed to the ground shivering its topmost branches into fragments in its fall. As if by the express will of God (for the brethren present had done nothing to cause it) the oak burst asunder into four parts, each part having a trunk of equal length. At the sight of this extraordinary spectacle the heathens who had been cursing ceased to revile and began, on the contrary, to believe and bless the Lord. Thereupon the holy bishop took counsel with the brethren, built an oratory from the timber of the oak and dedicated it to St. Peter the Apostle.

He then set out on a journey to Thuringia, having accomplished by the help of God all the things we have already mentioned. Arrived there, he addressed the elders and the chiefs of the people, calling on them to put aside their blind ignorance and to return to the Christian religion which they had formerly embraced. For, after the sovereignty of their kings came to an end, Theobald and Heden had seized the reins of government. Under their disastrous sway, which was founded more upon tyranny and slaughter than upon the loyalty of the people, many of the counts had been put to death or seized and carried off into captivity, whilst the remainder of the population, overwhelmed by all kinds of misfortunes, had submitted to the domination of the Saxons. Thus when the power of the dukes, who had protected religion, was destroyed, the devotion of the people to

---

[33]Charles Martel (688–741) was the natural son of Pippin of Heristal. He received the appellation Martel ("the Hammer") from his victory over the Saracens at Tours, which stopped the Islamic expansion into Christian Europe.

[34]Gregory II (r. 715–731). This long-standing special relationship with Frankish kings was renewed by Pope Gregory III in 731.

[35]There are several places in present-day Germany with the name Geismar.

Christianity and religion died out also, and false brethren were brought in to pervert the minds of the people and to introduce among them under the guise of religion dangerous heretical sects. Of these men the chief were Torchtwine, Zeretheve, Eaubercht and Hunraed, men living in fornication and adultery, whom, in the words of the Apostle, God has already judged. These individuals stirred up a violent conflict against the man of God; but when they had been unmasked and shown to be in opposition to the truth, they received a just penalty for their crimes.

When the light of faith had illumined the minds of the people and the population had been loosed from its bonds of error, when also the devil's disciples and the insidious seducers of the people, whom we have already mentioned, had been banished, Boniface, assisted by a few helpers, gathered in an abundant harvest. At first he suffered from extreme want and lacked even the necessaries of life, but, though in straitened circumstances and in deep distress, he continued to preach the Word of God. Little by little the number of believers increased, the preachers grew more numerous, church buildings were restored and the Word of God was published far and wide. At the same time the servants of God, monks of genuinely ascetic habits, were grouped together in one body and they established a monastery[36] with their own hands like the Apostles, procuring food and raiment for their needs. . . .

This, then, is how he traversed the whole of Frisia, destroying pagan worship and turning away the people from their heathen errors by his preaching of the Gospel. The heathen temples and gods were overthrown and churches were built in their stead. Many thousands of men, women and children were baptized by him, assisted by his fellow missionary and suffragan [i.e., assistant] bishop Eoban, who, after being consecrated and appointed to the diocese of Utrecht, was summoned to Frisia to help Boniface in his old age. He was also assisted in his labors by a number of priests and deacons whose names are subjoined: Wintrung, Walthere, Ethelhere, priests; Hamrind, Scirbald and Bosa, deacons; Wachar, Gundaecer, Illehere and Hathowulf, monks. These in company with St. Boniface preached the Word of God far and wide with great success and were so united in spirit that, like the Apostles, they had but one heart and one soul, and thus deserved to share in the same crown of martyrdom and the same final and eternal reward.

When, as we have already said, the faith had been planted strongly in Frisia and the glorious end of the saint's life drew near, he took with him a picked number of his personal followers and pitched a camp on the banks of the river Bordne[37] which flows through the territories called Ostor and Westeraeche and divides them. Here he fixed a day on which he would confirm by the laying-on of hands all the neophytes and those who had recently been baptized; and because the people were scattered far and wide over the countryside, they all returned to their homes, so that, in accordance with the instructions laid down by the holy bishop, they could meet together again on the day appointed for their confirmation.

But events turned out otherwise than expected. When the appointed day arrived and the morning light was breaking through the clouds after sunrise, enemies came instead of friends, new executioners in place of new worshippers of the faith. A vast number of foes armed with spears and shields rushed into the camp brandishing their weapons. In the twinkling of an eye the attendants sprang from the camp to meet them and snatched up arms here and there to defend the holy band of martyrs (for that is what they were to be) against the insensate fury of the mob. But the man of God, hearing the shouts and the onrush of the rabble, straightway called the clergy to his side, and, collecting together

---

[36]Ohrdruf, near Gotha (in east-central Germany). This monastery was governed for some years by Wigbert, abbot of Fritzlar, on the orders of Boniface.

[37]Now called the Boorne, in the present-day Dutch province of Friesland.

the relics of the saints, which he always carried with him, came out of his tent. At once he reproved the attendants and forbade them to continue the conflict, saying: "Sons, cease fighting. Lay down your arms, for we are told in Scripture not to render evil for good but to overcome evil by good. The hour to which we have long looked forward is near and the day of our release is at hand. Take comfort in the Lord and endure with gladness the suffering He has mercifully ordained. Put your trust in Him and He will grant deliverance to your souls." And addressing himself like a loving father to the priests, deacons and other clerics, all trained to the service of God, who stood about him, he gave them courage, saying: "Brethren, be of stout heart, fear not them who kill the body, for they cannot slay the soul, which continues to live for ever. Rejoice in the Lord; anchor your hope in God, for without delay He will render to you the reward of eternal bliss and grant you an abode with the angels in His heaven above. Be not slaves to the transitory pleasures of this world. Be not seduced by the vain flattery of the heathen, but endure with steadfast mind the sudden onslaught of death, that you may be able to reign evermore with Christ."

Whilst with these words he was encouraging his disciples to accept the crown of martyrdom, the frenzied mob of heathens rushed suddenly upon them with swords and every kind of war-like weapon, staining their bodies with their precious blood.[38]

When they had sated their lust for blood on the mortal remains of the just, the heathenish mob seized with exultation upon the spoils of their victory (in reality the cause of their damnation) and, after laying waste the camp, carried off and shared the booty; they stole the chests in which the books and relics were preserved and, thinking that they had acquired a hoard of gold and silver, carried them off, still locked, to the ships. Now the ships were stocked with provisions for the feeding of the

clerics and attendants and a great deal of wine still remained. Finding this goodly liquor, the heathens immediately began to slake their sottish appetites and to get drunk. After some time, by the wonderful dispensation of God, they began to argue among themselves about the booty they had taken and discussed how they were to share out the gold and silver which they had not even seen. During the long and wordy discussion about the treasure, which they imagined to be considerable, frequent quarrels broke out amongst them until, in the end, there arose such enmity and discord that they were divided into two angry and frenzied factions. It was not long before the weapons which had earlier murdered the holy martyrs were turned against each other in bitter strife.

After the greater part of the mad freebooters had been slain, the survivors, surrounded by the corpses of their rivals for the booty, swooped down upon the treasure which had been obtained by so much loss of life. They broke open the chests containing the books and found, to their dismay, that they held manuscripts instead of gold vessels, pages of sacred texts instead of silver plate. Disappointed in their hope of gold and silver, they littered the fields with the books they found, throwing some of them into reedy marshes, hiding away others in widely different places. But by the grace of God and through the prayers of the archbishop and martyr St. Boniface the manuscripts were discovered, a long time afterwards, unharmed and intact, and they were returned by those who found them to the monastery,[39] in which they are used with great advantage to the salvation of souls even at the present day.

Disillusioned by the loss of the treasure on which they had reckoned, the murderers returned to their dwellings. But after a lapse of

---

[38]Thirty of his disciples were martyred along with him, including his suffragan bishop Eoban.

[39]Probably the cathedral of Fulda. Three books, the so-called *Codices Bonifatiani*, are preserved in the Landesbibliothek at Fulda. One of these, almost cut through, is traditionally identified with the book mentioned in the *Life of Boniface*.

three days they were visited with a just retribution for their crimes, losing not only all their worldly possessions but their lives also. For it was the will of the omnipotent Creator and Savior of the world that He should be avenged of His enemies; and in His mercy and compassion he demanded a penalty for the sacred blood shed on His behalf. Deeply moved by the recent act of wicked savagery, He deigned to show the wrath He had concealed so long against the worshippers of idols. As the unhappy tidings of the martyr's death spread rapidly from village to village throughout the whole province and the Christians learned of their fate, a large avenging force, composed of warriors ready to take speedy retribution, was gathered together and rushed swiftly to their neighbors' frontiers. The heathens, unable to withstand the onslaught of the Christians, immediately took to flight and were slaughtered in great numbers. In their flight they lost their lives, their household goods and their children. So the Christians, after taking as their spoil the wives and children, men and maid-servants of the pagan worshippers, returned to their homes. As a result, the pagans round about, dismayed at their recent misfortune and seeking to avoid everlasting punishment, opened their minds and hearts to the glory of the faith. Struck with terror at the visitation of God's vengeance, they embraced after Boniface's death the teaching which they had rejected whilst he still lived.

The bodies of the holy bishop and of the other martyrs were brought by boat across the water called Aelmere, an uneventful voyage of some days, to the city of Utrecht, which we mentioned earlier. There the bodies were deposited and interred until some religious and trustworthy men of God arrived from Mainz. From there they had been sent in a ship by Bishop Lull, the successor of our holy bishop and martyr, to bring the body of the saint to the monastery built by him during his lifetime on the banks of the river Fulda. Of these men there was one named Hadda, remarkable for his continence and chastity, who planned the journey and organized the party. On him particularly and on all the brethren who accompanied him Lull imposed the obligation of setting out on the journey and of bringing back the sacred body in order that greater honor and reverence might be paid to the holy man and greater credence might be given to all the facts they saw and heard.

---

b. LETTER OF BISHOP DANIEL OF WINCHESTER[40] TO BONIFACE (c. 723)

To Boniface, honored and beloved leader, Daniel, servant of the people of God.

Great is my joy, brother and colleague in the episcopate, that your good work has received its reward. Supported by your deep faith and great courage, you have embarked upon the conversion of heathens whose hearts have hitherto been stony and barren; and with the Gospel as your ploughshare you have labored tirelessly day after day to transform them into harvest-bearing fields. Well may the words of the prophet be applied to you: "A voice of one crying in the wilderness, etc." [Isa 40:3, Mt 3:3, Mk 1:3, etc.]

Yet not less deserving of reward are they who give what help they can to such a good and deserving work by relieving the poverty of the laborers, so that they may pursue unhampered the task of preaching and begetting children to Christ. And so, moved by affection and good will, I am taking the liberty of making a few suggestions, in order to show you how, in my opinion, you may overcome with the least possible trouble the resistance of this barbarous people.

[40]Daniel of Winchester (d. 745) was one of the most learned, energetic, and influential bishops of the era.

Do not begin by arguing with them about the genealogies of their false gods. Accept their statement that they were begotten by other gods through the intercourse of male and female and then you will be able to prove that, as these gods and goddesses did not exist before, and were born like men, they must be men and not gods. When they have been forced to admit that their gods had a beginning, since they were begotten by others, they should be asked whether the world had a beginning or was always in existence. There is no doubt that before the universe was created there was no place in which these created gods could have subsisted or dwelt. And by "universe" I mean not merely heaven and earth which we see with our eyes but the whole extent of space which even the heathens can grasp in their imagination. If they maintain that the universe had no beginning, try to refute their arguments and bring forward convincing proofs; and if they persist in arguing, ask them, Who ruled it? How did the gods bring under their sway a universe that existed before them? Whence or by whom or when was the first god or goddess begotten? Do they believe that gods and goddesses still beget other gods and goddesses? If they do not, when did they cease and why? If they do, the number of gods must be infinite. In such a case, who is the most powerful among these different gods? Surely no mortal man can know. Yet man must take care not to offend this god who is more powerful than the rest. Do they think the gods should be worshipped for the sake of temporal and transitory benefits or for eternal and future reward? If for temporal benefit let them say in what respect the heathens are better off than the Christians. What do the heathen gods gain from the sacrifices if they already possess everything? Or why do the gods leave it to the whim of their subjects to decide what kind of tribute shall be paid? If they need such sacrifices, why do they not choose more suitable ones? If they do not need them, then the people are wrong in thinking that they can placate the gods with such offerings and victims.

These and similar questions, and many others that it would be tedious to mention, should be put to them, not in an offensive and irritating way but calmly and with great moderation. From time to time their superstitions should be compared with our Christian dogmas and touched upon indirectly, so that the heathens, more out of confusion than exasperation, may be ashamed of their absurd opinions and may recognize that their disgusting rites and legends have not escaped our notice.

This conclusion also must be drawn: If the gods are omnipotent, beneficent and just, they must reward their devotees and punish those who despise them. Why then, if they act thus in temporal affairs, do they spare the Christians who cast down their idols and turn away from their worship the inhabitants of practically the entire globe? And whilst the Christians are allowed to possess the countries that are rich in oil and wine and other commodities, why have they left to the heathens the frozen lands of the north, where the gods, banished from the rest of the world, are falsely supposed to dwell?

The heathens are frequently to be reminded of the supremacy of the Christian world and of the fact that they who still cling to outworn beliefs are in a very small minority.

If they boast that the gods have held undisputed sway over these people from the beginning, point out to them that formerly the whole world was given over to the worship of idols until, by the grace of Christ and through the knowledge of one God, its Almighty Creator and Ruler, it was enlightened, vivified and reconciled to God. For what does the baptizing of the children of Christian parents signify if not the purification of each one from the uncleanness of the guilt of heathenism in which the entire human race was involved?

It has given me great pleasure, brother, for the love I bear you, to bring these matters to your notice. Afflicted though I am with bodily infirmities, I may well say with the psalmist: "I know, O Lord, that thy judgment is just and that in truth thou hast afflicted me" [Ps

118:75]. For this reason, I earnestly entreat Your Reverence and those with you who serve Christ in the spirit to pray for me that the Lord who made me taste of the wine of compunction may quickly aid me unto mercy, that as He has punished me justly, so He may graciously pardon and mercifully enable me to sing in gratitude the words of the prophet: "According to the number of my sorrows, thy consolations have comforted my soul" [Ps 93:19].

I pray for your welfare in Christ, my very dear colleague, and beg you to remember me.

---

c. LETTER OF BONIFACE TO BISHOP DANIEL (c. 744)

To Bishop Daniel, beloved in the Lord, [from] Boniface, a servant of the servants of God, affectionate greetings in Christ.

It is the usual custom for men who are in trouble and anxiety to seek the consolation and advice of those on whose wisdom and affection they can rely. And so it is with me. Relying on your friendship and your experience, I come to lay before you all my difficulties and vexations of mind and beg you to support me with your comfort and advice. To quote the Apostle, all is conflict without and anxiety within [2 Cor 7:5]; but in my case there are also conflicts within and anxiety without. This is caused in particular by false priests and hypocrites who set God at defiance, thereby rushing to their own damnation and leading the faithful astray by their scandals and errors. They say, in the words of the prophet, Peace, peace, but there is no peace. They strive to sow cockle among the wheat, to choke with weeds or pervert into a poisonous weed the Word of God, which we received from the Catholic and Apostolic Church and which, to the best of our ability, we endeavor to disseminate. But what we plant they make no attempt to water in order that it may grow; in order, rather, that it may wither away they use every effort to root it out by proposing to the faithful new sects and new falsehoods.

Some of them refrain from eating food which God created for our sustenance; others live on milk and honey whilst rejecting bread and other food; some, and these do most harm to the people, say that murderers and adulterers can be accepted for the priesthood even if they persist in their crimes. The people, as the Apostle says, grow tired of sound doctrine and provide themselves with a succession of new teachers as the whim takes them [cf. 2 Tim 4].

In our visits to the Frankish court to obtain assistance and protection, it is not possible, as required by canon law, wholly to avoid the company of such men. We are careful, however, not to communicate with them in the sacred body and blood of the Lord during the celebration of Mass. We also avoid taking their advice or asking their consent, for to such men, mixing with heathens and common people, our toils and struggles are quite incomprehensible. When a priest, a deacon, a cleric or a monk, or any of the faithful, leaves the bosom of the Church, then he joins the heathens in abusing the members of the Church, and this raises terrible obstacles to the spread of the Gospel.

On all these matters we seek your help. We ask you particularly to intercede with God that we may fulfil our duties and our ministry without detriment to our soul. We beg you with most earnest prayer to intercede for us that God, the loving Consoler of those in distress, may deign to keep our souls amidst such trials unharmed and free from sin.

As regards my contacts with the priests already mentioned, I am anxious to have and to follow your considered advice. Without the patronage of the Frankish prince I can neither govern the faithful of the Church nor protect the priests, clerics, monks and nuns of God, nor can I forbid the practice of heathen rites and the worship of idols in Germany without his orders and the fear he inspires. When I come into his presence to secure his support for measures of this kind I cannot, as canon law requires, avoid personal contact with such men. All I can do is to avoid condoning their conduct. I am afraid of contracting sin by associating with them, for I remember that at the time of my consecration I took an oath over the body of St. Peter at Pope Gregory's command, promising that if I was unsuccessful in bringing them back to the right path I would avoid their company. On the other hand, if, in avoiding them, I fail to approach the Frankish prince, I fear that my missionary work amongst the people will greatly suffer.

Pray, resolve my doubts and hesitations by your advice, judgment and precept. For my own part, I feel that if I dissociate myself from them, especially in cases where their manner of life is not in conformity with the canons of the Church, and if I refrain from seeking their advice, from agreeing with their views and from taking part with them in the services of the Church, I shall have done enough.

There is one other comfort for my missionary labors that I should like to ask from you. May I be so bold as to beg of you to send me the *Book of the Prophets* which Winbert, of revered memory, my former abbot and teacher, left behind when he departed this life? It contains the text of the six prophets bound together in one volume, all written out in full with clear letters. Should God inspire you to do this for me, no greater comfort could be given me in my old age, nor could any greater reward be earned by yourself. A *Book of the Prophets*, such as I need, cannot be procured in this country, and with my failing sight it is impossible for me to read small, abbreviated script. I am asking for this particular book because all the letters in it are written out clearly and separately.

In the meantime I am sending you by the priest Forthere a letter and a small gift as a token of affection, a towel, not of pure silk but mixed with rough goat's hair, for drying your feet. . . .

News was brought to me recently by a priest who came to Germany from your parts that you had lost your sight. You, my Lord, are more aware than I am who it is who said: "Where he loves, he bestows correction" [Prov 13:24]. And St. Paul says: "When I am weakest, then I am strongest of all" [2 Cor 12:10]; and: "My strength is increased in infirmity" [2 Cor. 12:9]. The author of the psalms adds: "Many are the trials of the innocent" [Ps 34:19], etc. You, my father, have eyes like those of Didimus, of whom Antony is related to have said that his eyes saw God and His angels and the blessed joys of the heavenly Jerusalem.[41] On this account, and because I know your wisdom and your patience, I believe that God has permitted you to be afflicted in this way so that your virtue and merit may increase and that you may gaze with the eyes of the spirit on those things which God loves and commands, whilst seeing less of the things God hates and forbids. What are our bodily eyes in this time of trial but the windows of sin through which we observe sins and sinners, or, worse still, behold and desire them and so fall into sin?

Farewell, my lord, and pray for me in Christ.

---

[41]The hermit St. Antony of Egypt (c. 251–356); see 2A1. Didymus "the Blind" of Alexandria (c. 309–394) was praised by Antony for his "inner light," which more than compensated for the loss of his vision.

---

2. Rudolf of Fulda
LIFE OF LEOBA (c. 836)

The *Life* of St. Leoba (c. 700–780) offers an indication of the important role that gifted women could play in the early medieval conversion effort. Like Boniface, Leoba was born in England and belonged to a monastery from a young age. She

too eventually left to become a missionary in Germany and likewise reputedly detested court life and much preferred contemplative reading and prayer. As a woman in a male-dominated church and society, however, Leoba was obliged to contribute to the conversion effort in an indirect rather than direct manner. Beginning with a group of thirty nuns, she founded a women's monastery at Bishofsheim, which was to prove the model for all future convents in Germany. Leoba herself provided a model for later abbesses—some of them proclaimed saints—both in her exemplary personal conduct and in her patient submission to the authority of her superiors. Her biographer, Rudolf of Fulda (d. 865), writing more than fifty years after Leoba's death, was still able to locate a few nuns and other associates, all of whom provided admiring details about her firm leadership, her voracious reading, and most important, her universally recognized piety. Already by the time of Rudolf's work, Leoba's much sought-after relics had been moved (or "translated") twice, a testament to the extent of posthumous veneration for this saint. Within the accepted female sphere, then, Leoba was as influential as Boniface and other male missionaries in transforming pagan Germany into a Christian land.

. . . [H]er parents were English, of noble family and full of zeal for religion and the observance of God's commandments. Her father was called Dynno, her mother Aebba. But as they were barren, they remained together for a long time without children. After many years had passed and the onset of old age had deprived them of all hope of offspring, her mother had a dream in which she saw herself bearing in her bosom a church bell, which on being drawn out with her hand rang merrily. When she woke up she called her old nurse to her and told her what she had dreamt. The nurse said to her: "We shall yet see a daughter from your womb and it is your duty to consecrate her straightway to God. And as Anna offered Samuel to serve God all the days of his life in the temple [cf. 1 Sam 1–2], so you must offer her, when she has been taught the Scripture from her infancy, to serve Him in holy virginity as long as she shall live." Shortly after the woman had made this vow she conceived and bore a daughter, whom she called Thrutgeba, surnamed Leoba because she was beloved, for this is what Leoba means. And when the child had grown up her mother consecrated her and handed her over to Mother Tetta[42] to be taught the sacred sciences. And because the nurse had foretold that she should have such happiness, she gave her freedom.

The girl, therefore, grew up and was taught with such care by the abbess and all the nuns that she had no interests other than the monastery and the pursuit of sacred knowledge. She took no pleasure in aimless jests and wasted no time on girlish romances, but, fired by the love of Christ, fixed her mind always on reading or hearing the Word of God. Whatever she heard or read she committed to memory, and put all that she learned into practice. She exercised such moderation in her use of food and drink that she eschewed dainty dishes and the allurements of sumptuous fare, and was satisfied with whatever was placed before her. She prayed continually, knowing that in the Epistles the faithful are counseled to pray without ceasing. When she was not praying she worked with her hands at whatever was commanded her, for she had learned that he who will not work should not eat. However, she spent more time in reading and listening to Sacred Scripture than she gave to manual labor. She took great care not to forget what she had heard or read, observing the commandments of the Lord

---

[42]Tetta of Wimbourne, sister of the king of Wessex and abbess of the Wimbourne monastery.

and putting into practice what she remembered of them. In this way she so arranged her conduct that she was loved by all the sisters. She learned from all and obeyed them all, and by imitating the good qualities of each one she modelled herself on the continence of one, the cheerfulness of another, copying here a sister's mildness, there a sister's patience. One she tried to equal in attention to prayer, another in devotion to reading. Above all, she was intent on practicing charity, without which, as she knew, all other virtues are void.

When she had succeeded in fixing her attention on heavenly things by these and other practices in the pursuit of virtue she had a dream in which one night she saw a purple thread issuing from her mouth. It seemed to her that when she took hold of it with her hand and tried to draw it out there was no end to it; and as if it were coming from her very bowels, it extended little by little until it was of enormous length. When her hand was full of thread and it still issued from her mouth she rolled it round and round and made a ball of it. The labor of doing this was so tiresome that eventually, through sheer fatigue, she woke from her sleep and began to wonder what the meaning of the dream might be. She understood quite clearly that there was some reason for the dream, and it seemed that there was some mystery hidden in it. Now there was in the same monastery an aged nun who was known to possess the spirit of prophecy, because other things that she had foretold had always been fulfilled. As Leoba was diffident about revealing the dream to her, she told it to one of her disciples just as it had occurred and asked her to go to the old nun and describe it to her as a personal experience and learn from her the meaning of it. When the sister had repeated the details of the dream as if it had happened to her, the nun, who could foresee the future, angrily replied: "This is indeed a true vision and presages that good will come. But why do you lie to me in saying that such things happened to you? These matters are no concern of yours: they apply to the beloved

chosen by God." In giving this name, she referred to the virgin Leoba. "These things," she went on, "were revealed to the person whose holiness and wisdom make her a worthy recipient, because by her teaching and good example she will confer benefits on many people. The thread which came from her bowels and issued from her mouth signifies the wise counsels that she will speak from the heart. The fact that it filled her hand means that she will carry out in her actions whatever she expresses in her words. Furthermore, the ball which she made by rolling it round and round signifies the mystery of the divine teaching, which is set in motion by the words and deeds of those who give instruction and which turns earthwards through active works and heavenwards through contemplation, at one time swinging downwards through compassion for one's neighbor, again swinging upwards through the love of God. By these signs God shows that your mistress will profit many by her words and examples, and the effect of them will be felt in other lands afar off whither she will go." That this interpretation of the dream was true later events were to prove.

[Boniface then requests that Leoba be released from the monastery to aid him in missionary work in Germany. Abbess Tetta unhappily complies, and Leoba is sent to him.]

In furtherance of his aims [Boniface] appointed persons in authority over the monasteries and established the observance of the [Benedictine] Rule: he placed Sturm[43] as abbot over the monks and Leoba as abbess over the nuns. He gave her the monastery at a place called Bischofsheim, where there was a large community of nuns. These were trained accord-

---

[43]Also known as St. Sturmi (d. 779); Bavarian-born aide to Boniface and first abbot of the new monastery at Fulda. Sturm was later banished for his resistance to greater episcopal control of the monastery and became active in Charlemagne's campaign to convert the pagan Saxons.

ing to her principles in the discipline of monastic life and made such progress in her teaching that many of them afterwards became superiors of others, so that there was hardly a convent of nuns in that part which had not one of her disciples as abbess. She was a woman of great virtue and was so strongly attached to the way of life she had vowed that she never gave thought to her native country or her relatives. She expended all her energies on the work she had undertaken in order to appear blameless before God and to become a pattern of perfection to those who obeyed her in word and action. She was ever on her guard not to teach others what she did not carry out herself. In her conduct there was no arrogance or pride; she was no distinguisher of persons, but showed herself affable and kindly to all. In appearance she was angelic, in word pleasant, clear in mind, great in prudence, Catholic in faith, most patient in hope, universal in her charity. But though she was always cheerful, she never broke out into laughter through excessive hilarity. No one ever heard a bad word from her lips; the sun never went down upon her anger. In the matter of food and drink she always showed the utmost understanding for others but was most sparing in her own use of them. She had a small cup from which she used to drink and which, because of the meager quantity it would hold, it was called by the sisters "the Beloved's little one."

So great was her zeal for reading that she discontinued it only for prayer or for the refreshment of her body with food or sleep: the Scriptures were never out of her hands. For, since she had been trained from infancy in the rudiments of grammar and the study of the other liberal arts, she tried by constant reflection to attain a perfect knowledge of divine things so that through the combination of her reading with her quick intelligence, by natural gifts and hard work, she became extremely learned. She read with attention all the books of the Old and New Testaments and learned by heart all the commandments of God. To these she added by way of completion the writings of the church Fathers, the decrees of the Councils and the whole of ecclesiastical law.

She observed great moderation in all her acts and arrangements and always kept the practical end in view, so that she would never have to repent of her actions through having been guided by impulse. She was deeply aware of the necessity for concentration of mind in prayer and study, and for this reason took care not to go to excess either in watching or in other spiritual exercises. Throughout the summer both she and all the sisters under her rule went to rest after the midday meal, and she would never give permission to any of them to stay up late, for she said that lack of sleep dulled the mind, especially for study. When she lay down to rest, whether at night or in the afternoon, she used to have the Sacred Scriptures read out at her bedside, a duty which the younger nuns carried out in turn without grumbling. It seems difficult to believe, but even when she seemed to be asleep they could not skip over any word or syllable whilst they were reading without her immediately correcting them. Those on whom this duty fell used afterwards to confess that often when they saw her becoming drowsy they made a mistake on purpose to see if she noticed it, but they were never able to escape undetected. Yet it is not surprising that she could not be deceived even in her sleep, since He who keeps watch over Israel and neither slumbers nor sleeps possessed her heart, and she was able to say with the spouse in the Song of Songs: "I sleep, but my heart watcheth" [5:2].

She preserved the virtue of humility with such care that, though she had been appointed to govern others because of her holiness and wisdom, she believed in her heart that she was the least of all. This she showed both in her speech and behavior. She was extremely hospitable. She kept open house for all without exception, and even when she was fasting gave banquets and washed the feet of the guests with her own hands, at once the guardian and the minister of the practice instituted by our Lord.

Whilst the virgin of Christ was acting in this way and attracting to herself everyone's affection, the devil, who is the foe of all Christians, viewed with impatience her own great virtue and the progress made by her disciples. He therefore attacked them constantly with evil thoughts and temptations of the flesh, trying to turn some of them aside from the path they had chosen. But when he saw that all his efforts were brought to nought by their prayers, fasting and chaste lives, the wily tempter turned his attention to other means, hoping at least to destroy their good reputation, even if he could not break down their integrity by his foul suggestions.

There was a certain poor little crippled girl, who sat near the gate of the monastery begging alms. Every day she received her food from the abbess's table, her clothing from the nuns and all other necessities from them; these were given to her from divine charity. It happened that after some time, deceived by the suggestions of the devil, she committed fornication, and when her appearance made it impossible for her to conceal that she had conceived a child she covered up her guilt by pretending to be ill. When her time came, she wrapped the child in swaddling clothes and cast it at night into a pool by the river which flowed through that place. In this way she added crime to crime, for she not only followed fleshly sin by murder, but also combined murder with the poisoning of the water. When day dawned, another woman came to draw water and, seeing the corpse of the child, was struck with horror. Burning with womanly rage, she filled the whole village with her uncontrollable cries and reproached the holy nuns with these indignant words: "Oh, what a chaste community! How admirable is the life of nuns, who beneath their veils give birth to children and exercise at one and the same time the function of mothers and priests, baptizing those to whom they have given birth. For, fellow-citizens, you have drawn off this water to make a pool, not merely for the purpose of grinding corn, but unwittingly for a new and unheard-of kind of Baptism. Now go and ask those women, whom you compliment by calling them virgins, to remove

this corpse from the river and make it fit for us to use again. Look for the one who is missing from the monastery and then you will find out who is responsible for this crime."

At these words all the crowd was set in uproar and everybody, of whatever age or sex, ran in one great mass to see what had happened. As soon as they saw the corpse they denounced the crime and reviled the nuns. When the abbess heard the uproar and learned what was afoot she called the nuns together, told them the reason, and discovered that no one was absent except Agatha, who a few days before had been summoned to her parents' house on urgent business: but she had gone with full permission. A messenger was sent to her without delay to recall her to the monastery, as Leoba could not endure the accusation of so great a crime to hang over them. When Agatha returned and heard of the deed that was charged against her she fell on her knees and gazed up to heaven, crying: "Almighty God, who knowest all things before they come to pass, from whom nothing is hid and who hast delivered Susanna from false accusations when she trusted in Thee, show Thy mercy to this community gathered together in Thy name and let it not be besmirched by filthy rumors on account of my sins; but do Thou deign to unmask and make known for the praise and glory of Thy name the person who has committed this misdeed."

On hearing this, the venerable superior, being assured of her innocence, ordered them all to go to the chapel and to stand with their arms extended in the form of a cross until each one of them had sung through the whole psalter, then three times each day, at Tierce, Sext and None,[44] to go round the monastic buildings in procession with the crucifix at their head, calling upon God to free them, in His mercy, from this accusation. When they had done this and they were going into the church at None, having completed two rounds, the blessed Leoba went straight to the altar and, standing before the cross, which was

---

[44]I.e., the third, sixth, and ninth hours after sunrise.

being prepared for the third procession, stretched out her hands towards heaven, and with tears and groans prayed, saying: "O Lord Jesus Christ, King of virgins, Lover of chastity, unconquerable God, manifest Thy power and deliver us from this charge, because the reproaches of those who reproached Thee have fallen upon us." Immediately after she had said this, that wretched little woman, the dupe and the tool of the devil, seemed to be surrounded by flames, and, calling out the name of the abbess, confessed to the crime she had committed. Then a great shout rose to heaven: the vast crowd was astounded at the miracle, the nuns began to weep with joy, and all of them with one voice gave expression to the merits of Leoba and of Christ our Savior.

So it came about that the reputation of the nuns, which the devil had tried to ruin by his sinister rumor, was greatly enhanced, and praise was showered on them in every place. But the wretched woman did not deserve to escape scot-free and for the rest of her life she remained in the power of the devil. Even before this God had performed many miracles through Leoba, but they had been kept secret. This one was her first in Germany and, because it was done in public, it came to the ears of everyone.

[Boniface then exhorts Leoba to continue her work abroad; shortly afterward he himself is martyred.]

The blessed virgin, however, persevered unwaveringly in the work of God. She had no desire to gain earthly possessions but only those of heaven, and she spent all her energies on fulfilling her vows. Her wonderful reputation spread abroad and the fragrance of her holiness and wisdom drew to her the affections of all. She was held in veneration by all who knew her, even by kings. Pippin, King of the Franks, and his sons Charles and Carloman treated her with profound respect, particularly Charles, who, after the death of his father and brother, with whom he had shared the throne for some years, took over the reins of government.[45] He was a man of truly Christian life, worthy of the power he wielded and by far the bravest and wisest king that the Franks had produced. His love for the Catholic faith was so sincere that, though he governed all, he treated the servants and handmaids of God with touching humility. Many times he summoned the holy virgin to his court, received her with every mark of respect and loaded her with gifts suitable for her station. Queen Hiltigard also revered her with a chaste affection and loved her as her own soul. She would have liked her to remain continually at her side so that she might progress in the spiritual life and profit by her words and example. But Leoba detested the life at court like poison. The princes loved her, the nobles received her, the bishops welcomed her with joy. And because of her wide knowledge of the Scriptures and her prudence in counsel they often discussed spiritual matters and ecclesiastical discipline with her. But her deepest concern was the work she had set on foot. She visited the various convents of nuns and, like a mistress of novices, stimulated them to vie with one another in reaching perfection.

Sometimes she came to the Monastery of Fulda to say her prayers, a privilege never granted to any woman either before or since, because from the day that monks began to dwell there entrance was always forbidden to women. Permission was only granted to her, for the simple reason that the holy martyr St. Boniface had commended her to the seniors of the monastery and because he had ordered her remains to be buried there. The following regulations, however, were observed when she came there. Her disciples and companions were left behind in a nearby cell and she entered the monastery always in daylight, with one nun older than the rest; and after she had finished her prayers and held a conversation with the brethren, she returned towards nightfall to her disciples whom

---

[45]Pepin the Short (d. 768), mayor of the Frankish palace, seized power from the king Childeric III in 751 and ruled until his death. His son Charles (a.k.a. Charlemagne) expanded the kingdom to an empire spanning most of western Europe by his death in 814.

she had left behind in the cell. When she was an old woman and became decrepit through age she put all the convents under her care on a sound footing and then, on Bishop Lull's[46] advice, went to a place called Scoranesheim, four miles south of Mainz. There she took up residence with some of her nuns and served God night and day in fasting and prayer. . . .

She died in the month of September, the fourth of the kalends [i.e., the 5th] of October [780]. Her body, followed by a long cortège of noble persons, was carried by the monks of Fulda to their monastery with every mark of respect. Thus the seniors there remembered what St. Boniface had said, namely, that it was his

last wish that her remains should be placed next to his bones. But because they were afraid to open the tomb of the blessed martyr, they discussed the matter and decided to bury her on the north side of the altar which the martyr St. Boniface had himself erected and consecrated in honor of our Savior and the twelve Apostles.

After some years, when the church had grown too small and was being prepared by its rectors for a future consecration, Abbot Eigil, with permission of Archbishop Heistulf, transferred her bones and placed them in the west porch near the shrine of St. Ignatius the martyr, where, encased in a tomb, they rest glorious with miracles. For many who have approached her tomb full of faith have many times received divine favors. . . .

---

[46]Bishop of Mainz, 754–785.

BIBLIOGRAPHY

Primary Sources

Anthologies and Readers

Bettenson, Henry, ed. and trans., *The Later Christian Fathers* (Oxford: Oxford University Press, 1970).

Hillgarth, J. N., *Christianity and Paganism, 350–750: The Conversion of Western Europe*, rev. ed. (Philadephia: University of Pennsylvania Press, 1986).

Kraemer, Ross, ed., *Maenads, Martyrs, Matrons, Monastics: A Sourcebook on Women's Religions in the Greco-Roman World* (Minneapolis: Fortress Press, 1988).

Norris, Richard, A., ed. and trans., *The Christological Controversy* (New Haven: Yale University Press, 1996).

Peterson, Joan M., trans., *Handmaids of the Lord: Contemporary Descriptions of Feminine Asceticism in the First Six Christian Centuries* (Kalamazoo, Mich.: Cistercian Publications, 1996).

Russell, Norman, trans., *The Lives of the Desert Fathers* (Kalamazoo, Mich.: Cistercian Publications, 1981).

Scheff, Philip, ed., *Acts of Council of Nicaea: Nicene and Post-Nicene Fathers*, XIV (Grand Rapids, Mich.: Eerdmans, 1977).

Stevenson, J., ed., *A New Eusebius* (London: SPCK, 1957).

———, ed., *Creeds, Councils and Controversies* (London: SPCK, 1989).

Talbot, C. H., ed., *Anglo-Saxon Missionaries in Germany* (Kansas City: Sheed & Ward, 1954).

Ward, Benedicta, trans., *Sayings of the Desert Fathers* (Kalamazoo, Mich.: Cistercian Publications, 1975).

White, Caroline, ed. and trans., *Early Christian Lives* (New York: Penguin, 1998).

Wimbush, V., ed., *Ascetic Behavior in Greco-Roman Antiquity: A Sourcebook.* (Minneapolis: Fortress Press, 1990).

Selected Authors

Athanasius, *The Life of Saint Anthony and the Letter to Marcellinus*, trans. Robert C. Gregg (Mahwah, N.J.: Paulist Press, 1980).

Augustine, St., *Confessions*, trans. Henry Chadwick (Oxford: Oxford University Press, 1992).

Augustine, St., *City of God*, trans. Gerald Walsh et al. (New York: Penguin, 1958).

Bede, *History of the Church in England* (New York: Penguin, 1968).

————, *Lives of the Abbots* (London: Loeb, 1930).

Benedict, *Benedict's Rule: A Translation and Commentary*, trans. Terence G. Kardong (Collegeville, Minn: Liturgical Press, 1996).

Ephrem the Syrian: Hymns, trans. Kathlen E. McVey (Mahwah, N.J.: Paulist Press, 1989).

Eusebius, *The History of the Church from Christ to Constantine,* trans. and ed. G. A. Williamson (New York: Penguin, 1965).

Gregory the Great, St., *Morals on the Book of Job* (London: J. H. Parker, 1850).

————, *Pastoral Practice*, trans. John Leinenweber (Harrisburg, Pa.: Trinity Press International, 1998).

Gregory of Tours, *The Glory of the Martyrs*, trans. R. Van Dam (Liverpool: Liverpool University Press, 1988).

————, *A History of the Franks*, trans. Lewis Thorpe (New York: Penguin Classic, 1974).

Life of Columba, ed. and trans. Alan Orr and Majorie Olgivie Anderson (Oxford: Oxford University Press, 1991).

Pelagius's Commentary on St. Paul's Epistle to the Romans, ed. Theodor de Bruyn (Oxford: Oxford University Press, 1993).

St. Patrick: His Writings and Muirchu's Life, ed. A. B. E. Hood (Savage, Md.: Rowman & Littlefield, 1978).

Secondary Works

Historical Overviews

Brown, Peter, *Late Antiquity* (Oxford: Oxford University Press, 1998).

Collins, Roger, *Early Medieval Europe* (New York: Macmillan, 1991).

Fox, Robin Lane, *Pagans and Christians* (New York: Alfred A. Knopf, 1987).

Herrin, Judith, *The Formation of Christendom* (Princeton, N.J.: Princeton University Press, 1987).

Pelikan, Jaroslav, *The Christian Tradition: A History of the Development of Doctrine, Vol. I: The Emergence of the Catholic Tradition (100–600)* (Chicago: University of Chicago, 1971).

Wolfram, Herwig, *The Roman Empire and Its Germanic Peoples* (Berkeley and Los Angeles: University of California Press, 1997).

Asceticism and Monasticism

Burton-Christie, Douglas, *The Word in the Desert: Scripture and the Quest for Holiness in Early Christian Monasticism* (Oxford: Oxford University Press, 1993).

Knowles, David, *Christian Monasticism* (New York: McGraw-Hill, 1969).

Arianism and the Council of Nicaea

Gregg, R. C., and D. E. Groh, *Early Arianism: A View of Salvation* (Philadelphia: Fortress Press, 1981).

Williams, Rowan, *Arius: Heresy and Tradition* (London: Darton, Longman & Todd, 1987).

Saint Augustine of Hippo

Brown, Peter, *Augustine of Hippo* (Berkeley and Los Angeles: University of California, 1969).
Evans, R. F., *Pelagius: Inquiries and Re-appraisals* (New York: Seabury Press, 1968).
Wills, Garry, *Saint Augustine* (New York: Viking, 1999).

Relic Veneration and the Cult of the Saints

Brown, Peter, *The Cult of the Saints: Its Rise and Function in Latin Christianity* (Chicago: University of Chicago, 1981).
Geary, Patrick, *Furta Sacra: Theft of Relics in the Central Middle Ages* (Princeton, N.J.: Princeton University Press, 1978).
Van Dam, Raymond, *Saints and Their Miracles in Late Antique Gaul* (Princeton, N.J.: Princeton University Press, 1993).

Barbarian Conversion

Fletcher, Richard, *The Barbarian Conversion: From Paganism to Christianity* (Berkeley and Los Angeles: University of California, 1998).
MacMullen, Ramsay, *Christianity and Paganism in the Fourth to Eighth Centuries* (New Haven: Yale University Press, 1997).
Mayr-Harting, Henry, *The Coming of Christianity to Anglo-Saxon England* (New York: Schocken, 1972).
Russell, James C., *The Germanization of Early Medieval Christianity* (Oxford: Oxford University Press, 1994).

CHAPTER 3
The High Middle Ages

INNOCENT III (r. 1198–1216), embodiment of the medieval papacy at its peak of power. As pope, the former canon lawyer made emperors and broke kings, crushed heresies, reformed the clergy, and in general expanded the "full power" of the Roman see to an unprecedented and subsequently unsurpassed degree. (*Archivi Alinari/Art Resource, New York*)

By the beginning of the period of European history known as the High Middle Ages—which lasted roughly from 1050 to 1300—almost all of western and central Europe was at least formally Christian. These three centuries were a time of growth and innovation throughout the continent. The population, largely stagnant since the decline of the Roman Empire, nearly tripled during this time, from about 30 million to more than 80 million. As the demand for arable land increased proportionately, Europeans cleared forests, drained marshes, and began to farm many formerly uninhabited areas. Towns and cities likewise grew and multiplied, spurred by a boom in commerce and small-scale manufacturing. The economic and demographic crises of the fourteenth century would later cause a temporary reversal of such expansion, but by then the remarkably fruitful period of the High Middle Ages had indelibly influenced all of European civilization and Western Christianity.

One of the most dramatic transformations of the High Middle Ages concerned the government of the church and the powers of the papacy in particular. Though the bishops of Rome had undoubtedly grown in stature since the days of the ancient church, it was not really until the eleventh century that a series of popes began to assert a new level of authority, claiming the right to appoint and govern all clergy throughout Europe, powers that had heretofore belonged to secular rulers. The goal of these popes was ecclesiastical autonomy from worldly authorities, in particular from the German emperors who at that time ruled over northern Italy and generally treated the popes as their vassals. But it was a goal that would not be easily attained. For centuries kings and princes had been accustomed to controlling both church property and clerical appointments (known as "benefices") within their realms, and they were willing to defend that power both through diplomatic stratagems and outright warfare. The ensuing papal-imperial conflict (known as the Investiture Crisis) raged throughout most of the High Middle Ages, with the popes gaining the upper hand by the beginning of the thirteenth century. After that time, however, the tide turned. Although princes and emperors continued to show great deference to the papacy, the political advantage—and the all-important control of benefices—remained firmly in the hands of secular heads of state.

The papacy itself had changed considerably during the same period. Although it would be misleading to say that the administration of the European church became centralized during the High Middle Ages, certainly the popes and their staffs had become increasingly involved in every aspect of church governance, doctrine, and piety. During this time, popes such as Clement II (r. 1046–1047), Leo IX (r. 1049–1054), and especially Gregory VII (r. 1073–1085) conducted campaigns to reform the clergy throughout Europe, thereby asserting their authority over the entire Western church. For example, the so-called Gregorian Reform of the eleventh century ambitiously sought to eliminate the well-entrenched and near universal practice of clerical concubinage or marriage. Though many priests resisted abandoning their wives or female companions, the attempt to make them do so was itself significant, as such widespread reforms of clergy or laity were unprecedented in Christian history. During the twelfth century, similar papal reforms were aided by the development of a sophisticated legal code, known as canon law, and by the establishment of diocesan courts throughout Europe, which were used to enforce canonical standards in church matters. Meanwhile, in order to carry out these greater ambitions, the popes were obliged to greatly expand the bureaucratic apparatus of the Vatican, known as the *curia* (Latin "court"). The reign of Pope Innocent III (r. 1198–1216) offers a graphic illustration of the extent of the papacy's growth and power during this period. Calling himself the "vicar (i.e., representative) of Christ," Innocent asserted the papacy's secular rule over most of central Italy, issued various decrees that shaped the still-developing canon law (i.e., church law), summoned the largest ecumenical council (Lateran IV) in the church's history (with over 1200 bishops and abbots in attendance), launched the unsuccessful Fourth Crusade, and was preparing the Fifth Crusade at the time of his death.

The growth of the papacy was accompanied by two other notable developments among the clergy. The first was a pivotal revival of learning and the arts, now called "the twelfth-century Renaissance" (not to be confused with the later Italian Renaissance). In the post-Carolingian ninth century, there were no more than twenty tiny cathedral and other "schools" in all of Europe. With the demographic and urban booms of the High Middle Ages, however, this number jumped to over two hundred by the beginning of the twelfth century. Most of the training at these small clerical institutions was practically oriented, covering the essentials of Latin grammar and rhetoric necessary to perform various administrative and pastoral tasks within the church. Over the course of the twelfth century, however, specialized faculties of teachers and students emerged, eventually coalescing into independent institutions with their own charters from kings and emperors. These "universities" (Latin *universitatis,* "the whole") offered undergraduate and graduate training in a variety of fields and were governed entirely by their own faculty and students. Some quickly developed reputations for excellence in certain disciplines, such as the University of Paris (founded c. 1200), which was famous for its teaching in theology. One immediate impact of the twelfth-century Renaissance was the controversial assimilation into religious learning of pagan philosophical methods, particularly those of Aristotle. Another was the resulting professionalization of theology and the development of an increasingly technical and specialized study of the church's teachings. Because of their great influence on church councils and popes, moreover, theologians and other university-educated clerics did not merely discuss and teach about doctrine, they helped to define it.

The other important clerical development of the High Middle Ages was the transformation of monasticism, the bulwark of Christian asceticism since ancient times. Until the eleventh century, the thousands of monasteries throughout western Europe had all operated as independent institutions, subject only to their respective abbots and to the demands of the Benedictine Rule (see 2A). Even the extremely influential monastery at Cluny (established in 910 in southeastern France) had only exercised an informal influence over its hundreds of imitators until the establishment of a Cluniac network under the Abbot Hugh of Sémur (1049–1109). Soon after, the Cluniac system of a mother house with hundreds of daughter monasteries was imitated by the monastery of Citeaux, founded in 1098. By the end of the twelfth century, the Cistercians, as the members of this new order were known, had established over 530 houses in every corner of Europe. This monastic boom also saw the establishment of several new orders, most significantly the two mendicant, or "begging," orders of the thirteenth century: the Dominicans and the Franciscans. These last two groups represented the most significant departure from the Benedictine tradition, in which most monks lived in seclusion from the world. For although Dominicans and Franciscans also maintained a daily monastic routine and Rule, they mixed regularly with the laity in the course of their preaching and teaching.

It is difficult to summarize the impact of all these clerical transformations and reforms on the piety of most ordinary European Christians. Certainly personal beliefs about religious matters varied widely, and were usually mingled with surviving legends and practices from pre-Christian times. Indeed the common medieval reference to "Christendom" glossed over the wide-ranging cultural diversity of the many peoples who constituted this body of believers. Still, some generalizations are possible. For example, prayer was important in most people's lives, even if it often merely took the form of requests for divine protection from bad weather or disease. In addition, during the High Middle Ages, several of the distinctive features of Western Christianity emerged for the first time, including the practice of kneeling to pray with the hands placed together; the cult of special reverence for the Virgin Mary and the crucified Christ; and the observance of many Christmas customs, such as the building of manger scenes and the telling of legends about the Three Wise Men. For most laypeople, true piety consisted of frequent (though not necessarily weekly) church attendance, acts of personal sacrifice such as fasting or pilgrimage, and participation in the various feasts and processions that dotted the church calendar. The sacraments, particularly baptism and the Eucharist, also played key roles in maintaining a human bond with the divine.

Thus the relative prosperity and fruitfulness of secular life in the High Middle Ages was matched by a simultaneous outpouring of creativity and growth within the church. From the new strength and independence of the popes, to the flowering of canon law and theological scholarship, from the growth of monasteries to the flourishing of new traditions of piety among ordinary Christians, the developments of the High Middle Ages would continue to influence the history of Christianity for centuries to come.

CHAPTER 3 CHRONOLOGY

	Politics	Literature	Individuals	Other
10th cent.	962 Pope crowns Otto I (the Great) emperor			910 Beginning of monastic reforms at Cluny; widely imitated
11th cent.	1056–1106 Henry IV emperor 1066 Norman invasion of England 1073–1085 Gregory VII pope 1095 Urban II declares First Crusade 1099 Crusaders take Antioch & Jerusalem	c. 1080 *Song of Roland* 1098 Anselm of Bec, *Cur Deus Homo*	1033–1109 Anselm of Bec	c. 1000 Peace of God & Truce of God movements 1054 Schism between western & eastern Churches 1077 Henry IV yields to Gregory VII at Canossa 1084 Carthusian monastic order founded
12th cent.	1152–1190 Frederick Barbarossa emperor 1154–1189 Henry II king of England	1122 Abelard, *Sic et Non* c. 1140 Gratian, *Decretum* c. 1155 Peter Lombard, *Four Sentences*	1079–1142 Peter Abelard 1090–1153 Benard of Clairvaux 1098–1179 Hildegard of Bingen 1118–1170 Thomas à Becket	1119 Templars founded 1122 Concordat of Worms on investiture 1145 St. Denis, begin. of Gothic architecture 1189–1192 Third Crusade
13th cent.	1198–1216 Innocent III pope 1215 Magna Carta in England 1226–1270 St. Louis king of France 1294–1303 Boniface VIII pope 1285–1314 Philip the Fair king of France	c. 1266 Aquinas, *Summa Theologica*	1170–1221 St. Dominic 1181–1226 St. Francis of Assisi 1193–1253 St. Clare c. 1265–1308 Duns Scotus	c. 1200 University of Paris founded 1215 Lateran IV Council 1232 Inquisition launched against Albigensian heresy 1291 Fall of Acre (last Crusader outpost)
14th cent.	1347 Beginning of Hundred Years' War between England and France	c. 1314 Dante, *Divine Comedy* c. 1387 Chaucer, *Canterbury Tales*	c. 1285–1349 William of Occam	1309–1377 Papacy in Avignon (Babylonian captivity) 1347–1350 Black Death rages in Europe

A. Investiture Crisis

For the most part, the relationship between church and state during the Middle Ages was characterized by close cooperation and mutual interest. This was especially true in the case of the Frankish kings, who ruled over a large territory that encompassed parts of present-day France and Germany. Because of their long-time political support for the bishops of Rome, they enjoyed a particularly close relationship with the papacy. In fact, the ascendance of the Frankish king Charlemagne (768–814) and his successors to the title of "emperor" was to some degree instigated by their papal allies. Later, after the Frankish emperor Otto I proclaimed his realm (which really encompassed only Germany and northern Italy) to be a reestablishment of the western Roman Empire in 962, the popes were for the most part delighted to give their support. At precisely the same time, however, a new reform movement within the church was preparing to undermine this strong alliance. At first its supporters, known as Cluniacs (after the French monastery of Cluny where the movement originated), focused primarily on monastic reform. Their main goal was to liberate monasteries from the "polluting" control of secular rulers and to restore those institutions to their purely otherworldly focus. As a result, hundreds of new and "independent" monasteries were established, initiating a new separation between church and state. By the middle of the eleventh century, the movement had expanded considerably in scope, with Cluniac sympathizers attempting to wrest control of a variety of ecclesiastical offices and functions from secular rulers such as the emperors. Even more significantly, some of its proponents had now risen as high as the papacy itself, and from this seat of power they were able to launch the more radical papal program known as the Gregorian Reform as well as to provoke the church-state political conflict called the Investiture Crisis.

The most controversial claim of the Gregorian Reform (named for its instigator Pope Gregory VII) concerned the investing, or appointment, of new bishops. According to Gregory and his supporters, the current situation of lay rulers choosing and ceremonially endowing new bishops with their authority was entirely unacceptable. Not only did such a worldly practice taint the bishops so chosen but it also effectively made those bishops and other clerical officeholders into vassals of secular lords. Only the pope, claimed Gregory, had true authority over the clergy, and all lay rulers should accordingly cease their interference in such matters. Of course by this time the office of bishop carried immense political power as well as income, and emperors and kings were not willing to give up their traditional power over such offices without a fight. Nor did they wish to forgo the fees often paid to them by clerical appointees, a practice decried as "simony" by Gregorian reformers. The resulting conflict, which became known as the Investiture Crisis, heated up to a fever pitch in 1076 when Pope Gregory excommunicated—or cut off from the church and its sacraments—the unbending emperor Henry IV. The ensuing battle between Gregory and Henry was ultimately resolved in the emperor's favor, but similar problems continued to plague the church-state relationship until a compromise was reached at Worms (in west-central Germany) in 1122. Under this agreement, the emperor was granted the power to nominate episcopal candidates, but the ultimate investiture of those candidates—including the granting of the bishop's staff and ring—was reserved to the pope. This edict did not prevent similar tensions from flaring up between the papacy and other rulers throughout the Middle Ages, nor did it eliminate other sources of conflict between the church and the empire. It was, however, a major step forward for a papacy intent on political independence.

1. CORRESPONDENCE OF POPE GREGORY VII AND EMPEROR HENRY IV (1073–1077)

At its most basic level, the Investiture Crisis often came down to a personal power struggle between two extremely strong-willed men. The showdown between the young German emperor Henry IV (1050–1106) and the recently consecrated Pope Gregory VII (r. 1073–1085) is the most memorable example of this struggle for precedence. Gregory, who had risen far beyond his peasant origins in Tuscany, was a determined reformer and advocate of a strong papacy. Henry, sole monarch of a vast and unruly empire since the age of fifteen, harbored equally high ambitions for his own secular realm. Already before Gregory's papal coronation in 1073, Henry's attempts to gain control of church appointments within his empire had spurred Pope Alexander II to excommunicate five imperial advisors and threaten the emperor himself with the same. Distracted by concurrent political rebellions in Saxony, Henry quickly made peace with Alexander and attempted to preserve the same relations with his successor, Gregory. As the following excerpts from their letters show, their initial cordiality soon descended into bitter condemnations, particularly as Gregory's more radical objectives became clear. When Henry furiously denounced Gregory as a "false pope," Gregory's response was swift and unprecedented: he immediately excommunicated Henry as well as all German bishops who placed loyalty to the emperor above their duty to the pope. At the same time, Gregory declared Henry a usurper, or illegitimate ruler, and released all subjects from their oaths of obedience to the "false king." Henry's German enemies rejoiced at this declaration and in October 1076 convinced all of the emperor's vassals to honor the pope's command. Taking advantage of the pope's one-year deadline for absolution, Henry rushed to Gregory's palace at Canossa (in northern Italy) in January 1077, hoping to gain forgiveness and thus undercut his political opponents at home. For three full days, the pope made the humbled emperor wait outside the castle gate in the snow, dressed only in the sackcloth rags of a penitent. Finally, at the behest of Henry's queen, Bertha of Saxony, Gregory lifted his excommunication—on the condition, of course, that Henry now recognize papal authority in the investiture of bishops and other church matters. The chastened emperor gladly did so, returning to fight his rebellious German princes with the blessing of the pope but never forgetting the humiliating price he had paid. Meanwhile, Gregory enjoyed what appeared to be the complete triumph of the Gregorian Reform and his own goals for the papacy; in the final selection below, he brags of his victory in a letter to the German princes who had supported him. The last word, however, belonged to Henry, who eventually crushed the rebellion in his empire and, after another excommunication by Gregory, laid siege to Rome itself. Finally, after three years under siege, Rome capitulated in 1083, and Gregory was forced to flee the city. He ultimately died in exile, while Henry had his own papal candidate installed in Gregory's place.

a. HENRY TO GREGORY (1073)

To the most watchful and zealous Lord Pope, Gregory, distinguished by heaven with the apostolic dignity, Henry, by the grace of God King of the Romans,[1] sends the most faithful expression of due subservence.

Since, in order to continue rightly administered in Christ, the kingship and the priesthood are always in need of the strength which He delegates, it is surely fitting for them, my lord and most loving father, not to disagree with one another, but rather to cleave to each other, inseparably joined with the bond of Christ. Thus and in no other way, the concord of Christian unity and the condition of the Church's religious life are preserved in the bond of perfect charity and peace.

With God's consent we have held the office of kingship for some time now, but we have not shown to the priesthood the proper justice and honor in all things. To be sure, we have not borne in vain the avenging sword of the power given us by God; yet we have not always unsheathed it justly in judicial punishment against wrongdoers. Now, however, through divine mercy, we have been stung in some measure by remorse, and having turned against ourself in self-accusation, we confess our former sins to you, Most Indulgent Father, placing our hopes in the Lord that absolved by your apostolic authority we may be worthy of forgiveness.

Alas, we are guilty and wretched! Partly through the inclination of youthful pleasure, partly through the license of our mighty and imperious power, partly also through the seductive deception of those whose counsels we have followed, all too easily misled, we have sinned against heaven and before you, and now we are not worthy to be called your son. For not only have we usurped ecclesiastical properties, but we have also sold the churches themselves to unworthy men—men embittered with the gall of simony—who entered not by the door but by some other way; nor have we defended the churches as we should have. And now, since alone, without your authority, we cannot reform the churches, we earnestly seek your counsel together with your help in these matters as well as in all our affairs. We stand ready to keep your commands most zealously in every respect. And now especially for the church in Milan, which has fallen into error through our fault,[2] we ask that it be corrected canonically by your apostolic stringency and that your authoritative judgment should then proceed to the correction of other churches.

Therefore, God willing, we will not fail you in anything, and we humbly beg you, O father, actively to stand beside us, showing mercy in all things. In a short time you will receive our letter with our most faithful men, from whom, God granting, you will hear more fully about those of our affairs which await further discussion.

---

[1]The regal title by now regularly adopted by kings of the Germans.

[2]This controversy began during the pontificate of Alexander II, when Atto, the candidate of the "popular party and of papal reformers was electerd to the Milan archepiscopacy, in opposition to Godfrey who had been elected in haste by the royalists and invested with ring and staff by Henry. Godfrey was forced to withdraw to Brebbia, where he was steadfastly supported by Henry.

b. GREGORY TO HENRY
(December 8, 1075)

Gregory, bishop, servant of God's servants, to King Henry, greeting and the apostolic benediction—but with the understanding that he obeys the Apostolic See as becomes a Christian king.

Considering and weighing carefully to how strict a judge we must render an account of the stewardship committed to us by St. Peter, prince of the Apostles, we have hesitated to send you the apostolic benediction, since you are reported to be in voluntary communication with men who are under the censure of the Apostolic See and of a synod. If this is true, you yourself know that you cannot receive the favor of God nor the apostolic blessing unless you shall first put away those excommunicated persons and force them to do penance and shall yourself obtain absolution and forgiveness for your sin by due repentance and satisfaction. Wherefore we counsel Your Excellency, if you feel yourself guilty in this matter, to make your confession at once to some pious bishop who, with our sanction, may impose upon you a penance suited to the offense, may absolve you and with your consent in writing may be free to send us a true report of the manner of your penance.

We marvel exceedingly that you have sent us so many devoted letters and displayed such humility by the spoken words of your legates, calling yourself a son of our Holy Mother Church and subject to us in the faith, singular in affection, a leader in devotion, commending yourself with every expression of gentleness and reverence, and yet in action showing yourself most bitterly hostile to the canons and apostolic decrees in those duties especially required by loyalty to the Church. Not to mention other cases, the way you have observed your promises in the Milan affair;[3] made through your mother

and through bishops, our colleagues, whom we sent to you, and what your intentions were in making them is evident to all. And now, heaping wounds upon wounds, you have handed over the sees of Fermo and Spoleto—if indeed a church may be given over by any human power—to persons entirely unknown to us, whereas it is not lawful to consecrate anyone except after probation and with due knowledge.

It would have been becoming to you, since you confess yourself to be a son of the Church, to give more respectful attention to the master of the Church, that is, to Peter, prince of the Apostles. To him, if you are of the Lord's flock, you have been committed for your pasture, since Christ said to him: "Peter, feed my sheep [Jn 21:17]," and again: "To thee are given the keys of Heaven, and whatsoever thou shalt bind on earth shall be bound in Heaven and whatsoever thou shalt loose on earth shall be loosed in Heaven [Mt 16:19]." Now, while we, unworthy sinner that we are, stand in his place of power, still whatever you send to us, whether in writing or by word of mouth, he himself receives, and while we read what is written or hear the voice of those who speak, he discerns with subtle insight from what spirit the message comes. Wherefore Your Highness should beware lest any defect of will toward the Apostolic See be found in your words or in your messages and should pay due reverence, not to us but to Almighty God, in all matters touching the welfare of the Christian faith and the status of the Church. And this we say although our Lord deigned to declare: "He who heareth you heareth me; and he who despiseth you despiseth me" [Lk 10:16]. . . .

This edict [against lay investiture], which some who place the honor of men above that of God call an intolerable burden, we, using the right word, call rather a truth and a light necessary for salvation, and we have given judgment that it is to be heartily accepted and obeyed, not only by you and your subjects but by all princes and peoples who confess and worship

---

[3]See note 2.

Christ—though it is our especial wish and would be especially fitting for you, that you should excel others in devotion to Christ as you are their superior in fame, in station and in valor.

Nevertheless, in order that these demands may not seem to you too burdensome or unfair we have sent you word by your own liegemen not to be troubled by this reform of an evil practice but to send us prudent and pious legates from your own people. If these can show in any reasonable way how we can moderate the decision of the holy fathers [at the Council] saving the honor of the eternal king and without peril to our own soul, we will condescend to hear their counsel. It would in fact have been the fair thing for you, even if you had not been so graciously admonished, to make reasonable inquiry of us in what respect we had offended you or assailed your honor, before you proceeded to violate the apostolic decrees. But how little you cared for our warnings or for doing right was shown by your later actions.

However, since the long-enduring patience of God summons you to improvement, we hope that with increase of understanding your heart and mind may be turned to obey the commands of God. We warn you with a father's love that you accept the rule of Christ, that you consider the peril of preferring your own honor to his, that you do not hamper by your actions the freedom of that Church which he deigned to bind to himself as a bride by a divine union, but, that she may increase as greatly as possible, you will begin to lend to Almighty God and to St. Peter, by whom also your own glory may merit increase, the aid of your valor by faithful devotion.

Now you ought to recognize your special obligation to them for the triumph over your enemies which they have granted you, and while they are making you happy and singularly prosperous, they ought to find your devotion increased by their favor to you. That the fear of God, in whose hand is all the might of kings and emperors, may impress this upon you more than any admonitions of mine, bear in mind what happened to Saul after he had won a victory by command of the prophet, how he boasted of his triumph, scorning the prophet's admonitions, and how he was rebuked by the Lord, and also what favor followed David the king as a reward for his humility in the midst of the tokens of his bravery.

Finally, as to what we have read in your letters and do not mention here we will give you no decided answer until your legates, Radbod, Adalbert and Odescalcus, to whom we entrust this, have returned to us and have more fully reported your decision upon the matters which we commissioned them to discuss with you.

---

c. HENRY TO GREGORY
(January 24, 1076)

Henry, King not by usurpation, but by the pious ordination of God, to Hildebrand, now not Pope, but false monk:

You have deserved such a salutation as this because of the confusion you have wrought; for you left untouched no order of the Church which you could make a sharer of confusion instead of honor, of malediction instead of benediction.

For to discuss a few outstanding points among many: Not only have you dared to touch the rectors of the holy Church—the archbishops, the bishops, and the priests, anointed of the Lord as they are—but you have trodden them under foot like slaves who know not what their lord may do. In crushing them you have gained for yourself acclaim from the mouth of the rabble. You have judged that all these know nothing, while you alone know everything. In any case, you have sedulously used this knowledge not for edification, but for destruction, so greatly that we may believe Saint Gregory, whose name you have arrogated to yourself, rightly made this prophesy of you when he said: "From the abundance of his subjects, the mind of the prelate is often exalted, and he thinks that he has more knowledge than anyone else, since he sees that he has more power than anyone else."[4]

And we, indeed, bore with all these abuses, since we were eager to preserve the honor of the Apostolic See. But you construed our humility as fear, and so you were emboldened to rise up even against the royal power itself, granted to us by God. You dared to threaten to take the kingship away from us—as though we had received the kingship from you, as though kingship and empire were in your hand and not in the hand of God.

Our Lord, Jesus Christ, has called us to kingship, but has not called you to the priesthood. For you have risen by these steps: namely, by cunning, which the monastic profession abhors, to money; by money to favor; by favor to the sword. By the sword you have come to the throne of peace, and from the throne of peace you have destroyed the peace. You have armed subjects against their prelates; you who have not been called by God have taught that our bishops who have been called by God are to be spurned; you have usurped for laymen the bishops' ministry over priests, with the result that these laymen depose and condemn the very men whom the laymen themselves received as teachers from the hand of God, through the imposition of the hands of bishops.

You have also touched me, one who, though unworthy, has been anointed to kingship among the anointed. This wrong you have done to me, although as the tradition of the holy Fathers has taught, I am to be judged by God alone and am not to be deposed for any crime unless—may it never happen—I should deviate from the Faith. For the prudence of the holy bishops entrusted the judgment and the deposition even of Julian the Apostate[5] not to themselves, but to God alone. The true pope Saint Peter also exclaims, "Fear God, honor the king" [1 Pet 2:17]. You, however, since you do not fear God, dishonor me, ordained of Him.

Wherefore, when Saint Paul gave no quarter to an angel from heaven if the angel should preach heterodoxy, he did not except you who are now teaching heterodoxy throughout the earth. For he says, "If anyone, either I or an angel from heaven, preach any other gospel unto you than that which we have preached unto you, let him be accursed" [Gal 1:18]. Descend, therefore, condemned by this anathema and by the common judgment of all our bishops and of ourself. Relinquish the Apostolic See which you have arrogated. Let another mount the throne of Saint Peter, another who will not cloak violence with religion but who will teach the pure doctrine of Saint Peter.

I, Henry, King by the grace of God, together with all our bishops, say to you: Descend! Descend!

---

[4]Gregory I "the Great" (c. 540–604) in his *Pastoral Rule.*

[5]Julian the Apostate was an ancient Roman emperor (r. 361–364) who attempted a pagan restoration in the Christianized empire; his changes were quickly undone after his premature death.

d. GREGORY TO THE GERMAN PRINCES (late 1077)

Whereas, for love of justice you have made common cause with us and taken the same risks in the warfare of Christian service, we have taken special care to send you this accurate account of the king's penitential humiliation, his absolution and the course of the whole affair from his entrance into Italy to the present time.

According to the arrangement made with the legates sent to us by you we came to Lombardy about twenty days before the date at which some of your leaders were to meet us at the pass and waited for their arrival to enable us to cross over into that region. But when the time had elapsed and we were told that on account of the troublous times—as indeed we well believe—no escort could be sent to us, having no other way of coming to you we were in no little anxiety as to what was our best course to take.

Meanwhile we received certain information that the king was on the way to us. Before he entered Italy he sent us word that he would make satisfaction to God and St. Peter and offered to amend his way of life and to continue obedient to us, provided only that he should obtain from us absolution and the apostolic blessing. For a long time we delayed our reply and held long consultations, reproaching him bitterly through messengers back and forth for his outrageous conduct, until finally, of his own accord and without any show of hostility or defiance, he came with a few followers to the fortress of Canossa where we were staying. There, on three successive days, standing before the castle gate, laying aside all royal insignia, barefooted and in coarse attire, he ceased not with many tears to beseech the apostolic help and comfort until all who were present or who had heard the story were so moved by pity and compassion that they pleaded his cause with prayers and tears. All marveled at our unwonted severity, and some even cried out that we were showing, not the seriousness of apostolic authority, but rather the cruelty of a savage tyrant.

At last, overcome by his persistent show of penitence and the urgency of all present, we released him from the bonds of anathema and received him into the grace of Holy Mother Church, accepting from him the guarantee described below, confirmed by the signatures of the abbot of Cluny, of our daughters, the Countess Matilda and the Countess Adelaide,[6] and other princes, bishops and laymen who seemed to be of service to us.

And now that these matters have been arranged, we desire to come over into your country at the first opportunity, that with God's help we may more fully establish all matters pertaining to the peace of the Church and the good order of the land. For we wish you clearly to understand that, as you may see in the written guarantees, the whole negotiation is held in suspense, so that our coming and your unanimous consent are in the highest degree necessary. Strive, therefore, all of you, as you love justice, to hold in good faith the obligations into which you have entered. Remember that we have not bound ourselves to the king in any way except by frank statement—as our custom is—that he may expect our aid for his safety and his honor, whether through justice or through mercy, and without peril to his soul or to our own.

---

[6]Sisters of Emperor Henry IV.

B. Crusade

One of the most dramatic consequences of Christianity's legitimization in the fourth century was the transformation of the church's teachings on war and violence. Earlier Christians had taken Jesus's admonitions about turning the other cheek to heart, embracing his pacifist ideals and, in a few instances, suffering violent martyrdoms as a consequence. Following toleration and the more thorough assimilation of Christianity into Roman political life, however, the church began to reconsider the possibility that force was necessary in some situations, particularly where the "common good" was concerned. St. Augustine (354–430) even articulated a theory of just war, whereby Christians might participate in military conflicts under certain conditions. During the centuries following the collapse of the western Roman Empire, however, the Christian princes of

Europe became embroiled in such frequent warfare that earlier theological distinctions between just and unjust wars were simply forgotten. All wars to support the aims of a Christian ruler began to be touted as just, and prayers for God to bestow his blessing on military campaigns became commonplace. By the beginning of the High Middle Ages, the once-central Christian ideal of pacifism had come to be seen as a mere relic of the age of the martyrs.

Nonetheless, the idea of a "holy" war, or crusade (from French *croix,* "cross") did not gain prominence until the very end of the eleventh century. In 1095, Pope Urban II (r. 1088–1099) called on the warriors of Europe to undertake a "pilgrimage" to assist their Byzantine brethren in freeing Jerusalem and the rest of the Holy Land from the "infidel" Muslims. During the next 175 years, Western Christians repeatedly took up his call, sending a series of expeditions from Europe to the Middle East. The First Crusade, involving both popular marches and organized war parties from France and southern Italy, was by far the most successful, capturing Antioch in June 1098 and Jerusalem itself by July of the following year. Europeans immediately established a number of new "Latin" states, including a Kingdom of Jerusalem and countships in Edessa and Tripoli. Within fifty years, however, the Seljuk Turks began to win back their lost territories, seizing Edessa in 1144 and thereby triggering a second, unsuccessful crusade. From this point on, all the conquests of the First Crusade were gradually lost, despite a number of subsequent campaigns by Europeans, including the disastrous "Children's Crusade" in 1212, in which thousands of children perished before even reaching the Holy Land. By 1291, the last remaining Latin state had fallen into Muslim hands. The use of the word "crusade" as a rallying cry did not disappear with this defeat, but instead came to be applied to struggles against heretical Christians within Europe. The Western dream of Christianizing the Holy Land through holy war, however, was never to be realized.

1. Fulcher of Chartres
THE FIRST CRUSADE (1101)

Fulcher of Chartres (c. 1059–1127) was a French cleric who actually witnessed Pope Urban II's famous call to arms at the Council of Clermont. Although clearly a believer in the cause of crusade, Fulcher attempted to provide an objective account of the entire enterprise. His description of Urban's speech, for instance, includes the various political as well as religious motives of pope and crusaders. Shortly thereafter, when he accompanied his lord Stephen of Blois on the First Crusade, he likewise noted the frequent instances of greed and cruelty among his fellow Western Christians in their dealings with the Byzantines and Turks. His account of the final storming of Jerusalem in the spring of 1099 provides a typical contrast in pious words and barbarous deeds, with the crusaders crying "Help, God" as they rush into the Holy City and massacre hundreds and perhaps thousands of civilians as well as warriors. Fulcher remained in conquered Jerusalem until his death almost thirty years later, gradually composing what he considered to be an honest tribute to a necessarily bloody "liberation."

... In the year 1095 from the Lord's Incarnation, with Henry reigning in Germany as so-called emperor, and with Philip as king in France,[7] manifold evils were growing in all parts of Europe because of wavering faith. In Rome ruled Pope Urban II, a man distinguished in life and character, who always strove wisely and actively to raise the status of the Holy Church above all things.

He saw that the faith of Christianity was being destroyed to excess by everybody, by the clergy as well as by the laity. He saw that peace was altogether discarded by the princes of the world, who were engaged in incessant warlike contention and quarreling among themselves. He saw the wealth of the land being pillaged continuously. He saw many of the vanquished, wrongfully taken prisoner and very cruelly thrown into foulest dungeons, either ransomed for a high price or, tortured by the triple torments of hunger, thirst, and cold, blotted out by a death hidden from the world. He saw holy places violated; monasteries and villas burned. He saw that no one was spared of any human suffering, and that things divine and human alike were held in derision.

He heard, too, that the interior regions of Romania, where the Turks ruled over the Christians, had been perniciously subjected in a savage attack. Moved by long-suffering compassion and by love of God's will, he descended the mountains to Gaul, and in Auvergne he called for a council to congregate from all sides at a suitable time at a city called Clermont.[8] Three hundred and ten bishops and abbots, who had been advised beforehand by messengers, were present.

Then, on the day set aside for it, he called them together to himself and, in an eloquent address, carefully made the cause of the meeting known to them. In the plaintive voice of an aggrieved Church, he expressed great lamentation, and held a long discourse with them about the raging tempests of the world, which have been mentioned, because faith was undermined.

One after another, he beseechingly exhorted them all, with renewed faith, to spur themselves in great earnestness to overcome the Devil's devices and to try to restore the Holy Church, most unmercifully weakened by the wicked, to its former honorable status.

"Most beloved brethren," he said, "by God's permission placed over the whole world with the papal crown, I, Urban, as the messenger of divine admonition, have been compelled by an unavoidable occasion to come here to you servants of God. I desired those whom I judged to be stewards of God's ministries to be true stewards and faithful, with all hypocrisy rejected [1 Cor 4:1, 2; Mt 24:45, 46].

"But with temperance in reason and justice being remote, I, with divine aid, shall strive carefully to root out any crookedness or distortion which might obstruct God's law. For the Lord appointed you temporarily as stewards over His family to serve it nourishment seasoned with a modest savor. Moreover, blessed will you be if at last the Overseer find you faithful. . . .

"Now that you, O sons of God, have consecrated yourselves to God to maintain peace among yourselves more vigorously and to uphold the laws of the Church faithfully, there is work to do, for you must turn the strength of your sincerity, now that you are aroused by divine correction, to another affair that concerns you and God. Hastening to the way, you must help your brothers living in the Orient, who need your aid for which they have already cried out many times.[9]

---

[7]The "so-called emperor" was Henry IV (see 3A), not recognized as rightful emperor by adherents of popes Gregory VII and Urban II. Philip I of France (1060–1108) was later excommunicated by Urban and thus was unable to participate in the crusade.

[8]Clermont-Ferrand, in Auvergne (southern France). The Council met November 18–28, 1095, with Urban's famous speech delivered November 27.

[9]The Byzantine patriarch Alexius Comnenus had called on Urban for help against the infidels in January and March of that year (1095).

"For, as most of you have been told, the Turks, a race of Persians, who have penetrated within the boundaries of Romania[10] even to the Mediterranean to that point which they call the Arm of Saint George [i.e., the Bosporous], in occupying more and more of the lands of the Christians, have overcome them, already victims of seven battles, and have killed and captured them, have overthrown churches, and have laid waste God's kingdom. If you permit this supinely for very long, God's faithful ones will be still further subjected.

"Concerning this affair, I, with suppliant prayer—not I, but the Lord—exhort you, heralds of Christ, to persuade all of whatever class, both knights and footmen, both rich and poor, in numerous edicts, to strive to help expel that wicked race from our Christian lands before it is too late.

"I speak to those present, I send word to those not here; moreover, Christ commands it. Remission of sins will be granted for those going thither, if they end a shackled life either on land or in crossing the sea, or in struggling against the heathen. I, being vested with that gift from God, grant this to those who go.

"O what a shame, if a people, so despised, degenerate, and enslaved by demons would thus overcome a people endowed with the trust of almighty God, and shining in the name of Christ! O how many evils will be imputed to you by the Lord Himself, if you do not help those who, like you, profess Christianity!

"Let those," he said, "who are accustomed to wage private wars wastefully even against Believers, go forth against the Infidels in a battle worthy to be undertaken now and to be finished in victory. Now, let those, who until recently existed as plunderers, be soldiers of Christ; now, let those, who formerly contended against brothers and relations, rightly fight barbarians; now, let those, who recently were hired for a few pieces of silver, win their eternal reward. Let those, who wearied themselves to the detriment of body and soul, labor for a twofold honor. Nay, more, the sorrowful here will be glad there, the poor here will be rich there, and the enemies of the Lord here will be His friends there.

"Let no delay postpone the journey of those about to go, but when they have collected the money owed to them and the expenses for the journey, and when winter has ended and spring has come, let them enter the crossroads courageously with the Lord going on before."

After these words were spoken, the hearers were fervently inspired. Thinking nothing more worthy than such an undertaking, many in the audience solemnly promised to go, and to urge diligently those who were absent. There was among them one Bishop of Puy, Ademar by name,[11] who afterwards, acting as vicar-apostolic, ruled the whole army of God wisely and thoughtfully, and spurred them to complete their undertaking vigorously.

So, the things that we have told you were well established and confirmed by everybody in the Council. With the blessing of absolution given, they departed; and after returning to their homes, they disclosed to those not knowing, what had taken place. As it was decreed far and wide throughout the provinces, they established the peace, which they call the Truce, to be upheld mutually by oath.

Many, one after another, of any and every occupation, after confession of their sins and with purified spirits, consecrated themselves to go where they were bidden.

Oh, how worthy and delightful to all of us who saw those beautiful crosses, either silken or woven of gold, or of any material, which the pilgrims sewed on the shoulders of their woolen cloaks or cassocks by the command of the Pope,

---

[10]Actually the Anatolian provinces of the Byzantine Empire, where the Seljuk Turks had founded a state called Rum.

[11]Ademar de Monteil, Bishop of Puy, was the first to take the cross after Urban's crusading message. Having made a pilgrimage to Jerusalem in 1086–1087, he was the only person of any repute and experience to join the crusade at this time, and thus Urban appointed him as leader of the expedition, which set forth on August 15, 1096.

after taking the vow to go. To be sure, God's soldiers, who were making themselves ready to battle for His honor, ought to have been marked and fortified with a sign of victory. And so by embroidering the symbol [of the cross] on their clothing in recognition of their faith, in the end they won the True Cross itself. They imprinted the ideal so that they might attain the reality of the ideal.

It is plain that good meditation leads to doing good work and that good work wins salvation of the soul. But, if it is good to mean well, it is better, after reflection, to carry out the good intention. So, it is best to win salvation through action worthy of the soul to be saved. Let each and everyone, therefore, reflect upon the good, that he makes better in fulfillment, so that, deserving it, he might finally receive the best, which does not diminish in eternity.

In such a manner Urban, a wise man and reverenced,
Mediated a labor, whereby the world florescenced.

For he renewed peace and restored the laws of the Church to their former standards; also he tried with vigorous instigation to expel the heathen from the lands of the Christians. And since he strove to exalt all things of God in every way, almost everyone gladly surrendered in obedience to his paternal care. . . .

In the year of the Lord 1097, with spring weather accompanying March, immediately Robert the Norman and Count Stephen of Blois, who had been waiting for favorable weather, accompanied by their men, again turned seaward. The fleet was prepared, and on the Nones [i.e., 5th] of April, which at that time fell on the Holy Day of Easter, they embarked at the port of Brindisi.

"How unsearchable are His judgments, and His ways past finding out!" [Rom 11:33] For we saw one boat among the others, which, while near the shore and apparently unhindered, suddenly cracked apart in the middle. Whereby four hundred of both sexes perished

by drowning, concerning whom joyful praise to God immediately sounded.

For when those who were standing around had collected as many of the dead bodies as they could, they discovered crosses actually imprinted in the flesh on the shoulders of some of them. For what those living bore on their garments, it was fitting, with the Lord willing, that the same victorious sign remain with them thus preoccupied in His service under a pledge of faith. And at the same time, reason made it plain to those reflecting on it, that it was appropriate that, by such a miracle, those dead had already by God's mercy obtained the peace of everlasting life in the clearly evident fulfillment of the prophecy which had been written: "The just, though taken prematurely by death, shall find peace" [Wis 4:7]. . . .

{THE SIEGE OF THE CITY OF JERUSALEM}

When the Franks viewed the city, and saw that it would be difficult to take, our princes ordered wooden ladders to be made. By erecting them against the wall they hoped to scale it, and by a fierce attack enter the city, with God helping.

After they had done this, when the leaders gave the signal and the trumpets sounded, in morning's bright light of the seventh day following [June 13, 1099] they rushed upon the city from all sides in an astonishing attack. But when they had rushed upon it until the sixth hour of the day, and were unable to enter by means of the scaling ladders because there were few of them, they sadly abandoned the assault.

After consultation [June 15], craftsmen were ordered to make machines, so that by moving them to the walls they might, with God's aid, obtain the desired end. So this was done.

Meanwhile they suffered lack of neither bread nor meat; but, because that place was dry, unirrigated, and without rivers, both the men and the beasts of burden were very much in need of water to drink. This necessity forced them to seek water at a distance, and daily they laboriously carried it in skins from four or five miles to the siege.

After the machines were prepared, namely, the battering-rams and the sows, they again prepared to assail the city. In addition to other kinds of siege craft, they constructed a tower from small pieces of wood, because large pieces could not be secured in those regions. When the order was given, they carried the tower piecemeal to a corner of the city. Early in the same morning, when they had gathered the machines and other auxiliary weapons, they very quickly erected the tower in compact shape not far from the wall. After it was set up and well covered by hides on the outside, by pushing it they slowly moved it nearer to the wall.

Then a few but brave soldiers, at a signal from the horn, climbed on the tower. Nevertheless the Saracens defended themselves from these soldiers and, with slings, hurled firebrands dipped in oil and grease at the tower and at the soldiers, who were in it. Thereafter death was present and sudden for many on both sides.

From their position on Mount Zion, Count Raymond [of Toulouse] and his men likewise made a great assault with their machines. From another position, where Duke Godfrey [of Bouillon], Robert, Count of the Normans, and Robert of Flanders, were situated, an even greater assault was made on the wall. This was what was done on that day.

On the following day, at the blast of the trumpets, they undertook the same work more vigorously, so that by hammering in one place with the battering-rams, they breached the wall. The Saracens had suspended two beams before the battlement and secured them by ropes as a protection against the stones hurled at them by their assailants. But what they did for their advantage later turned to their detriment, with God's providence. For when the tower was moved to the wall, the ropes, by which the aforesaid beams were suspended, were cut by falchions [i.e., swords], and the Franks constructed a bridge for themselves out of the same timber, which they cleverly extended from the tower to the wall.

Already one stone tower on the wall, at which those working our machines had thrown flaming firebrands, was afire. The fire, little by little replenished by the wooden material in the tower, produced so much smoke and flame that not one of the citizens on guard could remain near it.

Then the Franks entered the city magnificently at the noonday hour on Friday [July 15, 1099], the day of the week when Christ redeemed the whole world on the cross. With trumpets sounding and with everything in an uproar, exclaiming: "Help, God!" they vigorously pushed into the city, and straightway raised the banner on the top of the wall. All the heathen, completely terrified, changed their boldness to swift flight through the narrow streets of the quarters. The more quickly they fled, the more quickly were they put to flight.

Count Raymond and his men, who were bravely assailing the city in another section, did not perceive this until they saw the Saracens jumping from the top of the wall. Seeing this, they joyfully ran to the city as quickly as they could, and helped the others pursue and kill the wicked enemy.

Then some, both Arabs and Ethiopians, fled into the Tower of David; others shut themselves in the Temple of the Lord and of Solomon,[12] where in the halls a very great attack was made on them. Nowhere was there a place where the Saracens could escape the swordsmen.

On the top of Solomon's Temple, to which they had climbed in fleeing, many were shot to death with arrows and cast down headlong from the roof. Within this Temple about ten thousand were beheaded.[13] If you had been there, your feet would have been stained up to the ankles with the blood of the slain. What more shall I tell? Not one of them was allowed

---

[12]Known to Muslims as the mosque of al-Aqsa; later headquarters of the crusader order of the Knights Templar.

[13]Another chronicler, Albert of Aix, places the count at three hundred, generally considered a more accurate estimate.

to live. They did not spare the women and children.

{THE SPOILS WHICH THE CHRISTIANS TOOK}

After they had discovered the cleverness of the Saracens, it was an extraordinary thing to see our squires and poorer people split the bellies of those dead Saracens, so that they might pick out besants[14] from their intestines, which they had swallowed down their horrible gullets while alive. After several days, they made a great heap of their bodies and burned them to ashes, and in these ashes they found the gold more easily.

Tancred [of Apulia] rushed into the Temple of the Lord, and seized much of the gold and silver and precious stones. But he restored it, and returned everything or something of equal value to its holy place. I say "holy," although nothing divine was practiced there at the time when the Saracens exercised their form of idolatry in religious ritual and never allowed a single Christian to enter.

With drawn swords, our people ran through
   the city;
Nor did they spare anyone, not even those
   pleading for mercy.
The crowd was struck to the ground, just as
   rotten fruit
Falls from shaken branches, and acorns from a
   wind-blown oak.

{THE SOJOURN OF THE CHRISTIANS IN THE CITY}

After this great massacre, they entered the homes of the citizens, seizing whatever they found in them. It was done systematically, so that whoever had entered the home first, whether he was rich or poor, was not to be harmed by anyone else in any way. He was to have and to hold the house or palace and whatever he had found in it entirely as his own. Since they mutually agreed to maintain this rule, many poor men became rich.

Then, going to the Sepulchre of the Lord and His glorious Temple, the clerics and also the laity, singing a new song [Ps. 33:3, 96:1] unto the Lord in a high-sounding voice of exultation, and making offerings and most humble supplications, joyously visited the Holy Place as they had so long desired to do.

Oh, time so longed for! Oh, time remembered among all others! Oh, deed to be preferred before all deeds! Truly longed for, since it had always been desired by all worshippers of the Catholic faith with an inward yearning of the soul. This was the place, where the Creator of all creatures, God made man, in His manifold mercy for the human race, brought the gift of spiritual rebirth. Here He was born, died, and rose. Cleansed from the contagion of the heathen inhabiting it at one time or another, so long contaminated by their superstition, it was restored to its former rank by those believing and trusting in Him.

And truly memorable and rightly remembered, because those things which the Lord God our Jesus Christ, as a man abiding among men on earth, practiced and taught have often been recalled and repeated in doctrines. And, likewise, what the Lord wished to be fulfilled, I believe, by this people so dear, both His disciple and servant and predestined for this task, will resound and continue in a memorial of all the languages of the universe to the end of the ages.

{THE CREATION OF KING AND PATRIARCH OF JERUSALEM AND THE FINDING OF THE LORD'S CROSS}

In the thousand and one hundred year less one
From the illustrious Lord's birth of the Virgin,
When Phoebus had lighted July fifteen times,
The Franks captured Jerusalem by strength of
   power;
And soon made Godfrey the ruler of the land.

---

[14]Gold coins, so called because they were originally Byzantine. Saracen besants were dinars of the same value as the Byzantine coins.

All the people of the army of the Lord elected him because of his noble excellence, the proven worth of his military service, his patient temperance, and also the elegance of his manners, as the ruler of the kingdom in the Holy City, to preserve and govern it.

At that time canons were appointed to serve in the Church of the Lord's Sepulchre and in His Temple. Then they decided not to elect a patriarch until they had asked the Roman Pope whom he wished to nominate.[15]

Meanwhile about five hundred Turks, Arabs, and black Ethiopians, who had fled into the Tower of David, requested Count Raymond, who sojourned near that tower, to permit as many as were alive to go away provided they leave their money in the tower. He granted this, and from that place they went to Ascalon.[16]

It was pleasing to God at that time, that a small piece of the Lord's Cross was found in a hidden place. [The particle was found August 5, 1099.] From ancient times until now it had been concealed by religious men, and now, God being willing, it was revealed by a certain Syrian. He, with his father as conspirator, had carefully concealed and guarded it there. This particle, reshaped in the style of a cross and artistically decorated with gold and silver, was first carried to the Lord's Sepulchre[17] and then to the Temple joyfully, with singing and giving thanks to God, who for so many days had preserved this treasure, His own and ours.

---

[15] Arnulf of Chocques, the chaplain of Robert of Normandy was elected patriarch pro tem.

[16] The last Muslim stronghold on the Palestinian coast, about forty miles southwest of Jerusalem. It was eventually conquered by crusaders in 1153 but was retaken by the Muslim army of Saladin in 1187.

[17] The supposed site of Christ's tomb, from which he rose on the third day after his crucifixion, the Holy Sepulchre was the sworn objective of all crusaders. The first Christian church built on the site was erected in the early fourth century; the present church dates from the early nineteenth century.

C. Scholastacism

By the time of the Protestant Reformation in the sixteenth century, the adjective "scholastic" more often than not carried a pejorative connotation, implying overly subtle distinctions in theology that were of interest only to academic specialists. The original sense of the term, however, was much more neutral, meaning simply "of the schools" or "of the universities." The criticisms associated with the much later sense of "scholastic" reflect two distinct but intertwined developments of the High Middle Ages: 1) the gradual emergence during the twelfth to fourteenth centuries of universities and the academic discipline known as theology ("study of God"); and 2) the gradual domination of theological faculties by an analytical method of argumentation that was drawn from the ancient Greek philosophers, especially the newly rediscovered Aristotle. Together, these university theologians and their "scientific" (Latin *scientia,* "knowing") methods virtually monopolized the intellectual inquiry of the high medieval church and profoundly influenced Christian doctrine and practice.

The scholastic method itself actually predated the founding of the first universities in the twelfth and thirteenth centuries. Church writers as early as St. Augustine and Boethius had made some use of philosophical argumentation in their writings. But it wasn't until shortly after the beginning of its second millennium that Western Christianity experienced a more systematic attempt to apply the techniques of dialectics, a type of logical analysis, to religious questions. Anselm of Bec (1033–1109), most famous for his work *Cur Deus Homo (Why God Became Man)*, was a pioneer in this respect. His goal, he explained, was to strengthen belief (*credere*) by improving understanding (*intellegere*). His method, imitated by subsequent "dialectical" theologians such as Peter Abelard and Thomas Aquinas, was to sort out apparent contradictions and inconsistencies in the Bible and church teachings with the aid of inductive and deductive reasoning. Over the next two hundred years, the compatibility of such reasoning with revealed teachings was consistently a hot issue, with several church leaders and later professional theologians fervently resisting the incursion of pagan philosophical methods, particularly those of Aristotle. By the end of the thirteenth century, however, both the universities and their "theological science" had prevailed.

1. Peter Abelard
HISTORY OF MY CALAMITIES (1140)

Peter Abelard (1079–1142) was probably the most famous and most controversial star of the early scholastic movement. Born to a minor noble family in Brittany (in northwest France), he studied in Paris and soon gained renown as a gifted teacher of dialectic. Unfortunately he was equally gifted at making enemies, including a certain powerful churchman named Fulbert, who had entrusted Abelard with the tutoring of his niece Eloise. Upon learning of the love affair and secret marriage between Eloise and her tutor, Fulbert ordered his henchman to castrate Abelard. Shortly after this brutal punishment, in 1121, Abelard's theological rivals succeeded in having his book on the Trinity condemned at the Council of Soissons. Abelard always claimed that the professional jealousy of theologians—who resented having a teacher of logic venture onto their turf—had been the cause of his persecution. Although he never wavered from his confidence in the compatibility of reason with faith, he did avoid public confrontations for the next fifteen years. Within three years of his resumption of teaching in 1136, though, he had again provoked a powerful alliance against him, this time including the celebrated preacher and mystic, Bernard of Clairvaux (1090–1153). In the following excerpt from his autobiography, Abelard describes the Council of Sens in 1140, where he was condemned for "unorthodox" teaching on the Trinity and forced to burn his own writings. Though clearly unbowed, Abelard was outmaneuvered, particularly by Bernard, who had persuaded Pope Innocent II (r. 1130–1143) to support the condemnation. Yet despite his personal "calamities," Peter Abelard did succeed in opening the door for the eventual acceptance of dialectic among the church's theologians.

On the last day of the council [of Sens], before the session convened, the legate [i.e., papal representative] and the archbishop [Henri de Sanglier] deliberated with my rivals and sundry others as to what should be done about me and my book, this being the chief reason for their having come together. And since they had discovered nothing either in my speech or in what I had hitherto written which would give them a case against me, they were all reduced to silence, or at the most to maligning me in whispers. Then Geoffroi, bishop of Chartres, who excelled the other bishops alike in the sincerity of his religion and in the importance of his see, spoke thus:

"You know, my lords, all who are gathered here, the doctrine of this man, what it is, and his ability, which has brought him many followers in every field to which he has devoted himself. You know how greatly he has lessened the renown of other teachers, both his masters and our own, and how he has spread as it were the offshoots of his vine from sea to sea. Now, if you impose a lightly considered judgment on him, as I cannot believe you will, you will know that even if [perhaps] you are in the right there are many who will be angered thereby, and that he will have no lack of defenders. Remember above all that we have found nothing in this book of his that lies before us whereon any open accusation can be based. Indeed it is true, as Jerome says: 'Fortitude openly displayed always creates rivals, and the lightning strikes the highest peaks.' Have a care, then, lest by violent action you only increase his fame, and lest we do more hurt to ourselves through envy than to him through justice. A false report, as that same wise man reminds us, is easily crushed, and a man's later life gives testimony as to his earlier deeds. If, then, you are disposed to take canonical action against him, his doctrine or his writings must be brought forward as evidence, and he must have free opportunity to answer his questioners. In that case, if he is found guilty or if he confesses his error, his lips can be wholly sealed. Consider the words of the blessed Nicodemus, who, desiring to free Our Lord Himself, said: 'Doth our law judge any man before it hear him and know what he doeth?'" [Jn 7:51]

When my rivals heard this they cried out in protest, saying: "This is wise counsel, woe that we should strive against the wordiness of this man, whose arguments, or rather, sophistries, the whole world cannot resist!" And yet, methinks, it was far more difficult to strive against Christ himself, for whom, nevertheless, Nicodemus demanded a hearing in accordance with the dictates of the law. When the bishop could not win their assent to his proposals, he tried in another way to curb their hatred, saying that for the discussion of such an important case the few who were present were not enough, and that this matter required a more thorough examination. His further suggestion was that my abbot, who was there present, should take me back with him to our abbey, in other words to the monastery of St. Denis,[18] and that there a large convocation of learned men should determine, on the basis of a careful investigation, what ought to be done. To this last proposal the legate consented, as did all the others.

Then the legate arose to celebrate mass before entering the council, and through the bishop sent me the permission which had been determined on, authorizing me to return to my monastery and there await such action as might be finally taken. But my rivals, perceiving that they would accomplish nothing if the trial were to be held outside of their own diocese, and in a place where they could have little influence on the verdict, and in truth having small wish that justice should be done, persuaded the archbishop that it would be a grave insult to him to transfer this case to another court, and that it would be dangerous for him if by chance I should thus be acquitted. They likewise went to the legate, and succeeded in so changing his opinion that finally they induced him to frame a new sentence, whereby he agreed to condemn my book without any further inquiry, to burn it forthwith in the sight of all, and to confine

---

[18]A Benedictine abbey just north of Paris, founded in 625.

me for a year in another monastery. The argument they used was that it sufficed for the condemnation of my book that I had presumed to read it in public without the approval of either the Roman pontiff or of the Church, and that, furthermore, I had given it to many to be transcribed. Methinks it would be a notable blessing to the Christian faith if there were more who displayed a like presumption. The legate, however, being less skilled in law than he should have been, relied chiefly on the advice of the archbishop, and he, in turn, on that of my rivals. When the Bishop of Chartres got wind of this, he reported the whole conspiracy to me, and strongly urged me to endure meekly the manifest violence of their enmity. He bade me not to doubt that this violence would in the end react upon them and prove a blessing to me, and counseled me to have no fear of the confinement in a monastery, knowing that within a few days the legate himself, who was now acting under compulsion, would after his departure set me free. And thus he consoled me as best he might, mingling his tears with mine.

Straightway upon my summons I went to the council, and there, without further examination or debate, did they compel me with my own hand to cast that memorable book of mine into the flames. Although my enemies appeared to have nothing to say while the book was burning, one of them muttered something about having seen it written therein that God the Father was alone omnipotent. This reached the ears of the legate, who replied in astonishment that he could not believe that even a child would make so absurd a blunder. "Our common faith," he said, "holds and sets forth that the Three are alike omnipotent." A certain Tirric, a schoolmaster, hearing this, sarcastically added the Athanasian phrase, "And yet there are not three omnipotent Persons, but only One."[19]

This man's bishop forthwith began to censure him, bidding him desist from such treasonable talk, but he boldly stood his ground, and said, as if quoting the words of Daniel: "'Are ye such fools, ye sons of Israel, that without examination or knowledge of the truth ye have condemned a daughter of Israel? Return again to the place of judgment' [Dan 13:48], and there give judgment on the judge himself. You have set up this judge, forsooth, for the instruction of faith and the correction of error, and yet, when he ought to give judgment, he condemns himself out of his own mouth. Set free today, with the help of God's mercy, one who is manifestly innocent, even as Susanna was freed of old from her false accusers."

Thereupon the archbishop arose and confirmed the legate's statement, but changed the wording thereof, as indeed was most fitting. "It is God's truth," he said, "that the Father is omnipotent, the Son is omnipotent, the Holy Spirit is omnipotent. And whosoever dissents from this is openly in error, and must not be listened to. Nevertheless, if it be your pleasure, it would be well that this our brother should publicly state before us all the faith that is in him, to the end that, according to its deserts, it may either be approved or else condemned and corrected."

When, however, I fain would have arisen to profess and set forth my faith, in order that I might express in my own words that which was in my heart, my enemies declared that it was not needful for me to do more than recite the Athanasian Symbol, a thing which any boy might do as well as I. And lest I should allege ignorance, pretending that I did not know the words by heart, they had a copy of it set before me to read. And read it I did as best I could for my groans and sighs and tears. Thereupon, as if I had been a convicted criminal, I was handed over to the Abbot of St. Médard, who was there present, and led to his monastery as to a prison. And with this the council was immediately dissolved.

The abbot and the monks of the aforesaid monastery, thinking that I would remain long

---

[19] The so-called Athanasian creed, attributed to the anti-Arian leader Athanasius (c. 293–373) but actually probably composed in the fifth century. It consists of about forty verses, which define the nature of the Trinity and the Incarnation and which by the time of Abelard had been incorporated into liturgies throughout Europe.

with them, received me with great exultation, and diligently sought to console me, but all in vain. O God, who dost judge justice itself, in what venom of the spirit, in what bitterness of mind, did I blame even Thee for my shame, accusing Thee in my madness! Full often did I repeat the lament of St. Anthony [the Great]: "Kindly Jesus, where wert Thou?" The sorrow that tortured me, the shame that overwhelmed me, the desperation that wracked my mind, all these I could then feel, but even now I can find no words to express them. Comparing these new sufferings of my soul with those I had formerly endured in my body,[20] it seemed that I was in very truth the most miserable among men. Indeed that earlier betrayal had become a little thing in comparison with this later evil, and I lamented the hurt to my fair name far more than the one to my body. The latter, indeed, I had brought upon myself through my own wrongdoing, but this other violence had come upon me solely by reason of the honesty of my purpose and my love of our faith, which had compelled me to write that which I believed.

—————

[20]A reference to his castration, ordered by Eloise's uncle.

2. Thomas Aquinas
SUMMA THEOLOGICA (c. 1267)

By the time Thomas Aquinas (c. 1225–1274) undertook to provide a "sum of all theology" in 1267, the dialectical method was no longer scorned as it had been a century earlier, in the time of Peter Abelard. Although the assimilation of philosophical methods into mainstream academic theology was by no means complete, thanks to the achievements of Aquinas in particular, the winds finally began to shift. Aquinas was from a prominent Neopolitan family and studied at the local university before moving on to graduate work in theology with the famed Albert the Great (1200–1280) at the University of Paris. In 1256 he was given a chair at the same institution and began to teach and write on scriptural exegesis, canon (church) law, and, most dangerously to his career, the philosophy of Aristotle. For the rest of his life, Aquinas would be active as the foremost spokesman for the incorporation of dialectics—and the methods of Aristotle in particular—into Christian theology. Like Abelard, he believed that rational inquiry and understanding aided faith and in no way contradicted or supplanted it. In the excerpt below from his *Summa Theologica,* Aquinas describes his theological method and acknowledges the ultimate superiority of revelation, particularly in those few instances where unaided human reason might lead one to mistaken conclusions. At the same time, the "scientific" structure and methods of his work leave no doubt about his profound admiration for the human intellect and its potential for probing the mysteries of Creation. Indeed, despite the *Summa*'s ultimate triumph, many theologians—particularly Duns Scotus (1266–1308) and his pupil William of Ockham (1285–1349)—believed that Thomistic scholasticism vastly overemphasized human reason at the expense of faith. Their resulting "Nominalist" approach to theology constituted the main rival to Aquinas's influence among scholastics for the next two centuries.

FIRST PART: TREATISE ON GOD

Question I: The Nature and Extent of Sacred Doctrine (In Ten Articles)

To place our purpose within proper limits, it is necessary first to investigate the nature and extent of this sacred doctrine. Concerning this there are ten points of inquiry.

(1) On the necessity of this doctrine? (2) Whether it is a science? (3) Whether it is one or many? (4) Whether it is speculative or practical? (5) How it is compared with other sciences? (6) Whether it is a wisdom? (7) What is its subject-matter? (8) Whether it is a matter of argument? (9) Whether it rightly employs metaphors and similes? (10) Whether the Sacred Scripture of this doctrine may be expounded in different senses?

Article 1: Whether, besides Philosophy, any further Doctrine is required?   *We proceed thus to the First Article:* It seems that, besides philosophical doctrine we have no need of any further knowledge.

Objection 1. For man should not seek to know what is above reason: *Seek not the things that are too high for thee* [Sir 3:22]. But those things which fall under reason are fully treated of in the philosophical sciences. Therefore any other knowledge besides philosophical science is superfluous.

Obj. 2. Further, knowledge can be concerned only with being, for nothing can be known except truth, and truth is convertible with being. But philosophical science treats of all being, even God Himself, so that there is a part of philosophy called theology, or the divine science, as Aristotle has proved.[21] Therefore, besides philosophical doctrine, there is no need of any further knowledge.

On the contrary, It is written: *All Scripture inspired of God is profitable to teach, to reprove, to cor-*

rect, to instruct in justice [2 Tim 3:16]. Now Scripture inspired of God is no part of the philosophical sciences, which have been built up by human reason. Therefore it is useful that besides philosophical doctrine there should be other knowledge that is, inspired of God.

I answer that, It was necessary for man's salvation that there should be a knowledge revealed by God, besides the philosophical sciences built up by human reason. First, indeed, because man is directed to God as to an end that surpasses the grasp of his reason: *The eye hath not seen, O God, besides Thee, what things Thou hast prepared for them that wait for Thee* [Isa 64:4]. But the end must first be known by men who are to direct their thoughts and actions to the end. Hence it was necessary for the salvation of man that certain truths which exceed human reason should be made known to him by divine revelation.

Even as regards those truths about God which human reason can discover, it was necessary that man should be taught by a divine revelation, because the truth about God such as reason could discover would only be known by a few, and that after a long time, and with the admixture of many errors. But man's whole salvation, which is in God, depends upon the knowledge of this truth. Therefore, in order that the salvation of men might be brought about more fitly and more surely, it was necessary that they should be taught divine truths by divine revelation.

It was therefore necessary that, besides the philosophical sciences discovered by reason there should be a sacred science obtained through revelation.

Reply Obj. 1. Although those things which are higher than man's knowledge may not be sought for by man through his reason, nevertheless, once they are revealed by God they must be accepted by faith. Hence the sacred text continues, *For many things are shown to thee above the understanding of man* [Sir 3:25]. And sacred doctrine consists in things of this kind.

Reply Obj. 2. Sciences are differentiated according to the different natures of knowable

---

[21]Referring to Aristotle's *Metaphysics,* a key source for Aquinas.

things. For the astronomer and the physicist both may prove the same conclusion—that the earth, for instance, is round; the astronomer by means of mathematics (that is, by abstracting from matter), but the physicist by means of matter itself. Hence there is no reason why those things which are dealt with in the philosophical sciences, so far as they can be known by natural reason, may not also be taught us by another science so far as they fall within revelation. Hence theology which pertains to sacred doctrine differs in genus from that theology which is part of philosophy.

Article 2. Whether Sacred Doctrine Is a Science? We proceed thus to the Second Article: It seems that sacred doctrine is not a science.

Objection 1. For every science proceeds from self-evident principles. But sacred doctrine proceeds from articles of faith which are not self-evident, since they are not admitted by all: *For all men have not faith* (2 Thess 3:2). Therefore sacred doctrine is not a science.

Obj. 2. Further, science is not of singulars. But sacred science treats of singulars, such as the deeds of Abraham, Isaac, and Jacob, and such like. Therefore sacred doctrine is not a science.

On the contrary, Augustine says, "to this science alone belongs that whereby saving faith is begotten, nourished, protected, and strengthened."[22] But this can be said of no science except sacred doctrine. Therefore sacred doctrine is a science.

I answer that, Sacred doctrine is a science. We must bear in mind that there are two kinds of sciences. There are some which proceed from a principle known by the natural light of the intellect, such as arithmetic and geometry and the like. There are some which proceed from principles known by the light of a higher science. Thus the science of perspective proceeds from principles established by geometry, and music from principles established by arithmetic. And in this way

sacred doctrine is a science, because it proceeds from principles established by the light of a higher science, namely, the science of God and the blessed. Hence, just as the musician accepts on authority the principles taught him by the mathematician, so sacred science believes the principles revealed to it by God.

Reply Obj. 1. The principles of any science are either in themselves self-evident, or reducible to the knowledge of a higher science. And such, as we have said, are the principles of sacred doctrine.

Reply Obj. 2. Singulars are not treated of in sacred doctrine because it is concerned with them principally, but they are introduced rather both as examples to be followed in our lives (as in moral sciences), and in order to establish the authority of those men through whom the divine revelation, on which this sacred scripture or doctrine is based, has come down to us. . . .

Article 4. Whether Sacred Doctrine Is a Practical Science? We proceed thus to the Fourth Article: It seems that sacred doctrine is a practical science.

Objection 1. For "a practical science is that which ends in action," according to the Philosopher [i.e., Aristotle]. But sacred doctrine is ordered to action: *Be ye doers of the word, and not hearers only* (Jas 1:22). Therefore sacred doctrine is a practical science.

Obj. 2. Further, sacred doctrine is divided into the Old and the New Law. But law pertains to moral science, which is a practical science. Therefore sacred doctrine is a practical science.

On the contrary, Every practical science is concerned with human operations, as for example moral science is concerned with human acts, and architecture with buildings. But sacred doctrine is chiefly concerned with God, of whom rather is man the handiwork. Therefore it is not a practical but a speculative science.

I answer that, Sacred doctrine, although it is one, as we have said (Art 3) extends to things which belong to different philosophical sciences, because it considers in each the same for-

---

[22]Augustine of Hippo (354–430) in his work *On the Trinity.*

mal aspect, namely so far as they can be known in the divine light. Hence, although among the philosophical sciences one is speculative and another practical, nevertheless sacred doctrine includes both, just as God, by one and the same knowledge, knows both Himself and His works.

Still, it is speculative rather than practical, because it is more concerned with divine things than with human acts, though it does treat even of these latter, according as man is ordered by them to the perfect knowledge of God, in which eternal Happiness consists. This is a sufficient *answer to the Objections.*

Article 5. Whether Sacred Doctrine Is Nobler Than Other Sciences? We proceed thus to the Fifth Article: It seems that sacred doctrine is not nobler than other sciences.

Objection 1. For the nobility of a science depends on the certitude it establishes. But other sciences, the principles of which cannot be doubted, seem to be more certain than sacred doctrine, for its principles—namely, articles of faith—can be doubted. Therefore other sciences seem to be nobler.

Obj. 2. Further, it is the sign of a lower science to depend upon a higher, as music depends upon arithmetic. But sacred doctrine receives from the philosophical sciences. For Jerome[23] observes, in his Epistle to Magnus, that "the ancient doctors so enriched their books with the doctrines and opinions of the philosophers, that thou knowest not what more to admire in them, their profane erudition or their scriptural learning." Therefore sacred doctrine is inferior to other sciences.

On the contrary, Other sciences are called the handmaidens of this one: *Wisdom sent her maids to invite to the tower* [Prov 9:3].

I *answer that,* Since this science is partly speculative and partly practical, it transcends all others whether speculative or practical. Now one speculative science is said to be nobler than another either by reason of its greater certitude or by reason of the higher worth of its subject-matter. In both these respects this science surpasses other speculative sciences: in point of greater certitude, because other sciences derive their certitude from the natural light of human reason, which can err, while this derives its certitude from the light of the divine knowledge, which cannot be deceived; in point of the higher worth of its subject-matter, because this science treats chiefly of those things which by their sublimity transcend human reason, while other sciences consider only those things which are within reason's grasp.

Of the practical sciences, that one is nobler which is ordered to a further end, as political science is nobler than military science, for the good of the army is directed to the good of the state. But the end of this science, in so far as it is practical, is eternal happiness, to which as to an ultimate end the purposes of every practical science are ordered. Hence it is clear that from every standpoint it is nobler than other sciences.

Reply Obj. 1. It may well happen that what is in itself the more certain may seem to us the less certain on account of the weakness of our intellect, "which is dazzled by the clearest objects of nature: as the owl is dazzled by the light of the sun."[24] Hence the fact that some happen to doubt about articles of faith is not due to the uncertain nature of the truths, but to the weakness of the human intellect. Yet the slenderest knowledge that may be obtained of the highest things is more desirable than the most certain knowledge obtained of lesser things, as is said in [Aristotle's] treatise *On the Parts of Animals.*

Reply Obj. 2. This science can in a sense take from the philosophical sciences, not as though it stood in need of them, but only in order to make its teaching clearer. For it takes its

---

[23]St. Jerome (341–420), one of the western fathers of the church and the translator of the Vulgate edition of the Bible.

[24]From Book II of Aristotle's *Metaphysics*

principles not from other sciences, but immediately from God, by revelation. Therefore it does not take from the other sciences as from the higher, but makes use of them as of the lesser, and as handmaidens; just as the master sciences make use of the sciences and supply their materials, as political of military science. That it thus uses them is not due to its own defect or insufficiency, but to the defect of our intellect, which is more easily led by what is known through natural reason (from which proceed the other sciences), to that which is above reason, such as are the teachings of this science. . . .

Article 8. Whether Sacred Doctrine Is a Matter of Argument?   We proceed thus to the Eighth Article: It seems this doctrine is not a matter of argument.

Objection 1. For Ambrose says:[25] "Put arguments aside where faith is sought." But in this doctrine faith especially is sought: *But these things are written that you may believe* [Jn 20:31]. Therefore sacred doctrine is not a matter of argument.

Obj. 2. Further, if it is a matter of argument, the argument is either from authority or from reason. If it is from authority, it seems unbefitting its dignity, for the proof from authority is the weakest form of proof according to Boethius.[26] But if from reason, this is unbefitting its end, because, according to Gregory,[27] "faith has no merit in those things of which human reason brings its own experience." Therefore sacred doctrine is not a matter of argument.

On the contrary, The Scripture says that a bishop should *embrace that faithful word which is according to doctrine, that he may be able to exhort in sound doctrine and to convince the gainsayers* [Tit 1:9].

I answer that, As other sciences do not argue in proof of their principles, but argue from their principles to demonstrate other truths in these sciences, so this doctrine does not argue in proof of its principles, which are the articles of faith, but from them it goes on to prove something else, as the Apostle from the resurrection of Christ argues in proof of the general resurrection [1 Cor 15].

However, it is to be borne in mind, in regard to the philosophical sciences, that the inferior sciences neither prove their principles nor dispute with those who deny them, but leave this to a higher science. But the highest of them, namely, metaphysics, can dispute with one who denies its principles only if the opponent will make some concession. But if he concede nothing, it can have no dispute with him, though it can answer his objections. Hence Sacred Scripture, since it has no science above itself, can dispute with one who denies its principles only if the opponent admits some at least of the truths obtained through divine revelation. Thus we can argue with heretics from texts in Holy Writ, and against those who deny one article of faith we can argue from another. But if our opponent believes nothing of divine revelation, there is no longer any means of proving the articles of faith by reasoning, but only of answering his objections—if he has any—against faith. Since faith rests upon infallible truth, and since the contrary of a truth can never be demonstrated, it is clear that proofs brought against faith cannot be demonstrations, but are arguments that can be answered.

Reply Obj. 1. Although arguments from human reason cannot avail to prove what must be received on faith, nevertheless this doctrine argues from articles of faith to other truths.

Reply Obj. 2. To argue from authority is most proper to this doctrine, since its principles are obtained by revelation, and thus we must believe the authority of those to whom the revelation has been made. Nor does this take away from the dignity of this doctrine, for although the argument from authority based on human reason is the weakest, yet the argument from authority based on divine revelation is the strongest.

---

[25]Ambrose of Milan (339–397), *On Faith.*
[26]Christian philosopher and Roman statesman (c. 480–c. 514), most famous as the author of *The Consolation of Philosophy,* written while he was in prison awaiting execution.
[27]Pope Gregory the Great (c. 540–604), in his *Homiletics.*

But sacred doctrine makes use even of human reason, not, indeed, to prove faith (for thereby the merit of faith would come to an end), but to make clear other things that are put forward in this doctrine. Since therefore grace does not destroy nature, but perfects it, natural reason should minister to faith as the natural bent of the will ministers to charity. And so the Apostle says: *Bringing into captivity every understanding unto the obedience of Christ* [2 Cor 10:5]. Hence sacred doctrine makes use also of the authority of philosophers in those questions in which they were able to know the truth by natural reason, as Paul quotes a saying of Aratus: *As some also of your own poets said; For we are also His offspring* [Acts 17:28].

Nevertheless, sacred doctrine makes use of these authorities as extrinsic and probable arguments. But it properly uses the authority of the canonical Scriptures as a necessary argument, and the authority of the doctors of the Church as one that may properly be used, though merely as probable. For our faith rests upon the revelation made to the apostles and prophets, who wrote the canonical books, and not on the revelations (if any such there are) made to other doctors. Hence Augustine says: "Only those books of Scripture which are called canonical have I learnt to hold in such honor as to believe their authors have not erred in any way in writing them. But other authors I so read as not to deem anything in their works to be true merely on account of their having so thought and written, whatever may have been their holiness and learning." . . .

Article 10. Whether in Holy Scripture a Word May Have Several Senses? *We proceed thus to the Tenth Article:* It seems that in Holy Writ a word cannot have several senses, historical or literal, allegorical, tropological [involving moral interpretations of figurative language] or moral, and anagogical [involving mystical interpretation].

Objection 1. For many different senses in one text produce confusion and deception and destroy all force of argument. Hence no proof, but only fallacies, can be deduced from a multiplic-

ity of propositions. But Holy Writ ought to be able to state the truth without any fallacy. Therefore there cannot be several senses to a word in Holy Writ.

Obj. 2. Further, Augustine says that "the Old Testament has a fourfold division namely, according to history, etiology, analogy, and allegory." Now these four seem altogether different from the four divisions mentioned in the first objection. Therefore it does not seem fitting to explain the same word of Holy Writ according to the four different senses mentioned above.

Obj. 3. Further, beside these senses, there is the parabolical, which is not one of these four.

On the contrary, Gregory [the Great] says: "Holy Writ by the manner of its speech transcends every science, because in one and the same sentence, while it describes a fact, it reveals a mystery."

I answer that, The author of Holy Writ is God, in whose power it is to signify His meaning not by words only (as man also can do), but also by things themselves. So, whereas in every other science things are signified by words, this science has the property that the things signified by the words have themselves also a meaning. Therefore that first meaning whereby words signify things belongs to the first sense, the historical or literal. That meaning whereby things signified by words have themselves also a meaning is called the spiritual sense, which is based on the literal and presupposes it.

Now this spiritual sense has a threefold division. For as the Apostle says [Heb 10:1] the Old Law is a figure of the New Law, and Dionysius[28] says the New Law itself is a figure of future glory. Again, in the New Law, whatever our Head has done is a type of what we ought to do. Therefore, so far as the things of the Old Law signify the things of the New Law, there is the allegorical sense. But so far as the things done in Christ, or so far as the things which signify Christ, are types of what we

---

[28]Dionysius the Pseudo-Areopagite, in his *Celestial Hierarchy* (c. 500), a work that includes a detailed exposition of the orders of angels between God and humans.

ought to do, there is the moral sense. But so far as they signify what relates to eternal glory, there is the anagogical sense.

Since the literal sense is that which the author intends, and since the author of Holy Writ is God, Who by one act comprehends all things by His intellect, it is not unfitting, as Augustine says if, even according to the literal sense, one word in Holy Writ should have several senses.

Reply Obj. 1. The multiplicity of these senses does not produce equivocation or any other kind of multiplicity, seeing that these senses are not multiplied because one word signifies several things, but because the things signified by the words can be themselves types of other things. Thus in Holy Writ no confusion results, for all the senses are founded on one—the literal—from which alone can any argument be drawn, and not from those intended in allegory, as Augustine says. Nevertheless, nothing of Holy Scripture perishes on account of this, since nothing necessary to faith is contained under the spiritual sense which is not elsewhere put forward by the Scripture in its literal sense.

Reply Obj. 2. These three—history, etiology, analogy—are grouped under the literal sense. For it is called history, as Augustine expounds

whenever anything is simply related; it is called etiology when its cause is assigned, as when Our Lord gave the reason why Moses allowed the putting away of wives—namely, on account of the hardness of men's hearts [Mt 19:8]; it is called analogy whenever the truth of one text of Scripture is shown not to contradict the truth of another. Of these four, allegory alone stands for the three spiritual senses. Thus Hugh of St. Victor[29] includes the anagogical under the allegorical sense, laying down three senses only—the historical, the allegorical, and the tropological.

Reply Obj. 3. The parabolical sense is contained in the literal, for by words things are signified properly and figuratively. Nor is the figure itself, but that which is figured, the literal sense. When Scripture speaks of God's arm, the literal sense is not that God has such a member, but only what is signified by this member, namely, operative power. Hence it is plain that nothing false can ever underlie the literal sense of Holy Writ.

---

[29]Theologian (d. 1142) from Augustinian monastery of St. Victor in Paris, particularly known for his biblical exegesis.

D. Sacrament

The ancient Christian church employed many sacred rituals during its public worship, or liturgy, as well as privately among believers. The Latin word *sacramentum,* which originally meant an oath of allegiance, had been appropriated by Christians as a term for some of these rites of the faithful. In translating the Bible from the Hebrew and Greek into Latin, St. Jerome (341–420) also chose this term as a translation for the Greek *mystērion,* or "mystery," which had been used by Paul to describe certain rituals that were considered to have a transformational power over the spirit, such as the marriage of a man and a woman (cf. Eph 5:32). Like his contemporary St. Augustine, however, Jerome and other ancient Christians spoke of "sacraments" in fairly general terms—a tradition still evident as late as the theologian Hugh of St. Victor (d. 1142), who enumerated over thirty "sacraments" within the church. Nevertheless, within Hugh's lifetime the theological meaning of "sacrament"—especially as enunciated by his contemporary Peter Lombard

(1100–1160)—began to be more narrowly defined. According to the church's doctrinal tradition from at least the twelfth century on, a sacrament was a specific visible sign or rite indicating a spiritual (and therefore invisible) change effected by the grace of God. Most significantly, Lombard and other scholastics argued that the ritual itself must have been ordained in the New Testament in order to be considered a sacrament. Lombard detected seven such sacraments in the Bible: baptism (normally as an infant), confirmation (of baptismal promises in the presence of the bishop), the eucharist, confession, marriage, priestly ordination (or "holy orders"), and last rites (also known as "extreme unction"). Though all of these rites had been long established among Christians, the scholastic singling out of these seven proved especially influential. The monumental Fourth Lateran Council of 1215 clearly supported the list, which was eventually officially confirmed by the Council of Florence in 1439. Lateran IV also made two equally important distinctions: first, that only ordained priests were empowered to administer most of the sacraments (with the notable exception of marriage, where the marrying couple themselves were considered to be the ministers); and second, that the proper performance of a sacramental ritual by an ordained priest was efficacious regardless of the personal character of the minister (*ex opere operato;* "from the work, worked"). It is nearly impossible to overstate the importance of the sacraments to medieval Christians, for whom these rites regulated life, death, and eternal life itself. For example, no person could be considered a Christian—and therefore eligible for eternal salvation—without undergoing the sacrament of baptism. Moreover, as only ordained ministers of the church could perform these vital rituals, the sacraments added a new aura of prestige to the priesthood.

1. Peter Lombard
FOUR BOOKS OF SENTENCES (c. 1155)

Peter Lombard (1100–1160) was one of the most influential luminaries of the socalled twelfth-century Renaissance. He studied with the greatest legal and theological minds of the times, first at Bologna, then at Rheims, and ultimately with the controversial Peter Abelard in Paris. While teaching at the cathedral school of Notre Dame, he wrote his *Four Books,* a monumental attempt to synthesize over a thousand years of church teachings and laws on a variety of subjects. The first three books deal respectively with God, his creation and creatures before Christ, and the coming of Christ. The fourth book pulls together all doctrinal tradition on the subject of the sacraments and the Final Judgment. As the work's structure indicates, Lombard considered the sacraments to be the key nourishment for Christians along the path to redemption during the time between Christ's first and second comings. In this excerpt he summarizes both the origins and nature of "the sacraments of the New Law" and explains the distinctions among them. This compilation and its conclusions exerted enormous influence on all subsequent theologians, and was surpassed in the medieval era only by the later *Summa Theologica* of Lombard's admirer Thomas Aquinas (1225–1274).

BOOK IV: *ON THE SACRAMENTS* DISTINCTION I: PART I

I. Of Sacraments

The Samaritan who tended the wounded man [Lk 10:30–37], applied for his relief the dressings of the sacraments, just as God instituted the remedies of the sacraments against the wounds of original and actual sin. Concerning the sacraments, four questions first present themselves for consideration: what a sacrament is, why it was instituted; wherein it consists, and how it is performed; and what the difference is between the sacraments of the old and the new covenants.

II. What a Sacrament Is

"A sacrament is the sign of a sacred thing (*res*)" [according to St. Augustine]. However, a *sacred mystery* is also called a sacrament, as the sacrament of divinity, so that a sacrament may be the *sign of something sacred,* and the *sacred thing signified;* but now we are considering a sacrament as a *sign.* —So, "A sacrament is the visible form of an invisible grace" [according to the theologian Berengar of Tours (d. 1088)].

III. What a Sign Is

"But a sign, is the thing (*res*) behind the form which it wears to the senses, which brings by means of itself something else to our minds" [Augustine].

IV. How a Sign and a Sacrament Differ

"Furthermore, some signs are *natural,* as smoke which signifies fire; others *conventional*" [wrote Augustine], and of those which are *conventional,* some are sacraments, some not. For every sacrament is a sign, but the converse is not true. A sacrament bears a resemblance to the thing, of which it is a sign. "For if sacraments did not bear a resemblance to the things of which they are the sacraments, they could not *properly* be called sacraments." For a sacrament is properly so called, because it is a sign of the grace of God and the expression of invisible grace, so that it bears its image and is its cause. Sacraments, therefore, were not instituted merely in order to signify something, but also as a means

of sanctification. For things which were instituted only to signify are signs only, and not sacraments; such as the sacrifices of flesh, and the ceremonial observances of the old law, which could never justify those who offered them; because, as the apostle says, "The blood of goats and of oxen and the ashes of an heifer, being sprinkled, sanctify such as are defiled, to the cleansing of the flesh" [Heb 9:13], but not of the spirit. Now this uncleanness was the touching of a dead body. Wherefore Augustine: "By that defilement which the law cleanses I understand merely the touching of a dead body, since anyone who had touched one, *was unclean seven days;* but he was purified according to the law on the third day and on the seventh, and was cleansed," so that he might enter the temple. These legal observances also cleansed sometimes from bodily leprosy; but no one was ever justified by the *works of the Law,* as says the apostle [Rom 3:20; Gal 2:16], even if he performed them in faith and charity. Why? because God has ordained them unto servitude, not unto justification, so that they might be *types of something to come,* wishing that these offerings should be made to him rather than to idols. They therefore were *signs,* yet also sacraments, although they are often called so incorrectly in the Scriptures, because they were rather signs of a sacred thing than availing anything themselves. These moreover the apostle calls *works of the Law,* which were instituted only to signify something, or as a yoke.

V. Why the Sacraments Were Instituted

The sacraments were instituted for a three-fold reason: for *humility, instruction,* and *exercise.* For *humility,* so that while man, by order of the Creator, abases himself in worship before insensible things, which by nature are beneath him, through this humility and obedience, he may become more pleasing to God, and more meritorious in his sight, at whose command he seeks salvation in things beneath him, yet not from them, but through them from God. For *instruction* also were the sacraments instituted, so that the mind might be taught by what it sees outside in visible form, to recognize the invisible virtue which is within. For man, who before sin saw God without a mediator, through sin has become so dulled that he is in no wise able to comprehend divine things, unless trained thereto by human things.—Likewise, the sacraments were instituted for exercise, because since man cannot be idle, there is offered him in the sacraments a useful and safe exercise by which he may avoid vain and harmful occupation. For he who devotes himself to good exercise is not easily caught by the tempter; wherefore Jerome warns us: "Always do some sort of work, that the devil may find you occupied." "There are, moreover, three kinds of *exercises*: one aims at the *edification of the soul,* another aims at the *nourishment of the body,* another at the *destruction of both*." And inasmuch as without a sacrament, to which God has not limited his power, he could have given grace to man, he has for the aforesaid reasons instituted the sacraments. "There are two parts of which a sacrament consists, namely *words* and *things: words,* as the invocation of the Trinity; *things,* as water, oil, and the like."

VI. Of the Difference Between the Old and the New Sacraments

Now it remains to note the difference between the old and the new sacraments; as we call sacraments what anciently they called sacred things, such as sacrifices and oblations and the like. The difference between these Augustine

indicated briefly when he said, "because the former only promised and signified salvation, while the latter give it." . . .

DISTINCTION II
I. Of the Sacraments of the New Law

Let us now come to the sacraments of the new covenant; which are baptism, confirmation, the blessing of bread, that is the eucharist, penance, extreme unction, ordination, marriage. Of these some offer a remedy for sin, and confer helping grace, as baptism; others are merely a remedy, as marriage; others strengthen us with grace and virtue, as the eucharist and ordination.

If indeed we are asked why these sacraments were not instituted immediately after the fall of man, since in them are justification and salvation; we say that before the advent of Christ, who brought grace, the sacraments of grace could not be granted, for they have derived their virtue from his death and passion. Now Christ was unwilling to come before man was convinced that he could find help in neither natural nor written law.

Marriage, however was instituted before sin, "not at all as a remedy, but as a sacrament and a duty" [according to the theologian Hugh of St. Victor (d. 1142)]; after sin indeed it became a remedy against the corruption of carnal concupiscence; of which we will treat in its place. . . .

---

2. STATUES OF BISHOP ROBERT GROSSETESTE FOR THE DIOCESE OF LINCOLN (1235)

The proposed reforms of an early thirteenth-century bishop reveal something of the difference that existed between theories about the sacraments and their actual use in everyday life. Robert Grosseteste (c. 1175–1253) was a celebrated Oxford scholar, renowned for his accomplishments in natural philosophy, or science. Immediately upon his election as bishop of Lincoln, the largest diocese in England, he undertook to reform all religious practice within his realm in conformance with church doctrine. The following statutes were among his first episcopal decrees, and, after issuing them, he made periodic official visits to see how his rules were being enforced. Grosseteste was scandalized by the level of ignorance and corruption among his own clergy, many of whom could not even recite such basics as the Ten Commandments or the Seven Deadly Sins. Just as troubling, in the case of the sacraments, many priests were apparently not performing the rituals correctly or were charging fees for administering them. These abuses did not diminish popular respect for the Eucharist and other sacraments, but they did endanger the rites' efficacy, because they had to be performed correctly in order to be legitimate. Moreover, because of priestly ignorance, many pagan beliefs and superstitions had come to be associated with the sacraments. Some Christians, for example, would take the Eucharistic bread home, break it up, and sprinkle it on their fields in the hope of improving crop yields. Eradicating such abuses and superstitions were the main concerns of Grosseteste, who, true to church doctrine on the sacraments, held that the right words and movement—as well as correct belief—mattered immensely.

Since we ought to render a good accounting concerning you which, according to Augustine, is to speak and not keep silent, to weep when we speak and are not heard, we cannot pass over in silence the things which we believe it necessary for you to know and observe.

(1) Therefore, because the safety of souls is not established without the observance of the decalogue, we exhort in the Lord, urgently enjoining each pastor of souls and parish priest to know the decalogue, that is, the ten commandments of the Mosaic Law, and frequently to preach and explain them to the people in his care. He should know also what are the seven deadly sins[30] and likewise preach that they must be avoided by the people. In addition, let him know, at least in simple form, the seven sacraments of the church, and most of all, those who are priests should know what things are required for a valid sacrament of confession and penance; and they should often teach the laity the form for baptizing in the common speech. Let each one also have at least a simple understanding of the faith as is contained in the creed, both the longer and the shorter, and that in the tract "Whoever wishes"[31] which is daily chanted in the church at Prime [i.e., before sunrise].

(2) Further, the eucharist which is the sacrament of the Lord's body is always to be kept respectfully, devoutly, and faithfully in a special place, clean and designated. Each priest should teach his people often that, when in the celebration of the mass the host of salvation is elevated,[32] they should bow reverently and do likewise when the priest carries it to the sick. Let him, properly vested, carry and return it with a clean covering placed over it, openly and respectfully before his breast with reverence and fear, with a little light always preceding, since it is *the brightness of eternal light* [Wis 7:26], so that by this faith and devotion may be increased among all people, as it is written in the general council. A bell as well as the light should always precede the host of the body of Christ, always to be venerated, so that by its sound the devotion of the faithful may be aroused to a due adoration of so great a sacrament. Let priests also diligently see to it that the holy eucharist does not become moist or moldy because of a defect in the vessel or from being kept too long, so that it become unpleasant in appearance and of disagreeable taste.

(3) Priests, moreover, must be especially prompt and ready not only during the day but also at night to visit the sick when they require it, lest a sick person, *quod absit* ["far be it!"] because of their

---

[30]Sloth, Avarice, Lust, Gluttony, Anger, Envy, and Pride.
[31]*"Quicunque vult,"* the opening words of the fifth-century creed of Athanasius concerning the Trinity and the Incarnation.

[32]The climactic moment of the church service, or mass, when the priest repeats the words of Christ at the Last Supper thereby changing the essences of the bread and wine into the body and blood of the Savior and raises the bread (host) and wine before the altar. Bread thus consecrated may then be distributed to the laity, though communion was generally infrequent during the Middle Ages.

negligence die without confession or communion of the body of the Lord or extreme unction.

(4) Also altar slabs are to be in good taste and of proper size and firmly attached to the surrounding wood so that they do not move from it, nor are they to be taken for any other use than for the celebration of the divine services; for example, colors are not to be ground on them or anything of that sort done.

(5) Chrism cloths[33] are not to be put to secular uses.

(6) Likewise, let the divine office be carried out in church fully and devoutly, so that, for example, readings, hymns, psalms, and other things which are recited in praise of God, may have the full pronunciation of the words and strict attention of the mind to the sense of the words, lest, *quod absit!* instead of a complete and living victim there is offered one mutilated or dead. . . .

(17) We most strictly forbid any rector of a church to make an agreement with his priests such that the priest will be able to receive, over and above the allotted stipend, payments for annual or triennial masses,[34] because such an agreement is clear indication that the priest, according to this, is being definitely underpaid. It also follows that he does not fulfill the annual or triennial anniversaries which he has accepted or that he does not properly carry out the religious observances in the parish church.

(18) An adequate and honest living must be given to these priests by the rectors of churches lest on account of inadequate living the churches should lack divine services or that these priests should covet dishonest money or beg their bread. . . .

(27) We have heard and are not a little grieved that certain priests exact money from the laity for penance or for administering other sacraments, and that certain priests enjoin penances with base profit attached: for example, that a woman known by her husband after childbirth and before her purification[35] should carry an offering to the altar with whatever woman in the same parish is to be purified; or that a murderer or anyone who encompassed the death of another offer for any dead person in the same parish. These and things of this kind which are filled with avarice we entirely forbid.

(28) And no priest is to charge for annual or triennial anniversaries with similar greediness so that he himself obviously makes profit.

(29) We have also heard that some priests make their deacons hear the confessions of the parishioners. It is not necessary to call to mind that this is out of place, since it is clearly true that the power of binding and loosing[36] is not bestowed on the deacon, and the priests themselves would not seek [to avoid] this unless they were intent on ease or time for secular affairs. Therefore, we firmly forbid deacons to hear confessions or impose penances or administer other sacraments which priests alone are allowed to administer. . . .

(35) The execrable custom which has been usual in certain churches of observing the Feast of Fools[37] we forbid altogether by the special authority of apostolic prescript, so that a house of sport may not be made out of the house of prayer, and the pain of the Circumcision of Our Lord Jesus Christ may not be mocked by jests and public shows.

(36) We also forbid any priests to celebrate [mass] with vinegar. . . .

(38) We also decree that in any church whatsoever the canon of the mass be set in proper order.

---

[33]Chrism, a mixture of olive oil and balsam, was used in the sacraments of baptism, confirmation, and holy orders, as well as the consecration of new churches and altars. The chrism cloth might refer to the baptismal gown of an infant.

[34]Masses offered on behalf of souls in purgatory, here meaning either every thirty days or thirty masses.

[35]Known as "churching," a common ritual required of every recently delivered (and therefore "polluted") mother before she could attend mass and rejoin the congregation at church.

[36]I.e., the forgiveness of sins through the sacrament of confession or penance, to be administered only by an ordained priest.

[37]Celebrated on New Year's, or the Feast of the Circumcision. During this feast, which probably originated in the previous century, members of the lower clergy were allowed to "rule over" and mock their superiors, in a riotous event usually accompanied by bawdy songs, gambling, and much drinking, all taking place within the cathedral and other churches.

E. Mendicants

The urban and intellectual revivals of the twelfth century eventually gave rise to a new type of clergy, known as mendicants. Unlike monks, who maintained separate communities and common property, members of the new mendicant orders sought a more literal imitation of Christ, disdaining possessions of any kind and practicing ministries in the world among laypeople. Unlike "secular" clergy such as parish priests, however, mendicants continued to observe a version of the monastic rule and were accountable only to the Superior General of their own order, rather than to the local bishop. Because these religious "brothers," or friars, had neither pastoral salaries nor common monastic property, they survived by their own labor as well as by begging, hence their designation (from Latin *mendicatio,* "begging").

The two great founders of mendicant orders were St. Dominic (1170–1221) and St. Francis of Assisi (1181–1226). Dominic was a Castilian who in 1206 began a mission of "evangelical preaching" against the French heretics known as Albigensians. Ten years later his "Order of Preachers"—also known as Dominicans or Black Friars (because of their garments) —was officially approved by the Pope. In drawing up a constitution for his new religious order, Dominic was considerably influenced by the preaching and ideals of his contemporary, Francis of Assisi. Like his hero Antony the Great (d. 355), Francis had been born to a wealthy merchant family and enjoyed a profligate youth before renouncing all of his possessions for a life of voluntary poverty and asceticism. After only a few years of wandering the Tuscan countryside as a pilgrim, he had acquired a handful of disciples that in 1210 was recognized by Pope Innocent III as a religious order, the Order of the Lesser Brothers. Like Dominic, Francis and his followers initially conceived of their mission of preaching and humility in the spirit of a crusade or pilgrimage among the laity. At the same time, both orders preserved the monk's daily litany of prayers, the Divine Office, as well as a fervent commitment to the ideal of apostolic poverty. These principles lay at the heart of the Rules that Francis and Dominic helped devise for their respective orders as well as for their sister communities, such as the order of religious women led by Francis's associate St. Clare (1193–1253). As both Dominicans and Franciscans grew in number over the course of the century, however, the practicality of a strict observance of poverty came into question. Dominicans, increasingly involved in teaching and other church "establishment" work, gradually abandoned the ban on property. Among the Franciscans, internal debates over the issue were much more violent, ultimately resulting in a schism between the majority of brothers, who favored some concessions to practical necessities, and radical adherents of absolute poverty, known as Spirituals. Though begging friars never disappeared from medieval Europe, they were at least officially discouraged by their own orders from the fourteenth century on.

1. DOCUMENTS ON ST. FRANCIS OF ASSISI

Though brief, the life of Francis of Assisi was filled with colorful and moving episodes that would become legendary among Christians ever after. It is no surprise that so many subsequent artists and writers were attracted to favorite scenes from the saint's tale, from his dramatic renunciation of all his possessions in the town square of Assisi to his preaching to the birds, fish, and even a ravenous wolf. His disciple Thomas Celano (c. 1180–c. 1252) provides one of our chief sources of information about Francis's life in his reverent biography written shortly after the saint's death. Many of the themes in Celano's account, which is excerpted in the first reading below, recall other saints' lives and even the gospels themselves. One characteristic of his portrait that seems particularly distinctive, however, is the joyful manner of Francis's preaching, even on the subject of penance. This generosity of spirit was widely attested and helps explain the saint's popularity both during his life and after his death. In his later years, Francis also fashioned the first Christmas manger scene, wrote poetry (excerpted in the readings below), and had a mystical experience in which the five wounds of the crucified Christ, known as the Stigmata, appeared on his body. This last phenomenon, which Francis characteristically attempted to conceal, provided his admirers with the ultimate proof of his sanctity. Within two years of his death, he was canonized by Pope Gregory IX, and shortly after that his body was interred in an immense basilica constructed to his memory in Assisi.

a. THOMAS CELANO, *LIFE OF ST. FRANCIS OF ASSISI* (1229)

In the city of Assisi, which lies at the edge of the Spoleto valley, there was a man by the name of Francis, who from his earliest years was brought up by his parents proud of spirit, in accordance with the vanity of the world; and imitating their wretched life and habits for a long time, he became even more vain and proud. . . .

These are the wretched circumstances among which the man whom we venerate today as a saint, for he is truly a saint, lived in his youth; and almost up to the twenty-fifth year of his age, he squandered and wasted his time miserably. Indeed, he outdid all his contemporaries in vanities and he came to be a promoter of evil and was more abundantly zealous for all kinds of foolishness. He was the admiration of all and strove to outdo the rest in the pomp of vainglory, in jokes, in strange doings, in idle and useless talk, in songs, in soft and flowing garments, for he was very rich, not however avaricious but prodigal, not a hoarder of money but a squanderer of his possessions, a cautious business man but a very unreliable steward. On the other hand, he was a very kindly person, easy and affable, even making himself foolish because of it; for because of these qualities many ran after him, doers of evil and promoters of crime. And thus overwhelmed by a host of evil companions, proud and high-minded, he walked about the streets of Babylon until the *Lord looked down from heaven* [Ps 32:13] and for his own name's sake removed his *wrath far off* and for his praise bridled Francis lest he should perish. *The hand of the Lord* therefore came *upon him* [Ezek 1:3] and a change was wrought by the right hand of the Most High, that through him an assurance might be granted to sinners that they had been restored to grace and that he might become an example to all of conversion to God. . . .

[After his conversion experience, Francis is locked up "in a dark place" for several days by his angry father.]

It happened, however, when Francis' father had left home for a while on business and the man of God remained bound in the basement of the house, his mother, who was alone with him and who did not approve of what her husband had done, spoke kindly to her son. But when she saw that he could not be persuaded away from his purpose, she was moved by motherly compassion for him, and loosening his chains, she let him go free. He, however, giving thanks to Almighty God, returned quickly to the place [i.e., a certain run-down church] where he had been before. But now, after he had been proved by temptations, he allowed himself greater liberty, and he took on a more cheerful aspect because of the many struggles he had gone through. From the wrongs done him he acquired a more confident spirit, and he went about everywhere freely with higher spirits than before. Meanwhile his father returned, and not finding Francis, he turned to upbraid his wife, heaping sins upon sins. Then, raging and blustering, he ran to that place hoping that if he could not recall him from his ways, he might at least drive him from the province. But, because it is true that *in the fear of the Lord is confidence* [Prov 14:26], when this child of grace heard his carnally minded father coming to him, confident and joyful he went to meet him, exclaiming in a clear voice that he cared nothing for his chains and blows. Moreover, he stated that he would gladly undergo evils for the name of Christ.

But when his father saw that he could not bring him back from the way he had undertaken, he was roused by all means to get his money back. The man of God had desired to offer it and expend it to feed the poor and to repair the buildings of that place. But he who had no love for money could not be misled by any aspect of good in it; and he who was not held back by any affection for it was in no way disturbed by its loss. Therefore, when the money was found, which he who hated the things of this world so greatly and desired the riches of heaven so much had thrown aside in the dust of the window sill, the fury of his raging father was extinguished a little, and the thirst of his avarice was somewhat allayed by the warmth of discovery. He then brought his

son before the bishop of the city, so that, renouncing all his possessions into his hands, he might give up everything he had. Francis not only did not refuse to do this, but he hastened with great joy to do what was demanded of him.

When he was brought before the bishop, he would suffer no delay or hesitation in anything; indeed, he did not wait for any words nor did he speak any, but immediately putting off his clothes and casting them aside, he gave them back to his father. Moreover, not even retaining his trousers, he stripped himself completely naked before all. The bishop, however, sensing his disposition and admiring greatly his fervor and constancy, arose and drew him within his arms and covered him with the mantle he was wearing. He understood clearly that the counsel was of God, and he understood that the actions of the man of God that he had personally witnessed contained a mystery. He immediately, therefore, became his helper and cherishing him and encouraging him, he embraced him in the bowels of charity. . . .

Meanwhile the holy man of God, having put on a new kind of habit and having repaired the aforesaid church, went to another place near the city of Assisi, where he began to rebuild a certain dilapidated and well-nigh destroyed church, and he did not leave off from his good purpose until he had brought it to completion.[38] Then he went to another place, which is called the Portiuncula,[39] where there stood a church of the Blessed Virgin Mother of God that had been built in ancient times, but was now deserted and cared for by no one. When the holy man of God saw how it was thus in ruins, he was moved to pity, because he burned with devotion toward the mother of all good; and he began to live there in great zeal. It was the third year of his conversion when he began to repair this church. At this time he wore a

---

[38]St. Pietro della Spina, about two miles southeast of Assisi and no longer extant.

[39]A tiny Benedictine church in the woods near Assisi, considered by Francis the cradle of his order, and now enclosed in the basilica of St. Mary of the Angels.

kind of hermit's dress, with a leather girdle about his waist; he carried a staff in his hands and wore shoes on his feet.

But when on a certain day the Gospel was read in that church, how the Lord sent his disciples out to preach, the holy man of God, assisting there, understood somewhat the words of the Gospel; after Mass he humbly asked the priest to explain the Gospel to him more fully. When he had set forth for him in order all these things, the holy Francis, hearing that the disciples of Christ should not possess gold or silver or money; nor carry along the way scrip, or wallet, or bread, or a staff; that they should not have shoes, or two tunics; but that they should preach the kingdom of God and penance,[40] immediately cried out exultingly: "This is what I wish, this is what I seek, this what I long to do with all my heart." Then the holy father, *overflowing with joy* [2 Cor 7:4], hastened to fulfill that salutary word he had heard, and he did not suffer any delay to intervene before beginning devoutly to perform what he had heard. He immediately put off his shoes from his feet, put aside the staff from his hands, was content with one tunic, and exchanged his leather girdle for a small cord. He designed for himself a tunic that bore a likeness to the cross, that by means of it he might beat off all temptations of the devil; he designed a very rough tunic so that by it he might crucify the flesh with all its vices and sins; he designed a very poor and mean tunic, one that would not excite the covetousness of the world. The other things that he had heard, however, he longed with the greatest diligence and the greatest reverence to perform. For he was not a deaf hearer of the Gospel, but committing all that he had heard to praiseworthy memory, he tried diligently to carry it out to the letter. . . .

From then on he began to preach penance to all with great fervor of spirit and joy of mind, edifying his hearers with his simple words and

his greatness of heart. His word was like a *burning fire* [Sir 23:22], penetrating the inmost reaches of the heart, and it filled the minds of all the hearers with admiration. He seemed completely different from what he had been, and, looking up to the heavens, he disdained to look upon the earth. This indeed is wonderful, that he first began to preach where as a child he had first learned to read and where for a time he was buried amid great honor,[41] so that the happy beginning might be commended by a still happier ending. Where he had learned he also taught, and where he began he also ended. In all his preaching, before he proposed the word of God to those gathered about, he first prayed for peace for them, saying: "The Lord give you peace." He always most devoutly announced peace to men and women, to all he met and overtook. For this reason many who had hated peace and had hated also salvation embraced peace, through the cooperation of the Lord, with all their heart and were made children of peace and seekers after eternal salvation.

Among these, a certain man from Assisi, of pious and simple spirit, was the first to devoutly follow the man of God. After him, Brother Bernard, embracing the delegation of peace, ran eagerly after the holy man of God to purchase the kingdom of heaven [cf. Mt 13:44]. He had often given the blessed father hospitality, and, having had experience of his life and conduct and having been refreshed by the fragrance of his holiness, he conceived a fear and brought forth the spirit of salvation. He noticed that Francis would pray all night, sleeping but rarely, praising God and the glorious Virgin Mother of God, and he wondered and said: "In all truth, this man is from God." He hastened therefore to sell all his goods and gave the money to the poor, though not to his parents; and laying hold of the title to the way of perfection, he carried out the counsel of the holy Gospel: *If thou wilt be perfect, go, sell what*

---

[40]The key gospel passages for Francis's conversion were Mt 10:9, Mk 6:8, 12, and Lk 9:2–30.

[41]The church of San Giorgio, where Francis was initially buried in 1226, before being reinterred in his newly constructed basilica in 1230.

thou hast, and give to the poor, and thou shalt have treasure in heaven; and come, follow me [Mt 19:21]. When he had done this, he was associated with St. Francis by his life and by his habit, and he was always with him until, after the number of the brothers had increased, he was sent to other regions by obedience to his kind father. His conversion to God was a model to others in the manner of selling one's possessions and giving them to the poor. St. Francis rejoiced with very great joy over the coming and conversion of so great a man, in that the Lord was seen to have a care for him by giving him a needed companion and a faithful friend.

But immediately another man of the city of Assisi followed him; he deserves to be greatly praised for his conduct, and what he began in a holy way, he completed after a short time in a more holy way. After a not very long time, Brother Giles followed him; he was *a simple and upright man,* and one *fearing* God [Job 1: 8]. He lived a long time, leading a holy life, *justly and piously,* and giving us examples of perfect obedience, manual labor, solitary life, and holy contemplation. After another one had been added to these, Brother Philip brought the number to seven. The Lord touched his lips with a purifying coal that he might speak pleasing things of him and utter sweet things. Understanding and interpreting the sacred Scriptures, though he had not studied, he became an imitator of those whom the leaders of the Jews alleged to be ignorant and unlearned. . . .

Meanwhile, while many were joining the brothers, as was said, the most blessed father Francis was making a trip through the Spoleto valley. He came to a certain place near Bevagna where a very great number of birds of various kinds had congregated, namely, doves, crows, and some others popularly called daws. When the most blessed servant of God, Francis, saw them, being a man of very great fervor and great tenderness toward lower and irrational creatures, he left his companions in the road and ran eagerly towards the birds. When he was close enough to them, seeing that they were waiting expectantly for him, he greeted

them in his usual way. But, not a little surprised that the birds did not rise in flight, as they usually do, he was filled with great joy and humbly begged them to listen to the word of God. Among the many things he spoke to them were these words that he added: "My brothers, birds, you should praise your Creator very much and always love him; he gave you feathers to clothe you, wings so that you can fly, and whatever else was necessary for you. God made you noble among his creatures, and he gave you a home in the purity of the air; though you neither sow nor reap, he nevertheless protects and governs you without any solicitude on your part" [cf. Mt 6:12, 66; 12:24]. At these words, as Francis himself used to say and those too who were with him, the birds, rejoicing in a wonderful way according to their nature, began to stretch their necks, extend their wings, open their mouths and gaze at him. And Francis, *passing through their midst, went on his way* [Lk 4:30] and returned, touching their heads and bodies with his tunic. Finally he blessed them, and then, after he had made the sign of the cross over them, he gave them permission to fly away to some other place. But the blessed father went his way with his companions, rejoicing and giving thanks to God, whom all creatures venerate with humble acknowledgement. But now that he had become simple by grace, not by nature, he began to blame himself for negligence in not having preached to the birds before, seeing that they had listened to the word of God with such great reverence. And so it happened that, from that day on, he solicitously admonished all birds, all animals and reptiles, and even creatures that have no feeling, to praise and love their Creator, for daily, when the name of the Savior had been invoked, he saw their obedience by personal experience.

When he came one day to a city called Alviano to preach the word of God, he went up to a higher place so that he could be seen by all and he began to ask for silence. But when all the people had fallen silent and were standing reverently at attention, a flock of swallows, chattering and making a loud noise, were building nests in that same place. Since the blessed Francis could not be heard by the people over the chattering of the birds, he spoke to them saying: "My sisters, swallows, it is now time for me to speak, for you have already spoken enough. Listen to the word of the Lord and be silent and quiet until the word of the Lord is finished." And those little birds, to the astonishment and wonder of the people standing by, immediately fell silent, and they did not move from that place until the sermon was finished. When these men therefore saw this miracle, they were filled with the greatest admiration and said: "Truly this man is a saint and a friend of the Most High." And they hastened with the greatest devotion to at least touch his clothing, *praising and blessing God* [Lk 24:53]. It is indeed wonderful how even irrational creatures recognized his affection for them and felt his tender love for them. . . .

He was moved by the same tender affection toward fish, too, which, when they were caught, and he had the chance, he threw back into the water, commanding them to be careful lest they be caught again. Once when he was sitting in a boat near a port in the lake of Rieti, a certain fisherman, who had caught a big fish popularly called a *tinca*,[42] offered it kindly to him. He accepted it joyfully and kindly and began to call it *brother;* then placing it in the water outside the boat, he began devoutly to bless the name of the Lord. And while he continued in prayer for some time, the fish played in the water beside the boat and did not go away from the place where it had been put until his prayer was finished and the holy man of God gave it permission to leave. For thus did the glorious father Francis, walking in the way of obedience and embracing perfectly the yoke of obedience to God, acquire great dignity in the sight of God in that creatures obeyed him. For even water was turned into wine for him, when on one occasion he was grievously ill at

the hermitage of St. Urban. At the taste of it he became well so easily that it was thought to be a miracle by all, as it really was. And truly he is a saint whom creatures obey in this way, and at whose nod the elements change themselves to other uses. . . .

At that time, when, as has been said, the venerable father Francis preached to the birds, going about the cities and towns and everywhere scattering the seeds of his blessings, he came to the city of Ascoli. There, when he preached the word of God very fervently, as was his custom, almost all the people were filled with such great grace and devotion, through a change brought about by the right hand of the Most High, that they trampled on one another in their eagerness to hear and see him. For at that time thirty men, clerics and lay, received the habit of religion from him.

So great was the faith of the men and women, so great their devotion toward the holy man of God, that he pronounced himself happy who could but touch his garment. When he entered any city, the clergy rejoiced, the bells were rung, the men were filled with happiness, the women rejoiced together, the children clapped their hands; and often, taking branches from the trees, they went to meet him singing. The wickedness of heretics was confounded, the faith of the Church exalted; and while the faithful rejoiced, the heretics slipped secretly away. For such great signs of sanctity were evident in him that no one dared to oppose his words, while the great assembly of people looked only upon him. In the midst of all these things and above everything else, Francis thought that the faith of the holy Roman Church was by all means to be preserved, honored, and imitated, that faith in which alone is found the salvation of all who are to be saved. He revered priests and he had a great affection for every ecclesiastical order. . . .

Also at Citta di Castello there was a woman obsessed by the devil. When the most blessed father Francis was in this city, the woman was brought to the house where he was staying. That woman, standing outside, began to gnash

---

[42]Probably a tench, member of the carp family.

her teeth and, her face twisted, she began to set up a great howl, as unclean spirits do. Many people of both sexes from that city came and pleaded with St. Francis in her behalf, for that evil spirit had long tormented and tortured her and had disturbed them with his loud cries. The holy father then sent to her a brother who was with him, wishing to discover whether it was really a devil or deception on the part of the woman. When that woman saw him, she began to deride him, knowing that it was not Francis who had come out. The holy father was inside praying. He came out when he had finished his prayer. But the woman, unable to stand his power, began to tremble and roll about on the ground. St. Francis called to her and said: "In virtue of obedience, I command you, unclean spirit, to go out of her." Immediately he left her, without injuring her, but departing in great anger. Thanks be to God, who does everything according to his will. . . .

The space of twenty years had now passed since Francis' conversion, according to what had been made known to him by the will of God. For when the blessed father and Brother Elias[43] were staying at one time at Foligno, one night when they had given themselves to sleep a certain white-garbed priest of a very great and advanced age and of venerable appearance stood before Brother Elias and said: "Arise, Brother, and say to Brother Francis that eighteen years are now completed since he renounced the world and gave himself to Christ, and that he will remain in this life for only two more years; then the Lord will call him to himself and he will go the way of all flesh." And thus it happened that the word of the Lord that had been made known long before was fulfilled at the appointed time.

When therefore he had rested for a few days in a place he greatly longed to be in and realized that the time of his death was at hand, he called to him two of his brothers and spiritual sons and commanded them to sing in a loud voice with joy of spirit the Praises of the Lord over his approaching death, or rather over the life that was so near. He himself, in as far as he was able, broke forth in that psalm of David: *I cried to the Lord with my voice: with my voice I made supplication to the Lord* [Ps 141:28] A certain brother, however, from among those standing about, whom the saint loved with a great affection, in his anxiety for all the brothers, said to him, when he saw those things and recognized that Francis was approaching his end: "Kind Father, alas, your sons are now without a father and are deprived of the true light of their eyes. Remember therefore your orphan sons whom you are now leaving; forgive them all their faults and give joy to those present and absent with your holy blessing." And the saint said to him: "Behold, my son, I am called by God; I forgive my brothers, both present and absent, all their offenses and faults, and, in as far as I am able, I absolve them; I want you to announce this to them and to bless them all on my behalf."

Finally he ordered the book of the Gospels to be brought and commanded that the Gospel according to St. John be read from that place where it begins: *Six days before the Passover, Jesus, knowing that the hour had come for him to pass from this world to the Father* [Jn 12:1]. The minister general [i.e., Brother Elias] had intended to read this Gospel, even before he had been commanded to do so; this passage had also appeared at the first opening of the book earlier, although the book was the whole and complete Bible in which this Gospel was contained. Francis then commanded that a hair shirt be put upon him and that he be sprinkled with ashes, for he was soon to become dust and ashes. Then, when many brothers had gathered about, whose father and leader he was, and while they were standing reverently at his side awaiting his blessed death and happy end, his most holy soul was freed from his body and received into the abyss of light, and his body *fell asleep* [Acts 7:60] in the Lord. One of his brothers and disciples, a man of some renown, whose name I think I should withhold here because

---

[43]Elias of Cortona (c. 1180–1253), an early companion of Francis and his successor as General of the Order.

while he lives in the flesh, he prefers not to glory in so great a privilege, saw the soul of the most holy father ascend over many waters directly to heaven. For it was like a star, having in some way the immensity of the moon, but to a certain extent the brightness of the sun, and it was born upward on a little white cloud.

b. FRANCIS OF ASSISI, "PRAYER" (1223)

Lord, make me an instrument of your peace;
where there is hatred, let me sow love;
where there is injury, pardon;
where there is doubt, faith;
where there is despair, hope;
where there is darkness, light;
and where there is sadness, joy;

Grant that I may not so much seek to be consoled as to console;
to be understood as to understand;
to be loved as to love;
for it is in giving that we receive;
it is in pardoning that we are pardoned;
and it is in dying that we are born to eternal life.

c. FRANCIS OF ASSISI, "THE CANTICLE OF BROTHER SUN" (1225)

Most high, all-powerful, all good, Lord!
All praise is yours, all glory, all honor
And all blessing.
To you, alone, Most High, do they belong.
No mortal lips are worthy
To pronounce your name.
All praise be yours, my Lord, through all that you have made,
And first my lord Brother Sun,
Who brings the day; and light you give to us through him.
How beautiful is he, how radiant in all his splendor!
Of you, Most High, he bears the likeness.
All praise be yours, my Lord, through Brothers Wind and Air,
And fair and stormy, all the weather's moods,
By which you cherish all that you have made.
All praise be yours, my Lord, through Sister Water,
So useful, lowly, precious and pure.

All praise be yours, my Lord, through Brother Fire,
Through whom you brighten up the night.
How beautiful is he, how gay! Full of power and strength.
All praise be yours, my Lord, through Sister Earth, our mother,
Who feeds us in her sovereignty and produces
Various fruits with colored flowers and herbs.
All praise be yours, my Lord, through those who grant pardon
For love of you; through those who endure Sickness and trial.
Happy those who endure in peace,
By you, Most High, they will be crowned.
All praise be yours, my Lord, through Sister Death,
From whose embrace no mortal can escape.
Woe to those who die in mortal sin!
Happy those She finds doing your will!
The second death can do no more harm to them.
Praise and bless my Lord, and give him thanks,
And serve him with great humility.

BIBLIOGRAPHY

Primary Sources

Anthologies and Readers

Hollister, C. Warren, ed., *The Twelfth Century Renaissance* (New York: Wiley, 1969).

Peters, Edward, ed., *The First Crusade: The Chronicle of Fulcher of Chartres and Other Source Materials* (Philadelphia: University of Pennsylvania Press, 1971).

————, ed., *Heresy and Authority in Medieval Europe* (Philadelphia: University of Pennsylvania Press, 1980).

Spade, Paul V., ed. and trans., *Five Texts on the Mediaeval Problem of Universals: Porphyry, Boethius, Abelard, Duns Scotus, Ockham* (Indianapolis: Hackett, 1994).

Thorndike, Lynn, ed., *University Records and Life in the Middle Ages* (New York: Columbia University Press, 1944).

Tierney, Brian, ed., *The Crisis of Church and State, 1050–1300* (Englewood Cliffs, N.J.: Prentice-Hall, 1964).

Tugwell, Simon, ed., *Early Dominicans: Selected Writings* (Mahwah, N.J.: Paulist Press, 1982).

Wakefield, Walter L., and Evans, Austin P., eds., *Heresies of the High Middle Ages* (New York: Columbia University Press, 1969).

Selected Authors

Abelard, Peter, *Ethical Writings,* trans. Paul V. Spade (Indianapolis: Hackett, 1995).

The Letters of Abelard and Heloise, trans. Bettey Radice (New York: Penguin Classics, 1974).

Thomas Aquinas, *Basic Writings of St. Thomas Aquinas,* ed. Anton C. Pegis, 2 vols. (New York: Random House, 1997).

————, *An Aquinas Reader,* ed. Mary T. Clark (Bronx, N.Y.: Fordham, 1972).

————, *Selected Philosophical Writings,* trans. Timothy McDermott (Oxford: Oxford University Press, 1993).

Anselm of Canterbury, *The Prayers and Meditations of St. Anselm,* ed. Benedicta Ward (New York: Penguin Classics, 1973).

Bernard of Clairvaux, *Selected Works,* trans. G. R. Evans (Mahwah, N.J.: Paulist Press, 1987).

Clare of Assisi, *Early Documents,* ed. and trans. Regis J. Armstrong (Mahwah, N.J.: Paulist Press, 1988).

Francis of Assisi, *Saint Francis of Assisi, Omnibus of Sources,* ed. Marion Haby (Chicago: Franciscan Herald Press, 1973).

Pope Gregory VII, *The Correspondence of Pope Gregory VII,* ed. Ephriam Emerton (New York: Columbia University Press, 1969).

Hildegard of Bingen, *The Letters of Hildegard of Bingen,* vol. I, ed. J. L. Baird and R. K. Ehrman (Oxford: Oxford University Press, 1998).

————, *Sciavis,* ed. Mother Columba Haut (Mahwah, N.J.: Paulist Press, 1992).

Joinville, Jean de, and Geoffroi de Villehardouin, *Chronicles of the Crusades,* ed. M.R.B. Shaw (New York: Penguin Classic, 1963).

Secondary Works

General

Hollister, C. Warren, *Medieval Europe: A Short History,* 7th ed. (New York: Viking, 1994).

Lynch, Joseph H., *The Medieval Church* (White Plains, N.Y.: Longman, 1992).

Pelikan, Jaroslav, *The Christian Tradition: A History of the Development of Doctrine, Vol. 2: The Growth of Medieval Theology (600–1300)* (Chicago: University of Chicago, 1978).

Southern, R.W., *Western Society and the Church in the Middle Ages* (New York: Penguin, 1990).

Tellenbach, Gerd, *The Church in Western Europe from the Tenth to the Early Twelfth Century* (Cambridge: Cambridge University Press, 1993).

Tierney, Brian, and Sidney Painter, *Western Europe in the Middle Ages, 300–1475* (New York: Knopf, 1983).

Investiture and the Papacy

Barraclough, Geoffrey, *The Medieval Papacy* (New York: Thames & Hudson, 1968).

Morris, C., *The Papal Monarchy: The Western Church, 1050–1250* (Oxford: Oxford University Press, 1989).

Ullmann, Walter, *A Short History of the Papacy in the Middle Ages* (London: Methuen, 1974).

Weinfurter, Stefan, *The Salian Century: Main Currents in an Age of Transition* (Philadelphia: University of Pennsylvania Press, 1994).

The Crusades

Madden, Thomas F., *A Concise History of the Crusades* (Savage, Md.: Rowman & Littlefield, 1999).

Riley-Smith, Jonathan, *The Oxford Illustrated History of the Crusades* (Oxford: Oxford University Press, 1997).

Scholasticism and the Twelfth-Century Renaissance

Brooke, Christopher, *The Twelfth Century Renaissance* (New York: Harcourt, Brace, & World, 1970).

Chenu, M. D., *Nature, Man and Society in the Twelfth Century* (Chicago: University of Chicago Press, 1983).

Clanchy, M. T., *Abelard: A Medieval Life* (Oxford: Blackwell, 1997).

Constable, Giles, *The Reformation of the Twelfth Century* (Cambridge: Cambridge University Press, 1998).

Leclerq, Jean, *The Love of Learning and the Desire for God* (New York: Mentor Omega, 1961).

Marenbon, John, *The Philosophy of Peter Abelard* (Cambridge: Cambridge University Press, 1997).

Pelikan, Jaroslav, *The Christian Tradition: A History of the Development of Doctrine, Vol. 3: The Growth of Medieval Theology (600-1300)* (Chicago: University of Chicago Press, 1978).

Wieruszowski, Helene, *The Medieval University* (New York: Van Nostrand, 1966).

Medieval Piety

Bynum, Caroline Walker, *Holy Feast and Holy Fast: The Religious Significance of Food to Medieval Women* (Berkeley and Los Angeles: University of California, 1987).

Brooke, Rosalind and Christopher, *Popular Religion in the Middle Ages* (New York: Thames & Hudson, 1984).

Flanagan, Sabina, *Hildegard of Bingen: A Visionary Life* (New York: Routledge, 1998).

Klauser, T., *A Short History of the Western Liturgy* (Oxford: Oxford University Press, 1969).

Ward, Benedicta, *Miracles and the Medieval Mind* (Philadelphia: University of Pennsylvania Press, 1982).

Medieval Heresy

Costen, Michael, *The Cathars and the Albigensian Crusade* (Manchester: Manchester University Press, 1997).

Lambert, Malcolm, *Medieval Heresies: Popular Movements from the Gregorian Reform to the Reformation* (Oxford: Blackwell, 1992).

Ladurie, Emmanuel LeRoy, *Montaillou: Promised Land of Error* (New York: George Braziller, 1978).

Franciscans and Dominicans

Bartoli, Marco, *Clare of Assisi* (Quincy, Ill.: Franciscan Press, 1993).

Moorman, John, *A History of the Franciscan Order: From Its Origins to the Year 1517* (Oxford: Oxford University Press, 1968; reprint 1997).

Robson, Michael, *St. Francis of Assisi: The Legend and the Life* (London: G. Chapman, 1997).

CHAPTER 4

The Late Middle Ages and Renaissance

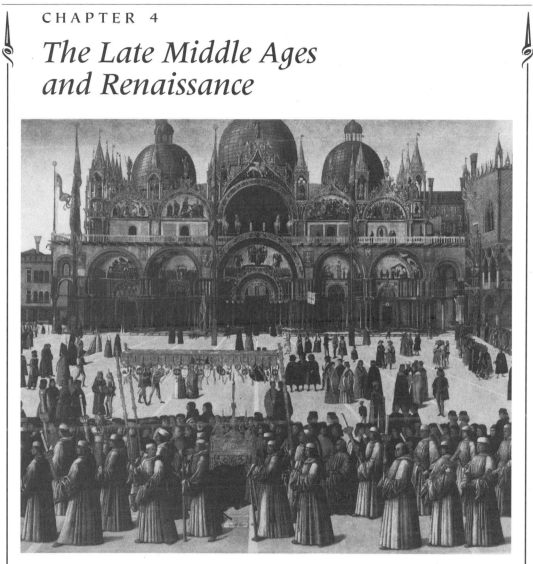

RELIGIOUS PROCESSION IN ST. MARK'S SQUARE, VENICE. During the later Middle Ages, the boundary between secular and religious public rituals was virtually nonexistent, with saints' feasts and other Christian holidays also providing occasions for the display of governmental authority, social status, and in this instance, civic pride. *(Archivi Alinari/Art Resource, New York.)*

It was long a commonplace to portray the fourteeth- and fifteenth-century church as corrupt and riven by dissatisfaction among the clergy and laity alike. Recent scholarship, however, has revealed a much more complicated picture of the era as a time when intense popular piety existed side by side with endemic problems of greed and hypocrisy at all levels of the church hierarchy. During the late Middle Ages, for instance, papal and priestly authority and prestige reached both new heights and new lows. The same might be said of the average Christian's understanding of and conformity to church doctrine. Clearly the Protestant and Catholic reformers of the sixteenth century, who would harshly criticize the late medieval church, had many grounds for complaint. But they also built on many of the pious beliefs and practices that emerged from the era. The violence of such contrasts was not surprising in an age devastated by prolonged warfare and the worst epidemic in the history of humanity yet also experiencing the great cultural flowering now known as the Renaissance. In that sense, the late Middle Ages marked both the culmination and the decline of medieval Christianity—a contradictory label for a contradictory time.

The papacy provides an excellent example of the extremes of the age. At the end of the thirteenth century, the popes were the strongest rulers in Europe, possessing undisputed authority over all church matters as well as the sophisticated legal and court system and the leading administrative bureaucracy of the day. Two hundred years later, the prestige of the papacy was at an all-time low, the corruption and immorality of the Roman court was infamous, and the popes themselves behaved like any other Italian princes, generally concerned more about territorial expansion and income than the governance of the Western church. Still, classifying the late Middle Ages as a period of complete papal decline would be a distortion. For while the effect of the papacy's degeneration on overall morale within the church cannot be ignored, the spiritual authority of the popes remained untouched, and lay and clerical piety thrived as never before. The key to this apparent contradiction lies in the long-standing distinction between papal politics and church administration. The very public humiliation of Pope Boniface VIII (r. 1294–1303) by the French king Philip IV (r. 1285–1314) weakened the pope considerably on the stage of international politics but did not directly affect the vibrance of the medieval church or his leadership of it. The same is true of the so-called Babylonian captivity of the church—seventy-two years during which the popes resided in Avignon under the influence of the French monarchy—and even the Great Schism of 1378–1417, when a series of two and eventually three claimants to the papal throne divided the loyalties of Western Christianity. The pope was hardly irrelevant to the smooth running of the church but neither was his relative political power or personal morality a particularly accurate gauge of the institution's vitality.

The most significant event of the late medieval period for most believers and the church in general was not the political decline of the papacy but the appearance of the Black Death in 1347. During the next three years alone, the pestilence killed at least one-third of all Europeans. There is no comparable event of this scope in Western history, and its impact on the lives of the survivors was immense and long-lasting. Some individuals apparently lost all faith in God or Christianity. Many more had exactly the opposite reaction, intensifying their practice of religious devotions, ranging from intercessory prayer to penitential self-flagellation. In the century and a half of demographic and economic recovery that followed the first outbreak of the plague, popular piety continued to boom and ordinary Christians preserved and creatively adapted these and other traditional practices. The cult of the saints was continually expanded to include new members, each of whom was then petitioned by Christians seeking divine intercession either for themselves or for a deceased loved one suffering in purgatory. Numerous shrines to the Virgin Mary rivaled the countless other sites of pilgrimage in medieval Europe, all bolstered by popular reports of miraculous healing or other successful petitions. Meanwhile, a complex cycle of church rituals—often including certain local additions to the mass and seven sacraments—continually reaffirmed the connection between the human and divine in every aspect of human existence.

The general thirst for pious fellowship led some individuals to form new associations with their fellow Christians. In urban areas, for instance, most craftsmen and professionals belonged to confraternities, voluntary religious groups that were active in philanthropic work as well as offering additional religious services for their members. Unlike neighborhood parish churches, where such men also participated, the confraternities maintained a membership usually restricted by trade (e.g., shoemakers or goldsmiths) and thus served a professional as well as religious function. Groups such as the Brothers and Sisters of the Common Life, also known as the Modern Devotion, by contrast, were open to all those who sought a more focused and contemplative religious experience. In any of their numerous meeting houses in northern Germany and the Netherlands, laypeople and clerics could come together for reading and discussion of the Bible as well as private meditation and prayer. Like the so-called tertiaries, or lay followers of religious orders, the members of the Modern Devotion remained completely orthodox in their attitude towards clerical leadership and church doctrine. Their goal was always to supplement rather than to replace the sacraments and other official rites of the church.

Given the vibrant diversity of religious beliefs and practices in late medieval Europe, it is perhaps surprising that there were not more instances of condemned teachings, or heresies, than actually occurred. In fact, the majority of heresies from this period—the Humilitati,

Waldensians, Beguines, Beghards, and others—merely represented intensifications of official church teachings on the ideal of apostolic poverty. The major distinction between such groups and the approved Franciscan and Dominican orders, which also embraced poverty, was the latter's unflinching recognition of the clerical hierarchy's authority. The same fatal mistake was also made by the heretical Wycliffites or Lollards of England and their Czech counterparts, the Hussites, although their radically different interpretations of certain key Bible passages were also among the reasons for their official condemnation. During the entire late medieval period, however, condemned or at least accused heretics never constituted more than a tiny fraction of all Christians. While it is true that inquisitional courts continued to grow in scope and frequency during this period, they remained a largely peripheral—if ominous—development.

Perhaps the greatest symbol of the internal contradictions of the age was the new fascination with Greek and Roman antiquity, which we now call the Renaissance. While the longing of Renaissance poets, painters, and sculptors to recreate the glories of the pagan world may seem antithetical to Christianity, almost all of these artists were in fact motivated by pious as well as aesthetic motives. Their frequent mixture of Christian and pagan themes and learning did not indicate any disrespect for their mother religion but rather a new admiration for the parallel teachings of many ancient nonbelievers. At the same time, however, Renaissance scholars were applying new historical and linguistic techniques to the writings of the church fathers and the Bible itself, yielding some interpretations that were perilously at odds with elements of traditional church doctrine. Much of this scholarship was supported, ironically, by the papacy itself. But discussions of its implications remained safely within the realm of academic speculation and had little effect on the church at large. In that sense, the fullest harvest of Renaissance biblical scholarship would not come until the sixteenth century, when leaders of the Protestant Reformation would use its findings to support their revolutionary break with the Catholic Church and inaugurate a dramatically new era in the history of Christianity.

CHAPTER 4 CHRONOLOGY

	Politics	Literature	Individuals	Other
14th cent.		1314 Dante, *Divine Comedy*	c. 1260–1327 Meister Eckhart	1305–1377 Papacy in Avignon (Babylonian captivity)
	1347–1453 Hundred Years' War between France and England	1343 Petrarch, *Secretum* c. 1350 Boccaccio, *Decameron* c. 1390 Chaucer, *Canterbury Tales*	c. 1330–1384 John Wycliffe 1347–1380 Catherine of Siena	1347–1350 First wave of Black Death in Europe 1378–1415 Papal schism 1381 Peasants' Revolt in England
15th cent.	1415 Battle of Agincourt 1453 Constantinople falls to Turks 1455–1485 English Wars of the Roses 1469–1492 Lorenzo the Magnificent ruler of Florence 1469 Marriage of Ferdinand of Aragon & Isabella of Castille 1494 Charles VIII of France invades Italy	c. 1418 Thomas à Kempis, *Initiation of Christ* c. 1450 Manetti, *On the Dignity of Man* 1487 Ficino, *Platonica Theologica*	1373–1415 Jan Hus 1412–1431 Jeanne d'Arc 1380–1444 Bernadino da Siena 1447–1510 Catherine of Genoa	1414–1418 Council of Constance 1421–1436 Hussite wars in Bohemia c. 1455 Gutenberg invents printing press 1462 Platonic Academy founded by Medicis 1478 Spanish Inquisition established 1492 Muslims and Jews expelled from Spain 1492 Columbus lands in New World 1494 Treaty of Tordesilla divides New World 1498 Burning of Savonarola & followers in Florence
16th cent.	1503–1513 Julius II pope 1509–1547 Henry VIII king of England 1515–1547 Francis I king of France 1519–1556 Charles V emperor	1513 Machiavelli, *The Prince* 1516 More, *Utopia*	1466–1536 Desiderius Erasmus 1483–1546 Martin Luther	1508 Michelangelo paints the Sistine Chapel 1512–1515 Lateran V council 1517 Luther posts 95 Theses in Wittenberg

A. Pilgrimage

Journeys to sacred places to seek supernatural help or to express piety were common in the ancient world. The earliest record of a Christian pilgrimage is a trip by a bishop from what is now eastern Turkey to Jerusalem in the early third century. By the time of Constantine, a century later, a network of Christian holy sites had emerged throughout the Mediterranean world. Most of these places—for example, the tombs of St. Peter and Paul in Rome—had been sanctified by the relics of a particular saint (see 2D), and as a result offered pilgrims special access to the divine. During the Middle Ages, the number of Christian pilgrimage sites multiplied, partly as a result of the increasing use of the journey as a form of penance to compensate for various individual sins. Hope for intercession (especially in the form of miraculous healing) and simple curiosity also played significant roles in the spread of this practice. In the sixteenth century, Protestants would officially abolish pilgrimages and relic veneration, but in Catholic areas both traditions have survived to the present day.

1. *THE PILGRIM'S GUIDE TO SANTIAGO DE COMPOSTELA (c. 1173)*

The shrine of St. James (Spanish *Santiago*) at Compostela in northwestern Spain was second only to Rome and Jerusalem in popularity with medieval Christian pilgrims. During the long Muslim occupation of most of Spain, the legend of the saint's mission to the peninsula had served as a rallying point for Spanish Christians. After the Christian *Reconquista* ("reconquest") of much of Spain in the eleventh century, a new church was built at Compostela for the supposed relics of St. James. From that point on, the site became a magnet for Christian pilgrims from all over Europe. This anonymous guidebook from the twelfth century conveys many of the reasons that pilgrimages continued to be so popular throughout the Middle Ages. In addition to the promise of divine forgiveness or intercession, a visit to Compostela offered a type of vacation from the tedium of the everyday. Although clothed simply and travelling light, medieval pilgrims took time to appreciate exotic people and places as well as "must-see" relics and churches. The guidebook accordingly provides the necessary practical information (directions, tolls, local customs) as well as historical and artistic descriptions of the various sites along the way.

CHAPTER VII: THE QUALITY OF THE LANDS AND THE PEOPLE ALONG THIS ROAD

On the road of the Blessed James by the route of Toulouse, having crossed the river Garonne, one enters first the land of Gascon; thereafter, having cleared the pass of Somport, one finds the country of Aragón and then, as far as the bridge on the Arga and beyond, the land of Navarra. If one takes the route of the pass of Cize, on the other hand, one finds, after Tours, the country of Poitou, a land well-managed, excellent and full of all blessing. The inhabitants of Poitou are vigorous and warlike; extraordinarily able users of bows, arrows and lances in times of war, they are daring on the battlefront, fast in running, comely in dressing, of noble features, of clever language, generous in the rewards they bestow and prodigal in the hospitality they offer. Then comes the country of Saintonge. Having crossed somehow a sea sound and the river Garonne, one arrives to the region of the Bordelais, excellent in wine, abundant in fishes, but of rustic language. Those of Saintonge have already a rustic language, but those of Bordelais prove to have an even more rustic one. Thence one needs three more days of march, for people already tired, to traverse the Landes of the Bordelais.

This is a desolate region deprived of all good: there is here no bread, wine, meat, fish, water or springs; villages are rare here. The sandy and flat land abounds none the less in honey, millet, panic-grass, and wild boars. If perchance you cross it in summertime, guard your face diligently from the enormous flies that greatly abound there and which are called in the vulgar wasps or horseflies; and if you do not watch your feet carefully, you will rapidly sink up to the knees in the sea-sand copiously found all over.

Having traversed this region, one comes to the land of Gascon rich in white bread and excellent red wine, and covered by forests and meadows, streams and healthy springs. The Gascons are fast in words, loquacious, given to mockery, libidinous, drunkards, prodigal in food, ill-dressed, and rather careless in the ornaments they wear. However, they are well-trained in combat and generous in the hospitality they provide for the poor.

Seated around the fire, they have the habit of eating without a table and of drinking all of them out of one single cup. In fact, they eat and drink a lot, wear rather poor clothes, and lie down shamelessly on a thin and rotten straw litter, the servants together with the master and the mistress.

On leaving that country, to be sure on the road of St. James, there are two rivers that flow near the village of Saint-Jean-de-Sorde, one to the right and one to the left, and of which one is called brook and the other river. There is no way of crossing them without a raft. May their ferrymen be damned! Though each of the streams is indeed quite narrow, they have the habit of demanding one coin from each man, whether poor or rich, whom they ferry over, and for a horse they ignominiously extort by force four. Now, their boat is small, made of a single tree, hardly capable of holding horses. Also, when boarding it one must be most careful not to fall by chance into the water. You will do well in pulling your horse by the reins behind yourself in the water, outside the boat, and to embark but with few passengers, for if it is overloaded it will soon become endangered.

Also, many times the ferryman, having received his money, has such a large troop of pilgrims enter the boat that it capsizes and the pilgrims drown in the waves. Upon which the boatmen, having laid their hands upon the spoils of the dead, wickedly rejoice.

Then, already near the pass of Cize, one reaches the Basque country, on the seashore of which, towards the north, lies the city of Bayonne. This land, whose language is barbarous, is wooded, mountainous, devoid of bread, wine, and all sorts of food for the body, except that, in compensation, it abounds in apples, cider, and milk.

In this land, that is to say near Port-de-Cize in the town called Ostabat and in those of Saint-Jean and Saint-Michel-Pied-de-Port, there are evil toll-gatherers who will certainly be damned through and through. In point of fact, they actually advance towards the pilgrims with two or three sticks, extorting by force an unjust tribute. And if some traveler refuses to hand over the money at their request, they beat him with the sticks and snatch away the toll-money while cursing him and searching even through his breeches. These are ferocious people; and the land in which they dwell is savage, wooded and barbarous. The ferociousness of their faces and likewise of their barbarous speech scares the wits out of those who see them. Though according to the rules and regulations they should not demand a tribute from anybody but merchants, they unjustly cash in from pilgrims and all sorts of travelers. Whenever they ought to receive, according to the usage, four or six coins for a certain service, they cash in eight or twelve, that is to say, double. . . .

In the Basque country there is on the road of St. James a very high mountain, which is called Port-de-Cize, either because that is the gate of Spain, or because it is by that mountain that the necessary goods are transported from one country to the other. Its ascent is eight miles long, and its descent, equally eight. In fact, its height is such that it seems to touch the sky: to him who climbs it, it seems as if he was able to touch the sky with his hand. From its summit one can see the sea of Bretagne and that of the west, as well as the boundaries of three regions, that is to say, Castilla, Aragón, and France. On the summit of this mountain there is a place called the Cross of Charles, because it was here that Charles [i.e., Charlemagne], setting out with his armies for Spain, opened up once a passageway with axes, hatchets, pickaxes and other implements, and that he first erected the sign of the cross of the Lord and, falling on his knees and turning towards Galicia, addressed a prayer to God and St. James. Wherefore the pilgrims, falling on their knees and turning towards the land of St. James, use to offer there a prayer while each planted his own cross of the Lord like a standard. Indeed, one can find there up to a thousand crosses; and that is why that place is the first station of prayer of St. James.

On that mountain, before Christianity had spread out on Spanish lands, the impious Navarrese and the Basques used not merely to rob the pilgrims going to St. James, but also to ride them as if they were asses and before long to slay them. Near this mountain, to be sure, towards the north, there is a valley called Valcarlos where Charles himself encamped together with his armies after his warriors had

been slain at Roncesvalles.[1] Many pilgrims proceeding to Santiago who do not want to climb the mountain go that way.

Afterwards, in descending from the summit, one finds the hospice and the church with the rock that Roland, the formidable hero, split with his sword in the middle, from top to bottom, in a triple stroke. Next, one comes to Roncesvalles, the site where, to be sure, once took place the big battle in which King Marsile, Roland, Olivier as well as forty thousand Christian and Saracen soldiers were slain.

After this valley lies the land of the Navarrese which abounds in bread, wine, milk, and livestock. The Navarrese and the Basques are very similar and show much the same characteristics in their food, garments, and language, though the Basques are easily recognized by their complexion, which is whiter than that of the Navarrese. The Navarrese wear black and short garments, only knee-long, in the Scottish fashion, and use a footwear which they call *lavarcas* made of uncured, hairy leather, attached around the foot with leather straps, which cover the bottom of the foot only, leaving the rest bare. They wear dark, elbow-long, wool cloaks, fringed in the manner of a cape and which they call *sayas*. They dress most poorly and eat and drink disgustingly. The whole household of a Navarrese, to be sure, the servant no less than the master, the maid no less than the mistress, eat from a single dish all the food mixed together; and they eat not with spoons but with their own hands and furthermore drink from a single cup. If you saw them eating, you would take them for dogs or pigs in the very act of devouring; if you heard them speaking, you would be reminded of the barking of dogs. Their language is, in fact, completely barbarous. They call God *Urcia;* the Mother of God, *Andrea Maria;* bread, *orgui;* wine, *ardum;* meat, *aragui;* fish, *araign;* house, *echea;* the master of the house, *iaona;* the mistress, *andrea;* the church, *elicera;* the priest, *belaterra,* which

---

[1] Legendary last stand of Charlemagne's nephew during the emperor's retreat from Spain; it inspired the medieval epic, *The Song of Roland.*

means beautiful land; grain, *gari;* water, *uric;* king, *ereguia;* St. James, *Iaona domne Jacue.*

This is a barbarous nation, distinct from all other nations in habits and way of being, full of all kind of malice, and of black color. Their face is ugly, and they are debauched, perverse, perfidious, disloyal and corrupt, libidinous, drunkard, given to all kind of violence, ferocious and savage, impudent and false, impious and uncouth, cruel and quarrelsome, incapable of anything virtuous, well-informed of all vices and iniquities. . . .

CHAPTER VIII: THE SAINTLY REMAINS ON THIS ROAD AND THE PASSION OF ST. EUTROPIUS
The Alyscamps

Subsequently, one should visit the cemetery next to the city of Arles, in a place called Alyscamps, and intercede there, as is customary, for the deceased with prayers, psalms, and alms. Its length and width are one mile each. In no cemetery anywhere, except in this one, can one find so many and so large marble tombs set upon the ground. They are of various workmanship and bear antique engravings in Latin letters but in an unintelligible language. The farther into the distance one looks, the lengthier the rows of sarcophagi become.

In the same cemetery there are seven churches. If in any of them a priest celebrates the Eucharist for the defunct, or if a layman has a priest celebrate it devoutly, or if a cleric recites the Psalter, he may be certain to have those pious deceased lying there intercede for his salvation in the presence of God at the final Resurrection. In effect, the remains of numerous holy martyrs and confessors are resting there, while their souls rejoice already in the paradisiacal realm. Their commemoration is celebrated, according to the usage, on Monday after the octave of Easter. . . .

Concerning the Body and the Altar of Saint James

Up to this point we have treated the characteristics of the church; now we ought to treat the venerable altar of the Apostle. In this revered basilica, under the high altar erected, with the greatest deference, in his honor rests, as it is reported, the venerated body of the Blessed James. It is enclosed in a marble casket placed in a most precious vaulted tomb of admirable workmanship and harmonious dimensions.

His body is immovable, according to what is asserted and furthermore as it is witnessed by Saint Theodemir [d. 847], bishop of the city, who had discovered it a long time ago and in no way could remove it from its place. May therefore the imitators from beyond the mountains blush who claim to possess some portion of him or even his entire relic. In fact, the body of the Apostle is here in its entirety, divinely lit by paradisiacal carbuncles, incessantly honored with immaculate and soft perfumes, decorated with dazzling celestial candles, and diligently worshipped by attentive angels.

Over his tomb there is a small altar which, as it is told, was made by his disciples and which, for the sake of the love for the Apostle and his disciples, nobody subsequently wanted to demolish. And above this there is a large and most admirable altar which measures five palms in height, twelve in length, and seven in width. So have I measured it with my own hands. The small altar is, consequently, enclosed under the large one on three sides—on the right, the left, and the back; but it is open on the front in such a way that, once the silver antependium [i.e., decorative altar covering] has been removed, one is able to clearly see the old altar.

If somebody would want to donate, out of devotion for the Blessed James, an altar-ornament or a linen-cloth in order to cover the apostolic altar, he must send it of nine palms in width and twenty-one palms in length. If, on the other hand, one would like to send, out of love for God and the Apostle, an ornamental linen-cloth to cover the front of the antependium, one must see to it that its width be seven palms and its length, thirteen. . . .

CHAPTER X: THE DISTRIBUTION OF THE OFFERINGS AT THE ALTAR OF ST. JAMES

Seventy-two canons, corresponding to the number of the seventy-two Disciples of Christ, are attached to this church; they follow the rule of the Blessed Doctor Isidore of Spain.[2] They divide among themselves, by successive weeks, the oblations of the altar of Saint James. To the first canon correspond the oblations of the first week; to the second, those of the second; to the third, those of the third; and so they share the oblations to the last one.

Each Sunday, tradition dictates that the oblations be shared out in three parts: the first is assigned to the hebdomadary[3] to whom it corresponds; the other two are first drawn together and are then divided in their turn into three parts; one of these is given to the canons for their communal meal; another, to the fabric of the basilica; and the third one, to the archbishop of the church. But the oblations of the week which goes from Palm to Easter must be given, according to accepted custom, to the poor pilgrims of Saint James lodged in the hospice. Furthermore, were the justice of God appropriately observed, one would be obliged to give at all times the tenth part of the oblations of the altar of Saint James to the poor who drop in at the hospice.

Indeed, all poor pilgrims must, the first night that follows the day of their arrival to the altar of the Blessed James, receive at the hospice, for the love of God and the Apostle, full hospitality. Those who are sick, to be sure, must be charitably taken care of there either until their death or until their complete recovery. So it is done at Saint Léonard: no matter how many poor pilgrims make it there, all receive subsistence. Furthermore, custom dictates that the leprous of the city be given the oblations that reach the altar each Sunday, from the beginning of the morning

until the hour of terce. And if a prelate of the same basilica committed fraud in this matter or changed in some way the destiny of the oblations, as we have just described it, may his sin stand between God and him.

CHAPTER XI: THE PROPER WELCOMING OF THE PILGRIMS OF ST. JAMES

Pilgrims, whether poor or rich, who return from or proceed to Santiago, must be received charitably and respectfully by all. For he who welcomes them and provides them diligently with lodging will have as his guest not merely the Blessed James, but the Lord himself, who in His Gospels said: "He who welcomes you, welcomes me" [Mt 10:40; Mk 9:37; Lk 9:48]. Many are those who in the past brought upon themselves the wrath of God because they refused to receive the pilgrims of Saint James or the indigent.

In Nantua, which is a city between Genève and Lyon, a weaver refused to hand out some bread to a pilgrim who had asked for it: all of a sudden some linen of his dropped to the ground torn in its middle. In Villeneuve, a woman kept some bread under hot ashes. A needy pilgrim of Saint James asked her for alms by the love of God and the Blessed James. When she answered that she had no bread, the pilgrim exclaimed: "May the bread you have turn into stone!" And when the pilgrim left her house and was already at a considerable distance, this vicious woman turned to the ashes with the idea of retrieving her bread, but found only a round stone instead. With contrite heart she set out to look for the pilgrim, but could not find him anymore.

Two valiant Frenchmen, returning one day from Santiago destitute of all, kept asking for lodging, by the love of God and Saint James, all about the city of Poitiers from the house of Jean Gautier and as far as Saint-Porchaire—and they could find none. And having finally been put up by some poor man in the last house of that street next to the basilica of Saint-

---

[2]St. Isidore of Seville (c. 560–636), theologian and scholar.
[3]The priest assigned to celebration of the mass for a given week.

Porchaire, by the effects of divine vengeance, a violent fire burned to the ground that very night the entire street, starting from the house where they first asked for lodging and up to the one which had welcomed them. And these were about one thousand houses in all. But the one in which the servants of God had been put up remained, by divine grace, untouched.

That is the reason why it should be known that the pilgrims of Saint James, whether poor or rich, have the right to hospitality and to diligent respect.

---

2. Desiderius Erasmus
A PILGRIMAGE FOR RELIGION'S SAKE (1526)

By the time the famed humanist Erasmus (1469–1536) published his satirical look at pilgrimage in 1526, the practice had already come under heavy criticism from all of the religious reformers later known as Protestants. Though Erasmus vehemently denounced the Lutheran cause, he did share the antipathy of the "heretics" toward the extremely popular custom of pilgrimage. In this dialogue the simple-minded pilgrim Ogygius unembarassedly describes all of the superstitions and abuses that Erasmus thought typical of pilgrims. His neighbor Menedemus ("stay-at-home") listens obligingly, asking supposedly innocent questions, which in fact aim at making Ogygius and his beliefs appear even more ridiculous. This representation of late medieval pilgrimage, therefore, should not be interpreted as a faithful description but rather as a highly polemical attack. The principal shrines discussed here, Our Lady of Walsingham (in Norfolk) and St. Thomas of Canterbury, were visited by Erasmus himself during one of his trips to England. When King Henry VIII broke with the Church of Rome shortly thereafter, both shrines were destroyed and the custom of pilgrimage officially prohibited in England.

Menedemus. What marvel is this? Don't I see my neighbor Ogygius, whom nobody's laid eyes on for six whole months? I heard he was dead. It's his very self, unless I'm losing my mind completely. I'll go up to him and say hello. — Greetings, Ogygius!

Ogygius. Same to you, Menedemus.

Menedemus. Where in the world do you turn up from, safe and sound? A sad rumor spread here that you'd sailed in Stygian waters.[4]

Ogygius. No, thank heaven; I've seldom enjoyed better health.

Menedemus. I hope you'll always be able to refute silly rumors of that sort! But what's this fancy outfit? You're ringed with scallop shells, choked with tin and leaden images on every side, decked out with straw necklaces, and you have snake eggs on your arms.[5]

Ogygius. I've been on a visit to St. James of Compostela and, on my way back, to the famous Virgin-by-the Sea, in England; or rather I revisited her, since I had gone there three years earlier.

Menedemus. Out of curiosity, I dare say.

---

[4]I.e., died. In Greek mythology, the river Styx marked the boundary between the worlds of the living and the dead.

[5]Shells, traditional symbols of pilgrims, were connected especially with St. James and the pilgrimage to Compostela. The "snake eggs" are beads, i.e., a rosary.

Ogygius. Oh, no: out of devotion.

Menedemus. Greek letters, I suppose, taught you that devotion.

Ogygius. My wife's mother had bound herself by a vow that if her daughter gave birth to a boy and he lived, I would promptly pay my respects to St. James and thank him in person.

Menedemus. Did you greet the saint only in your own name and your mother-in-law's?

Ogygius. Oh, no, in the whole family's.

Menedemus. Well, I imagine your family would have been no less safe even if you had left James ungreeted. But do please tell me: what answer did he make when you thanked him?

Ogygius. None, but he seemed to smile as I offered my gift, nodded his head slightly, and at the same time held out these scallop shells.

Menedemus. Why does he give these rather than something else?

Ogygius. Because he has plenty of them; the sea nearby supplies them.

Menedemus. O generous saint, who both delivers those in labor and gives presents to callers! But what new kind of vowing is this, that some lazy person lays the work on others? If you bound yourself by a vow that, should *your* affairs prosper, *I* would fast twice a week, do you think I'd do what you had vowed?

Ogygius. No, I don't, even if you'd sworn in your own name. For you enjoy mocking the saints. But she's my mother-in-law; custom had to be kept. You're acquainted with women's whims, and besides I had an interest in it, too.

Menedemus. If you hadn't kept her vow, what risk would there have been?

Ogygius. The saint couldn't have sued me at law, I admit, but he could have been deaf thereafter to my prayers, or secretly have brought some disaster upon my family. You know the ways of the mighty.

Menedemus. Tell me, how is the excellent James?

Ogygius. Much colder than usual.

Menedemus. Why? Old age?

Ogygius. Joker! You know saints don't grow old. But this newfangled notion that pervades the whole world {i.e., Protestantism} results in

his being greeted more seldom than usual. And if people do come, they merely greet him; they make no offering at all, or only a very slight one, declaring it would be better to contribute that money to the poor.

Menedemus. An impious notion!

Ogygius. And thus so great an Apostle, accustomed to shine from head to foot in gold and jewels, now stands a wooden figure with hardly a tallow candle to his name.

Menedemus. If what I hear is true, there's danger that other saints may come to the same pass.

Ogygius. More than that: a letter is going round which the Virgin Mary herself wrote on this very theme.

Menedemus. Which Mary?

Ogygius. The one called Mary a Lapide.

Menedemus. At Basel, unless I'm mistaken.

Ogygius. Yes.

Menedemus. Then it's a stony saint you tell me of. But to whom did she write?

Ogygius. She herself gives the name in the letter.

Menedemus. Who delivered the letter?

Ogygius. Undoubtedly an angel, who placed it on the pulpit from which the recipient preaches. And to prevent suspicion of fraud, you shall see the very autograph.

Menedemus. So you recognize the hand of the angel who is the Virgin's secretary?

Ogygius. Why, of course.

Menedemus. By what mark?

Ogygius. I've read Bede's epitaph, which was engraved by an angel.[6] The shape of the letters agrees entirely. Also I've read the manuscript message to St. Giles.[7] They agree. Aren't these facts proof enough?

Menedemus. Is one allowed to see it?

Ogygius. Yes, if you'll promise to keep your mouth shut about it.

---

[6]In the abbey church at Durham. The word *venerabilis* was said to have been added to the epitaph of the scholar Bede (c. 673–735) by the hand of an angel.
[7]Legend said that when St. Giles (eighth century) interceded with God for the remission of the king's sins, an angel appeared and placed on the altar a scroll, which announced that the sins were forgiven.

Menedemus. Oh, to tell me is to tell a stone.

Ogygius. But some stones[8] are notorious for giving secrets away.

Menedemus. Then tell it to a deaf man, if you don't trust a stone.

Ogygius. On that condition I'll read it. Lend me your ears.

Menedemus. I've lent them.

Ogygius. "Mary, Mother of Jesus, to Glaucoplutus:[9] greetings. Know that I am deeply grateful to you, a follower of Luther, for busily persuading people that the invocation of saints is useless. For up to this time I was all but exhausted by the shameless entreaties of mortals. They demanded everything from me alone, as if my Son were always a baby (because he is carved and painted as such at my bosom), still needing his mother's consent and not daring to deny a person's prayer; fearful, that is, that if he did deny the petitioner something, I for my part would refuse him the breast when he was thirsty. And sometimes they ask of a Virgin what a modest youth would hardly dare ask of a bawd—things I'm ashamed to put into words. Sometimes a merchant, off for Spain to make a fortune, commits to me the chastity of his mistress. And a nun who has thrown off her veil and is preparing to run away entrusts me with her reputation for virtue—which she herself intends to sell. A profane soldier, hired to butcher people, cries upon me, 'Blessed Virgin, give me rich booty.' A gambler cries, 'Help me, blessed saint; I'll share my winnings with you!' And if they lose at dice, they abuse me outrageously and curse me, because I wouldn't favor their wickedness. A woman who abandons herself to a life of shame cries, 'Give me a fat income!' If I refuse anything, they protest at once, 'Then you're no mother of mercy.'

"Some people's prayers are not so irreverent as absurd. An unmarried girl cries, 'Mary, give me a rich and handsome bridegroom.' A married one, 'Give me fine children.' A pregnant woman, 'Give me an easy delivery.' An old woman, 'Give me a long life without a cough or a thirst.' A doddering old man, 'Let me grow young again.' A philosopher, 'Give me power to contrive insoluble problems.' A priest, 'Give me a rich benefice.' A bishop, 'Preserve my church.' A sailor, 'Give me prosperous sailings.' A governor, 'Show me thy Son before I die.' A courtier, 'Grant that at point of death I may confess sincerely.' A countryman, 'Give me a heavy rain.' A country woman, 'Save the flock and herd from harm.' If I deny anything, straightway I'm cruel. If I refer to my Son, I hear, 'He wills whatever you will.' So am I alone, a woman and a virgin, to assist those who are sailing, fighting, trading, dicing, marrying, bearing children; to assist governors, kings, and farmers?

"What I've described is very little in comparison with what I endure. But nowadays I'm troubled much less by these matters. For this reason I would give you my heartiest thanks, did not this advantage bring a greater disadvantage along with it. I have more peace, but less honor and wealth. Formerly, I was hailed as 'Queen of Heaven, mistress of the world'; now I hear scarcely an 'Ave Maria' even from a few. Formerly I was clothed in gold and jewels; I had many changes of dress; I had golden and jeweled offerings made to me. Now I have hardly half a cloak to wear, and that one is mouse-eaten. My annual income is scarcely enough to keep the wretched sacristan who lights the little lamp or tallow candle. And yet all these hardships I could have borne, if you weren't said to be plotting even greater ones. You're trying, they say, to remove from the churches whatever belongs to the saints. Now just consider what you're doing. Other saints have means of avenging injuries. If Peter is ejected from a church, he can in turn shut the gate of heaven against you. Paul has a sword; Bartholomew is armed with a knife. Under his

[8]Touchstones, which tell whether supposed gold is true or not. [9]"Owl-rich," a play on the first name of Ulrich Zwingli (1484–1531), the Swiss religious reformer. When this letter was later censured by the theology faculty of the Sorbonne, Erasmus replied that it had been directed against the Protestant Zwinglians.

monk's robe William is completely armed, nor does he lack a heavy lance. And what could you do against George, with his horse and his coat of mail, his spear and his terrible sword? Anthony's not defenseless, either: he has his sacred fire.[10] Others likewise have weapons or mischiefs they direct against anybody they please. But me, however defenseless, you shall not eject unless at the same time you eject my Son whom I hold in my arms. From him I will not be parted. Either you expel him along with me, or you leave us both here, unless you prefer to have a church without Christ. I wanted you to know this. Think carefully what to answer, for my mind's absolutely made up. From our stony house, on the Calends of August, in the year of my Son's passion 1524. I, the Virgin a Lapide, have signed this with my own hand."

Menedemus. A dreadful, threatening letter, indeed! I imagine Glaucoplutus will take warning.

Ogygius. If he's wise.

Menedemus. Why didn't the excellent James write to him on this same subject?

Ogygius. I don't know, except that he's rather far away, and all letters are intercepted nowadays.

Menedemus. But what fortune brought you back to England?

Ogygius. An unexpectedly favorable breeze carried me there, and I had virtually promised the saint-by-the-sea that I would pay her another visit in two years.

Menedemus. What were you going to ask of her?

Ogygius. Nothing new, just the usual things: family safe and sound, a larger fortune, a long and happy life in this world, and eternal bliss in the next.

Menedemus. Couldn't the Virgin Mother here at home see to those matters? At Antwerp she has a church much grander than the one by the sea.

Ogygius. I can't deny that, but different things are bestowed in different places, either because she prefers this or (since she is obliging) because she accommodates herself in this respect to our feelings.

[Ogygius then describes his pilgrimage to Virgin-by-the-sea in England.]

Menedemus. Did you overlook Thomas, Archbishop of Canterbury?[11]

Ogygius. By no means. No pilgrimage is more devout.

Menedemus. I long to hear about it, if that's not too much trouble.

Ogygius. Oh, no, I want you to hear. There's a section of England called Kent, facing France and Flanders. Its chief city is Canterbury. In it are two monasteries, almost adjacent, both of them Benedictine houses. That named for St. Augustine is evidently the older; the one now called after St. Thomas appears to have been the Archbishop's seat, where he used to live with a few chosen monks; just as today, too, bishops have residences adjoining the churches but apart from the houses of other canons. (In old time both bishops and canons were usually monks; evidence abounds to prove that.) The church sacred to St. Thomas rises to the sky so majestically that it inspires devotion even in those who see it from afar. Thus by its splendor it now dims the glory of the neighboring one and, so to speak, overshadows the spot that was anciently the most sacred. It has two huge towers, as though greeting visitors a long way off and making the region ring far and wide with the wonderful sound of its bronze bells. At the south entrance of the church are stone statues of three armed men, who with sacrilegious hands murdered the blessed saint. Their surnames are added: Tusci, Fusci, Berri.[12]

---

[10]St. William of Gellone, called Duke of Aquitaine, was a soldier in the service of Charlemagne, who fought against the Saracens. According to various traditions, St. Peter held the keys to the kingdom of heaven (cf. Mt. 16:19); Saints Paul and Bartholomew displayed emblems representing the method of their execution, a sword and a knife (for flaying), respectively; St. George, the patron saint of England, slew a dragon; and St. Anthony was credited with the maritime weapon of erysipelas, a fire sprayed on enemy ships and crews.

[11]Thomas à Becket (1118–1178), English martyr and focus of a hugely popular saint's cult during the late Middle Ages.
[12]William de Tracy, Reginald Fitzurse, and Richard le Breton or Brito. Erasmus omits the name of the fourth, Hugh de Morville.

Menedemus. Why is so much honor paid to impious men?

Ogygius. Obviously they have the same honor as Judas, Pilate, and Caiaphas,[13] that band of wicked soldiers whom you see carefully carved on gilded altars. The surnames are added lest anybody in the future speak well of them. Attention is called to them in order that hereafter no courtier lift a hand against bishops or Church property. For those three conspirators went mad after committing their crime, and would not have recovered had they not begged help of the most holy Thomas.

Menedemus. O the everlasting mercy of martyrs!

Ogygius. When you enter, the spacious grandeur of the building is disclosed. This part is open to the public.

Menedemus. Is there nothing to see there?

Ogygius. Nothing but the mass of the structure, and some books—among them the Gospel of Nicodemus—fastened to pillars, and a tomb, I don't know whose.

Menedemus. Then what?

Ogygius. Iron screens prevent you from going any farther, but they permit a view of the space between the end of the building and the choir, as it is called. This is ascended by many steps, under which a certain vault gives access to the north side. A wooden altar sacred to the Holy Virgin is shown there; a very small one, not worth seeing except as a monument of antiquity, a rebuke to the luxury of our times. There the holy man is said to have spoken his last farewell to the Virgin when death was at hand. On the altar is the point of the sword with which the crown of the good bishop's head was cut off, and his brain evident smashed to make death come more quickly. Out of love for the martyr we reverently kissed the sacred rust of this sword.

Leaving this place, we went into the crypt. It has its own custodians. First is shown the mar-

tyrs' skull,[14] pierced through. The top of the cranium is bared for kissing, the rest covered with silver. Along with this is displayed a leaden plate with "Thomas of Acre"[15] carved on it. The hair shirt, girdle, and drawers by which the bishop used to subdue his flesh hang in the gloom there—horrible even to look at, and a reproach to our softness and delicacy.

Menedemus. Perhaps to the monks themselves, too.

Ogygius. I can neither affirm nor deny that, nor is it any of my business.

Menedemus. Very true.

Ogygius. From here we return to the choir. On the north side mysteries are laid open. It is wonderful how many bones were brought forth—skulls, jaws, teeth, hands, fingers, whole arms, all of which we adored and kissed.[16] This would have gone on forever if my fellow pilgrim, a disagreeable chap, had not cut short the enthusiasm of the guide.

Menedemus. Who was this?

Ogygius. An Englishman named Gratian Pullus,[17] a learned and pious man but less respectful toward this side of religion than I liked.

Menedemus. Some Wycliffite,[18] I suppose.

Ogygius. I don't think so, though he had read his books. Where he got hold of them isn't clear.

Menedemus. Did he offend the guide?

Ogygius. An arm was brought forth, with the bloodstained flesh still on it. He shrank from kissing this, looking rather disgusted. The custodian soon put his things away. Next we viewed the altar table and ornaments; then the

---

[13]The apostle, Roman procurator, and Sanhedrin judge responsible for the death of Jesus, thus a parallel to the assassination of Becket.

[14]Probably the newly acquired relic of St. Dunstan (c. 909–988), which had recently been enclosed in a mitred bust of silver.

[15]There was a legend that the saint's mother was a Saracen.

[16]The relics, we are told, included part of the table at which the Last Supper was eaten and some of the clay out of which God made Adam.

[17]Pullus ("colt") is undoubtedly John Colet (c. 1466–1519), the dean of St. Paul's and a friend and patron of Erasmus.

[18]I.e., one of the followers of the condemned English heretic John Wycliffe (c. 1330–1384), popularly known by the sixteenth century as Lollards.

objects that were kept under the altar—all of them splendid; you'd say Midas and Croesus were beggars if you saw the quantity of gold and silver.

Menedemus. No kisses here?

Ogygius. No, but a different sort of desire came to my mind.

Menedemus. What was it?

Ogygius. I was sad because I had no such relics at home.

Menedemus. A sacrilegious wish!

Ogygius. Admitted, and I begged the saint's forgiveness before I left the church. After this we were conducted to the sacristy. Good Lord, what an array of silk vestments there, what an abundance of gold candelabra! There, too, we saw St. Thomas' staff. It looked like a cane plated with silver. It was not at all heavy, had no ornamentation, and was no more than waist-high.

Menedemus. No cross?[19]

Ogygius. None that I saw. We were shown a pallium, silk to be sure, but coarse, without gold or jewels, and there was a facecloth, soiled by sweat from his neck and preserving obvious spots of blood. These memorials of the plain living of olden times we gladly kissed.

Menedemus. They're not shown to everyone?

Ogygius. Certainly not, my good friend.

Menedemus. How did you manage to make such an impression of devoutness that no secrets were kept from you?

Ogygius. I had some acquaintance with the Reverend Father William Warham,[20] the Archbishop. He gave me a note of recommendation.

Menedemus. I hear from many persons that he is a man of remarkable kindness.

Ogygius. More than that: you would call him kindness itself if you knew him. His learning, integrity, and holiness of life are so great that you would find him lacking in no quality befit-

ting a perfect prelate. Next we were led up above, for behind the high altar you ascend as though into a new church. There, in a small chapel, is shown the entire face of the saint, gilded, and ornamented with many jewels. Here a certain unlooked-for accident almost upset all our good luck.

Menedemus. I'm waiting to hear what misfortune you mean.

Ogygius. My friend Gratian made a *faux pas* here. After a short prayer, he asked the keeper, "I say, good father, is it true, as I've heard, that in his lifetime Thomas was most generous to the poor? "Very true," the man replied, and began to rehearse the saint's many acts of kindness to them. Then Gratian: "I don't suppose his disposition changed in this matter, unless perhaps for the better." The custodian agreed. Gratian again: "Since, then, the saint was so liberal towards the needy, although he was still poor himself and lacked money to provide for the necessities of life, don't you think he'd gladly consent, now that he's so rich and needs nothing, if some poor wretched woman with hungry children at home, or daughters in danger of losing their virtue because they have no money for dowries, or a husband sick in bed and penniless—if, after begging the saint's forgiveness, she carried off a bit of all this wealth to rescue her family, as though taking from one who wanted her to have it, either as a gift or a loan?" When the keeper in charge of the gilded head made no reply to this, Gratian, who's impulsive, said, "For my part, I'm convinced the saint would even rejoice that in death, too, he could relieve the wants of the poor by his riches." At this the custodian frowned and pursed his lips, looking at us with Gorgon eyes, and I don't doubt he would have driven us from the church with insults and reproaches had he not been aware that we were recommended by the archbishop. I managed to placate the fellow by smooth talk, affirming that Gratian hadn't spoken seriously, but liked to joke; and at the same time I gave him some coins.

Menedemus. I quite approve of your sense of duty. But seriously, I wonder sometimes what

---

[19]I.e., "No cross on the staff?" An archbishop's staff is surmounted by a cross.

[20]Archbishop of Canterbury from 1504 to 1532. Erasmus, who owed much to his patronage, dedicated his edition of the New Testament (1516) to Warham.

possible excuse there could be for those who spend so much money on building, decorating, and enriching churches that there's simply no limit to it. Granted that the sacred vestments and vessels of the church must have a dignity appropriate to their liturgical use; and I want the building to have grandeur. But what's the use of so many baptisteries, candelabra, gold statues? What's the good of the vastly expensive organs, as they call them? (We're not content with a single pair, either.) What's the good of that costly musical neighing when meanwhile our brothers and sisters, Christ's living temples, waste away from hunger and thirst?

Ogygius. Every decent, sensible man favors moderation in these matters, of course. But since the fault springs from excessive devotion, it merits applause, especially when one thinks of the opposite vice in those who rob churches of their wealth. These gifts are generally given by kings and potentates, and would be worse spent on gambling and war. And removal of anything from there is, in the first place, regarded as sacrilege; next, those who are regular contributors stop their giving; above all, men are incited to robbery. Hence churchmen are custodians of these things rather than owners of them. In short, I'd rather see a church abounding in sacred furnishings than bare and dirty, as some are, and more like stables than churches.

Menedemus. Yet we read that in former times bishops were praised for selling the sacred vessels and using the money to relieve the poor.

Ogygius. They're praised today, too, but only praised. In my judgment, to imitate them is neither allowable nor agreeable. . . .

Menedemus. I long to hear the rest of the tale, so expect me as a guest for dinner. You'll tell it more comfortably there.

Ogygius. Well, thanks very much for inviting yourself, since so many who are pressed to come decline. But my thanks will be doubled if you'll dine at home today, for my time will be taken up with greeting my family. Besides, I have a plan more convenient for us both. Have lunch at *your* home tomorrow for me and my wife. Then I'll talk until dinner—until you admit you're satisfied; and if you like, we won't desert you even at dinner. What are you scratching your head for? You get dinner ready; we'll be sure to come.

Menedemus. I'd prefer stories I wouldn't have to pay for. All right: I'll furnish a bit of lunch, only it will be tasteless unless you season it with good stories.

Ogygius. But look here! Don't you itch to go on these pilgrimages?

Menedemus. Maybe I'll itch after you've finished talking. As matters stand now, I have enough to do by going on my Roman stations.[21]

Ogygius. Roman? You, who've never seen Rome?

Menedemus. I'll tell you. Here's how I wander about at home. I go into the living room and see that my daughter's chastity is safe. Coming out of there into my shop, I watch what my servants, male and female, are doing. Then to the kitchen, to see if any instruction is needed. From here to one place and another, observing what my children and my wife are doing, careful that everything be in order. These are my Roman stations.

Ogygius. But St. James will look after these affairs for you.

Menedemus. Sacred Scripture directs me to take care of them myself. I've never read any commandment to hand them over to saints.

---

[21]Processions to certain churches in Rome on certain days.

B. Contemptus Mundi

As many religious writers of the Middle Ages were fond of recalling, Jesus himself taught that "those who hate their life in this world will keep it for eternal life" [Jn 12:25]. Following the first outbreak of the devastating Black Death in the mid fourteenth century, this belief in the transitoriness of the world took on a new dimension for European Christians. In works of art, religious contempt for worldly things (*contemptus mundi*) found expression in rotting corpses or skeletons graphically reminding the viewer "once I was as you were; soon you will be as I am." The principal objective of these so-called macabre paintings and statues was to provoke a meditation on one's own death (*memento mori*) that would spur the Christian to cast off the pleasures and preoccupations of the world and instead embrace the spiritual pursuits that insured eternal happiness. Travelling mendicant preachers and other clerics preached a similar message, particularly to the prospering residents of wealthy city-states like Florence and Sienna. Although such reformers undoubtedly had less of an impact than they hoped to, they did succeed in promulgating a new degree of monastic-inspired piety among the laity. Through various methods of self-denial and discipline—such as self-flagellation and fasting—laypeople were thus able to "hate the world" even while they continued to live immersed in it.

1. Thomas à Kempis
THE IMITATION OF CHRIST (c. 1418)

One of the enduring products of the fourteenth-century *contemptus mundi* spirit was the growth of new voluntary religious societies among laypeople and clerics. One of these groups, the Brothers and Sisters of the Common Life (also known as the Modern Devotion) consisted of small communities of lay and clerical Christians, who hoped to escape from the lures of the world and sought spiritual perfection through prayer, reading of Scripture, and contemplation. Active in northern Germany and the Netherlands, the Brothers and Sisters of the Common Life established communal homes for members as well as elementary schools for their children. It was typical of their supreme dedication to humility that their most famous composition, *The Imitation of Christ,* written by group member Thomas à Kempis (c. 1380–1471), was first published anonymously. À Kempis argued that the worldly achievements of great learning, wealth, or fame, along with a variety of simpler physical appetites, were all barriers to attaining true piety. The genuine imitation of Christ, according to him, required an all-consuming contempt of the world at every level. His practical guide, combining consolation and admonition, was one of the most popular works of the fifteenth and sixteenth centuries. Even after the Reformation brought on the decline of the group's houses and elementary schools, *The Imitation of Christ* continued to attract Protestant and Catholic admirers alike.

BOOK ONE: COUNSELS ON THE SPIRITUAL LIFE

Chapter 1: On the Imitation of Christ

"He who follows Me shall not walk in darkness," says Our Lord [Jn 8: 12].

In these words Christ counsels us to follow His life and way if we desire true enlightenment and freedom from all blindness of heart. Let the life of Jesus Christ, then, be our first consideration.

The teaching of Jesus far transcends all the teachings of the Saints, and whosoever has His spirit will discover concealed in it heavenly manna. But many people, although they often hear the Gospel, feel little desire to follow it, because they lack the spirit of Christ. Whoever desires to understand and take delight in the words of Christ must strive to conform his whole life to Him.

Of what use is it to discourse learnedly on the Trinity, if you lack humility and therefore displease the Trinity? Lofty words do not make a man just or holy; but a good life makes him dear to God. I would far rather feel contrition than be able to define it. If you knew the whole Bible by heart, and all the teachings of the philosophers, how would this help you without the grace and love of God? "Vanity of vanities, and all is vanity" [Eccl 1: 2], except to love God and serve Him alone. And this is supreme wisdom—to despise the world, and draw daily nearer the kingdom of heaven.

It is vanity to solicit honors, or to raise oneself to high station. It is vanity to be a slave to bodily desires, and to crave for things which bring certain retribution. It is vanity to wish for long life, if you care little for a good life. It is vanity to give thought only to this present life, and to care nothing for the life to come. It is vanity to love things that so swiftly pass away, and not to hasten onwards to that place where everlasting joy abides.

Keep constantly in mind the saying, "The eye is not satisfied with seeing, nor the ear filled with hearing" [Eccl 1:8]. Strive to withdraw your heart from the love of visible things, and direct your affections to things invisible. For those who follow only their natural inclinations defile their conscience, and lose the grace of God.

Chapter 2: On Personal Humility

Everyone naturally desires knowledge, but of what use is knowledge itself without the fear of God? A humble countryman who serves God is more pleasing to Him than a conceited intellectual who knows the course of the stars, but neglects his own soul. A man who truly knows himself realizes his own worthlessness, and takes no pleasure in the praises of men. Did I possess all knowledge in the world, but had no love [cf. 1 Cor 13:2], how would this help me before God, who will judge me by my deeds?

Restrain an inordinate desire for knowledge, in which is found much anxiety and deception. Learned men always wish to appear so, and desire recognition of their wisdom. But there are many matters, knowledge of which brings little or no advantage to the soul. Indeed, a man is unwise if he occupies himself with any things save those that further his salvation. A spate of words does nothing to satisfy the soul, but a good life refreshes the mind, and a clean conscience brings great confidence in God.

The more complete and excellent your knowledge, the more severe will be God's judgment on you, unless your life be the more holy. Therefore, do not be conceited of any skill or knowledge you may possess, but respect the knowledge that is entrusted to you. If it seems to you that you know a great deal and have wide experience in many fields, yet remember that there are many matters of which you are ignorant. So do not be conceited, but confess your ignorance. Why do you wish to esteem yourself above others, when there are many who are wiser and more perfect in the Law of God? If you desire to know or learn anything to your advantage, then take delight in being unknown and unregarded.

A true understanding and humble estimate of oneself is the highest and most valuable of all lessons. To take no account of oneself, but always to think well and highly of others is the highest wisdom and perfection. Should you see another person openly doing evil, or carrying out a wicked purpose, do not on that account consider yourself better than him, for you cannot tell how long you will remain in a state of grace. We are all frail; consider none more frail than yourself. . . .

Chapter 5: On Reading the Holy Scriptures

In the holy Scriptures, truth is to be looked for rather than fair phrases. All sacred scriptures should be read in the spirit in which they were written. In them, therefore, we should seek food for our souls rather than subtleties of speech, and we should as readily read simple and devout books as those that are lofty and profound. Do not be influenced by the importance of the writer, and whether his learning be great or small, but let the love of pure truth draw you to read. Do not inquire, "Who said this?" but pay attention to what is said.

Men pass away, but the word of the Lord endures forever [Ps 117:2].

God speaks to us in different ways, and is no respecter of persons. But curiosity often hinders us in the reading of the Scriptures, for we try to examine and dispute over matters that we should pass over and accept in simplicity. If you desire to profit, read with humility, simplicity, and faith, and have no concern to appear learned. Ask questions freely, and listen in silence to the words of the Saints; hear with patience the parables of the fathers, for they are not told without good cause.

Chapter 6: On Control of the Desires

Whenever a man desires anything inordinately, at once he becomes restless. A proud and avaricious man is never at rest; but a poor and humble man enjoys the riches of peace. A man who is not yet perfectly dead to self is easily tempted, and is overcome even in small and trifling things. And he who is weak in spirit, and still a prey to the senses and bodily passions, can only with great

difficulty free himself from worldly lusts. Therefore he is sad when he does so withdraw himself, and is quickly angered when anyone opposes him. Yet, if he obtains what he desires, his conscience is at once stricken by remorse, because he has yielded to his passion, which in no way helps him in his search for peace. True peace of heart can be found only by resisting the passions, not by yielding to them. There is no peace in the heart of a worldly man, who is entirely given to outward affairs; but only in a fervent, spiritual man.

Chapter 7: On Avoiding Vain Hope and Conceit

Whoever puts his confidence in men or in any creature is very foolish. Do not be ashamed to be the servant of others for love of Jesus Christ, and to appear poor in this world. Do not trust in yourself, but put your whole confidence in God. Do what you are able and God will bless your good intention. Do not trust in your own knowledge, nor in the cleverness of any man living, but rather in the grace of God, who aids the humble, and humbles the proud.

Do not boast of your possessions, if you have any, nor of the influence of your friends; but glory in God, who gives all things and desires above all things to give you Himself. Do not be vain about your beauty or strength of body, which a little sickness can mar and disfigure. Take no pleasure in your own ability and cleverness, lest you offend God, who has Himself bestowed on you all your natural gifts.

Do not esteem yourself better than others, lest you appear worse in the eyes of God, who alone knows the heart of man. Do not be proud of your good deeds, for God does not judge as men; and what delights men often displeases God. If you have any good qualities, remember that others have more; and so remain humble. It does you no harm when you esteem all others better than yourself, but it does you great harm when you esteem yourself above others. True peace dwells only in the heart of the humble: but the heart of the proud is ever full of pride and jealousy. . . .

Chapter 10: On Avoiding Talkativeness

Avoid public gatherings as much as possible, for the discussion of worldly affairs becomes a great hindrance, even though it be with the best of intentions, for we are quickly corrupted and ensnared by vanity. Often I wish I had remained silent, and had not been among men. But why is it that we are so ready to chatter and gossip with each other, when we so seldom return to silence without some injury to our conscience? The reason why we are so fond of talking with each other is that we think to find consolation in this manner, and to refresh a heart wearied with many cares. And we prefer to speak and think of those things which we like and desire, or of those which we dislike. Alas, however, all this is often to no purpose, for this outward consolation is no small obstacle to inner and divine consolation.

We must watch and pray, that our time may not be spent fruitlessly. When it is right and proper to speak, speak to edify. Evil habits and neglect of spiritual progress are the main cause of our failure to guard the tongue. But devout conversation on spiritual matters greatly furthers our spiritual progress, especially with those who are heart and soul with us in the service of God.

Chapter 11: On Peace, and Spiritual Progress

We could enjoy much peace if we did not busy ourselves with what other people say and do, for this is no concern of ours. How can anyone remain long at peace who meddles in other people's affairs; who seeks occasion to gad about, and who makes little or no attempt at recollection? Blessed are the single-hearted [cf. Mt 5:8], for they shall enjoy much peace.

How were some of the Saints so perfect and contemplative? It is because they strove with all their might to mortify in themselves all worldly desires, and could thus cling to God in their inmost heart, and offer themselves freely and wholly to Him. But we are held too firmly by our passions, and are too much concerned with the passing affairs of the world. We seldom completely master a single fault, and have little zeal for our daily progress; therefore we remain spiritually cold or tepid.

If only we were completely dead to self, and free from inner conflict, we could savor spiritual things, and win experience of heavenly contemplation. But the greatest, and indeed the whole obstacle to our advance is that we are not free from passions and lusts, nor do we strive to follow the perfect way of the Saints. But when we encounter even a little trouble, we are quickly discouraged, and turn to human comfort.

If we strove to stand firm in the struggle like men of valor, we should not fail to experience the help of our Lord from heaven. For He is ever ready to help all who fight, trusting in His grace; He also affords us occasions to fight that we may conquer. If we rely only on the outward observances of religion, our devotion will rapidly wane. But let us lay the axe to the root that, being cleansed from our passions, we may possess our souls in peace.

If each year we would root out one fault, we should soon become perfect. But, alas, the opposite is often the case, that we were better and purer in the beginning of our conversion than after many years of our profession. Our zeal and virtue should grow daily; but it is now held to be a fine thing if a man retains even a little of his first fervor. If only we would do a little violence to ourselves at first, we would later be enabled to do everything easily and gladly.

It is hard to give up old habits, and harder still to conquer our own wills. But if you cannot overcome in small and easy things, how will you succeed in greater? Resist your evil inclinations in the beginning, and break off evil habits, lest they gradually involve you in greater difficulties. Oh, if you could only know how great a peace for yourself and how great a joy for your fellows your good endeavor would win, you would have greater care for your spiritual progress.

Chapter 12: On the Uses of Adversity

It is good for us to encounter troubles and adversities from time to time, for trouble often compels a man to search his own heart. It reminds him that he is an exile here, and that he can put his trust in nothing in this world. It is good, too, that we sometimes suffer opposition, and that men think ill of us and misjudge us, even when we do and mean well. Such things are an aid to humility, and preserve us from pride and vainglory. For we more readily turn to God as our inward witness, when men despise us and think no good of us.

A man should therefore place such complete trust in God, that he has no need of comfort from men. When a good man is troubled, tempted, or vexed by evil thoughts, he comes more clearly than ever to realize his need of God, without whom he can do nothing good. Then, as he grieves and laments his lot, he turns to prayer amid his misfortunes. He is weary of life, and longs for death to release him, that he may be dissolved, and be with Christ. It is then that he knows with certainty that there can be no complete security nor perfect peace in his life. . . .

Chapter 14: On Avoiding Rash Judgments

Judge yourself, and beware of passing judgment on others. In judging others, we expend our energy to no purpose; we are often mistaken, and easily sin. But if we judge ourselves, our labor is always to our profit. Our judgment is frequently influenced by our personal feelings, and it is very easy to fail in right judgment when we are inspired by private motives. Were God Himself the sole and constant object of our desire, we should not be so easily distressed when our opinions are contradicted.

Very often some inner impulse or outward circumstance draws us to follow it, while many people are always acting in their own interest, although they are not conscious of it. Such appear to enjoy complete tranquillity of mind so long as events accord with their wishes, but at once become distressed and disconsolate when things fall out otherwise. Similarly, differences of opinions and beliefs only too often give rise to quarrels among friends and neighbors, and even between religious and devout people.

Old habits are hard to break, and no one is easily weaned from his own opinions; but if you rely on your own reasoning and ability rather than on the virtue of submission to Jesus Christ, you will but seldom and slowly attain wisdom. For God wills that we become perfectly obedient to Himself, and that we transcend mere reason on the wings of a burning love for Him. . . .

Chapter 20: On the Love of Solitude and Silence

Choose a suitable time for recollection and frequently consider the loving-kindness of God. Do not read to satisfy curiosity or to pass the time, but study such things as move your heart to devotion. If you avoid unnecessary talk and aimless visits, listening to news and gossip, you will find plenty of suitable time to spend in meditation on holy things. The greatest Saints used to avoid the company of men whenever they were able, and chose rather to serve God in solitude.

A wise man once said "As often as I have been among men, I have returned home a lesser man."[22] We often share this experience, when we spend much time in conversation. It is easier to keep silence altogether than not to talk more than we should. It is easier to remain quietly at home than to keep due watch over ourselves in public. Therefore, whoever is resolved to live an inward and spiritual life must, with Jesus, withdraw from the crowd. No man can live in the public eye without risk to his soul, unless he who would prefer to remain obscure. No man can safely speak unless he who would gladly remain silent. No man can safely com-

---

[22]A reference to the ancient Roman statesman and philosopher, Seneca (4 B.C.E.–65 C.E.).

mand, unless he who has learned to obey well. No man can safely rejoice, unless he possesses the testimony of a good conscience.

The security of the Saints was grounded in the fear of God, nor were they less careful and humble because they were resplendent in great virtues and graces. But the security of the wicked springs from pride and presumption, and ends in self-deception. Never promise yourself security in this life, even though you seem to be a good monk or a devout hermit. . . .

Chapter 23: A Meditation on Death

Very soon the end of your life will be at hand: consider, therefore, the state of your soul. Today a man is here; tomorrow he is gone. And when he is out of sight, he is soon out of mind. Oh, how dull and hard is the heart of man, which thinks only of the present, and does not provide against the future! You should order your every deed and thought, as though today were the day of your death. Had you a good conscience, death would hold no terrors for you; even so, it were better to avoid sin than to escape death. If you are not ready to die today, will tomorrow find you better prepared? Tomorrow is uncertain; and how can you be sure of tomorrow?

Of what use is a long life, if we amend so little? Alas, a long life often adds to our sins rather than to our virtue!

Would to God that we might spend a single day really well! Many recount the years since their conversion, but their lives show little sign of improvement. If it is dreadful to die, it is perhaps more dangerous to live long. Blessed is the man who keeps the hour of his death always in mind, and daily prepares himself to die. If you have ever seen anyone die, remember that you, too, must travel the same road.

Each morning remember that you may not live until evening; and in the evening, do not presume to promise yourself another day. Be ready at all times, and so live that death may never find you unprepared. Many die suddenly and unexpectedly; for at an hour that we do not know the Son of Man will come. When your last hour strikes, you will begin to think very differently of your past life, and grieve deeply that you have been so careless and remiss. . . .

Dear soul, from what peril and fear you could free yourself, if you lived in holy fear, mindful of your death. Apply yourself so to live now, that at the hour of death, you may be glad and unafraid. Learn now to die to the world, that you may begin to live with Christ. Learn now to despise all earthly things, that you may go freely to Christ. Discipline your body now by penance, that you may enjoy a sure hope of salvation.

Foolish man, how can you promise yourself a long life, when you are not certain of a single day? How many have deceived themselves in this way, and been snatched unexpectedly from life! You have often heard how this man was slain by the sword; another drowned; how another fell from a high place and broke his neck; how another died at table; how another met his end in play. One perishes by fire, another by the sword, another from disease, another at the hands of robbers. Death is the end of all men; and the life of man passes away suddenly as a shadow.

Who will remember you when you are dead? Who will pray for you? Act now, dear soul; do all you can; for you know neither the hour of your death, nor your state after death. While you have time, gather the riches of everlasting life. Think only of your salvation, and care only for the things of God. Make friends now, by honoring the Saints of God and by following their example, that when this life is over, they may welcome you to your eternal home.

Keep yourself a stranger and pilgrim upon earth, to whom the affairs of this world are of no concern. Keep your heart free and lifted up to God, for here you have no abiding city. Daily direct your prayers and longings to Heaven, that at your death your soul may merit to pass joyfully into the presence of God. . . .

2. Bernadino da Siena

ON THE VANITY OF THE WORLD AND ESPECIALLY OF WOMEN (1425)

Bernadino da Siena (1380–1444) was perhaps the most popular preacher of the fifteenth century. During more than thirty years of travels throughout north and central Italy, he spread a message of repentance and moral reform to hundreds of thousands of eager listeners. As an Observant Franciscan, Bernadino felt nothing but contempt for the riches and conceits of the world. The usual targets of his sermons were usurers and other "cheats," heretics, unconverted Jews, and—as in this case—vain women. For Bernadino, trying to improve on nature in any way, whether through cosmetics or intellectual curiosity, was as serious a sin as adultery or blasphemy. His sermon combines humorous and occasionally crude anecdotes with scriptural exegesis to construct a powerful tirade against the seemingly innocuous subject of women's fashion. San Bernadino, as he was later known, personally played an enormous role in the spread of the *contemptus mundi* sentiment in Italy, in many respects paving the way for the brief theocracy of Savonarola in Florence during the 1490s. At the same time, his phenomenal success helped his own religious order, the Franciscans, grow from 20 small communities in Italy to 230 at the time of his death.

This is the Sermon on Worldly Vanity, Particularly among Women.

Odisti observantes vanitates supervacue [Ps 31:6]. These are the words of David the prophet. In the vernacular they say: "You have hated those who needlessly observe vanities."

What these words mean is that God has always borne a hatred for those men and women who, through vanity, dress better than they should or who [think more about their dress] than about anything else. Oh men! Oh women! When you think about the evil you have committed, you will abstain from it, and in the future you will do no more. Many men and many women think they have done just this. But still God hated them in three ways, and for three reasons God now hates us.

In particular, God abhors:

First, curiosity: *observantes*
Second, the vanity in us: *vanitates*
Third, superfluousness: *supervacue*

First, God abhors us for our curiosity—for example, *observantes*, when men and women turn to new fashions. Don't you know that harlots are the first to have all fashions? Isn't this what David says? *Ibunt in inventione sua* ["I left them to follow their own counsels" Ps 81:12].

However, [the psalmist] says *observantes* [about the] great amounts of cloth that are tossed into sleeves and puffs and ruffles and broad fringes. Or about the *berzi* [elaborate braided hairstyles] on your heads. What is a *berzo*? It is something that will bounce you into hell. You will bounce right in just as a cricket sometimes jumps into the hearthfire. That's why he says *vanitates*. Many women will tell me, "I just do so to please my husband. I don't want him to take it badly if I don't do what he wants, and I'm just trying to keep him happy as best as I can." I answer, "You must help him, but not to ruin himself, and yourself too." And remember that a custom that takes hold of others will seem of great importance. Here is an example: There once was a man who emptied privies: that was his trade and his profession. It happened that once when he was in Venice, he passed by the druggists' shops. Surrounded by these shops and their many perfumes, he unexpectedly fell to the ground in a dead faint. A doctor was sent for right away, but he couldn't tell what was wrong with him. Other doctors were fetched, and finally one of them asked what his trade was. When he heard that the man was a privy cleaner, this doctor said, "Bring in some stable manure or some other stinking stuff." He put it to the man's nose and on his wrists and the man came to immediately because this was what he was used to. You laugh, but this is something to weep about! This is the stink of the woman who gets all dressed up, and who stinks to her own husband, but still she's never satisfied with him. This is [the stink of] the sodomite, who has no odor only among the dregs of society of sodomy. And I tell you, I am here to admonish you for your sins, men and women alike.

[God's] second abhoration: *supervacue*, [superfluous] assiduously. Take a look at the women: over and above all her other vices, look at the *cioppe* [overdresses] in her coffers and hanging from her clothes poles, and all the coffers and the poles are groaning under their loads. You can see the poor, naked man, dying of the cold, and you're busy clothing your clothes poles! You will answer to God for this. . . .

These are the reasons—vanity, curiosity, and superfluousness—for God's hatred toward you, because [such behavior] spites heaven, because it harms you yourself, and because it brings harm to your neighbor.

First, because it spites heaven. You will hear the seven reasons why you are all heading for damnation and are an offense to God:

First, by trying to improve on God

Second, by willfully refusing to conform to His will

Third, by buzzing in the temple of God

Fourth, by offending God

Fifth, by besmirching Mary in your praise of her

Sixth, by provoking the angels

Seventh, by setting the archangels against you

First, by trying to improve on God in his good and holy works. I am speaking generally, to men and women, young and old, humble and great, but more particularly to women than to men.

What do you think, woman: is it a sin or an insult to God to make yourself into something that you are not? As Cyprian and Scotus say, according to Augustine in Book 4 of *On Christian Doctrine*:[23] *Si quis pingendi artifex vultum aut speciem* ["If an artist had depicted the face and form of a man"], etc., if there were a most renowned and skillful master painter who made a portrait of Our Lady, or else a [picture] of her with her son in her arms—beautiful, well composed, pleasing and of pious aspect, and someone of less skill or who didn't know what he was doing attempted to improve upon the portrait by adding something, and if he then took an oven whiskbroom or his bare hands and set about rubbing the face, how much would he be wronging the master who painted [the face]? For He is the first painter and you, who know nothing about painting, are spoiling it. And you set yourself up against the will of God when you make a shame of the face he gave you, spoiling it with your smearings. Where you're white, you make yourself red, where you're red, you make yourself white. Where you're yellow, you color yourself, where you're curly, you make yourself cleanshaven. If you're big you belt yourself in until you burst, and if you're thin you pad yourself with cotton batting, and if you're short, you want high *pianelle* [wooden clogs]. Whether you're dark or fair or however you are, you spoil the image that God gave you. And then they tell their confessors, "We do it to please our husbands." You're lying in your throats! And the confessors are fooled by you if they believe it, and

---

[23]Obviously, Augustine (354–430) could not have cited an opinion of the fourteenth-century Franciscan theologian Duns Scotus. "Scote" is probably a scribal corruption of Ambrose (c. 339–397), whose teaching, together with Cyprian's, was cited by Augustine.

they are fooling you by their generosity to you. That's why I beg you—so that you won't have to confess something that seems shameful to you—don't ever dirty up your face, either in your bedroom or in any other place. Don't make yourself appear beautiful in public and ugly at home. Do the opposite and I'll believe that you are trying to please your husband. Be ugly when you're outside your house, and make yourself beautiful at home for love of your husband, and you will please him and content him in every way. And if you do the contrary, every bit of disgust you raise in him will push him into shame, to the harm and discontent of your soul and his own. When he sees that you get all dressed up to go out, he will immediately become suspicious and think that you aren't faithful to him, and then he'll fall into all the sins of sodomy, etc. This is why David says, *Abstitit regina a dextris tuis in vestitu deaurato, circumdata varietate* ["The princess is decked in her chamber with gold-woven robes; in many-colored robes she is led to the king" Ps 45:31]. Thus every star is in its proper place and often little is better than a lot. You can see that a peppercorn is intrinsically better than a whole heap of dung. I can also tell you that I know of few beautiful women who are loved—and who perhaps also love—or whose husbands are not always suspicious and jealous. So don't make yourself otherwise than the way God made you. If God made you beautiful, God gave you a great misfortune, if you only knew it; but if you know how to behave properly, you will be greatly rewarded in eternal life.

I'm talking about beautiful and ugly women alike. Certainly, God does not care more about the great than the humble, about young women more than the old; God loves without measure all who do his will. So don't try to improve on God. This is what Augustine says (just like Ambrose and Jerome[24]) in Book 4 of *Christian Doctrine* to those who change the face God gave them. How will you dare to appear before God? God won't even recognize you. As

Saint Matthew says, *Amen dico vobis, nescio vos,* "truly, I say to you, I do not know you," [Mt 25:12] because you don't have the face I gave you, because you have smeared it and dirtied it up to seem more beautiful than I made you.

Second, not conforming to God's will. When you say the "Our Father," pay attention to the phrase that says, *Fiat voluntas tua.* One woman says, "Thy will be done on earth as it is in heaven." She may say so, but see how she spoils what He has made. *Omnia in sapientia fecisti* ["In wisdom hast thou made them all." Ps 104:24]. Therefore, since you have been made by the will of God, why do your actions contradict what you say you want? Don't you see that in what you say—in the prayer you say that God's will should be done in earth as in heaven—you are twisting that prayer around? So you don't want [God's will] to be done, even in heaven. If your hair is falling out, it is perhaps all right to fix it so you don't look bald. Go ahead and do it, but don't overdo it. If it's the custom to go around with a full head of hair, you don't have to do so. However, don't deceive yourself. And don't change your hair color to gold or white: have the amount of hair and the kind of hair that looks like your own. And if you have [plenty of] hair on your head, why do you set yourself to making it blond, smearing it with so much stuff, drying your head in the sun, wetting it and drying it, wetting it and drying it? Don't you see how much harm this does? It leads to headaches, deafness, rotted teeth, and bad breath. Be content, like the canary, who may be tiny but still doesn't envy the ass, who is so big. Each of them sings in his own way, too, and the ass doesn't envy the nightingale for his song or the canary either.

Third, you make God hate you for your buzzing about in the temple of God. In church there is so much competition among these women, who are so tense that they seem to have mattress-beaters up their spines, each thinking herself the most beautiful. Oxen go plowing up and down and they all pull together, but each mother is just delighted when her daughter is courted. Oh you mothers! If you behave this way,

---

[24]Other church fathers of the fourth century.

remember that you will lead this daughter of yours to perdition, and perhaps you have already done so. Now just think how many evils were committed during the three holy days of Holy Week, when everyone ought to be weeping, and you were glowering at one another. Oh, how embarrassed I was! It seemed that these things were going on to spite God. You will say, "I wanted to show off my daughter." [Listen to this] example. There is in the world a city in which barefooted women are displayed and measured against a wall to see how tall they are. A man once came to take [a wife] there, and everybody measured her as was the custom, and when he had seen her, they asked him if she pleased him. He answered that he would think about it. At this point the woman said, "So this man says he'll think about it? He can just go and think about it all he wants, for I have thought about it and I don't want him, since he looks first and then thinks about it." To be sure, he was a short man and she was half a *braccio* [roughly an arm's length] taller than he.

Another man was interested in marrying his sister to someone, so he brought her to him so he could see her. Her charms were artificial, and when he realized it, he drew a knife and killed her.

Oh woman! You have already killed hundreds of souls with your face smearings, perhaps thousands. When will you ever repent? You there, you've sucked in perhaps a hundred young men; when will you repent? Solomon in chapter 7 says of the woman dressed like a harlot that she is wily of heart [Prov 7:10] and lies in wait [Prov 7:12], just as the Church attracts souls: *Ad capiendas animas*. She snared men like nightingales and chaffinches. And it doesn't even bother your conscience.

Fourth, don't you believe that Christ, the son of God, loves his father? Oh, when he sees so many great offenses to his magnificence, don't you think that grieves him? Why should that grieve God? Just because it is an offense to the Father. [Christ] came into this world to make peace between you and God, and you do just the opposite. You have been the cause of many shameful sins: usury, homicides, fornications, adulteries, and so forth.

Fifth, offense to the Virgin Mary if you have ever [profaned] a church or any other sanctified place: cathedrals, hospitals, etc. Don't you see that a church is [the same thing as] the saint to which the church is dedicated? Some who have been in the Holy Land say that no woman ever enters into a Saracen's temple while a man is inside, and when the men have left, the women come in. And all the men go barefoot and the women with their faces covered so they cannot be seen. And they pray to the devil with so much faith that they are sometimes off the ground in contemplation. When they hear of our ways they burst out laughing, and they're not far wrong. For my part, I think that more evil is committed in the cathedral on a solemn feast day than in a public place the whole week long. However, the minute they enter into the church, the Virgin Mary gives them her malediction when they act this way. It's the same for you, woman, when you enter the church with vanity: Mary immediately curses you. And let me warn you, don't ever go to a convent to amuse some nun, because when you leave the convent, she will swear at you and curse father, mother, and herself. For this reason, it's better not to go. Furthermore, you shouldn't put anyone into a convent who isn't eighteen years old; and if someone [younger] were put there, you should pay a certain amount [of dowry] for her. I don't want you meddling in these matters. Don't lay your hands on other people's forage, for it belongs to God. Leave to God what is God's, and you be master of your own affairs. Furthermore, I beg you, when country people come here, don't have them arrested for their debts. They come to the sermons to hear the word of God, and you have them hauled away for their debts! Be merciful!

Sixth, the angels despise you. Everyone has a guardian angel to watch over his soul, and when you do so much evil, your angel curses you. [All the angels] leave you and go away from you, and they curse the woman who was the cause of your bad actions as well. Souls are snared just like pigeons and doves, and the angels are just as sad about it as they are joyful over good [actions].

God, the saints, the apostles, and the angels all curse you for opposing the will of God; it is just as in this world when people love one another and one of them is hurt and they all despise the one who did the harm.

[My] second principal part [speaks of] you yourself. Now I want to give you the real medicine; what you have had so far is syrup. Regarding yourself, you will see seven ills.

First, the soul as the chamber of sins. If a woman is vain, she is a chamber of haughty superiority. Oh, how long they look at themselves before they leave the house! If she is haughty, it leads to the sin of vainglory as she preens and plucks herself. When she sees that someone else is more beautiful than she, envy is born, and if she cannot rival her beauty, she is bitter. Then she wants more clothes than she has, and if she doesn't get them, she gets angry. Thus she wears herself out, and she loses weight because she doesn't get to the [social] rank she would like. Then she stimulates [her appetite] with things to eat and drink, she warms up to the idea, and then comes gluttony. One thing follows another and every sin is born in her.

Second, the waste of time. If you thought of how much time is wasted and put that much effort into the salvation of your soul, you would be better off than Mary Magdalen. Saint Paul says, *Dum tempus habemus, operemur in bonum,* "while we have time let us do good" [Gal 6:10]. Job says, *Breves dies hominis sunt,* "Brief are men's days" [Job 14:5]. He has but a short time to be saintly and good. . . .

Third, you lose every prayer that you say. Every church office, every psalm, and every mass. Paul says to Timothy, *Non in tortis crinibus et vestitu pretioso* ["Women should adorn themselves modestly and sensibly in seemly apparel, not with braided hair, or gold, or pearls, or costly attire." 1 Tim 2:9]. All Lombardy has borrowed the custom of curly hair from Siena. Oh, woe to the person who started this fashion!

Fourth, you get yourselves all excited. Just like a bitch—when a bitch needs a dog, all the dogs come following along behind her. And when she doesn't, they don't. This is like a woman who can be known by her eyes, and you had better get it straight that more can be understood by acts than by words. David the prophet says of this, *Illi maledicent et tu benedices* ["They will curse and you will bless." Ps 108:28]. [For] example, when you want to sell a horse in the piazza, you put straw on his head. This seems crazy to someone who sees this sign but asks "Is that horse for sale?" Someone who understands it will ask how much you want for the horse. This is what happens when a woman dresses in finery and adorns herself: she is for sale to lovers. Sometimes it's the mother who beautifies her and dresses her up, and that beautifying is what arouses love in the girl's lover. And the mother is a procuress for having beautified her that way.

Fifth, when a woman is vain, what you should do is think about providing a dowry, not satisfy her [wishes] with all the clothes she wants. And if her husband has only meager earnings, he won't be able to eat except by her dowry, if it's a good one. So if she keeps all her dowry in her clothes chests, she may force her husband to enter into unfavorable contracts, because she has pushed him to spend beyond his capabilities.

Sixth, vanity often makes your will vacillate, for often it's like the blowfly that flies into a lamp and buzzes around and around. That's what a lover does: he buzzes around the vain woman until he finally makes her fall by promising, "I'll take you to wife; I love you so; you're the one I'm yearning for," etc. So don't ever believe anyone, because they'll all trick you and then tell everyone about it. And if in any way you give in, everywhere you go you'll be ashamed. Don't listen to a single word, for he will say, "I'll keep it a secret," but it won't be true. As it has been said, *Nihil occultum quod non reveletur,* "There is no secret that will not be revealed" [Lk 12:2]. There are many mothers who'll be happy with their daughters [when this happens] because then they will be married. . . .

The third principal part is out of respect for your neighbor, and it concerns your husband's soul. [God] says, "I will make him a helper fit for him" [Gen 2:18] and he put [Adam's] body to profit. This is what happens when a man loves [his wife] too much. Likewise, you will see a woman is beautiful, but she is [as sharp] as Solomon's [two-edged] sword in Proverbs [5:4]. Thus she doesn't make up for the sin of not giving a good example. Thus she contaminates the other women with her scandal, for when one sees another wearing some new exaggeration, she immediately gets one for herself, just like a sheep.

[For] example, a man had to take some sheep across the sea, and when they had been far from land for quite a few days [the ship] arrived at a port. As they were approaching the port the sheep saw the land, and as ill luck would have it, one of them gave a jump and fell into the sea. All the others followed along behind and they were all drowned. This is what females do: if one could not do just what another does, she would die.

If you have loved your wife, she may say to you, "This is what I want! That's what so-and-so has! You don't love me! Now I see where your mind is! She's this and she's that! I'm prettier than she is! What kind of beauty do you call that? Now we'll see if what I've heard is true: don't you have enough troubles at home? You'd be a fine match for her! Now I'll just see what you think of me and if you love me!"

Similarly, if someone has stolen because of a woman, the woman who caused it all will have her share in the punishment. Do you know why? Because of those wide sleeves, without which you wouldn't dream of going out. And do you know what the devil says? He says, "I made him steal to make broad sleeves for my woman here." Another devil says, "I'll hold him fast so he won't give it back. Just leave it to me!"

Women's vanity is the destruction of a city, ruined by velvets and woolens, for if the same money were put into merchandise it would turn a good profit. But you keep it in your coffers along with your pearls, your other jewelry, your silver, and so forth. You know I speak the truth. Whole families are undone by the inordinate dowries that are given and that men taking a wife demand; if the dowry is not to their liking, they refuse to take her. This is why they give themselves over to the vice of sodomy, some to one kind of ribaldry, some to another, and every sort of vice is practiced. In this way, the population shrinks little by little. And in this way you lose your soul, your body, and your goods, as you have seen. This is why David says, *"Odisti observantes vanitates supervacue."*

So, my brothers, work for the common good and for the welfare of our city, so that you will have grace here and glory in eternal life. Amen.

C. Inquisition

During the first twelve hundred years of the Church's existence, the ultimate punishment for Christians deemed "heretics" (from Greek *haireisthai,* "to choose") was excommunication, or severance from the body of believers. Beginning in the early thirteenth century, though, a new method of detecting and punishing heretics was created. In 1208, as part of a crusade against dualist Cathar heretics in northern Italy and southern France, Pope Innocent III established special church courts known as "inquisitions" (Latin *inquisitio,* "investigation"). Initially these travelling courts relied on voluntary admissions or the testimony of at least two witnesses for conviction and usually prescribed some sort of penance, such as fasting, alms, or a pilgrimage. From 1252 on, however, the special investigators in charge, or inquisitors, were permitted to use torture with particularly obstinate subjects. After a suspect's coerced confession, the court's sentence was then announced in a "general sermon," known in Spain as the *auto da fé*. Even then, severe punishments such as confiscation of property, imprisonment, or execution remained more the exception than the rule. Throughout most of the Middle Ages, inquisitions operated on an ad hoc basis, and they had fallen into general disuse by the end of the fourteenth century. In 1479, though, the Spanish monarchies established their own standing inquisition, thereafter mostly used against recently converted Jews and Muslims. In 1542 Pope Paul III set up a permanent Roman Inquisition, known as the Holy Office, which served as the final instance of appeal for all heresy cases in the Catholic Church. The Spanish Inquisition was finally suppressed in 1834, and the Holy Office was reorganized in 1908 and again in 1965 to become the modern Congregation for the Propagation of the Faith.

1. Bernard Gui
MANUAL OF THE INQUISITOR (1323)

Bernard Gui (c. 1262–1331) was a Dominican friar and extremely successful inquisitor in southern France, personally presiding over the condemnation of more than 930 Cathar heretics, 42 of whom were "abandoned to the secular arm" for execution. Before returning he composed a manual for others of his profession. Most of his advice is eminently practical: know your foe, be ready for all types of tricks and evasions, always get as much information as possible out of each witness. Gui also provides guidelines for determining the proper punishment, thereby illustrating the range from the most common penances imposed (often pilgrimages) to the much rarer execution at the hands of secular authorities. At the outset of his work he describes "the five [heretical] sects," though in fact two of the groups he mentions—superficially converted Jews and magicians—were not really organized sects of any kind. The other three groups, however—the Waldensians, the Beguines, and the Cathars (known in France as Albigensians)—did pose an organized threat to the authority of the Catholic Church and thus were actively pursued by Gui and his fellow inquisitors. Though Waldensians and Beguines in fact survived into modern times, the inquisition's main nemesis, the Cathars, were effectively disbanded by the mid fourteenth century.

GENERAL INSTRUCTION

... It is very difficult to seize heretics if they do not confess their error openly, but conceal it, or if there is no certain and sufficient testimony against them. In that case the inquisitor is troubled on all sides. For, on one side, his conscience troubles him if someone is punished who has neither confessed nor been convicted. But if, on the other, people of whose falsity, cunning, and malice he has repeatedly been informed escape with the cleverness of foxes to do more damage to the faith, his heart is even more troubled, because as a result they are only strengthened, multiply, and acquire still more cunning. On yet another side, it scandalizes faithful laymen if an inquisition is undertaken against someone and then abandoned in frustration, as it were. When they see that learned men are duped by uneducated, base people, their faith weakens a little. They believe that we are able at any moment to explain the faith so lucidly and clearly that no one could withstand us without our being able instantly to refute him so clearly that even the laymen could understand why. This is why it is not profitable to dispute the faith in front of laymen with heretics as clever as this.

One should also point out that the same medicine does not heal all illnesses, because each illness has its own specific medicine. In the same way no unvarying method of interrogation, investigation, and examination should be used for every one of the heretics of the different sects. A method unique and specific to each must rather be used for individuals as well as for groups of people. Like a prudent doctor of souls, the inquisitor should consider the quality, condition, status, illness, and place of the people whom, or about whom, he is investigating. He should proceed cautiously in inquiring into and examining these matters, should not put, or persist in putting, all of the following questions in the same way and the same order to all people, and in the case of some people he should not be satisfied with having asked these particular questions, not even all of them, but should bridle the heretic's cunning with the harness of his discretion so that, with God's help, he can act the midwife and drag the winding snake from a bottomless bilge of errors.

A single, infallible rule can really not be given in these matters, or else the sons of darkness will have time to become familiar with the procedure, foresee it, avoid it the more easily, like a trap, and even manage to take precautions against it. A knowledgeable inquisitor will therefore carefully take his cue from the answers of the deponents, from the statements of the accusers, from what experience has taught him, from his own good judgment, or from the following questions or interrogations, whichever God may provide.

In order to familiarize the reader briefly with the method of examining the five sects, i.e., the Manichaeans, the Waldensians, also known as the Poor of Lyons, the pseudo-Apostles, those who are popularly known as the Beguines,[25] and Jewish converts to Christianity who return to the vomit of Judaism, as well as fortune-tellers, magicians, and those who pray to demons, pests which gravely interfere with the purity of the faith, we shall on the following pages methodically add certain observations, first describing the general substance of each sect's error, then adding the proper method of examination. This will become clear in the following. . . .

HOW TO AVOID THE CUNNING OF THE BEGUINES

. . . One must, therefore, safeguard oneself in one's investigation against the malice and the astuteness of such people. They must in all circumstances be forced to swear, simply and absolutely, without any conditions or reservations, that they will say the full truth, and nothing but the truth, about themselves as well as about their accomplices, believers, favorers, hosts, and defenders, according to the meaning of the inquisitor's questions, without bad faith or deceit, regardless whether they are confessing on their own or responding to the inquisitor's questions, about themselves or others, in the affirmative or negative, and all of this for the entire length of the inquisition. Otherwise they shall automatically bring perjury and the penalty thereof upon themselves.

One must avoid accepting an oath from them which is accompanied by any conditions

---

[25]"Manichaeans" refers to the Cathars, also known in southern France as Albigensians. Waldensians were followers of Peter Valdes (d. c. 1210) who rejected the authority of many clerics and believed in lay preaching. The Beguines and Beghards were found principally in the Netherlands and northern France and were suspect to Gui and others because of their close association with the outlawed Spiritual Franciscans and other advocates of radical apostolic poverty.

or reservations, or by a protestation like the one mentioned above. One must explain to them that, contrary to what they say they believe, it does not amount to offending God, and that God is in fact not offended, if a judge seeks the truth in order to discover error and heresy, and that they must stand by the judgment of the inquisitor in this matter, and not their false opinion.

Contrary to what they say, it really has nothing to do with wounding, or inflicting damage or injury on, a neighbor, but rather with helping him to his good and the salvation of his soul, when people who are infected by, and embroiled in, errors are denounced so that they can be corrected, turned back from their error to the way of truth, and better themselves, lest they become even more corrupt and infect and corrupt others with their errors.

But if they pertinaciously refuse to swear without said conditions and reservations, if, that is to say, they have not precisely sworn to say the full truth and nothing but the truth in the trial in which they are being charged, as has already been explained, they should first be admonished according to the rule of canon law. Someone who has been admonished and still refuses to swear shall be sentenced to excommunication in writing, unless he immediately swears the desired oath precisely, or at least swears at the hour, the day, or the time which the investigating judge may, out of his kindness or equity, have thought fit to give him as a last chance, even though legally he is obliged to swear precisely, simply, immediately, and without any delay. When the sentence of excommunication has been ordered, formulated, and issued, it shall be entered into the proceedings.

When someone has incurred a sentence of excommunication and has pertinaciously borne it with a hardened heart for several days, he shall be called back to trial and be asked if he considers himself excommunicated and bound by said sentence. If he answers that he does not consider himself excommunicated and bound by said sentence, he proves *ipso facto* that he obviously scorns the keys of the Church. This is a

definite case of error and heresy, and someone who pertinaciously perseveres in this belief must be considered a heretic. Both the question and his response shall be entered in the proceedings, and one should go on to prosecute him as the law demands, admonish him canonically, and warn him one last time to abandon and abjure such error and heresy. Otherwise he will from that time on be judged a heretic, will be condemned, and as such will be relinquished to the judgment of a secular court.

Note also that, in order to prove his malice, to make his error more obvious, and to justify the process against him, another, new sentence of excommunication may be issued in writing against him for contumacy in matters of faith, inasmuch as he pertinaciously refuses to swear simply and precisely, to answer questions concerning the faith and to abjure an express heretical error, thus manifestly dodging obedience, no less than one who has been summoned for some other reason and contumaciously absents himself. He shall be informed in writing that another sentence has been issued against him. Because, furthermore, he has been excommunicated for contumacy in matters of faith, he must and can be legally condemned as a heretic as soon as he has endured said sentence for more than one year with a stubborn heart.

Note, moreover, that, if anybody is willing to testify, one may proceed to hear witnesses against such a person, and that, in order to draw out the truth, he may be starved, imprisoned, or chained, and that, on the advice of experts, he may also be questioned, to the degree which the nature of the affair and the condition of his person may require.

ON THE INQUISITORS' SERMON IN GENERAL

When the confessions and depositions about heresy, harboring heretics, favoring heretics, regarding themselves or others, or whatever else may be within the competence of the inquisition, have been received from the confessors; when the defense of the dead and the living has been stated and been brought to a conclusion; when all statements of confession or defense have also been carefully and faithfully examined; and when advice has been sought and obtained from prelates and lawyers, then the inquisitors will proceed with the necessary solemnity to pronounce the sermon in which thanks are given, penances enjoined, and sentences issued according to the merits and demerits of everyone.

At a suitable time before the sermon, however, the inquisitors will seek advice from the aforementioned persons. First, a brief summary of offenses shall be compiled, in which the substance of everybody's confession concerning his own offense shall be completely dealt with, without mentioning any names, in order to ensure that the counsellors' decision on the penance to be imposed for every offense will be free of any personal regard. It is true that their advice would be more to the point if everything were recounted in detail. This procedure should therefore be followed where and when counsellors to whom these things can be revealed without any risk can be found. The risk of calumny would then also be smaller. But, because of the just mentioned danger, this has from the beginning not been the habit of the inquisition. A fully detailed account of everybody's confession, however, is given to the bishop or his vicar beforehand, in the presence of a few experts, secretaries, and jurors.

For one or two days before the sermon, furthermore, and in the presence of a notary and several witnesses, the inquisitor will read to everyone individually and separately a vernacular version of the summary of his offenses. He will likewise read it in the public sermon, addressing the person concerned and saying: "You such and such, from such and such a place, as is proved by your confession, have done such and such."

Likewise, on the day before the sermon, the inquisitor himself or his representative, whichever may seem better, will order each and everyone to appear the following day in the place where the public sermon will be given,

where they will receive their penance or hear their sentence, according to the nature of their offense. On the following day he will begin with the sermon early in the morning.

The following order applies to what should be done in the general sermon of inquisitors for heresy in the regions of Toulouse and Carcassone:

First of all, a sermon shall be given, which, considering how much is to be done, should be brief. Then the customary indulgence shall be granted.[26]

Second, the oath of the officers of the royal court, of the consuls, and of others present with temporal jurisdiction shall be received.

Third, crosses shall be taken off those to whom that grace is due.

Fourth, the men and women for whom it is judged expedient shall be led out of the prison, and crosses and pilgrimages shall be imposed on them.

Fifth, the offenses of those on whom penances or sentences are to be imposed shall be recounted and read in the vernacular in the following order: first, of those on whom discretionary penances are to be imposed, like going on pilgrimage, bearing the cross, and living according to certain general rules; then those who are to be immured simply; then those who must do penance for bearing false testimony and be immured; then, if there are any, the priests and clerics who are to be deposed and immured; then the dead of whom it must be made known that they would have had to be immured had they been alive; then those who died without repenting of their heresy, whose bodies are to be exhumed;[27] then fugitives who are to be condemned as heretics; then heretics who relapsed into a heresy which they had abjured in a trial, who are to be relinquished to the secular arm, first the laymen, then the

---

[26]Usually involving some form of penance and/or monetary fine.

[27]I.e., removed from the hallowed ground of a Christian cemetery and usually cremated, just as live heretics were burnt at the stake.

clerics, if there are any; then the perfect heretics, who refuse to turn away from heresy and to return to the unity of the Church, whether they are Manichaeans, Waldensians, or belong to the heretical sect of those who call themselves Beguines or the Poor of Christ, keep themselves separate from the community of the others, and weaken the power of Pope and Church; finally those who had confessed heresy in a previous trial and later revoked their confession, or whom witnesses overwhelmingly convicted of heresy and who still refuse to admit the truth even though they are unable to defend themselves against it, or clear themselves of it, in a trial, who are to be relinquished to the secular court as impenitent heretics.

Sixth, when the offenses have been recounted and before penances are to be imposed, penitents shall abjure their heresy and swear an oath to obey the orders of the Church and the inquisitors. Then they shall be absolved from the sentences of excommunication which have been promulgated by the law against such people in general, and which they are known in fact to have incurred because of their heretical offenses.

Seventh, the sentences shall be first read in Latin and then briefly explained in the vernacular, in the same order in which the offenses were read, if that is convenient to do. The number of people on whom penances, punishments, or sentences are to be imposed, however, is occasionally so great that such an order cannot very well be observed, but must be altered in some respects and within reasonable limits. It depends on the discretion of the judge to decide which order seems the most fitting and expedient to be observed. . . .

WHAT TO DO ABOUT HERETICS WHO REPENT AT THE MOMENT OF PUNISHMENT

If it happens, as has already more than once been the case, that someone has been relinquished and handed over to the secular arm and court, was re-

ceived by that court, has been led to the place of execution, and then says and asserts that he wants to do penance and to renounce his errors, then such a person must be kept alive and given back to the inquisitors. Unless he has perhaps relapsed again, the inquisitors must receive him, so as to put equity above rigor in this matter and avoid scandalizing those of little faith by the Church's denial of the sacrament of penance to someone seeking it. The office of the inquisition is known to have done something like this several times already.

In such a case the inquisitors must, however, exercise the greatest caution and carefully observe whether the conversion is true or simulated, since those who are converted on the point of death may well be suspected of having only acted out of fear of punishment. Let them be tested, to show whether they walk in darkness or in light, lest they act the wolf in sheep's clothing.

Whether or not they are honest can be reliably determined by the following methods and trials: they are, if they promptly and voluntarily denounce and reveal all their accomplices to the inquisitors; likewise, if they persecute their sect in signs, words, and actions, and humbly confess their old errors one by one and execrate and abjure them all in the same way. All of this can be evidently ascertained by examining them and reading their confession, which should be taken down in writing.

After such people have been received and have confessed in trial, they must with their own mouths revoke and execrate all the errors they held before, abjure each individual error as well as the whole of their heresy in public trial, confess the Catholic faith, and promise and swear whatever else is customary in the case of people received back from heresy. Finally, they shall be incarcerated forever in order to do penance, with the power to mitigate the sentence being reserved,[28] as is the custom.

---

[28]This power was usually reserved to the inquisition itself, although secular authorities sometimes also mitigated sentences.

Even though it is not common law to save them and receive them into penance after their sentence has been issued, as it has just been described, the office of the inquisition has nevertheless observed this procedure previously in several similar cases. Because it has the greatest privileges, and seeks the salvation of souls and the purity of the faith above all else, it is also the first to receive heretics into penance who wish to be converted and return to the unity of the Church. Through their confessions, moreover, accomplices and more errors are often discovered, the truth is found thereby and error revealed, and the office prospers.

But if such conversion seems more likely to be feigned or simulated to the inquisitors, the aforesaid procedures shall be stopped so that the sentence which has been issued may take effect.

D. Mysticism

Mysticism, a direct experience of the divine or ultimate reality, is by no means limited to any one era in the church's history or even to Christianity itself. Certainly many prominent members of the ancient church, most notably St. Augustine, described mystical experiences of their own, as did prominent figures of the High Middle Ages such as Hildegard of Bingen (1098–1179) and Bernard of Clairvaux (1090–1153). The mysticism of the fourteenth and fifteenth centuries, however, deserves special attention because it seems to have played a much greater role than ever before in the piety of many laypeople. While this was by no means a widespread phenomenon, the era did see an increasing number of ordinary Christians from all social backgrounds who expressed a desire to "know" God directly, a development that may have accounted for the great popularity of a work such as Thomas à Kempis's *Imitation of Christ,* with its step-by-step approach to the question. In most instances, though, the ineffable, or indescribable, nature of ecstatic union between Creator and created forced mystics to rely on allegories and poetic language in their attempts to convey the experience to others. Though the church hierarchy did not prohibit such personal quests, it also did not actively encourage them, particularly given the danger that an individual seeking mystical union with God might stray into heresy without proper clerical guidance. Rather, the mystical experiences of such remarkable individuals as Meister Eckhart and St. Catherine of Siena (1347–1380) were greeted as genuine but truly rare occurrences.

1. Meister Eckhart
SERMON (c. 1320)

Meister Eckhart (c. 1260–1327) came to his mystical approach to God slowly, only after having spent many years in more traditional intellectual pursuits. After studying theology at the universities of Paris and Cologne, he continued his quest for divine "knowledge" through a series of administrative posts in the Dominican Order. Eventually, while back in his native Germany, he decided that all efforts to "know" or even imagine God, no matter how learned, were doomed to failure because of the limitations of the human senses and mind. Instead, he argued that only through "unknowing," a type of self-annihilation and emptying, could the soul truly experience the indescribable divine spark, that "being" which every soul shared with the eternal God. While Meister Eckhart's vernacular sermons were very popularly received, some of his theological enemies detected a pantheistic taint to his teachings and succeeded in having him tried for heresy. Eckhart protested his orthodoxy, but he died before the trial was over. Upon completion of the trial, he was posthumously excommunicated, and all of his writings were ordered destroyed. Fortunately, although the bulk of his work was probably lost, some of Eckhart's dedicated followers, known as the Friends of God, were able to preserve a number of his sermons and other writings.

THIS IS MEISTER ECKHART FROM WHOM GOD NOTHING HID

Dum medium silentium tenerent omnia et nox in suo cursu medium iter haberet etc. [Wis 18:14]. "For while all things were in quiet silence and the night was in the midst of her course, etc." Here in time we make holiday because the eternal birth which God the Father bore and bears unceasingly in eternity is now born in time, in human nature. St. Augustine says this birth is always happening. But if it happen not in me what does it profit me? What matters is that it shall happen in me.

We intend therefore to speak of this birth as taking place in us: as being consummated in the virtuous soul, for it is in the perfect soul that God speaks his Word. What I shall say is true only of the perfected man, of him who has walked and is still walking in the way of God; not of the natural undisciplined man who is entirely remote from and unconscious of this birth.

There is a saying of the wise man: "When all things lay in the midst of silence then leapt there down into me from on high, from the royal throne, a secret word." This sermon is about this word.

Concerning it three things are to be noted. The first is, whereabouts in the soul God the Father speaks his Word, where she is receptive of this act, where this birth befalls. It is bound to be in the purest, loftiest, subtlest part of the soul. Verily, and God the Father in his omnipotence had endowed the soul with a still nobler nature, had she received from him anything yet more exalted, then must the Father have delayed this birth for the presence of this greater excellence. The soul in which this birth shall come to pass must be absolutely pure and must live in gentle fashion, quite peaceful and wholly introverted: not running out through the five senses into the manifoldness of creatures, but altogether within and harmonized in her summit. That is its place. Anything inferior is disdained by it.

The second part of this discourse has to do with man's conduct in relation to this act, this interior speaking, this birth: whether it is more profitable to cooperate in it—perhaps by creating in the mind an imaginary image and disciplining oneself thereon by reflecting that God is wise, omnipotent, eternal, or whatever else one is able to excogitate about God—so that the birth may come to pass in us through our own exertion and merit; or whether it is more profitable and conducive to this birth from the Father to shun all thoughts, words and deeds as well as all mental images and empty oneself, maintaining a wholly God-receptive attitude, such that one's own self is idle letting God work. Which conduct subserves this birth best?

The third point is the profit and how great it is, which accrues from this birth.

Note in the first place that in what I am about to say I intend to avail myself of natural proofs that ye yourselves can grasp, for though I put more faith in the scriptures than myself, nevertheless it is easier and better for you to learn by means of arguments that can be verified.

First we will take the words: "In the midst of the silence there was spoken in me a secret word."

—But, Sir, where is the silence and where the place in which the word is spoken?

As I said just now, it is in the purest part of the soul, in the noblest, in her ground, [indeed] in the very essence of the soul. That is mid-silence for thereinto no creature did ever get, nor any image, nor has the soul there either activity or understanding, therefore she is not aware of any image either of herself or any creature. Whatever the soul effects she effects with her powers. When she understands she understands with her intellect. When she remembers she does so with her memory. When she loves she does so with her will. She works then with her powers and not with her essence. Now every exterior act is linked with some means. The power of seeing is brought into play only through the eyes; elsewhere she can neither do nor bestow such a thing as seeing. And so with all the other senses: their operations are always effected through some means or other. But there is no activity in the essence of the soul; the faculties she works with emanate from the ground of the essence but in her actual ground there is mid-stillness; here alone is rest and a habitation for this birth, this act, wherein God the Father speaks his Word, for it is intrinsically receptive of naught save the divine essence, without means. Here God enters the soul with his all, not merely with a part. God enters the ground of the soul. None can touch the ground of the soul but God only. No creature is admitted into her ground, it must stop outside in her powers. There it sees the image whereby it has been drawn in and found shelter. For when the soul-powers contact a creature they act to make of the creature an image and likeness which they absorb. By it they know the creature. Creatures cannot go into the soul, nor can the soul know anything about a creature which she has not willingly taken the image of into herself. She approaches creatures through their present images; an image being a thing that the soul creates with her powers. Be it a stone, a rose, a man, or anything else that she wants to know about, she gets out the image of it which she has already taken in and is thus enabled to unite herself with it. But an image received in this way must of necessity enter from without through the senses.

Consequently there is nothing so unknown to the soul as herself. The soul, says a philosopher, can neither create nor absorb an image of herself. So she has nothing to know herself by. Images all enter through the senses, hence she can have no image of herself. She knows other things but not herself. Of nothing does she know so little as of herself, owing to this arrangement. Now thou must know that inwardly the soul is free from means and images, that is why God can freely unite with her without form or similitude. Thou canst not but attribute to God without measure whatever power thou dost attribute to a master. The wiser and more powerful the master the more immediately is his work effected and the simpler it is. Man requires many instruments for his external works; much preparation is needed [before] he can bring them forth as he has imagined them. The sun and moon whose work is to give light, in their mastership perform this very swiftly: the instant their radiance is poured forth, all the ends of the world are full of light. More exalted are the angels, who need less means for their works and have fewer images. The highest Seraph[29] has but a single image. He seizes as a unity all that his inferiors regard as manifold. Now God needs no image and has no image: without image, likeness or means does God work in the soul, aye, in her ground whereinto no image did ever get but only himself with his own essence. This no creature can do.

---

[29]A member of the highest of the nine orders of angels.

—How does God the Father give birth to his Son in the soul: like creatures, in image and likeness?

No, by my faith! but just as he gives him birth in eternity and no otherwise.

—Well, but how does he give him birth there?

See. God the Father has perfect insight into himself, profound and thorough knowledge of himself by means of himself, not by means of any image. And thus God the Father gives birth to his Son, in the very oneness of the divine nature. Mark, thus it is and in no other way that God the Father gives birth to his Son in the ground and essence of the soul and thus he unites himself with her. Were any image present there would not be real union and in real union lies thy whole beatitude.

Now haply thou wilt say: "But there is nothing innate in the soul save images." No, not so! If that were true the soul would never be happy, for God cannot make any creature wherein thou canst enjoy perfect happiness, else were God not the highest happiness and final goal, whereas it is his will and nature to be the alpha and omega of all. No creature can be happiness. And here indeed can just as little be perfection, for perfection (perfect virtue that is to say) results from perfection of life. Therefore verily thou must sojourn and dwell in thy essence, in thy ground, and there God shall mix thee with his simple essence without the medium of any image. No image represents and signifies itself: it stands for that of which it is the image. Now seeing that thou hast no image save of what is outside thee, therefore it is impossible for thee to be beatified by any image whatsoever.

The second point is, what does it behove a man to do in order to deserve and procure this birth to come to pass and be consummated in him: is it better for him to do his part towards it, to imagine and think about God, or should he keep still in peace and quiet so that God can speak and act in him while he merely waits on God's operation? At the same time I repeat that this speaking, this act, is only for the good and perfect, those who have so absorbed and assimilated the essence of virtue that it emanates from them naturally, without their seeking; and above all there must live in them the worthy life and lofty teaching of our Lord Jesus Christ. Such are permitted to know that the very best and utmost of attainment in this life is to remain still and let God act and speak in thee. When the powers have all been withdrawn from their bodily forms and functions, then this Word is spoken. Thus he says: "in the midst of the silence the secret word was spoken to me." The more completely thou art able to in-draw thy faculties and forget those things and their images which thou hast taken in, the more, that is to say, thou forgettest the creature, the nearer thou art to this and the more susceptible thou art to it. If only thou couldst suddenly be altogether unaware of things, [indeed], couldst thou but pass into oblivion of thine own existence as St. Paul did when he said: "Whether in the body I know not, or out of the body I know not, God knoweth!" [2 Cor 12:2] Here the spirit had so entirely absorbed the faculties that it had forgotten the body: memory no longer functioned, nor understanding, nor the senses, nor even those powers whose duty it is to govern and grace the body; vital warmth and energy were arrested so that the body failed not throughout the three days during which he neither ate nor drank. Even so fared Moses when he fasted forty days on the mount and was none the worse for it: on the last day he was as strong as on the first [cf. Ex 34:29]. Thus a man must abscond from his senses, invert his faculties and lapse into oblivion of things and of himself, concerning which a philosopher apostrophised the soul: "Withdraw from the restlessness of external activities!" And again: "Flee away and hide thee from the turmoil of outward occupations and inward thoughts for they create nothing but discord!" If God is to speak his Word in the soul she must be at rest and at peace; then he speaks in the soul his Word and himself: not an image but himself. Dionysius[30] says: "God has no image nor likeness of himself seeing that he is intrinsically all good, truth and being." God performs all his works, in himself and outside himself, simultaneously. Do not fondly imagine that God, when he created the heavens and the earth and all creatures, made one thing one day and another the next. Moses describes it thus it is true, nevertheless he knew better: he did so merely on account of those who are incapable of understanding or conceiving otherwise. All God did was: he willed and they were. God works without instrument and without image. And the freer thou art from images the more receptive thou art to his interior operation; and the more introverted and oblivious thou art the nigher thou art thereto. Dionysius exhorted his disciple Timothy in this sense saying: "Dear son Timothy, do thou with untroubled mind swing thyself up above thyself and above thy powers, above all modes and all existences, into the secret, still darkness, that thou mayest attain to the knowledge of the unknown super-divine God." All things must be forsaken. God scorns to work among images.

Now haply thou wilt say: "What is it that God does without images in the ground and essence?" That I am incapable of knowing, for my soul-powers can receive only in images; they have to recognize and lay hold of each thing in its appropriate image: they cannot recognize a bird in the image of a man. Now since images all enter from without, this is concealed from my soul, which is most salutary for her. Not-knowing makes her wonder and leads her to eager pursuit, for she knows clearly *that* it is but knows not *how* nor *what* it is. No sooner does a man know the reason of a thing than immediately he tires of it and goes to casting about for something new. Always clamoring to know, he is ever inconstant. The soul is constant only to his unknowing knowing which keeps her pursuing.

The wise man said concerning this: "In the middle of the night when all things were in quiet silence there was spoken to me a hidden word." It came like a thief, by stealth. What does he mean by a word that was hidden? The nature of a word is to reveal what is hidden. It appeared before me, shining out with intent to reveal and giving me knowledge of God. Hence it is called a word. But what it was remained hidden from me. That was its stealthy coming "in a whispering stillness to reveal itself." It is just because it is hidden that one is and must be always after it. It appears and disappears: we are meant to yearn and sigh for it.

St. Paul says we ought to pursue this until we [find] it and not stop until we grasp it. When he returned after having been caught up into the third heaven where God was made known to him and where he beheld all things, he had forgotten nothing, but it was so deep down in his ground that his intellect could not reach it: it was veiled from him. He was therefore obliged to pursue it and search for it in himself, not outside himself. It is not outside, it is inside: wholly within. And being convinced of this he said, "I am sure that neither death nor any affliction can separate me from what I find within him" [cf. Rom 8:38–39].

There is a fine saying of one heathen philosopher to another about this, he says: "I am aware of something in me which sparkles in my intelligence; I clearly perceive that it is somewhat but *what* I cannot grasp. Yet methinks if I could only seize it I should know all truth." To which the other philosopher replied: "Follow it boldly! for if thou canst seize it thou wilt possess the sum-total of all good and have eternal life!" St. Augustine expresses himself in the same sense: "I am conscious of something within me that plays before my soul and is as a light dancing in front of it; were this brought to steadiness and perfection in me it would surely be eternal life!" It hides yet it shows. It comes, but after the manner of a thief, with

---

[30]Dionysius the Pseudo-Areopagite (fl. c. 500), a mystical theologian who similarly taught enlightenment through unknowing.

intent to take and to steal all things from the soul. By emerging and showing itself somewhat it purposes to decoy the soul and draw it towards itself to rob it and take itself from it. As saith the prophet: "Lord take from them their spirit and give them instead thy spirit" [cf. Ps 104:29–30]. This too the loving soul meant when she said: "My soul dissolved and melted away when Love spoke his word: when he entered I could not but fail." And Christ signified it by his words: "Whosoever shall leave aught for my sake shall be repaid an hundredfold, and whosoever will possess me must deny himself and all things and whosoever will serve me must follow me nor go any more after his own" [cf. Mt 16:24–25; Mk 8:34; Lk 9:23–27].

Now haply thou wilt say: "But, Sir, you are wanting to change the natural course of the soul! It is her nature to take in through the senses, in images. Would you upset this arrangement?"

No! But how knowest thou what nobility God has bestowed on human nature, what perfections yet uncatalogued, aye yet undiscovered? Those who have written of the soul's nobility have gone no further than their natural intelligence could carry them: they never entered her ground, so that much remained obscure and unknown to them. "I will sit in silence and hearken to what God speaketh within me," said the prophet. Into this retirement steals the Word in the darkness of the night. St. John says, "The light shines in the darkness: it came unto its own and as many as received it became in authority sons of God: to them was given power to become God's sons" [Jn 1:5, 11–12].

Mark now the fruit and use of this mysterious Word and of this darkness. In this gloom which is

his own the heavenly Father's Son is not born alone: thou too art born there a child of the same heavenly Father and no other, and to thee also he gives power. Observe how great the use. No truth learned by any master by his own intellect and understanding, or ever to be learned this side the day of judgment, has ever been interpreted at all according to this knowledge, in this ground. Call it an thou wilt an ignorance, an unknowing, yet there is in it more than in all knowing and understanding without it, for this outward ignorance lures and attracts thee from all understood things and from thyself. This is what Christ meant when he said: "Whosoever denieth not himself and leaveth not father and mother and is not estranged from all these, he is not worthy of me" [Mt 10:37–38; Lk 14:26–27]. As though to say: he who abandons not creaturely externals can neither be conceived nor born in this divine birth. But divesting thyself of thyself and of everything external thereto does indeed give it thee. And in very truth I believe, nay I am sure, that the man who is established herein can in no wise be at any time separated from God. I hold he can in no wise lapse into mortal sin. He would rather suffer the most shameful death, as the saints have done before him, than commit the least of mortal sins. I hold that he cannot willingly commit, nor yet consent to, even a venial sin, whether in himself or in another. So strongly is he drawn and attracted to this way, so much is he habituated to it, that he could never turn to any other: to this way are directed all his senses, all his powers.

May the God who has been born again as man assist us in this birth, continually helping us, weak man, to be born again in him as God. Amen.

---

2. Catherine of Genoa
PURGATION AND PURGATORY (c. 1490)

Catherine Fieschi (1447–1510) was born to a noble family in Genoa and carefully groomed for a suitable marriage in Genoese society. From an early age, she exhibited exceptional piety; she even attempted to enter a convent at the age of thirteen but eventually surrendered to her parents' wishes and married three years later, at sixteen. After about ten years of luxurious living, however, she experienced a mystical conversion and rejected her worldly life for one of contemplation and service to the poor and sick. Eventually her husband also converted and joined her in her work in a Genoese women's hospital. During her lifetime she was credited with many miracles as well as with continuing mystical visions, such as the one she describes below. Like many other mystics, Catherine turned to poetry to approximate her experience of the fiery and all-consuming divine love, which she describes as both exhilarating and purgative. Her subject here is the afterlife's "middle place" of Purgatory, where the souls of the departed who are not yet ready for Heaven must be cleansed of their sin and guilt.

These souls cannot think,
"I am here, and justly so because of my sins,"
or "I wish I had never committed such sins
for now I would be in paradise,"
or "That person there is leaving before me,"
or "I will leave before that other one."
They cannot remember the good and evil
in their past nor that of others.
Such is their joy in God's will, in His pleasure,
that they have no concern for themselves
but dwell only on their joy in God's ordinance,
in having Him do what He will.
They see only the goodness of God,
His mercy toward men.
Should they be aware of other good or evil,
theirs would not be perfect charity.
They do not see that their suffering
is due to their sins,
for that awareness would be a want of perfection,
and in purgatory souls cannot sin.
Only once do the souls understand
the reason for their purgatory:
the moment in which they leave this life.
After that moment, that knowledge disappears.
Immersed in charity, incapable of deviating
    from it,
they can only will or desire pure love.
There is no joy save that in paradise
to be compared to the joy of the souls in purga-
    tory.
This joy increases day by day
because of the way in which the love of God
corresponds to that of the soul,
since the impediment to that love is worn away
    daily.

This impediment is the rust of sin.
As it is consumed
the soul is more and more open to God's love.
Just as a covered object left out in the sun
cannot be penetrated by the sun's rays, in the
    same way,
once the covering of the soul is removed,
the soul opens itself fully to the rays of the sun.
The more rust of sin is consumed by fire,
the more the soul responds to that love,
and its joy increases.
Not that all suffering disappears,
 but the duration of that suffering diminishes.
The souls in purgatory
do not consider that punishment as suffering
for, content in God's will,
they are one with Him in pure charity.
In contrast to this joy,
this harmony with God's will
also brings about a very great suffering.
Its comprehension is beyond all words or
    thought.
God's grace, a spark of His light,
has illuminated this for me,
but I cannot express that revelation in words.
That vision, which the Lord granted me,
will never leave me.
I will say of it what I can
and leave the understanding of it
to those for whom God wills it.
The source of all suffering is sin,
either original or actual.
The soul in its creation is pure and simple,
free from all stain,
and endowed with a certain instinct for God.

Original sin weakens that instinct.
Once actual sin weighs down the soul still
    more,
the distance between the soul and God
becomes greater yet;
and it increases still more
as the soul,
moving even further away from Him, becomes
    evil.
All goodness
is a participation in God and His love for His
    creatures.
 God loves irrational creatures
and His love provides for them;
in the case of mankind, however,
His love manifests itself in greater or lesser
    degree
according to the impediments that block His
    love.
When a soul is close to its first creation,
pure and unstained,
the instinct for beatitude asserts itself
with such impetus and fiery charity
that any impediment becomes unbearable.
The more the soul is aware of that impediment,
the greater its suffering.
The souls in purgatory have no sin in them,
nor is there any impediment between them and
    God.
Their only suffering lies in what holds them
    back,
that instinct which has not as yet
fully manifested itself. . . .

Let us imagine
that in the whole world there was but one
    bread
and that it could satisfy the hunger of all.
Just to look at it would be to nourish oneself.
That bread
is what a healthy man, with an appetite, would
    seek;
and when he could not find it or eat it,
his hunger would increase indefinitely.
Aware that that bread alone could assuage his
    hunger,
he would also know

that without it his hunger could never abate.
Such is the hell of the hungry
who, the closer they come to this bread,
the more they are aware that they do not as yet
    have it.
Their yearning for that bread increases,
because that is their joy.
Were they to know that they would never see
    the bread,
that would be perfect hell,
the case of the damned souls
who no longer hope to see
the true bread and the true God.
The hungry souls in purgatory, however,
though they do not see as much of the bread
as they would wish,
hope to see it and fully enjoy it one day.
This, then, is their suffering,
the waiting for the bread
that will take away their hunger.
I see also that just as the cleansed soul
can find no rest but in God,
having been created for that,
just so the sinful soul has no proper place for it
    but hell
—that is the place that God has ordained for it.
At the moment of death, therefore,
the soul goes to its appointed place
with no other guide for it but the nature of its
    sins;
and—in case of mortal sin—hell is its proper
    place.
Were the sinful soul not there
where the justice of God wills it,
the soul would be in a still greater hell.
Then it would be out of that divine order
which is a part of God's mercy;
the soul would not be suffering as much as it
    ought to.
This is why, finding no other place more fit-
    ting,
the soul of its own volition
flings itself into its proper place. . . .

Having seen all this in the divine light,
I would want to frighten people, to cry out to
    each and

every one,
"O wretches who let yourselves be blinded in
this world
and make no provision
for this one most important need,
even when you are aware of it!
You seek refuge under the mercy of God,
which you claim to be great—
but do you not see that the great goodness of
God
will judge you for having gone against His will?"
His goodness must force us to do what He
wills,
not encourage us to commit evil.
His justice will not be wanting
and we must meet its demands.
Do not rely on yourself and say,
"I will confess myself, receive a plenary indulgence,
and with that be cleansed of all my sins."
The confession and contrition that is required
for the
plenary indulgence
is such, and so demanding, that were you to
realize it
you would tremble in terror,
more fearful of not having that grace
than confident of being able to obtain it. . . .
I see my soul alienated from all spiritual things
that could give it solace and joy.
It has no taste
for the things of the intellect, will, or memory,
and in no manner tends more to one thing
than to another.
Quite still and in a state of siege,
the me within finds itself gradually stripped
of all those things that in spiritual or bodily
form
gave it some comfort;
and once the last of them has been removed
the soul, understanding that they were at best
supportive,
turns its back on them completely.
So vehement is the soul's instinct to rid itself
of all that impedes its own perfection
that it would endure hell itself to reach that
end.

For that reason the soul tenaciously sets about
casting aside all those things
that could give the inner self specious comfort.
It casts out the least imperfection.
Cutting itself off from all
except those who seem to walk the way of
perfection,
the soul concentrates itself,
preferring not to frequent places where those
persons
find their pleasure.
With respect to the exterior, the soul, however,
still felt itself besieged
since the spirit could be of little help to it,
for it could find no place on earth
from which it could draw strength
such as would please its human instincts.
Its only comfort was in God,
who did all this out of love and mercy
in order to satisfy His justice;
and the contemplation of this truth gave
the soul contentment and peace.
Nonetheless, the soul
does not leave its prison or seek to do so
until God has done all that is necessary.
Its only pain
would be in being excluded from His ordinance,
which above all things it finds just and
merciful.
And she [Catherine] would add:
All this I saw as clearly as if I touched them,
but I cannot find the words to express them.
These things that I speak about work within
me
in secret and with great power.
The prison in which I seem to be
is the world, the body its bonds;
and they weigh upon the lesser me within,
which is impeded from making its way to its
true end.
To assist it in its weakness,
God's grace has allowed the soul
to participate in His life,
to become one with Him,
in the sharing of His goodness.
Since it is impossible for God to suffer,

the more souls immerse themselves in Him
the more they participate in His joyful Being.
Thus, the pain that remains is for the final
consummation,
the full actualization of the soul.
The more sinless the soul,
the more it knows and enjoys God,
in Whose presence it comes to rest.
He who would rather die than offend God
would still suffer the pangs of death;
he would be sustained, however, by the light of
  God,
Whom he honors.

Similarly, the soul, no matter how intense its
  sufferings,
values the ordinance of God above all things,
for He is above and beyond
whatever may be felt or conceived.
Such knowledge does not come through intellect or will,
as I have said. It comes from God, with a
  rush.
God busies the soul with Himself,
in no matter how slight a way,
and the soul, wrapped up in God,
cannot but be oblivious to all else.

E. Humanism

The *studia humanitatis* ("study of things human") and the so-called humanists who pursued it lay at the heart of an intellectual and cultural turning point we now know as the Renaissance. A relatively tiny movement, humanism was initially confined to the city-states of northern Italy, but its revival of interest in the literature and art of classical antiquity eventually had implications for every aspect of European civilization. Like the sophists of ancient Athens and the great orators of bygone Rome, humanists placed great value on the skill of rhetoric, or literary persuasion. Scorning the style of contemporary scholastics, whose Latin the humanists considered "barbarous" and overly technical, they looked instead to the speeches and poems of ancient masters such as Cicero and Seneca for inspiration. Within a few generations of the movement's mid-fourteenth-century beginnings, however, humanist scholars had broadened their scope of interest from its initial focus on the rhetorical skill of ancient Latin texts to include all aspects of "things human" in Greek and Roman literature: history, philosophy, philology, etc. Their devotion to these and other "humanities," however, should not be construed as being in any way anti-Christian or even anti-religious. To the contrary, almost all humanists shared the same overriding goal of moral self-improvement through study, a tradition of religious purposefulness that stretches from Francesco Petrarch (1304–1374), the "father of humanism," to Desiderius Erasmus (1466–1536), the "prince of humanists." In fact, the humanists' closer attention to the precise language and context of ancient sources even gave birth to a new "science" of biblical criticism and translation. This led several scholars to question the accuracy of the Vulgate (the church-sanctioned Latin translation of the Bible) and to offer new translations of their own, based on the original Greek and Hebrew texts of the Scriptures. Of course, not all Christians agreed with the humanists' confident blending of pagan and sacred learning, nor did all Christians share the typical humanist optimism about humankind's potential for improvement. Nonetheless, by the beginning of the sixteenth century, the humanist slogan of *Ad fontes* ("back to the sources") had become a commonplace of European learning and one that would be shared by Protestant and Catholic thinkers alike during the turbulent years to come.

1. Giannozzo Manetti
ON THE DIGNITY OF MAN (c. 1450)

Giannozzo Manetti (1396–1450) was a prolific Florentine humanist, who authored at least twenty-two books on a variety of subjects. In this excerpt from his most famous work, *On the Dignity of Man,* he has undertaken to defend the nobility of the human intellect and body, vigorously rejecting the *contemptus mundi* tradition (see 4B) and attacking its intellectual underpinnings. His chief target is the medieval classic *De Miseria Humanae Conditionis* (On the Wretchedness of the Human Condition), written by the influential pope Innocent III (r. 1198–1216), who was the very embodiment of high medieval learning. The result is a document that points up the startling contrast between the scholastic method and conclusions favored by Innocent and other theologians of his time and the methods and conclusions of humanist thinkers such as Manetti. Though both Innocent and Manetti share a reverence for the church fathers and other ancient Christian authorities, Manetti displays a typical humanist disdain for subsequent commentaries and prefers to go straight to the sources themselves for evidence. His defense of human dignity also mixes pagan and Christian authors freely, citing arguments from the Bible and St. Augustine side by side with the opinions of Aristotle, Seneca, and Josephus. Likewise typical of the humanist approach is the exceptional attention Manetti pays to words themselves, whether he is constructing an etymological proof or swaying the reader with his flowing prose and historical examples. Thanks to this rhetorical skill, Manetti's optimistic appraisal of the human condition was hailed as a convincing repudiation of the dominant pessimistic and "scientific" tradition represented by Pope Innocent and many scholastic theologians.

So far all of those things which seemed to me to pertain to the eminent dignity and excellence of man in the highest degree, I have treated in a general but clear manner (insofar as the limitations of our modest talent permitted) in the first three books of this work. Now I think that an opportune and suitable time has come to put the finishing touches to this work, which I certainly would have already done except that I thought it important to refute what has been written by many ancient and modern writers on the goodness of death and the misery of human life. What they wrote is somewhat repugnant. In refuting the aforesaid opinions—forgive me

if I call them frivolous and false—I have decided to follow a certain order so that the matter may be treated rather more seriously and precisely. First of all, I will reply briefly to the objections they pose concerning the fragility of the human body; secondly, to their objections concerning the baseness of the soul; finally, to the difficulties they raise about the whole person of man. . . .

[Manetti then surveys classical philosophy and the Bible on the question of human dignity before focusing on Innocent's *De Miseria*.]

The primary tenet which our worthy [Pope] Innocent seems to have based the whole sorry work which it pleased him to call "on misery" is evidently what concerns the birth of every man in the process of being born, a principle he laid down almost at the beginning of his book, as well he might, where he treats of human misfortunes in these words: "We are all born wailing that we might express the misery of our nature. For the new born male says 'ha' and the female 'he'—saying 'he' or 'ha' all who are born of Eve. And what is 'Eva' but *heu ha?* In either case the interjection does but express the depth of the pain of the one who suffers it. Hence she, who before her sin was called 'virago' (made of man), deserved to be called Eve after her sin, and so forth."

He develops his argument from this starting point, where he thinks he has laid excellent foundations for his projected edifice. But these foundations are such that were I not restrained, as our poet says,[31] by the reverence I owe to the Sovereign Pontiff, I should strongly maintain them to be shallow, childish and far from being consonant with pontifical and apostolic dignity. However, because of our very great reverence for his deceased Holiness, we will be content with a few honest refutations of his pretentions by which it will be seen, however, that we have accomplished at least fairly well our professed purpose of refuting and disproving them. And so before all else we must consider briefly the quality and strength of his supposed "firm" and "solid" and "adamant" foundations to be able the more easily to take cognizance of and the more clearly to understand—after diligently and carefully applying ourselves to it— what quality and strength the rest of the structure will have that rests on foundations that are in truth weak and fragile, made of sand rather than of adamantine rock.

In the first place, the sacred words of Holy Scripture clearly show how false and repugnant to real truth are his attempts to construe the natural interjections "he" and "ha" as evident expressions of the wretchedness of man. For Moses, under the inspiration of the Spirit of God, says in the beginning of Genesis: "The man called his wife's name Eve, because she was the mother of all the living" (Gen 3:20). And so she was called "Eve" because she was to be the mother and origin and principle of all men who would descend from her as from an original root. This is clear enough in the sacred words of the Latin text but it is still clearer in the Hebrew for the great prophet, describing the origin and growth of all things in this book says, among other things: "And he called the name of his wife Aia"; and wishing to show the reason for such a name, he at once adds; "because she was to be the mother of all the living," that is, of all men, who, because of the excellence of human nature, and, as the Greeks say more explicitly, because of autonomasia,[32] inherently deserved to be called "living," as they are indeed designated by the Hebrew word. But in place of this term our Jerome, the most precise of all interpreters whether Greek or Latin, always puts Eve for the sake of euphony.

The other instance of Innocent's errors is like the first—namely, what he says of the term "woman" when he affirms that before sin she deserved to be called "woman" and after sin "Eve." This will be shown to be just as false as the first, especially if the very words of the prophet are examined a little more attentively and accurately: "Then the man said: This at last is bone of my bones and flesh of my flesh; she shall be called woman, because she was taken out of man" (Gen 2:23). This is easy enough to understand in the Latin and is still clearer and more evident in the Hebrew, which puts it thus: "She shall be called 'Misca' because she was taken out of "Misc" (a word which means what 'vir' means in Latin)." Now Jerome, in order to maintain as faithfully as possible the etymology of the word in his translation,

---

[31]Dante Alighieri (1265–1321), in the *Inferno,* part one of his *Divine Comedy.*

[32]Lit., "self-naming," or calling something by a simpler name based on its most significant function.

substituted for the Hebrew "Misca" the word "viragine" which means derived from "vir" (or man). Josephus in the first book of his *Jewish Antiquities*[33] supports our contention in these words: "For thus, he says, woman was called Misca in the Hebrew language. But their name for woman was Eve, which means mother of all the living."

If in view of the above our worthy Innocent is proven to be so obviously wrong in his principles and fundamentals, what shall we expect him to do in the rest of the structure that is erected upon the aforesaid errors? It is not likely that a man who, as we know, has gone wrong from the outset will grasp the truth as he proceeds with the work. Of course, he would never have fallen into such serious and manifest errors if he had not been completely ignorant of Hebrew literature. Let us take a short look at some of the details of his work and arraign before the tribunal of truth, in order to refute them, a number of his chapters on the individual misfortunes of men—namely, those concerned with nakedness, the fruits of men and trees, the disability of old age, the brevity of life, the toil of mortals, the various preoccupations of men, their diverse anxieties and other matters of the kind which for the sake of brevity we will pass over—although Innocent had a great deal to say about all of them.

To proceed with some order in our refutation, let us begin at the beginning by setting down a few points concerning nakedness. When he speaks of it, Innocent says: "Man comes naked into the world and naked will he depart. He comes forth possessing nothing and possessing nothing will he depart." To this we answer that it behooved man to be so born for the sake of dignity and beauty. For in the first place, if we were born like the brutes with hairy pelts of one sort or another there is no saying how shameful and ugly we would appear. Because of the excellence of our make-up, the result of the delicacy of the human seed, the

manner of our birth could not eventuate otherwise. But, supposing it could have been otherwise, certainly nature would never have hidden the human body, her most beautiful and most marvelously shaped work, under a foreign garment lest she cover its beauties with unsuitable and unworthy veils.

We might give a different answer concerning the natural covering of all men at their birth; and we are determined to make such reply because in the same place Innocent decries the natural garment in which we are all born in these words: "If, however, man is born clothed let him consider how he is clothed—in a garment that is shameful to mention, more shameful still to hear described, most shameful of all to look upon: a filthy hide streaming with blood." We rightly interpret him to mean the after-birth, this is what physicians call the kind of membrane with which infants are born. It is by natural necessity that everyone must bear this during birth, to be laid aside after birth. What shall we say of his attempt to compare the fruits of men and trees to each other? A little after he spoke of nakedness, he attempted a comparison in these words: "Consider the grasses and the trees; out of their substance they produce flowers, leaves and fruit. But man brings forth lice-eggs, lice and stomach worms. They yield oil, wine and balsam whereas man spews forth sputum, urine and excrement. They breathe forth a sweet odor; but man is redolent of an abominable stink." And so he goes on with great flourish and an abundance of detail, regaling us with other broadsides of filthiness and malodorousness, which in the name of dignity and good morals we will pass over at this time.

To these objections of the sovereign Pontiff, so cunningly conceived and aptly expressed, the reply can be given that the very choice of such a comparison is evidently absurd for that fruit is truly said to be peculiar to any tree which that tree produces of its own nature. Now the fruits proper to man are not those shameful and incidental kinds of filthiness and malodorousness mentioned above; rather our human fruits

[33]Flavius Josephus (c. 37–100).

are to be deemed the many operations of intelligence and will. It is these to which man is born by nature just as the tree is born to produce fruit. And although nature does not intend those incidental things in man (they come from a certain necessary excess of food and drink) yet it is altogether marvelous and even unbelievable to observe how much service many of the things which are called incidental in man seem to render in many areas. Consider, for example, what has been written by physicians on the subject of saliva, urine, excrement and hair. The saliva of a fasting man cures the poisonous sting of snakes and eye troubles; his urine contributes to easing the stomach and to the preservation of the sight in a wonderful fashion; wax from human ears smeared on the nostrils seems to induce sleep for insomniacs; human excrement and hair (we learn from the reading of the Gospel that not even one hair will perish) fertilize the fields more copiously and abundantly than any other kind of excrement.

What shall we say about the afflictions of old age and the brevity of life? There can be no doubt that just as we found suitable answers to the above objections we are rightly convinced that opportune replies will not fail in this case. For if in the beginning of the human condition our ancient forefathers lived so long that some of them reached around 900 years of age—Innocent seems to adduce reasons to show that our human life is unworthy of esteem since he argues that it is by comparison excessively brief—to my mind God is to be thought of as having at that time fairly consulted the interests of human circumstances and as having wisely provided for them. If God had done otherwise the human race, given only the narrow span of our present life, would not have been able to increase and multiply or to build cities or to develop the arts and sciences. But after those things which were necessary to men were discovered and developed, thanks to the protracted life span, and at length emerged in a mature state, human life little by little became

shorter and finally reached this comparative brevity which we now experience.

Josephus in the above mentioned *Jewish Antiquities* clearly supports this view when he says that God in the beginning granted such a long and lasting life to the early ancestors of our religion; and a little later when he speaks of the death of Tare, the father of Abraham, after having said that Tare lived 205 years, he immediately adds this: "For at this time the life of men was being shortened and continued to become shorter until the time of Moses after whom the term of life was set at 120 years." After men had built many cities and developed the useful arts and propagated the race it was not at all necessary for the conservation and well being of the human race that there be a longer life than is now commonly lived. For the purpose of the knowledge we have to acquire and the works we have to perform and for the purpose of living well and happily, both the life span man once lived and that he now lives are sufficient as Seneca[34] shows in *De Brevitate Vitae* where he refutes the well-known adage: "Art is long but life is short." Let us emphasize that to the above mentioned infirmities of old age ought to be compared not only the pleasures of youth but also the pleasures of old age; if this were done we are rightly convinced that many more and much greater pleasures than afflictions accrued to men who lived in ancient times and do accrue to men living presently.

We can give the same answer concerning the labor of mortals as we just gave concerning the afflictions of old age. It is our opinion that many more pleasures than labors arise from human activity for those engaged in it. If we consider carefully each and every activity of man it seems clear that just as some toil is involved in every activity, just as surely do we find pleasure equal to and even greater than the labor in any one of our pursuits. According to the celebrated opinion of Aristotle men ought necessarily to find enjoy-

---

[34]Ancient Roman statesman and author (4 B.C.E.–65 C.E.).

ment while they are living; nay, that philosopher, speaking of pleasure in the 10th book of his *Ethics,* proves that it can never be separated or disjoined from human activity. And, what is more admirable, he avows that pleasure is so firmly rooted in human life that nothing can separate it. These are his very words: "It is clear that pleasure arises through each and every one of the senses: for we say that acts of seeing and hearing bring pleasure." And further on when he had proved that pleasure is sought after by all men, he speaks thus: "But let the question, whether we seek to live for the sake of pleasure or seek pleasure for the sake of life, remain where it is at present; for these things appear to go together and suffer no separation; without activity there is no pleasure and pleasure is the fine point of all activity."

It follows from this that man is in a state of continuous pleasure throughout his life, at every moment from birth to death. If this is the case then it is evident that there are more pleasures than labors. We spoke of this and explained it in fuller detail earlier. It is our opinion that the same reply applies to objections about the various preoccupations and anxieties of men. In discussing matters that are so evident let us not be more lengthy than the nature and terms of the matter require. We say this especially in view of the fact that all the objections expressed above, as well as any new ones that might be made concerning human afflictions, are easily dealt with and abundantly refuted in virtue of the resurrection of bodies at the end of time. For when we rise again our bodies will be restored to us in a most glorious manner. They will be renewed, lacking all sin, all corruption, all weakness, all deformity—in short, our bodies will be completely freed of all infirmities and other vexations which we experience from every quarter in this life and, further, they will be clothed in all the ornaments of singular beauty. At this point we will give a short proof of this by reference to the many marvelous traits of glorified bodies.

The first of these qualities is a continuous and abiding health which no kind of illness will be able to obstruct or interfere with. The psalmist appears to speak of this health in many passages, especially in the following song where he says: "Bless the Lord, O my soul, who heals all your diseases" [Ps 103:3]. The second quality is a youthfulness that knows no aging. For that abiding integrity of body would not be so much of an advantage to him were it not accompanied by the happiness of continuous youth; neither would there be much gained if he who was always in health was nevertheless burdened by the weight of years and in need of some sort of staff to support him. For we shall all arise in the perfect and complete age of just 30 years. As the Apostle says: "Until we all attain to the unity of the faith and of the knowledge of the Son of God, to mature manhood, to the measure of the stature of the fulness of Christ" [Eph 4:13]. Although in His 33rd year Christ underwent His passion yet it was in His 30th year that He came forth from the desert where He had so long hidden Himself in prayer and meditation and appeared in full view of the world. Because of this we shall rise at the suitable age of thirty. And, at the resurrection we shall be present not only in the age of Christ but also, *mirabile dictu* ["wonderful to relate"], with His bodily stature as the Apostle testifies in his own words when he says: "For those whom He foreknew He also predestined to be conformed to the image of His Son" [Rom 8:29]. The third freedom to be enjoyed by bodies is this: our bodies which in this present state experience the oppression of so many needs, so many burdens, so much corruption resulting from sin, will then become light and subtle and resplendently free of all stain. The fourth quality is a beauty without blemish; for if the white beauty of a spotless body consists in the proportion of parts accompanied by a certain agreeableness of color, surely in that state there can be no disproportion of parts, so to speak, nor a lack of such an accompanying sweetness of color as will ornament the whole body. For so it is plainly written in the Scriptures: "Then the righteous will shine like the sun in the Kingdom of the Father" [Mt 13:43].

The fifth quality adds to the others an immunity to suffering and immortality; for those who dwell there will be bothered by neither heat, cold, hunger, thirst, old age nor any sort of toil. The sixth quality will be in the form of rest without interruption; for there the whole man will find rest and, indeed, continuous rest. The seventh quality will bestow on man an abiding and everlasting joy that knows no grief; for God will so completely wipe away and cleanse every tear from the eye of His saints that never again will a tear ever make an appearance, with the result that no pain will ever again be felt, no cry or lament ever again be heard; the travails of this life will disappear altogether along with the mortal life of this world [cf. Rev 7:17; 21:4].

What we have said, therefore, is a refutation of all possible objections to our praiseworthy view of the dignity and excellence of man. But there remains for us to advance some noteworthy points about the rewards and joys of the blessed and, at the same time, say something about the pains and punishments of the damned. No one with even a passing knowledge of Scripture is unaware that the joys of the saints are many and great and practically infinite. In the first place they will enjoy the Beatific Vision, full of glory and sweetness. That is why we say with the apostle Paul: "For we now see in a mirror dimly, but then face to face" [1 Cor 13:12]. And with John the Evangelist: "When he appears we shall be like him, for we shall see him as he is" [1 Jn 3:2]. Matthew also clearly confirms this in his record of the famous sermon on the Mount which we are all familiar with—a sermon delivered to the apostles after the Lord has taken them apart from the crowd: "Blessed are the pure in heart, for they shall see God" [Mt 5:8]. We could mention 600 further places in Scripture which prove our assertion that the just, once arrived in their true homeland, look upon the face of God. But, lest we be too lengthy, we have of set purpose avoided this—all the more since the matter is so obvious that no one can justifiably be in doubt or confusion about it.

---

2. Florentino Vespasiano da Bisticci
LIVES OF ILLUSTRIOUS MEN, "POPE NICHOLAS V" (c. 1485)

As one of Florence's most prominent booksellers, Vespasiano da Bisticci (1421–1498) was well acquainted with most of the notable humanists of the day. He was also aware of the indispensable role that powerful patrons played in all aspects of intellectual life, from sponsoring individual scholars to assembling great libraries. Much of his career was spent in the service of wealthy collectors such as Cosimo di Medici and the king of Naples, locating and purchasing books on every subject imaginable. Yet of all the 105 "illustrious men" he describes in his memoirs, none stands out as a greater bibliophile than Pope Nicholas V (r. 1447–1455), founder of the Vatican Library, who is profiled in the following excerpt. Vespiano's affection for Nicholas comes through clearly as he chronicles the pope's legendary generosity in supporting the work of humanist scholars. He also conveys some of the ravenous intellectual curiosity that fueled Nicholas's lifelong—and typically humanist—fascination with ideas and learning. Modern observers sometimes forget the pivotal role that the Renaissance popes played in the subsidizing of humanist studies at a variety of levels. As a former tutor himself, Nicholas, like Vespasiano, understood that without such patronage, all hopes for a true revival of ancient learning would forever remain but a dream.

In all matters his merit made itself apparent, and, notwithstanding the high esteem of his position, his carriage towards all those who knew him was most amiable. He was very witty, he had a pleasant word for everyone, and all those who held converse with him were afterwards friendly to him, by reason of his admirable manner and of his marvelous natural gifts. His negotiations with the courts of all the nations of the world gave him an honorable position, and in these he had always met men of worth and worship. He behaved most liberally to all, not regarding what he possessed as really his own. He did not know what avarice was; indeed, if he retained anything of his own, it was simply because no one had asked him for it. He spent money beyond his power, as at that time he maintained a large number of clerks, the best he could find, and never considered their wage. He had full trust in his own ability, knowing that he would never want, and he used to say that there were two things he would do, if he had the money to spend, that is to say, buy books and build houses. During his pontificate he did both. And although at this time he was poor, he was determined that all the books which were produced for him should be of the very finest in every respect. He had books in every branch of learning, and amongst them the works of St. Augustine in twelve fine volumes, all newly edited in the best style: likewise the works of ancient and modern doctors, nearly all of which he had read and annotated with his own hand; for, taking both the ancients and the moderns, he was one of the finest scribes that ever lived, and in these books of his, where he could find no notes, he added some of his own. And today in Santo Spirito, in a library called after Boccaccio which forms part of the library of the friars and was built by Nicolao Nicoli, who placed therein certain of Boccaccio's books in order that they might not be lost, there is a book which Maestro Tomaso

[i.e., the future Pope Nicholas V] gave to the friars, the treatise by St. Augustine, *Contra Julianum pelagianistam* ["Against Julianus the Pelagian"] and against other heretics, which is throughout annotated by him.[35] Whenever he went with the cardinal out of Italy, he never returned without bringing back some book hitherto unknown, such as the Sermons of Pope Leo [the Great], the notes of St. Thomas [Aquinas] on St. Matthew, a most excellent work, and many others. There was no Latin or Greek writer in any of the faculties with whom he was not acquainted; and as to the arranging of a library there was no one to equal him, and for this reason Cosimo dei Medici,[36] when he was about to set in order the library of St. Marco, wrote to Maestro Tomaso begging him to send direction as to how a library should be formed. And who is there who has not gone through this trouble before bringing some such a scheme into working order? Maestro Tomaso wrote the instructions with his own hand, and sent them to Cosimo; moreover, he did the same with the libraries of Santo Marco, of the Badia of Fiesole, of the Duke of Urbino and of Signor Alessandro Sforza.

All men of letters are under heavy obligation to Pope Nicholas for the favor he extended to them, and for the high estimation he gained for books and for writers everywhere. It often happened to Maestro Tomaso that he found himself without money, so he had to buy books on credit; and, in order to pay his scribes and miniature painters, he borrowed as much as it seemed he could afterwards repay. He was by nature generous: this liberality of nature is indeed a blessing, and, on the other hand, avarice is accursed. It was said by St. John Chrysos-

---

[35]Giovanni Boccaccio (1313–1375), author of the *Decameron*, and Nicolao Nicoli (c. 1364–1437) were both early influential proponents of humanist studies in Florence.
[36]Ruler of the city-state of Florence (1364–1437).

tom[37] that if all the world, transmuted to gold, should be placed before a miser, his greed would be so great that he would still be unsatiated, and that a man could more easily fly through the air than a miser could become liberal. Avarice is expressly contrary to nature. Maestro Tomaso had the widest experience, and besides the seven liberal arts, was supremely gifted as a politician, as if he had never applied himself to anything else, but had been brought up in the administration of important matters of state, on which indeed his judgment was marvelously clear. All who might talk with him on any subject of learning, would imagine that he must have studied it exclusively. His natural talent had something of the Divine, as had also his mental impressions of what had befallen him. . . .

A vast amount was sent to the apostolic seat in Peter's pence,[38] whereupon the Pope began to build, and searched for Latin and Greek books in all places where they might be found, never regarding the price. He collected many of the best scribes and gave them continual employ. He brought together a number of learned men and set them to produce new books, and also to translate others not in the libraries, rewarding them liberally; and when the books were translated and brought to him he would hand over ample sums of money in order that the translators might go to their work with a good will. He spent much in supporting men of letters, and at his death it was found by inventory that since the time of Ptolemy,[39] there had never been collected such a store of books. He caused copies to be made of all, not reckoning the cost; indeed, if he could not procure a particular work, he would have it copied. After he had induced a great company of learned men to repair to Rome on liberal payment, he wrote to Messer Giannozzo

Manetti[40] at Florence to come also to practice as a writer and translator. Manetti left Florence for Rome, where he was received by the Pope with the highest honor. Nicolas granted to him, besides the office of secretary, six hundred ducats, exhorting him to undertake the translation of the books of the Bible and Aristotle, and to finish the books himself he had already begun, *Contra Judæos et gentes* ["Against the Jews and Gentiles"], a wonderful work indeed, had it ever been finished; but no more than ten books of it were written. He translated the New Testament and the Psalter, *De Hebraica veritate* ["On Hebrew Truth"], with five books of apologetics in defense of the Psalter aforementioned, showing that in all the Scripture there is not a syllable without a hidden meaning.

It was the design of Pope Nicholas to found a library at St. Peter's for the general use of the Roman court, and this would have been a wonderful work could he have accomplished it; but, forestalled by death, he left it unfinished. For the elucidation of the Holy Scriptures he caused quantities of books to be translated: likewise many pagan writings and certain works of grammar necessary for the study of Latin.[41] The *Ortografia* of Messer Giovanni Tortello, whom His Holiness made his librarian, a valuable and useful book amongst grammarians: the *Iliad* of Homer: *De Situ Orbis* of Strabo were translated for him by Guarino, to whom he gave five hundred florins for each part, Asia, Africa and Europe, making one thousand five hundred florins in all. Herodotus and Thucydides were translated by Messer Lorenzo Valla, whom he paid most generously for his pains: Xenophon and Diodorus by Messer Poggio: Polybius by Nicoli Perotto, to whom, when he was presented to the Pope, Nicholas gave five hundred papal ducats, newly minted, in a purse, and told him that this was not the reward he merited, but that in due time he should receive one which would content

---

[37]Ancient church father (c. 347–407).
[38]An ecclesiastical tax paid to the pope by all secular rulers and religious houses.
[39]Ancient Egyptian astronomer (fl. second century C.E.), best known for his descriptions of a geocentric solar system.

[40]Famed Florentine humanist (1396–1459); see also 4E1.
[41]Almost all of the works named subsequently are those of ancient Greek and Latin authors.

him. The works of Philo, a Jew of the greatest merit, unknown in Latin.[42] The *De Plantis* of Theophrastus and the *Problemata Aristotelis* were both translated by Theodore, a Greek of great learning and eloquence. The *Republica* of Plato, together with the *Leges,* the *Posteriora,* the *Ethica* and *Physica,* the *Magna Moralia,* the *Metaphysica* and the *Rhetorica* were done by Trabizonda. The *De Animalibus* of Aristotle, a very valuable work, by Theodore. Amongst sacred writings the works of Dionisias the Areopagite, a marvelous book, was translated by Fra Ambrogio, the most of the translations hitherto made having been very barbarous. I heard Pope Nicholas say that this translation was excellent, and that he understood it better in this simple text than in the others with the numberless comments and notes they contained. The wonderful book, *De preparatione evangelica,* of Eusebius Panfilus, a work of most profound learning. Many works of St. Basil,

of St. Gregory Nazianzen, about eighty homilies of Chrysostom on St. Matthew, which had been lost five hundred years and more. Twenty-five of these had been translated by Orontius more than five hundred years ago, and this work was much in use, both by ancients and moderns, for it is on record that when St. Thomas Aquinas was on his way to Paris, and before he arrived there, he was shown these homilies, whereupon he exclaimed, "I would rather have St. John Chrysostom on St. Matthew, than the city of Paris," so highly did he esteem it. This was now translated by Trabizonda, as well as Cyril on Genesis and on St. John, works worthy of all praise. There were many others translated or written at the request of His Holiness of which I have no report. I have written only about those known to me.

Pope Nicholas was the ornament and the light of literature and of learned men, and if after him there had appeared another Pope following in his footsteps, letters would have achieved a position worthy of them, but after him they fell into evil case through want of bounty. . . .

---

[42] See 132.

BIBLIOGRAPHY

Primary Sources

Anthologies and Readers

Bondanella, Julia Conaway and Mark Musa, eds., *The Italian Renaissance Reader* (New York: Meridian, 1987).

Cassirer, Ernst, et al., eds., *The Renaissance Philosophy of Man* (Chicago: University of Chicago Press, 1948).

Crowder, C. M. D., *Unity, Heresy, and Reform, 1378–1460* (New York: St. Martin's Press, 1977).

Peters, Edward, ed., *Heresy and Authority* (Philadelphia: University of Pennsylvania Press, 1980).

Petroff, Elizabeth A., ed., *Medieval Women's Visionary Literature* (Oxford: Oxford University Press, 1986).

Strauss, Gerald, ed., *Manifestations of Discontent in Germany on the Eve of the Reformation* (Indianapolis: Indiana University Press, 1971).

Swanson, R. N., *Catholic England: Faith, Religion, and Observance Before the Reformation* (Manchester: University of Manchester Press, 1993).

Van Engen, John, ed., *Devotio Moderna* (Mahwah, N.J.: Paulist Press, 1988).

Wakefield, W. L. and A. P. Evans, *Heresies of the High Middle Ages* (New York: Columbia University Press, 1968).

Select Authors

Anonymous, *The Pilgrim's Guide to Santiago de Compostela,* trans. William Melczer (New York: Italica Press, 1993).

Geoffrey Chaucer, *Canterbury Tales,* trans. Nevill Coghill (London: Penguin, 1952).

Dante Aligheiri, *The Divine Comedy*, Vol I: *Inferno,* trans. Mark Musa (New York: Penguin Classics, 1971).

Thomas à Kempis, *The Imitation of Christ,* trans. Leo Sherley-Price (London: Penguin, 1952).

Catherine of Genoa, *Purgation and Purgatory,* trans. Serge Hughes (Mahwah, N.J.: Paulist Press, 1979).

Catherine of Siena, *The Dialogue,* trans. Susanne Noffke (Mahwah, N.J.: Paulist Press, 1980).

Meister Eckhart, *The Essential Sermons, Commentaries, Treatises and Defense,* ed. Edmund Colledge and Bernard McGinn (Mahwah, N.J.: Paulist Press, 1981).

Desiderius Erasmus, *In Praise of Folly and Other Writings,* ed. Robert Adams (New York: Norton, 1989).

————, *Ten Colloquies,* trans. Craig Thompson (Toronto: University of Toronto Press, 1997).

Pico Della Mirandola, *On the Dignity of Man,* trans. Charles G. Wallis et al. (Indianapolis: Hackett, 1998).

Francesco Petrarch, *Petrarch's Secretum,* ed. Davy A. Carozza and H. James Shey (New York: Peter Lang, 1989).

Florentino Vespasiano de Bisticci, *Renaissance Prince, Popes, and Prelates,* trans. William George and Emily Waters (New York: Harper & Row, 1963).

Jacobus de Voragine, *The Golden Legend,* trans. William Granger Ryan, 2 vol. (Princeton, N.J.: Princeton University Press, 1993).

Secondary Works

General

Huizinga, Johan, *The Autumn of the Middle Ages* (Chicago: University of Chicago Press, 1996).

Oakley, Francis, *The Western Church in the Late Middle Ages* (Ithaca, N.Y.: Cornell University Press, 1979).

Ozment, Steven, *The Age of Reform, 1250–1550: An Intellectual and Religious History of Late Medieval and Reformation Europe* (New Haven: Yale University Press, 1980).

Swanson, Robert N., *Religion and Devotion in Europe, c. 1215–1515* (Cambridge: Cambridge University Press, 1995).

Thomson, John A. F., *Popes and Princes, 1417–1519: Politics and Polity in the Late Medieval Church* (Boston: Allen & Unwin, 1980).

Waley, Daniel, *Later Medieval Europe,* 2nd ed. (White Plains, N.Y.: Longman, 1985).

Pilgrimage and Popular Piety

Aston, Margaret, *Faith and Fire: Popular and Unpopular Religion, 1350–1600* (Rio Grande, Ohio: Hambledon Press, 1993).

Christian, William A., Jr., *Apparitions in Late Medieval and Renaissance Spain* (Princeton, N.J.: Princeton University Press, 1981).

Finucane, Ronald C., *Miracles and Pilgrims: Popular Beliefs in Medieval England* (Savage, Md.: Rowman & Littlefield, 1977).

Kendall, Alan, *Medieval Pilgrims* (New York: Putnam, 1970).

Tentler, Thomas N., *Sin and Confession on the Eve of the Reformation* (Princeton, N.J.: Princeton University Press, 1977).

Devotio Moderna and Contemptus Mundi

Post, R. R., *The Modern Devotion: Confrontation with Reformation and Humanism* (Leiden, the Netherlands: Brill, 1968).

Inquisition and Heresy

Kamen, Henry, *The Spanish Inquisition: An Historical Revision* (London: Weidenfeld & Nicolson, 1997).

Lambert, Malcolm, *Medieval Heresy: Popular Movements from the Gregorian Reform to the Reformation* (Oxford: Oxford University Press, 1992).

Moore, R. I., *The Formation of a Persecuting Society* (Oxford: Oxford University Press, 1987).

Mysticism

Szarmach, Paul E., ed., *An Introduction to the Medieval Mystics of Europe* (Albany, N.Y.: State University of New York, 1984).

Underhill, Evelyn, *Mysticism* (New York: Image/Doubleday, 1990).

Humanism and the Renaissance

Hay, Denys, *The Renaissance* (Cambridge: Cambridge University Press, 1977).

Kristeller, Paul Oskar, *Renaissance Thought and Its Sources* (New York: Columbia University Press, 1979).

Trinkaus, Charles,*"In Our Image and Likeness": Humanity and Divinity in Italian Humanist Thought,* 2 vols. (Chicago: University of Chicago Press, 1970).

The Reformation Era

TEMPLE DE LYON, NOMMÉ PARADIS.

A CALVINIST CHURCH IN LYONS, FRANCE. Unlike the Catholic mass, with its focus on the priestly celebrant and his sacramental transformation of the Eucharistic bread and wine, the Calvinist service revolved around the preached Word, hence the centrality of the pulpit in this converted house. Some other social conventions such as segregation of the sexes and better seats for the wealthy, however, remained intact among sixteenth-century Protestants. *(Giraudon/Art Resource, New York)*

The history of Western Christianity is a history of perpetual reform. Throughout the Middle Ages, *reformatio*—either of persons or institutions—was accomplished without rupturing the unity of the Catholic Church. This too was the initial goal of sixteenth-century reformers such as Erasmus of Rotterdam and Martin Luther. Their calls for a return to the purity of the early church and improved preaching of the gospel were intended to restore unity to a church they saw as torn by ignorance and self-interest. The irony was that both men contributed to the greatest schism in the history of Western Christianity, the basic rift between Protestants and Catholics, which we now call the Reformation.

The history of the Reformation may be divided into three overlapping phases. The first comprised the twenty years or so before actual schism, during which *reformatio* was indeed associated with internal housecleaning efforts, ranging from improved discipline of immoral clerics and laypeople to several humanist projects to revise existing translations of the Bible. Activists in this sphere included the leader of the Spanish monarchies' reform efforts, Cardinal Jiménez de Cisneros, as well as the internationally renowned scholar and popular writer Desiderius Erasmus. As a result of the efforts of these and other pre-Reformation reformers, many fiscal abuses of the Church were curbed, several lay piety movements thrived, and a reform Council, Lateran V (1512–1517), was convened. Reform, all of its advocates conceded, was a slow process, but it was not a futile hope.

Before he launched the second and most important phase of the Reformation, Martin Luther no doubt agreed. Certainly his many years as an austere Augustinian monk and later as a theology professor demonstrated the depth of his commitment to the Christian traditions he inherited as well as a firm determination to see these ideals realized. Even his most famous attack on religious corruption, his nailing of 95 theses for debate to the door of the Wittenberg cathedral in 1517, was motivated more by a desire to eliminate such abuses as indulgence sales than by a wish to found a new church. Only three years later, however, Luther's fundamental theological disagreements with the church hierarchy had become so profound that he was excommunicated as a heretic. The Reformation had begun.

Many contemporaries thought Luther's excommunication by the church and later ban by the Holy Roman emperor would be the final nails in his coffin. Unlike earlier dissidents, however, Luther possessed a distinct advantage in his secular patron, Elector Frederick of Saxony. The electors of Saxony were among the most powerful rulers in the Holy Roman Empire and among the few capable of defying the emperor's outlawing of Luther in 1521. For the next twenty-five years, Frederick and his successors shielded Luther and his followers from their Catholic enemies and also provided a base at Wittenberg from which to spread Luther's version of Christianity. Known by its adherents as Evangelical Christianity (implying that it was the original faith of the gospel, Greek *evangelion*) and by its detractors as Lutheranism (implying that it was an invented "religion" of one man), the new faith spread rapidly throughout German and Scandinavian lands. (Luther's followers eventually became known as Protestants because they protested against the Holy Roman emperor's banning of their faith. Later the term came to refer to all non-Catholic denominations in the West.) Principal differences with the "Romanist" church were enunciated in a creed presented at the 1530 imperial assembly at Augsburg and thus known as the Augsburg Confession. The most important distinction was Luther's doctrine of justification by faith and grace alone (*sola fide* and *sole gratia*). This meant that individual Christians could attain salvation only by having faith in God's gracious gift of forgiveness as offered through Christ. Unlike Catholic teaching, this belief relegated all "good works" to the status of pious acts of thanksgiving for the gift of salvation rather than seeing them as necessary steps toward the attainment of salvation. This and all of Luther's teachings were based on his foundational premise of *sola scriptura,* the belief that the guidance of the Scriptures, when read in "the spirit of the gospel," was sufficient for salvation and that the biblical interpretations and priestly intercessions of the "papist" church were not only unnecessary but "hypocritical and corrupt."

The doctrine of *sola scriptura* in turn helped launch the third and final phase of the Reformation, namely, the growth of Protestant diversity. If, as Luther preached, there was no privileged priesthood among true believers, then no human intercessors were necessary in an individual's relationship with God. Christ alone was the intermediary who conveyed divine grace and forgiveness for sin. Some Christians interpreted this to mean that any group of like-minded believers could worship God and seek salvation in their own way, guided only by Holy Scripture, and indeed many such groups began to appear. Already, reform movements in various Swiss and imperial cities had begun forging different definitions of Christianity on the basis of *sola scriptura.* While most of these relied on support from secular rulers and governments, some groups and individuals sought a less worldly church and worship. A few of these, such as the Anabaptists, rejected entirely all practices they considered secular and instead formed separatist communes with only the minimal amount of "government" deemed necessary. Unfortunately, these largely pacifist congregations were generally lumped together with more violent rejecters of governmental and ecclesiastical authority and treated just as harshly.

The suppression of various politically radical interpretations of Luther's preaching did not spell the end of Protestant diversity, however. In fact, the growth of a new movement under John Calvin in the 1540s is sometimes termed by historians "the Second Reformation." Though very similar to Lutheranism in most doctrinal matters, Calvinism (or Reformed Christianity) placed a much greater emphasis on eliminating all practices and beliefs that were not demonstrably Christian (i.e., scripturally based). Like Lutheran pastors, Calvinist ministers made extensive use of both oral and published sermons and other forms of spreading the gospel. Calvin also established local ecclesiastical courts known as consistories to help in instilling godly behavior in congregations. These bodies, composed of both ministers and prominent laypeople (elders, or presbyters), investigated a wide range of "ungodly" activities and were occasionally empowered to mete out the punishment of suspension or excommunication.

The second half of the sixteenth century also saw the organized response of the Catholic Church to the Protestant schism, a movement known alternately as the Counter Reformation or Catholic Reformation. From 1545 to 1563 a church council met three times at the northern Italian city of Trent to consider the meaning of *reformatio* for pious Catholics. The result was a reform movement that effected wide-ranging corrections of fiscal and moral abuses but made very few changes in doctrine. For example, the doctrine of justification by faith *and* good works was upheld, as were the pivotal roles of ordained priests and the sacraments. Like Protestants, reform Catholics enlisted the mass medium of the printing press in their cause and also made aggressive new pedagogical and missionary efforts, in this case with the aid of religious orders as the Society of Jesus, or Jesuits.

This occasionally violent mode of seeking converts was common among all sixteenth-century denominations in the war for souls. As in the days of the ancient church, the rivalry among different Christian groups inevitably led to bloody conflicts. After all, each side firmly believed that its opponent churches were dragging the souls of millions into hell, and in such a case even the most violent response seemed justified. In the sixteenth century, moreover, only a few Christian groups such as the Anabaptists were without secular force. The remainder—whether Lutheran or Calvinist or Catholic—had no shortage of coercive tools at their disposal nor any scruples about using them to defend their religious truth. The resulting climate of interdenominational hatred—and even warfare—thus cast a dark shadow over the early days of an era that was otherwise remarkable for its religious revitalization.

CHAPTER 5 CHRONOLOGY

	Politics	Literature	Individuals	Other
15th cent.	1494 Charles VIII of France invades Italy		1469–1536 Desiderius Erasmus	1492 Columbus lands in New World
16th cent.	1509–1547 Henry VIII king of England 1515–1547 Francis I king of France 1519–1556 Charles V emperor 1520–1566 Suleiman the Magnificent sultan of Ottoman Turks 1534 Act of Supremacy in England 1547–1584 Ivan the Terrible czar 1548–1555 Augsburg Interim following Charles V's victory at Mühlberg 1553–1558 Mary I and Catholic restoration in England 1555 Peace of Augsburg in H.R.E. 1556–1598 Philip II king of Spain 1558–1603 Elizabeth I queen of England 1561–1593 Religious wars in France 1571 Turkish fleet defeated at Lepanto 1588 Spanish Armada defeated by England 1589/94–1610 Henry IV king of France 1598 Edict of Nantes in France	1513 Machiavelli, *The Prince* 1516 Erasmus, *Novum Instrumentum* 1516 More, *Utopia* 1522 Luther translates N.T. into German 1525 Tyndale translates N.T. into English 1532/34 Rabelais, *Gargantua & Pantagruel* 1536 Calvin, *Institutes* (1st ed.) 1543 Copernicus, *On the Revolutions . . .* 1547 Book of Common Prayer 1557 First papal *Index of Prohibited Books* 1563 Heidelberg catechism 1571–1588 Montaigne, *Essays* 1590–1616 Shakespeare active	1483–1546 Martin Luther 1484–1531 Ulrich Zwingli 1491–1551 Martin Bucer 1491–1556 Ignatius Loyola 1496–1561 Menno Simmons 1506–1552 Francis Xavier 1509–1564 John Calvin 1513–1572 John Knox 1516–1605 Theodore Beza 1515–1582 Theresa of Avila	1511–1517 Fifth Lateran Council 1517 Luther posts 95 theses in Wittenberg 1521 Luther outlawed at Diet of Worms 1524–1525 German Peasants' Revolt 1527 Sacking of Rome by rioting Habsburg troops 1530 Augsburg Confession of Faith 1534–1535 Anabaptist kingdom in city of Münster 1540 Society of Jesus approved by pope 1545–1563 Council of Trent ca. 1550–1650 Witch craze in Europe 1553 Anti-Trinitarian Servetus executed in Geneva 1572 St. Bartholomew's Day massacre 1582 Gregorian calendar introduced in most Catholic areas
17th cent.	1618–1648 Thirty Years' War	1605/16 Cervantes, *Don Quixote*		1605 Gunpowder Plot uncovered in England

A. Evangelicalism

The Greek word *evangelion* means "good news." In the ancient church, the good news of Christ's redemption was conveyed throughout the Roman Empire first by a handful—and eventually by thousands—of preaching missionaries. From the beginning, however, the good news was also spread by an important alternate medium—the written word. Accounts of Jesus' life and teaching, as well as letters of instruction and encouragement, were read aloud at the gatherings of the early Christian communities and eventually became a standard element of worship services. Gradually, over the course of the next three centuries, all of the officially approved writings about Jesus were gathered by church leaders into what is now known as the New Testament. Even so, a variety of translations from the original Greek into the then-universal language of Latin generated confusion and even disputes. In 382, at the request of Pope Damasus, the scholarly St. Jerome (342–420) began work on a new Latin translation of both the Old and New Testaments, using the oldest Greek and Hebrew manuscripts he could locate. This magnum opus, completed more than twenty-five years later, was eventually recognized by church officials as the authoritative version of the Christian Bible and came to be known as the Vulgate edition (because it was written in the "vulgar," or common, tongue of Latin). The Vulgate went on to serve as Europe's only recognized Latin translation of Holy Scripture for more than 1,100 years.

In the early sixteenth century, however, the Vulgate began to come under attack from some Christians who saw it as an impediment rather than an aid in the spread of Christ's message. Their movement, which came to be known as evangelicalism, grew from two types of concern about biblical authority . First, an increasing number of scholars throughout Europe had begun to question the accuracy of Jerome's translation. Since the pioneering work of the Italian humanist Lorenzo Valla (1406–1457), philology, or the study of language, had become an increasingly sophisticated discipline. Valla himself had used his knowledge of Greek and Latin to point out some of Jerome's more questionable translations as well as a few of the "spurious" interpretations they had engendered among theologians. The second and much more sweeping offensive against the Vulgate began, though, with Desiderius Erasmus's publication of his own Greek-Latin version of the New Testament in 1516. Like Jerome, Erasmus (1469–1536) remained limited by the possibilities of a solo project of such scope. His work, however, ignited a controversy over the Vulgate that expanded far beyond scholarly quibbles about linguistics into schismatic differences over doctrine itself. For Erasmus, the frequent mistranslation of "mystery" as "sacrament," for instance, along with many other such "mistakes" had helped distort what he considered to be the true teachings of Jesus and the apostles. Although Erasmus later backed away from some of the more radical assertions that Martin Luther and others were to draw from his translation of "the good news," he could not undo the furor that these interpretations caused nor the Reformation they enabled.

1. Desiderius Erasmus of Rotterdam
PARACLESIS: OR, AN EXHORTATION (1516)

Erasmus of Rotterdam has been called "the prince of the humanists" and the most cosmopolitan scholar since antiquity. To his mind, however, scholarly learning was only valuable to the extent that it strengthened piety. His religious commitment was reflected in his determination to produce an edited version of the New Testament in Greek, accompanied by his own Latin translation. In the following excerpt from his preface to that influential work, Erasmus pleads with his fellow Christians to go back to the biblical sources themselves (*ad fontes,* a humanist motto) to discover the true "good news," and not to rely on the "hypo-critical" and "impious" secondhand versions of Scriptures offered by professional theologians. The Light of the World, which shone forth in the gospels, he writes, should not be kept hidden under a bushel. At the same time, he argues that no special expertise is needed to read with profit from the Bible and thus—logically—calls for Scripture to be translated into all vernaculars and to be proclaimed as widely as possible.

. . . I absolutely dissent from those people who don't want the holy scriptures to be read in translation by the unlearned—as if, forsooth, Christ taught such complex doctrine that hardly anyone outside a handful of theologians could understand it, or as if the chief strength of the Christian religion lay in people's ignorance of it. Perhaps the state secrets of kings have to be concealed, but Christ wanted his mysteries to be disseminated as widely as possible. I should prefer that all women, even of the lowest rank, should read the evangelists and the epistles of Paul, and I wish these writings were translated into all the languages of the human race, so that they could be read and studied, not just by the Irish and the Scots, but by the Turks as well, and the Saracens. The first step is simply to understand. Many will ridicule, no doubt, but some will be intrigued. As a result, I would hope that the farmer might chant a holy text at his plow, the spinner sing it as she sits at her wheel, the traveler ease the tedium of his journey with tales from the scripture. Let all conversation between Christians draw from this source, for almost all of us are as our daily conversation forms us. Let each individual grasp what he can, and give expression to what he feels. Let the slowest not envy the quickest, and let the leader encourage the follower, not despair of him. Why should we restrict the allegiance of all to just a few? It makes no sense when baptism (in which we all first profess the Christian religion) along with the sacraments and the final reward of immortality are open equally to all, that doctrine should be confined to just a handful. I mean those to whom common opinion nowadays assigns the names of theologians and monks; not only are they a tiny minority of the Christian populace, but I could wish they were more like what their names signify. For among the theologians I fear too many can be found who betray the title they bear by dealing in earthly affairs, not divinity; and among the monks who profess the poverty of Christ and contempt for the world can be found something even worse than worldliness.

In my opinion he is truly a theologian who teaches, not by contorted syllogisms, but by his very demeanor and facial expression, by his eyes and the tenor of his whole life, that riches are to be despised, that the Christian should not rely on the protections of this world, but put his entire trust in heaven. He should not revenge injuries done him, should pray for those who wish him ill, should seek to do good to those who have done wrong, should choose as his special friends good men, wherever found, since they are all members of the same corporation, and should tolerate evildoers if he cannot correct them. He should believe that those who are stripped of their goods, spoiled of their belongings, and acquainted with grief are truly blessed, and not at all to be pitied; he should even think that death itself will be welcomed by the truly devout, since it is nothing but a passage to immortality. If anyone stirred by the spirit of Christ preaches doctrine of this sort and not only inculcates it but encourages, animates, and incites others to it, then indeed he is truly a theologian, whether he is a ditch-digger or a weaver. If anyone in his person and in his daily life exemplifies these doctrines, he is in truth a great doctor. Someone else, perhaps not even a Christian, may discourse more elegantly on the process by which the angels achieve understanding; but persuading us to live an angelic life, free from all stain, in the here and now—that in brief is the true task of a Christian theologian.

Someone may complain that these ideas are obvious and stupid; I can only answer that these obvious ideas are what Christ particularly taught, they are what the apostles repeat, these ideas (however stupid they may be) begot for us a multitude of true Christians and attracted a swarm of illustrious martyrs. This philosophy, unlearned as it appears to some, has brought under its sway the highest kings in the world, and nations and peoples without number—as neither mere force nor philosophical erudition could do. Certainly I don't object to that abstract philosophy being discussed by the learned, if they think it worth doing. But just as surely common Christian folk can content themselves with that general name, since the apostles and the church fathers, whether they understood these subtleties or not, certainly did not teach them. If princes put into daily practice these principles which I've described as plebeian, if preachers in their sermons set them forth, if schoolmasters would convey them to their pupils instead of that pompous erudition they derive from Averroes[1] and Aristotle—then Christendom might not be convulsed by these all-but-endless wars, people might not be racked by such an insane fury to pile up riches any which way, sacred and profane business alike would not be torn up by such furious litigation, and finally we should not quarrel so much over mere manners and ceremonies with those who do not profess the philosophy of Christ.

The business of founding or advancing the Christian religion has been assigned to three classes of men in particular; to the princes and the magistrates who act in their behalf, to the bishops and their delegate priests, and to those teachers who inspire the young to seek knowledge. If these men, setting aside their own personal interests, were to work together heartily in behalf of Christ, we should no doubt see emerging everywhere not too many years hence an authentic and (as Paul says) a *genuine*[2] variety of Christians, people who would restore the philosophy of Christ not just in ceremonies and logical propositions but in the human heart and in the total life of the individual. By these weapons the enemies of the Christian name will be attracted to the faith of Christ far more quickly than by threats or weapons. To join all our energies together no force is more powerful than the truth itself. He is no Platonist who does not read the books of Plato—how can he be a theologian, let alone a Christian, who has not read the book of Christ? *"Who loves me,"* he said, *"keeps my word"* [Jn 14, 15, 23]; it is the very mark that he himself designated. Well, then, if we are really Christians in our hearts, if we actually believe he was sent from heaven to teach us what the philosophers could not, if we really expect from him rewards such

[1]Spanish Muslim philosopher (1126–1198), also known as Ibn Rushd of Córdoba, through whose commentaries the works of Aristotle reached the West. Until the fall of Constantinople in 1453, Averroes was practically the only conduit of Aristotle's thought; he thus had great, though often unavowed, influence on the scholastic philosophies.
[2]*Genuine* is given in the Greek.

as no prince however opulent could ever give us, why is anything more precious to us than this text? How can anything carry weight which is not in harmony with these teachings? Why, in dealing with these sacred texts, do we allow ourselves liberties such as, or even greater than, those assumed by profane interpreters in their discussions of secular laws or medical textbooks? Like performers on a public stage, we twist the text around, saying about it whatever comes to mind, distorting it and obscuring its sense. We drag down the teachings of heaven and force them like a Lydian rule[3] to fit our own life-patterns and while we make great shows of erudition by gathering together scraps of pagan literature, we—I won't say we corrupt the main point of Christian religion, but—we restrict to a very few men matters that Christ wanted to be diffused as widely as possible; and that nobody can deny. The Christian philosophy is seated more deeply in the emotions than in learned syllogisms; for it, life is more than logic, inspiration is more than erudition, transfiguration more than argumentation. Very few can be learned, but no man is denied permission to be a Christian, no man is forbidden to be pious, and, I will add boldly, nothing prevents any man from being a theologian.

Our philosophy sinks easily into the human mind because it is so largely in accord with human nature. What else is this philosophy of Christ, which he himself calls being born again [Jn 3:3], but renewal of a human nature originally well formed? By the same token, though nobody taught this philosophy more authoritatively and effectively than Christ himself, many things can be found in the books of the pagans that agree with his teachings. No philosophical school ever existed so crass as to teach that money makes a man happy. None was ever so impudent as to place the final good of life in the vulgar honors and pleasures. The Stoics recognized that no man was wise unless he was also good; they knew that nothing was truly good or honest except real virtue, nothing evil or shameful except dishonor alone. In Plato's dialogues Socrates repeatedly teaches that an injury should not be repaid with an injury; he also teaches that since the soul is immortal, those men are not to be bewailed who depart this life for a better one with a clear consciousness of having behaved virtuously. He taught besides that the soul should be freed in every possible way from the claims of the body, and led toward those things which truly exist though they are not seen. Aristotle in his *Politics* wrote that nothing can be pleasant to us which is not in one degree or another degrading, with the solitary exception of virtue. Even Epicurus concedes that nothing in man's life can be pleasurable unless he possesses a mind conscious of no wrong in itself—from which alone, as from a fountain, true delight gushes forth. What shall we say of this, that a great part of Christ's doctrine is to be found in some of the philosophers, notably Socrates, Diogenes, and Epictetus? But since Christ taught his doctrine much more fully, and exemplified it even better, is it not monstrous that his teachings are ignored, neglected, or even mocked by Christians? Whatever in these writers of antiquity coincides closely with Christianity, let us follow by all means. But if there are certain things which alone can make a proper Christian, why do we look on them as almost more archaic and obsolete than the books of Moses?

The first step is to know what he taught, the second to put it in practice. I don't think anyone should consider himself a Christian simply because he can carry on a dispute about instances, relations, quiddities, and formalities, involving the question in a thicket of thorny abstractions—but only if he holds to the lessons that Christ taught and exemplified, holds to them, and exemplifies them himself. Not that I want to condemn the industry of those who exercise their mental powers in perfectly praiseworthy arguments of an abstract nature; it's no part of my intent to offend anyone. But it's my opinion—and a proper one, unless I'm badly mistaken—that the pure and genuine philosophy of Christ is

---

[3]The Lydian rule was made of lead, therefore flexible; it was used to model curves and irregular surfaces.

drawn from no other source than the evangelical books and the letters of the apostles. Any man who piously reflects on these writings, praying rather than disputing, and seeking to be transformed within rather than armed for battle, will certainly find that there is nothing pertaining to the felicity of man, nothing relating to our conduct in this world, nothing about the great problems of life, that is not treated here, explained and resolved. If we want to learn something, why should any author be more agreeable than Christ himself? If we want a pattern for living, what model is more suitable than Christ the archetype? If we crave some medication against the foul lusts of the mind, why do we suppose a better remedy can be found somewhere else? If we want reading to stir up a soul grown torpid and weary, where, I ask you, will you find sparks so lively and vital? If you want to raise your mind above the vexations of this life, why should you suppose other delights will prove more alluring? Why have we regularly preferred to learn the lessons of Christ from the writings of men other than Christ himself? And because he promised to be with us even to the end of time [Mt 28:20], he is present most especially in these writings in which even now he lives, breathes, and speaks to us, more forcefully (I might almost say) than when he lived among men. The Jews saw less and heard less than you see and hear in these evangelical writings, if you will only bring to them eyes to see and ears to hear him. . . .

May all of us who in baptism pledged ourselves in the very words of Christ, if we did so sincerely, imbibe the teachings of Christ even amid the embraces of our parents and the caresses of our nurses. For whatever the new-formed soul first receives sinks deeply and clings tenaciously. May the first babblings of children be of Christ, may the first stages of infancy be modeled on the example of one whom I should like babes to know from their infancy and toddlers to love even as little children. For just as the strictness of some teachers causes students to hate good letters even before they know them, so there are some preachers who make the philosophy of Christ seem grim and

sour, though really there is nothing more delightful. Let young people be trained in these studies, then, until by the silent passage of time they have matured into vigorous adults in Christ. Other men's writings are such that the effort devoted to them has often seemed vain in the end, and it happens that after devoting their entire lives to supporting some last-ditch cause, men change their minds and at the final moment defect. But happy the man whom death overtakes in the act of meditating this philosophy of Christ. Let us all, then, immerse ourselves in it, embrace it, practice it night and day, kiss it greedily, and die in it after we have been transformed into it, thus confirming the saying that "studies culminate in manners."[4] Anyone who cannot follow this path (but whoever really wants to can do it) may worship these writings as a treasure bequeathed by that divine bosom. If someone should show us the footprints of Christ, how eagerly would we Christians bow down in worship before them! Why then don't we venerate his living and breathing image in these writings? Should anyone produce a tunic worn by Christ, we would hurry to the ends of the earth to kiss it. But you might assemble his entire wardrobe, and it would contain nothing that Christ did not express more explicitly and truly in the evangelic books. To show our love of Christ we lavish gold and precious stones on a statue of stone or wood. But why wouldn't it be better to use these gems and golden ornaments—or anything else, more precious still, if it can be imagined—to adorn these writings which bring Christ before us more effectively by far than any graven image? An image, if it represents anything at all, represents only the form of the body, but these writings set before you the living picture of his sacred mind, Christ as he actually spoke, healed, died, and rose from the grave, rendering him so completely present that you would see less of him if you had him directly in front of your eyes.

---

[4]The saying *Abeunt studia in mores* comes from Ovid's *Heroides*, "Sappho to Phaon."

2. Martin Luther
PREFACE TO THE NEW TESTAMENT (1522)

Erasmus's call for new translations was answered, but he was not always happy with the result. Most famously, one of his admirers, a theology professor named Martin Luther (1483–1546), carried the Dutch reformer's evangelicalism much further than the master would have wished. The more Luther compared the church's interpretation of the Bible with the texts themselves, the more he became convinced that many theologians and councils had distorted the true Christian message. His eventual rejection of the church hierarchy and insistence on teaching "scriptures alone" (*sola scriptura*) brought Luther into heated conflict with the Catholic Church. As a consequence, he was excommunicated by the pope and was also banned by the Holy Roman emperor, a sentence that meant that if his opponents chose to murder him they would not face any legal punishment. Immediately thereafter, Luther was spirited away by his allies to the Saxon castle of the Wartburg, where he began a translation of the entire New Testament into German. Like Erasmus, he considered the spirit of the gospels self-evident, yet both reformers were aware that anyone, even the devil, might "pervert" the meaning of Scriptures. For this reason, Luther very carefully chose the German words that he considered most appropriate to this self-evident spirit. Even then, though, he could not resist heavily annotating, introducing, and explaining, as he does in the preface to his New Testament translation. He also could not resist having favorites—particularly Paul's letter to the Romans—as well as dislikes. The latter predictably included the New Testament letter of James—which says nothing of justification by faith (the pivotal Lutheran doctrine) and is rather "full of straw"—as well as the Old Testament in general. Luther eventually translated the Old Testament into German, but he considered both it and the Jewish religion it described mainly as demonstrations of the inadequacy of good works and the absolute need for Christ's intervention and grace.

[It would be right and proper that this book should appear without preface and without any other name than that of its authors, and convey only its own name and its own language. But many wild interpretations and prefaces have driven the thought of Christians to a point where no one any longer knows what is Gospel or Law, Old Testament or New. Necessity demands, therefore, that it should have an announcement, or preface, by which the simple man can be brought back from the old notions to the right road, and taught what he is to expect in this book, so that he may not seek laws and commandments where he ought to be seeking the Gospel and God's promises.

Therefore it should be known, in the first place, that the idea must be given up that there are four Gospels and only four Evangelists. The division of the New Testament books into legal, historical, prophetic and wisdom books, is also to be rejected entirely. Some make this division, thinking that by it they are somehow comparing the New with the Old Testament. On the contrary, it is to be held firmly that,]

Just as the Old Testament is a book in which are written God's laws and commandments, together with the history of those who kept and of those who did not keep them; so the New Testament is a book in which are written the

Gospel and the promises of God, together with the history of those who believe and of those who do not believe them. For Gospel is a Greek word, and means in Greek, a good message, good tidings, good news, a good report, which one sings and tells with rejoicing. So, when David overcame the great Goliath, there came among the Jewish people the good report and encouraging news that their terrible enemy had been smitten and they had been rescued and given joy and peace; and they sang and danced and were glad for it [1 Sam 18:6].

So the Gospel, too, is a good story and report, sounded forth into all the world by the apostles, telling of a true David who strove with sin, death, and devil, and overcame them, and thereby rescued all those who were captive in sin, afflicted with death, and overpowered by the devil; He made them righteous, gave them life, and saved them, so that they were given peace and brought back to God. For this they sing, and thank and praise God, and are glad forever, if only they believe firmly and are steadfast in faith.

This report and encouraging tidings, or evangelical and divine news, is also called a New Testament, because it is a testament, when a dying man bequeaths his property, after his death, to heirs whom he names, and Christ, before His death commanded, and bequeathed this Gospel, to be preached into all the world, and thereby gave to all who believe, as their possession, everything that He had, that is, His life, in which He swallowed up death; His righteousness, by which He blotted out sin; His salvation, with which He overcame everlasting damnation. A poor man, dead in sin and tied for hell, can hear nothing more comforting than this precious and tender message about Christ, and from the bottom of his heart, he must laugh and be glad over it, if he believes it true.

Now to strengthen this faith, God promised this Gospel and testament in many ways, by the prophets in the Old Testament, as St. Paul says, in Romans 1:1f, "I am separated to preach the Gospel of Christ, which He promised before through His prophets in the Holy Scrip-

ture, concerning His Son, who was born of the seed of David, etc."

To indicate some of these places:—He gave the first promise, when He said to the serpent, in Genesis 3:15, "I will put enmity between thee and the woman, and between thy seed and her seed; he shall tread on thy head and thou shalt sting his heel." Christ is the seed of this woman, and He has trodden upon the devil's head, i.e., sin, death, hell, and all his power, for without this seed, no man can escape sin, death, or hell.

Again, in Genesis 22:18, He promised Abraham, "Through thy seed shall all the nations of the earth be blessed." "Christ is the seed of Abraham," says St. Paul, in Galatians 3:16, and He has blessed all the world through the Gospel, for where Christ is not, there is still the curse that fell upon Adam and his children when he had sinned, so that all of them together are guilty of sin, death, and hell, and must belong to them. Against this curse the Gospel blesses all the world by the public announcement, "He that believeth in this seed shall be blessed," that is, rid of sin and righteous, and shall remain alive and be saved forever; as Christ Himself says in John 11:26, "He that believeth in me shall never die."

Again, He made this promise to David, in 2 Samuel 7:12ff, when He said, "I will raise up thy seed after thee, who shall build a house to my name, and I will establish the throne of his kingdom forever." That is the kingdom of Christ, of which the Gospel speaks, an everlasting kingdom, a kingdom of life, salvation, and righteousness, and all those who believe shall enter into it from out of the prison of sin and death.

There are many more such promises of the Gospel in the other prophets also, for example, in Micah 5:2, "And thou Bethlehem, Ephratah, though thou art small in comparison with the thousands of Judah, out of thee shall come for me Him who is Lord in Israel"; and again in Hosea 13:14, "I will redeem them from hell and rescue them from death; death, I will be to thee a poison; hell, I will be to thee a pestilence."

The Gospel, then, is nothing but the preaching about Christ, Son of God and of David, true God and man, who by His death and resurrection has overcome all men's sin, and death and hell, for us who believe in Him. Thus the Gospel can be either a brief or a lengthy message; one can describe it briefly, another at length. He describes it at length, who describes many works and words of Christ,—as do the four Evangelists; he describes it briefly who does not tell of Christ's works, but indicates shortly how by His death and resurrection He has overcome sin, death, and hell for those who believe in Him, as do St. Peter and St. Paul.

See to it, therefore, that you do not make of Christ a second Moses or of the Gospel a book of laws and doctrines, as has been done heretofore; and certain prefaces, even those of St. Jerome, speak for this. For the Gospel does not really demand works of ours by which we become righteous and are saved, nay, it condemns such works; but it does demand faith in Christ, that He has overcome for us sin, death, and hell, and thus makes us righteous, and gives us life and salvation, not through our works, but through His own works, death, and suffering, in order that we may avail ourselves of His death and victory, as though they were our own.

To be sure, Christ, in the Gospel, and St. Peter and St. Paul besides, do give many commandments and doctrines, and expound the law, but these are to be counted like all Christ's other works and benefits. To know His works and the things that happened to Him, is not yet a knowledge of the Gospel, for if you know only these things, you do not yet know that He has overcome sin, death, and devil. So, too, it is not yet knowledge of the Gospel, when you know these doctrines and commandments, but only when the voice comes that says, "Christ is your own, with His life, teaching, works, death, resurrection, and all that He is, has, does, and can do."

We see, also, that He does not compel us but invites us kindly and says, "Blessed are the poor, etc."; and the apostles use the words, "I exhort," "I entreat," "I beg." Thus one sees on every hand that the Gospel is not a book of law, but really a preaching of the benefits of Christ, shown to us and given to us for our own, if we believe. But Moses, in his books, drives, compels, threatens, smites and rebukes terribly; for he is a law-giver and driver.

Hence it comes that to a believer no law is given by which he becomes righteous before God, as St. Paul says in 1 Timothy 1:9, because he is alive and righteous and saved by faith, and he needs nothing more, except to prove his faith by works. Nay, if faith is there, he cannot hold himself back; he shows himself, breaks out into good works, confesses and teaches this Gospel before people, and risks his life for it. Everything that he lives and does is directed to his neighbor's profit, in order to help him, not only to the attainment of this grace, but in body, property, and honor. He sees that this is what Christ has done for him, and he follows Christ's example.

That is what Christ meant when He gave, at last, no other commandment than love, by which men were to know who were His disciples and true believers. For where works and love do not break forth, there faith is not right, the Gospel does not take hold, and Christ is not rightly known. See, then, that you so approach the books of the New Testament as to learn to read them in this way.

[From all this you can now judge all the books and decide among them which are the best. John's Gospel and St. Paul's Epistles, especially that to the Romans, and St. Peter's first Epistle are the true kernel and marrow of all the books. They ought rightly be the first books and it would be advisable for every Christian to read them first and most, and by daily reading, make them as familiar as his daily bread.

In them you find not many works and miracles of Christ described, but you do find it depicted, in masterly fashion, how faith in Christ overcomes sin, death, and hell, and gives life, righteousness, and salvation. This is the real nature of the Gospel, as you have heard.

If I had to do without one or the other,— either the works or preaching of Christ,—I would rather do without His works than His preaching; for the works do not help me, but His words give life, as He Himself says [Jn 5:51]. Now John writes very little about the works of Christ, but very much about His preaching, while the other Evangelists write much of His works and little of His preaching; therefore John's Gospel is the one, tender, true chief Gospel, far, far to be preferred to the other three and placed high above them. So, too, the Epistles of St. Paul and St. Peter far surpass the other three Gospels,—Matthew, Mark and Luke.

In a word, St. John's Gospel and his first Epistle, St. Paul's Epistles, especially Romans, Galatians and Ephesians, and St. Peter's first Epistle are the books that show you Christ and teach you all that it is necessary and good for you to know, even though you were never to see or hear any other book or doctrine. Therefore St. James' Epistle is really an epistle of straw, compared to them; for it has nothing of the nature of the Gospel about it. But more of this in other prefaces.]

---

3. William Tyndale
PREFACE TO THE PENTATEUCH (1530)

William Tyndale (c. 1494–1536) was not the first translator of the Bible into English. He was, however, the first to do so directly from Greek and Hebrew sources, rather than from the Vulgate. Since he could not publish his version of the New Testament in his native England, he left for the continent and in 1525 published his work in a more sympathetic German state. Like Erasmus and Luther, he prefaces his later translation to the Pentateuch, or first five books of the Old Testament, with a refutation of all of the arguments against a vernacular translation and the dangers of misinterpretation. Unfortunately, Tyndale's evangelical fervor eventually resulted in his execution for heresy in 1536 in Flanders (modern Belgium). His translation lived on, however, revived in Henry VIII's authorized version three years after Tyndale's death and later providing the basis for the King James Version (1611) and the modern Revised Standard Version.

When I had translated the New Testament, I added an epistle unto the latter end, in which I desired them that were learned to amend if ought were found amiss. But our malicious and wily hypocrites, which are so stubborn and hard-hearted in their wicked abominations, that it is not possible for them to amend any thing at all (as we see by our daily experience, when both their livings and doings are rebuked with the truth), say, some that it is not lawful for the lay-people to have it in their mother-tongue; some, that it would make them all heretics, as it would, no doubt, from many things which they of long time has falsely taught; and that is the whole cause wherefore they forbid it, though they other cloaks pretend: and some, or rather every one, say that it would make them rise against the king, whom they themselves (unto their damnation) never yet obeyed. And lest the temporal rulers should see their falsehood, if the scripture came to light, causeth them so to lie.

And as for my translation, in which they affirm unto the lay-people (as I have heard say) to be I [know] not how many thousand heresies, so that it cannot be mended or correct; they have yet taken so great pain to examine it, and to compare it unto that they would fain have it, and to their own imaginations and juggling terms, and to have somewhat to rail at, and under that cloak to blaspheme the truth; that they might with as little labour (as I suppose) have translated the most part of the bible. For they which in times past were wont to look on no more scripture than they found in their Duns,[5] or such like devilish doctrine, have yet now so narrowly looked on my translation, that there is not so much as one *i* therein, if it lack a tittle over his head, but they have noted it, and number it unto the ignorant people for an heresy. Finally, in this they be all agreed, to drive you from the knowledge of the scripture, and that ye shall not have the text thereof in the mother-tongue, and to keep the world still in darkness, to the intent they might sit in the consciences of the people, through vain superstition and false doctrine, to satisfy their filthy lusts, their proud ambition, and unsatiable covetousness, and to exalt their own honour above king and emperor, yea, and above God himself.

A thousand books had they [rather] to put forth against their abominable doings and doctrine, than that the scripture should come to light. For as long as they may keep that down, they will so darken the right way with the mist of their sophistry, and so tangle them that either rebuke or despise their abominations, with arguments of philosophy, and with worldly similitudes and apparent reasons of natural wisdom, and with wresting the scripture unto their own purpose, clean contrary unto the process, order, and meaning of the text; and so delude them in descanting upon it with allegories, and amaze them, expounding it in many senses before the unlearned lay-people (when it hath but one simple, literal sense, whose light the owls cannot abide), that, though thou feel in thine heart, and art sure, how that all is false that they say, yet couldst thou not solve their subtle riddles.

Which thing only moved me to translate the new Testament. Because I had perceived by experience, how that it was impossible to establish the lay-people in any truth, except the scripture were plainly laid before their eyes in their mother-tongue, that they might see the process, order, and meaning of the text: for else, whatsoever truth is taught them, these enemies of all truth quench it again, partly with the smoke of their bottomless pit, whereof thou readest in Apocalypse, chap. ix [Rev 9] (that is, with apparent reasons of sophistry, and traditions of their own making, founded without ground of scripture) and partly in juggling with the text, expounding it in such a sense as is impossible to gather of the text, if thou see the process, order, and meaning thereof.

---

[5]John Duns Scotus (c. 1266–1308) was a Franciscan Realist philosopher and later the symbol of subtle, and even overly complex, scholastic theology. He was especially unpopular among English reformers because of his strong defense of the papacy against the divine right of kings. Among contemporary Roman Catholics, however, his following in the universities rivaled that of Aquinas.

B. Justification

All Christians since Jesus have accepted as a basic tenet of faith that human beings are not by nature righteous or just. St. Paul held that alienation from God the Creator was the result of Adam and Eve's rejection of Yahweh in the Garden of Eden. By the fifth century, the conflicts between Pelagius and St. Augustine over human nature had resulted in a much more precise orthodox definition of "original sin" as well as its effects on Christians seeking righteousness and re-union with God (see 2C). Most importantly, all Catholic theologians for the next thousand years agreed that justification, or the process of becoming worthy of salvation in God's eyes, always required two essential elements: first, the grace, or unearned help of God himself; and second, voluntary cooperation, effort, and merit on the part of the individual sinner. While many other aspects of the the-ology of salvation remained open to debate, these two assumptions did not—at least until Martin Luther and the Protestant Reformation.

1. Martin Luther
PREFACE TO THE EPISTLE OF ST. PAUL TO THE ROMANS (1522)

As a young monk, Martin Luther wholeheartedly accepted the doctrine that sal-vation required not only God's grace but also an individual's effort and merit. Unfortunately, as he later recounted, his attempts to make himself just—and thus worthy of salvation—not only consistently failed but caused him immense consternation. About the time of his 1515 university lectures on the Epistle of St. Paul to the Romans, however, he experienced a personal and theological break-through (the so-called tower experience) that alleviated his suffering. The right-eousness of God, he decided, was in no way earned but rather was freely given by the Creator himself. Original sin was much too deep in human nature for any individual to gain salvation except through God's help alone (*sola gratia*). Justifi-cation, consequently, was better described as an extrinsic declaration by a merci-ful divine judge rather than a laborious (and ultimately futile) process of human self-purification and self-justification. This radical definition of original sin led in turn to a radical redefinition of the very essence of being a Christian. The defining Christian act, according to Luther, was not the performance of good works but rather an acceptance of God's gift of salvation through faith. As St. Paul wrote in Rom 1:17, "the just live by faith (*fide*)"—to which Luther added the word "alone" (hence the term *sola fide* justification). This sentence and this epistle, Luther believed, were the heart and entire guiding spirit of Jesus' "good news."

This Epistle is really the chief part of the New Testament and the very purest Gospel, and is worthy not only that every Christian should know it word for word, by heart, but occupy himself with it every day, as the daily bread of the soul. It can never be read or pondered too much, and the more it is dealt with the more precious it becomes, and the better it tastes.

Therefore, I, too, will do my best, so far as God has given me power, to open the way into it through this preface, so that it may be the better understood by everyone. For heretofore it has been evilly darkened with commentaries and all kinds of idle talk, though it is, in itself, a bright light, almost enough to illumine all the Scripture.

To begin with we must have knowledge of its language and know what St. Paul means by the words, law, sin, grace, faith, righteousness, flesh, spirit, etc., otherwise no reading of it has any value.

The little word "law," you must not take here in human fashion, as a teaching about what works are to be done or not done. That is the way it is with human laws,—the law is fulfilled by works, even though there is no heart in them. But God judges according to what is at the bottom of the heart, and for this reason, His law makes its demands on the inmost heart and cannot be satisfied with works, but rather punishes works that are done otherwise than from the bottom of the heart, as hypocrisy and lies. Hence all men are called liars, in Psalm 116:11, for the reason that no one keeps or can keep God's law from the bottom of the heart, for everyone finds in himself displeasure in what is good and pleasure in what is bad. If, then, there is no willing pleasure in the good, then the inmost heart is not set on the law of God, then there is surely sin, and God's wrath is deserved, even though outwardly there seem to be many good works and an honorable life.

Hence St. Paul concludes, in chapter 2, that the Jews are all sinners, and says that only the doers of the law are righteous before God [Rom 2:13]. He means by this that no one is, in his works, a doer of the law; on the contrary, he speaks to them thus, "Thou teachest not to commit adultery, but thou committest adultery" [Rom 2:22]; and "Wherein thou judgest another, thou condemnest thyself, because thou doest the same thing that thou judgest" [Rom 2:2]; as if to say, "You live a fine outward life in the works of the law, and judge those who do not so live, and know how to teach everyone; you see the splinter in the other's eye, but of the beam in your own eye you are not aware" [Mt 7:3].

For even though you keep the law outwardly, with works, from fear of punishment or love of reward, nevertheless, you do all this without willingness and pleasure, and without love for the law; but rather with unwillingness, under compulsion; and you would rather do otherwise, if the law were not there. The conclusion is that at the bottom of your heart you hate the law. What matter, then, that you teach others not to steal, if you are a thief at heart, and would gladly be one outwardly, if you dared? Though, to be sure, the outward work is not far behind such hypocrites! Thus you teach others, but not yourself; and you yourself know not what you teach, and have never yet rightly understood the law. Nay, the law increases sin, as he says in chapter 5, for the reason that the more the law demands what men cannot do, the more they hate the law [Rom 5:20].

For this reason he says, in chapter 7, "The law is spiritual" [Rom 7:14]. What is that? If the law were for the body, it could be satisfied with works; but since it is spiritual, no one can satisfy it, unless all that you do is done from the bottom of the heart. But such a heart is given only by God's Spirit, who makes a man equal to the law, so that he acquires a desire for the law in his heart, and henceforth does nothing out of fear and compulsion, but everything out of a willing heart. That law, then, is spiritual which will be loved and fulfilled with such a spiritual heart, and requires such a spirit. Where that spirit is not in the heart, there sin remains, and displeasure with the law, and enmity toward it; though the law is good and just and holy.

Accustom yourself, then, to this language, and you will find that doing the works of the law and fulfilling the law are two very different things. The work of the law is everything that one does, or can do toward keeping the law of his own free will or by his own powers. But since under all these works and along with them there remains in the heart dislike for the law and the compulsion to keep it, these works are all wasted and have no value. That is what St. Paul means in chapter 3, when he says, "By the works of the law no man becomes righteous before God" [Rom 3:20]. Hence you see that the wranglers and sophists are deceivers, when they teach men to prepare themselves for grace by means of works. How can a man prepare himself for good by means of works, if he does no good works without displeasure and unwillingness of heart? How shall a work please God, if it proceeds from a reluctant and resisting heart?

To fulfil the law, however, is to do its works with pleasure and love, and to live a godly and good life of one's own accord, without the compulsion of the law. This pleasure and love for the law is put into the heart by the Holy Ghost, as he says in chapter 5 [Rom 5:5]. But the Holy Ghost is not given except in, with, and by faith in Jesus Christ, as he says in the introduction; and faith does not come, save only through God's Word or Gospel, which preaches Christ, that He is God's Son and a man, and has died and risen again for our sakes, as he says in chapters 3, 4, and 10 [Rom 3:25, 4:25, 10:9].

Hence it comes that faith alone makes righteous and fulfils the law; for out of Christ's merit, it brings the Spirit, and the Spirit makes the heart glad and free, as the law requires that it shall be. Thus good works come out of faith. That is what he means in chapter 3 [Rom 3:31], after he has rejected the works of the law, so that it sounds as though he would abolish the law by faith; "Nay," he says, "we establish the law by faith," that is, we fulfil it by faith.

Sin, in the Scripture, means not only the outward works of the body, but all the activities that move men to the outward works, namely, the inmost heart, with all its powers. Thus the little word "do" ought to mean that a man falls all the way into sin and walks in sin. This is done by no outward work of sin, unless a man goes into sin altogether, body and soul. And the Scriptures look especially into the heart and have regard to the root and source of all sin, which is unbelief in the inmost heart. As, therefore, faith alone makes righteous, and brings the Spirit, and produces pleasure in good, eternal works, so unbelief alone commits sin, and brings up the flesh, and produces pleasure in bad external works, as happened to Adam and Eve in Paradise [Gen 3:6].

Hence Christ calls unbelief the only sin, when he says, in John 16:8ff., "The Spirit will rebuke the world for sin, because they believe not on me." For this reason, too, before good or bad works are done, which are the fruits, there must first be in the heart faith or unbelief, which is the root, the sap, the chief power of all sin. And this is called in the Scriptures, the head of the serpent and of the old dragon, which the seed of the woman, Christ, must tread under foot, as was promised to Adam, in Genesis 3:15.

Between grace and gift there is this difference. Grace means properly God's favor, or the good-will God bears us, by which He is disposed to give us Christ and to pour into us the Holy Ghost, with His gifts. This is clear from chapter 5 [Rom 5:15], where he speaks of "the grace and gift in Christ." The gifts and the Spirit increase in us every day, though they are not yet perfect, and there remain in us the evil lust and sin that war against the Spirit, as he says in Romans 7:14 and Galatians 5:17, and the quarrel between the seed of the woman and the seed of the serpent is foretold in Genesis 3:15. Nevertheless, grace does so much that we are accounted wholly righteous before God. For His grace is not divided or broken up, as are the gifts, but it takes us entirely into favor, for the sake of Christ our Intercessor and Mediator, and because of that the gifts are begun in us.

In this sense, then, you understand chapter 7, in which St. Paul still calls himself a sinner, and yet says, in chapter 8 [Rom 8:1], that there is nothing condemnable in those are in Christ on account of the incompleteness of the gifts and of the Spirit. Because the flesh is not yet slain, we still are sinners; but because we believe and have a beginning of the Spirit, God is so favorable and gracious to us that He will not count the sin against us or judge us for it, but will deal with us according to our faith in Christ, until sin is slain.

Faith is not that human notion and dream that some hold for faith. Because they see that no betterment of life and no good works follow it, and yet they can hear and say much about faith, they fall into error, and say, "Faith is not enough; one must do works in order to be righteous and be saved." This is the reason that, when they hear the Gospel, they fall to—and make for themselves, by their own powers, an idea in their hearts, which says, "I believe." This they hold for true faith. But it is a human imagination and idea that never reaches the depths of the heart, and so nothing comes of it and no betterment follows it.

Faith, however, is a divine work in us. It changes us and makes us to be born anew of God (Jn 1:13); it kills the old Adam and makes altogether different men, in heart and spirit and mind and powers, and it brings with it the Holy Ghost. O, it is a living, busy, active, mighty thing, this faith; and so it is impossible for it not to do good works incessantly. It does not ask whether there are good works to do, but before the question rises; it has already done them, and is always at the doing of them. He who does not these works is a faithless man. He gropes and looks about after faith and good works, and knows neither what faith is nor what good works are, though he talks and talks, with many words, about faith and good works.

Faith is a living, daring confidence in God's grace, so sure and certain that a man would stake his life on it a thousand times. This confidence in God's grace and knowledge of it makes men glad and bold and happy in dealing with God and with all His creatures; and this is the work of the Holy Ghost in faith. Hence a man is ready and glad, without compulsion, to do good to everyone, to serve everyone, to suffer everything, in love and praise of God, who has shown him this grace; and thus it is impossible to separate works from faith, quite as impossible as to separate heat and light from fire. Beware, therefore, of your own false notions and of the idle talkers, who would be wise enough to make decisions about faith and good works, and yet are the greatest fools. Pray God to work faith in you; else you will remain forever without faith, whatever you think or do.

Righteousness, then, is such a faith and is called "God's righteousness," or "the righteousness that avails before God," because God gives it and counts it as righteousness for the sake of Christ, our Mediator, and makes a man give to every man what he owes him. For through faith a man becomes sinless and comes to take pleasure in God's commandments; thus he gives to God the honor that is His and pays Him what he owes Him; but he also serves man willingly, by whatever means he can, and thus pays his debt to everyone. Such righteousness nature and free will and all our powers cannot bring into existence. No one can give himself faith, and no more can he take away his own unbelief; how, then, will he take away a single sin, even the very smallest? Therefore, all that is done apart from faith, or in unbelief, is false; it is hypocrisy and sin, no matter how good a show it makes (Rom 14:23).

You must not so understand flesh and spirit as to think that flesh has to do only with unchastity and spirit only with what is inward, in the heart; but Paul, like Christ, in John 3:6, calls "flesh" everything that is born of the flesh; viz., the whole man, with body and soul, mind and senses, because everything about him longs for the flesh. Thus you should learn to call him "fleshly" who thinks, teaches, and talks a great deal about high spiritual matters, but without grace. From the "works of the flesh," in Galatians 5:20, you can learn that Paul calls heresy and hatred "works of the flesh," and in Romans 8:3, he says that "the law was weak through the flesh," and this does not refer to unchastity, but to all sins, above all to unbelief, which is the most spiritual of all vices. On the other hand, he calls him a spiritual man who is occupied with the most external kind of works, as Christ, when He washed the disciples' feet, and Peter, when he steered his boat, and fished. Thus "the flesh" is a man who lives and works, inwardly and outwardly, in the service of the flesh's profit and of this temporal life; "the spirit" is the man who lives and works, inwardly and outwardly, in the service of the Spirit and the future life.

Without such an understanding of these words, you will never understand this letter of

St. Paul, or any other book of Holy Scripture. Therefore, beware of all teachers who use these words in a different sense, no matter who they are, even Jerome, Augustine, Ambrose, Origen, and men like them, or above them. Now we will take up the Epistle.

It is right for a preacher of the Gospel first, by a revelation of the law and of sin, to rebuke everything and make sin of everything that is not the living fruit of the Spirit and of faith in Christ, so that men may be led to know themselves and their own wretchedness, and become humble and ask for help. That is what St. Paul does. He begins in chapter 1 and rebukes the gross sin and unbelief that are plainly evident, as the sins of the heathen, who live without God's grace, were and still are. He says: The wrath of God is revealed from heaven, through the Gospel, upon all men because of their godless lives and their unrighteousness. For even though they know and daily recognize that there is a God, nevertheless, nature itself, without grace, is so bad that it neither thanks nor honors Him, but blinds itself, and goes continually from bad to worse, until at last, after idolatry, it commits the most shameful sins, with all the vices, and is not ashamed, and allows others to do these things unrebuked.

In chapter 2, he stretches this rebuke still farther and extends it to those who seem outwardly to be righteous, but commit sin in secret. Such were the Jews and such are all the hypocrites, who, without desire or love for the law of God, lead good lives, but hate God's law in their hearts, and yet are prone to judge other people. It is the nature of all the hypocrites to think themselves pure, and yet be full of covetousness, hatred, pride, and all uncleanness (Mt 23:25, 27). These are they who despise God's goodness and in their hardness heap wrath upon themselves. Thus St. Paul, as a true interpreter of the law, leaves no one without sin, but proclaims the wrath of God upon all who live good lives from nature or free will, and makes them appear no better than open sinners; indeed he says that they are hardened and unrepentant.

In chapter 3, he puts them all together in a heap, and says that one is like the other; they are all sinners before God, except that the Jews have had God's Word. Not many have believed on it, to be sure, but that does not mean that the faith and truth of God are exhausted; and he quotes a saying from Psalm 51:4, that God remains righteous in His words. Afterwards he comes back to this again and proves by Scripture that they are all sinners and that by the works of the law no man is justified, but that the law was given only that sin might be known.

Then he begins to teach the right way by which men must be justified and saved, and he says, They are all sinners and without praise from God, but they must be justified, without merit, through faith in Christ, who has earned this for us by His blood, and has been made for us a mercy-seat by God, Who forgives us all former sins, proving thereby that were we aided only by His righteousness, which He gives in faith, which is revealed in this time through the Gospel and "testified before by the law and the prophets." Thus the law is set up by faith, though the works of the law are put down by it, together with the reputation that they give.

After the first three chapters, in which sin is revealed and faith's way to righteousness is taught, he begins, in chapter 4, to meet certain objections. And first he takes up the one that all men commonly make when they hear of faith, that it justifies, without works. They say, "Are men, then, to do no good works?" Therefore he himself takes up the case of Abraham, and asks, "What did Abraham accomplish, then, with his good works? Were they all in vain? Were his works of no use?" He concludes that Abraham was justified by faith alone, without any works; nay, the Scriptures, in Genesis 15:16, declare that he was justified by faith alone, even before the work of circumcision. But if the work of circumcision contributed nothing to his righteousness, though God commanded it and it was a good work of obedience; then, surely, no other good work will contribute anything to righteousness. On the other hand, if Abraham's circumcision was an external sign by which he showed the righteousness that was already his in faith, then all good works are only external signs which follow out of faith, and show, like good fruit, that a man is already inwardly righteous before God.

With this powerful illustration, out of the Scriptures, St. Paul establishes the doctrine of faith which he had taught before, in chapter 3. He also brings forward another witness, viz, David, in Psalm 32:1f, who says that a man is justified without works, although he does not remain without works when he has been justified. Then he gives the illustration a broader application, and concludes that the Jews cannot be Abraham's heirs merely because of their blood, still less because of the works of the law, but must be heirs of Abraham's faith, if they would be true heirs. For before the law—either the law of Moses or the law of circumcision—Abraham was justified by faith and called the father of believers; moreover, the law works wrath rather than grace, because no one keeps it out of love for it and pleasure in it, so that what comes by the works of the law is disgrace rather than grace. Therefore faith alone must obtain the grace promised to Abraham, for these examples were written for our sakes, that we, too, should believe.

In chapter 5, he comes to the fruits and works of faith, such as peace, joy, love to God and to every man, and confidence, boldness, joy, courage, and hope in tribulation and suffering. For all this follows, if faith be true, because of the over-abundant goodness that God shows us in Christ, so that He caused Him to die for us before we could ask it, nay, while we were still His enemies. Thus we have it that faith justifies without any works; and yet it does not follow that men are, therefore, to do no good works, but rather that the true works will not be absent. Of these the work-righteous saints know nothing, but feign works of their own in which there is no peace, joy, confidence, love, hope, boldness, nor any of the qualities of true Christian works and faith.

After this, he breaks out, and makes a pleasant excursion, and tells whence come both sin and righteousness, death and life, and compares Adam and Christ. He says that Christ had to come, a second Adam, to bequeath His righteousness to us, through a new spiritual birth in faith, as the first Adam bequeathed sin to us, through the old, fleshly birth. Thus he declares, and confirms it, that no one, by his own works, can help himself out of sin into righteousness, any more than he can prevent the birth of his own body. This is proved by the fact that the divine law—which ought to help to righteousness, if anything can—has not only not helped, but has even increased sin; for the reason that the more the law forbids, the more our evil nature hates it, and the more it wants to give rein to its own lust. Thus the law makes Christ all the more necessary, and more grace is needed to help our nature.

In chapter 6, he takes up the special work of faith, the conflict of the spirit with the flesh, for the complete slaying of the sin and lust that remain after we are justified. He teaches us that by faith we are not so freed from sin that we can be idle, slack, and careless, as though there were no longer any sin in us. There is sin; but it is no longer counted for condemnation, because of the faith that strives against it. Therefore we have enough to do all our life long in taming the body, slaying its lusts, and compelling its members to obey the spirit and not the lusts, thus making our lives like the death and resurrection of Christ and completing our baptism—which signifies the death of sin and the new life of grace—until we are entirely pure of sins, and even our bodies rise again with Christ and live forever.

And that we can do, he says, because we are in grace and not in the law. He himself explains that to mean that to be without the law is not the same thing as to have no laws and be able to do what one pleases; but we are under the law when, without grace, we occupy ourselves in the work of the law. Then sin assuredly rules by the law, for no one loves the law by nature; and that is great sin. Grace, however, makes the law dear to us, and then sin is no more there, and the law is no longer against us, but with us.

This is the true freedom from sin and the law, of which he writes, down to the end of this chapter, saying that it is liberty only to do good with pleasure and live a good life without the compulsion of the law. Therefore this liberty is a spiritual liberty, which does not abolish the law, but presents what the law demands; namely, pleasure and love. Thus the law is quieted, and no longer drives men or makes demands of them. It is just as if you owed a debt to your overlord and could not pay it. There are two ways in which you could rid yourself of debt,—either he would take nothing from you and would tear up the account; or some good man would pay it for you, and give you the means to satisfy the account. It is in this latter way that Christ has made us free from the law. Our liberty is, therefore, no fleshly liberty, which is not obligated to do anything, but a liberty that does many works of all kinds, and thus is free from the demands and the debts of the law.

In chapter 7, he supports this with a parable of the married life. When a man dies, his wife is single, and thus the one is released from the other; not that the wife cannot or ought not take another husband, but rather that she is now really free to take another, which she could not do before she was free from her husband. So our conscience is bound to the law, under the old man; when he is slain by the Spirit, then the conscience is free; the one is released from the other; not that the conscience is to do nothing, but rather that it is now really free to cleave to Christ, the second husband, and bring forth the fruit of life.

Then he sketches out more broadly the nature of sin and the law, showing how, by means of the law sin now moves and is mighty. The old man hates the law the more because he cannot pay what the law demands, for sin is his nature and by himself he can do nothing but sin; therefore the law is death to him, and torment. Not that the law is bad, but his evil nature cannot endure the good, and the law demands good of him. So a sick man cannot endure it when he is required to run and jump and do the works of a well man.

Therefore St. Paul here concludes that the law, rightly understood and thoroughly comprehended, does nothing more than remind us of our sin, and slay us by it, and make us liable to eternal wrath; and all this is taught and experienced by our conscience, when it is really smitten by the law. Therefore a man must have something else than the law, and more than the law, to make him righteous and save him. But they who do not rightly understand the law are blind; they go ahead, in their presumption, and think to satisfy the law with their works, not knowing what the law demands, viz., a willing and happy heart. Therefore they do not see Moses clearly, the veil is put between them and him, and covers him [2 Cor 3:13f].

Then he shows how spirit and flesh strive with one another in a man. He uses himself as an example, in order that we may learn rightly to understand the work of slaying sin within us. He calls both spirit and flesh "laws," for just as it is the nature of the divine law to drive men and make demands of them, so the flesh drives men and makes demands and rages against the spirit, and will have its own way. The spirit, too, drives men and makes demands contrary to the flesh, and will have its own way. This contention within us lasts as long as we live, though in one man it is greater, in another less, according as spirit or flesh is stronger. Nevertheless, the whole man is both spirit and flesh and he fights with himself until he becomes wholly spiritual.

In chapter 8, he encourages these fighters, telling them not to condemn the flesh; and he shows further what the nature of flesh and spirit is, and how the spirit comes from Christ, Who has given us His Holy Spirit to make us spiritual and subdue the flesh. He assures us that we are still God's children, however hard sin may rage within us, so long as we follow the spirit and resist sin, to slay it. Since, however, nothing else is so good for the mortifying of the flesh as the cross and suffering, he comforts us in suffering with the support of the Spirit of love, and of the whole creation. For the Spirit sighs within us and the creation longs with us that we may be rid of the flesh and of sin [Rom 8:23f]. So we see that these three chapters (6–8) deal with the one work of faith, which is to slay the old Adam and subdue the flesh.

In chapters 9, 10, and 11, he teaches concerning God's eternal predestination, from which it originally comes that one believes or not, is rid of sin or not rid of it. Thus our becoming righteous is taken entirely out of our hands and put in the hand of God. And that is most highly necessary. We are so weak and uncertain that, if it were in our power, surely not one man would be saved, the devil would surely overpower us all; but since God is certain, and His predestination cannot fail, and no one can withstand Him, we still have hope against sin.

And here we must set a boundary for those audacious and high-climbing spirits, who first bring their own thinking to this matter and begin at the top to search the abyss of divine predestination, and worry in vain about whether they are predestinate. They must have a fall; either they will despair, or else they will take long risks.

But do you follow the order of this epistle. Worry first about Christ and the Gospel, that you may recognize your sin and His grace; then fight your sin, as the first eight chapters here have taught; then, when you have reached the eighth chapter, and are under the cross and suffering, that will teach you the right doctrine of predestination, in the ninth, tenth and eleventh chapters, and how comforting it is. For in the absence of suffering and the cross and the danger of death, one cannot deal with predestination without harm and without secret wrath against God. The old Adam must die before he can endure this subject and drink the strong wine of it. Therefore beware not to drink wine while you are still a suckling. There is a limit, a time, an age for every doctrine.

In chapter 12, he teaches what true worship is; and he makes all Christians priests, who are to offer not money and cattle, as under the law, but their own bodies, with a slaying of the lusts. Then he describes the outward conduct of Christians, under spiritual government, telling how they are to teach, preach, rule, serve, give, suffer, love, live, and act toward friend, foe and all men. These are the works that a Christian does; for, as has been said, faith takes no holidays.

In chapter 13, he teaches honor and obedience to worldly government, which accomplishes much, although it does not make its people righteous before God. It is instituted in order that the good may have outward peace and protection, and that the wicked may not be free to do evil, without fear, in peace and quietness. Therefore the righteous are to honor it, though they do not need it. In the end he comprises it all in love, and includes it in the example of Christ, Who has done for us what we also are to do, following in His footsteps.

In chapter 14, he teaches that weak consciences are to be led gently in faith and to be spared, so that Christians are not to use their liberty for doing harm, but for the furtherance of the weak. If that is not done, then discord follows and contempt for the Gospel; and the Gospel is the all-important thing. Thus it is better to yield a little to the weak in faith, until they grow stronger, than to have the doctrine of the Gospel come to nought. This is a peculiar work of love, for which there is great need even now, when with meat-eating and other liberties, men are rudely and roughly shaking weak consciences, before they know the truth.

In chapter 15, he sets up the example of Christ, to show that we are to suffer those who are weak in other ways,—those whose weakness lies in open sins or in unpleasing habits. These men are not to be cast off, but borne with till they grow better. For so Christ has done to us, and still does every day; He bears with our many faults and bad habits, and with all our imperfections, and helps us constantly.

Then, at the end, he prays for them, praises them and commends them to God; he speaks of his office and his preaching, and asks them gently for a contribution to the poor at Jerusalem; all that he speaks of or deals with is pure love.

The last chapter is a chapter of greetings, but he mingles with them a noble warning against doctrines of men, which are put in alongside the doctrine of the Gospel and cause offense. It is as though he had foreseen that out of Rome and through the Romans would come the seductive and offensive canons and decretals and the whole squirming mass of human laws and commandments, which have now drowned the whole world and wiped out this Epistle and all the Holy Scriptures, along with the Spirit and with faith, so that nothing has remained there except the idol, Belly, whose servants St. Paul here rebukes. God release us from them. Amen.

Thus in this Epistle we find most richly the things that a Christian ought to know; namely, what is law, Gospel, sin, punishment, grace, faith, righteousness, Christ, God, good works, love, hope, the cross, and also how we are to conduct ourselves toward everyone, whether righteous or sinner, strong or weak, friend or foe. All this is ably founded on Scripture and proved by his own example and that of the prophets. Therefore it appears that St. Paul wanted to comprise briefly in this one epistle the whole Christian and evangelical doctrine and to prepare an introduction to the entire Old Testament; for, without doubt, he who has this epistle well in his heart, has the light and power of the Old Testament with him. Therefore let every Christian exercise himself in it habitually and continually. To this may God give His grace. Amen.

2. John Calvin
INSTITUTES OF THE CHRISTIAN RELIGION (1536/1559)

Justification by faith and grace alone was not immediately embraced by all early Protestants. Many of the Swiss reformers, particularly Ulrich Zwingli, continued to stress the importance of both faith and good works in salvation, albeit in greatly revised form. By the middle of the sixteenth century, however, it was clear that Luther's doctrine of justification had won over the great majority of Protestant churches. His emphasis on human frailty and divine sovereignty was taken to new heights by the leader of the second generation of Protestant reformers, John Calvin (1509–1564) of Geneva. In his theological masterpiece, *Institutes of the Christian Religion,* Calvin went into much greater detail than Luther about the workings of God's plan for salvation. The doctrine he is most often associated with—predestination—in fact was just one aspect of his approach to the greater issue of divine providence. Like Luther, Calvin considered the radical sinfulness of human nature as proof that: 1) all people were deserving of eternal damnation; and 2) only divine grace could intervene to prevent this "natural" course of events. His doctrine of predestination stated that God had chosen only a few "elect" humans for salvation, a decision that was made before time began and that could not be affected by human prayer or action. This was "a horrible decree," Calvin conceded, but once the veil of human vanity was pulled aside, humankind's complete reliance on God's grace for justification allowed no other conclusion.

BOOK ONE: THE KNOWLEDGE OF GOD THE CREATOR
Chapter 1: The Knowledge of God and That of Ourselves Are Connected. How They Are Interrelated.

1. Without knowledge of self there is no knowledge of God.　Nearly all of the wisdom we possess, that is to say, true and sound wisdom, consists of two parts: the knowledge of God and of ourselves. But, while joined by many bonds, which one precedes and brings forth the other is not easy to discern. In the first place, no one can look upon himself without immediately turning his thoughts to the contemplation of God, in whom he "lives and moves" [Acts 17:28]. For, quite clearly, the mighty gifts with which we are endowed are hardly from ourselves; indeed, our very being is nothing but subsistence in the one God. Then, by these benefits shed like dew from heaven upon us, we are led as by rivulets to the spring itself. Indeed, our very poverty better discloses the infinitude of benefits reposing in God. The miserable ruin, into which the rebellion of the first man cast us, especially compels us to look upward. Thus, not only will we, in fasting and hungering, seek thence what we lack; but, in being aroused by fear, we shall learn humility. For, as a veritable world of miseries is to be found in mankind, and we are thereby despoiled of divine raiment, our shameful nakedness exposes a teeming horde of infamies. Each of us must, then, be so stung by the consciousness of his own unhappiness as to attain at least some knowledge of God. Thus, from the feeling of our own ignorance, vanity, poverty, infirmity, and—what is more—depravity and corruption, we recognize that the true light of wisdom, sound virtue, full abundance of every good, and purity of righteousness rest in the Lord alone. To this extent we are prompted by our own ills to contemplate the good things of God; and we cannot seriously aspire to him before we begin to become displeased with ourselves. For what man in all the world would not gladly remain as he is—what man does not remain as he is—so long as he does not know himself, that is, while content with his own gifts, and either ignorant or unmindful of his own misery? Accordingly, the knowledge of ourselves not only arouses us to seek God, but also, as it were, leads us by the hand to find him.

2. Without knowledge of God there is no knowledge of self.　Again, it is certain that man never achieves a clear knowledge of himself unless he has first looked upon God's face, and then descends from contemplating him to scrutinize himself. For we always seem to ourselves righteous and upright and wise and holy—this pride is innate in all of us—unless by clear proofs we stand convinced of our own unrighteousness, foulness, folly, and impurity. Moreover, we are not thus convinced if we look merely to ourselves and not also to the Lord, who is the sole standard by which this judgment must be measured. For, because all of us are inclined by nature to hypocrisy, a kind of empty image of righteousness in place of righteousness itself abundantly satisfies us. And because nothing appears within or around us that has not been contaminated by great immorality, what is a little less vile pleases us as a thing most pure—so long as we confine our minds within the limits of human corruption. Just so, an eye to which nothing is shown but black objects judges something dirty white or even rather darkly mottled to be whiteness itself. Indeed, we can discern still more clearly from the bodily senses how much we are deluded in estimating the powers of the soul. For if in broad daylight we either look down upon the ground or survey whatever meets our view round about, we seem to ourselves endowed with the strongest and keenest sight; yet when we look up to the sun and gaze straight at it, that power of sight which was particularly strong on earth is at once blunted and confused by a great brilliance, and thus we are compelled to admit that our keenness in looking upon things earthly is sheer dullness when it comes to the sun. So it happens in estimating our spiritual goods. As long as we do not look beyond the earth, being quite content with our own righteousness, wisdom, and virtue, we flatter ourselves most sweetly, and fancy ourselves all but demigods. Suppose we but once begin to raise our thoughts to God, and to ponder his nature, and how completely perfect are his righteousness, wisdom, and power—the straightedge to which we must be shaped. Then, what masquerading earlier as righteousness was pleasing in us will soon grow filthy in its consummate wickedness. What wonderfully impressed us under the name of wisdom will stink in its very foolishness. What wore the face of power will prove itself the most miserable weakness. That is, what in us seems perfection itself corresponds ill to the purity of God.

3. Man before God's majesty. Hence that dread and wonder with which Scripture commonly represents the saints as stricken and overcome whenever they felt the presence of God. Thus it comes about that we see men who in his absence normally remained firm and constant, but who, when he manifests his glory, are so shaken and struck dumb as to be laid low by the dread of death—are in fact overwhelmed by it and almost annihilated. As a consequence, we must infer that man is never sufficiently touched and affected by the awareness of his lowly state until he has compared himself with God's majesty. . . .

BOOK THREE: THE WAY WE RECEIVE THE GRACE OF CHRIST
Chapter 2: Faith: Its Definition Set Forth, and Its Properties Explained

(The object of faith is Christ) 1. But it will be easy to understand all these matters after a clearer definition of faith has been presented, to enable our readers to grasp its force and nature. We may well recall here what was explained before: First, God lays down for us through the law what we should do; if we then fail in any part of it, that dreadful sentence of eternal

death which it pronounces will rest upon us. Secondly, it is not only hard, but above our strength and beyond all our abilities, to fulfill the law to the letter; thus, if we look to ourselves only, and ponder what condition we deserve, no trace of good hope will remain; but cast away by God, we shall lie under eternal death. Thirdly, it has been explained that there is but one means of liberation that can rescue us from such miserable calamity: the appearance of Christ the Redeemer, through whose hand the Heavenly Father, pitying us out of his infinite goodness and mercy, willed to help us; if, indeed, with firm faith we embrace this mercy and rest in it with steadfast hope.

But now we ought to examine what this faith ought to be like, through which those adopted by God as his children come to possess the Heavenly Kingdom, since it is certain that no mere opinion or even persuasion is capable of bringing so great a thing to pass. And we must scrutinize and investigate the true character of faith with greater care and zeal because many are dangerously deluded today in this respect. Indeed, most people, when they hear this term, understand nothing deeper than a common assent to the gospel history. In fact, when faith is discussed in the schools, they call God simply the object of faith, and by fleeting speculations as we have elsewhere stated, lead miserable souls astray rather than direct them to a definite goal. . . .

Chapter 11: Justification by Faith: First the Definition of the Word and of the Matter

. . . *2. The concept of justification.* But that we may not stumble on the very threshold—and this would happen if we should enter upon a discussion of a thing unknown—first let us explain what these expressions mean: that man is justified in God's sight, and that he is justified by faith or works. He is said to be justified in God's sight who is both reckoned righteous in God's judgment and has been accepted on account of his righteousness. Indeed, as iniquity is abominable to God, so no sinner can find favor in his eyes in so far as he is a sinner and so long as he is reckoned as such. Accordingly, wherever there is sin, there also the wrath and vengeance of God show themselves. Now he is justified who is reckoned in the condition not of a sinner, but of a righteous man; and for that reason, he stands firm before God's judgment seat while all sinners fall. If an innocent accused person be summoned before the judgment seat of a fair judge, where he will be judged according to his innocence, he is said to be "justified" before the judge. Thus, justified before God is the man who, freed from the company of sinners, has God to witness and affirm his righteousness. In the same way, therefore, he in whose life that purity and holiness will be found which deserves a testimony of righteousness before God's throne will be said to be justified by works, or else he who, by the wholeness of his works, can meet and satisfy God's judgment. On the contrary, justified by faith is he who, excluded from the righteousness of works, grasps the righteousness of Christ through faith, and clothed in it, appears in God's sight not as a sinner but as a righteous man.

Therefore, we explain justification simply as the acceptance with which God receives us into his favor as righteous men. And we say that it consists in the remission of sins and the imputation of Christ's righteousness. . . .

Chapter 14: The Beginning of Justification and Its Continual Progress

. . . 6. *Man can contribute nothing to his own righteousness.* The thought repeatedly returns to my mind that there is danger of my being unjust to God's mercy when I labor with such great concern to assert it, as if it were doubtful or obscure. But since our ill will is such that it never yields to God that which is his, unless it is powerfully compelled, I am obliged to dwell on this a little longer. Now as Scripture is sufficiently clear on this matter, I shall contend by means of its words rather than my own. Isaiah, when he has described the universal destruction of mankind, beautifully adds the order of restoration: "The Lord saw it, and it appeared evil

in his sight. . . . He saw that there was no man, and wondered that there was no one to intervene; and he entrusted salvation to his own arm, and with his own righteousness strengthened himself" [Is 59:15–16]. If a covenant of this sort, which is clearly the first union of us with God, depends upon God's mercy, no basis is left for our righteousness.

And I should like to learn from those who pretend that man goes to meet God with some work of righteousness whether they think there can be any other righteousness at all than that which is accepted by God. If it is mad to think so, what acceptable thing can come to God from his enemies, all of whom he spurns with all their doings? Truth testifies that all of us, I say, are mortal and open enemies of our God until we are justified and received into friendship. If justification is the beginning of love, what righteousness of works will precede it? To turn aside that pestilent arrogance, John faithfully reminds us how we did not first love Him [1 Jn 4:10]. And the Lord had at an earlier time taught this very thing through his prophet. "I will love them with a willing love," he says, "for my anger has turned from them" [Hos 14:4]. If his love has willingly inclined itself to us, surely it is not aroused by works.

But the ignorant mass of men suppose this to mean only that no one has deserved Christ's completion of our redemption but that in entering into possession of redemption we are aided by our own works. Nay, rather, however we may have been redeemed by Christ, until we are engrafted into his fellowship by the calling of the Father, we are both the heirs of darkness and death and the enemies of God. For Paul teaches that we are not cleansed and washed of our uncleanness by Christ's blood except when the Spirit works that cleansing in us [1 Cor 6:11]. Peter, meaning to say the same thing, asserts that the sanctification of the Spirit is effectual "for obedience and for sprinkling with the blood of Christ" [1 Pet 1:2]. If we are sprinkled through the Spirit with the blood of Christ for purification, let us not think that before this cleansing we were anything other than is a sinner without Christ. Therefore let this be regarded as a fact: the beginning of our salvation is a sort of resurrection from death into life, because when it has been granted to us to believe in Christ for his sake [Phil 1:29], then at last we begin to pass over from death into life. . . .

Chapter 21: Eternal Election, By Which God Has Predestined Some to Salvation, Others to Destruction

1. Necessity and beneficial effect of the doctrine of election; danger of curiosity. In actual fact, the covenant of life is not preached equally among all men, and among those to whom it is preached, it does not gain the same acceptance either constantly or in equal degree. In this diversity the wonderful depth of God's judgment is made known. For there is no doubt that this variety also serves the decision of God's eternal election. If it is plain that it comes to pass by God's bidding that salvation is freely offered to some while others are barred from access to it, at once great and difficult questions spring up, explicable only when reverent minds regard as settled what they may suitably hold concerning election and predestination. A baffling question this seems to many. For they think nothing more inconsistent than that out of the common multitude of men some should be predestined to salvation, others to destruction.[7] But how mistakenly they entangle themselves will become clear in the following discussion. Besides, in the very darkness that frightens them not only is the usefulness of this doctrine made known but also its very sweet fruit. We shall never be clearly persuaded, as we ought to be, that our salvation flows from the wellspring of God's free mercy until we come to know his eternal election, which illumines God's grace by this contrast: that he does not indiscriminately adopt all into the hope of salvation but gives to some what he denies to others.

How much the ignorance of this principle detracts from God's glory, how much it takes away from true humility, is well known. Yet Paul denies that this which needs so much to be known can be known unless God, utterly disregarding works, chooses those whom he has decreed within himself. "At the present time," he says, "a remnant has been saved according to the election of grace. But if it is by grace, it is no more of works; otherwise grace would no more be grace. But if it is of works, it is no more of grace; otherwise work would not be work" [Rom 11:5–6]. If—to make it clear that our salvation comes about solely from God's mere generosity—we must be called back to the course of election, those who wish to get rid of all this are obscuring as maliciously as they can what ought to have been gloriously and vociferously proclaimed, and they tear humility up by the very roots. Paul clearly testifies that, when the salvation of a remnant of the people is ascribed to the election of grace, then only is it acknowledged that God of his mere good pleasure preserves whom he will, and moreover that he pays no reward, since he can owe none.

They who shut the gates that no one may dare seek a taste of this doctrine wrong men no less than God. For neither will anything else suffice to make us humble as we ought to be nor shall we otherwise sincerely feel how much we are obliged to God. And as Christ teaches, here is our only ground for firmness and confidence: in order to free us of all fear and render us victorious amid so many dangers, snares, and mortal struggles, he promises that whatever the Father has entrusted into his keeping will be safe [Jn 10:28–29]. From this we infer that all those who do not know that they are God's own will be miserable through constant fear. Hence those who by being blind to the three benefits we have noted[8] would wish the foundation of our salvation to be removed from our midst, very badly serve the interests of themselves and of all other believers. How is it that the church

---

[7]Of the many who took this attitude, Calvin may have had chiefly in mind Erasmus, Johann Eck, and Albert Pighius, each of whom had written a treatise on free will attacking Luther's doctrine of predestination.

[8]I.e., God's free mercy, God's glory, and the devout Christian's sincere humility.

becomes manifest to us from this, when, as Bernard rightly teaches, "it could not otherwise be found or recognized among creatures, since it lies marvelously hidden . . . both within the bosom of a blessed predestination and within the mass of a miserable condemnation?"[9]

But before I enter into the matter itself, I need to mention by way of preface two kinds of men.

Human curiosity renders the discussion of predestination, already somewhat difficult of itself, very confusing and even dangerous. No restraints can hold it back from wandering in forbidden bypaths and thrusting upward to the heights. If allowed, it will leave no secret to God that it will not search out and unravel. Since we see so many on all sides rushing into this audacity and impudence, among them certain men not otherwise bad, they should in due season be reminded of the measure of their duty in this regard.

First, then, let them remember that when they inquire into predestination they are penetrating the sacred precincts of divine wisdom. If anyone with carefree assurance breaks into this place, he will not succeed in satisfying his curiosity and he will enter a labyrinth from which he can find no exit. For it is not right for man unrestrainedly to search out things that the Lord has willed to be hid in himself, and to unfold from eternity itself the sublimest wisdom, which he would have us revere but not understand that through this also he should fill us with wonder. He has set forth by his Word the secrets of his will that he has decided to reveal to us. These he decided to reveal in so far as he foresaw that they would concern us and benefit us.

2. Doctrine of predestination to be sought in Scripture only. . . . Let this, therefore, first of all be before our eyes: to seek any other knowledge of predestination than what the Word of God discloses is not less insane than if one should purpose to walk in a pathless waste, or to see in darkness. And let us not be ashamed to be ignorant of something in this matter, wherein there is a certain learned ignorance.[10] Rather, let us willingly refrain from inquiring into a kind of knowledge, the ardent desire for which is both foolish and dangerous, nay, even deadly. But if a wanton curiosity agitates us, we shall always do well to oppose to it this restraining thought: just as too much honey is not good, so for the curious the investigation of glory is not turned into glory [Prov 25:27]. For there is good reason for us to be deterred from this insolence which can only plunge us into ruin. . . .

---

[9]St. Bernard of Clairvaux (1090–1153), Cistercian monk and influential preacher, in his *Sermons on the Song of Songs.*

[10]*"Docta ignorantia."* The phrase is from St. Augustine of Hippo (354–430) and was revived a century before Calvin as the title of an important philosophical study of the knowledge of God by Nicolas of Cusa (1401–1464), *De docta ignorantia.*

3. St. Teresa of Ávila
LIFE (1565)

The Catholic response to Lutheran and Calvinist teachings on justification was in many ways typical of the Counter Reformation's answer to Protestantism. On the one hand, many Catholic polemicists ridiculed the "lazy" Lutheran doctrine of salvation by faith alone, arguing that only those who feared the hard work of salvation could propose such an "unscriptural" and "antitraditional" escape. The reform Council of Trent echoed this sentiment and reaffirmed the "ancient" teaching of justification through faith and good works. On the other hand, the same council also introduced moral reforms, particularly among the clergy, intended to eliminate abuses of the sacraments and other "good works," and to promote behavior closer to its ascetic ideal. The writings and life of the Spanish mystic and nun St. Teresa of Ávila (1515–1582) truly embodied both of these responses. The gardening metaphor she uses in her autobiographical *Life,* excerpted below, eloquently encapsulates the Catholic teaching on justification, illustrating the ultimate reliance on divine grace while at the same time demonstrating the necessity of cooperation and constant work by the soul's gardener. Famed for her mystical writings, Teresa was also known as a reformer. Believing that her order, the Carmelites, had strayed too far from its beginnings as a strictly ascetic group, she founded many new convents of "discalced" or shoeless nuns, based on the order's older, more austere rule.

. . . Now to speak of those who are beginning to be servants of love—for this, I think, is what we become when we decide to follow along the way of prayer Him who loved us so greatly. It is so high an honor that even the thought of it brings a strange joy. Servile fear vanishes immediately, if we act as we should in this first stage. . . . For the perfect possession of this true love of God brings all blessings with it. We are so niggardly and so slow to give ourselves entirely to God that we do not prepare ourselves to secure that precious thing, which His Majesty does not wish us to enjoy if we have not paid a high price first. . . .

We resolve to be poor, and that is a great merit. But very often we resume our precautions and take care not to be short of necessities, also of superfluities, and even to collect friends who will supply us. In this way we take greater pains and, perhaps, expose ourselves to greater danger in our anxiety not to go short than we did before, when we had possession of our estates. Presumably we also gave up all thought of our own importance when we became nuns, or when we began to lead a spiritual life and to pursue perfection. Yet the moment our self-importance is wounded we forget that we have given ourselves to God. We want to snatch it up and tear it out of His very hands, as they say, even after we have, to all appear-

ances, made Him lord over our will. And it is the same with everything else.

That is a fine way of seeking God's love! We expect it by the handful, as they say, and yet we want to keep our affections for ourselves! We make no attempt to carry our desires into effect, and fail to raise them above the earth, and yet we want great spiritual comforts. This is not good, for the two aims are, as I see it, irreconcilable. So, since we do not manage wholly to give ourselves up, we never receive the whole of this treasure. May it please the Lord to give it us drop by drop, even though receiving it may cost us all the labors in the world. . . .

Here I shall have to make use of a comparison though, being a woman and writing only what I have been commanded to write, I should like to avoid it. But this spiritual language is so difficult to use for those like myself who have no learning, that I must find some other means of expression. It may be that my comparisons will not very often be effective, in which case your Reverence[11] will be amused at my stupidity. It strikes me that I have read or heard this one before. But as I have a bad memory I do not

---

[11]Teresa's confessors had asked her to prepare this statement of her beliefs in order to ward off any accusations of unorthodoxy by an overly zealous Spanish Inquisition.

know where it occurred or what it illustrated. But for the present it will serve my purpose.

A beginner must look on himself as one setting out to make a garden for his Lord's pleasure, on most unfruitful soil which abounds in weeds. His Majesty roots up the weeds and will put in good plants instead. Let us reckon that this is already done when a soul decides to practice prayer and has begun to do so. We have then, as good gardeners, with God's help to make these plants grow, and to water them carefully so that they do not die, but produce flowers, which give out a good smell, to delight this Lord of ours. Then He will often come to take His pleasure in this garden and enjoy these virtues.

Now let us see how this garden is to be watered, so that we may understand what we have to do, and what labor it will cost us, also whether the gain will outweigh the effort, or how long it will take. It seems to me that the garden may be watered in four different ways. Either the water must be drawn from a well, which is very laborious; or by a water-wheel and buckets, worked by a windlass—I have sometimes drawn it in this way, which is less laborious than the other, and brings up more water—or from a stream or spring, which waters the ground much better, for the soil then retains more moisture and needs watering less often, which entails far less work for the gardener; or by heavy rain, when the Lord waters it Himself without any labor of ours; and this is an incomparably better method than all the rest.

Now to apply these four methods of watering, by which this garden is to be maintained and without which it will fail. This is my purpose, and will, I think, enable me to explain something about the four stages of prayer, to which the Lord has, in His kindness, sometimes raised my soul. May he graciously grant that I may speak in such a way as to be of use to one of the persons who commanded me to write this,[12] whom the Lord has advanced in four months far beyond the point that I have reached in seven-

teen years. He prepared himself better than I, and therefore, without any labor on his part, his garden is watered by all these four means; although it only receives the last water drop by drop. But, as things are going, with the Lord's help, his garden will soon be submerged. If my way of explaining all this seems crazy to him, he is welcome to laugh at me.

We may say that beginners in prayer are those who draw the water up out of the well; which is a great labor, as I have said. For they find it very tiring to keep the senses recollected, when they are used to a life of distraction. Beginners have to accustom themselves to pay no attention to what they see or hear, and to put this exercise into practice during their hours of prayer, when they must remain in solitude, thinking whilst they are alone of their past life. Although all must do this many times, the advanced as well as the beginners, all need not do so equally, as I shall explain later. At first they are distressed because they are not sure that they regret their sins. Yet clearly they do, since they have now sincerely resolved to serve God. They should endeavor to meditate on the life of Christ, and thus the intellect will grow tired. Up to this point we can advance ourselves, though with God's help of course, for without it, as everyone knows, we cannot think one good thought.

This is what I mean by beginning to draw water from the well—and God grant that there may be water in it! But at least this does not depend on us, who have only to draw it up and do what we can to water the flowers. But God is so good that when for reasons known to His Majesty—and perhaps for our greater profit— He wishes the well to be dry, we, like good gardeners, must do what we can ourselves. Meanwhile He preserves the flowers without water, and in this way He makes our virtues grow. Here by water I mean tears, or if there be none, a tenderness and inward feeling of devotion. But what shall a man do here who finds that for many days on end he feels nothing but dryness, dislike, distaste and so little desire to go and draw water that he would give it up

---

[12]Father Pedro Ibañez, a Dominican theologian and also longtime confidant and correspondent of Teresa.

altogether if he did not remember that he is pleasing and serving the Lord of the garden; if he did not want all his service to be in vain, and if he did not also hope to gain something for all the labor of lowering the bucket so often into the well and bringing it up empty? It will often happen that he cannot so much as raise his arms to the task, or think a single good thought. For by this drawing of water I mean, of course, working with the understanding. . . .

It is of especial note—and I say this because I know it from experience—that the soul which begins resolutely to tread this path of mental prayer, and can manage not greatly to care about consolations and tenderness in devotion, neither rejoicing when the Lord gives them nor being discouraged when He withholds them, has already gone a large part of the way. Though it may often stumble, it need have no fear of falling back, for its building has been begun on firm foundations. The love of the Lord does not consist in tears or in these consolations and tendernesses which we so much desire and in which we find comfort, but in our serving Him in justice, fortitude, and humility. Anything else seems to me rather an act of receiving than of giving on our part.

As for a poor woman like myself, a weak and irresolute creature, it seems right that the Lord should lead me on with favors, as He now does, in order that I may bear certain afflictions with which He has been pleased to burden me. But when I hear servants of God, men of weight, learning, and understanding, worrying so much because He is not giving them devotion, it makes me sick to listen to them. I do not say that they should not accept it if God grants it to them, and value it too, for then His Majesty will see that it was good for them, but they should not be distressed when they do not receive it. They should realize that since the Lord does not give it to them they do not need it. They should exercise control over themselves and go right ahead. Let them take it from me that all this fuss is a mistake, as I have myself seen and proved. It is an imperfection in them; they are not advancing in freedom of spirit but hanging back through weakness. . . .

I repeat my warning that it is most important not to raise the spirit if the Lord does not raise it for us; and if He does, we know it immediately. This straining is especially harmful to women, because the devil can delude them. I am quite certain, however, that the Lord will never allow anyone to be harmed who endeavors to approach Him with humility. On the contrary, such a person will derive great gain and advantage from the attack by which Satan intended to destroy him.

I have dwelt for so long on this way of prayer because it is the commonest with beginners and because the advice I offer is very important. I admit that it has been better expressed by others in other places, and that I have felt some shame and confusion in writing this, though not enough. Blessed be the Lord for it all, whose will and pleasure it is that a woman like myself should speak of things that are His, and of such a sublime nature. . . .

C. Anabaptists

Amid all of the religious bigotry and violence that characterized sixteenth-century Europe, no denomination was so universally hated and persecuted as the people known to their opponents as "Anabaptists," or "Rebaptizers." In fact, the people referred to by this derogatory label—who included such groups as the Mennonites and Hutterites—represented a diversity of Christian beliefs, and were united only in two very basic principles: 1) the individual's right to read

Scriptures under no tutelage other than that of the Holy Spirit; and 2) the necessity of informed consent to become a member of "the true Church," a doctrine they believed was self-evident in the biblically ordained bond between personal conversion and baptism. For such individuals, the baptism of a still babbling infant could not be seen as having any spiritual effect, because it was impossible for a newborn truly to understand and accept Christ's sacrifice. Since, however, each of them had already received such baptism shortly after birth, their subsequent adult baptisms were viewed by opponents as a second baptism—an act that had been considered a capital offense since the days of the late Roman Empire. It was this practice that provided the pretext for the relentless and often violent campaigns against Anabaptists that were waged throughout the sixteenth century by Protestant and Catholic rulers alike.

1. LETTER FROM CONRAD GREBEL TO THOMAS MÜNTZER (September 5, 1524)

Although Anabaptists were called "fanatics" by their contemporaries and have been dubbed "radical Protestants" by modern historians, they saw themselves simply as Christians, or Brothers and Sisters. One of the earliest Anabaptist groups began as the result of a disagreement between the Zurich-based Protestant reformer Ulrich Zwingli, and certain members of his congregation, led by Conrad Grebel (1498–1526) and Michael Sattler (1490–1527). Grebel and his supporters fully agreed with Zwingli's reform of the Eucharist and other Catholic rituals but thought him too conservative in his belief that a close alliance should exist between church and state. In 1523 they called on Zwingli to repudiate the city council and to form a new Christian community that would resemble the earliest Christian churches in its communal values and clear separation from the worldliness of the state. When Zwingli rejected their vision, Grebel and his group turned to the presumably more sympathetic pastor Thomas Müntzer (1490–1525) in Saxony, who was similarly alienated from Luther and other Reformation leaders. The resulting letter, excerpted below, reveals the values and goals of an early Anabaptist community, including not just adult baptism, but total withdrawal from the state modeled on the ancient Christians' relationship to the Roman Empire. After receiving no reply from Müntzer (who may never have received the letter), Sattler and his "brethren" went ahead with their plan and began baptizing adult converts in Zurich.

Peace, grace, and mercy from God our Father and Jesus Christ our Lord be with us all, Amen.

Dear Brother Thomas,

For the sake of God, please do not let it surprise you that we address you without title and ask you as a brother henceforth to exchange ideas with us by correspondence, and that we, unsolicited and unknown to you, have dared to initiate such future dialogue. God's Son, Jesus Christ, who offers himself as the only Master and Head to all who are to be saved and commands us to be brethren to all brethren and believers through the one common Word, has moved and impelled us to establish friendship and brotherhood and to bring the following theses to your attention. Also the fact that you have written two booklets on phony faith has led us to write to you. Therefore, if you will accept it graciously for the sake of Christ our Savior, it may, if God wills, serve and work for the good. Amen. . . .

Therefore we ask and admonish you as a brother in the name, power, Word, Spirit, and salvation which comes to all Christians through Jesus Christ our Master and Savior, to seek earnestly to preach only God's Word unflinchingly, to establish and defend only divine practices, to esteem as good and right only what can be found in definite clear Scripture, and to reject, hate, and curse all the schemes, words, practices, and opinions of all men, even your own. . . .

[Grebel then offers a twenty-five-point criticism of Müntzer's translation of the mass into German and of his continuing use of hymns, priestly vestments, and other rituals not supported by Scripture.]

With this, since you are much better informed about the Lord's Supper, and we have merely indicated our understanding, if we are incorrect, teach us better, and be willing yourself to drop chanting and the mass, and act only in accord with the Word, and proclaim and establish the practices of the apostles with the Word. If that cannot be done it would be better to leave everything in Latin, unchanged and uncompromised. If that which is right cannot be established, then still do not administer after your own or the antichristian priestly rites, and at least teach how it ought to be, as Christ does in John 6, teaching how one should eat and drink his flesh and blood. Pay no attention to the apostasy or to the unchristian forbearance, which the very learned foremost evangelical preachers established as an actual idol and planted throughout the world. It is far better that a few be correctly instructed through the Word of God and believe and live

right in virtues and practices than that many believe deceitfully out of adulterated false doctrine. Although we admonish and implore you, we do hope that you will do it of your own accord and are therefore admonishing you in deepest affection because you listened so kindly to our brother and have confessed to him that you have been too lax, and because you and Carlstadt[13] are regarded among us as the purest proclaimers and preachers of the purest Word of God. And if you both properly impugn those who mix human word and practice with the divine, you should also logically break away from the priesthood, benefices, and all kinds of new and ancient practices and from your own and ancient opinions and become completely pure. If your benefices, like ours, are based on interest and tithes, both of which are actual usury, and if you are not supported by one entire congregation, we hope you will withdraw from the benefices. You know well enough how a shepherd is to be supported. . . .

March forward with the Word and create a Christian church with the help of Christ and his rule such as we find instituted in Matthew 18 [:15–20] and practiced in the epistles. Press on in earnest with common prayer and fasting, in accord with faith and love without being commanded and compelled. Then God will help you and your lambs to all purity, and the chanting and the tablets will fall away. There is more than enough wisdom and counsel in the Scripture on how to teach, govern, direct, and make devout all classes and all men. Anyone who will not reform or believe and strives against the Word and acts of God and persists therein, after Christ and his Word and rule have been preached to him, and he has been admonished with the three witnesses before the church [Mt 18:15–17], such a man we say on the basis of God's Word shall not be put to death but regarded as a heathen and publican and left alone.

---

[13]Andreas Bodenstein von Karlstadt (c. 1480–1541), an early associate of Luther in Wittenberg, who was later denounced by his mentor for his violent iconoclasm and other radical tendencies.

Moreover, the gospel and its adherents are not to be protected by the sword,[14] nor [should] they [protect] themselves, which as we have heard through our brother is what you believe and maintain. True believing Christians are sheep among wolves, sheep for the slaughter. They must be baptized in anguish and tribulation, persecution, suffering, and death, tried in fire, and must reach the fatherland of eternal rest not by slaying the physical but the spiritual. They use neither worldly sword nor war, since killing has ceased with them entirely, unless indeed we are still under the old law, and even there (as far as we can know) war was only a plague after they had once conquered the Promised Land. No more of this.

On the subject of baptism, your writing pleases us well, and we ask for further instruction from you. We are taught that without Christ's rule of binding and loosing, even an adult should not be baptized. The Scriptures describe baptism for us, that it signifies the washing away of sins by faith and the blood of Christ (that the nature of the baptized and believing one is changing before and after), that it signifies one has died and shall (die) to sin and walks in newness of life and Spirit and one will surely be saved if one through the inward baptism lives the faith according to this meaning, so that the water does not strengthen and increase faith and give a very great comfort and last resort on the deathbed, as the scholars at Wittenberg say. Also that it does not save, as Augustine, Tertullian, Theophylact, and Cyprian taught,[15] thus dishonoring faith and the suffering of Christ for mature adults and dishonoring the suffering of Christ for un-

baptized infants. On the basis of the following Scriptures—Genesis 8, . . . Romans 1, 2, 7, 10; Matthew 18–19; Mark 9–10; Luke 18, etc.[16] —we hold that all children who have not attained the knowledge to discern between good and evil and have not eaten of the tree of knowledge are surely saved through the suffering of Christ, the new Adam, who has restored the life that has been distorted, because they would have been subject to death and damnation only if Christ had not suffered, not afterward risen to the infirmity of our broken nature, unless it can be proved to us that Christ did not die for children. But in answer to the charge that faith is required of all who are to be saved, we exclude children and on the basis of the above texts accept that they will be saved without faith and that they do not believe; and we conclude from the description of baptism and from Acts (according to which no child was baptized) and also from the above texts, which are the only ones which deal with the subject of children, and all other Scriptures which do not concern children, that infant baptism is a senseless, blasphemous abomination contrary to all Scripture and even contrary to the papacy, for we learn through Cyprian and Augustine that for many years after the time of the apostles, for six hundred years, believers and unbelievers were baptized together, etc. Since you know this ten times better than we, and have published your protestation against infant baptism, we hope that you will not act contrary to God's eternal Word, wisdom, and command, according to which only believers should be baptized and will not baptize children. If you or Carlstadt do not adequately write against infant baptism and all that pertains to it, how and why one is to baptize, etc., I (Conrad Grebel) will try my hand at it and will finish writing out what I have begun against all (except for

---

[14]According to Rom 13:4, "worldly sword" refers to the office of government.

[15]Tertullian (c. 160–c. 225) and Cyprian (d. 258) were church fathers whose contributions to a Catholic orthodoxy predated the Council of Nicaea in 325 C.E. The writings of Augustine (354–430) postdated the Council of Nicaea. It is uncertain to which of several churchmen by the name of Theophylact Grebel was referring. Among the four writers listed by Grebel, it is Augustine (in fact a proponent of infant baptism) who is best known for the doctrine of baptism to which he refers.

---

[16]The verses dealing with the subject of children cited by Grebel were Gen 8:21; Deut 1:39; 30; 6; 31:13; 1 Cor 14:20; Wis 12:19; 1 Pet 2:2; Mt 18:1–6, 10; 19:13–15; Mk 9:33–37; 10: 13–16; Lk 18:15–17. The texts in Romans are uncertain.

you) who have thus far written misleadingly and knowingly about baptism, and who have translated into German the senseless, blasphemous form of infant baptism, like Luther, Leo, Osiander, and the Strasbourgers,[17] and some who have acted even more shamefully. Unless God averts it, I together with all of us are and shall be more certain of persecution by the scholars, etc., than by other people. We beg you not to use or adopt the old rites of the antichrist, such as sacrament, mass, signs, etc. Hold to the Word alone and administer as all emissaries should, especially you and Carlstadt,

and you will be doing more than all the preachers of all nations. . . .

Greet all the brethren for us, the shepherds and the sheep, who accept the Word of faith and salvation with deep desire and hunger, etc. One thing more. We desire a reply from you; and if you publish anything, send it to us by this messenger or another. We would also like to know whether you and Carlstadt are of one mind. We hope and believe you are. We commend to you this messenger, who has also carried letters from us to our dear brother Carlstadt. And if you should go to Carlstadt so that you would reply jointly, that would be a great joy to us. The messenger is to return to us. Whatever we have not adequately paid him will be reimbursed when he returns.

---

[17]The reference here is to Luther's German translation of the baptismal liturgy (1523), which in turn influenced the 1524 versions of Leo Jud, Andreas Osiander (1498–1552), and the Strasbourg city council.

2. *THIRTEEN STATEMENTS OF THE ORDER OF LIFE* AND *A CODE FOR PUBLIC BEHAVIOR* [IN MÜNSTER] (1534)

Violent persecution of the Anabaptists did not spring solely from their attachment to adult baptism. The radical separation of church and state demanded by Sattler and the early Brethren also gave their movement a threatening political dimension. Though the majority of the Swiss Brethren were fervent pacifists (known as *Stäbler,* or "shepherds"), some Anabaptists believed that force was justified in establishing the "true" church's independence from the secular authority of nonbelievers. Some of these so-called "sword-bearers" (*Schwertler*), such as the revolutionary Thomas Müntzer, became involved in the German Peasants' Revolt of 1524–1525, a massive uprising that cost thousands of people their lives. The backlash against all Anabaptists—*Stäbler* or *Schwertler*—was especially severe, with Grebel and several of the early Zurich brethren being executed and the remaining Anabaptist communities being scattered throughout what is now southern Germany and the Czech Republic.

While many other communities were wiped out entirely, one group of refugees was successful in establishing a safe haven in the north German city of Münster. Under the leadership of Jan Mattijs (d. 1534) and later the more apocalyptic Jan Beukelsz (c. 1509–1536), the Münster Anabaptists took control of the city and attempted to establish the New Jerusalem in preparation for the Last Days. Like the executed apologist Balthasar Hübmaier (c. 1487–1528), these *Schwertler* held the minority opinion among Anabaptists that violence was at times justified. Starting in February 1534, Mattijs and Beukelsz issued a series of ordinances establishing capital punishment for blasphemy and a variety of offenses and instituting communalization of all property and eventually polygamy. A joint Protestant-Catholic siege of the city finally succeeded in mid 1535, and hundreds of the inhabitants of Münster were ruthlessly slaughtered while their leaders were slowly tortured to death. The latter's mutilated bodies were then displayed in cages at the top of the main church's tower. Their bones were finally removed in the nineteenth century, but the cages can still be seen today, the final remnants of the *Schwertler* Anabaptist movement.

Although all of us in this holy church of Münster, in whose hearts the law and the will of God are inscribed by the finger of God . . . should readily fulfill them, we, twelve elders of the nation, shall nevertheless summarize them briefly in a list in order that the new state may be protected so that each one may see what to do and what not to do. . . .

The Scripture directs that those who are disobedient and unrepentant regarding several sins shall be punished with the sword:

1. Whoever curses God and his holy Name or his Word shall be killed [Lev 24].

2. No one shall curse governmental authority [Ex 22, Deut 17], on pain of death.

3. Whoever does not honor or obey his parents [Ex 21:21] shall die.

4. Servants must obey their masters, and masters be fair to their servants [Eph 6].

5. Both parties who commit adultery shall die [Ex 20, Lev 20, Mt 5].

6. Those who commit rape, incest, and other unclean sexual sins should die [Ex 22, Lev 20]. . . .

7. Avarice is the root of all evil [1 Tim 6].

8. Concerning robbery, you shall not steal [Ex. 20, Deut 27]: Cursed be he who narrows his neighbor's boundary.

9. Concerning fraud and overcharging [1 Thes 4]: The Lord will judge this.

10. Concerning lying and defamation [Wis 1]: A lying mouth destroys a soul.

11. Concerning disgraceful speech and idle words [Mt 12]: Men must account for every idle word they speak, on the Day of Judgment.

12. Concerning strife, disputes, anger, and envy [Gal 5, 1 Jn 4]: Whoever hates his brother is a murderer.

13. Concerning slander, murmuring, and insurrection among God's people [Lev 19]: There shall be no slanderer or flatterer among the people.

. . . Whoever disobeys these commandments and does not truly repent, shall be rooted out of the people of God, with ban and sword, through the divinely ordained governmental authority.

---

3. LETTER FROM A DUTCH ANABAPTIST MARTYR TO HER DAUGHTER (1573)

From the beginning, most Anabaptists had adopted the *Stäbler,* or pacifist, approach toward secular authority, refusing to go to war, do violence of any kind, or take oaths of political allegiance. (Most of their modern descendants have continued to espouse pacifism, and a few—notably the Amish—have also maintained total separation from the state as a core belief.) These beliefs did not prevent their enemies from painting all Anabaptists as violent revolutionaries, particularly given the association of some of their brethren with the German Peasants' Revolt and the Anabaptist kingdom at Münster. Throughout the remainder of the sixteenth century, their consistent attitude of nonresistance made Anabaptists especially easy targets for religious as well as civic persecution. The Dutch martyr Elisabeth Muntsdorp was probably a member of either a Mennonite (after Menno Simmons, 1496–1561) or Melchiorite (after Melchior Hoffmann, 1498–1543) congregation. Her moving farewell letter to her infant daughter became part of a collection of Anabaptist "testimonies" published during the seventeenth century, when at last violent persecutions of the sect had come to an end.

[Testament] written to Janneken my own dearest daughter, while I was (unworthily) confined for the Lord's sake, in prison, at Antwerp, A.D. 1573.

The true love of God and wisdom of the Father strengthen you in virtue, my dearest child; the Lord of heaven and earth, the God of Abraham, the God of Isaac, and the God of Jacob, the Lord in Israel, keep you in His virtue, and strengthen and confirm your understanding in His truth. My dear little child, I commend you to the almighty, great and terrible God, who only is wise, that He will keep you, and let you grow up in His fear, or that He will take you home in your youth, this is my heart's request of the Lord: you who are yet so young, and whom I must leave here in this wicked, evil, perverse world.

Since, then, the Lord has so ordered and foreordained it, that I must leave you here, and you are here deprived of father and mother, I will commend you to the Lord; let Him do with you according to His holy will. He will govern you, and be a Father to you, so that you shall have no lack here, if you only fear God; for He will be the Father of the orphans and the Protector of the widows.

Hence, my dear lamb, I who am imprisoned and bound here for the Lord's sake, can help you in no other way; I had to leave your father for the Lord's sake, and could keep him only a short time. We were permitted to live together only half a year, after which we were apprehended, because we sought the salvation of our souls. They took him from me, not knowing my condition, and I had to remain in imprisonment, and see him go before me; and it was a great grief to him, that I had to remain here in prison. And now that I have abided the time, and borne you under my heart with great sorrow for nine months, and given birth to you here in prison, in great pain, they have taken you from me. Here I lie, expecting death every morning, and shall now soon follow your dear father. And I, your dear mother, write you, my dearest child, something for a remembrance, that you will thereby remember your dear father and your dear mother.

Since I am now delivered up to death, and must leave you here alone, I must through these lines cause you to remember, that when you have attained your understanding, you endeavor to fear God, and see and examine why and for whose name we both died; and be not ashamed to confess us before the world, for you must know that it is not for the sake of any evil. Hence be not ashamed of us; it is the way which the prophets and the apostles went, and the narrow way which leads into eternal life, for there shall no other way be found by which to be saved.

Hence, my young lamb, for whose sake I still have, and have had, great sorrow, seek, when you have attained your understanding, this narrow way, though there is sometimes much danger in it according to the flesh, as we may see and read, if we diligently examine and read the Scriptures, that much is said concerning the cross of Christ. And there are many in this world who are enemies of the cross, who seek to be free from it among the world, and to escape it. But, my dear child, if we would with Christ seek and inherit salvation, we must also help bear His cross; and this is the cross which He would have us bear: to follow His footsteps, and to help bear His reproach; for Christ Himself says: "Ye shall be persecuted, killed, and dispersed for my name's sake" [Mt 10:17–22; Lk 21:12–13]. Yea, He Himself went before us in this way of reproach, and left us an example, that we should follow His steps; for, for His sake all must be forsaken, father, mother, sister, brother, husband, child, yea, one's own life. . . .

Thus, my dear child, it is now fulfilled in your dear father and mother. It was indeed prophesied to us beforehand, that this was awaiting us; but not everyone is chosen hereunto, nor expects it; the Lord has chosen us hereunto. Hence, when you have attained your understanding, follow this example of your father and mother. And, my dear child, this is my request of you, since you are still very little and young; I wrote this when you were but one month old. As I am soon now to offer up my sacrifice, by the help of the Lord, I leave you this: "That you fulfill my request, always uniting with them that fear God; and do not regard the pomp and boasting of the world, nor the great multitude, whose way leads to the abyss of hell, but look at the little flock of Israelites, who have no freedom anywhere, and must always flee from one land to the other, as Abraham did; that you may hereafter obtain your fatherland; for if you seek your salvation, it is easy to perceive which is the way that leads to life, or the way that leads into hell. Above all things, seek the kingdom of heaven and His righteousness; and whatever you need besides shall be added unto you. Mt 6:33."

Further, my dear child, I pray you, that wherever you live when you are grown up, and

begin to have understanding, you conduct yourself well and honestly, so that no one need have cause to complain of you. And always be faithful, taking good heed not to wrong any one. Learn to carry your hands always uprightly, and see that you like to work, for Paul says: "If any will not work, neither shall he eat." 2 Thes 3:10. And Peter says: "He that will love life, and see good days, let him refrain his tongue from evil." 1 Pet 3:10.

Hence, my dear Janneken, do not accustom your mouth to filthy talk, nor to ugly words that are not proper, nor to lies; for a liar has no part in the kingdom of heaven; for it is written: "The mouth that lieth slayeth the soul" [Wis 1:11]. Hence beware of this, and run not in the street as other bad children do; rather take up a book, and learn to seek there that which concerns your salvation.

And where you have your home, obey those whose bread you eat. If they speak evil, do you speak well. And learn always to love to be doing something; and do not think yourself too good for anything, nor exalt yourself, but condescend to the lowly, and always honor the aged wherever you are.

I leave you here; oh, that it had pleased the Lord, that I might have brought you up; I should so gladly have done my best with respect to it; but it seems that it is not the Lord's will. And though it had not come thus, and I had remained with you for a time, the Lord could still take me from you, and then, too, you should have to be without me, even as it has now gone with your father and myself, that we could live together but so short a time, when we were so well joined since the Lord had so well mated us, that we would not have forsaken each other for the whole world, and yet we had to leave each other for the Lord's sake. So I must also leave you here, my dearest lamb; the Lord that created and made you now takes me from you, it is His holy will. I must now pass through this narrow way which the prophets and martyrs of Christ passed through, and many thousands who put off the mortal clothing, who died here for Christ, and now they wait under the altar till their number shall be fulfilled, of which number your dear father is one. And I am now on the point of following him, for I am delivered up to death, as it appears in the eyes of man; but if it were not the will of the Lord (though it seems that I am delivered up to death), He could yet easily deliver me out of their hands and give me back to you, my child. Even as the Lord returned to Abraham his son Isaac [Gen 22], so He could still easily do it; He is still the same God that delivered Daniel out of the lion's den, and the three young men out of the fiery furnace; [cf. Dan 3ff.] He could still easily deliver me out of the hands of man. . . .

O my dearest lamb, that you might know the truth when you have attained your understanding, and that you might follow your dear father and mother, who went before you; for your dear father demonstrated with his blood that it is the genuine truth, and I also hope to attest the same with my blood, though flesh and blood must remain on the posts and on the stake, well knowing that we shall meet hereafter. Do you also follow us my dear lamb, that you too may come where we shall be, and that we may find one another there, where the Lord shall say: "Come, ye blessed of my Father, inherit the kingdom prepared for you from the beginning." . . .

I leave you here among my friends; I hope that my father, and my stepmother, and my brothers, and my sisters will do the best with you as long as they live. Be subject and obedient to them in everything, so far as is not contrary to God. I leave you what comes from my mother's death, namely, thirty guilders and over; I do not know how much it is, since I have been long imprisoned here, and do not know what it has all cost. But I hope that Grietge, my dear sister, who has shown me so much friendship, will do her best to give you what belongs to you. And as to what may come to you from your father, I do not know, since I can learn nothing about his parents, because it is so far from here; if they should inquire after you, my friends may do the best in the matter.

And so, Janneken, my dear lamb, who are yet very little and young, I leave you this letter, together with a gold real, which I had with me in prison, and this I leave you for a perpetual adieu, and for a testament; that you may remember me by it, as also by this letter. Read it, when you have understanding, and keep it as long as you live in remembrance of me and of your father, if peradventure you might be edified by it. And I herewith bid you adieu, my dear Janneken Munstdorp, and kiss you heartily, my dear lamb, with a perpetual kiss of peace. Follow me and your father, and be not ashamed to confess us before the world, for we were not ashamed to confess our faith before the world, and this adulterous generation; hence I pray you, that you be not ashamed to confess our faith, since it is the true evangelical faith, another than which shall never be found.

Let it be your glory, that we did not die for any evil doing, and strive to do likewise, though they should also seek to kill you. And on no account cease to love God above all, for no one can prevent you from fearing God. If you follow that which is good, and seek peace, and ensue it, you shall receive the crown of eternal life; this crown I wish you and the crucified, bleeding, naked, despised, rejected and slain Jesus Christ for your bridegroom.

D. Indoctrination

Indoctrination was not a pejorative word in the sixteenth century. In fact, the inculcation of correct Christian teaching was a common, if often frustrated, goal of all religious reformers, Catholic as well as Protestant. What was unique to the era of the Reformation was both the new diversity of Christian creeds and the development of new methods for conveying these creeds within a competitive marketplace of ideas. Without a doubt the most important technological development in this respect was the emergence of the printing press during the second half of the fifteenth century. In their first forty years of existence, European presses published more books (over six million) than the combined total that had been produced during the previous one thousand years. By the time of the Reformation, no city or small town was untouched by the constant influx of new titles and authors that this thriving industry produced. Driven by new Protestant (and later Catholic) campaigns to educate the laity, such publications constituted a dramatic transformation of evangelizing techniques unsurpassed in all of Christian history.

1. WOODCUTS

The first wave of evangelical propaganda, during the 1520s, consisted mainly of attacks on the leadership of the Catholic Church. A few early pamphlets delved into more sophisticated theological issues, but the majority aimed at demonstrating the numerous deviations of the Roman church from the "true" Christianity described in the Bible. Amid the numerous literary forms adopted for this purpose, one of the most popular was the dialogue, which allowed readers to witness the contrast between truth and lies in the personifications of the "true" and "false" Christian. The latter was often a scheming priest or monk, bent on distorting God's word to his own corrupt ends. In a society with a literacy rate of only 10–15%, most of these publications reached people only indirectly, through a public reading or word of mouth, if at all. Woodcuts and engravings, on the other hand, were accessible to everyone. What they lacked in depth of message they made up for in directness and succinctness. Over time, the simple images depicted on the earliest woodcuts—such as a picture of a fat, richly robed and corrupt pope contrasted with a view of a poor and suffering Christ—evolved into a more sophisticated art form, featuring images that ranged from crude, grotesque, and scatological caricatures of the Roman Antichrist and his clerical minions to highly detailed visual comparisons of "true" and "false" faith.

(i)

(ii)

(iii)

(iv)

Lucas Cranach, pamphlet (1521)
A simple but effective evangelical contrast between Christ and his alleged earthly representative, the pope. While Jesus washes the feet of his apostles **(i)**, the pope makes kings and emperors kiss his own feet **(ii)**. Jesus drives the moneychangers out of the temple **(iii)**; the pope himself acts as a moneychanger by selling indulgences and religious dispensations **(iv)**. *(Pierpont Morgan Library, New York)*

Unknown Artist, pamphlet (1522)
Another example of anticlerical satire. The wolfish pope (with tiara), together with his cardinals, bishops, and monks, have used their nets to entrap the foolish leaders of the world and their wealth (the crowned geese with pearls). *(Herzog August Bibliothek, Wolfenbuttel)*

Lucas Cranach, pamphlet (1545)
The rhymed caption to this crude attack reads, "The pope has done to the kingdom of Christ/What is here being done to his own crown/Do it two at a time, says the Spirit/Fill it up confidently; in God we trust." *(Brieg Gymnasialbibliothek)*

Bapſt hat dem reich Chriſti gethon
Wie man hie handelt ſeine Cron.
Machts jr zweifeltig: ſpricht der geiſt
Schenckt getroſt ein: Gott iſts ders heiſt.
Mart: Luth: D.

2. HYMNS

Evangelical hymns, almost invariably in the vernacular, both instructed and fortified the faithful. The ancient Christian theme of conflict between the forces of light and darkness was revived by Martin Luther in his famous hymn "A Mighty Fortress Is Our God." Such violent apocalyptic imagery was in fact typical of many early evangelical hymns, which purposely recalled the steely resolve of ancient martyrs in the face of persecution and their undying faith in the imminence of Christ's Second Coming. Paul Speratus's hymn, "Salvation unto Us Has Come," by comparison, moves well beyond a battle-cry of the faithful to propagate the Lutheran doctrine of justification through faith alone, packing an astonishing number of theological details into a few stanzas. It is a capsulated form of the most important Protestant innovation in religious indoctrination—the published catechism (see 5D3). The hymn's use of rhyme and meter and the emotional power of music were all thought to aid in impressing churchgoers with the basic tenets of the faith as they worshipped.

a. MARTIN LUTHER, "A MIGHTY FORTRESS IS OUR GOD" (1527–1528)

1. A mighty fortress is our God,
A sword and shield victorious;
He breaks the cruel oppressor's rod
And wins salvation glorious.
The old satanic foe
Has sworn to work us woe!
With craft and dreadful might
He arms himself to fight.
On earth he has no equal.

2. No strength of ours can match his might!
We would be lost, rejected.
But now a champion comes to fight,
Whom God himself elected.
You ask who this may be?
The Lord of hosts is he!
Christ Jesus, mighty Lord,
God's only Son, adored.
He holds the field victorious.

3. Though hordes of devils fill the land
All threat'ning to devour us,
We tremble not, unmoved we stand;
They cannot overpow'r us,
Let this world's tyrant rage;
In battle we'll engage!
His might is doomed to fail;
God's judgment must prevail!
One little word subdues him.

4. God's Word forever shall abide,
No thanks to foes, who fear it;
For God himself fights by our side
With weapons of the Spirit.
Were they to take our house,
Goods, honor, child, or spouse,
Though life be wrenched away,
They cannot win the day.
The Kingdom's ours forever!

b. PAUL SPERATUS, "SALVATION UNTO US HAS COME" (1524)

1. Salvation unto us has come
By God's free grace and favor;
Good works cannot avert our doom,
They help and save us never.
Faith looks to Jesus Christ alone,
Who did for all the world atone;
He is our mediator.

2. Theirs was a false, misleading dream
Who thought God's law was given
That sinners might themselves redeem
And by their works gain heaven.
The Law is but a mirror bright
To bring the inbred sin to light
That lurks within our nature.

3. And yet the Law fulfilled must be,
Or we were lost forever;

Therefore God sent his Son that he
Might us from death deliver.
He all the Law for us fulfilled,
And thus his Father's anger stilled
Which over us impended.

4. Faith clings to Jesus' cross alone
And rests in him unceasing;
And by its fruits true faith is known,
With love and hope unceasing.
For faith alone can justify;
Works serve our neighbor and supply
The proof that faith is living.

5. All blessing, honor, thanks, and praise
To Father, Son, and Spirit,
The God who saved us by his grace;
All glory to his merit.
O triune God in heav'n above,
You have revealed your saving love;
Your blessed name we hallow.

3. THE HEIDELBERG CATECHISM (1563)

Luther first published a small book of religious questions and answers for children in 1529. Intended as an instructional guide for parents and pastors, the new catechism was wildly popular, spawning numerous imitations, including some authored by Catholics and Calvinists. The most famous of the latter was the so-called Heidelberg catechism, drawn up by Reformed (Calvinist) theologians under the sponsorship of the Elector of the Rhineland-Palatinate in western Germany. Unlike the primitive anti-papist woodcuts and other polemics of the early Reformation, the Heidelberg catechism aimed at a more thorough and uniform indoctrination, be it of an unformed child or an ignorant (and possibly obstinate) adult. Most catechisms were organized as a series of weekly lessons, each based on a theme that would, ideally, be similar to that Sunday's homily. In this way, the questions and answers memorized in Sunday school, together with the sermons explaining them, could be internalized in digestible bits.

PART III: THANKFULNESS

Lord's Day 32

Q. 86. *Since we are redeemed from our sin and its wretched consequences by grace through Christ without any merit of our own, why must we do good works?*

A. Because just as Christ has redeemed us with his blood he also renews us through his Holy Spirit according to his own image, so that with our whole life we may show ourselves grateful to God for his goodness and that he may be glorified through us; and further, so that we ourselves may be assured of our faith by its fruits and by our reverent behavior may win our neighbors to Christ.

Q. 87. *Can those who do not turn to God from their ungrateful, impenitent life be saved?*

A. Certainly not! Scripture says, "Surely you know that the unjust will never come into possession of the kingdom of God. Make no mistake; no fornicator or idolater, none who are guilty either of adultery or of homosexual perversion, no thieves or grabbers or drunkards or slanderers or swindlers, will possess the kingdom of God" [1 Cor 6:9–10].

Lord's Day 33

Q. 88. *How many parts are there to the true repentance or conversion of man?*

A. Two: the dying of the old self and the birth of the new.

Q. 89. *What is the dying of the old self?*

A. Sincere sorrow over our sins and more and more to hate them and to flee from them.

Q. 90. *What is the birth of the new man?*

A. Complete joy in God through Christ and a strong desire to live according to the will of God in all good works.

Q. 91. *But what are good works?*

A. Only those which are done out of true faith, in accordance with the Law of God, and for his glory, and not those based on our own opinion or on the traditions of men.

Lord's Day 34

Q. 92. *What is the Law of God?*

A. God spoke all these words saying: [recitation of the Ten Commandments].

Q. 93. *How are these commandments divided?*

A. Into two tables, the first of which teaches us in four commandments how we ought to live in relation to God; the other, in six commandments, what we owe to our neighbor.

Q. 94. *What does the Lord require in the first commandment?*

A. That I must avoid and flee all idolatry, sorcery, enchantments, invocation of saints or other

creatures because of the risk of losing my salvation. Indeed, I ought properly to acknowledge the only true God, trust in him alone, in humility and patience expect all good from him only, and love, fear and honor him with my whole heart. In short, I should rather turn my back on all creatures than do the least thing against his will.

Q. 95. *What is idolatry?*

A. It is to imagine or possess something in which to put one's trust in place of or beside the one true God who has revealed himself in his Word.

Lord's Day 35

Q. 96. *What does God require in the second commandment?*

A. That we should not represent him or worship him in any other manner than he has commanded in his Word.

Q. 97. *Should we, then, not make any images at all?*

A. God cannot and should not be pictured in any way. As for creatures, although they may indeed be portrayed, God forbids making or having any likeness of them in order to worship them, or to use them to serve him.

Q. 98. *But may not pictures be tolerated in churches in place of books for unlearned people?*

A. No, for we must not try to be wiser than God who does not want his people to be taught by means of lifeless idols, but through the living preaching of his Word.

Lord's Day 36

Q. 99. *What is required in the third commandment?*

A. That we must not profane or abuse the name of God by cursing, by perjury, or by unnecessary oaths. Nor are we to participate in such horrible sins by keeping quiet and thus giving silent consent. In a word, we must not use the holy name of God except with fear and reverence so that he may be rightly confessed and addressed by us, and be glorified in all our words and works.

Q. 100. *Is it, therefore, so great a sin to blaspheme God's name by cursing and swearing that God is also angry with those who do not try to prevent and forbid it as much as they can?*

A. Yes, indeed; for no sin is greater or provokes his wrath more than the profaning of his name. That is why he commanded it to be punished with death.

Lord's Day 37

Q. 101. *But may we not swear oaths by the name of God in a devout manner?*

A. Yes, when the civil authorities require it of their subjects, or when it is otherwise needed to maintain and promote fidelity and truth, to the glory of God and the welfare of our neighbor. Such oath-taking is grounded in God's Word and has therefore been rightly used by God's people under the Old and New Covenants.

Q. 102. *May we also swear by the saints or other creatures?*

A. No; for a lawful oath is a calling upon God, as the only searcher of hearts, to bear witness to the truth, and to punish me if I swear falsely. No creature deserves such honor.

Lord's Day 38

Q. 103. *What does God require in the fourth commandment?*

A. First, that the ministry of the gospel and Christian education be maintained, and that I diligently attend church, especially on the Lord's day, to hear the Word of God, to participate in the holy Sacraments, to call publicly upon the Lord, and to give Christian service to those in need. Second, that I cease from my evil works all the days of my life, allow the Lord to work in me through his Spirit, and thus begin in this life the eternal Sabbath. . . .

---

4. LETTER FROM DUTCH CALVINIST MINISTER ON RURAL IGNORANCE AND APATHY (1602)

Despite the great publishing success of catechisms and other religious works, the actual progress of denominational indoctrination should not be overstated. When Lutheran, Calvinist, and Catholic authorities sent out inspectors to check on the success of their respective reform programs, most were disappointed by the continuing ignorance and even popular resistance their clergy faced. Clergy often found that the best they could do was to accept ill-informed members into their congregations; otherwise they faced empty pews and a surrounding community that was either indifferent or openly hostile to their efforts. The resistance of laypeople to religious indoctrination was a particular frustration to the new and much more ambitious ministers and priests of the late sixteenth century, who—in contrast to their pre-Reformation predecessors—were themselves generally very well educated in their denominations' respective teachings. Their morale was not helped by a continuing shortage of clerical recruits as well as low pay and assignments to communities that often did not welcome outsiders. The following complaints of a young Reformed (Calvinist) minister posted in the Dutch countryside were disappointingly familiar to all religious leaders of the times.

To the Reverend and Most Renowned Master Franciscus Junius, Doctor of Sacred Theology and Professor at the university of Leiden. (I will pay the boatman who brings your reply.)

Greeting many times over, most Reverend, Renowned and Esteemed Doctor, Pardon my boldness, that I should interrupt you so boldly, involved as you are in the concerns of the university of Leiden and of the Church and immersed in the controversies with the Jesuits: necessity compels me and the care for my church to which my God has destined me. It is now two months since I undertook the ministry of the Word of God in this village of Aarlanderveen. I have quite shocked the rustics, simple souls, who can scarcely tell A from B. This is not surprising for they have been without a minister for a good two years and they are all devoted either to Lutheranism or to the Papists. The church consists of only six men and seven women; there are no elders and only a single deacon. In general the village is quite populous and many here would wish to join the church, but they fear the mocking laughter of the Lutherans (of whom there is here a huge number). Hear, most renowned master, the state of the church and entertain briefly the reason for my writing. Whitsuntide[18] is at hand when the Lord's Supper is administered in all the villages. When therefore I now summon even those who are outside the church and invite these with more kindly words to Holy Communion, I cause offense to many. These say that they are indeed convinced in their hearts of the truth of our religion, but are, however, too little advanced in the fundamentals of religion and cannot advance sufficiently on account of their agricul-

tural pursuits. Nevertheless they seek to be received into the church, saying that they believe in Christ crucified, that they renounce their works except [those performed] by the sole merit of Christ. I ask whether this profession is adequate and whether I am allowed to admit such to the church, when their outward life coincides with this confession. I ask you, Reverend Doctor, in the name of Jesus Christ to the increase of whose Church I devote myself, to reply to me at once, if you are able, for they press me greatly. Once I have admitted them, the Lutherans will say that they too can profess the same [things] and are similarly not to be excluded in future from the service or else (for they are embittered) they will say sarcastically, "behold, these are the Reformed." On the other hand, if I exclude these (since the people here are simple souls), no one, who is conscious of his ignorance, will ever join the church. As I am beset on all sides I eagerly await your judgement. I ask you urgently to free me from my difficulties with a few words, or else, if you are unable to do so because you are busy, to prevail on Master Gomarus or Master Trelcatius to write me. For those who wish to join the church press for an answer. May the perfect and almighty God keep you safe for a long time for the sake of the churches of Holland, the University and the Commonwealth to the glory of His name. 3 May 1602.

Most humble servant of Christ and admirer of your learning, Johannes Lydius, minister of the Word of God in Aarlanderveen.

---

[18]Also known as pentecost, marking the descent of the Holy Spirit upon the Apostles and celebrated fifty days after Easter.

5. St. Ignatius Loyola
SPIRITUAL EXERCISES (1533)

In most methods of indoctrination—as with many other reform issues—Catholics followed and imitated Protestant successes. One of the few Catholic trailblazers in this arena was Ignatius Loyola (1491–1556), founder of the Society of Jesus, or Jesuits. Until he was wounded at the 1520 battle of Pamplona, Loyola had been committed to a military and court career in his native Spain.

While convalescing, however, he experienced a religious conversion and began to write the earliest drafts of his *Spiritual Exercises.* This document underwent many revisions during Loyola's subsequent experiences as a pilgrim in the Holy Land and student at the University of Paris. It took on a fresh significance following the pope's approval of his new religious order in 1540. Novices as well as seasoned Jesuits thereafter regularly employed the *Exercises* as a guide in the cultivation of their own consciences with the goal of strengthening their resolve to do God's will. As in Teresa of Ávila's garden, the cultivation that Loyola describes is most laborious at the beginning and requires both hard work and close supervision. Thus it is important for each aspirant (or "exercitant") to have a skilled Spiritual Director to monitor progress and judge when the next level of exercise should be attempted. According to Loyola, the seeds of doctrine should only be planted once the soil of the aspirant's soul has been sufficiently prepared, in particular by making sure that the spiritual beginner has achieved an intensely personalized sense of sin and hell. This first stage, or "week," is an absolute prerequisite to the exercitant's voluntarily embracing Christ and his church during the second, third, and fourth weeks. The rigorous discipline involved in Loyola's *Spiritual Exercises* and the thorough indoctrination that resulted has led some historians to compare the experience to basic training in the military. Certainly, sixteenth-century Jesuits treasured their reputation as highly motivated and focused missionaries, reveling in the hardships they faced both in European lands and in Asia and the Americas.

PRINCIPLE AND FOUNDATION

Man was created to praise, reverence, and serve God our Lord, and by this means to save his soul. The other things on the face of the earth were created for man's sake, and in order to aid him in the prosecution of the end for which he was created. Consequently, man ought to make use of them just so far as they help him to attain his end; he ought to withdraw himself from them just so far as they hinder him. It is therefore necessary that we should make ourselves indifferent to all created things, in all that is left to the liberty of our free will and is not forbidden, so that we do not for our part wish for health rather than sickness, for wealth rather than poverty, for honor rather than dishonor, for a long life rather than a short one, and so in all other things, desiring and choosing only that which leads us more directly to the end for which we were created.

THE PARTICULAR EXAMINATION—

to be made three times daily, and an examination of oneself to be made twice.

1. In the morning: Immediately on rising, the man ought to resolve to guard himself carefully against that particular sin or defect which he desires to correct and amend.

2. After the midday meal: He ought to ask of God our Lord that which he desires, i.e., grace to remember how often he has fallen into that particular sin or defect and to make amends in the future. After this, let him make the first examination, demanding an account from his soul concerning the particular matter which he desires to correct or amend, reviewing the time elapsed hour by hour, or period by period, beginning from the time when he rose till the moment of the present examination. Let him

mark on the first line of the diagram[19] as many points as there are times when he has fallen into that particular sin or defect. Afterwards let him resolve anew to amend himself until the second examination that he will make.

3. After supper: The second examination will be made in the same way, going through the interval hour by hour from the first examination to the present one, and marking on the second line of the same diagram as many points as there are times he has again fallen into that same particular sin or defect. . . .

GENERAL EXAMINATION OF CONSCIENCE
In Order to Purify Oneself and to Confess Better

I presuppose that there are within me three kinds of thoughts: one my own, which springs entirely from my own liberty and will; and two others, which come from without, one from the good spirit and the other from the evil.

Of Thoughts
There are two ways of gaining merit from an evil thought which comes from without.

1. For example, a thought comes of committing a mortal sin, which thought I resist promptly, and it remains conquered.

2. When the same evil thought comes to me, and I resist it, and it returns time after time, and I always resist it, until it goes away conquered; and this second way is much more meritorious than the first.

A venial sin is committed when the same thought of sinning mortally comes and one gives ear to it, dwelling a few moments on it, or receiving some slight sensual delectation, or when there is some negligence in rejecting such a thought.

There are two ways of sinning mortally:

1. When a man gives consent to an evil thought with the intention of acting afterwards according to this consent, or with the desire of doing so if he could.

2. When that sin is carried out in action; and this is a more grievous sin for three reasons: first, on account of the longer time; secondly, on account of the greater intensity; thirdly, on account of the greater injury to both persons. . . .

THE SECOND EXERCISE

A meditation upon sins; it contains, after the preparatory prayer and two preludes, five points and a colloquy. PREPARATORY PRAYER. Let the preparatory be the same.

FIRST PRELUDE. The first prelude will be the same [as in the first exercise].

SECOND PRELUDE. The second prelude is to ask for that which I desire; it will be here to beg great and intense sorrow and tears for my sins.

FIRST POINT. The first point is the review of the sins, that is to say to recall to memory all the sins of my life, contemplating them from year to year, or from period to period. Three things help in this: first, to behold the place and the house where I have lived; second, to recall the intercourse I have had with others; third, the occupation in which I have been engaged.

SECOND POINT. The second, is to weigh the sins, considering the foulness and malice that each mortal sin committed has in itself, even supposing that it were not forbidden.

THIRD POINT. The third, is to consider who I am, abasing myself by comparisons: 1st, what am I in comparison with all men; 2nd, what are all men in comparison with the angels and saints in heaven; 3rd, to consider what is all creation in comparison with God—therefore, myself alone, what can I be? 4th, to consider all my corruption and bodily foulness; 5th, to behold myself as an ulcer and abscess whence have issued so many sins and iniquities and such vile poison.

FOURTH POINT. The fourth point, is to consider who God is, against Whom I have sinned, contemplating His attributes and comparing

---

[19]Designed for tallying sins.

them with their contraries in myself: His wisdom with my ignorance, His omnipotence with my weakness, His justice with my iniquity, His goodness with my perversity.

FIFTH POINT. The fifth point, is an exclamation of wonder, with great affection running through all creatures in my mind, and thinking how they have suffered me to live, and have preserved me in life; how the angels, who are the sword of the divine justice, have borne with me and guarded me and prayed for me; how the saints have been interceding and entreating for me; and the heavens, sun, moon, stars, and elements, fruits, birds, fishes, and beasts (have ministered to me); and the earth, how it has not opened to swallow me up, creating new hells that I might suffer in them forever.

COLLOQUY. To end with a colloquy of mercy, reasoning and giving thanks to God our Lord, that He has given me life until now, and resolving with his grace to amend for the future. *Our Father. . . .*

THE FIFTH EXERCISE

A meditation on hell: it contains, after the preparatory prayer and two preludes, five points and one colloquy. PREPARATORY PRAYER. Let the preparatory prayer be the usual one.

FIRST PRELUDE. The first prelude is a composition of place, which is here to see with the eyes of the imagination the length, breadth and depth of hell.

SECOND PRELUDE. To ask for that which I desire. It will be here to ask for an interior sense of the pain which the lost suffer, in order that if through my faults I should forget the love of the eternal Lord, at least the fear of punishment may help me not to fall into sin.

FIRST POINT. To see with the eyes of the imagination those great fires, and the souls as it were in bodies of fire.

SECOND POINT. To hear with the ears the wailings, the groans, the cries, the blasphemies against Christ our Lord, and against all His saints.

THIRD POINT. To smell with the sense of smell, the smoke, the brimstone, the filth, and the corruption.

FOURTH POINT. To taste with the sense of taste, bitter things, such as tears, sadness, and the worm of conscience.

FIFTH POINT. To feel with the sense of touch how those fires touch and burn the souls.

COLLOQUY. To make a colloquy with Christ our Lord, to bring to memory the souls that are in hell, some because they did not believe in His coming; others because, though believing, they did not act according to His commandments. Making three classes:

1. (Those who were lost) before His coming.
2. (Those who were lost) during His life in the world.
3. (Those who have been lost) since that time; and herewith to give Him thanks that He has not, by putting an end to my life, permitted me to fall into any of these classes. In like manner, to consider how until now He has always treated me with so great pity and mercy; ending with an *Our Father.*

The First Exercise is to be made at midnight; the second immediately on rising in the morning; the third before or after Mass, but so that it be made before dinner[20]; the fourth at the hour of Vespers[21]; the fifth one hour before supper. This arrangement of hours, more or less, is to be observed in all the four Weeks, so far as age, disposition, and constitution enable the retreatant to make the five Exercises a day, or fewer.

ADDITIONS

For the purpose of helping the retreatant to make the Exercises better, and to find more surely what he desires.

1. After having gone to bed, when I wish to go to sleep, to think, for the space of a *Hail*

---

[20]I.e., midday.
[21]I.e., late afternoon.

Mary, of the hour when I ought to rise, and for what purpose, recapitulating the Exercise which I have to make.

2. When I awake, not admitting other thoughts, at once to turn my mind to that which I am going to contemplate in the first Exercise at midnight, exciting myself to confusion for my many sins, setting before myself examples, e.g. as if a knight were to find himself in the presence of his king and all his court, covered with shame and confusion because he has grievously offended him from whom he has first received many gifts and favors. Likewise in the second Exercise, considering myself a great sinner, bound with chains and about to appear before the supreme eternal Judge, taking as an example how prisoners in chains, and worthy of death appear before their temporal judge; and with these thoughts, or with others, according to the subject matter, to dress myself.

3. One or two paces from the place in which I am about to meditate, I will stand for the space of an *Our Father,* with my mind raised on high, considering how God our Lord sees me, etc., and make an act of reverence or humiliation.

4. To enter upon the contemplation, at one time kneeling, at another prostrate on the ground, or lying face upwards, or seated, or standing, always intent on seeking that which I desire. Here we will make two observations: first, if kneeling I find that which I desire, I will not change to another position; and if prostrate, in like manner, etc.; secondly, in the point in which I find that which I desire there will I rest without being anxious to proceed farther, until I have satisfied myself.

5. After the Exercise is finished, for the space of a quarter of an hour, either sitting or walking, I will examine how it has gone with me in the contemplation or meditation; if badly, I will look over the cause whence it proceeds, and when I have discovered it I will be sorry for it, so as to amend in future. If well, I will thank God our Lord, and proceed in the same manner another time.

6. To refuse to think of pleasant and joyful things, as of glory, the Resurrection, etc.; because any consideration of joy and delight hinders the feeling of pain, sorrow, and tears for our sins; but rather to keep before my mind that I desire to be sorry and to feel the pain, remembering rather death and judgment.

7. For the same purpose to deprive myself of all light, closing the shutters and doors while I am in my room, except to say prayers, to read, or to take food.

8. Not to laugh, nor to say anything that may provoke laughter.

9. To restrain my eyes, except in receiving or taking leave of the person with whom I shall speak.

10. Penance, divided into interior and exterior: Interior penance consists in grieving for one's sins, with a firm resolution not to commit the same or any others. Exterior penance, which is the fruit of the former, consists in chastisement for sins committed. . . .

E. Religious Toleration

Unlike most ancient religions, early Christianity was from the beginning an exclusive and thus dogmatically intolerant religion. By the time of Christianity's legalization in the fourth century, the vehemence normally reserved for pagan competitors was increasingly evident in intra-ecclesiastical disputes, occasionally leading to violent suppression, as in the case of the Donatists and the Pelagians (see 2C). Still, it was not until the Middle Ages that state coercion was regularly applied in cases of "false teaching," or heresy (see 4D). The Protestant Reformation and its fracturing of the Western church merely exacerbated this long-standing reliance on "the sword" to settle serious doctrinal dissent. All European states had an official religion—be it Catholic, Lutheran, or Calvinist—and the governments of these states did not hesitate to discipline, expel, and sometimes even execute obstinate adherents to other "heretical" denominations. Inquisitorial methods and censorship were ubiquitous in the sixteenth century, as were popular riots and lynchings of persecuted minorities.

Religious toleration, consequently, was a contradiction in terms in Reformation Europe. In Germany the 1555 Peace of Augsburg established a truce among Protestant and Catholic states, allowing each ruler to choose the official religion in his territory. This principle of *"cuius regio, eius religio"* ("whose region, his religion") eliminated interterritorial conflicts between German Protestants and Catholics for a time but did not address the problem of religious pluralism within a state; indeed, it exacerbated the internal conflicts that were also raging in England, Holland, and especially France. Soon these religious tensions led to the unprecedented Europewide conflict known today as the Thirty Years' War (1618–1648). This war, which was fought across the vast expanse of kingdoms, principalities, and other territories that are now known as Germany, involved all the major European powers of the day. While all of the combatants claimed to be fighting for religious reasons, most were equally—if not more strongly—motivated by the desire for territorial and political gain. Even at the end of this extremely bloody "religious" war, the only progress toward Protestant and Catholic coexistence was the establishment of a universal principle of *cuius regio, eius religio.* Full religious tolerance and pluralism, which require the separation of church and state, would not come to most of Europe until the early nineteenth century and, in some places, even later.

1. TWO LETTERS ON THE ST. BARTHOLOMEW'S DAY MASSACRE

The St. Bartholomew's Day Massacre (August 24, 1572) has become emblematic of the hatred and barbarity unleashed by religious intolerance during the centuries following the Reformation. Ironically, the days immediately before the massacre were filled with great hope as French Protestant and Catholic leaders gathered in Paris to celebrate the wedding of Henri of Bourbon, king of Navarre, to the princess Marguerite. Henri was a Protestant—or Huguenot, as they were known in France—while Marguerite was the sister of the Catholic king of France, Charles IX of the House of Valois. At some point during the several days of post-wedding festivities, however, the Queen Mother was persuaded by the arch-Catholic faction to seize the opportunity to have the Huguenot leader, Admiral Coligny, assassinated. The initial botched attempt was followed by the slaughter of at least 10,000 Huguenots in Paris and thousands more in the provinces. Protestant leaders such as Théodor Beza (1519–1605) were understandably stunned by news of the massacre. In the first reading below, Beza speculates that it was part of a larger Catholic conspiracy hatched at the reform Council of Trent (1545–1563). Meanwhile, Catholics throughout the continent rejoiced at a decisive blow against dangerous heretics, celebrating the event with *Te Deum* masses and huge festivals. In the second letter excerpted below, a Jesuit named Joachim Opser greets the massacre triumphantly as a vindication of the Catholic Church.

Predictably, the massacre only embittered both sides further and ushered in another twenty years of religiously motivated assassinations and battles throughout France. In 1593 the same Henri of Navarre was at last able to end this period of civil war by publicly embracing Catholicism (with his now famous words, "Paris is worth a mass"), thus gaining recognition from all sides as the new king, Henri IV. Shortly after his ascension to the throne, he issued the famous Edict of Nantes, granting religious toleration to Huguenots within certain walled cities of France. Although Henri's 1598 decree would be scaled back by later rulers— and eventually revoked by King Louis XIV in 1685—it did succeed in preserving the peace for a time. Along with its German counterpart, the Peace of Augsburg (1555), the Edict of Nantes represented the closest thing to religious tolerance that Europe would see during the sixteenth century.

a. THÉODOR BEZA TO CHRISTOPH HARDESHEIM[22] (SEPTEMBER 4, 1572)

I write without collecting my wits, stricken in spirit, and with a sense of tragic foreboding, to inform you of the events which have taken place, as they were reported to me, and which I can hardly grasp in my mind, let alone describe in writing or in speech.

On the fourth day after the wedding celebrations of the King of Navarre,[23] which passed off peacefully enough, the Lord Admiral[24] (whom even his enemies admit to have been the wisest and most outstanding of men, on account of the integrity of his mind) was returning from the King's Court to his lodging, reading on the way certain letters that had been handed to him, when two bullets fired by a hired marksman from the window of a house wounded him in such a way that although his body was not injured, one of the bullets took away his right thumb and the other went right through his left arm.

When this happened there was complete confusion, some of those present being in a state of shock, others breaking their way into the house to find the marksman, who made his escape, however, through a small doorway. A maidservant and a boy were taken for questioning, and the Admiral was carried home. The King himself,[25] together with his brother and several leading noblemen, hastened to call on him and pretended to show concern. No effort was to be spared, it was said, to track down the evildoer as speedily as possible, the King swearing that if such a deed was not punished with the greatest severity, he was no King. The very next day (the 23rd of last month) he himself ordered his very own bodyguards to watch the Admiral's house day and night so that he should not be attacked by his enemies.

During the evening of the 23rd it became clear that the wounds were not going to prove

---

[22]Nuremberg jurist and friend of Beza's, also called Herdesianus and Hessiander (d. 1586).

[23]Henri de Navarre (1553–1610), son of Antoine de Bourbon and Jeanne d'Albert, later crowned as Henri IV of France (1589–1610).

[24]Gaspard de Coligny (1519–1572), one of the most prominent French nobles to convert to Calvinism and leader of the Huguenot movement after the death of Louis de Condé in 1569.

[25]Charles IX (1550–1574), Valois successor to Francis I and ruler in his own right since 1563.

fatal, and it was after this that assassins were sent, before dawn on the 24th, from the town to the lodging of our people, an easy way for them to get in having been planned in advance. They cruelly hacked many to death as they slept, and then they all fell at once upon the Admiral, inflicting upon him so many wounds that he fell to the floor semi-conscious. As for the guards posted by the King, not only did they fail to resist, they made the assassination possible, and took a leading part in it, killing without exception all those who did not manage to escape, noblemen, domestics, and others. They hacked the Admiral, inflicting many wounds. Not content with this they threw his body out of the window for the crowd to tear apart. Then the whole town became a scene of massacre. So great was the mad rage that no distinction was made of age, sex or condition. Navarre and Condé[26] only just managed to escape, and there is a rumor, still unconfirmed, that they have been poisoned. Some of the assembled noblemen tried to put up a resistance but in the end a great many were killed, only a very few escaping by making their way into the suburbs and taking flight. It is reported that thirty-two noblemen of the first rank, the most prominent of the leaders of our party, as well as eighty gentlemen of lower rank lost their lives: simply because they attended the wedding festivities of the King of Navarre. And out of the rest of the population, if what is being said is true, no less than 8,000 were slain.

As the news of this atrocity spread rapidly through the provinces, city-gates everywhere were closed, and in case someone resorted to treachery our people were assured in solemn proclamations that they had no need to be afraid (for in many places they could have overcome their enemies in an open fight). And then, that very same night, in almost every town, our people were detained without warning and cast into prison. We still do not know what will happen in most places. They say that in Lyons at least 3,000 people have died, some cruelly put to the sword, some strangled. Others were thrown into the Saône to drown, but some of them managed to struggle ashore and to make their way here.

It is said that the King's brother[27] was not merely a spectator of this horrific tragedy but an actor in it, and that he is soon going to ride with an army to join the Duke of Alva.[28] Many believe that the French fleet, recently assembled at Bordeaux, has sailed to England to commit similar atrocities there, using the money recently injected into the sworn confederation and with greater help from the Pope than has been available before. No one can doubt that these events are the result of a plot worked out at the Council of Trent.[29] In this city, hated as it is by everybody and especially by its neighbors, we have no choice but to behave as if we were in the front line of the battle. I am afraid that all one can hope is that we will go down bravely, unless the merciful Lord makes his presence known to us in some special way and fortifies our inadequacy and our weakness. My thoughts run more upon death than upon life at this time, and I write to you, most honored friend and dear brother, for what may well be the last time.

The papers you entrusted to me, more precious than any treasure, I am returning to you since it is impossible to have them printed here at the moment because of the unexpected death of Crespin.[30] I will take care somehow, if I can, to see that they get back either to you yourself or to our brother Master Bullinger in Zurich.[31]

---

[26]The two leading Protestant heirs in France: Henri de Navarre (then aged nineteen) and Henri de Condé (1552–1588).

[27]The future Henri III (1551–1589), who succeeded Charles IX two years later and was eventually assassinated.
[28]Fernando Álvarez de Toledo y Pimentel (1507–1582), third Duke of Alba and leader of the Spanish military occupation of the rebellious (and largely Calvinist) Netherlands from 1567 to 1573.
[29]The Catholic reform council, which met in three sessions between 1545 and 1563.
[30]Jean Crespin (d. 1572), Huguenot printer and martyrologist who had died a few months before the massacre.
[31]Heinrich Bullinger (1504–1575), successor to Zwingli as the leading reformer in Zurich.

I have told you a story of unprecedented perfidy and cruel barbarity; from such events may our Lord God preserve us.

Farewell, my brother. Continue to pray to the Lord for us all. May I ask you to communicate to my esteemed brethren Masters Durnhofer and Camerarius the news of all this for it hurts me to describe repeatedly all this sorrow.[29] One thing only consoles me, the hope that my future life will be but brief, so that I may soon draw nearer to my God.

---

[29]Lorenz Durnhofer (1532–1594), Wittenberg theologian and later pastor in Nuremberg, and Philip Camerarius (1537–1624), Protestant jurist at the University of Altdorf, near Nuremberg.

b. JOACHIM OPSER, S.J.,[32] TO THE ABBOT OF ST. GALLEN MONASTERY (AUGUST 26, 1572)

I think that I shall not bore you if I mention in detail an event as unexpected as it is useful to our cause, and which not only delights the Christian world with admiration, but brings it to a peak of rejoicing. Concerning this you will hear what the Captain has to say.[33] Rejoice in advance, but do not for that disdain or reject as superfluous the lines I write with more satisfaction perhaps than seems quite proper, for I affirm nothing I have not got from authoritative sources.

The Admiral has perished miserably on August 24, with all the heretical French nobility. (One can say it without exaggeration.) What immense carnage! I shuddered at the sight of this river [the Seine] full of naked and horribly mutilated corpses. Up to the present, the King has spared none but the King of Navarre. In effect, today August 26, towards one o'clock, the King of Navarre attended Mass with the King Charles, so that all conceive the greatest hopes of seeing him change his religion. . . . Everyone agrees in praising the prudence and magnanimity of the King who, after having by his kindness and indulgence fattened, as it were, the heretics like cattle, has suddenly had them slaughtered by his soldiers. . . . All heretical booksellers that one could find have been massacred and cast naked into the river.

Ramus,[34] who had jumped out of his bedroom, quite high up, still lies naked on the river bank, pierced by numerous dagger-blows. In a word, there is no one (even women not excepted) who has not been either killed or wounded.

One more thing as concerns the massacre of the Admiral; I hold these details from the man who gave him the third blow with his battle axe, from that Conrad Burg who used to be groom at Steward Joachim Waldemann's at Wyl. When the Swiss, under the orders of the Duc D'Anjou, had broken in the doors, Conrad, followed by Leonhard Grunenfelder of Glaris and Martin Koch of Fribourg, reached the Admiral's room which was the third in the house. The servant was killed first. The Admiral was in a dressing gown and none at first wanted to lay hands on him; but Martin Koch, more daring than the others, struck the wretch with his halberd; Conrad gave him the third blow, and at the seventh at last he fell dead against the chimney of his room. By order of the Duc de Guise[35] his corpse was thrown out of the window and, after tying a rope round his neck as in the way with criminals, he was offered in display for all the people by dragging him to the Seine. Such was the end of that pernicious man, who not only brought a great many to the brink in his lifetime, but who, dying, swept a crowd of heretical nobles into hell with him.

---

[32]Society of Jesus; a member of the Jesuit order.
[33]The captain commanding the detachment of Swiss mercenaries that broke into the house of the Huguenot leader, Admiral Coligny, and murdered the admiral.
[34]Pierre Ramée, or Ramus (1515–1572), best known as a humanist and pedagogical reformer.
[35]Henri de Lorraine, Duke of Guise (1550–1588), then leader of the anti-Huguenot faction in France, ultimately assassinated on royal orders in 1588.

2. Sebastian Castellio
CONCERNING HERETICS (1562)

The case of Miguel Servedo, better known as Servetus (1511–1553), is a classic example of sixteenth-century religious intolerance. Servetus was a contentious Spanish physician, most famous for his 1531 book denying the Trinity. He narrowly escaped the Catholic Inquisition in Vienna and was instead burned in effigy. Next, despite having just published an attack on Calvin's *Institutes,* Servetus inexplicably fled to the Calvinist stronghold of Geneva, where he was promptly arrested and, after a lengthy trial, burned for real as a heretic. Calvin, who had in fact sought the milder execution of decapitation, nonetheless defended the magistrates' actions in his *Defense of the Orthodox Faith* (1554). This work particularly enraged Sebastian Castellio (1515–1563), a former associate of Calvin, who had been expelled from Geneva in 1545 after his disagreement with the reformer over the definition of "essential doctrines." His 1562 response to Calvin's *Defense* was circulated only in manuscript and not published until 1612 in Holland (and even then it appeared under the pseudonym of Vaticanus). Castellio's work is constructed as a "dialogue" and in fact consists of various excerpts culled from Calvin's writings, followed by Castellio's imagined responses. His rejoinder to Calvin's justification for executing heretics is a highly personalized argument for religious tolerance, which stresses both the subjectivity of Calvin's interpretations and the reformer's fear of letting opponents speak. In addition, Castellio's document lays a philosophical foundation for the much later concepts of freedom of speech and freedom of religion.

REPLY TO CALVIN'S BOOK
IN WHICH HE ENDEAVORS
TO SHOW THAT HERETICS
SHOULD BE COERCED BY
THE RIGHT OF THE SWORD

Calvin 1. Defense of the Orthodox Faith Concerning the Sacred Trinity against the prodigious errors of the Spaniard Michael Servetus,[36] where it is shown that heretics are to be punished with the sword and in particular that this so impious man was justly and properly punished at Geneva.

Vaticanus.[37] Calvin defines heresy in terms of error, as if he said, I will write against the errors of Servetus and will show that those who err, that is, heretics, are to be punished with the sword as Servetus, who erred, was punished by the sword. We shall see that this is the mind of Calvin. He wishes all those who grievously err to be killed unless they endorse the opinion of Calvin. . . . If this were done, all who bear the Christian name would be killed, except Calvinists. . . .

Calvin 2. . . . I did not at first think it necessary to make a direct reply to this man. The absurdity of his delirium seemed to me so great that I hoped it would go up in smoke without opposition.

---

[36]Published in 1554 in Geneva, after the execution of Servetus for heresy.

[37]Pseudonym for Castellio.

Vaticanus. . . . And it would have gone up in smoke had it been absurd delirium. . . .

Calvin 14. When warning and exhortation were of no avail I was unwilling to exceed the rule of our Lord to avoid a heretic who sins, being self-condemned, as the Apostle Paul puts it [Tit 3:10].

Vaticanus. . . . The rule of our Lord is to admonish a sinner first in private, then to take with thee one or two witnesses, and finally to tell the Church [Mt 18:15–17]. Calvin's first admonition has been described above; the second was prison; and the third, the rod of the magistrate.

Calvin 17. What preposterous humanity is it, I ask you, to cover with silence the crime of one man and to prostitute a thousand souls to the snares of Satan?

Vaticanus. If the errors of Servetus are snares, then you prostitute a thousand souls to the wiles of Satan by stirring them up. . . . Although you misrepresent and mutilate much in Servetus, nevertheless many are seduced by the excerpts in your book. . . . I know a man who has been so taken by the reasoning of Servetus concerning infant baptism, cited by you [in your book], as to assert that nothing could be more cogent. . . .

Calvin 18. Would that the errors of Servetus were buried, but when I see them circulating I cannot be silent without the guilt of perfidy.

Vaticanus. You have only yourself to blame. There was almost no mention of the first book of Servetus and the subsequent works could have been sold like the others without disturbance, but now that the man has been burned with his books, everybody is burning with a desire to read them. . . .

Vaticanus [in reply to Calvin 20]. . . . [Calvin] wishes to kill all heretics and wishes to hold as heretics all who disagree with him. His program would call for the extermination of all the Papists, Lutherans, Zwinglians, Anabaptists, and the rest. There would survive only Calvinists, Jews, and Turks, whom he excepts. . . .

Calvin 25. Prove that the coming of Christ has mitigated penalties against heresy.

Vaticanus. How mitigated? Before the coming of Christ there is no mention of heretics in the whole law. . . . I do not deny that there were heretics, but I do not find that the law prescribes any penalty for them. In the New Testament I find that they are to be avoided. So the penalty is not mitigated, but altered. . . .

Calvin 26. Another fanatic . . . calls Servetus his best brother and for that reason denies that heretics are to be punished on the ground that each may forge the sense of Scripture to his liking, since the certain truth lies hidden in clouds.

Vaticanus. He is wroth that anyone should declare the Scriptures obscure. He thinks them clear. He contradicts Zwingli[38] who considers them obscure, and contradicts himself who writes so many commentaries to explain what is so clear. . . .

Calvin 41. The fact that the sword has been used for persecution does not prevent the pious magistrate from using his rod to defend the afflicted Church, nor do the crosses of the martyrs impede the just aid of the laws that the faithful may worship God in tranquillity.

Vaticanus. . . . If Servetus had attacked you by arms, you had rightly been defended by the magistrate; but since he opposed you in writings, why did you oppose them with iron and flame? Do you call this the defense of the pious magistrate? Does your piety consist only in hurrying to the fire strangers passing peacefully through your city? And do you dare to upbraid the Papists? Produce a single instance in which the Papists dragged a Lutheran or Calvinist from Mass to prison as Servetus among you was dragged from a sermon. . . .

Vaticanus [in reply to Calvin 55]. . . . Calvin boasts that he did not cut out Servetus's tongue. But he did cut off his life and burn his books lest Servetus be able after his death to defend his cause before the world, even with books. Yet Calvin thinks that everyone should

---

[38]Ulrich Zwingli (1484–1531), first Protestant reformer of Zurich and early leader of the so-called Swiss Sacramentarians, who were later led by Calvin.

accept his judgment about Servetus and make no further inquiry after our master has made his pronouncement. Why did he burn the books? He feared, I suppose, that men would be corrupted. Then why did he not entertain the same fear formerly, when he himself took care to print the *Interim* at Geneva in his refutation?[39] Why did he not do the same for Servetus, unless because Servetus exposed Calvin more successfully than did the *Interim?* Calvin may say that he was not in a position to suppress the *Interim.* Why did he not at least banish it from his city? Why does he not prohibit the printing and sale of other pernicious books at Geneva? Aristotle is allowed, though he denies the foremost article of the creed, the creation of the world. The Koran is permitted and Apuleius, Martial, Plautus, Terence, Horace, Catullus, Tibullus, Propertius, and other nefarious corrupters of morals. Ovid's *Art of Love*—that is, of Adultery—is allowed, as well as the works of his imitator Clement Marot.[40] A refugee from France wrote back from Geneva a few years ago: "I have escaped from Babylon. Please send me all the works of Ovid with commentaries." They call the papacy "Babylon." What is Jerusalem? What shall I say of the trash which is printed there? Beza's *Zoographia* and *Passavant*, or Viret's book *On the Death of His Wife?*[41] These books are full of nothing but scurrility and triviality. . . .

Calvin 77. Now we see that the ministers of the Gospel must be prepared to bear the cross and enmity and whatever pleases the world, and the Lord equipped them with no other arms than patience. Nevertheless, kings are commanded to protect the doctrine of piety by their support.

Vaticanus. To kill a man is not to defend a doctrine, but to kill a man. When the Genevans killed Servetus they did not defend a doctrine; they killed a man. The defense of doctrine is not the affair of the magistrate but of the doctor. What has the sword to do with doctrine? . . .

Calvin 78. Our critics say that nothing is more inappropriate than to force men to the faith which consists in free obedience. . . .

Vaticanus. "No man can come to me, except the Father which hath sent me draw him" [Jn 6:44]. These persecutors wish the magistrate to draw men who are unwilling to be drawn by God, as if the magistrate could accomplish more than God. . . .

Calvin 79. We grant that the magistrate is not in a position to penetrate the hearts of men by edicts that they should embrace the doctrine of salvation obediently and submit themselves to God, but the calling of the magistrate does require that impure and petulant tongues should not be allowed to lacerate the sacred name of God and trample upon His worship.

Vaticanus. . . . This is said in a captious and malicious spirit. An impure and petulant tongue is not to be ascribed to anyone who differs from Calvin on the Lord's Supper, infant baptism, predestination, and persecution, provided one believes in the truth of Sacred Scripture.

Calvin 80. A private man, who does not exercise the power of life and death, would not be guiltless if he suffered his home to be polluted by sacrilege. How much more craven would it be in the magistrate if he connived at the unbridled violation of piety? . . .

Vaticanus. This is more rhetorical than Christian. . . . What does Calvin consider "an unbridled violation of piety"? . . . Servetus denied that infants should be baptized. Did Servetus believe what he said or did he not? Calvin calls this an unbridled violation. By what right? An unbridled violation calls for conscious sin. But Servetus, if he sinned, sinned unconsciously. Did you then, Calvin, kill Servetus because he so believed or because he so spoke? If you killed him

---

[39]Castellio is referring to a lengthy refutation of Servetus's writings in Calvin's work on ecclesiastical government, *The True Method of Reforming the Church* (1548).

[40]French poet and translator (1496–1544), twice exiled from France for his Protestant sympathies and once exiled from Geneva (over Calvin's objections) for gambling at backgammon.

[41]The books cited are the works of the leading Calvinist missionaries to France, Théodor Beza (1519–1605) and Pierre Viret (1511–1571).

because he so spoke, you killed him on account of the truth, for the truth is to say what you believe, even though you are in error. . . . But if you killed him because he so believed, then you should teach him to believe otherwise, and you should show from Scripture that those who err and believe incorrectly are to be killed. . . .

Calvin 82. . . . If the Son of God drove out those who on the pretext of religion sold sacrifices in the temple, why may not the pious magistrate use the sword committed to him to coerce perfidious apostates who profane and violate the temple of God with open contumely?

Vaticanus. We, too, may argue after Calvin's fashion: if the Son of God did not condemn the adulteress, why should the magistrate condemn adulterers? If Calvin replies that Christ was not the judge of adultery, we say the same with regard to the whip of cords. There was no law—and if Christ had acted as a magistrate He ought to have followed the law—there was no law that the whip of cords should be used on the money changers. Moreover, if Christ drove them out, He did not kill them; and if Christ did it with His own hand, the magistrate should do the like and not leave the office to the executioner. If Christ drove them out of a temple made with hands, the magistrate should do the same. If Calvin answers that the temple was a figure of the temple not made with hands, that is, of the heart of man . . . we say by the same right that the whip made by hand was a spiritual whip, that is, of the Word of God, which Word is given not to the magistrate, but to the minister. . . . If Christ did not command that the money changers be cast out of the temple of God by the magistrate, and did not make Himself an accuser against them, but with His own hand cast them out, then Calvin who wishes to be the vicar of Christ should not have sent Servetus to the magistrate to be cast out and killed, nor should he have employed his cook as an accuser, but should have cast out Servetus with his own hand, his own weapon, that is, with the word. . . .

BIBLIOGRAPHY

Primary Sources

Anthologies and Readers

Baylor, Michael, ed., *The Radical Reformation* (Cambridge: Cambridge University Press, 1991).

Bray, Gerald, ed., *Documents of the English Reformation* (Minneapolis: Fortress Press, 1994).

Cocrane, Arthur C., *Reformed Confessions of the Sixteenth Century* (Louisville, Ky.: Westminster Press, 1966).

Dixon, C. Scott, ed., *The Continental Reformation: The Essential Readings* (Malden, Mass.: Blackwell, 1998).

Duke, Alastair, Gillian Lewis, and Andrew Pettegree, eds., *Calvinism in Europe, 1540–1610: A Collection of Documents*, (Manchester: Manchester University Press, 1992).

Harder, Leland, ed., *Sources of Swiss Anabaptism* (Scottdale, Pa.: Herald Press, 1983).

Olin, John, ed., *The Catholic Reformation: From Savonarola to Ignatius Loyola* (New York: Harper & Row, 1990).

Rummel, E., ed., *Scheming Papists and Lutheran Fools: Five Reformation Satires* (Bronx, N.Y.: Fordham University Press, 1993).

Ziegler, Donald J., ed., *Great Debates of the Reformation* (New York: Random House, 1969).

Zuck, Lowell, ed., *Christianity and Revolution; Radical Christian Testimonies, 1520–1650* (Philadelphia: Temple University Press, 1975).

Select Authors

Calvin, John, *Institutes of the Christian Religion,* ed. J. T. McNeill (Louisville, Ky.: Westminster Press, 1975).

———, *John Calvin and Jacopo Sadoleto: A Reformation Debate: Sadoleto's Letter to the Genevans and Calvin's Reply,* ed. John C. Olin (New York: Harper Torchbooks, 1966).

Castellio, Sebastian, *Concerning Heretics,* trans. Roland Bainton (New York: Columbia University Press, 1935).

Erasmus, Desiderius, *The Essential Erasmus,* ed. J. P. Dolan (New York: Mentor, 1964).

———, *In Praise of Folly and Other Writings,* ed. R. M. Adams (New York: Norton, 1989).

Loyola, Ignatius, *Spiritual Exercises and Selected Works,* ed. George E. Ganss (Mahwah, N.J.: Paulist Press, 1991).

———, *The Autobiography of St. Ignatius Loyola,* ed. John C. Olin (New York: Harper Torchbooks, 1974).

Luther, Martin, *Martin Luther: Selections from his Writings,* ed. J. Dillenberger (New York: Anchor/Doubleday, 1962).

———, *Three Treatises* (Minneapolis: Fortress Press, 1973).

Schleitheim Confession, ed. John H. Yoder (Scottdale, Pa.: Herald Press, 1977).

Teresa of Ávila, *The Life of Saint Teresa of Ávila By Herself,* trans. J. M. Cohen (London: Penguin Classic, 1957).

———, *Interior Castle* (New York: Image/Doubleday, 1972).

Tyndale, William, *Tyndale's New Testament,* ed. David Daniell (New Haven: Yale University Press, 1989).

———, *Tyndale's Old Testament,* ed. David Daniell (New Haven: Yale University Press, 1992).

Secondary Works

General

Jensen, De Lamar, *Reformation Europe,* 2nd ed. (Lexington, Mass.: D.C. Heath, 1992).

Marshall, Sherrin, ed., *Women of the Reformation and Counter-Reformation: Public and Private Worlds* (Bloomington, Ind.: Indiana University Press, 1989).

McGrath, Alister, *Reformation Thought: An Introduction,* 2nd ed. (Malden, Mass.: Blackwell, 1993).

Ozment, Steven, *The Age of Reform, 1250–1550: An Intellectual and Religious History of Late Medieval and Reformation Europe* (New Haven: Yale University Press, 1980).

Rice, Eugene, *The Foundations of Early Modern Europe, 1460–1559,* 2nd ed. (New York: Norton, 1994).

Northern Humanism

Bainton, Roland, *Erasmus of Christendom* (San Francisco: Collins, 1969).

Marius, Richard, *Thomas More: A Biography* (Cambridge: Harvard University Press, 1984).

Spitz, Lewis, *The Religious Renaissance of the German Humanists* (Cambridge: Harvard University Press, 1967).

The German and Swiss Reformations

Bainton, Roland, *Here I Stand: A Life of Martin Luther* (Nashville, Tenn.: Abingdon-Cokesbury, 1950).

Bouwsma, William, *John Calvin: A Sixteenth Century Portrait* (Oxford: Oxford University Press, 1988).

Oberman, Heiko, *Luther: Man Between God and the Devil* (New York: Image/Doubleday, 1992).

Scribner, Robert, *For the Sake of Simple Folk: Popular Propaganda for German Reformation* (Oxford: Oxford University Press, 1994).

Williams, George, *The Radical Reformation,* 2nd ed. (Kirksville, Mo.: Sixteenth Century Journal Publishers, 1992).

The English Reformation

Cowan, Ian B., *The Scottish Reformation* (New York: St. Martin's, 1982).

Daniell, David, *William Tyndale: A Biography* (New Haven: Yale University Press, 1994).

Duffy, Eamon, *The Stripping of the Altars* (New Haven: Yale University Press, 1992).

Haigh, Christopher, *English Reformations* (Oxford: Oxford University Press, 1993).

The Catholic Reformation

Bilinkoff, Jodi, *The Avila of Saint Teresa* (Ithaca, N.Y.: Cornell University Press, 1989).

Eire, Catlos, *From Madrid to Purgatory* (Cambridge: Cambridge University Press, 1995).

Jedin, Hubert, *History of the Council of Trent,* 2 vols. (St. Louis: B. Herder, 1957–61).

Meisner, W. W., *Ignatius of Loyola: The Psychology of a Saint* (New Haven: Yale University Press, 1992).

O'Connell, Marvin R., *The Counter Reformation, 1560–1610* (New York: Harper & Row, 1974).

O'Malley, John W., *The First Jesuits* (Cambridge: Harvard University Press, 1993).

French Religious Wars

Diefendorf, Barbara, *Beneath the Cross: Catholics and Huguenots in Sixteenth-Century Paris* (Oxford: Oxford University Press, 1991).

Holt, Mack, *The French Wars of Religion, 1562–1629* (Cambridge: Cambridge University Press, 1995).

Kingdon, Robert, *Myths About the St. Bartholomew's Day Massacres* (Cambridge: Harvard University Press, 1988).

Religious Toleration

Bainton, Roland, *Hunted Heretic: The Life and Death of Michael Servetus* (Magnolia, Mass: P. Smith, 1978).

Laursen, John Christian, and Cary J. Nederman, eds., *Beyond the Persecuting Society: Religious Toleration Before the Enlightenment* (Philadelphia: University of Pennsylvania, 1998).

Scribner, Bob, and Ole Peter Grell, eds., *Tolerance and Intolerance in the European Reformation* (Cambridge: Cambridge University Press, 1996).

The Confessional Age

GEORGE WHITEFIELD PREACHING TO MOORFIELDS, ENGLAND. Eighteenth-century "Methodists" such as Whitefield and John Wesley preached the gospel wherever they could find an audience, including at popular festivals, prisons, and even public executions. Their self-assured enthusiasm won the Anglican evangelists many converts as well as some enemies among congregations in Great Britain and its colonies. *(Corbis/Bettmann)*

The profound effects of the Reformation on Western Christianity have yet to be fully measured. The most visible consequence during the period from the mid sixteenth to late eighteenth century was the emergence of many different churches across Europe, each claiming to represent the true Christian tradition. This growth of denominationalism and the systematic division of Western Christianity into various creeds, or confessions, is referred to by historians as confessionalization. Initially the pressure for greater doctrinal standardization came as much from within denominations as from without. Bitter divisions within each of the main three churches—Roman Catholic, Lutheran, and Reformed—soon gave rise to definitive theologies and other marks of confessional distinctiveness. The Lutheran Formula of Concord (1577), signed by most of the church's German leaders, thus clearly distinguished Lutheran teachings from those of the Catholic Church, as articulated at the Council of Trent (1545–1563). The Second Helvetic Confession (1566) and the Synod of Dort (1619) performed similar functions for the Swiss and Dutch Reformed churches, respectively. The process of making average people doctrinally correct Lutherans, or Calvinists, or Catholics, on the other hand, often required several generations of education and social transformation. It was also never entirely successful, sometimes resulting in new splinter churches or conversely in individual indifference and skepticism. Nevertheless, by the end of the eighteenth century, the confessionalization of Western Christianity was largely complete, resulting in a Europe that was a mosaic of distinctive Protestant and Catholic faiths, all maintaining their own doctrines, worship practices, and authority structures.

The price of confessionalization, particularly during the seventeenth century, was often high. Most infamously, the religious wars and other violence that plagued Europe for over a century after Martin Luther's Ninety-five Theses took an enormous toll in human lives and property. Because of the ancient tradition of the church-state alliance, every state, large or small, had only one official religion, with all other faiths considered both heretical and subversive to the state's authority. In France, for instance, the Valois monarchs chose to remain Catholic, and thereby obliged all of their Protestant subjects (up to 30% of the population in some areas) to maintain outward conformity to Catholicism. Attempted compromises for the Huguenot (Calvinist) minority were consistently undermined by dynastic politics and religious bigotry. As a result, tens of thousands of French Protestants and Catholics died during three decades of religious violence and upheaval, a period that ended only when a Huguenot noble, Henry of Navarre, succeeded to the throne and converted to Catholicism. His later decree of toleration for French Huguenots, proclaimed in the Edict of Nantes in 1598, appeared to solve the problem of the new Christian pluralism but in fact was gradually eroded by his royal successors and ultimately revoked by Louis XIV in 1685. Thus through a combination of political force and doctrinal instruction, France was fully confessionalized as Catholic by the beginning of the eighteenth century.

Other European states varied in their experience of religious violence but not in the overall pattern of politically directed confessionalization. In Catholic Spain and Italy, Protestant minorities always remained small and politically insignificant. Though some "heretics" were imprisoned or even executed for their beliefs, governmental enforcement of religious orthodoxy in these regions tended to focus more on the superficial conversion of Jews and Muslims. Meanwhile, Germany, the home of the Reformation, at first appeared to have the best luck in avoiding religious violence. After the Catholic emperor Charles V unsuccessfully attempted to impose his religion on the many Protestant cities and states of his realm, he agreed to the famous compromise agreement of the Peace of Augsburg in 1555. This treaty enshrined the concept of *cuius regio, eius religio* ("whose region, his religion"), meaning that the official religion of each of Germany's myriad principalities and other territories would be determined by the creed of its ruler or governing body. For the next sixty-three years, confessionalization continued relatively peacefully in the hundreds of Catholic, Lutheran, and Calvinist states of the German empire, but in 1618 the most devastating religiously-inspired war of all broke out: the Thirty Years' War. At first the Catholic imperial forces were victorious, but as fellow Protestant armies from Denmark and Sweden entered the conflict, the fighting and destruction dragged on. By 1648, the year that a peace treaty was finally concluded, every state in Europe had directly or indirectly contributed to the bloodshed, which had left much of Germany in ruins and many governments deep in debt. The only unmitigated good that emerged from the catastrophe was a Europewide exhaustion with religious violence and a grudging acceptance of Christian pluralism as an unalterable fact. The Peace of Westphalia, signed in 1649, thus marked a definitive end to large-scale religious warfare between European states.

Confessional conflict within European states was an entirely different matter, however, and many states continued to be plagued by schisms and religiously inspired violence into the early eighteenth century, with isolated conflicts continuing even up to the present day. England provides an especially dramatic example of this phenomenon. Here, the official state church was Protestant, and Catholicism was therefore outlawed. During the seventeenth century, though, a perceived drift towards Catholic teachings and practices led some English Christians (known as Puritans) to dissent from the Church of England and attempt to reform or leave it. Once again, the ultimate consequence was religious violence, although (as everywhere in Europe) various other political motives played a part in the strife as well. Even after the Puritans and their allies had won the English Civil War, the problem of Christian pluralism persisted. When the monarchy was restored in 1660, punitive laws against nonconforming minority faiths were intensified, just as in contemporary Catholic France. Throughout Europe, in fact, a policy of coerced conversions or expulsions remained the norm in many confessionalized Protestant and Catholic states, a practice that was supposedly aimed at preserving religious homogeneity and thus social harmony. One of the most infamous examples of "confessional cleansing" was the forced exile of thousands of Protestants from the Catholic bishopric of Salzburg in 1731. Although limited religious toleration, such as that articulated in England's Act of Toleration in 1689, was making headway by the beginning of the eighteenth century, full toleration and the granting of political rights for religious minorities remained more than a hundred years away in most regions.

The Confessional Age was not only a period of religious coercion and strife, however. One of the most acclaimed consequences of greater religious instruction was a general intensification of personal piety, in various forms and in every denomination. This is not to suggest that such acts were lacking among pre-Reformation Christians, but rather that corporate acts of worship were previously more emphasized than the typically post-Reformation practices of individual Bible reading and extended private prayer. Similarly, the emphasis on personal conversion, while also common among medieval Christians, received an especially important boost from Protestant teachings on the primacy of individual faith and the elimination of the necessity for any human intermediaries between the believer and God. This tendency is also evident among Catholics, in its most extreme form among French Jansenists and Quietists, who preferred austere contemplation and self-scrutiny to communal worship and rituals. Though the various denominations of the Confessional Age remained adamantly separated on many questions of doctrine and practice, the increased "privatization" of Christianity was one feature shared by all.

Sometimes such interiorization of faith led to schisms with established churches and doctrines. English Nonconformists such as the Quakers are the most obvious example, but every denomination experienced the same internal conflicts. In other instances, though, the intensification of personal devotion led to spiritual revivals within the confessions themselves. German Pietists, in particular, sought to revive the flame of the Holy Spirit, which they feared was near extinction among their fellow Lutherans amid the unenthusiastic conformism of the day. Eighteenth-century Methodists similarly aimed at reinvigorating faith on the individual level, though their movement did eventually break away from its parent Church of England. Finally, the focus on individual conscience, combined with a growing confidence in the methods of empirical science and philosophy, led some Christians to reject all organized religion whatsoever. Calling themselves Deists or Rationalists, these "enlightened" thinkers taught that Nature and

Reason, rather than the churches and their doctrines, provided access to the divine and that all else was superstition and mythology. Though other Christians accused them of blasphemy or atheism, the Deists maintained that they alone truly revered the Creator and his plan for humanity.

The Confessional Age of Western Christianity embodied many conflicting tendencies. While institutional centralization and doctrinal standardization within the main churches intensified, the number of denominations and sects continued to grow exponentially. While more Christians were educated in their faith than in perhaps any previous period of history, ancient superstitions and hatred towards Jews, Gypsies, and various suspected witches led to countless bloody pogroms and witch-hunts. And while the church-state alliance was stronger than at any other time in history, the seeds of its dissolution had already been planted with the growth of religious nonconformity and skepticism. Truly the full impact of the Reformation was just beginning to be realized.

CHAPTER 6 CHRONOLOGY

	Politics	Literature	Individuals	Other
16th cent.	1598 Edict of Nantes in France		1575–1624 Jakob Böhme	1580–1650 Worst years of witch craze
17th cent.	1603 James I and Stuart dynasty in England 1610 Henry IV of France assassinated 1618–1648 Thirty Years' War 1624–1642 Richelieu shapes French policy 1642–1648 English Civil War 1640–1688 Friedrich Wilhelm elector of Brandenburg-Prussia 1643/50–1715 Louis XIV king of France 1649–1660 English Commonwealth (Cromwell) 1683 Turkish siege of Vienna fails 1687 Turks defeated at Mohacs 1688–1689 Glorious Revolution in England 1689–1725 Peter the Great czar	1611 King James Bible 1620 Bacon, *Novum Organum* 1632 Galileo, *Dialogue* 1637 Descartes, *Discourse on Method* 1639 Jansen, *Augustinius* 1651 Hobbes, *Leviathan* 1667 Milton, *Paradise Lost* 1670 Spinoza, *Tractatus Theologica-Politicus* 1675 Spener, *Pia Desideria* 1687 Newton, *Principia* 1689 Locke, *Two Treatises* 1696 Toland, *Christianity Not Mysterious*	1599–1658 Oliver Cromwell 1624–1691 George Fox 1623–1662 Blaise Pascal 1627–1704 Bishop Bossuet 1635–1705 P. J. Spener	1618 Synod of Dort condemns Arminianism 1619 First African slaves in N. America 1629 Edict of Restitution in H.R.E. 1659–1661 Europewide famines 1685 Edict of Nantes revoked by Louis XIV
18th cent.	1740–1780 Maria Theresa Austrian empress 1740–1786 Frederick the Great king of Prussia 1756–1763 Seven Years' War 1780–1790 Joseph II Austrian emperor 1776–1781 American War of Independence 1789 Beginning of French Revolution 1792–1794 Jacobin Terror in France 1799 Napoleon and the Consulate in France	1726 Swift, *Gulliver's Travels* 1751–1772 *Encyclopédie* 1759 Voltaire, *Candide* 1762 Rousseau, *Émile*	1688–1772 E. Swedenborg 1700–1760 Count Zinzendorf 1703–1758 Jonathan Edwards 1694–1788 Voltaire 1712–1778 J.-J. Rousseau 1703–1791 John Wesley 1724–1804 Immanuel Kant	1722–1743 Zinzendorf founds Herrnhut colony of Moravian Pietists 1734–1743 Great Awakening in British America 1742 First performance of Handel's *Messiah* 1773 Society of Jesus dissolved 1774 First Unitarian Church, London

A. Nonconformists

One of the most wide-ranging effects of the Reformation was the establishment of state churches by various Protestant rulers. This was particularly true in England, where, by casting off papal authority, Henry VIII and his successors assumed control over all clerics, ecclesiastical property, and doctrine within the now independent Church of England. Though a Catholic restoration was attempted during the brief reign of Queen Mary (r. 1553–1558), the Protestant Church of England was immediately reestablished by her half-sister Elizabeth (r. 1558–1603) and secured thereafter by several official acts of religious uniformity.

Some English Protestants, however, remained dissatisfied with the doctrinal conservatism of the Anglican Church, and instead preferred rituals, teachings, and authority structures that were closer to those of the Calvinists and other Reformed continental churches. With the ascendancy of King James I (r. 1603–1625), a conservative in religious matters, the hopes of such Nonconformists were dashed. Some dissenters, later known as Pilgrims, emigrated to the Netherlands and the New World. Others continued their resistance and attempts at reform within the Church of England, though the reign of Charles I (r. 1625–1649) and his archconservative primate, Archbishop Laud, led to even greater religious strife and persecution of dissenters. Eventually, the conflict between Arminian forces (those who advocated a ceremonial and hierarchical church) and Puritan proponents (who were more Calvinist and who wanted a more Protestant church structure) contributed to the eruption of the English Civil War (1642–1648). In addition to these religious differences, the conflict was fueled by political tensions between the royalists, who favored rule by a quasi-absolutist monarch, and the militant antiroyalists (known as Roundheads) who wanted to restrict the monarchy and establish a more parliamentary form of government. The Puritan, antiroyalist contingent eventually prevailed, a triumph that resulted in the beheading of the English king for treason in 1649 and the establishment of a republican Commonwealth under the leadership of its "Lord Protector," Oliver Cromwell (1599–1658).

Congregationalists predominated among the Nonconformists in the new Commonwealth, but a number of other Nonconformist groups also blossomed amidst the new religious toleration, including so-called Independents, Baptists, Quakers, the radical democratic Levellers, and many others. Unfortunately for all of these dissenting groups, the Commonwealth fell into disarray under Cromwell's successor, his son Richard, and in 1660 the Stuart monarchy was restored under Charles II. During the next decade, several penal laws were passed against Nonconformists, stripping all Nonconformist ministers of their positions and incomes, forbidding any private religious meetings apart from established churches, and banning anyone with Nonconformist religious beliefs from serving in government office. Finally, in 1688, Charles's successor, James II, was forced to abdicate in the Glorious Revolution, and Parliament passed a Bill of Rights and Toleration Act which allowed Nonconformists to maintain their own places of worship and ministers. The Church of England retained its official status, as it does to this day, but all coercive attempts to enforce religious conformity were definitively abandoned.

1. THE LIFE OF MRS. LUCY HUTCHINSON, WRITTEN BY HERSELF (1665)

For the Calvinist-inspired Nonconformists known to their detractors as Puritans, persecution by the Church of England under Archbishop Laud merely provided a greater opportunity for the godly to prove their devotion to "the true covenant." Their subsequent victory in the Civil War, moreover, convinced them that they were indeed the instruments of divine providence, and that England itself played a pivotal role in the historical drama of human salvation. In this autobiographical "testament" addressed to her children, Lucy Apsley Hutchinson (1620–c. 1690) effectively conveys how Puritan zeal and English chauvinism were interwoven among Roundhead supporters during and after the war. Her husband, Colonel John Hutchinson (1616–1664), served as one of the judges at Charles I's treason trial; later advised Oliver Cromwell during the Commonwealth; and, upon the Restoration of the Stuart monarchy, was imprisoned and executed in 1664. Despite the ups and downs of her familial and religious fortunes, Lucy Hutchinson remained convinced that divine providence had been at work in Britain since Roman times and that the light of the gospel, though often dimmed, would never be extinguished. Her brief description of the hand of providence at work in her own life also provides some fascinating glimpses of the author as an intensely pious and studious young girl, "outstripping" her brothers at school and disdaining the "frivolous" play of other children.

The Almighty Author of all beings, in his various providences, whereby he conducts the lives of men from the cradle to the tomb, exercises no less wisdom and goodness than he manifests power and greatness, in their creation; but such is the stupidity of blind mortals, that instead of employing their studies in these admirable books of providence, wherein God daily exhibits to us glorious characters of his love, kindness, wisdom, and justice, they ungratefully regard them not, and call the most wonderful operations of the great God the common accidents of human life, especially if they be such as are usual, and exercised towards them in ages wherein they are not very capable of observation, and whereon they seldom employ any reflection; for in things great and extraordinary, some, perhaps, will take notice of God's working, who either forget or believe not that he takes as well a care and account of their smallest concernments, even the hairs of their heads.

Finding myself in some kind guilty of this general neglect, I thought it might be a means to stir up my thankfulness for things past, and to encourage my faith for the future, if I recollected as much as I have heard or can remember of the passages of my youth, and the general and particular providences exercised to me, both in the entrance and progress of my life. Herein I meet with so many special indulgences as require a distinct consideration, they being all of them to be regarded as talents intrusted to my improvement for God's glory. The parents by whom I received my life, the places where I began and continued it, the time when I was brought forth to be a witness of God's wonderful workings in the earth, the rank that was given me in my generation, and the advantages I received in my person, each of them carries along with it many mercies which are above my utterance, and as they give me infinite cause of glorifying God's goodness, so I cannot reflect on them without deep humiliation for the small improvement I have made of so rich a stock; which, that I may yet by God's grace better employ, I shall recall and seriously ponder: and, first, as far as I have since learnt, set down the condition of things in the place of my nativity, at that time when I was sent into the world. It was on the 29th day of January, in the year of our Lord [1620], that in the Tower of London, the principal city of the English Isle, I was, about four of the clock in the morning, brought forth to behold the ensuing light. My father was Sir Allen Apsley, lieutenant of the Tower of London; my mother, his third wife, was Lucy, the youngest daughter of Sir John St. John, of Lidiard Tregooze, in Wiltshire, by his second wife. My father had then living a son and a daughter by his former wives, and by my mother three sons, I being her eldest daughter. The land was then at peace (it being towards the latter end of the reign of King James [I]), if that quietness may be called a peace, which was rather like the calm and smooth surface of the sea, whose dark womb is already impregnated with a horrid tempest.

Whoever considers England will find it no small favour of God to have been made one of its natives, both upon spiritual and outward accounts. The happiness of the soil and air contribute all things that are necessary to the use or delight of man's life. The celebrated glory of this isle's inhabitants, ever since they received a mention in history, confers some honour upon every one of her children, and with it an obligation to continue in that magnanimity and virtue, which hath famed this island, and raised her head in glory higher than the great kingdoms of the neighbouring continent. Britain hath been as a garden enclosed, wherein all things that man can wish, to make a pleasant life, are planted and grow in her own soil, and whatsoever foreign countries yield, to increase admiration and delight, are brought in by her fleets. The people, by the plenty of their country, not being forced to toil for bread, have ever addicted themselves to more generous employments, and been reckoned, almost in all ages, as

valiant warriors as any part of the world sent forth: insomuch, that the greatest Roman captains thought it not unworthy of their expeditions, and took great glory in triumphs for imperfect conquests. Lucan[1] upbraids Julius Caesar for returning hence with a repulse, and it was two hundred years before the land could be reduced into a Roman province, which at length was done, and such of the nation, then called Picts, as scorned servitude, were driven into that barren country of Scotland, where they have ever since remained a perpetual trouble to the successive inhabitants of this place. The Britons, that thought it better to work for their conquerors in a good land, than to have the freedom to starve in a cold or barren quarter, were by degrees fetched away, and wasted in the civil broils of these Roman lords, till the land, almost depopulated, lay open to the incursions of every borderer, and were forced to call a stout warlike people, the Saxons, out of Germany, to their assistance. These willingly came at their call, but were not so easily sent out again, nor persuaded to let their hosts inhabit with them, for they drove the Britons into the mountains of Wales, and seated themselves in those pleasant countries which from the new masters received a new name, and ever since retained it, being called England; and on which the warlike Dane made many attempts, with various success, but after about two or three hundred years' vain contest, they were for ever driven out, with shame and loss, and the Saxon Heptarchy melted into a monarchy, which continued till the superstitious prince, who was sainted for his ungodly chastity, left an empty throne to him that could seize it. He who first set up his standard in it, could not hold it, but with his life left it again for the Norman usurper, who partly by violence, partly by falsehood, laid here the foundation of his monarchy, in the people's blood, in which it hath swam about five hundred years, till the flood that bore it was ploughed into such deep

---

[1]Marcus Annaleus Lucanus (39–65 C.E.), author of a historical epic on the civil war between Caesar and Pompey.

furrows as had almost sunk the proud vessel. Of those Saxons that remained subjects to the Norman conqueror, my father's family descended; of those Normans that came in with him, my mother's was derived; both of them, as all the rest in England, contracting such affinity, by mutual marriages, that the distinction remained but a short space; Normans and Saxons becoming one people, who by their valour grew terrible to all the neighbouring princes, and have not only bravely acquitted themselves in their own defence, but have showed abroad how easily they could subdue the world, if they did not prefer the quiet enjoyment of their own part above the conquest of the whole.

Better laws and a happier constitution of government no nation ever enjoyed, it being a mixture of monarchy, aristocracy, and democracy, with sufficient fences against the pest of every one of those forms—tyranny, faction and confusion; yet is it not possible for man to devise such just and excellent bounds, as will keep in wild ambition, when prince's flatterers encourage that beast to break his fence, which it hath often done, with miserable consequences both to the prince and people; but could never in any age so tread down popular liberty, but that it arose again with renewed vigour, till at length it trod on those that trampled it before. And in the just bounds, wherein our kings were so well hedged in, the surrounding princes have with terror seen the reproof of their usurpations over their free brethren, whom they rule rather as slaves than subjects, and are only served for fear, but not for love; whereas this people have ever been as affectionate to good, as unpliable to bad sovereigns.

Nor is it only valour and generosity that renown this nation; in arts we have advanced equal to our neighbours, and in those that are most excellent, exceeded them. The world hath not yielded men more famous in navigation, nor ships better built or furnished. Agriculture is as ingeniously practised; the English archers were the terror of Christendom, and their clothes the ornament; but those low things bounded not their great spirits, in all ages it hath yielded men as famous in all kinds of learning, as Greece or Italy can boast of.

And to complete the crown of all their glory, reflected from the lustre of their ingenuity, valour, wit, learning, justice, wealth, and bounty, their piety and devotion to God, and his worship, hath made them one of the most truly noble nations in the Christian world. God having as it were enclosed a people here, out of the waste common of the world, to serve him with a pure and undefiled worship. Lucius[2] the British king was one of the first monarchs of the earth that received the faith of Christ into his heart and kingdom; Henry the Eighth,[3] the first prince that broke the antichristian yoke off from his own and his subjects' necks. Here it was that the first Christian emperor received his crown; here began the early dawn of Gospel light, by Wickliffe[4] and other faithful witnesses, whom God raised up after the black and horrid midnight of antichristianism; and a more plentiful harvest of devout confessors, constant martyrs, and holy worshippers of God, hath not grown in any field of the church, throughout all ages, than those whom God hath here glorified his name and gospel by. Yet hath not this wheat been without its tares; God in comparison with other countries hath made this as a paradise, so, to complete the parallel, the serpent hath in all times been busy to seduce, and not unsuccessful; ever stirring up opposers to the infant truths of Christ.

No sooner was the faith of Christ embraced in this nation, but the neighbouring heathens invaded the innocent Christians, and slaughtered multitudes of them; and when, by the mercy of God, the conquering Pagans were afterwards converted, and there were none left to oppose the

---

[2]According to legend, the first Christian king in Britain, sometime during the second century.

[3]Tudor king of England (r. 1509–1547) and initiator of the English Reformation with his Act of Supremacy in 1534.

[4]John Wycliffe (1330–1384), English theologian, reformer, and condemned heretic. Wycliffe's Bible-centered teachings challenged the role and authority of the established church hierarchy.

name of Christ with open hostility, then the subtle serpent put off his own horrid appearance, and comes out in a Christian dress, to persecute Christ in his poor prophets, that bore witness against the corruption of the times. This intestine quarrel hath been more successful to the devil, and more afflictive to the church, than all open wars; and, I fear, will never happily be decided, till the Prince of Peace come to conclude the controversy, which at the time of my birth was working up into that tempest, wherein I have shared many perils, many fears, and many sorrows; and many more mercies, consolations, and preservations, which I shall have occasion to mention in other places.

From the place of my birth I shall only desire to remember the goodness of the Lord, who hath caused my lot to fall in a good ground; who hath fed me in a pleasant pasture, where the well-springs of life flow to all that desire to drink of them. And this is no small favour, if I consider how many poor people perish among the heathen, where they never hear the name of Christ; how many poor Christians spring up in countries enslaved by Turkish and antichristian tyrants, whose souls and bodies languish under miserable slavery. None know what mercy it is to live under a good and wholesome law, that have not considered the sad condition of being subject to the will of an unlimited man; and surely it is too universal a sin in this nation, that the common mercies of God to the whole land are so slightly regarded, and so inconsiderately passed over; certainly these are circumstances which much magnify God's loving-kindness and his special favour to all that are of English birth, and call for a greater return of duty from us than from all other people of the world.

Nor is the place only, but the time of my coming into the world, a considerable mercy to me. It was not in the midnight of popery, nor in the dawn of the gospel's restored day, when light and shades were blended and almost undistinguished, but when the Sun of truth was exalted in his progress, and hastening towards a meridian glory. It was, indeed, early in the morning, God being pleased to allow me the privilege of beholding the admirable growth of gospel light in my days: and oh! that my soul may never forget to bless and praise his name for the wonders of power and goodness, wisdom and truth, which have been manifested in this my time.

The next blessing I have to consider in my nativity is my parents, both of them pious and virtuous in their own conversation, and careful instructors of my youth, not only by precept but example; which, if I had leisure and ability, I should have transmitted to my posterity, both to give them the honour due from me in such a grateful memorial, and to increase my children's improvement of the patterns they set them; but since I shall detract from those I would celebrate, by my imperfect commemorations, I shall content myself to sum up some few things for my own use, and let the rest alone, which I either knew not, or have forgotten, or cannot worthily express. . . .

As soon as I was weaned a French woman was taken to be my dry-nurse, and I was taught to speak French and English together. My mother, while she was with child of me, dreamed that she was walking in the garden with my father, and that a star came down into her hand, with other circumstances, which, though I have often heard, I minded not enough to remember perfectly; only my father told her, her dream signified she should have a daughter of some extraordinary eminency; which thing, like such vain prophecies, wrought as far as it could its own accomplishment: for my father and mother fancying me then beautiful, and more than ordinarily apprehensive, applied all their cares, and spared no cost to improve me in my education, which procured me the admiration of those that flattered my parents. By the time I was four years old I read English perfectly, and having a great memory, I was carried to sermons; and while I was very young could remember and repeat them exactly, and being caressed, the love of praise tickled me, and made me attend more heedfully. When I was about seven years of age, I remember I had at one time eight tutors in several qualities, languages, music, dancing, writing, and needlework; but my genius was quite averse from all but my book, and that I was so eager of, that my mother thinking it prejudiced my health, would moderate me in it; yet this rather animated me than kept me back, and every moment I could steal from my play I would employ in any book I could find, when my own were locked up from me. After dinner and supper I still had an hour allowed me to play, and then I would steal into some hole or other to read. My father would have me learn Latin, and I was so apt that I outstripped my brothers who were at school, although my father's chaplain, that was my tutor, was a pitiful dull fellow. My brothers, who had a great deal of wit, had some emulation at the progress I made in my learning, which very well pleased my father; though my mother would have been contented if I had not so wholly addicted myself to that as to neglect my other qualities. As for music and dancing, I profited very little in them, and would never practise my lute or harpsichord but when my masters were with me; and for my needle I absolutely hated it. Play among other children I despised, and when I was forced to entertain such as came to visit me, I tired them with more grave instructions than their mothers, and plucked all their babies to pieces, and kept the children in such awe, that they were glad when I entertained myself with elder company; to whom I was very acceptable, and living in the house with many persons that had a great deal of wit, and very profitable serious discourses being frequent at my father's table and in my mother's drawing-room, I was very attentive to all, and gathered up things that I would utter again, to great admiration of many that took my memory and imitation for wit. It pleased God that, through the good instructions of my mother, and the sermons she carried me to, I was convinced that the knowledge of God was the most excellent study, and accordingly applied myself to it, and to practise as I was taught. I used to exhort my mother's maids much, and to turn their idle discourses to good subjects; but I thought, when I had done this on the Lord's day, and every day performed my due tasks of reading and praying, that then I was free to anything that was not sin; for I was not at that time convinced of the vanity of conversation which was not scandalously wicked. I thought it no sin to learn or hear witty songs and amorous sonnets or poems, and twenty things of that kind, wherein I was so apt that I became the confidant in all the loves that were managed among my mother's young women; and there was none of them but had many lovers, and some particular friends beloved above the rest. Among these I have. . . .

[at this point in the manuscript there is a great gap, many leaves being torn out, apparently by the writer herself]

Five years after me my mother had a daughter that she nursed at her own breast, and was infinitely fond of above all the rest; and I being of too serious a temper was not so pleasing to my. . . .

[here the story of herself abruptly ends]

---

2. John Milton
POETRY

John Milton (1608–1674), most famous for his epic *Paradise Lost,* was one of the greatest poets to write in the English language. He was also a fervent Nonconformist, who considered sects and schisms to be signs of a healthy body politic and was thus staunchly opposed to the High Church politics of Charles I and

Archbishop Laud. Prior to and during the English Civil War, he wrote many tracts in defense of the antiroyalist Parliamentarians, earning much enmity among royal supporters and much favor among the eventually victorious Roundheads. Cromwell honored Milton by appointing him Secretary of Foreign Tongues in the Commonwealth, but the poet remained somewhat wary of the Protector's autocratic tendencies. Still, when Parliament considered limiting religious toleration, an alarmed Milton turned without hesitation to Cromwell, who shared his inclinations towards denominational diversity. The sonnet he dedicated to the Lord Protector, "To the Lord General Cromwell," was thus an appeal to preserve the Nonconformist ideal of private conviction rather than replace it with a new imposed conformity, this time Puritan in nature. This personal liberty was a sacred matter for Milton, who had, a year earlier, been dealt a blow that severely tested his own convictions, namely, complete blindness at the age of 43. In Milton's sonnet "On His Blindness," written a few years later, he movingly describes how such an affliction consistently frustrated him yet perhaps also strengthened his faith through perseverance.

a. JOHN MILTON, "TO THE LORD GENERAL CROMWELL" (1652)

Cromwell, our chief of men, who through a
    cloud
  Not of war only, but detractions rude,
  Guided by faith and matchless fortitude,
  To peace and truth thy glorious way hast
    ploughed,
And on the neck of crownéd fortune
    proud
  Hast reared God's trophies, and his work
    pursued,

While Darwen[5] stream with blood of Scots
  imbrued,
  And Dunbar field re-sounds thy praises loud;
And Worcester's laureate wreath. Yet much remains
  To conquer still; peace hath her victories
  No less renowned than war; new foes arise
Threatening to bind our souls with secular chains:
  Help us to save free conscience from the paw
  Of hireling wolves, whose gospel is their maw.

---

[5]Darwen, Dunbar, and Worcester were all famous victories of Cromwell against the rebellious Scots.

b. JOHN MILTON, "ON HIS BLINDNESS" (1655)

When I consider how my light is spent
  Ere half my days in this dark world and
    wide,
  And that one talent which is death to hide
  Lodged with me useless, though my soul
    more bent
To serve therewith my Maker, and present
  My true account, lest he returning chide,

"Doth God exact day-labor, light denied?"
  I fondly ask. But Patience, to prevent
That murmur, soon replies, "God doth not
    need
  Either man's work or his own gifts. Who
    best
  Bear his mild yoke, they serve him best. His
    state
Is kingly: thousands at his bidding speed,
  And post o'er land and ocean without rest;
  They also serve who only stand and wait."

3. George Fox
JOURNAL (1635–1675)

It is perhaps ironic that the only thoroughly pacifist Nonconformist sect of seventeenth-century England probably aroused the most hostility among Christians of the day. Mocked as "Quakers" because they visibly trembled when the spirit of God moved them, the Society of Friends (as they called themselves) possessed no dogma as such and an extremely loose institutional structure. It is likely that they might have gone the way of other now-extinct seventeenth-century Nonconformist groups were it not for the charismatic leadership and organizational skills of their founder, George Fox (1624–1691). Fox was an intensely introspective "seeker," whose public criticisms of contemporary religious teachings and social mores resulted in frequent beatings as well as imprisonment at least six times during his life, once for two and a half years. Stubbornly undeterred, he continued preaching the primacy of the "Inner Light," or divine element within every person, as well as the irrelevance of all sacraments and formalized worship. His followers also opposed church tithes, oaths of any kind, military service, and all hierarchical social conventions, from the mandatory doffing of a hat to a social "superior," to the making of any distinctions in personal address. In this excerpt from his journal, Fox describes his earliest struggles as well as his radical notions of equality among Christians (calling everyone by the informal "thou," even the Lord Protector himself). Though his enemies decried him as anarchic, immoral, and even unchristian, his movement spread within and beyond England, prompting one follower to donate a huge tract of land in the American colonies as a haven and "Holy Experiment" for fellow Quakers. The result was the colony of Pennsylvania, founded in 1682 by William Penn. Even then hundreds of Friends continued to languish in English prisons until finally in 1689 the Act of Toleration guaranteed religious freedom in England and put an end to the persecution of Nonconformists.

1635   That all may know the dealings of the Lord with me, and the various exercises, trials, and troubles through which he led me.

I was born in the month called July in the year 1624, at Drayton-in-the-Clay in Leicestershire. My father's name was Christopher Fox; he was by profession a weaver, an honest man, and there was a Seed of God in him. The neighbours called him "Righteous Christer." My mother was an upright woman; her maiden name was Mary Lago, of the family of the Lagos and of the stock of the martyrs.[6] . . .

When I came to eleven years of age, I knew pureness and righteousness; for while I was a child I was taught how to walk to be kept pure. The Lord taught me to be faithful in all things,

---

[6]A reference to the persecution of Protestants during the brief Catholic restoration in England under Queen Mary I (r. 1553–1558).

and to act faithfully two ways, viz., inwardly to God and outwardly to man, and to keep to "yea" and "nay" in all things. For the Lord showed me that though the people of the world have mouths full of deceit and changeable words, yet I was to keep to "yea" and "nay" in all things; and that my words should be few and savoury, seasoned with grace; and that I might not eat and drink to make myself wanton but for health, using the creatures in their service, as servants in their places, to the glory of him that hath created them. . . .

Afterwards, as I grew up, my relations thought to have me a priest, but others persuaded to the contrary; whereupon I was put to a man, a shoemaker by trade, and that dealt in wool, and used grazing, and sold cattle; and a great deal went through my hands. While I was with him, he was blessed; but after I left him he broke, and came to nothing. I never wronged man or woman in all that time, for the Lord's power was with me and over me, to preserve me. While I was in that service, I used in my dealings the word "verily," and it was a common saying among people that knew me, "If George says 'Verily' there is no altering him." When boys and rude people would laugh at me, I let them alone and went my way, but people had generally a love to me for my innocency and honesty. . . .

1644 Now during the time that I was at Barnet[7] a strong temptation to despair came upon me. And then I saw how Christ was tempted, and mighty troubles I was in. And sometimes I kept myself retired in my chamber, and often walked solitary in the Chase there, to wait upon the Lord. And I wondered why these things should come to me, and I looked upon myself and said, "Was I ever so before?". . .

1646 When I was come down into Leicestershire, my relations would have had me married, but I told them I was but a lad, and I must get wisdom. Others would have had me into the auxiliary band among the soldiery, but I refused; and I was grieved that they proffered such things to me, being a tender youth. Then I went to Coventry,[8] where I took a chamber for a while at a professor's house till people began to be acquainted with me, for there were many tender[9] people in that town.

And after some time I went into my own country again, and was there about a year, in great sorrows and troubles, and walked many nights by myself. . . .

I went to another ancient priest at Mancetter in Warwickshire and reasoned with him about the ground of despair and temptations, but he was ignorant of my condition; and he bid me take tobacco and sing psalms. Tobacco was a thing I did not love and psalms I was not in an estate to sing; I could not sing. Then he bid me come again and he would tell me many things, but when I came again he was angry and pettish, for my former words had displeased him. . . .

1647 Now after I had received that opening from the Lord that to be bred at Oxford or Cambridge was not sufficient to fit a man to be a minister of Christ, I regarded the priests less, and looked more after the dissenting people. And among them I saw there was some tenderness, and many of them came afterwards to be convinced, for they had some openings. But as I had forsaken all the priests, so I left the separate preachers also, and those called the most experienced people; for I saw there was none among them all that could speak to my condition. And when all my hopes in them and in all men were gone, so that I had nothing outwardly to help me, nor could tell what to do, then, Oh then, I heard a voice which said, "There is one, even Christ Jesus, that can speak to thy condition," and when I heard it my heart did leap for joy. Then the Lord did let me see why there was none upon the earth that could speak to my

---

[7]A northern borough of Greater London.

[8]A city and borough in the West Midlands.

[9]I.e., receptive to Fox's preaching of the Holy Spirit.

condition, namely, that I might give him all the glory; for all are concluded under sin, and shut up in unbelief as I had been, that Jesus Christ might have the pre-eminence, who enlightens, and gives grace, and faith and power. Thus, when God doth work who shall let [prevent] it? And this I knew experimentally. . . .

And one day, when I had been walking solitarily abroad and was come home, I was taken up in the love of God, so that I could not but admire the greatness of his love. And while I was in that condition it was opened unto me by the eternal Light and power, and I therein saw clearly that all was done and to be done in and by Christ, and how he conquers and destroys this tempter, the Devil and all his works, and is atop of him, and that all these troubles were good for me, and temptations for the trial of my faith which Christ had given me. And the Lord opened me that I saw through all these troubles and temptations. My living faith was raised, that I saw all was done by Christ, the life, and my belief was in him. And when at any time my condition was veiled, my secret belief was stayed firm, and hope underneath held me, as an anchor in the bottom of the sea, and anchored my immortal soul to its Bishop, causing it to swim above the sea, the world where all the raging waves, foul weather, tempests, and temptations are. But oh, then did I see my troubles, trials and temptations more than ever I had done! . . .

And therefore none can be a minister of Christ Jesus but in the eternal Spirit, which was before the Scriptures were given forth; for if they have not his Spirit, they are none of his. . . .

1648   In the year 1648, as I was sitting in a Friend's house in Nottinghamshire (for by this time the power of God had opened the hearts of some to receive the word of life and reconciliation), I saw there was a great crack to go throughout the earth, and a great smoke to go as the crack went; and that after the crack there should be a great shaking. This was the earth in people's hearts, which was to be shaken before the Seed of God was raised out of the earth. And it was so; for the Lord's power began to

shake them, and great meetings we began to have, and a mighty power and work of God there was amongst people, to the astonishment of both people and priests. . . .

After this I went again to Mansfield, where was a great meeting of professors and people, and I was moved to pray, and the Lord's power was so great that the house seemed to be shaken. When I had done, some of the professors said it was now as in the days of the apostles, when the house was shaken where they were. . . .

Moreover when the Lord sent me forth into the world, he forbade me to put off my hat to any, high or low; and I was required to "thee" and "thou" all men and women, without any respect to rich or poor, great or small. And as I travelled up and down, I was not to bid people "good morrow" or "good evening," neither might I bow or scrape with my leg to any one, and this made the sects and professions to rage. But the Lord's power carried me over all to his glory, and many came to be turned to God in a little time, for the heavenly day of the Lord sprang from on high, and brake forth apace by the light of which many came to see where they were. . . .

1649   Oh, the rage and scorn, the heat and fury that arose! Oh, the blows, punchings, beatings and imprisonments that we underwent for not putting off our hats to men! For that soon tried all men's patience and sobriety, what it was. Some had their hats violently plucked off and thrown away so that they quite lost them. The bad language and evil usage we received on this account are hard to be expressed, besides the danger we were sometimes in of losing our lives for this matter, and that, by the great professors of Christianity. . . .

1653   And the next day we came through that country into Cumberland again where we had a general meeting of many thousands of people atop of a hill, near Langlands. Heavenly and glorious it was and the glory of the Lord did shine over all, and there were as many as one could well speak over, there was such a multitude. Their eyes were kept to Christ their teacher and they came to sit under their vine, that afterwards a Friend in the ministry, Francis Howgill,[10] went amongst them, and when he was moved to stand up amongst them he saw they had no need of words for they was all sitting down under their teacher Christ Jesus; so he was moved to sit down again amongst them without speaking anything.

So great a convincement there was in Cumberland, Bishoprick, Northumberland, Yorkshire, Westmorland, and Lancashire, and the plants of God grew and flourished so by heavenly rain, and God's glory shined upon them, that many mouths the Lord opened to his praise, yea to babes and sucklings he ordained strength. . . .

But at the first convincement, when Friends could not put off their hats to people nor say "you" to a particular, but "thee" and "thou"; and could not bow nor use the world's salutations, nor fashions, nor customs, many Friends, being tradesmen of several sorts lost their custom at the first; for the people would not trade with them nor trust them and for a time Friends that were tradesmen could hardly get enough money to buy bread. But afterwards people came to see Friends' honesty and truthfulness and "yea" and "nay" at a word in their dealing, and their lives and conversations did preach and reach to the witness of God in all people, and they knew and saw that for conscience sake towards God, they would not cozen and cheat them, and at last that they might send any child and be as well used as themselves, at any of their shops.

So then things altered so that all the enquiry was, where was a draper or shopkeeper or tailor or shoemaker or any other tradesman that was a Quaker; insomuch that Friends had double the trade, beyond any of their neighbours. And if there was any trading they had it, insomuch that then the cry of all the professors and others was "If we let these people alone they will take the trading of the nation out of our hands." . . .

1655 . . . And when I was at London [Colonel Hacker[11]] left me at the Mermaid and went and told Oliver Cromwell of me.

And I gave forth a paper and bid him carry it to Oliver, which is here as followeth: . . .

[Fox quotes a brief note of introduction to Cromwell.]

And after a few days I was had before Oliver Cromwell by Captain Drury.

Upon the Fifth-day of the First-month Captain Drury who brought George Fox up to London by order from Colonel Hacker did come to the inn into the chamber where George Fox lay and said that it was required of George Fox from Oliver Cromwell that he would promise that he would not take up a sword against the Lord Protector or the Government as it is now; and that George Fox would write down the words in answer to that which the Protector required, and for George Fox to set his hand to it.

The Fifth-day of the First-month George Fox was moved of the Lord to give out these words following which were given to Oliver Cromwell. And George Fox was then presently brought before him by Captain Drury.

George Fox to Oliver Cromwell, 1654[12]

I, who am of the world called George Fox, do deny the carrying or drawing of any carnal sword against any, or against thee, Oliver Cromwell, or any man. In the presence of the Lord I declare it.

God is my witness, by whom I am moved to give this forth for the Truth's sake, from him whom the world calls George Fox; who is the son of God who is sent to stand a witness against all violence and against all the works of darkness, and to turn people from darkness to the light, and to bring them from the occasion

---

[10]A farmer-preacher who became one of the early leaders of the Quaker movement.

[11]Colonel Francis Hacker (d. 1660), a supporter of the Lord Protector Cromwell, had Fox brought to London under armed guard.
[12]1655 (by the modern calendar).

of the war and from the occasion of the magistrate's sword, which is a terror to the evil doers who act contrary to the light of the Lord Jesus Christ, which is a praise to them that do well, a protection to them that do well and not evil. Such soldiers as are put in that place no false accusers must be, no violence must do, but be content with their wages; and the magistrate bears not the sword in vain.

From under the occasion of that sword I do seek to bring people. My weapons are not carnal but spiritual, and "my kingdom is not of this world" [Jn 18:36], therefore with a carnal weapon I do not fight, but am from those things dead; from him who is not of the world, called of the world by the name George Fox. And this I am ready to seal with my blood. . . .

From him who to all your souls is a friend, for establishing of righteousness and cleansing the land of evil doers and a witness against all wicked inventions of men and murderous plots, which answered shall be with the light in all your consciences, which makes no covenant with death, to which light in you all I speak, and am clear.

G. F.

who is of the world called George Fox, who a new name hath which the world knows not.

We are witnesses of this testimony, whose names in the flesh are called

Thomas Aldam
Robert Craven

He brought me in before him before he was dressed, and one Harvey[13] (that had come amongst Friends but was disobedient) waited upon him.

And so when I came before him [on March 6, 1655] I was moved to say, "Peace be on this house"; and I bid him keep in the fear of God that he might receive wisdom, that by it he might be ordered, that with it he might order all things under his hand to God's glory. And I spake much to him of Truth, and a great deal of discourse I had with him about religion, wherein he carried himself very moderately; but he said we quarrelled with the priests, whom he called ministers. . . .

And I told him the prophets, Christ, and the apostles declared freely; and they declared against them that did not declare freely; such as preached for filthy lucre and divined for money and preached for hire and were covetous and greedy like the dumb dogs that could never have enough; and such priests as did bear rule by their means and the people that loved to have it so. Now they that have the same spirit that Christ, and the prophets, and apostles had could not but declare against all such now as they did then. And several times he said it was very good, and truth, and I told him that all Christendom so called had the Scriptures but they wanted the power and spirit that they had that gave them forth; and therefore they were not in fellowship with the Son, nor with the Father, nor with the Scriptures, nor one with another.

And many more words I had with him. And many people began to come in, that I drew a little backward, and as I was turning he catched me by the hand and said these words with tears in his eyes, "Come again to my house; for if thou and I were but an hour in a day together we should be nearer one to the other," and that he wished me no more ill than he did to his own soul. And I told him if he did he wronged his own soul; and so I bid him hearken to and hear God's voice that he might stand in his counsel and obey it; if he did so, that would keep him from hardness of heart, and if he did not hear God's voice his heart would be hardened. And he said it was true. So I went out, and he bid me come again. And then Captain Drury came out after me and told me his Lord Protector said I was at liberty and might go whither I would, "And," says he, "my Lord says you are not a fool," and said he never saw such a paper in his life as I had sent him before by him. Then I was brought into a great hall, where the Protector's gentlemen were to dine; and I asked them what they did bring me thither for. They said, it was by the Protector's

---

[13]Charles Harvey, groom of the bed-chamber.

order, that I might dine with them. I bid them let the Protector know I would not eat a bit of his bread, nor drink a sup of his drink. When he heard this, he said that there was a people risen, meaning us, that he could not win either with honour, high places, nor gifts, but all other people he could. For we did not seek any of their places, gifts, nor honours, but their salvation and eternal good, both in this nation and elsewhere. But it was told him again that we had forsook our own, and were not like to look for such things from him. . . .

1670 . . . And at this time there were great persecutions and there had been searching for me at London, and some meetinghouses plucked down and broken up with soldiers. Sometimes they would come with a troop of horse and a company of foot, and they would break their swords and muskets, carbines and pikes, with beating Friends and wounding abundance, so that the blood stood like puddles in the street. . . .

1675 . . . The Truth sprang up first, to us so as to be a people to the Lord, in Leicestershire in 1644, in Warwickshire in 1645, Not-tinghamshire in 1646, in Derbyshire in 1647, and in the adjacent counties in 1648, 1649, and 1650; and in Yorkshire in 1651, and in Lancashire and Westmorland in 1652, and in Cumberland, Bishoprick, and Northumberland in 1653, in London and most parts of the nation and Scotland and Ireland in 1654. And in 1655 many went beyond seas, where Truth also sprang up. And in 1656 Truth broke forth in America and in many other places.

And the Truth stood all the cruelties and sufferings that were inflicted upon Friends by the Long Parliament[14] and then by Oliver Protector, and all the Acts that Oliver Protector made, and his Parliaments, and his son Richard after him, and the Committee of Safety.

And after, it withstood and lasted out all the Acts and Proclamations, since 1660 that the King came in. And still the Lord's Truth is over all and his Seed reigns and his Truth exceedingly spreads unto this year 1676.

------

[14]The Long Parliament met from November 3, 1640, to April 20, 1653, when it was dissolved by Cromwell.

B. Witch-Hunt

Religious violence during the Confessional Age was by no means limited to conflicts between Protestants and Catholics, or between established churches and Nonconformists. All early modern Christians in fact shared at least one acknowledged common enemy, Satan, and were convinced that a conspiracy of the evil one's followers was afoot throughout Europe. This at least was the common justification for the torture and execution of at least 60,000 individuals from 1550 to 1700 for the crime of witchcraft. Beliefs in witches had been common since ancient times, but by the beginning of the sixteenth century, three distinct developments had given birth to a new social phenomenon now known as the great witch craze, or witch-hunt. The first was the 1486 compilation of all theological and "scientific" opinions about witches in the *Malleus Maleficarum* ("Hammer of Witches") by the Austrian Dominicans Jakob Sprenger and Heinrich Kramer. This oft-reprinted and widely distributed work served as the authoritative handbook for Protestants and Catholics alike in identifying and questioning suspected witches. The notion of a Satanic conspiracy was nourished by a second event, namely, the outbreak of the Reformation and the common Protestant and Catholic labeling of heretical opponents as diabolical and dangerous to true Christianity. Finally, the concurrent increase in legal codification and criminal prosecution in general provided a third and decisive element in the witch-hunt formula. As a result of these developments, the various personal animosities and loose rumors of witchcraft that had always existed among ordinary people were given new theological and legal support. This encouraged many individuals to make more frequent official accusations of witchcraft against each other, a trend that—when combined with the low threshold of physical evidence required for conviction and the great reliance on tortured confessions—yielded the thousands of "witches" that Sprenger and Kramer had predicted. There is no real evidence of any organized Satanism or even paganism during this period, but belief in the existence of witches was apparently genuine and widespread until at least the mid seventeenth century in most parts of Europe. Eventually learned opinion turned against legal prosecution of witches—if not against the belief in witches itself—and the witch craze gradually drew to a close. The last officially sanctioned European witch-burning took place in Switzerland in 1782.

1. WITCHES AT CHELMSFORD (1589)

One of the most influential contributions of the *Malleus Maleficarum* to the witch craze was its consolidation of many popular notions about witches into one stereotyped image, which gradually came to be accepted by people across Europe. By the end of the sixteenth century, most accusations of witchcraft included the common elements of a compact with the devil, the witches' sabbath, the ability to fly, and black magic. This contemporary published account of a witch-hunt in Chelmsford (in southeastern England) predictably contains most of these details, as well as the presence of certain witches' "familiars," or demons in animal form (in this instance a ferret and two frogs named Jack and Jill). Lurid details from the trial records were the bread and butter of the thriving tabloids of the day, yet it is not irrelevant that the accused women in these cases had bad local reputations. Sexual impropriety or simple unfriendliness were more than grounds enough to suspect such individuals of involvement, magical or otherwise, in every misfortune in the neighborhood. The pamphlet excerpted below describes only those few cases of the Chelmsford witch-hunt where accusations (even from a child) actually led to execution. Still, it is worth noting, even in these cases, the almost complete absence of any material evidence and the self-confirming reliance on tortured confessions.

THE ARRAIGNMENT AND EXECUTION OF JOAN CUNNY OF STISTED IN THE COUNTY OF ESSEX, WIDOW, OF THE AGE OF FOURSCORE YEARS OR THEREABOUTS, WHO WAS BROUGHT BEFORE ANTHONY MILDMAY, ESQUIRE, THE LAST DAY OF MARCH 1589.

Imprimis, this examinate saith and confesseth that she hath knowledge and can do the most detestable art of witchcraft, and that she learned this her knowledge in the same of one Mother Humphrey of Maplestead, who told her that she must kneel down upon her knees and make a circle on the ground, and pray unto Satan the chief of the devils (the form of which prayer that she then taught her this examinate hath now forgotten), and that then the spirits would come unto her.

The which she put in practice about twenty years since, in the field of John Wiseman of Stisted, gentleman, called Cowfen Field; and there making a circle as she was taught, and kneeling on her knees, said the prayer now forgotten; and invocating upon Satan, two spirits did appear unto her within the said circle, in the similitude and likeness of two black frogs, and there demanded of her what she would have, being ready to do for her what she would desire, so that she would promise to give them her soul for their travail, for otherwise they would do nothing for her.

Whereupon she did promise them her soul, and then they concluded with her so to do for her what she would require, and gave themselves several names—that is to say, the one Jack and the other Jill, by the which names she did always after call them. And then taking them up, she carried them home in her lap and put them in a box, and gave them white bread and milk.

And within one month after, she sent them to milk Hurrell's beasts [i.e., cows], which they did, and they would bring milk for their own eating and not for her. And further, she saith that her spirits never changed their colour since they first came unto her, and that they would familiarly talk with her when she had anything to say or do with them, in her own language.

And likewise she confesseth that she sent her said spirits to hurt the wife of John Sparrow the elder of Stisted, which they did, and also that where Master John Glascock of Stisted aforesaid had a great stack of logs in his yard, she by her said spirits did overthrow them.

And further saith that she hath hurt divers persons within this sixteen or twenty years, but how many she now knoweth not. Furthermore,

she confesseth that she sent her spirits unto William Unglee of Stisted, miller, and because they could not hurt him, she sent them to hurt one Barnaby Griffin his man[-servant], which they did.

Likewise, she confesseth that she sent her said spirits to hurt Master Kirchin, minister of the said town, and also unto one George Coe of the said town, shoemaker, to hurt him likewise. But they could not, and the cause why they could not, as the said spirits told her, was because they had at their coming a strong faith in God, and had invocated and called upon Him, that they could do them no harm.

And further, she saith that Margaret Cunny her daughter did fall out with Father Hurrell and gave him cursed speeches, and thereupon she thinketh she sent her spirits to her.

Also she doth utterly deny that she sent her said spirits to Finch's wife, Devenish's wife, and Reynold Ferrer, or any of them to hurt them. And being further examined, she confesseth that although her said spirits at some time can have no power to hurt men, yet they may have power to hurt their cattle.

This Joan Cunny living very lewdly, had two lewd daughters no better than naughty [sluts] who had two bastard children: being both boys, these two children were chief witnesses and gave in great evidence against their grandam and mothers, the eldest being about 10 or 12 years of age.

Against this Mother Cunny the elder boy gave in this evidence, which she herself after confessed: that she going to Braintree market came to one Harry Finch's house to demand some drink; his wife being busy and a-brewing told her she had no leisure to give her any. Then Joan Cunny went away discontented, and at night Finch's wife was grievously taken in her head, and the next day in her side, and so continued in most horrible pain for the space of a week, and then died. Mother Cunny confessed that she sent her spirit Jill to torment her.

The same boy confessed that he was commanded by his grandmother to fetch a burden of wood, which he gathered, but another boy stole it from him, and he came home without and told his grandam; and she commanded her spirit to prick the same boy in the foot, which was done, and the same boy came to the bar lame, and gave evidence against her.

Again the same boy confessed that his grandam, when he had lost his wood, said she would have wood enough, and bade him go into Sir Edward Huddlestone's ground (being High Sheriff of the shire) and to take with him Jack the spirit; and so he did, who went unseen to anybody but to the boy, and when they came to a mighty oak tree, the spirit went about it, and presently the tree blew up by the roots and no wind at all stirring at this time; which Master High Sheriff acknowledged to be blown down in a great calm.

THE CONFESSION OF JOAN UPNEY OF DAGENHAM IN THE COUNTY OF ESSEX, WHO WAS BROUGHT BEFORE SIR HENRY GRAY, KNIGHT, THE THIRD OF MAY 1589.

This examinate saith that one Fustian Kirtle, otherwise called Whitecoat, a witch of Barking, came to her house about seven or eight years ago and gave her a thing like a mole, and told her if she owed anybody any ill will, if she did bid it, it would go [strike] them.

She saith that mole tarried not above a year with her but it consumed away, and then she gave her another mole and a toad, which she kept a great while, and was never without some toads since, till her last going away from her house, when she confesseth she ran away because she heard John Harrold and Richard Foster say she was a witch, and such other words.

She saith that one day she left a toad under the groundsill at Harrold's house, and it pinched his wife and sucked her till she died, but it never came to her the said Joan Upney again.

She saith that one day another toad went over her threshold as Richard Foster's wife was coming that way, and it went and pinched her

and never returned again. Other two toads she left at home when she ran away, but they consumed away.

She saith that her eldest daughter would never abide to meddle with her toads, but her youngest daughter would handle them and use them as well as herself.

THE EXAMINATION OF JOAN PRENTICE, ONE OF THE WOMEN OF THE ALMSHOUSE OF SIBLE HEDINGHAM WITHIN THE SAID COUNTY, BEING TAKEN THE 29 OF MARCH, IN THE 31ST YEAR OF THE REIGN OF OUR SOVEREIGN LADY ELIZABETH.

Imprimis, this said examinate saith and confesseth, that about six years last past, between the feasts of All Saints and the birth of our Lord God, the Devil appeared unto her in the almshouse aforesaid about ten of the clock in the night time, being in the shape and proportion of a dunnish coloured ferret, having fiery eyes; and the said examinate being alone in her chamber, and sitting upon a low stool preparing herself to bedward, the ferret standing with his hinder legs upon the ground and his forelegs settled upon her lap, and settling his fiery eyes upon her eyes, spake and pronounced unto her these words following, namely: "Joan Prentice, give me thy soul."

To whom this examinate, being greatly amazed, answered and said, "In the name of God, what art thou?" The ferret answered, "I am Satan; fear me not, my coming unto thee is to do thee no hurt but to obtain thy soul, which I must and will have before I depart from thee." To whom the said examinate answered and said that he demanded that of her which is none of hers to give, saying that her soul appertained only unto Jesus Christ by whose precious blood-shedding it was bought and purchased.

To whom the said ferret replied and said, "I must then have some of thy blood," which she willingly granting, offered him the forefinger of her left hand; the which the ferret took into his mouth and, setting his former feet upon that hand, sucked blood thereout, insomuch that her finger did smart exceedingly. And the said examinate demanding again of the ferret what his name was, it answered "Bid"; and then presently the said ferret vanished out of her sight suddenly.

Item, the said examinate saith further that about one month after, the said ferret came again unto her in the night time as she was sitting upon a little stool, preparing herself to bedward, as is above said. "Joan, wilt thou go to bed?" to whom she answered "Yea, that I will by God's grace"; then presently the ferret leapt up upon her lap, and from thence up to her bosom, and laying his former feet upon her left shoulder, sucked blood out of her left cheek, and then he said unto her, "Joan, if thou wilt have me do anything for thee, I am and will be always ready at thy commandment." And thereupon she, being a little before fallen out with William Adams his wife of Sible Hedingham aforesaid, willed the ferret to spoil her drink which was then in brewing, which he did accordingly.

Item, the said examinate furthermore saith and confesseth that the said ferret divers times after appeared unto her, always at the time when she was going to bed; and the last time he appeared unto her was about seven weeks last past, at which time she going to bed, the ferret leaped upon her left shoulder and sucked blood out of her left cheek and, that done, he demanded of her what she had for him to do? To whom she answered, "Go unto Master Glascock's house, and nip one of his children a little, named Sara, but hurt it not."

And the next night he resorted unto her again and told her that he had done as she willed him, namely, that he had nipped Sara Glascock and that she should die thereof. To whom she answered and said, "Thou villain! What has thou done? I bid thee to nip it but a little and not to hurt it, and hast thou killed the child?" Which speech being uttered, the ferret vanished away suddenly, and never came to her since.

Item, she affirmeth that the occasion why she did will her ferret to nip the said child was for that she being the day before at the house of the said Master Glascock to beg his alms, answer was made to her by one of his maiden servants that both her master and mistress were from home, and therefore desired her to be contented for that time, and thereupon the examinate departed greatly discontented, and that night sent her ferret to nip the child as is aforesaid.

Item, she saith and affirmeth that at what time soever she would have her ferret do anything for her, she used the words "Bid, Bid, Bid, come Bid, come Bid, come Bid, come suck, come suck, come suck," and that presently he would appear as is aforesaid and sucked blood out of her left cheek, and then performed any mischief she willed or wished him to do for her unto or against any of her neighbours.

Lastly, the said examinate saith and confesseth that one Elizabeth Whale, the wife of Michael Whale of Sible Hedingham aforesaid, labourer, and Elizabeth Mott, the wife of John Mott of the said town, cobbler, are as well acquainted with her Bid as herself is, but knoweth not what hurt they or any of them have done to any of their neighbours.

When their inditements were read, and their examinations also, they stood upon their terms to prolong life. Yet to make the matters more apparent, sundry witnesses were produced to give evidence against them; and first the judge of the circuit very wisely with a great foresight called in the two bastard children before mentioned, and commended them greatly for telling the truth of that which he should ask them concerning their grandam and their mothers (which they did). And having said what they could, together with the depositions of sundry other witnesses, they having confessed sufficient matter to prove the inditements, the jury found these bad women guilty, and that they had slain men, women and children, and committed very wicked and horrible actions, divers and sundry times, and thereupon the judge proceeded and pronounced the sentence of death against them, as worthily they had deserved.

After they had received their judgments, they were conveyed from the bar back again to prison, where they had not stayed above two hours but the officers prepared themselves to conduct them to the place of execution. To which place they led them, and being come thither, one Master Ward, a learned divine, being desired by the justices did exhort these wicked women to repentance, and persuaded them that they would show unto the people the truth of their wickedness, and to call upon God for mercy with penitent hearts, and to ask pardon at His hands for the same. Some few

prayers they said after the preacher, but little else more than this, that they had deserved to die in committing those wicked sins, and so took their deaths patiently.

Note that Mother Upney being inwardly pricked, and having some inward feeling in conscience, cried out saying that she had grievously sinned, that "the Devil had deceived her, the Devil had deceived her," and that she had twice given her soul to the Devil; yet by the means of God's spirit working in her, and the pains which Master Ward took with her, she seemed very sorry for the same, and died very penitent, asking God and the world forgiveness even to the last gasp, for her wicked and detestable life.

---

2. RECANTATION OF CORNELIUS LOOS (1593)

Not all Christians of the Confessional Age, learned or otherwise, accepted the prevailing belief in witches. Johann Weyer (1515–1588), a Lutheran physician, was one of the most prominent early skeptics on the question, arguing not only that no diabolical conspiracy existed but also that certain "witches" were, at worst, malevolent poisoners, not magicians of any kind. Such opinions did not sit well with fervent witch-hunters, of course. The German Archbishopric of Trier was one of the most active regions for witch prosecution in Europe, and when its officials learned that a local theologian had publicly endorsed Weyer's arguments, the offender was forced to recant or face heresy charges. In this coerced statement, Cornelius Loos (1546–1595) renounced all of his previous denials of witchcraft and reaffirmed the "truths" of the *Malleus Maleficarum*. As the postscript notes, however, Loos later recanted his recantation and barely escaped another heresy charge after he again questioned the existence of witches. Such would repeatedly be the fate of dissenters such as Weyer and Loos until governmental authorities eventually came to share their opinion a half century later.

I, Cornelius Losæus Callidius, born at the town of Gouda in Holland, but now (on account of a certain treatise *On True and False Witchcraft*, rashly and presumptuously written without the knowledge and permission of the superiors of this place, shown by me to others, and then sent to be printed at Cologne) arrested and imprisoned in the Imperial Monastery of St. Maximin, near Trier, by order of the Most Reverend and Most Illustrious Lord, the Papal Nuncio, Octavius, Bishop of Tricarico: whereas I am informed of a surety that in the aforesaid book and also in certain letters of mine on the same subject sent clandestinely to the clergy and town council of Trier, and to others (for the purpose of hindering the execution of justice against the witches, male and female), are contained many articles which are not only erroneous and scandalous, but also suspected of heresy and smacking of the crime of treason, as being seditious and foolhardy, against the common opinion of theological teachers and the decisions and bulls of the Supreme Pontiffs, and contrary to the practice and to the statutes and laws of the magistrates and judges, not only of this Archdiocese of Trier, but of other provinces and principalities, I do therefore revoke, condemn, reject, and repudiate the said articles, in the order in which they are here subjoined.

1. In the first place, I revoke, condemn, reject, and censure the idea (which both in words and writing I have often and before many persons pertinaciously asserted, and which I wished to be the head and front of this my disputation) that the things which are written about the bodily transportation or translation of witches, male and female, are altogether fanciful and must be reckoned the figments of an empty superstition; [and this I recant] both because it smacks of rank heresy and because this opinion partakes of sedition and hence savors of the crime of treason.

2. For (and this in the second place I recant), in the letters which I have clandestinely sent to sundry persons, I have pertinaciously, without solid reasons, alleged against the magistracy that the [aerial] flight of witches is false and imaginary; asserting, moreover, that the wretched creatures are compelled by the severity of the torture to confess things which they have never done, and that by cruel butchery innocent blood is shed and by a new alchemy gold and silver coined from human blood.

3. By these and by other things of the same sort, partly in private conversations among the people, partly in sundry letters addressed to both the magistracies,[15] I have accused of tyranny to their subjects the superiors and the judges.

4. And consequently, inasmuch as the Most Reverend and Most Illustrious Archbishop and Prince-Elector of Trier not only permits witches, male and female, to be subjected in his diocese to deserved punishment, but has also ordained laws regulating the method and costs of judicial procedure against witches, I have with heedless temerity tacitly insinuated the charge of tyranny against the aforesaid Elector of Trier.

5. I revoke and condemn, moreover, the following conclusions of mine, to wit: that there are no witches who renounce God, pay worship to the Devil, bring storms by the Devil's aid, and do such like things, but that all these things are dreams.

6. Also, that magic (*magia*) ought not to be called witchcraft (*maleficium*), nor magicians (*magi*) witches (*malefici*), and that the passage of Holy Scripture, "Thou shalt not suffer a witch to live" (*Maleficos non patieris vivere*) [Ex 22:18] is to be understood of those who by a natural use of natural poisons inflict death.

7. That no compact does or can exist between the Devil and a human being.

8. That devils do not assume bodies.

9. That the life of Hilarion written by St. Jerome is not authentic.

10. That there is no sexual intercourse between the Devil and human beings.

11. That neither devils nor witches can raise tempests, rain-storms, hail-storms, and the like, and that the things said about these are mere dreams.

12. That spirit and form apart from matter cannot be seen by man.

13. That it is rash to assert that whatever devils can do, witches also can do through their aid.

14. That the opinion that a superior demon can cast out an inferior is erroneous and derogatory to Christ.[16]

15. That the Popes in their bulls do not say that magicians and witches perpetrate such things (as are mentioned above).

---

[15] I.e., both secular and ecclesiastical courts.

[16] A marginal note here cites Lk 11.

16. That the Roman Pontiffs granted the power to proceed against witches, lest if they should refuse they might be unjustly accused of magic, just as some of their predecessors had been justly accused of it.

These assertions, all and singular, with many calumnies, falsehoods, and sycophancies, toward the magistracy, both secular and ecclesiastical, spitefully, immodestly, and falsely poured forth, without cause, with which my writings on magic teem, I hereby expressly and deliberately condemn, revoke, and reject, earnestly beseeching the pardon of God and of my superiors for what I have done, and solemnly promising that in future I will neither in word nor in writing, by myself or through others, in whatsoever place it may befall me to be, teach, promulgate, defend, or assert any of these things. If I shall do to the contrary, I subject myself thenceforward, as if it were now, to all the penalties of the law against relapsed heretics, recusants, seditious offenders, traitors, backbiters, sycophants, who have been openly convicted, and also to those ordained against perjurers. I submit myself also to arbitrary correction, whether by the Archbishop of Trier or by any other magistrates under whom it may befall me to dwell, and who may be certified of my relapse and of my broken faith, that they may punish me according to my deserts, in honor and reputation, property and person.

In testimony of all which I have, with my own hand, signed this my recantation of the aforesaid articles, in presence of notary and witnesses.

(*Signed*)   CORNELIUS LOOSÆUS CALLIDIUS

[Followed by the names and signatures of various theologians and other attesting churchmen, as well as this postscript from the town secretary of Antwerp:]

Here you have the Recantation in full. And yet afterwards again at Brussels, while serving as curate in the church of Notre Dame de la Chapelle, he was accused of relapse, and was released only after a long imprisonment, and being again brought into suspicion (whence you may understand the pertinacity of his madness) escaped a third indictment through a premature death; but (much the pity!) left behind not a few partisans, men so imperfectly versed in medicine and sound theology as to share this stupid error. Would that they might be wise, and seriously realize at last how rash and noxious it is to prefer the ravings of a single heretic, Weyer,[17] to the judgment of the Church!

---

[17]Johann Weyer (1515–1588); see document introduction.

3. Cotton Mather
WITCHES (1689)

The notorious witch trials of Salem, Massachusetts, were almost as shocking to European contemporaries as they are to us today. For many foreign observers this relatively late outburst of witch fever merely confirmed the religious and intellectual backwardness of New World colonies. The role of clerics in this panic was certainly significant, and the popular New England preacher Cotton Mather (1663–1728) was particularly active. In this tract, based on a sermon he delivered in Boston earlier the same year, Mather reaffirms practically every witch stereotype known, especially the notion of a diabolical conspiracy, which he believed was at work in his congregation's very midst. His defensive posture throughout is perhaps indicative of the skepticism of many of his readers, who shared the attitudes of their European cousins. Nevertheless, Mather's mix of scriptural references and "the testimony of experience" (i.e., forced confessions) was apparently a powerful catalyst in the series of witchcraft accusations and trials that took place three years later in nearby Salem. Public opinion eventually put an end to the mass hysteria that gripped Salem during this time, but only after nineteen people had been executed for consorting with the devil. Four years later, the colony's legislature adopted a resolution of repentance for the trials, and shortly after that one of the chief judges of Salem admitted that the executions had been unjust.

Such an Hellish thing there is as *Witchcraft* in the World. There are Two things which will be desired for the advantage of this Assertion. It should *first* be show'd WHAT *Witchcraft* is;

My Hearers will not expect from me an accurate *Definition* of the *vile Thing;* since the Grace of God has given me the Happiness to speak without *Experience* of it. But from Accounts both by *Reading* and *Hearing* I have learn'd to describe it so.

WITCHCRAFT is the Doing of *Strange* (and for the most part *Ill*) Things by the help of *evil Spirits, Covenanting* with (and usually *Representing* of) the woeful children of men.

This is the *Diabolical Art* that *Witches* are notorious for.

First. *Witches* are the Doers of *Strange* Things. They cannot indeed perform any proper *Miracles;* those are things to be done only by the *Favourites* and *Embassadours* of the *Lord.* But *Wonders* are often produced by them, though chiefly such Wonders as the Apostle calls in 2 *Thes.* 2, 9. *Lying wonders.* There are *wonderful Storms* in the *great* world, and *wonderful Wounds* in the *little* World, often effected by these *evil Causes.* They do things which transcend the ordinary *Course* of Nature, and which puzzle the ordinary *Sense* of Mankind. Some *strange* things are done by them in a way of *Real Production.* They do really *Torment,* they do really *Afflict* those that their Spite shall extend unto. Other *Strange* Things are done by them in a way of *Crafty Illusion.* They do craftily make of the *Air,* the *Figures* and *Colours* of things that never can be truly created by them.

All men might *see,* but, I believe, no man could *feel,* some of the Things which the *Magicians* of *Egypt* exhibited of old.

Secondly. They are not only *strange* Things, but *Ill* Things, that *Witches* are the Doers of. In this regard also they are not the Authors of *Miracles:* those are things *commonly* done for the *Good* of Man, *alwaies* done for the *Praise* of *God.* But of these *Hell-hounds* it may in a special manner be said, as in *Psal.* 52, 3. *Thou lovest evil more than good.* For the most part they labour to robb *Man* of his *Ease* or his *Wealth;* they labour to wrong *God* of His *Glory.* There is Mention of Creatures that they call *White Witches,* which do only *Good-Turns* for their Neighbours. I suspect that there are none of that sort; but rather think, *There is none that doeth good, no, not one.* If they *do good,* it is only that they *may do hurt.*

Thirdly. It is by virtue of *evil Spirits* that *Witches* do what they do. We read in *Ephes.* 2, 2. about the *Prince of the power of the air.* There is confined unto the *Atmosphere* of our *Air* a vast *Power,* or *Army of Evil Spirits,* under the Government of a Prince who employs them in a continual Opposition to the Designs of GOD: The Name of that *Leviathan,* who is the *Grand-Seigniour of Hell,* we find in the Scripture to be *Belzebub.* Under the Command of that mighty Tyrant, there are vast *Legions & Myriads* of Devils, whose *Businesses & Accomplishments* are not all the same. Every one has his *Post,* and his *Work;* and they are all glad of an opportunity to be *mischievous* in the World. These are they by whom *Witches* do exert their *Devillish* and malignant Rage upon their *Neighbours:* And especially Two Acts concur hereunto. The *First* is, Their *Covenanting* with the Witches. There is a most hellish *League* made between them, with various *Rites* and *Ceremonies.* The *Witches* promise to serve the *Devils,* and the *Devils* promise to *help* the witches; *How?* It is not convenient to be related. The *Second* is, their *Representing* of the witches. And hereby indeed these are drawn into *Snares* and *Cords* of Death. The Devils, when they go upon the *Errands* of the *Witches,* do bear their *Names;* and hence do *Harmes* to come to be carried from the *Devils* to the *Witches.* We need not suppose such a wild thing as the *Transforming* of those Wretches into *Bruits* or *Birds,* as we too often do.

It should next be proved *THAT* Witchcraft *is.*

The *Being* of such a thing is denied by many that place *a great part* of their *small wit* in derideing the Stories that are told of it. Their chief Argument is, That they never *saw* any Witches, therefore there are *none.* Just as if you or I should say, We never met with any *Robbers* on the Road, therefore there never was any *Padding* [i.e., highway robbery] there.

Indeed the *Devils* are loath to have true Notions of *Witches* entertained with us. I have beheld them to put out the eyes of an enchaunted Child, when a Book that proves, *There is Witchcraft,* was laid before her. But there are especially Two Demonstrations that evince the Being of that Infernal mysterious thing.

First. We have the Testimony of *Scripture* for it. We find *Witchcrafts* often mentioned, sometimes by way of *Assertion,* sometimes by way of *Allusion,* in the Oracles of God. Besides that, We have there the History of diverse *Witches* in these infallible and inspired Writings. Particularly,

the Instance of the *Witch* at *Endor,* in 1 *Sam.* 28. 7. is so plain and full that *Witchcraft* itself is not a more amazing thing, than any *Dispute* about the Being of it, after this. The Advocates of *Witches* must use more *Tricks* to make Nonsense of the *Bible,* than ever the *Witch* of *Endor* used in her Magical Incantations, if they would evade the Force of that famous History. They that will believe no *witches,* do imagine that *Jugglers* only are meant by them whom the Sacred Writ calleth so. But what do they think of that law in *Exod.* 22.18. *Thou shalt not suffer a Witch to live?* Methinks 'tis a little too hard to punish every silly *Juggler* with so great Severity.

Secondly. We have the *Testimony* of *Experience* for it. What will those *Incredulous,* who must be the only *Ingenious* men, say to This? Many *Witches* have like those in *Act.* 19. 18. *Confessed and shewed their deeds.* We see those things done, that is impossible any *Disease* or any *Deceit* should procure. We see some hideous *Wretches* in hideous *Horrours* confessing, *That they did the Mischiefs.* This *Confession* is often made by them that are owners of as much Reason as the people that laugh at all *Conceit* of *Witchcraft:* the exactest Scrutiny of skilful Physicians cannot find any *Distraction* in their minds. This *Confession* is often made by them that are apart One from another, and yet they *agree* in all the Circumstances of it. This *Confession* is often made by them that at the same time will produce the *Engines* and *Ensignes* of their *Hellish Trade,* and give the standers-by an *Ocular Conviction* of *what* they do, and *how.* There can be no Judgment left of any *Humane Affairs,* if such *Confessions* must be Ridiculed: all the *Murders,* yea, and all the *Bargains* in the World must be mere *Imaginations* if such *Confessions* are of no Account.

C. Deism

The Confessional Age, we must remember, coincided almost exactly with the so-called Scientific Revolution and later Enlightenment. During the century and a half between the publication of Copernicus's *On Heavenly Bodies* (1543) and

Newton's *Principia* (1687), a virtual flood of scientific discoveries and new theories profoundly transformed the human view of the natural world, at least among educated people. Newton himself, like many scientists of the day, remained deeply pious, but his descriptions of a largely mechanistic universe did cause some contemporaries to reconsider the role of God and of organized religions such as Christianity in human affairs. At the same time, the Scientific Revolution inspired many philosophers and other intellectuals with an ever-growing confidence in the near infallibility of human reason, whether in matters social, material, or metaphysical. By the end of the seventeenth century, some thinkers tentatively applied the rationalist method to Christianity itself, arguing that the best way to know the Creator was through his creation, Nature, rather than through the creeds of organized churches. Their wariness towards all claims of special revelation probably also owed something to the painful memory of not-too-distant religious wars, as well as to new knowledge of various non-Christian religions. At their most extreme, some of these Deists, as they were known, relegated God to the distant, transcendent role of a cosmic watchmaker, who had constructed the universe and humans and then retreated after starting everything in motion. Deists' supreme confidence in their own deductive abilities was criticized by many contemporaries, most famously by the philosophers David Hume (1711–1776) and Bishop Butler (1692–1752). Many devout Protestant and Catholic adherents were similarly put off by their "arrogant" dismissal of all organized religions. Still, Deism remained an influential movement throughout the eighteenth century, spreading far beyond its origins in France and England to every corner of Europe as well as to the New World, in the last instance numbering many of the American founding fathers among its followers.

1. Isaac Newton
MATHEMATICAL PRINCIPLES OF NATURAL PHILOSOPHY (PRINCIPIA) (1687)

Sir Isaac Newton (1642–1727) is best known as the brilliant formulator of several physical laws, most notably the law of gravitation. Throughout all of his studies of the natural universe, however, Newton remained acutely conscious of what he considered to be the divine source of nature's harmony. In the conclusion to his *Principia,* his masterwork on physics, the great scholar attempts to articulate the place of God within the carefully ordered universe he has just described. Comparing the human mind's attempt to understand God to a blind man's attempt to understand color, Newton concludes that the only way for our limited intellect to know the eternal one is indirectly, through his creation. For although the exquisite cosmic ballet of the heavenly bodies leaves no doubt that an omniscient deity is at work, Newton says, the characteristics of the Supreme Being himself remain elusive at best. The implications of such beliefs for organized religion are not discussed in the *Principia,* but many admirers of Newton's work used his findings to support their own Deist criticisms of Christian churches and clergy, particularly during the early eighteenth century.

The six primary planets are revolved about the sun in circles concentric with the sun, and with motions directed towards the same parts, and almost in the same plane. Ten moons are revolved about the earth, Jupiter, and Saturn, in circles concentric with them, with the same direction of motion, and nearly in the planes of the orbits of those planets; but it is not to be conceived that mere mechanical causes could give birth to so many regular motions, since the comets range over all parts of the heavens in very eccentric orbits; for by that kind of motion they pass easily through the orbs of the planets, and with great rapidity; and in their aphelions,[18] where they move the slowest, and are detained the longest, they recede to the greatest distances from each other, and hence suffer the least disturbance from their mutual attractions. This most beautiful system of the sun, planets, and comets, could only proceed from the counsel and dominion of an intelligent and powerful Being. And if the fixed stars are the centers of other like systems, these, being formed by the like wise counsel, must be all subject to the dominion of One; especially since the light of the fixed stars is of the same nature with the light of the sun, and from every system light passes into all the other systems: and lest the systems of the fixed stars should, by their gravity, fall on each other, he hath placed those systems at immense distances from one another.

This Being governs all things, not as the soul of the world, but as Lord over all; and on account of his dominion he is wont to be called Lord God *Pantokraton,* or *Universal Ruler;* for *God* is a relative word, and has a respect to servants; and *Deity* is the dominion of God not over his own body, as those imagine who fancy God to be the soul of the world, but over servants. The Supreme God is a Being eternal, infinite, absolutely perfect; but a being, however perfect, without dominion, cannot be said to be Lord God; for we say, my God, your God, the God of Israel, the God of Gods, and the Lord of Lords; but we do not say, my Eternal, your Eternal, the Eternal of Israel, the Eternal of Gods; we do not say, my Infinite, or my Perfect: these are titles which have no respect to servants. The word *God* usually signifies *Lord;* but every lord is not a God. It is the dominion of a spiritual being which constitutes a God: a true, supreme, or imaginary dominion makes a true, supreme, or imaginary God.

And from his true dominion it follows that the true God is a living, intelligent, and powerful Being; and, from his other perfections, that he is supreme, or most perfect. He is eternal and infinite, omnipotent and omniscient; that is, his duration reaches from eternity to eternity; his presence from infinity to infinity; he governs all things, and knows all things that are or can be done. He is not eternity and infinity, but eternal and infinite; he is not duration or space, but he endures and is present. He endures forever, and is everywhere present; and, by existing always and everywhere, he constitutes duration and space. Since every particle of space is *always,* and every indivisible moment of duration is *everywhere,* certainly the Maker and Lord of all things cannot be *never* and *nowhere.* Every soul that has perception is, though in different times and in different organs of sense and motion, still the same indivisible person. There are given successive parts in duration, coexistent parts in space, but neither the one nor the other in the person of a man, or his thinking principle; and much less can they be found in the thinking substance of God. Every man, so far as he is a thing that has perception, is one and the same man during his whole life, in all and each of his organs of sense. God is the same God, always and everywhere. He is omnipresent not *virtually* only, but also *substantially;* for virtue cannot subsist without substance. In him are all things contained and moved; yet neither affects the other: God suffers nothing from the motion of bodies; bodies find no resistance from the omnipresence of God. It is allowed by all that the Supreme God exists necessarily; and by the same necessity he exists *always* and *everywhere.*

[18]The point on the orbit of a celestial body that is farthest from the sun.

Whence also he is all similar, all eye, all ear, all brain, all arm, all power to perceive, to understand, and to act; but in a manner not at all human, in a manner not at all corporeal, in a manner utterly unknown to us. As a blind man has no idea of colors, so have we no idea of the manner by which the all-wise God perceives and understands all things. He is utterly void of all body and bodily figure, and can therefore neither be seen, nor heard, nor touched; nor ought he to be worshiped under the representation of any corporeal thing. We have ideas of his attributes, but what the real substance of anything is we know not. In bodies, we see only their figures and colors, we hear only the sounds, we touch only their outward surfaces, we smell only the smells, and taste the savors; but their inward substances are not to be known either by our senses, or by any reflex act of our minds: much less, than, have we any idea of the substance of God. We know him only by his most wise and excellent contrivances of things, and final causes; we admire him for his perfections; but we reverence and adore him on account of his dominion: for we adore him as his servants; and a god without dominion, providence, and final causes, is nothing else but Fate and Nature. Blind metaphysical necessity, which is certainly the same always and everywhere, could produce no variety of things. All that diversity of natural things which we find suited to different times and places could arise from nothing but the ideas and will of a Being necessarily existing. But, by way of allegory, God is said to see, to speak, to laugh, to love, to hate, to desire, to give, to receive, to rejoice, to be angry, to fight, to frame, to work, to build; for all our notions of God are taken from the ways of mankind by a certain similitude, which, though not perfect, has some likeness, however. And thus much concerning God; to discourse of whom from the appearances of things, does certainly belong to natural philosophy. . . .

---

2. Voltaire
PHILOSOPHICAL DICTIONARY (1764)

No one person better embodied the spirit of the Enlightenment, either to contemporaries or to posterity, than the French philosopher François Marie Arouet (1694–1778), better known by his pen name of Voltaire. Throughout his long life, Voltaire wrote incessantly in defense of a multitude of rationalist causes and reforms. Always controversial and witty, he took particular pride in using his Jesuit education against what he considered the greatest enemy of truth and freedom in his day, the Catholic Church. His massive *Philosophical Dictionary*, composed during the twelve years Voltaire spent at the court of Frederick the Great of Prussia, was intended to be the crowning achievement of his literary career. The essay-style "definitions" display all of his trademark erudition and sarcasm. They also make clear his contempt for the "mythological" aspects of all Christian churches, as well as his conviction that there is but one Truth, accessible to all rational and open-minded people. Voltaire enjoyed ridiculing the Catholic Church and its "irrational superstitions," but he always claimed that his polemic served a higher purpose. In the reading below, drawn from his definitions of religious terms, his goal is the defense of the Deist "faith"—which of course required no faith whatsoever, according to Voltaire, only simple reason.

"MIRACLES"

A miracle, according to the real meaning of the word, is something admirable. Then everything is a miracle. The marvelous order of nature, the rotation of a hundred million globes around a million suns, the activity of light, the life of animals—these are perpetual miracles.

According to accepted notions, we call *miracle* the violation of these divine and eternal laws. Let there be an eclipse of the sun during a full moon, let a dead man walk five miles carrying his head in his arms, and we'll call that a miracle.

Some natural scientists maintain that there are no miracles in this sense of the word; and here are their arguments.

A miracle is the violation of mathematical, divine, immutable, eternal laws. By this very statement, a miracle is a contradiction in terms. A law cannot be immutable and violable at the same time. But, they may be asked, can't a law be suspended by its author, since it was established by God himself? They have the insolence to answer, No, that it is impossible for the infinitely wise Being to make laws in order to violate them. They say that he might unsettle his machine, but only to make it go better; however, it is clear that, being God, he made this immense machine as best he could: if he had seen some imperfections resulting from the nature of the material, he would have attended to that in the beginning; so he will never change anything in it.

Moreover, God cannot do anything without reason; now what reason could make him temporarily disfigure his own work?

For the sake of men, they will be told. Then, they reply, it would be at least for the sake of all men; for it is impossible to conceive Divine Nature working for some men in particular, and not for the whole human race; and even the human race is quite unimportant: it is much less than a small anthill in comparison with all the beings that fill infinity. Now isn't it the most absurd piece of folly to imagine that the infinite Being would reverse the eternal working of the immense activity which makes the whole universe move, all for the sake of three or four hundred ants on this little mud pile?

But let's suppose that God had wanted to single out a small number of men by special favors: would he need to change what he had established for all times and places? Surely he has no need for this change, this inconstancy, to favor his creatures: his favors are in his very laws. He has foreseen everything, arranged everything, for them; all obey irrevocably the force that he has impressed on nature forever.

Why should God perform a miracle? To realize a certain plan concerning a few living beings! He would then be saying: "I could not complete a certain plan, with the universe ordered as it now is according to my divine decrees, my eternal laws; I am going to change my eternal ideas, my immutable laws, to try to execute what I could not do with them." This would be an admission of his weakness, not his power. It would seem to be the most inconceivable contradiction in him. Therefore, to dare palm off miracles on God is really to insult him (if men can insult God); it's to tell him: "You are a weak and inconsistent being." It is therefore absurd to believe in miracles—in one way or another it dishonors Divinity.

These philosophers are pressed hard; they are told: "In vain do you exalt the immutability of the supreme Being, the eternity of his laws, the regularity of his infinite worlds: our little mud heap proliferates with miracles; the histories are as full of prodigies as of natural events. The daughters of the high priest Anius changed everything they wanted to into wheat, wine, or oil; Athalide, Mercury's daughter, came back to life several times, Aesclepius revived Hippolytus; Hercules tore Alcestis from the grasp of death; Er came back to the world after spending two weeks in hell; Romulus and Remus were the children of a god and a vestal virgin; the Palladium fell from heaven in the city of Troy; Berenice's hair became a constellation; the hut of Baucis and Philemon was changed into a superb temple; Orpheus' head spoke oracles after his death; the walls of Thebes built themselves at the sound of the flute, in the presence of the Greeks; the cures performed in the temple of Aesclepius were innumerable, and we still have documents containing the names of eye-witnesses of Aesclepius' miracles."[19]

Give me the name of a nation where incredible prodigies have not been performed, above all in times when they could hardly read or write.

The philosophers reply to these objections merely by laughing and shrugging their shoulders; but Christian philosophers say: "We believe in the miracles performed in our holy religion; we believe them with faith, and not with our reason, which we take care not to listen to; for, as everybody knows, when faith speaks, reason must hold its tongue. We believe in the miracles of Jesus Christ and his apostles firmly and absolutely, but allow us to doubt a little those of some others; for example, permit us to suspend our judgment on the things reported by a simple man to whom the title 'great' has been given. He maintains that a little monk was so accustomed to perform miracles that finally the prior prohibited him from exercising his talent. The little monk obeyed; but, when he saw a poor tiler falling from the top of a roof, he hesitated between the desire to save his life and holy obedience. He merely ordered the tiler to stay in the air until he had fresh instructions, and he ran quickly to inform his prior about the matter. The prior absolved him of the sin he had committed in starting a miracle without permission, and permitted him to finish it, provided he remained content with it and did nothing further. We will grant the philosophers that they may distrust this story a little."

But how dare you deny, the philosophers are further asked, that St. Gervasius and St. Protasius appeared to St. Ambrose in a dream, informing him of the place where their relics could be found?[20] That St. Ambrose had them dug up, and that they cured a blind man? St. Augustine was then in Milan; it is he who reports this miracle: *Immenso populo teste* ["with a huge crowd of witnesses"], he writes in his *City of God,* book XXII. This is one of the best-confirmed of miracles. The philosophers reply that they don't believe a word of it; that Gervasius and Protasius appeared to nobody; that it matters precious little to mankind whether it knows where the remains of their carcasses are; that they have no more faith in this little blind man than in Vespasian's;[21] that it is a useless miracle; that God does nothing useless; and they hold firmly to their principles. My respect for St. Gervasius and St. Protasius doesn't permit me to share the opinion of these philosophers: I merely report on their incredulity. They make much of the passage in Lucian, which is in *The Death of Peregrinus:* "When an adroit juggler turns Christian, he is sure to make his fortune." But, since Lucian is a secular author, he should have no influence over us.[22]

These philosophers cannot bring themselves to believe in the miracles performed in the second century. In vain have eyewitnesses written that when St. Polycarp, bishop of Smyrna,[23] was condemned to be burned and thrown into the flames, they heard a voice from heaven which exclaimed: "Courage, Polycarp! Be strong, show yourself a man!" that then the flames of the stake turned aside from his body and formed a pavilion of fire around his head, and a dove flew out of the

---

[19]Most of the stories Voltaire mentions are from ancient Greek and Roman myths about miraculous returns from the dead, especially through the intervention of the Greek god of healing, Aesclepius. Er is the Pamphylian in Plato's *Republic* who returns to life to report what he has seen in the other world.

[20]On the event of founding his new cathedral in Milan in 386, St. Ambrose received a "presentiment" about the relics of two second-century martyrs, Gervasius and Protasius. Two large skeletons were subsequently excavated in a nearby church, and after being reinterred in the cathedral the relics were credited with several miraculous healings.
[21]The Roman emperor Vespasian (r. 69–79) supposedly healed a blind man.
[22]Lucian of Samosata (c. 120–180), Greek satirist, best known for his witty dialogues. Peregrinus was a Cynic in search of a true religion who ended his life by walking into a flaming pyre. Lucian's obvious scorn in the tale for Christian gullibility and ignorance undoubtedly struck a responsive chord in Voltaire.
[23]Voltaire remained skeptical about Polycarp's "supposed martyrdom" c. 167.

midst of the stake; finally, they had to cut off Polycarp's head. "What is this miracle good for?" ask the unbelievers. "Why did the flames lose their power, and why didn't the executioner's ax lose its power? How is it that so many martyrs emerge safe and sound from burning oil, and they cannot resist the edge of the sword?" The reply is that it was the will of God. But the philosophers want to see all this with their own eyes before they believe it.

Those who fortify their arguments with science will tell you that the Fathers of the Church themselves often admitted that no more miracles were being performed in their time. St. Chrysostom[24] expressly says: "The extraordinary gifts of the spirit were given even to the unworthy, because then the Church had need of miracles; but today they are not given even to the worthy, because the Church no longer needs them." Later he admits that there is no longer anybody who resurrects the dead, nor even anybody who cures the sick.

Despite the miracle of St. Gervasius and of Protasius, St. Augustine himself says in his *City of God*: *Cur, inquiunt, nunc illa miracula quae praedicatis facta esse non fiunt?* —"Why, they ask, are the miracles which, you boast, used to be performed no longer performed today?" And he gives the same reason for it: *Possem quidem dicere necessaria prius fuisse quam crederet mundus, ad hoc ut crederet mundus.* —"Indeed, I might say that miracles were necessary before the world believed, so that it might believe."

It is objected against the philosophers that in spite of this admission, St. Augustine still mentions an old cobbler of Hippo who went to pray in the chapel of the twenty martyrs after he had lost his clothes; when he came home he found a fish with a gold ring in its body, and the cook who cooked the fish said to the cobbler: "Here's what the twenty martyrs have given you."

To this the philosophers reply that there is nothing in the story that contradicts the laws of nature, that physical laws are in no way violated by a fish swallowing a gold ring and a cook giving this ring to a cobbler; there is no miracle here.

If one reminds these philosophers that according to St. Jerome, in his *Life of the Hermit Paul*, this hermit had several conversations with satyrs and fauns, that a raven brought him half a loaf for dinner for thirty years, and a whole loaf on the day St. Anthony came to see him, they would still reply that all this is not entirely against the laws of nature, that satyrs and fauns might have existed, and that in any case, if a tale is a piece of childishness, it has nothing in common with the true miracles of the Savior and his apostles.[25] Several good Christians have objected to the history of St. Simeon Stylites, written by Theodoret.[26] Many miracles the Greek Church accepts as authentic have been called in question by several Latins, just as Latin miracles have been suspect to the Greek Church; finally came the Protestants who have handled the miracles of both Churches very roughly.

A learned Jesuit,[27] who preached in India for many years, complains that neither he nor his brethren could ever perform a miracle. Xavier laments in several of his letters that he doesn't have the gift of tongues; he says that among the Japanese he was like a mute statue. True, the Jesuits have written that he brought eight dead men back to life: that's a great deal; but we must also take into account that he brought them back to life fifteen thousand miles from here. Since then, there have been people who claim that the abolition of the Jesuits in France has been a much greater miracle than those of Xavier and Ignatius.[28]

---

[24]St. John Chrysotom (c. 347–407), early church father.

[25]Voltaire is citing episodes from two extremely popular biographies of Egyptian desert fathers, both written in the fourth century.

[26]Theodoret (c. 393–466) was a condemned Nestorian bishop whose *Religious History* comprised a collection of monastic biographies, including that of the famed ascetic Simeon Stylites (c. 390–459) (see 2A).

[27]Francis Xavier (1506–1552), Jesuit missionary to India and Japan.

[28]Ignatius Loyola (1494–1556), founder of the Jesuit order. In 1764 the Society of Jesus was banned in France and in 1773 suppressed altogether by Pope Clement XIV. It was formally restored by Pope Pius VII in 1814.

Be that as it may, all Christians agree that the miracles of Jesus Christ and his apostles are incontestably true, but that we may strongly doubt some miracles performed in recent times, which have not been fully authenticated.

For instance, it would be desirable that a miracle, for the sake of being fully verified, should be performed in the presence of the Academy of Sciences in Paris, or the Royal Society in London, and the Faculty of Medicine, assisted by a detachment of the regiment of Guards to keep back the crowd of the common people, whose impertinence might interfere with the performance of the miracle.

One day a philosopher was asked what he would say if he saw the sun stop; that is, if the movement of the earth around that star ceased, if all the dead came back to life, and if all the mountains threw themselves into the ocean together—all this to prove some important truth, like, say, versatile grace. "What would I say?" replied the philosopher. "I'd turn Manichean;[29] I'd say that there is one principle that unmakes what the other principle has made." . . .

"SECT"

Every sect, of whatever kind, is the rallying point for doubt and error. Scotists, Thomists, Realists, Nominalists, Papists, Calvinists, Molinists, Jansenists, are nothing but assumed names.[30]

There are no sects in geometry; we don't say, a Euclidian, an Archimedian.[31]

When the truth is evident, it is impossible for parties and factions to arise. People have never argued over whether it was daytime at noon.

Once the part of astronomy which determines the course of the stars and the recurrence of eclipses was known, there were no longer any disputes among astronomers.

People don't say in England: "I am a Newtonian, I am a Lockian, Halleyian";[32] why? Because whoever has done some reading cannot refuse his assent to truths taught by these three great men. The more Newton is revered, the less people call themselves Newtonians; this word would suggest that there are anti-Newtonians in England. Perhaps we still have some Cartesians in France; that's simply because the system of Descartes is a tissue of erroneous and ridiculous fancies.

The same thing holds true of the small number of truths of fact which are well established. The documents in the Tower of London have been authoritatively collected by Rymer;[33] there are no Rymerians, because nobody takes it into his head to question his collection. It contains no contradictions, no absurdities, no prodigies, nothing that revolts reason, consequently nothing that sectarians strain to sustain or overthrow with absurd arguments. Hence everybody agrees that Rymer's *Acts* are worthy of confidence.

You are a Mahometan [i.e., Muslim], hence there are people who are not, hence you might well be wrong.

Which would be the true religion if Christianity didn't exist? The one in which there were no sects; the one about which all minds would inevitably agree.

Now on what dogma do all minds agree? On the worship of a God, and on probity. All the philosophers on earth who had a religion have said at all times: "There is a God, and men must be just." This, then, is the universal religion established in all times and for all men.

---

[29]The dualist Christian heresy of the ancient church, named after its leader Mani. Among its unorthodox doctrines, Manicheanism taught the existence of two nearly equal universal forces of good and evil.

[30]Successive pairings of philosophical/theological rivals from the thirteenth through seventeenth centuries.

[31]Referring to the "fathers" of geometry: Euclid (fl. c. 300 B.C.E.) and Archimedes (c. 287–212 B.C.E.).

[32]By this contrast, Voltaire implies that practitioners of rational and "objective" pursuit of truth—such as Isaac Newton (1643–1727), John Locke (1632–1704), or Edmund Halley (1656–1742)—inspire no divisive rivalries or schools.

[33]Twenty volumes of transcriptions of British foreign treaties, edited by English literary critic Thomas Rymer (1641–1713), again a supposed example of objective, obvious facts.

Hence, the point on which they all agree is true, and hence the systems by which they disagree are false.

"My sect is the best," a Brahmin [i.e., Hindu] tells me. But, my friend, if your sect is good, it is necessary; for were it not absolutely necessary, you would admit to me that it was useless; if it is absolutely necessary, it is so to all men; how then can it be that all men don't possess what is absolutely necessary to them? How can it be that the rest of the world laughs at you and your Brahma?

When Zoroaster, Hermes, Orpheus, Minos,[34] and all great men say: "Let us worship God and be just," nobody laughs; but the whole world hisses the man who claims that we can please God only by holding a cow's tail when we die, and the man who insists that we should have the end of our foreskin cut off, and the man who consecrates crocodiles and onions, and the man who makes eternal salvation depend on the bones of the dead which he wears under his shirt, or to a plenary indulgence which he buys in Rome for two and a half sous.

What causes this unanimous laughing and hissing from one end of the universe to the other? It must be that the things the world laughs at are not obvious truths. What would we say to a secretary of Sejanus who dedicated to Petronius a book, written in a bombastic style, entitled: "The truths of the Sybilline oracles, proved by the facts"?[35] At the outset the secretary proves to you that it was necessary for God to send several sybils into the world, one after the other; for there were no other means of instructing mankind. It is demonstrated that God spoke to these sybils, for the word *sybil* signifies *council of God*. They must have lived a long time, for this is the least of the privileges

due to those to whom God speaks. Their number was twelve, for that number is sacred. They certainly predicted all the events of the world, for Tarquinus Superbus[36] bought three of their books for a hundred écus from an old woman. What unbeliever, adds the secretary, dares to deny all these evident facts which occurred in a corner of the world's surface? Who could deny that their prophecies were fulfilled? Didn't Vergil[37] himself quote the predictions of the sybils? If we don't have the sybilline books in the original, written at a time when no one could read and write, don't we have authentic copies? Impiety must fall silent before such proofs. Thus spoke Houttevillus to Sejanus. He hoped to get the post of augur, which would have been worth fifty thousand livres to him, and he got nothing.

"What my sect teaches is obscure, I admit it," says a fanatic, "and it is by virtue of this obscurity that it must be believed; for it says itself that it is full of obscurities. My sect is absurd, therefore it is divine; for how could what seems so mad be embraced by so many nations if it were not divine? It's precisely like the Koran, which, the Sunnites[38] say, has the face of an angel and the face of a beast; don't be shocked by the snout of the beast, and revere the face of the angel." That's how this madman talks; but a fanatic of another sect replied to this fanatic: "You're the one who is the beast, and I'm the angel."

Now who will judge this contest? Who will decide between these two enthusiasts? The man who is reasonable, impartial, learned in a science which is not merely verbal, the man liberated from prejudices, and a lover of truth and justice; in a word, the man who is not a beast and doesn't think he is an angel.

---

[34]Legendary founders of widespread and influential religious cults in the ancient world.

[35]A satirical reference to *The Christian Religion, proved by the facts,* a rationalist defense of Christianity written by the priest A.-C.-F. Houtteville (1686–1742) and despised by Voltaire. The Sibylline Oracles were an ancient collection of Jewish and Christian prophecies written in imitation of the pagan Sibylline Books, also oracular in nature.

[36]Last (and worst) Roman king (sixth century B.C.E.), who repeatedly refused to purchase the Sybilline Books until only the last three books were left undestroyed.

[37]The Roman poet Virgil (d. 19 B.C.E.), author of the *Aeneid,* who supposedly predicted the coming of the Christian Messiah.

[38]The Sunni branch of Islam, noted for its tradition of mystical poetry.

D. Methodism

John Wesley (1703–1791), founder of the Methodist movement, never intended to create a new Christian denomination. Initially, the small "Holy Club" he organized with his brother Charles in 1729 while a teacher at Oxford University was merely a Bible-reading group of like-minded students, modeled on the devotions of Moravian Pietists, a German Lutheran sect. Ridiculed by outsiders as "Bible moths" or "methodists" (because of their programmatic approach to piety), Wesley and his followers gradually grew more estranged from the Church of England over the next sixty years. By the time of Wesley's death, Methodists had already begun appointing their own "superintendents" (later called bishops in the colonies), regularly meeting in their own "chapels" (rather than established churches), and deciding doctrine and other ecclesiastical matters in their own conferences. In the time between, however, the overriding mission of Wesley and all Methodists had been simply evangelization within the Anglican Church itself. Even his detractors marveled at Wesley's energy in this ministry. Since preaching in the churches was not permitted him, he began "riding the circuit," giving sermons in open fields, public squares, coal mines, and even prisons. Over the course of fifty years, he is estimated to have traveled over 8,000 miles annually by horse, delivering a total of 40,000 sermons in his lifetime. His fervor and popularity were matched by those of several other Methodist missionaries, most notably his associate George Whitefield (1714–1770), who played such an instrumental role in the American Great Awakening of the 1740s (see 7B). Eventually Whitefield and some other Methodists broke away from Wesley because of his unorthodox belief in free will, but the movement as a whole continued to thrive, claiming over 120,000 members by the time of Wesley's death. This following increased severalfold during the next century, particularly among the working classes of the United Kingdom and United States.

1. John Wesley
MINUTES OF SOME LATE CONVERSATIONS BETWEEN THE REV. MESSRS. WESLEY AND OTHERS (1747)

Like many other Christians of his time, the young John Wesley was greatly troubled by the question "Am I saved?" Though ordained as a priest in the Church of England, Wesley increasingly turned to the mystical approach of the Moravian Pietists for consolation in this matter. Shortly before a return visit to the Moravian settlement at Herrnhut (near Berlin), he began reading Martin Luther's preface to Paul's Epistle to the Romans, and on May 24, 1738, experienced a profound conversion, or second birth. Thereafter, he later wrote, his anxiety about death and punishment left him, and he wanted only to spread the divine message of forgiveness. As Wesley makes clear in the following "dialogues" from the first Methodist conference, the "rebirth" of justification through faith alone (*sole fide*) marks only the beginning of the much longer—and reversible—process known as sanctification. In other words, justification through God's grace both liberates a Christian from the damnation of original sin and restores the individual's ability to strive for sanctification by conforming to the godly ideal of the Scriptures. This process, according to Wesley, is long and perilous, often involving "backsliding" into sinful behavior, and for many the goal of sanctification would not be realized until shortly before death. This interpretation had the singular effect of making Wesley appear Calvinist to many members of the Anglican Church (because of his emphasis on *sole fide* justification) and quasi-Catholic to Lutherans and Calvinists, who denied that free will played any role whatsoever in the salvation process. The Methodist definition of sanctification, moreover, helps explain the urgency of Wesley's evangelization; he wanted his listeners to understand that justification was only the beginning of salvation and that there remained much work to be done. The doctrine of sanctification also helps account for the Methodist insistence on such tenets of "godly living" as total abstinence from alcohol and constant charity toward one's fellows.

CONVERSATION I.

Monday, June 25th, 1744

Q. 1. What is it to be justified?

A. To be pardoned and received into God's favour; into such a state, that, if we continue therein, we shall be finally saved.

Q. 2. Is faith the condition of justification?

A. Yes; for every one who believeth not is condemned; and every one who believes is justified.

Q. 3. But must not repentance, and works meet for repentance, go before this faith?

A. Without doubt; if by repentance you mean conviction of sin; and by works meet for repentance, obeying God as far as we can, forgiving our brother, leaving off from evil, doing good, and using his ordinances, according to the power we have received.

Q. 4. What is faith?

A. Faith in general is a divine, supernatural [evidence or conviction] of things not seen; that is, of past, future, or spiritual things: it is a spiritual sight of God and the things of God.

First. A sinner is convinced by the Holy Ghost, "Christ loved me, and gave himself for me" [Eph 5:2]. This is that faith by which he is justified, or pardoned, the moment he receives it. Immediately the same Spirit bears witness, "Thou art pardoned; thou hast redemption in his blood" [Eph 1:7]. And this is saving faith, whereby the love of God is shed abroad in his heart.

Q. 5. Have all Christians this faith? May not a man be justified and not know it?

A. That all true Christians have such a faith as implies an assurance of God's love, appears from Rom 8:15; Eph 4:32; 2 Cor 13:5; Heb 8:10; 1 Jn 4:10, and 19. And that no man can be justified and not know it, appears farther from the nature of the thing: for faith after repentance is ease after pain, rest after toil, light after darkness. It appears also from the immediate, as well as distant, fruits thereof.

Q. 6. But may not a man go to heaven without it?

A. It does not appear from holy writ that a man who hears the Gospel can [Mk 16:16], whatever a Heathen may do: Rom 2:14. . . .

On Tuesday morning, June 26th, was considered the doctrine of Sanctification:

Q. 1. What is it to be sanctified?

A. To be renewed in the image of God, in righteousness and true holiness.

Q. 2. Is faith the condition, or the instrument, of sanctification?

A. It is both the condition and instrument of it. When we begin to believe, then sanctification begins. And as faith increases, holiness increases, till we are created anew.

Q. 3. What is implied in being a perfect Christian?

A. The loving the Lord our God with all our heart, and with all our mind, and soul, and strength; Deut 6:5 30:6; Ezek 36:25–29.

Q. 4. Does this imply that all inward sin is taken away?

A. Without doubt; or how could we be said to be saved "from all our uncleannesses?" verse 29.

Q. 5. Can we know one who is thus saved? What is a reasonable proof of it?

A. We cannot, without the miraculous discernment of spirits, be infallibly certain of those who are thus saved. But we apprehend, these would be the best proofs which the nature of the thing admits: (1) If we had sufficient evidence of their unblamable behaviour preceding. (2) If they gave a distinct account of the time and manner wherein they were saved from sin, and of the circumstances thereof, with such sound speech as could not be reproved. And, (3) If, upon a strict inquiry afterward from time to time, it appeared that all their tempers, and words, and actions, were holy and unreprovable.

Q. 6. How should we treat those who think they have attained this?

A. Exhort them to forget the things that are behind, and to watch and pray always, that God may search the ground of their hearts. . . .

Friday, August 2nd {1745}

Q. 20. Should we not have a care of depreciating justification, in order to exalt the state of full sanctification?

A. Undoubtedly we should beware of this; for one may insensibly slide into it.

Q. 21. How shall we effectually avoid it?

A. When we are going to speak of entire sanctification, let us first describe the blessings of a justified state, as strongly as possible.

Q. 22. Does not the truth of the Gospel lie very near both to Calvinism and Antinomianism?[39]

A. Indeed it does; as it were, within a hair's breadth: so that it is altogether foolish and sinful, because we do not quite agree either with one or the other, to run from them as far as ever we can.

Q. 23. Wherein may we come to the very edge of Calvinism?

A. (1) In ascribing all good to the free grace of God. (2) In denying all natural free-will, and all power antecedent to grace. And (3) In excluding all merit from man; even for what he has or does by the grace of God.

Q. 24. Wherein may we come to the edge of Antinomianism?

A. (1) In exalting the merits and love of Christ. (2) In rejoicing evermore.

Q. 25. Does faith supersede (set aside the necessity of) holiness or good works?

A. In no wise. So far from it, that it implies both, as a cause does its effects.

About ten, we began to speak of Sanctification: with regard to which, it was inquired:

Q. 1. When does inward sanctification begin?

A. In the moment we are justified. The seed of every virtue is then sown in the soul. From that time the believer gradually dies to sin, and grows in grace. Yet sin remains in him; yea, the seed of all sin, till he is sanctified throughout in spirit, soul, and body.

Q. 2. What will become of a Heathen, a Papist, a Church of England man, if he dies without being thus sanctified?

A. He cannot see the Lord. But none who seeks it sincerely shall or can die without it; though possibly he may not attain it, till the very article of death.

---

[39]A religion "without laws"; in other words, entirely subjective.

Q. 3. Is it ordinarily given till a little before death?

A. It is not, to those that expect it no sooner, nor consequently ask for it, at least, not in faith.

Q. 4. But ought we to expect it sooner?

A. Why not? For although we grant, (1) That the generality of believers whom we have hitherto known were not so sanctified till near death: (2) That few of those to whom St. Paul wrote his Epistles were so at the time he wrote: (3) Nor he himself at the time of writing his former Epistles: yet this does not prove that we may not today.

Q. 5. But would not one who was thus sanctified be incapable of worldly business?

A. He would be far more capable of it than ever, as going through all without distraction.

Q. 6. Would he be capable of marriage?

A. Why should he not?

Q. 7. Should we not beware of bearing hard on those who think they have attained?

A. We should. And the rather, because if they are faithful to the grace they have received, they are in no danger of perishing at last. No, not even if they remain in luminous faith, as some term it, for many months or years; perhaps till within a little time of their spirits returning to God.

Q. 8. In what manner should we preach entire sanctification?

A. Scarce at all to those who are not pressing forward. To those who are, always by way of promise; always drawing, rather than driving.

Q. 9. How should we wait for the fulfilling of this promise?

A. In universal obedience; in keeping all the commandments; in denying ourselves and taking up our cross daily. These are the general means which God hath ordained for our receiving his sanctifying grace. The particular are, prayer, searching the Scripture, communicating, and fasting. . . .

Wednesday, June 17th {1747}

. . . Q. 9. But how does it appear that this [sanctification] is to be done before the article of death?

A. First. From the very nature of a command, which is not given to the dead, but to the living. Therefore, "Thou shalt love God with all thy heart," [Mt 22:37; Mk 12:30; Lk 10:27] cannot mean, Thou shalt do this when thou diest, but while thou livest.

Secondly. From express texts of Scripture: (1) "The grace of God that bringeth salvation hath appeared to all men, teaching us that, having renounced ungodliness and worldly lusts, we should live soberly, righteously, and godly, in this present world; looking for—the glorious appearing of our Saviour Jesus Christ; who gave himself for us, that he might redeem us from all iniquity, and purify unto himself a peculiar people, zealous of good works" [Tit 2:11–14]. (2) "He hath raised up a horn of salvation for us,—to perform the mercy promised to our fathers; the oath which he sware to our father Abraham, that he would grant unto us, that we, being delivered out of the hand of our enemies, should serve him without fear, in holiness and righteousness before him, all the days of our life," [Lk 1:69–75].

Q. 10. Is there any example in Scripture of persons who had attained to this?

A. Yes. St. John, and all those of whom he says in his First Epistle, "Herein is our love made perfect, that we may have confidence in the day of judgment: because as he is, so are we in this world," 4:17.

Q. 11. But why are there not more examples of this kind recorded in the New Testament?

A. It does not become us to be peremptory in this matter. One reason might possibly be, because the Apostles wrote to the Church while it was in a state of infancy. Therefore they might mention such persons the more sparingly, lest they should give strong meat to babes.

Q. 12. Can you show one such example now? Where is he that is thus perfect?

A. To some who make this inquiry one might answer, "If I knew one here, I would not tell you. For you do not inquire out of love. You are like Herod. You only seek the young child to slay it."

But more directly we answer, there are numberless reasons why there should be few (if any indisputable) examples. What inconveniences would this bring on the person himself, set as a mark for all to shoot at! What a temptation would it be to others, not only to men who knew not God, but to believers themselves! How hardly would they refrain from idolizing such a person! And yet, how unprofitable to gainsayers! "For if they hear not Moses and the Prophets," Christ and his Apostles, "neither would they be persuaded, though one rose from the dead" [Lk 16:21].

Q. 13. Suppose one had attained to this, would you advise him to speak of it?

A. Not to them who know not God. It would only provoke them to contradict and blaspheme: nor to any without some particular reason, without some particular good in view. And then they should have an especial care to avoid all appearance of boasting.

Q. 14. Is it a sin, not to believe those who say they have attained?

A. By no means, even though they said true. We ought not hastily to believe, but to suspend our judgment, till we have full and strong proof.

Q. 15. But are we not apt to have a secret distaste to any who say they are saved from all sin?

A. It is very possible we may, and that on several grounds; partly from a concern for the honour of God, and the good of souls, who may be hurt, yea, or turned out of the way, if these are not what they profess; partly from a kind of implicit envy at those who speak of higher attainments than our own; and partly from our slowness and unreadiness of heart to believe the works of God.

Q. 16. Does not the harshly preaching perfection tend to bring believers into a kind of bondage, or slavish fear?

A. It does; therefore we should always place it in the most amiable light, so that it may excite only hope, joy, and desire.

Q. 17. Why may we not continue in the joy of faith even till we are made perfect?

A. Why indeed! since holy grief does not quench this joy; since, even while we are under the cross, while we deeply partake of the sufferings of Christ, we may rejoice with joy unspeakable.

Q. 18. Do we not discourage believers from rejoicing evermore?

A. We ought not so to do. Let them all their life long rejoice unto God, so it be with reverence. And even if lightness or pride should mix with their joy, let us not strike at the joy itself, (this is the gift of God,) but at that lightness or pride, that the evil may cease and the good remain.

Q. 19. Ought we to be anxiously careful about perfection, lest we should die before we have attained?

A. In no wise. We ought to be thus careful for nothing, neither spiritual nor temporal.

Q. 20. But ought we not to be troubled on account of the sinful nature which still remains in us?

A. It is good for us to have a deep sense of this, and to be much ashamed before the Lord: but this should only incite us the more earnestly to turn unto Christ every moment, and to draw light, and life, and strength from him, that we may go on conquering and to conquer. And, therefore, when the sense of our sin most abounds, the sense of his love should much more abound.

Q. 21. Will our joy or our trouble increase as we grow in grace?

A. Perhaps both. But without doubt our joy in the Lord will increase as our love increases.

Q. 22. Is not the teaching believers to be continually poring upon their inbred sin the ready way to make them forget that they were purged from their former sins?

A. We find by experience it is; or to make them undervalue and account it a little thing; whereas, indeed, (though there are still greater gifts behind,) this is inexpressibly great and glorious.

2. METHODIST HYMNS

Hymns played a vital role in the Methodist quest for sanctification. Like the Nonconformists and Pietists of the previous century, Wesley and his followers believed that the powerful combination of poetry and music was especially effective in reviving the enthusiasm of the justified soul, thus strengthening the individual's resolve to become more godly. Hymns were also especially efficient vehicles for doctrinal instruction. Many Methodist hymns were so popular as to be quickly adopted by other Protestant denominations and eventually even among Catholics. The following excerpts come from a 1780 collection, which contains 539 hymns, most written in conformance with the Church of England's annual liturgical calendar. The majority, including the famous "Hark the Herald Angels Sing," were written by Charles Wesley (1707–1788), brother of the great evangelizer, who also studied at Oxford and preached the Methodist message in Bristol and London.

a. JOHN WESLEY, PREFACE TO *A COLLECTION OF HYMNS FOR THE USE OF THE PEOPLE CALLED METHODISTS* (1779)

1. For many years I have been importuned to publish such a hymn-book as might be generally used in all our congregations throughout Great Britain and Ireland. I have hitherto withstood the importunity, as I believed such a publication was needless, considering the various hymn-books which my brother and I have published within these forty years last past; so that it may be doubted whether any religious community in the world has a greater variety of them.

2. But it has been answered, "Such a publication is highly needful upon this very account: for the greater part of the people, being poor, are not able to purchase so many books; and those that have purchased them are, as it were, bewildered in the immense variety. A proper Collection of Hymns for general use, carefully made out of all these books, is therefore still wanting; and one comprised in so moderate a compass as to be neither cumbersome nor expensive."

3. It has been replied, "You have such a Collection already, (entitled 'Hymns and Spiritual Songs') which I extracted several years ago from a variety of hymn-books." But it is objected, "This is in the other extreme: it is far too small. It does not, it cannot, in so narrow a compass, contain variety enough; not so much as we want, among whom *singing* makes so considerable a part of the public service. What we want is, a Collection not too large, that it may be cheap and portable; nor too small, that it may contain a sufficient variety for all ordinary occasions."

4. Such a Hymn-Book you have now before you. It is not so large as to be either cumbersome or expensive; and it is large enough to contain such a variety of hymns as will not soon be worn threadbare. It is large enough to contain all the important truths of our most holy religion, whether speculative or practical; yea, to illustrate them all, and to prove them both by Scriptures and reason; and this is done in a regular order. The hymns are not carelessly jumbled together, but carefully ranged under proper heads, according to the experience of real Christians. So that this book is, in effect, a little body of experimental and practical divinity.

5. As but a small part of these hymns is of my own composing, I do not think it inconsis-

tent with modesty to declare, that I am persuaded no such hymn-book as this has yet been published in the English language. In what other publication of the kind have you so distinct and full an account of Scriptural Christianity? such a declaration of the heights and depths of religion, speculative and practical? so strong cautions against the most plausible errors; particularly those that are now most prevalent? and so clear directions for making your calling and election sure; for perfecting holiness in the fear of God?

6. May I be permitted to add a few words with regard to the *poetry*? Then I will speak to those who are judges thereof, with all freedom and unreserve. To these I may say, without offence, 1. In these hymns there is no doggerel; no botches; nothing put in to patch up the rhyme; no feeble expletives. 2. Here is nothing turgid or bombast, on the one hand, or low and creeping, on the other. 3. Here are no *cant* expressions; no words without meaning. Those who impute this to us know not what they say. We talk common sense, both in prose and verse, and use no word but in a fixed and determinate sense. 4. Here are, allow me to say, both the purity, the strength, and the elegance of the English language; and, at the same time, the utmost simplicity, and plainness, suited to every capacity. Lastly, I desire men of taste to judge (these are the only competent judges) whether there be not in some of the following hymns the true spirit of poetry, such as cannot be acquired by art and labour, but must be the gift of nature. By labour a man may become a tolerable imitator of Spenser, Shakespeare, or Milton; and may heap together pretty compound epithets, as "pale-eyed," "meek-eyed," and the like; but unless he be *born* a poet, he will never attain the genuine spirit of poetry.

7. And here I beg leave to mention a thought which has been long upon my mind, and which I should long ago have inserted in the public papers, had I not been unwilling to stir up a nest of hornets. Many gentlemen have done my brother and me (though without naming us) the honour to reprint many of our hymns. Now, they are perfectly welcome so to do, provided they print them just as they are. But I desire they would not attempt to mend them; for they really are not able. None of them is able to mend either the sense or the verse. Therefore, I must beg of them one of these two favours; either to let them stand just as they are, to take them for better for worse; or to add the true reading in the margin, or at the bottom of the page; that we may no longer be accountable either for the nonsense or for the doggerel of other men.

8. But to return. That which is of infinitely more moment than the spirit of poetry, is the spirit of piety. And I trust all persons of real judgment will find *this* breathing through the whole Collection. It is in this view chiefly, that I would recommend it to every truly pious reader, as a means of raising or quickening the spirit of devotion; of confirming his faith; of enlivening his hope; and of kindling and increasing his love to God and man. When Poetry thus keeps its place, as the handmaid of Piety, it shall attain, not a poor perishable wreath, but a crown that fadeth not away.

JOHN WESLEY

LONDON, *Oct.* 20, 1779

---

b. CHARLES WESLEY, "COME, SINNERS, TO THE GOSPEL FEAST" (1747)

Come sinners, to the gospel feast;
Let every soul be Jesus' guest:
Ye need not one be left behind,
For God hath bidden all mankind.

Sent by my Lord, on you I call;
The invitation is to all:
Come all the world! come, sinner, thou!
All things in Christ are ready now.

Come, all ye souls by sin oppressed,
Ye restless wanderers after rest;
Ye poor, and maimed, and halt, and blind,
In Christ a hearty welcome find.

My message as from God receive;
Ye all may come to Christ and live:

O let his love your hearts constrain
Nor suffer him to die in vain.

See him set forth before your eyes,
That precious, bleeding sacrifice:
His offered benefits embrace,
And freely now be saved by grace.

---

c. CHARLES WESLEY, "O FOR A THOUSAND TONGUES TO SING!" (1740)

O for a thousand tongues to sing
    my dear Redeemer's praise,
The glories of my God and King,
    the triumphs of his grace!

My gracious Master and my God,
    assist me to proclaim
And spread through all the earth abroad
    the honors of thy Name.

Jesus! the Name that charms our fears
    and bids our sorrows cease;
'tis music in the sinner's ears,
    'tis life and health and peace.

He speaks; and, listening to his voice,
    new life the dead receive,
The mournful broken hearts rejoice,
    the humble poor believe.

Hear him, ye deaf, ye voiceless ones,
    your loosened tongues employ;
Ye blind, behold your Savior comes;
    and leap, ye lame, for joy!

Glory to God and praise and love
    be now and ever given
by saints below and saints above,
    the Church in earth and heaven.

BIBLIOGRAPHY

Primary Sources

Anthologies and Readers

Cressy, David, and Lori Anne Ferrell, eds., *Religion and Society in Early Modern England: A Sourcebook* (New York: Routledge, 1996).

Erb, Peter C., *The Pietists: Selected Writings* (Mahwah, N.J.: Paulist Press, 1983).

Gay, Peter, ed., *The Enlightenment: A Comprehensive Anthology* (New York: Simon & Schuster, 1985).

Kors, Alan C., and Edward Peters, eds., *Witchcraft in Europe, 1100–1700* (Philadelphia: University of Pennsylvania, 1977).

Steere, Douglas V., ed., *Quaker Spirituality: Selected Writings* (Mahwah, N.J.: Paulist Press, 1984).

Waring, E. Graham, ed., *Deism and Natural Religion* (New York: F. Ungar, 1967).

Yolton, John W., *Philosophy, Religion, and Science in the Seventeenth and Eighteenth Centuries* (Rochester, N.Y.: University of Rochester, 1990).

Selected Authors

Donne, John, *Selections from Divine Poems, Sermons, Devotions and Prayers,* ed. John E. Booty (Mahwah, N.J.: Paulist Press, 1990).

Fox, George, *The Journal of George Fox,* ed. John L. Nickalls (Cambridge: Cambridge University Press, 1952).

Hutchinson, Lucy, *Memoirs of the Life of Colonel Hutchinson,* ed. James Sutherland (Oxford: Oxford University Press, 1973).

Krämer, Heinrich, and Jakob Sprenger, *Malleus Maleficarum,* trans. & ed. Montague Summers (Mineola, N.Y.: Dover, 1971).

Milton, John, *The Portable Milton*, ed. Douglas Bush (London: Penguin, 1949).

Newton, Isaac, *Mathematical Principles of Natural Philsophy* (London: Encyclopedia Britannica, 1972).

Pascal, Blaise, *Pensées and Other Writings,* trans. Honor Levi (Oxford: Oxford Univeristy Press, 1995).

Spener, Philip Jakob, *Pia Desideria,* trans. and ed. Theodore Tappert (Minneapolis: Fortress Press, 1964).

Voltaire, *Philosophical Dictionary,* 2 vols., trans. and ed. Peter Gay (New York: Basic Books, 1962).

————, *The Portable Voltaire*, ed. Ben Ray Redman (London: Penguin Classic, 1949).

Wesley, John, *John and Charles Wesley: Selected Prayers, Hymns, Journal Notes, Sermons, Letters, and Treatises,* ed. Frank Whaley (Mahwah, N.J.: Paulist Press, 1981).

Secondary Works

General

Black, Jeremy, *Eighteenth Century Europe, 1700–1789* (New York: Macmillan, 1990).

Cragg, Gerald R., *The Church and the Age of Reason (1648–1789)* (New York: Penguin, 1960).

Dunn, Richard S., *The Age of Religious Wars, 1559–1715* (New York: Norton, 1979).

Thomas, Keith, *Religion and the Decline of Magic: Studies in Popular Beliefs in Sixteenth and Seventeenth Century England* (1971; reissued by Oxford University Press, 1997).

English Civil War and Nonconformism

Adair, John, *Puritans: Religion and Politics in Seventeenth-Century England and America* (Stroud, Gloucestershire: Sutton, 1998).

Ball, Bryan W., *The Seventh-Day Men: Sabbatarians and Sabbatarianism in England and Wales, 1600–1800* (Oxford: Oxford University Press, 1994).

Hill, Christopher, *The World Turned Upside Down* (New York: Viking, 1972).

————, *Oliver Cromwell: God's Englishman* (New York: Dial Press, 1970).

Todd, Margo, ed. *Reformation to Revolution: Politics and Religion in Early Modern England* (New York: Routledge, 1995).

Watts, Michael R., *The Dissenters, Vol. I: From the Reformation to the French Revolution* (Oxford: Clarendon Press, 1978).

European Witch-Hunts

Briggs, Robin, *Witches and Neighbors: A History of European Witchcraft* (New York: Viking, 1996).

Levack, Brian, *The Witch-Hunt in Early Modern Europe,* 2nd ed. (Longman, 1995).

Midelfort, H. C. Erik, *Witchhunting in Southwestern Germany, 1562–1684* (Stanford, Calif.: Stanford University Press, 1972).

Pietism and Methodism

Brown, Dale, *Understanding Pietism* (Grand Rapids, Mich.: Eerdmans, 1978).

Heitzenrater, Richard P., *Wesley and the People Called Methodists* (Nashville, Tenn.: Abingdon Press, 1995).

Rack, Henry D., *Reasonable Enthusiast: John Wesley and the Rise of Methodism,* 2nd ed. (Nashville, Tenn.: Abingdon Press, 1993).

Stoeffler, R. E., *The Rise of Evangelical Pietism* (Leiden, The Netherlands: Brill, 1970).

Deism, Skepticism, and Atheism

Ayer, A. J., *Voltaire* (New York: Random House, 1986).

Brooks, John, *Science and Religion: Some Historical Perspectives* (Cambridge: Cambridge University Press, 1991).

Gay, Peter, *The Enlightenment: An Interpretation,* 2 vols. (New York: Vintage, 1966, 1968).

Hunter, Michael, and David Wooton, eds., *Atheism from the Reformation to the Enlightenment* (Oxford: Oxford University Press, 1992).

Popkin, Richard H., *The History of Skepticism from Erasmus to Spinoza* (Berkeley and Los Angeles: University of California Press, 1979).

CHAPTER 7

North American Christianity to 1860

AN EARLY NINETEENTH-CENTURY CAMP MEETING ON THE AMERICAN FRONTIER. Following the Great Awakening of the 1730s and 1740s, outdoor religious revivals—characterized by fervent preaching, enthusiastic hymn-singing, and ecstatic personal conventions—became the staple of North American Christianity, growing in frequency and size with every subsequent generation. *(Corbis/Bettmann)*

The history of Christianity in the United States and Canada reflects a larger history of both cultural continuity and cultural rupture with Europe. From the earliest Spanish missionaries of the sixteenth century to the native-born visionaries and church founders of the nineteenth and twentieth centuries, North American Christianity has been shaped by a combination of Old World tradition and New World innovation. The potent mix of old and new has spawned an astonishing diversity of Christian beliefs and denominations, including more than 1,200 groups in the contemporary United States alone. Though most churches of European origin have continued to thrive in Canada and the United States, the plethora of new denominations—combined with a very different tradition of church-state relations—has produced a religious history in North America quite different from that of Europe.

The origins of North America's denominational diversity are not hard to detect. In large part, the confessional variety of the New World reflects the religious diversity of its Old World immigrants. Until the eighteenth century, this diversity for the most part corresponded to clear patterns of European colonization. For example, the native and immigrant populations of the Spanish territories of southern and western North America, like those in South America, were entirely Catholic. The same was eventually true of large parts of eastern Canada and the Great Lakes region, settled and evangelized by French Catholics. On the other hand, New England and the eastern seaboard of what is now the United States were mostly colonized by English and Dutch Protestants, including large numbers of Puritan Congregationalists in Massachusetts, many Dutch Reformed (Calvinist) settlers in modern New York and New Jersey, and Quaker dissenters in the colonies of Pennsylvania and Rhode Island. Until the mid eighteenth century, the Church of England maintained the undisputed upper hand in all of the southern colonies. But with the nondenominational revival movement of the 1740s and the American Revolution of the 1770s, that ecclesiastical dominance began to fade. In the years after the British recognition of American independence in 1783, the same decline in influence also became evident among the other leading American denominations, Congregationalists and Presbyterians.

What weakened the mainstream churches, ironically, was not a decline in Christian faith but an explosion of religious fervor that drew Christians to new beliefs and new churches. Fervent revivals and evangelization contributed to enormous growth in membership among Baptists and Methodists, with the latter becoming the largest American Protestant denomination by the early nineteenth century and remaining so until the 1920s. Smaller and completely new churches also blossomed during the nineteenth century, yielding a plethora of new Christian denominations. Some, such as the Unitarians, represented a transcendentalist approach to worship and belief. Leaders such as Ralph Waldo Emerson (1803–1882) sought to escape the divisiveness of all doctrines and dogma (including belief in the Trinity) and instead focus on personal and social betterment. Others sought a restoration of the "primitive" church of the New Testament. For example, the churches of the Disciples of Christ held that all of the mainstream churches had forsaken the earliest Christians' teachings on congregational organization, forms of worship, and adult baptism. Their "restorationist" approach sought to reestablish the purity of New Testament discipline and worship.

This same goal was in fact common among many new Christian denominations of the nineteenth century, albeit with somewhat different interpretations of what a return to the ancient church actually meant. The Seventh Day Adventists believed that divine revelations to their leader, Ellen Gould White, had explained certain hidden meanings of the Scriptures. Meanwhile, the Mormons (formally the Church of Jesus Christ of Latter Day Saints) held that a heavenly messenger had provided their leader with divinely inspired supplements to the canonical Bible. Groups such as these based many of their beliefs on key passages in the Bible, which, according to their interpretation, revealed special information on the date and nature of the Second Coming, or Advent, of Jesus. Some publicized their beliefs widely. For example, the crusading Adventist William Miller (1782–1848) attracted nationwide attention with his predictions that Christ would return sometime in the year 1843 or 1844. Often, however—as among the Mormons and members of the Church of Christ Scientist, founded by Mary Baker Eddy (1821–1910)—some prophecies and teachings were restricted only to the church's faithful, lest outsiders ridicule or distort them. Each of these new churches, as well as the hundreds of other new cults and sects of the century, aggressively sought converts wherever they could find them, competing with all of the older Protestant denominations, as well as the Catholic Church, for the souls of the American people.

Throughout the nineteenth century (and into the twentieth century), immigration from Europe continued to play an important role in sustaining and augmenting the denominational diversity of both the United States and Canada. Irish immigrants, for example, streamed into both countries, especially during the great potato famine of the 1840s, thereby bolstering the Catholic population of each nation. In Canada, these Catholic refugees merely further solidified the large Catholic bloc in place since the days of the earliest French missionaries. In the overwhelmingly Protestant United States, however, Catholics from Ireland (along with those from Germany) transformed a minority religion into a church with larger membership than that of most major Protestant denominations. During the nineteenth century, this influx of "foreign-spirited papists" triggered a political backlash among so-called Protestant nativists, such as the Know-Nothings. Attempted restrictions of Catholic immigration were generally unsuccessful, though, and by 1870 Roman Catholicism had become the largest single Christian denomination in the United States. Nonetheless, social segregation between Catholics and Protestants remained the norm, with members of the denominations usually attending separate schools, living in separate neighborhoods, and joining separate social service clubs. Only after World War II did cultural assimilation and mixing finally yield the climate of toleration that made possible the election of John F. Kennedy as the first Roman Catholic president in 1960.

In addition to immigration and the founding of multiple new churches, the issue of slavery marked the early history of Christianity in North America, and particularly the United States, setting it apart from European religious history. Until the early nineteenth century, most slaves shared the same denomination as their masters and worship services were usually segregated. Beginning with the founding of the African Methodist Episcopal Church in 1816 by the freed slave Richard Allen, however, many free blacks began to form their own churches, separate from those that were dominated by white leadership. Meanwhile, some of those same white church leaders began to call for the abolition of slavery, a stance that caused controversy and even schism within several denominations. In 1845, for example, a number of slavery-tolerant congregations left the Baptist mainstream to form the Southern Baptist Convention. The American Civil War resolved the question of slavery but did not heal the continuing divisions among Christians over racial questions. If anything, the segregation of black and white U.S. Christians became even more pronounced in the century following the war, a pattern particularly evident in the growth of all-black Holiness and Pentecostal congregations during the beginning of the twentieth century. Even today, almost a century and a half after the Emancipation Proclamation, the legacy of racial division continues to shape American Christianity.

By the time of the American Civil War and of Canadian independence, the distinctiveness of North American Christianity was an undisputed fact. Though many churchgoers maintained ties with European-based denominations—most notably in the Roman Catholic and Anglican churches—the rapidly growing new Christian sects seemed poised to overtake most of the established churches by the end of the nineteenth century. In fact, both older and more recent denominations have survived into the twenty-first century, and the dynamic North American tradition of Christian diversity continues unabated.

	Politics	Literature	Individuals	Other
16th cent.	1565 St. Augustine founded			
17th cent.	1607 Jamestown colony founded 1620 Plymouth colony established 1634 Catholic colony of Maryland founded 1675–1676 King Philip's War 1681 Pennsylvania colony founded	1630 Winthrop, *A Model of Christian Charity*	1591–1643 Anne Hutchinson 1593–1649 J. de Brébeuf, S.J. 1603–1683 Roger Williams 1607–1646 Isaac Jogues, S.J. 1644–1718 William Penn 1656–1680 Catherine Tegahkouita	1619 First African slaves in N. America 1636 Harvard University founded 1692 Salem witch trials
18th cent.	1756–1763 French and Indian Wars 1776–1781 American Revolution 1788 U.S. Constitution ratified 1789 First Amendment adopted	1741 Edwards, *Sinners in the Hands of an Angry God*	1703–1758 Jonathan Edwards 1713–1784 Junípero Serra 1714–1770 George Whitefield	1734–1742 Great Awakening in New England 1773 First Methodist Conference in N. America 1776 Separation of church & state in Virginia
19th cent.	1861–1865 Civil War	1838 Emerson, "Divinity School Address" 1850 Hawthorne, *The Scarlet Letter*	1782–1849 William Miller 1805–1844 Joseph Smith 1801–1877 Brigham Young 1821–1910 Mary Baker Eddy 1837–1899 Dwight L. Moody 1827–1915 Ellen G. White	1844 Millerites expect Second Coming 1847 Mormons move to Utah

A. New World Missions

The European discovery of the Americas at the end of the fifteenth century marked the beginning of a new period of worldwide expansion for Christianity. Driven by a thirst for new territory and riches, European soldiers, speculators, and settlers flocked to the New World. But along with those bent on conquest came missionaries whose mandate was to convert the native peoples of the Americas to Christianity. Most of these missionaries—and some of the rulers who sent them—were motivated by a sincere belief that they were saving the souls of indigenous Americans from certain damnation. Unfortunately, conversion, as in the Europe of the Middle Ages, was sometimes forced and often superficial. At the same time, however, clerical missionaries were instrumental in curbing some of the worst cruelties against the peoples of the New World, as well as in providing education and other services for Indians throughout the Americas. From the early sixteenth through the eighteenth centuries, this New World missionary activity was dominated by the Catholic monarchies of Spain, Portugal, and France, who sent numerous Franciscans and Dominicans, and later Jesuits, on demanding and often dangerous missions to bring Christianity to every corner of North and South America. In 1622, Pope Gregory XV (r. 1621–1623) placed all Catholic missionary activity under the control of an agency called Sacred Congregation for the Propagation of the Faith, a move that gave proselytizing clerics greater independence from secular colonial authorities. During the next two centuries, hundreds of mission outposts were founded throughout North and South America, thereby establishing a firm Catholic foothold among the indigenous peoples of the New World. The membership rolls of Protestant churches in the Americas, by contrast, were swelled primarily by emigrants from England, Germany, and the Netherlands rather than by organized missionary activity. Not until the early eighteenth century did Protestant foundations such as the Society for Promoting Christian Knowledge (S.P.C.K.) and various Pietist groups begin to use missionary work to make significant inroads among the native populations.

1. Jean de Brébeuf
"INSTRUCTIONS FOR THE FATHERS OF OUR SOCIETY WHO SHALL BE SENT TO THE HURONS" (1637)

The exploits of European missionaries among American Indians made for inspirational reading among the faithful in the Old World. Ironically, the more that missionaries such as the Jesuit Jean de Brébeuf (1593–1649) emphasized the tedium and hardship of such work, the more their religious orders' recruitment numbers rose. Brébeuf was clearly aware that many young Frenchmen would be entranced by the challenge of dying for the faith, and his practical advice to would-be missionaries was intended as an antidote to unrealistic and romantic expectations. The true fortitude of the missionary, he writes, is the ability to endure long periods of confusion, neglect, insult, and physical discomfort. Learned theological debates have no place in this world, where the main goal is to gain trust among a foreign and suspicious people and only then to begin the laborious work of religious instruction. Brébeuf's instructions were the fruit of his own long experience with the Hurons, which included an initial two-year stint without a single convert. During the twenty-odd years of his New World ministry, though, the Frenchman did eventually succeed in making hundreds of Indian converts as well as in recruiting several new missionaries to carry on his work. Like his compatriot Isaac Jogues (1607–1646), Brébeuf was finally tortured and killed by the Iroquois. Both men were later canonized by the Catholic Church, and together with other executed missionaries of present-day Canada and the northeastern United States, they are known collectively as the North American Martyrs.

Easy as may be a trip with the Savages, there is always enough to greatly cast down a heart not well under subjection. The readiness of the Savages does not shorten the road, does not smooth down the rocks, does not remove the dangers. Be with whom you like, you must expect to be, at least, three or four weeks on the way, to have as companions persons you have never seen before; to be cramped in a bark Canoe in an uncomfortable position, not being free to turn yourself to one side or the other; in danger fifty times a day of being upset or of being dashed upon the rocks. During the day, the Sun burns you; during the night, you run the risk of being a prey to Mosquitoes. You sometimes ascend five or six rapids in a day; and, in the evening, the only refreshment is a little corn crushed between two stones and cooked in fine clear water; the only bed is the earth, sometimes only the rough, uneven rocks, and usually no roof but the stars; and all this in perpetual silence. If you are accidentally hurt, if you fall sick, do not expect from these Barbarians any assistance, for whence could they obtain it? And if the sickness is dangerous, and you are remote from the villages, which are here very scattered, I would not like to guarantee that they would not abandon you, if you could not make shift to follow them.

When you reach the Hurons, you will indeed find hearts full of charity; we will receive you with open arms as an Angel of Paradise, we shall have all the inclination in the world to do you good; but we are so situated that we can do very little. We shall receive you in a Hut, so mean that I have scarcely found in France one wretched enough to compare it with; that is how you will be lodged. Harassed and fatigued as you will be, we shall be able to give you nothing but a poor mat, or at most a skin, to serve as a bed; and, besides, you will arrive at a season when miserable little insects that we call here *Taouhac,* and, in good French, *pulces* [fleas], will keep you awake almost all night, for in these countries they are incomparably more troublesome than in France; the dust of the Cabin nourishes them, the Savages bring them to us, we get them in their houses; and this petty martyrdom, not to speak of Mosquitoes, Sandflies, and other like vermin, lasts usually not less than three or four months of the Summer.

Instead of being a great master and great Theologian as in France, you must reckon on being here a humble Scholar, and then, good God! with what masters!—women, little children, and all the Savages,—and exposed to their laughter. The Huron language will be your saint Thomas and your Aristotle[1]; and clever man as you are, and speaking glibly among learned and capable persons, you must make up your mind to be for a long time mute among the Barbarians. You will have accomplished much, if at the end of a considerable time, you begin to stammer a little.

And then how do you think you would pass the Winter with us? After having heard all that must be endured in wintering among the Montagnets[2] Savages, I may say that that is almost the life we lead here among the Hurons. I say it without exaggeration, the five and six months of Winter are spent in almost continual discomforts,—excessive cold, smoke, and the annoyance of the Savages. . . .

"But is that all?" some one will exclaim. "Do you think by your arguments to throw water on the fire that consumes me, and lessen ever so little the zeal I have for the conversion of these Peoples? I declare that these things have served only to confirm me the more in my vocation; that I feel myself more carried away than ever by my affection for New France, and that I bear a holy jealousy towards those who are already enduring all these sufferings; all these labors seem to me nothing, in comparison with what I am willing to endure for God; if I knew a place under Heaven where there was yet more to be suffered, I would go there." Ah! whoever you are to whom God gives these sentiments and this light, come, come, my dear Brother, it is workmen such as you that we ask for here; it is to souls like yours that God has appointed the conquest of so many other souls whom the Devil holds yet in his power; apprehend no difficulties,—there will be none for you, since it is your whole consolation to see yourself crucified with the Son of God. . . .

The Fathers and Brethren whom God shall call to the Holy Mission of the Hurons ought to exercise careful foresight in regard to all the hardships, annoyances, and perils that must be encountered in making this journey, in order to be prepared betimes for all emergencies that may arise.

You must have sincere affection for the Savages,—looking upon them as ransomed by the blood of the son of God, and as our brethren with whom we are to pass the rest of our lives.

To conciliate the Savages, you must be careful never to make them wait for you in embarking.

You must provide yourself with a tinder box or with a burning mirror, or with both, to furnish them fire in the daytime to light their pipes, and in the evening when they have to encamp; these little services win their hearts.

You should try to eat their *sagamité* or salmagundi[3] in the way they prepare it, although it may be dirty, half-cooked, and very tasteless. As to the other numerous things which may be unpleasant, they must be endured for the love of God, without saying anything or appearing to notice them.

It is well at first to take everything they offer, although you may not be able to eat it all; for, when one becomes somewhat accustomed to it, there is not too much.

You must try and eat at daybreak unless you can take your meal with you in the canoe; for the day is very long, if you have to pass it without eating. The Barbarians eat only at Sunrise and Sunset, when they are on their journeys.

You must be prompt in embarking and disembarking; and tuck up your gowns so that they will not get wet, and so that you will not carry either water or sand into the canoe. To be properly dressed, you must have your feet and legs bare; while crossing the rapids, you can wear your shoes, and, in the long portages, even your leggings.

You must so conduct yourself as not to be at all troublesome to even one of these Barbarians.

It is not well to ask many questions, nor should you yield to your desire to learn the language and to make observations on the way; this may be carried too far. You must relieve those in your canoe of this annoyance, espe-

---

[1]The "angelic doctor," Thomas Aquinas (1225–1274), and his philosophical hero, Aristotle (384–322 B.C.E.).
[2]Members of the Algonquin tribe.

[3]A mixture of chopped meat and vegetables.

cially as you cannot profit much by it during the work. Silence is a good equipment at such a time.

You must bear with their imperfections without saying a word, yes, even without seeming to notice them. Even if it be necessary to criticize anything, it must be done modestly, and with words and signs which evince love and not aversion. In short, you must try to be, and to appear, always cheerful.

Each one should be provided with half a gross of awls, two or three dozen little knives, called *jambettes* [pocket-knives], a hundred fish-hooks, with some beads of plain or colored glass, with which to buy fish or other articles when the tribes meet each other, so as to feast the Savages; and it would be well to say to them in the beginning, "Here is something with which to buy fish." Each one will try, at the portages, to carry some little thing, according to his strength; however little one carries, it greatly pleases the Savages, if it be only a kettle.

You must not be ceremonious with the Savages, but accept the comforts they offer you, such as a good place in the cabin. The greatest conveniences are attended with very great inconvenience, and these ceremonies offend them.

Be careful not to annoy anyone in the canoe with your hat; it would be better to take your nightcap. There is no impropriety among the Savages.

Do not undertake anything unless you desire to continue it; for example, do not begin to paddle unless you are inclined to continue paddling. Take from the start the place in the canoe that you wish to keep; do not lend them your garments, unless you are willing to surrender them during the whole journey. It is easier to refuse at first than to ask them back, to change, or to desist afterwards.

Finally, understand that the Savages will retain the same opinion of you in their own country that they will have formed on the way and one who has passed for an irritable and troublesome person will have considerable difficulty afterwards in removing this opinion. You have to do not only with those of your own canoe, but also (if it must be so stated) with all those of the country; you meet some to-day and others to-morrow, who do not fail to inquire, from those who brought you, what sort of man you are. It is almost incredible how they observe and remember even the slightest fault. When you meet the Savages on the way, as you cannot yet greet them with kind words, at least show them a cheerful face, and thus prove that you endure gaily the fatigues of the voyage. You will thus have put to good use the hardships of the way, and already advanced considerably in gaining the affection of the Savages.

This is a lesson which is easy enough to learn, but very difficult to put into practice; for, leaving a highly civilized community, you fall into the hands of barbarous people who care little for your Philosophy or your Theology. All the fine qualities which might make you loved and respected in France are like pearls trampled under the feet of swine, or rather of mules, which utterly despise you when they see that you are not as good pack animals as they are. If you go naked and carry the load of a horse upon your back, as they do, then you would be wise according to their doctrine, and would be recognized as a great man, otherwise not. Jesus Christ is our true greatness; it is He alone and His cross that should be sought in running after these people, for, if you strive for anything else, you will find naught but bodily and spiritual affliction. But having found Jesus Christ in His Cross, you have found the roses in the thorns, sweetness in bitterness, all in nothing.

2. Pierre François Xavier Charlevoix
"THE CONVERSION AND HOLY DEATH
OF CATHERINE TEGAHKOUITA" (1744)

The spread of Christianity in North America was not solely the work of European-born missionaries. Since the first proselytizing of the sixteenth century, hard-working and often charismatic natives played equally important roles in persuading their respective peoples to embrace the new religion. Local cult figures, such as the enormously popular Catherine Tegahkouita (1656–1680), also exercised considerable influence in the mission of Christian conversion. Though her Algonquin mother was Christian, Catherine learned about the new religion mostly from various French missionaries, particularly the Jesuit Jacques de Lamberville, whom she first encountered in 1676, at the age of twenty. Her story is reminiscent of those of the earliest Christian martyrs, including such elements as an unpopular refusal to marry (for reasons of chastity), extreme fasting, persecution and near death because of her faith, and various charitable works of caring for the sick and aged. Like many cult figures throughout the ages, she died young. All of these attributes, combined with several miracles attributed to her, resulted in widespread veneration of Catherine among both native and European-born residents of New France, a tradition that continues to this day in Quebec. In 1980 she was beatified by the Catholic Church, an honor that often leads to canonization as a saint.

New France has had her apostles and her martyrs, and has given the church saints in all conditions, and I do not hesitate to say that they would have done honor to the primitive ages of Christianity. Several I have made known so far as the course of this history permitted me. The lives of some have been published; but God, who exalted his glory during their life-time by the great things which he effected through them; by the luster which their sanctity has diffused over this vast continent; by the courage with which he inspired them to found with untold toil a new Christendom amid the most fearful barbarism, and to cement it with their blood, chose none of these to display on their tombs, all the riches of his power and mercy; but conferred this honor on a young neophyte, almost unknown to the whole country during her life. For more than sixty years she has been regarded as the Protectress of Canada, and it

has been impossible to oppose a kind of *cultus* publicly rendered to her.

This holy virgin, so celebrated under the name of Catharine Tegahkouita, was born in 1656, at Gandahouhagué,[4] a town in the Mohawk canton, of a heathen Iroquois father and a Christian Algonquin mother. She lost her mother at the age of four, and was still quite young when her father died, leaving her to the care of one of her aunts, and under the control of an uncle who had the chief authority in his village. The smallpox which she had in her infancy having weakened her sight, she was long compelled as it were to remain in the corner of a cabin, her eyes being unable to stand the light, and this retirement was the first source of her happiness. What she did at first from necessity, she continued to do from choice, thereby

---

[4]Fonda, New York.

avoiding whatever could cause her to lose that moral purity so hard to preserve amid idolatrous and then very dissolute youth.

As soon as she saw herself of age to act, she took on herself all the toil of the household; and this shielded her from two dangers, fatal to most Indian girls; I mean, private conversations and idleness. Her relatives however wished her to use the decorations common to young persons of her sex, and although she yielded from simple compliance with their wishes, and with all possible repugnance, it was a matter of much scruple to her, when, favored by the light of faith, she learned how dangerous it is to seek to please men.

The first knowledge that she acquired of Christianity, was imparted by some missionaries sent to the Iroquois after M. de Tracy's expedition.[5] On their way they passed through the town where she lived and were received at her cabin. She was appointed to take care of them, and waited on them in a manner that surprised them. She had herself, on beholding them, been moved by an impulse that excited sentiments in her heart, regarded subsequently by her as the first spark of the heavenly fire, by which she was in the sequel so completely inflamed. The fervor and recollection of those religious in their devotions, inspired her with the desire of praying with them, and she informed them of it. They understood much more than she expressed; they instructed her in the Christian truth, as far as the short stay which they made in that town permitted them, and left her with a regret that on her side was heartily reciprocated. Some time after a marriage was proposed to her; as she showed strong opposition, her relatives did not press it; but they soon returned to the charge, and to save themselves the trouble of overcoming her resistance, they without mentioning it to her, betrothed her to a young man, who at once went to her cabin and sat down beside her. To ratify the marriage, it only required that she should remain near the husband selected for her, such being the way of these tribes; but she abruptly left the cabin, and protested that she would not return till he withdrew. This conduct drew on her much ill treatment, which she endured with unalterable patience. She was more sensible to the reproach made that she had no affection for her kindred, that she hated her tribe and gave all her attachment to that to which her mother belonged. Nothing however could overcome her repugnance for the state of life in which they sought to involve her.

Meanwhile Father Jacques de Lamberville[6] arrived at Gaudahouhagué with orders to found a mission there. Tegahkouita then felt her former desires to become a Christian revive; but she was still for some time without mentioning it, either from respect to her uncle, who did not relish our religion, or from simple timidity. At last an opportunity came for avowing her conviction, and she was not wanting. A wound in the foot which she had received, kept her in the cabin, while all the other women were busy harvesting the Indian corn. Father de Lamberville, compelled to suspend his public instructions, which no one would attend, took this time to visit the cabins, and instructed those whom age or infirmity detained there. One day he entered that where Tegahkouita was.

Unable to dissemble the joy which this visit caused her, she did not hesitate to open her mind to the missionary in the presence of two or three women, who were in company with her, on her design of embracing Christianity. She added that she would have great obstacles to overcome, but that nothing appalled her. The energy with which she spoke, the courage she displayed, a certain modest yet resolute air, that lighted up her countenance, at once told the missionary that his new proselyte would

---

[5]The French commander, Alexandre de Prouville, Marquis de Tracy (1603–1670), had cleared the way for the missionaries by leading a western military expedition against the hostile Iroquois in 1666.

[6]Jesuit missionary (1641–1710).

not be an ordinary Christian. He accordingly carefully taught her many things, which he did not explain to all preparing for baptism. God doubtless infuses into hearts, of which he has especially reserved possession, a sort of purely spiritual sympathy, forming even in this life the sacred bond which will unite them hereafter in the abode of glory. Father de Lamberville, whom I knew well, was one of the most holy missionaries of New France, where he died, at Sault Saint Louis,[7] spent with toil and austerity, and, if I may use the expression, in the arms of Charity. He often declared that in his first interview with Tegahkouita, he thought he could discern that God had great designs as to that virgin; yet he would not exercise any haste in conferring baptism on her, and he adopted in her case all the precautions that experience has counseled as necessary to make sure of the Indians, before administering the sacrament of regeneration.

The whole winter was spent in these trials, and on her side the young catechumen employed this precious time in rendering herself worthy of a grace, whose importance she fully comprehended. Before granting it to adults, the missionaries took great pains to inquire privately into their conduct and morality. Father de Lamberville asked all who knew Tegahkouita, and was greatly surprised to find that there was not one, even among those who had given her most to suffer, but sounded her praises. This was all the more glorious for her, as Indians are much given to slander, and naturally inclined to put an evil interpretation on the most innocent actions. The missionary accordingly no longer hesitated to grant her what she solicited with such earnestness. She was baptized on Easter Sunday, 1676, and received the name of Catharine.

The grace of the sacrament received into a heart which her uprightness and innocence had so well prepared, produced wondrous effects. Whatever idea the missionary had already conceived of the young Iroquois maiden, he was as-

tonished to find in her, immediately after baptism, not a neophyte needing to be confirmed in the faith, but a soul filled with the most precious gifts of heaven, and whom he too would have to guide in the most sublime spiritual ways. In the outset her virtue excited the admiration of those even who were least inclined to imitate her, and those on whom she depended, left her free to follow every impulse of her zeal, but this did not last long. The innocence of her life, the precautions which she took to avoid all that could in the least affect it, and especially her extreme reserve as to whatever could in the slightest degree offend purity, appeared to the young men of her village as a reproach on the dissolute life they led, and many laid snares with the sole view of dimming a virtue which dazzled them.

On the other hand, although she had relaxed nothing in her domestic occupations, and was ever found ready to give her services to all, her relatives were displeased to see her give to prayer all the time left her, and to prevent her suspending on Sundays and holidays the work which the church forbids on those days consecrated to the Lord, they made her pass them without food. Seeing, however, that they gained nothing by this course, they had recourse to still more violent means; they often ill-treated her in a most unbecoming manner; when she went to the chapel, they sent young men to pursue her with hooting and pelt her with stones; men either really drunk or pretendedly drunk rushed upon her, as though they designed to take her life; but, undismayed by these artifices and acts of violence, she continued her devotions as though she enjoyed the most perfect liberty.

One day when she was in her cabin, a young man entered abruptly, with flashing eyes, brandishing his hatchet as if intending to tomahawk her. At this sight she displayed no emotion, and bowed down her head to receive the blow; but the madman, seized at the instant by a panic fear, fled as precipitately as though pursued by a war-party. These first storms were succeeded by a still more dangerous persecution. Catharine's aunt

---

[7] In southern Quebec, along the St. Lawrence Seaway.

was a woman of morose disposition, who was displeased with all that her niece did to satisfy her, for the simple reason that she could find nothing to reprove. One day the virtuous neophyte happened to call the husband of this woman by his own name, instead of calling him Father, as usual; her aunt imagined, or pretended to believe, that this familiar mode of speaking showed an improper connection between the uncle and the niece, and she hastened on the spot to Father de Lamberville to assert that she had surprised Catharine soliciting her husband to sin. The missionary promised to examine the case, and when he learned on what this atrocious accusation rested, he gave the slanderer a rebuke that covered her with confusion; but which ultimately increased the annoyance of the innocent girl.

Had all this involved merely suffering, than which nothing was more to her taste, she would never have thought of changing her position; but she feared that she could not always hold firm against the seduction of bad example, or escape being overcome gradually by human respect, so powerful in the Indian mind. She accordingly began to look for an asylum, where her innocence and religion would be shielded from danger. La Prairie de la Magdeleine,[8] where several Iroquois Christians began to settle, seemed to her well adapted, and she felt an ardent desire to remove thither; but this was not easily done.

Her uncle beheld with great displeasure the depopulation of his canton, and he declared himself the avowed enemy of all who contributed to it. It was therefore apparently impossible to obtain his consent, and it was not easy for Catharine to leave him without it. But God, who had destined her to be the example and ornament of this transplanted Christian colony, facilitated what had at first seemed impossible. She had an adopted sister, a neophyte like herself, married to a Christian very zealous for the conversion of his countrymen. This man had already taken up his abode at La Prairie de la Magdeleine, and he was one of those who

under various pretexts, traversed the Iroquois towns in order to make proselytes. He knew that the greater favor he could do to Catharine would be to take her to his home: he spoke of the matter to his wife, who confirmed him in his design, and earnestly exhorted him to give her sister this consolation. . . .

[The brother-in-law then persuades Catherine's uncle to release her to his charge.]

She had not yet made her first communion when she arrived in the colony, and it is not usual in these missions to grant this favor to neophytes till after long trials. Catharine was fearful that she would be subjected to this rule, but her virtue, far more than her repeated entreaties, soon induced her director to make an exception in her favor; nor had he any reason to repent. The frequent communions, which she was permitted to receive, did not diminish in the least her fervor in preparing for them. It was enough to see her in her most ordinary actions to be roused to devotion; but when she partook of the divine mysteries, it was impossible to be near her, and not be filled with the most tender love for God. . . .

She was at last attacked by a malady, which was at once deemed mortal; and that at a time when the labors in the field so engaged all, that she could scarcely expect care from any one. She remained alone whole days with a platter of Indian corn, and a little water beside her bed. Delighted to behold herself thus forsaken of men, she communed constantly with her God, and found the days only too short. On Tuesday in Holy Week, 1678 [1680], she grew worse and received Holy Viaticum. The missionary wished also to administer Extreme Unction[9] at once, but she assured him that it could be

---

[8]A Christian village near what is now Montreal, Canada.

[9]Holy Viaticum refers to the reception of communion by a dying person; the term literally means "food for the journey." It is normally followed by the sacrament of Extreme Unction, also known as the last rites, a final anointing with oil.

deferred till next day. She spent all the ensuing night in a loving colloquy with her divine Savior, and with His Holy Mother, whom she had always singularly honored, regarding herself as a spouse of Christ, and as attached to the retinue of the Queen of Virgins.

On Wednesday morning she received the sacred anointing, and about three o'clock in the afternoon she expired after a gentle agony of half an hour, retaining her complete consciousness and sound judgment till her last sigh. . . . Her countenance, extremely attenuated by aus-

terity and by her last illness, suddenly changed as soon as she ceased to live. It was seen assuming a rosy tint that she had never had; nor were her features the same. Nothing could be more beautiful, but with that beauty which love of virtue inspires. The people were never weary gazing on her, and each retired, his heart full of the desire to become a saint. As a distinction her body was placed in a coffin, and her tomb soon became celebrated by the concourse of the faithful, who flocked from all parts of Canada, and by the miracles wrought there. . . .

---

3. Junípero Serra
ANNUAL RECORDS OF THE MISSION OF SAN CARLOS DE MONTEREY (1770–1784)

The success of early Catholic missionary work among the North American Indians owed far more to the patient day-to-day ministering of reliable community builders such as Junípero Serra (1713–1784) than to any dramatic mass conversions. Serra was a Spanish Franciscan who first came to the New World in 1750, at the age of thirty-six. After almost twenty years of work in Mexico he moved north with Spanish troops in their occupation of Upper California. From 1769 to 1782 he founded nine missions within the present-day state of California, including San Diego (1769), San Francisco (1776), Santa Clara (1777), and his headquarters at San Carlos de Monterey (1770). In these two excerpts from his annual records for San Carlos, we glimpse how much of his missionary work involved clearing ground, planting crops, and building walls, as well as administering the sacraments and preaching to recently converted natives. His tendency to mix numbers of baptisms and marriages with grain and livestock inventories should not be misinterpreted, however. Serra was interested in much more than the mounting number of conversions recorded in his ledger. He was also a spirited preacher and advocate of his parishioners, genuinely concerned about their spiritual and physical health. His popularity among Christian Native Americans, in fact, helped secure Spanish control of Upper California well into the nineteenth century. He is known as the Apostle of California and was beatified by the Catholic Church in 1985, the first step toward being made a saint.

[1770]
HAIL JESUS, MARY, JOSEPH!

On the most solemn feast of the Holy Spirit, Pentecost Sunday, June 3, 1770, this mission of San Carlos de Monterey was founded to the joy

of the sea and land expeditions. In a short time the rejoicing was shared by the entire kingdom and eagerly celebrated in both Spains.

On that day, after imploring the assistance of the Holy Spirit, the sacred standard of the cross was blessed, raised, and adored by all. The ground was blessed, an altar set up, and a sort of chapel formed with naval flags. The holy sacrifice of the Mass was sung, a sermon was preached, and, at the end, the *Te Deum*[10] was intoned. With these (ceremonies), possession was duly taken of Monterey for (our) holy Church and the crown of Spain. A legal document covering all was drawn up and will be found where it belongs. All this occurred on the beach at the landing place of the said port, the same spot on which one hundred sixty-seven years before, as it is written, the expedition of Don Sebastián Vizcaino had celebrated Mass.[11]

The following day, after choosing the most likely spot on that plain, the construction of the presidio[12] was enthusiastically begun by the men of both sea and land forces. By the fourteenth of the same month, the most solemn feast of Corpus (Christi), a chapel had been built as well as it could be, at the spot in the presidio which it still occupies, and a high Mass was sung with the Blessed Sacrament exposed in its monstrance.[13] After the Mass there was a procession, in which His Sacramental Majesty passed over the ground that till then had been so heathen and miserable. It was a day of great consolation for all of us who were Christians.

So the presidio was begun but the troop was too small to be divided into two bodies. Thus we, the religious, were forced to establish ourselves in and remain incorporated with this presidio until further arrangements [could be made], even though we knew that there we could do no sowing or any other kind of work.

We remained like this for one year, spending the time putting in order our residence and the most necessary storerooms for our supplies and in making friends with the Indians who were coming to see us; and we tried to win some children. In fact, within a short time, we baptized three and when the boat returned at the end of the year [1771], we had already twenty new Christians at Monterey. As ten religious came on this vessel, we were then twelve. We all dressed in rich chasubles and had a most solemn procession for Corpus (Christi). We had here the vestments for future missions, the men from the ship, and those of the land force, etc. Thanks be to God! . . .

YEAR 1783

We can consider this the happiest year of the mission because the number of baptisms was one hundred seventy-five and of marriages thirty-six.

The sowing of all grains amounted to eighty-four bushels, eight pecks. This included one bushel and a half of wheat, half a bushel of corn, and two pecks of beans, which were sown for the [Lower] California Indians, who had moved here and were married in this mission.

And the harvest, less the amount of forty-seven bushels which belonged to these Indians and other concessions made to the people such as a portion of the barley which they might reap and some twenty bushels of wheat from the chaff of the threshing, which was stored in the mission granaries amounted to twenty-six hundred fourteen and a half bushels, that is, of measured barley six hundred seventy bushels, eight hundred thirty-five of wheat, only two hundred according to our estimate are kept in the ear. There were nine hundred seventy-one bushels of corn of both kinds according to our estimate, sixty-three bushels of peas, sixteen bushels of horse beans, four bushels of lentils, and fifty-three bushels of various kinds of beans.

Today the new Christians of this mission number six hundred fourteen living persons, even though some of them take a leave of absence from time to time. They have been maintained and are maintained without any scarcity and we supplied the quartermaster of the

---

[10]*Te Deum Laudamus* ("Thee, God, we praise"), an ancient hymn of rejoicing, usually sung in celebration of some great event.
[11]Don Sebastián Vizcaino (1550?–1615) and his exploring party entered Monterey Bay on December 16, 1602.
[12]I.e., fort.
[13]The monstrance is a large and often ornate receptacle with a small glass chamber in its center for displaying the host, or sanctified bread.

presidio of San Carlos with one hundred thirty bushels of Indian corn; because they did not ask for more, also with thirty bushels of beans. The escort of this mission, at the request of the ensign quartermaster, received rations in those two kinds of grain. There have not been other deliveries of consequence so that in our prudent judgment of the two chief commodities, wheat and corn, about half the amount harvested may still remain.

The value of the food supplied to the presidio has been paid already in cloth, which now covers the Indians who grew the crops, but at that we are still distressed at the sight of so much nudity among them.

We do not get clothing new from the soldiers, as we did formerly, not even from those who have debts to us no matter how small. The wool, which in some of the missions is enough to cover Indian nakedness, here has not been any help to us so far, because the thefts of sheep are so numerous that already for more than three years, we can not exceed two hundred head between goats and sheep, and from shearing the few that we have we get nothing worthwhile.

The condition, then, of the Mission in things spiritual is that up to this day in the Mission:

Baptisms..1,006
Confirmations..936
    And since those of the other missions
    belong in some way to this it is noted
    in passing that their number is........5,307
Marriages in this mission......................259
Burials...356

The number of Christian families living at the mission and eating jointly, as well as widowers, single men, and children of both sexes, is evident from the enclosed census lists and so is omitted here.

They pray twice daily with the priest in the church. More than one hundred twenty of them confess in Spanish and many who have died used to do it as well. The others confess as best they can. They work at all kinds of mission labor, such as farm hands, herdsmen, cowboys, shepherds, milkers, diggers, gardeners, carpenters, farmers, irrigators, reapers, blacksmiths, sacristans, and they do everything else that comes along for their corporeal and spiritual welfare.

The work of clearing the fields once, sometimes twice, or even three times a year, is considerable because the land is very fertile. When we clear new land great hardship is required. Altogether there is sufficient land cleared for sowing more than one hundred bushels of wheat, and it is sowed in that grain, barley, vegetables, and corn. Every year we clear a little more.

To the seven months' work required to take water from the river for irrigation, as mentioned above, we must add the labor of bringing it to the lagoon near the mission residence. In some years, this lagoon used to be dry. Now it is always full, making it a great convenience and a delight to the mission. Some salmon have been placed in the pool and so we have it handy.

The timber palisade was inadequate to protect the seed grain because they steal the paling for firewood. So we dug a circular trench many thousands of varas[14] long. This was a two years' labor and withal nothing sufficed to prevent losses every year.

Some of the land which we cleared for farming was not only covered with long tough grasses and thickets but also with great trees, willows, alders, and so forth, and it has been hard work, as we have already noted, but we hope that it will pay off at a profit. We also have a sizable walled garden [which produces] abundant vegetables and some fruit.

MISSION BUILDINGS

In the first few years we worked hard and well on the church and the rest of the buildings. [They were made] of paling with flat earthen roofs to minimize fire danger, but no matter what we did they always leaked like a sieve and

---

[14]The Spanish *vara* was equivalent to about 2.8 feet.

between that and the humidity everything would rot. So we decided to build of adobe and thus today all buildings are [of that material]. They are as follows:

An adobe church, forty by eight varas, with a thatched roof.

Likewise, the three-room residence of the three priests. One [room is] large, with an alcove for a bed. The floor is plain earth and the roof thatched.

Also, a granary about twenty varas long with several small compartments, a porch, and a thatched roof.

Likewise, another granary about thirty varas long with its porch and four wooden barred windows. The floor is plain earth and the roof thatched.

Also, another adobe house, thirty varas long, divided for the present into only three sections: one serves as a storeroom, another at the opposite end is used as a dormitory for the girls; the center section is a large room with two barred windows and doors. It is white-washed and clean and is used as a guest chamber for the ships' officers and for some other occasions. It is going to be divided into two rooms for which we already have the two doors with their hinges.

Likewise, another adobe building with an earthen roof and with its own shed and key. It houses the forge where the blacksmith works. It has a porch and window.

Also, next to this building is another which we call the carpenter shop. It has a room with a separate door and key for safeguarding the tools. It has two windows with bars and a door.

Likewise, another building next to the ones just mentioned where the women grind [grain], make cheese, and where different tools are kept.

Also, another building, larger than the preceding ones, where for the present the family of the Mexican blacksmith lives.

Likewise, four adobe buildings a little further on, which are [a place for] five carts, the wood shed, kitchen, and a hen house.

Also, there is a serviceable adobe corral with sections for sheep and goats and next to this a separate pen for pigs. The rest of the corrals for horses and cattle, with their corresponding stud and bull stalls, are all made of paling and from time to time give us quite a bit of repair trouble.

THE ANIMALS

number today:

Cattle, large and small 500
Sheep and goats, about the same number
    of each 220
Riding and draft mules 18
Tame and broken horses 20
Four herds of mares with their colts 90
    Also with them, two young mules
    from the time we had a jack
One old ass that may be with foal 1
Pigs 25

ACCOUNTS

Regarding the remainder of the status of the mission, [we note] that when the vessels arrive from Mexico with the supplies we know whether we have credits or debits from our stipends. This year the [boats] have not yet reached here, so we do not have this information.

We know of no local debts but there may be some hidden or unexpected debt like those we have had in the past.

The mission paid Lieutenant Ortega[15] eighteen pesos for a tent from the King's stores, which was given the father president for use when he was at San Buenaventura Mission, and while he assisted at the foundation of the new presidio of Santa Barbara. He did not think such a debt existed until they came to collect it.

Not long ago this mission paid fifteen pesos as a donation for the war, more than a year after the conflict ended,[16] as a result of misinformation given the commandancy general to the effect that the father president had excluded from the count some Indians who had run away from the

---

[15]José Francisco Ortega (d. 1798) was a Mexican-born soldier who rose to the rank of brevet captain in the Spanish colonial forces.
[16]The preliminary articles of peace between Great Britain and Spain were signed on January 20, 1783.

mission after the lists had been completed. This was not true, for when we made the lists everyone of them had been apostates for at least two years and some for more than three. He mentioned them only as an incentive so that they might return them [to the mission] for me.

We did not even think about mentioning those who ran away, nor those who died, after the lists were made, nor did we discount them but just the same we paid the fifteen pesos and the [entire] donation amounted to over one hundred pesos, the sum they finally asked for. At the beginning of the year when the governor showed me these [directions for] reports, inventories, and census lists, of the mission [that were] to be sent to the commandancy general, I told him that I would care for it gladly, since the reverend father guardian of my holy college[17] had given me the same order.

But, that it had to be on condition, that the papers and letters for those documents would be post free, for I had received a letter from the commander general of much less bulk than any of these reports and it bore the notation: eleven reales. What would so many papers cost?

He answered me that yes [they were post free] and, in fact, the ensign always urged me to accept [such] letters saying, even in writing, that

the figures in question had reference to other accounts and that I would not have to pay it.

With that assurance, I went ahead certain that the envelope which came from San Gabriel entitled: "Reports, Inventories, and Census List of San Gabriel Mission" [was free even though] there was a notation, twenty reales, which I have kept by accident. Despite this, a few days ago we received a bill from the quartermaster for twenty-five pesos, two reales for [postage on] letters sent to the mission. They were the creditors and they collected. All we need now is some other arbitrary debt unknown to us.

What we get in the annual distributions purchased in Mexico with our stipends is known already. After using enough for our clothing, chocolate, wine, and candles for Mass, and some minor objects for the church, the rest goes for the Indians, especially for clothing to cover them. So far as we can see, nothing more need be said on this point.

If anything else should be made known about the administration and state of the mission, it can be asked of us specifically and with assurance that we will hide nothing, for thanks to the goodness of God we do not fear the light, and, since what has been said so far is true, we the ministers of the mission sign it, July 1, 1784.

Fray Junípero Serra—Fray Mathías Antonio de Santa Cathalina Noreiga [rubrica].

---

[17]The College of San Fernando in Mexico City had been formally established in 1733.

B. Great Awakening

The Great Awakening of 1734–1742 was probably the single most significant religious event in colonial North America. An effort to restore religious enthusiasm and win new converts to the faith, it began with a series of prayer gatherings led by the Puritan preacher Jonathan Edwards (1703–1758) in Northampton, Massachusetts. Inspired by Methodist and Pietist revivals in Europe (see 6D), Edwards and the fellow revivalists who followed in his wake proclaimed the Protestant doctrine of justification by faith (see 5B) and believed in the power of the preached word to effect conversion. From its first stirrings in Massachusetts, the movement set off a chain reaction of local "revivals" that quickly spread throughout the colonies. The peak of religious excitement came in 1740, when the famed English preacher George Whitefield (1714–1770) made a speaking tour of New England and the southern colonies, attracting huge crowds and bolstering sagging church attendance. The Great Awakening eventually subsided, but not before it had created a new and popular alternative to the established churches' more somber form of worship. With its large outdoor gatherings of Christians from various denominations spurred on by powerful preachers to religious remorse, rejoicing, and often "rebirth," this first and greatest American revival also established a pattern that Christian revivalists in this country have continued to follow to the present day (see 9B).

1. ACCOUNTS OF THE GREAT AWAKENING

Most historians credit the Puritan preacher Jonathan Edwards as the instigator of the Great Awakening, although many other Reformed, or Calvinist, pastors also played important roles in spreading the movement. Edwards was the preeminent American theologian of his day, and in 1734–1735 he had succeeded in generating a small religious revival in his own town of Northampton, Massachusetts. Five years later, he learned of the planned colonial tour of Englishman George Whitefield, whom he knew only by reputation. In the first reading below, Edwards enthusiastically writes the great Anglican homilist, inviting him to visit Northhampton, an invitation that Whitefield accepted several months later. At this time Whitefield was far and away the most famous preacher in the English-speaking world. His decision to tour the colonies came in the wake of a painful break with his friend and colleague John Wesley, who would go on to found the Methodist church. Though he disagreed with Wesley on the doctrine of predestination, Whitefield shared many of his friend's other goals and beliefs. Like Wesley, he was convinced that the spoken word (as well as music) had the ability to awaken dormant souls and in many cases effect a Christian rebirth.

Whitefield's first American tour, which he describes in passages from his diary quoted below, prompted a wide variety of reactions. Edwards and other influential Congregationalist ministers warmly endorsed his sermons, both for their theological content and their persuasive crowd appeal. Even the normally skeptical Benjamin Franklin (1706–1790) admitted to being so moved by Whitefield's preaching in Philadelphia that he ended up emptying his pockets for a proposed orphanage in Georgia. In the third reading below, drawn from his *Autobiography,* Franklin also describes using "scientific" methods to calculate the size of some of Whitefield's outdoor audiences, concluding that the preacher was comfortably heard (without any amplification) by up to 30,000 people at once. Other accounts estimate that in one month alone, Whitefield spoke every day to crowds of 7,000–8,000 each—at a time when the total population of New England was under 300,000. The contagious excitement preceding each of Whitefield's visits is obvious in the fourth reading, taken from the diary of a New Jersey farmer who traveled to hear the famous man and claimed a conversion experience as the result. Meanwhile, Whitefield also drew opponents such as the Anglican churchman Timothy Cutler, whose letters are excerpted in the final reading and who lamented the many calamities brought about by the revivalist's tour. Not only did Whitefield criticize the Church hierarchy, Cutler claimed, but he also spread a "mass hysteria" that undermined the rituals and the very essence of organized religion. Though Whitefield in fact never left or denied his own Anglican Church, it is true that the Great Awakening and revivalism in general did help break down denominational barriers.

a. JONATHAN EDWARDS, LETTER TO GEORGE WHITEFIELD (1740)

Northampton in New England, Feb. 12, 1739/40

Reverend Sir,

My request to you is, that in your intended journey through New England the next summer, you would be pleased to visit Northampton. I hope it is not wholly from curiosity that I desire to see and hear you in this place; but I apprehend, from what I have heard, that you are one that has the blessing of heaven attending you wherever you go: and I have a great desire, if it may be the will of God, that such a blessing as attends your desire, if it may be the will of God, that such a blessing as attends your person & labors may descend on this town, and may enter mine own house, and that I may receive it in my own soul. Indeed I am fearful whether you will not be disappointed in New England, and will have less success here than in other places: we who have dwelt in a land that has been distinguished with light, and have long enjoyed the gospel, and have been glutted with it, and have despised it, are I fear more hardened than most of those places where you have preached hitherto. But yet I hope in that power and mercy of God that has appeared so triumphant in the success of your labors in other places, that he will send a blessing with you even to us, though we are unworthy of it. I hope, if God preserves my life, to see something of that salvation of God in New England which he has now begun, in a benighted, wicked and miserable world and age and in the most guilty of all nations. It has been with refreshment of soul that I have heard of one raised up in the Church of England to revive the mysterious,

spiritual, despised and exploded doctrines of the gospel, and full of a spirit of zeal for the promotion of real vital piety, whose labors have been attended with such success. Blessed be God that hath done it! who is with you, and helps you, and makes the weapons of your warfare mighty. We see that God is faithful, and never will forget the promises that he has made to his church; and that he will not suffer the smoking flax to be quenched, even when the floods seem to be overwhelming it; but will revive the flame again, even in the darkest times. I hope this is the dawning of a day of God's mighty power and glorious grace to the world of mankind. May you go on reverend sir! and may God be with you more and more abundantly, that the work of God may be carried on by a blessing on your labors still, with that swift progress that it has been hitherto, and rise to a greater height, and extend further and further, with an irresistible power bearing down all opposition! And may the gates of hell never be able to prevail against you! and may God send forth more laborers into his harvest of a like spirit, until the kingdom of Satan shall shake, and his proud empire fall throughout the earth, and the kingdom of Christ, that glorious kingdom of light, holiness, peace and love, shall be established from one end of the earth unto the other!

Give my love to Mr. Seward:[18] I hope to see him here with you. I believe I may venture to say that what has been heard of your labors and success has not been taken notice of more in any place in New England than here, or received with fuller credit. I hope therefore if we have opportunity, we shall hear you with greater attention. The way from New York to

---

[18]William Seward, Whitefield's associate and publicist.

Boston through Northampton is but little further than the nearest that is; and I think leads through as populous a part of the country as any. I desire that you and Mr. Seward would come directly to my house. I shall account it a great favor and smile of providence to have opportunity to entertain such guests under my roof, and to have some acquaintance with such persons.

I fear it is too much for me to desire a particular remembrance in your prayers, when I consider how many thousands do doubtless desire it, who can't all be particularly mentioned; and I am far from thinking myself worthy to be distinguished. But pray, sir, let your heart be lifted up to God for me among others, that God would bestow much of that blessed Spirit on me that he has bestowed on you, and make me also an instrument of his glory.

I am, reverend sir,
unworthy to be called your
fellow laborer,
Jonathan Edwards

---

b. GEORGE WHITEFIELD, *DIARY* (1740)
Philadelphia

Thursday, May 8. Had what my body much wanted, a thorough night's repose. Was called up early in the morning, as I always am, to speak to poor souls under convictions. The first who came was an Indian trader, whom God was pleased to bring home by my preaching when here last. He is just come from the Indian nation, where he has been praying with and exhorting all he met who were willing to hear. He has hopes of some of the Indians; but his fellow-traders endeavoured to prejudice them against him. However, he proposes to visit them again in the autumn, and I humbly hope the Lord will open a door amongst the poor heathen. The conversion of one of their traders, I take to be one great step towards it. Lord, carry on the work begun. Fulfil Thy ancient promises, and let Thy Son have the heathen for His inheritance, and the utmost parts of the earth for His possession.

I conversed also with a poor negro woman, who has been visited in a very remarkable manner. God was pleased to convert her by my preaching last autumn; but being under dejections on Sunday morning, she prayed that salvation might come to her heart, and that the Lord would be pleased to manifest Himself to her soul that day. Whilst she was at meeting, hearing Mr. M———n, a Baptist preacher, the Word came with such power to her heart, that at last she was obliged to cry out; and a great concern fell upon many in the congregation. The minister stopped, and several persuaded her to hold her peace; but she could not help praising and blessing God. Many since this have called her mad, and said she was full of new wine; but the account she gave me was rational and solid, and, I believe in that hour the Lord Jesus took a great possession of her soul. Such cases, indeed, have not been very common; but when an extraordinary work is being carried on, God generally manifests Himself to some souls in this extraordinary manner. I doubt not, when the poor negroes are to be called, God will highly favour them, to wipe off their reproach, and shew that He is no respecter of persons, but that whosoever believeth in Him shall be saved.

Preached, at eleven, to six or seven thousand people, and cleared myself from some aspersions that had been cast upon my doctrine, as though it tended to Antinomianism.[19] I believe God has much people in the city of Philadelphia. The congregations are very large and serious, and I have scarce preached this time amongst them without stirring amongst the

---

[19] A rejection of all rules or laws, in this instance implying a radically subjective experience of Christianity.

dry bones.[20] At five in the evening I preached again, but to a rather larger audience; and, after sermon, rode ten miles to a friend's house, that I might be in readiness to preach the next morning, according to appointment. How differently am I treated from my Master! He taught people by day, and abode all night upon the Mount of Olives. He had not where to lay His head; but go where I will, I find people receiving me into their houses with great gladness. . . .

Boston

Friday, September 19. I was visited by several gentlemen and ministers, and went to the Governor's with Esquire Willard, the Secretary of the Province, a man fearing God, and with whom I have corresponded some time, though before unknown in person. The Governor received me with the utmost respect, and desired me to see him as often as I could. At eleven, I went to public worship at the Church of England, and afterwards went home with the Commissary,[21] who had read prayers. He received me very courteously; and, it being a day whereon the clergy of the Established Church met, I had an opportunity of conversing with five of them together. I think, one of them began with me for calling "that Tennent[22] and his brethren *faithful* ministers of Jesus Christ." I answered, "I believed they were." They then questioned me about "the validity of the Presbyterian ordination." I replied, "I believed it was valid." They then urged against me a passage in my first *Journal,* where I said, "That a Baptist minister at Deal did not give a satisfactory answer concerning his mis-

sion." I answered, "Perhaps my sentiments were altered." "And is Mr. Wesley[23] altered in his sentiments?" said one; "for he was very strenuous for the Church, and rigorous against all other forms of government when he was at Boston." I answered, "He was then a great bigot, but God has since enlarged his heart, and I believed he was now likeminded with me in this particular." I then urged, "That a catholic spirit was best, and that a Baptist minister had communicated lately with me at Savannah." "I suppose," said another, "you would do him a good turn, and would communicate with him." I answered, "Yes," and urged "that it was best to preach the new birth, and the power of godliness, and not to insist so much on the form: for people would never be brought to one mind as to that; nor did Jesus Christ ever intend it." "Yes, but He did," said Dr. Cutler. "How do you prove it?" "Because Christ prayed, 'That all might be one, even as Thou Father and I are One' [Jn 17:21]." I replied, "That was spoken of the inward union of the souls of believers with Jesus Christ, and not of the outward Church." "That cannot be," said Dr. Cutler, "for how then could it be said, 'that the world might know that Thou hast sent Me?' [Jn 17:21]" He then (taking it for granted that the Church of England was the only true apostolical Church) drew a parallel between the Jewish and our Church, urging how God required all things to be made according to the pattern given in the Mount. I answered, "That before the parallel could be just, it must be proved, that every thing enjoined in our Church was as much of a Divine institution as any rite or ceremony under the Jewish dispensation." I added further, "That I saw regenerate souls among the Baptists, among the Presbyterians, among the Independents, and among the Church folks,—all children of God, and yet all born again in a different way of worship: and who can tell which is the most evangelical?" "What, can you see regeneration with your eyes?" said the Commissary, or words to that effect.

---

[20]Cf. Ezek 37:11 and its description of the wind resurrecting the dry bones into warriors for the Lord, a favorite metaphor among eighteenth-century preachers for reviving the parched soul.

[21]Dr. Timothy Cutler (1684–1761), Anglican rector of Boston and fierce opponent of Whitefield's revival; see 7B1e.

[22]Gilbert Tennent (1703–1764), an itinerant Presbyterian preacher eventually banned in Connecticut for his unorthodox methods and arrested when he defied the ban. He was accused of inciting a riot at his arrest; later he served as a minister in New Brunswick, New Jersey.

---

[23]John Wesley (1703–1791), founder of Methodism and an associate of Whitefield's.

Soon after, we began to talk of the Righteousness of Christ, and the Commissary said, "Christ was to make up for the defects of our righteousness." I asked him, "Whether conversion was not instantaneous?" He was unwilling to confess it, but he having just before baptised an infant at public worship, I asked him, "Whether he believed that very instant in which he sprinkled the child with water, the Holy Ghost fell upon the child?" He answered, "Yes." "Then," said I, "according to your own principles, regeneration is instantaneous, and since you will judge of the new birth by the fruits, pray watch that child, and see if it brings forth the fruits of the Spirit. I also said, "That if every child was really born again in baptism, then every baptised infant would be saved." "And so they are," said Dr. Cutler. "How do you prove that?" "Because the Rubric[24] says, 'that all infants dying after baptism before they have committed actual sin, are undoubtedly saved.'" I asked, "What text of Scripture was there to prove it?" "Here," said he, (holding a Prayer Book in his hand) "the Church says so." We then just hinted at predestination. I said, "I subscribed to the seventeenth Article of the Church[25] in its literal sense with all my heart." We then talked a little about falling away finally from grace. I said, "A true child of God, though he might fall foully, yet could never fall finally." "But," said he, the Article says, "'Men may fall away from grace given.'" I answered, "But then observe what follows 'and by the grace of God they may rise again.'" Several other things of less consequence passed between us. Finding how inconsistent they were, I took my leave, resolving they should not have an opportunity of denying me the use of their pulpits. However, they treated me with more civility than any of our own clergymen have done for a long while. The Commissary very kindly urged me to dine with them; but, being pre-engaged, I went to my lodgings, and in the afternoon, preached to about four thousand people in Dr. Colman's meeting-house; and afterwards exhorted and prayed with many who came to my lodgings, rejoicing at the prospect there was of bringing many souls in Boston to the saving knowledge of the Lord Jesus Christ. Grant this, O Father, for Thy dear Son's sake! Amen.

---

[24]The ritual instructions and interpretations of the Church of England, highlighted in red ("rubric") in the *Book of Common Prayer,* were often a focus of controversy between "High Church" and "Low Church" (especially Methodist) Anglicans.

[25]A reference to the Thirty-nine Articles (1563), which together with the *Book of Common Prayer* constitute the doctrinal statements of the Church of England. The seventeenth article expressed a Reformed understanding of divine election, which Whitefield accepted while his colleague John Wesley did not. All Anglican clergy and laity of this period were required to subscribe to the statements in their entirety.

---

c. BENJAMIN FRANKLIN, *AUTOBIOGRAPHY* (1771)

Mr. Whitfield, in leaving us, went preaching all the Way thro' the Colonies to Georgia. The Settlement of that Province had lately begun; but instead of being made with hardy industrious Husbandmen accustomed to Labour, the only People fit for such an Enterprise, it was with Families of broken Shopkeepers and other insolvent Debtors, many of indolent and idle habits, taken out of the Gaols, who being set down in the Woods, unqualified for clearing Land, and unable to endure the Hardships of a new Settlement, perished in Numbers, leaving many helpless Children unprovided for. The Sight of their miserable Situation inspired the benevolent Heart of Mr. Whitfield with the Idea of building an Orphan House there, in which they might be supported and educated. Returning northward he preach'd up this Charity, and made large Collections; for his Eloquence had a wonderful Power over the Hearts and Purses of his Hearers, of which I myself was an Instance. I did not disapprove of the Design, but as Georgia was then destitute of Materials and Workmen, and it was propos'd to send them from Philadelphia at a great Expence, I thought it would have been better to have built the House here and brought the Children to it. This I advis'd, but he was resolute in his first Project, and rejected my Counsel, and I thereupon refus'd to contribute. I happened soon after to attend one of his Sermons, in the Course of which I perceived he intended to finish with a Collection, and I silently resolved he should get nothing from me. I had in my Pocket a Handful of Copper Money, three or four Silver Dollars, and five Pistoles in Gold. As he proceeded I began to soften, and concluded to give the Coppers. Another Stroke of his Oratory made me asham'd of that, and determin'd me to give the Silver; and he finish'd so admirably, that I empty'd my Pocket wholly into the Collector's Dish, Gold and all. At this Sermon there was also one of our Club, who being of my Sentiments respecting the Building in Georgia, and suspecting a Collection might be intended, had by Precaution emptied his Pockets before he came from home; towards the Conclusion of the Discourse, however, he felt a strong Desire to give, and apply'd to a Neighbour who stood near him to borrow some Money for the Purpose. The Application was unfortunately to perhaps the only Man in the Company who had the firmness not to be affected by the Preacher. His Answer was, *At any other time, Friend Hopkinson, I would lend to thee freely; but not now; for thee seems to be out of thy right Senses.*

Some of Mr. Whitfield's Enemies effected to suppose that he would apply these Collections to his own private Emolument; but I, who was intimately acquainted with him, (being employ'd in printing his Sermons and Journals, &c.) never had the least Suspicion of his Integrity, but am to this day decidedly of the Opinion that he was in all his Conduct, a perfectly *honest Man*. And methinks my Testimony in his Favour ought to have the more Weight, as we had no religious Connection. He us'd indeed sometimes to pray for my Conversion, but never had the Satisfaction of believing that his

Prayers were heard. Ours was a mere civil Friendship, sincere on both Sides, and lasted to his Death. . . .

The last time I saw Mr. Whitfield was in London, when he consulted me about his Orphan House Concern, and his Purpose of appropriating it to the Establishment of a College.

He had a loud and clear Voice, and articulated his Words and Sentences so perfectly that he might be heard and understood at a great Distance, especially as his Auditories, however numerous, observ'd the most exact Silence. He preach'd one Evening from the Top of the Court House Steps, which are in the Middle of Market Street, and on the West Side of Second Street which crosses it at right angles. Both Streets were fill'd with his Hearers to a considerable Distance. Being among the hindmost in Market Street, I had the Curiosity to learn how far he could be heard, by retiring backwards down the Street towards the River, and I found his Voice distinct till I came near Front-Street, when some Noise in that Street, obscur'd it. Imagining then a Semi-Circle, of which my Distance should be the Radius, and that it were fill'd with Auditors, to each of whom I allow'd two square feet, I computed that he might well be heard by more than Thirty-Thousand. This reconcil'd me to the Newspaper Accounts of his having preach'd to 25,000 People in the Fields, and to the ancient Histories of Generals haranguing whole Armies, of which I had sometimes doubted.

By hearing him often I came to distinguish easily between Sermons newly compos'd, and those which he had often preach'd in the Course of his Travels. His Delivery of the latter was so improv'd by frequent Repetitions, that every Accent, every Emphasis, every Modulation of Voice, was so perfectly well turn'd and well plac'd, that without being interested in the Subject, one could not help being pleas'd with the Discourse, a Pleasure of much the same kind with that receiv'd from an excellent Piece of Musick. This is an Advantage itinerant Preachers have over those who are stationary: as the latter cannot well improve their Delivery of a Sermon by so many Rehearsals.

d. NATHAN COLE, *DIARY* (1740)

Now it pleased god to send mr. whitfeld into this land & my hearing of his preaching at philadelphia like one of the old aposles, & many thousands flocking after him to hear ye gospel and great numbers were converted to Christ, i felt the spirit of god drawing me by conviction i longed to see & hear him & wished he would come this way and i soon heard he was come to new york & ye jases [Jerseys] & great multitudes flocking after him under great concern for their Soule & many converted which brought on my concern more & more hoping soon to see him but next i herd he was on long iland & next at boston & next at northampton & then one morning all on a Suding about 8 or 9 o Clock there came a messenger & said mr. whitfeld preached at hartford & weathersfield yesterday & is to preach at middeltown this morning at 10 o clock i was in my field at work i dropt my tool that i had in my hand & run home & run throu my house & bad my wife get ready quick to goo and hear mr. whitfield preach at middeltown & run to my pasture for my hors with all my might fearing i should be too late to hear him i brought my hors home & soon mounted & took my wife up & went forward as fast as i thought ye hors could bear, & when my hors began to be out of breath i would get down & put my wife on ye Saddel & bid her ride as fast as she could & not Stop or Slak for me except I bad her & so i would run untill i was almost out of breth & then mount my hors again & so i did severel times to favour my hors we improved every moment to get along as if we was fleeing for our lives all this while fearing we should be too late to hear ye Sarmon for we had twelve miles to ride dubble in littel more then an hour & we went round by the upper housen parish & when we came within about a half a mile of ye road that comes down from hartford weathersfield & stepney to middeltown on high land i saw before me a Cloud or fog rising i first thought off

from ye great river but as i came nearer ye road i heard a noise something like a low rumbling thunder & i presently found it was ye rumbling of horses feet coming down ye road & this Cloud was a Cloud of dust made by ye running of horses feet it arose some rods into ye air over the tops of ye hills & trees & when i came within about twenty rods of ye road i could see men & horses Sliping along in ye Cloud like shadows & when i came nearer it was like a stedy streem of horses & their riders scarcely a horse more than his length behind another all of a lather and some with swet ther breath rooling out of their noistrels in ye cloud of dust every jump every hors semed to go with all his might to carry his rider to hear ye news from heaven for ye saving of their Souls it made me trembel to see ye Sight how ye world was in a strugle i found a vacance between two horses to Slip in my hors & my wife said law our cloaths will be all spoiled see how they look for they was so covered with dust that thay looked allmost all of a coler coats & hats & shirts & horses We went down in ye Streem i herd no man speak a word all ye way three mile but evry one presing forward in great hast & when we gat down to ye old meating house thare was a great multitude it was said to be 3 or 4000 of people asembled together we gat of from our horses & shook off ye dust and ye ministers was then coming to the meating house i turned and looked toward ye great river & saw the fery boats running swift forward & backward bringing over loads of people ye ores roed nimble & quick every thing men horses & boats all seamed to be struglin for life ye land & ye banks over ye river lookt black with people & horses all along ye 12 miles i see no man at work in his field but all seamed to be gone—when i see mr. whitfield came up upon ye Scaffil he looked almost angellical a young slim slender youth before some thousands of people & with a bold undainted countenance & my hearing how god was with him every where as he came along its solumnized my mind & put me in a trembling fear before he began to preach for he looked as if he was Cloathed with authority from ye great god, & a sweet sollome Solemnity sat upon his brow & my hearing him preach gave me a heart wound by gods blessing my old foundation was broken up & i saw that my righteousness would not save me then i was convinced of ye doctrine of Election & went right to quareling with god about it because all that i could do would not save me & he had decreed from Eternity who should be saved & who not i began to think i was not Elected & that god made some for heaven & me for hell & i thought god was not Just in so doing i thought i did not stand on even Ground with others if as i thought i was made to be damned my heart then rose against god exceedigly for his making me for hell now this distress lasted almost two years.

---

e. TIMOTHY CUTLER, LETTERS (1740, 1742)

{To the Secretary of the Society for the Propagation of the Gospel, 11 December 1740}

... The whole Church in this Town and the adjacent parts, with all the Church both at home and abroad, hath felt the ill effects of Mr. Whitefield's visits. Our sufferings here are very particular, being but an handful to the dissenters, who of all orders and degrees were highly fond of his coming, and gave him a most hearty and distinguishing welcome, and strived to excell one another in it, and to be cold or differently effected is with them a pretty strong mark of reprobation. The clergy of this Town never invited him into their Pulpits, nor did he ask them, nor ever attended any one of our Churches, saving one Friday at Prayers, upon his first entrance, to make himself known to us, tho' he tarried over three Sundays in Town, daily preaching in our Meeting Houses, and in open places, and was an hearer among the Dissenters[26] on one part of two Sundays. Bishops, Divines, Churchmen and Christians are with us, good or bad, as he describes them, and nothing but a conformity to his notions and rules will give us a shining character. The Idea he gives us of the present Church (and too many receive it) is Heterodoxy, Falsehood to our articles and rules, Persecution, and never more so. The principals, and books and practices of this Country are applauded and preferred to everything now in the Church, and People are exhorted to adhere to their Dissenting Pastors.

Too many unhappy Feuds and Debates are owing to Mr. Whitfield's being among us; and we have even disobliged the Dissenters in suffering them to engross him, but I hope the Fury and Ferment is subsiding, and that we shall at length be tolerably sweetened towards one another. What may hinder it are the enthusiastic Notions very much kindled among us and like to be propagated by his Writings, dispersed everywhere, with Antinomianism revived, and I fear also, Infidel and Libertine Principles, which some express a particular fondness for at this time. Our labours among our people would be very much assisted by suitable Books on these subjects, and the Society's bounty in this kind never wants good effects, tho' not so large as good men wish.

{To the Bishop of London, 14 January 1742}

... [Since my earlier letter], Enthusiasm has swell'd to much higher degrees of madness; and nothing is too bad wherewith to stigmatize those who disapprove of it so that should the Friends of it encrease much more, their Bitterness, Fury & Rage might well make us tremble. They assemble People in Towns and frequently enter Meeting Houses without the knowledge or Liking of the Proper Teachers, who commonly think it safest for them to stifle their Resentments. Those who could not act that Prudence have many of them had Parties made among them to their great Vexation, and some Laymen or other have started up, and Strengthened the Schism in the Exercise of their Gifts of

---

[26]Nonconformists to the Church of England, in this instance referring mainly to Methodists.

Praying and Preaching, and indeed the Times are fruitful of many such Ruling Elders, Deacons, and other illiterate Mechanics, who neglect or lay aside their callings for this Purpose, and are much admired and followed by the People. Two of them have enter'd this Town and affected multitudes; and one of them has had the Liberty of sundry Dissenting Pulpits; here as well as elsewhere, we have new Lectures in abundance, stated and occasional, by Day and Night. Here Children and Servants stroll, withdrawing themselves from Family care and Subjection; and Day Labourers spend much of their Time, expecting notwithstanding full Wages. In some Places (this Town not excepted), Lectures, especially Evening ones, are attended with hideous Yellings, and shameful Revels, continuing till Midnight, and till Break of Day, and much Wickedness is justly feared to be the Consequence of Them.

C. Premillennialism

Ever since the resurrected Jesus promised his apostles that he would return to them (cf. Mt 24, 25; Mk 13:24 ff.; Lk 21:25 ff.), Christians have looked with expectation to the Second Coming. For most ancient Christians, this was apparently considered to be an imminent event, often conflated with the Final Judgment and end of the world. The Book of Revelation, or Apocalypse, offers a vivid and dramatic description of the cataclysms and other consequences associated with Christ's return to earth. Since the days of the early church, a minority of Christians—known in modern times as premillennialists—have believed that the Second Coming (especially as prophesied in the Book of Revelation) would mark the beginning of one thousand years, or a millennium, of peace and prosperity among true Christians. During the Middle Ages and Reformation era, this belief was held only by a few tiny sects, such as the heretical Waldensians or persecuted Münster Anabaptists. By the start of the nineteenth century, however, carefully calculated predictions of the apocalyptic beginning of the millennium had become increasingly popular. The most famous prediction, based on an elaborate decoding of several biblical prophecies, was that of the American William Miller (1782–1848). For Miller, the key Scriptural passage was Daniel 8:14, in which a predicted restoration of the temple of Jerusalem in 2,300 days was interpreted to mean the Second Coming of the embodiment of the Temple, Jesus himself, in 2,300 years. Dating the prophecy from 457 B.C.E., Miller came up with an estimate that Christ would return between March 1843 and March 1844. When neither Christ nor the millennium arrived during this period or by a later recalculated 1844 date, Miller and his thousands of followers were thrown into the despair of "the Great Disappointment." Nevertheless, by the end of the nineteenth century, several other premillennial or Adventist groups emerged, each predicated on a somewhat different understanding of the Second Coming's timing and consequences. The most successful of these denominations have been the Seventh Day Adventists and the Jehovah's Witnesses, each claiming millions of adherents today. Because of their extensive missionary work, both churches have gained more converts abroad than any other American-based church (with the possible exception of the Mormons).

1. Ellen G. White
THE GREAT CONTROVERSY (1888)

Ellen Gould White (1827–1915) came from a family of Millerite premillennialists who endured "the Great Disappointment" of 1844. In the years immediately following, she and her husband, James V. White, gathered a small number of other Millerites to form a new church known as Sabbatarian Adventists. Like Miller, the group based its interpretation of the Second Coming on Dan 8:14. According to a vision of Ellen White's, however, 1844 marked the beginning of a new age for Christians (when Jesus entered a heavenly Holy of Holies) rather than the imminent bodily return of Christ. During the course of her long life, White would experience many other visions, eventually filling nine published volumes and touching on issues ranging from proper dress and hygiene (White advocated complete abstention from alcohol, tobacco, and meat) to the doctrine of "soul sleep," a belief that the soul dies with the body and that only the souls of true Christians will be resurrected during the Second Coming. In the following excerpt, White discusses the calculation for the "opening of the sanctuary" in 1844 as well as the key Adventist teaching of Sabbatarianism. The traditional Christian designation of Sunday, the first day of the week, as the Lord's Day was in White's eyes a direct violation of the Bible's commandment to keep holy the Sabbath, or the seventh day. Only by purifying the church of this and other "papist" corruptions, she wrote, could true Christians hope to be counted among the 144,000 "saints" the Book of Revelation said would be granted eternal life when Christ eventually did return.

The prophecy which seemed most clearly to reveal the *time* of the second advent was that of Dan 8:14: "Unto two thousand and three hundred days; then shall the sanctuary be cleansed." Following his rule of making Scripture its own interpreter, Miller learned that a day in symbolic prophecy represents a year [Num 14:34; Ezek 4:6]; he saw that the period of 2,300 prophetic days, or literal years, would extend far beyond the close of the Jewish dispensation, hence it could not refer to the sanctuary of that dispensation. Miller accepted the generally received view, that in the Christian age the earth is the sanctuary, and he therefore understood that the cleansing of the sanctuary foretold in Dan 8:14 represented the purification of the earth by fire at the second coming of Christ. If, then, the correct starting-point could be found for the 2,300 days, he concluded that the time of the second advent could be readily ascertained. Thus would be revealed the time of that great consummation, the time when the present state, with "all its pride and power, pomp and vanity, wickedness and oppression, would come to an end;" when the curse would be "removed from off the earth, death be destroyed, reward be given to the servants of God, the prophets and saints, and them who fear His name, and those be destroyed that destroy the earth."[27] . . .

The angel had been sent to Daniel for the express purpose of explaining to him the point which he had failed to understand in the vision of the eighth chapter, the statement relative to time,—"Unto two thousand and three hundred days; then shall the sanctuary be cleansed." After bidding Daniel "understand the matter, and consider the vision," the very first words of

---

[27]White is quoting the *Memoirs of William Miller* (1849).

the angel are, "Seventy weeks are determined upon thy people and upon thy holy city." The word here translated "determined," literally signifies "cut off." Seventy weeks, representing 490 years, are declared by the angel to be cut off, as specially pertaining to the Jews. But from what were they cut off? As the 2,300 days was the only period of time mentioned in chapter eight, it must be the period from which the seventy weeks were cut off; the seventy weeks must therefore be a part of the 2,300 days, and the two periods must begin together. The seventy weeks were declared by the angel to date from the going forth of the commandment to restore and build Jerusalem. If the date of this commandment could be found, then the starting-point for the great period of the 2,300 days would be ascertained.

In the seventh chapter of Ezra the decree is found [Ezra 7:12–26]. In its completest form it was issued by Artaxerxes, king of Persia, B.C. 457. But in Ezra 6:14 the house of the Lord at Jerusalem is said to have been built "according to the commandment of Cyrus, and Darius, and Artaxerxes king of Persia." These three kings, in originating, re-affirming, and completing the decree, brought it to the perfection required by the prophecy to mark the beginning of the 2,300 years. Taking B.C. 457, the time when the decree was completed, as the date of the commandment, every specification of the prophecy concerning the seventy weeks was seen to have been fulfilled.

"From the going forth of the commandment to restore and to build Jerusalem unto the Messiah the Prince shall be seven weeks, and three-score and two weeks,"—namely, sixty-nine weeks, or 483 years. The decree of Artaxerxes went into effect in the autumn of B.C. 457. From this date, 483 years extend to the autumn of A.D. 27. At that time this prophecy was fulfilled. The word "Messiah" signifies "the Anointed One." In the autumn of A.D. 27, Christ was baptized by John, and received the anointing of the Spirit. The apostle Peter testifies that "God anointed Jesus of Nazareth with the Holy Ghost and with power" [Acts 10:38].

And the Saviour Himself declared, "The Spirit of the Lord is upon Me, because He hath anointed Me to preach the gospel to the poor" [Lk 4:18]. After His baptism He went into Galilee, "preaching the gospel of the kingdom of God, and saying, *The time* is fulfilled" [Mk 1:14, 15].

"And He shall confirm the covenant with many for one week." The "week" here brought to view is the last one of the seventy; it is the last seven years of the period allotted especially to the Jews. During this time, extending from A.D. 27 to A.D. 34, Christ, at first in person and afterward by His disciples, extended the gospel invitation especially to the Jews. As the apostles went forth with the good tidings of the kingdom, the Saviour's direction was, "Go not into the way of the Gentiles, and into any city of the Samaritans enter ye not: but go rather to the lost sheep of the house of Israel" [Mt 10:5, 6]. . . .

Thus far every specification of the prophecies is strikingly fulfilled, and the beginning of the seventy weeks is fixed beyond question at B.C. 457, and their expiration in A.D. 34. From this data there is no difficulty in finding the termination of the 2,300 days. The seventy weeks—490 days—having been cut off from the 2,300, there were 1,810 days remaining. After the end of 490 days, the 1,810 days were still to be fulfilled. From A.D. 34, 1,810 years extend to 1844. Consequently the 2,300 days of Dan 8:14 terminate in 1844. At the expiration of this great prophetic period, upon the testimony of the angel of God, "the sanctuary shall be cleansed" [Dan 8:14]. Thus the time of the cleansing of the sanctuary—which was almost universally believed to take place at the second advent—was definitely pointed out.

Miller and his associates at first believed that the 2,300 days would terminate in the *spring* of 1844, whereas the prophecy points to the *autumn* of that year. The misapprehension of this point brought disappointment and perplexity to those who had fixed upon the earlier date as the time of the Lord's coming. But this did not in the least affect the strength of the argument showing that the 2,300 days terminated in the year 1844, and that the great event represented by the cleansing of the sanctuary must then take place. . . .

But clearer light came with the investigation of the sanctuary question. They now saw that they were correct in believing that the end of the 2,300 days in 1844 marked an important crisis. But while it was true that that door of hope and mercy by which men had for eighteen hundred years found access to God, was closed, another door was opened, and forgiveness of sins was offered to men through the intercession of Christ in the most holy. One part of His ministration had closed, only to give place to another. There was still an "open door" to the heavenly sanctuary, where Christ was ministering in the sinner's behalf.

Now was seen the application of those words of Christ in the Revelation, addressed to the church at this very time: "These things saith He that is holy, He that is true, He that hath the key of David, He that openeth, and no man shutteth; and shutteth, and no man openeth; I know thy works: behold, I have set before thee an open door, and no man can shut it" [Rev 3:7, 8]. . . .

The passing of the time in 1844 was followed by a period of great trial to those who still held the advent faith. Their only relief, so far as ascertaining their true position was concerned, was the light which directed their minds to the sanctuary above. Some renounced their faith in their former reckoning of the prophetic periods, and ascribed to human or satanic agencies the powerful influence of the Holy Spirit which had attended the Advent Movement. Another class firmly held that the Lord had led them in their past experience; and as they waited and watched and prayed to know the will of God, they saw that their great High Priest had entered upon another work of ministration, and following Him by faith, they were led to see also the closing work of the church. . . .

The papacy has attempted to change the law of God. The second commandment, forbidding image worship, has been dropped from the law, and the fourth commandment has been so changed as to authorize the observance of the first instead of the seventh day as the Sabbath. But papists urge, as a reason for omitting the second commandment, that it is unnecessary, being included in the first, and that they are giving the law exactly as God designed it to be understood. This cannot be the change foretold by the prophet. An intentional, deliberate change is presented: "He shall *think* to change the times and the law." The change in the fourth commandment exactly fulfils the prophecy. For this the only authority claimed is that of the church. Here the papal power openly sets itself above God.

While the worshipers of God will be especially distinguished by their regard for the fourth commandment,—since this is the sign of His creative power, and the witness to His claim upon man's reverence and homage—the worshipers of the beast will be distinguished by their efforts to tear down the Creator's memorial, to exalt the institution of Rome. It was in behalf of the Sunday that popery first asserted its arrogant claims; and its first resort to the power of the state was to compel the observance of Sunday as "the Lord's day." But the Bible points to the seventh day, and not to the first, as the Lord's day. Said Christ, "The Son of man is Lord also of the Sabbath" [Mt 12:8; Mk 2:28; Lk 6:5]. The fourth commandment declares, "The seventh day is the Sabbath of the Lord" [Ex 16:26]. And by the prophet Isaiah the Lord designates it, "My holy day" [Mk 2:28; Isa 58:13].

The claim so often put forth, that Christ changed the Sabbath, is disproved by His own words. In His sermon on the mount He said: "Think not that I am come to destroy the law, or the prophets: I am not come to destroy, but to fulfil. For verily I say unto you, Till heaven and earth pass, one jot or one tittle shall in no wise pass from the law, till all be fulfilled. Whosoever therefore shall break one of these least commandments, and shall teach men so, he shall be called the least in the kingdom of heaven: but whosoever shall do and teach them, the same shall be called great in the kingdom of heaven" [Mt 5:17–19].

It is a fact generally admitted by Protestants, that the Scriptures give no authority for the change of the Sabbath. This is plainly stated in publications issued by the American Tract Society and the American Sunday-school Union. One of these works acknowledges "the complete silence of the New Testament so far as any explicit command for the Sabbath [Sunday, the first day of the week] or definite rules for its observance are concerned."

Another says: "Up to the time of Christ's death, no change had been made in the day;" and, "so far as the record shows, they [the apostles] did not . . . give any explicit command enjoining the abandonment of the seventh-day Sabbath, and its observance on the first day of the week."

Roman Catholics acknowledge that the change of the Sabbath was made by their church, and declare that Protestants, by observing the Sunday, are recognizing her power. In the "Catholic Catechism of Christian Religion," in answer to a question as to the day to be observed in obedience to the fourth commandment, this statement is made: "During the old law, Saturday was the day sanctified; but *the church*, instructed by Jesus Christ, and directed by the Spirit of God, has substituted Sunday for Saturday; so now we sanctify the first, not the seventh day. Sunday means, and now is, the day of the Lord."

As the sign of the authority of the Catholic Church, papist writers cite "the very act of changing the Sabbath into Sunday, which Protestants allow of; . . . because by keeping Sunday, they acknowledge the church's power to ordain feasts, and to command them under sin." What then is the change of the Sabbath, but the sign, or mark, of the authority of the Roman Church—"the mark of the beast"? [cf. Rev 13 ff.]

The Roman Church has not relinquished her claim to supremacy; and when the world and the Protestant churches accept a sabbath of her creating, while they reject the Bible Sabbath, they virtually admit this assumption. They may claim the authority of tradition and of the Fathers for the change; but in so doing they ignore the very principle which separates them from Rome,—that "the Bible, and the Bible only, is the religion of Protestants." The papist can see that they are deceiving themselves, willingly closing their eyes to the facts in the case. As the movement for Sunday enforcement gains favor, he rejoices, feeling assured that it will eventually bring the whole Protestant world under the banner of Rome. . . .

In the issue of the contest, all Christendom will be divided into two great classes,—those who keep the commandments of God and the faith of Jesus, and those who worship the beast and his image and receive his mark. Although church and state will unite their power to compel "all, both small and great, rich and poor, free and bond," to receive "the mark of the beast" [Rev 13:16], yet the people of God will not receive it. The prophet of Patmos beholds "them that had gotten the victory over the beast, and over his image, and over his mark, and over the number of his name, stand on the sea of glass, having the harps of God," and singing the song of Moses and the Lamb [Rev 15:2, 3].

D. Abolitionism

Slavery was ubiquitous in the ancient world and was apparently tolerated by St. Paul and other early Christians, who nonetheless urged converted masters to free their slaves. After the fall of the western Roman Empire, slavery was gradually transformed into a milder form of servitude, sometimes known as serfdom, which itself had virtually disappeared in western Europe by the dawn of the

Reformation. At the very same time, however, Europeans living in the Americas began a new chapter in the history of slavery, buying and selling captive Africans—and, for a short time, American Indians—who were put to work on the vast plantations of the New World. Many churchmen and Catholic missionaries in particular condemned the practice. But a subsequent prohibition by the Spanish crown applied only to Native Americans, and the importation of black slaves to New World colonies grew by leaps and bounds over the course of the next three centuries totaling thirteen million African captives by the end of the eighteenth century. In 1619 the first African slaves were brought into the English colonies, and by the time of the American colonial rebellion in 1776, the institution of slavery had become indispensable to the economic prosperity of most of the southern colonies. A minority of American Quakers and Puritans had spoken out against the practice as fundamentally unchristian and had outlawed it in Pennsylvania and elsewhere. When it came time to write a constitution for the newly created United States of America, however, the Founding Fathers bowed to pressure from slaveowners and traders and, in contradiction to their claim that "all men are created equal," continued to permit slavery in the new nation. By the beginning of the nineteenth century, though, the chorus of voices demanding the abolition of slavery had grown much louder. Freed blacks joined with white northerners in the abolitionist crusade, and by the 1850s the United States appeared poised to join the majority of European nations that had already prohibited slavery. Tragically, however, the tensions over slavery and other issues led instead to a bloody civil war. It was only at the war's conclusion in 1865 that the abolitionists' goal was achieved with the freedom and enfranchisement of African-American slaves in the Thirteenth and Fourteenth amendments to the U.S. Constitution.

1. Samuel Sewall
THE SELLING OF JOSEPH: A MEMORIAL (1700)

Samuel Sewall (1652–1730) was a devout Puritan and a judge of the Supreme Court of Massachusetts. His argument against slavery was at its core a religious one, though it remained a minority opinion among Puritans and other American Christians until well into the nineteenth century. Most Christians of the day considered the many references to slavery in the Old and New Testaments as justification for continuing the practice in modern times. Sewall, however, saw the injustices and cruelties described in the very same passages as conclusive biblical evidence that the institution of slavery always had been and always would be wrong and against God's wishes. His celebration of personal liberty as a gift second only to life itself has much in common with John Locke's famous formulation of human rights as well as with key passages in the much later Declaration of Independence. Sewall's combination of a biblical interpretation and natural law creates what might seem to the modern reader to be a powerful argument against slavery. Yet he was a man ahead of his time. It would be another one hundred years before a significant number of Americans would share his beliefs.

Forasmuch as Liberty *is in real value next unto* Life: *None ought to part with it themselves, or deprive others of it, but upon most mature consideration.*

The Numerousness of Slaves at this Day in the Province, and the Uneasiness of them under their Slavery, hat put many upon thinking whether the Foundation of it be firmly and well laid; so as to sustain the Vast Weight that is built upon it. It is most certain that all Men, as they are the Sons of Adam, are Co-heirs, and have equal Right unto Liberty, and all other outward Comforts of Life. God *hath given the Earth {with all its commodities} unto the Sons of Adam. Ps 115, 16. And hath made of one Blood all nations of Men, for to dwell on all the face of the Earth and hath determined the Times before appointed, and the bounds of their Habitation: That they should seek the Lord. Forasmuch then as we are the Offspring of God, &c.* Acts 17, 26, 27, 29. Now, although the Title given by the last Adam doth infinitely better Men's Estates, respecting God and themselves; and grants them a most beneficial and inviolable Lease under the Broad Seal of Heaven, who were before only Tenants at Will; yet through the Indulgence of God to our First Parents after the Fall, the outward Estate of all and every of their Children, remains the same as to one another. So that Originally, and Naturally, there is no such thing as Slavery. Joseph was rightfully no more a Slave to his Brethren, than they were to him; and they had no more Authority to Sell him, than they had to Slay him. And if they had nothing to do to sell him; the Ishmaelites bargaining with them, and paying down Twenty pieces of Silver, could not make a Title. Neither could Potiphar have any better Interest in him than the Ishmaelites had. Gen 37, 20, 27, 28. For he that shall in this case plead Alteration of Property, seems to have forfeited a great part of his own claim to Humanity. There is no proportions between Twenty Pieces of Silver and Liberty. The Commodity itself is the Claimer. If Arabian Gold be imported in any quantities, most are afraid to meddle with it, though they might have it an easy rates; lest it should have been wrongfully taken from the Owners, it should kindle a fire to the Consumption of their whole Estate. 'Tis pity there should be more Caution used in buying a Horse, or a little lifeless dust, than there is in purchasing men and Women. . . .

And all things considered, it would conduce more to the Welfare of the Province, to have White Servants for a Term of Years, than to have Slaves for Life. Few can endure to hear of a Negro's being made free; and indeed they can seldom use their Freedom well; yet their continual aspiring after their forbidden Liberty, renders them Unwilling Servants. And there is such a disparity in their Conditions, Colour, and Hair, that they can never embody with us, & grow up in orderly Families, to the Peopling of the Land, but still remain in our Body Politick as a kind of extravasat[28] Blood. As many Negro Men as there are among us, so many empty Places are there in our Train Bands, and the places taken up of Men that might make Husbands for our Daughters. And the Sons and Daughters of New England would become more like Jacob and Rachel, if this Slavery were thrust quite out of Doors. Moreover it is too well known what Temptations masters are under, to connive at the Fornication of their Slaves, lest they should be obliged to find them Wives, or pay their Fines. It seems to be practically pleaded that they might be lawless; 'tis thought much of, that the Law should have satisfaction for their Thefts, and other Immoralities; by which means, Holiness to the Lord is more rarely engraved upon this sort of Servitude. It is likewise most lamentable to think, how in taking Negroes out of Africa, and selling of them here, That which God has joined together, Men do boldly rend assunder; men from their Country, Husbands from their Wives, Parents from their Children. How horrible is the Uncleanness, Mortality, if not Murder, that the Ships are guilty of that bring great Crouds of these miserable Men and Women. Methinks when we are bemoaning the

---

[28]Blood that is ready to erupt or be drawn into the surrounding body tissue.

barbarous Usage of our Friends and Kinsfolk in Africa, it might not be unreasonable to enquire whether we are not culpable in forcing the Africans to become Slaves amongst ourselves. And it may be a question whether all the Bene-

fit received by Negro Slaves will balance the Accompt of Cash laid out upon them; and for the Redemption of our own enslaved Friends out of Africa.

2. David Walker
FOUR ARTICLES (1829)

The abolitionist movement of the nineteenth century relied as much on emancipated slaves and other free blacks as it did on white activists. David Walker (1785–1830) was born to a slave father and free black mother in North Carolina. Assuming the free status of his mother, he moved to Boston, where he operated a used clothing store and became an outspoken proponent of abolitionism. Like most abolitionists, Walker felt extreme disgust at the hypocrisy of white Christians—especially clerics—who were busy converting foreign "heathens" but cared little for the salvation or liberty of the African-American slaves in their midst. His writings also contained apocalyptic warnings of destruction, which led many slaveholders—as well as many fellow abolitionists—to believe that Walker advocated a slave revolt. His death soon after publishing the following tract remains shrouded in mystery, with historians unable to confirm or deny rumors that Walker was poisoned by one of his numerous enemies. A year after his death, however, slaveowners' worst fears were realized in the violent slave uprising led by the slave preacher Nat Turner in Virginia. Turner and his followers were eventually caught and executed, but only after more than 250 people, most of them black, had lost their lives.

ARTICLE III: OUR WRETCHEDNESS IN CONSEQUENCE OF THE PREACHERS OF RELIGION

Religion, my brethren, is a substance of deep consideration among all nations of the earth. The Pagans have a kind, as well as the Mahometans, the Jews and the Christians. But pure and undefiled religion, such as was preached by Jesus Christ and his apostles, is hard to be found in all the earth. God, through his instrument, Moses, handed a dispensation of his divine will to the children of Israel after they had left Egypt for the land of Canaan, or of Promise, who through hypocrisy, oppression, and unbelief, departed from the faith. He then,

by his apostles handed a dispensation of his, together with the will of Jesus Christ, to the Europeans in Europe, who, in open violation of which, have made *merchandize* of us, and it does appear as though they take this very dispensation to aid them in their infernal depredations upon us. Indeed, the way in which religions was and is conducted by the Europeans and their descendants, one might believe it was a plan fabricated by themselves and the *devils* to oppress us. But hark! my master has taught me better than to believe it—he has taught me that his gospel as it was preached by himself and his apostles remains the same, notwithstanding Europe has tried to mingle blood and oppression with it.

It is well known to the Christian world that Bartholomew Las Casas [1474–1556], that very notoriously avaricious Catholic priest or preacher, and adventurer with Columbus in his second voyage, proposed to his countrymen, the Spaniards in Hispaniola, to import Africans from the Portuguese settlement in Africa, to dig up gold and silver, and work their plantations for them, to effect which, he made a voyage thence to Spain, and opened the subject to his master, Ferdinand, then in declining health, who listened to the plan; but who died soon after, and left it in the hands of his successor, Charles V. This wretch ("Las Cassas, the Preacher,") succeeded so well in his plans of oppression, that in 1503, the first blacks had been imported into the new world. Elated with this success, and stimulated by sordid avarice only, he importuned Charles V, in 1511, to grant permission to a Flemish merchant to import 4,000 blacks at one time. Thus we see, through the instrumentality of a pretended preacher of the gospel of Jesus Christ our common master, our wretchedness first commenced in America—where it has been continued from 1503 to this day, 1829. A period of three hundred and twenty-six years. But two hundred and nine, from 1620—when twenty of our fathers were brought into Jamestown, Virginia, by a Dutch man-of-war, and sold off like brutes to the highest bidders; and there is not a doubt in my mind, but that tyrants are in hopes to perpetuate our miseries under them and their children until the final consummation of all things. But if they do not get dreadfully deceived, it will be because God has forgotten them.

The Pagans, Jews and Mahometans try to make proselytes to their religions, and whatever human beings adopt their religions, they extend to them their protection. But Christian Americans not only hinder their fellow creatures, the Africans, but thousands of them will *absolutely beat a coloured person nearly to death, if they catch him on his knees, supplicating the throne of grace.* This barbarous cruelty was by all the heathen nations of antiquity, and is by the Pagans, Jews and Mahometans of the present day, left entirely to Christian Americans to inflict on the Africans and their descendants that their cup which is nearly full may be completed. I have known tyrants or usurpers of human liberty in different parts of this country take their fellow creatures, the colored people, and beat them until they would scarcely leave life in them; what for? Why they say, "The black devils had the audacity to be found *making prayers and supplications to the God who made them!!!*" Yes, I have known small collections of coloured people to have convened together, for no other purpose than to worship God Almighty, in spirit and in truth, to the best of their knowledge; when tyrants, calling themselves *patrols*, would also convene and wait almost in breathless silence for the poor coloured people to commence singing and praying to the Lord our God, and as soon as they had commenced the wretches would burst I upon them and drag them out and commence beating them as they would rattle-snakes—many of whom, they would beat so unmercifully, that they would hardly be able to crawl for weeks and sometimes for months.—Yet the American ministers send out missionaries to convert the heathen, while they keep us and our children sunk at their feet in the most abject ignorance and wretchedness that ever a people was afflicted with since the world began. Will the Lord suffer this people to proceed much longer? Will he not stop them in their career? Does he regard the heathens abroad, more than the heathens among the Americans? Surely the Americans must believe that God is partial, notwithstanding his Apostle Peter, declared before Cornelius and others that he has no respect to persons, but in every nation he that feareth God and worketh righteousness is accepted with him.—"The word," said he, "which God sent unto the children of Israel, preaching peace, by Jesus Christ, (he is the Lord of all)" [Acts 10:36].

Have not the Americans the Bible in their hands? Do they believe it? Surely they do not. See how they treat us in open violation of the Bible!! They no doubt will be greatly offended with me, but if God does not awaken them, it will be, because they are superior to other men, as they have represented themselves to be. Our divine Lord and Master said "all things whatsoever ye would that men should do unto you, do ye even so unto them" [Mt 25:40]. But an American minister, with the Bible in his hand, holds us and our children in the most abject slavery and wretchedness. Now I ask them, would they like for us to hold them and their children in abject slavery and wretchedness? No says one, that never can be done—you are too abject and ignorant to do it—you are not men—you were made to be slaves to us, to dig up gold and silver for us and our children. Know this, my dear sirs, that although you treat us and our children now, as you do your domestic beasts—yet the final result of all future events are known but to God Almighty alone, who rules in the armies of heaven and among the inhabitants of the earth, and who dethrones one earthly king and sits up another, as it seemeth good in his holy sight. We may attribute these vicissitudes to what we please, but the God of armies and of justice rules in heaven and in earth, and the whole American people shall see and know it yet, to their satisfaction. I have known pretended preachers of the gospel of my master, who not only held us as their natural inheritance, but treated us with as much rigor as any Infidel or Deist in the world—just as though they were intent only on taking our blood and groans to glorify the Lord Jesus Christ. The wicked and ungodly, seeing their preachers treat us with so much cruelty, they say: our preachers, who must be right, if any body are, treat them like brutes, and why cannot we?—They think it is no harm to keep them in slavery and put the whip to them, and why cannot we do the same!—They being preachers of the gospel of Jesus Christ, if it were any harm, they would surely preach against their oppression and do their utmost to erase it from the country; not only in one or two cities, but one continual cry would be raised in all parts of this confederacy, and would cease only with the complete overthrow of the system of slavery, in every part of the country.

But how far the American preachers are from preaching against slavery and oppression,

which have carried their country to the brink of a precipice; to save them from plunging down the side of which, will hardly be effected, will appear in the sequel of this paragraph, which I shall narrate just as it transpired. I remember a Camp Meeting in South Carolina, for which I embarked in a Steam Boat at Charleston, and having been five or six hours on the water, we at last arrived at the place of hearing, where was a very great concourse of people, who were no doubt, collected together to hear the word of God, (that some had collected barely as spectators to the scene, I will not here pretend to doubt, however, that is left to themselves and their God.) Myself and boat companions, having been there a little while, we were all called up to hear; I among the rest, went up and took my seat—being seated, I fixed myself in a complete position to hear the word of my Saviour and to receive such as I thought was authenticated by the Holy Scriptures; but to my no ordinary astonishment, our Reverend gentleman got up and told us (colored people) that slaves must be obedient to their masters—must do their duty to their masters or be whipped—the whip was made for the backs of fools, &c.

Here I pause for a moment, to give the world time to consider what was my surprise, to hear such preaching from a minister of my Master, whose very gospel is that of peace and not of blood and whips, as this pretended preacher tried to make us believe. What the American preachers can think of us, I aver this day before my God, I have never been able to define. They have newspapers and monthly periodicals, which they receive in continual succession, but on the pages of which, you will scarcely ever find a paragraph respecting slavery, which is ten thousand times more injurious to this country than all the other evils put together; and which will be the final overthrow of its government, unless something is very speedily done; for their cup is nearly full.—

Perhaps they will laugh at, or make light of this; but I tell you Americans! that unless you speedily alter your course, *you* and *your Country are gone!!!!!!* For God Almighty will tear up the very face of the earth!!!! Will not that very remarkable passage of Scripture be fulfilled on Christian Americans? Hear it Americans!! "He that is unjust, let him be unjust still:—and he which is filthy, let him be filthy still; and he that is righteous, let him be righteous still; and he that is holy, let him be holy still" [Rev 22:11]. I hope that the Americans may hear, but I am afraid that they have done us so much injury, and are so firm in the belief that our Creator made us to be an inheritance to them forever, that their hearts will be hardened, so that their destruction may be sure.—This language, perhaps is too harsh for the American's delicate ears. But Oh Americans! Americans!! I warn you in the name of the Lord, (whether you will hear, or forbear,) to repent and reform, or you are ruined!!!!!! Do you think that our blood is hidden from the Lord, because you can hide it from the rest of the world by sending out missionaries, and by your charitable deeds to the Greeks, Irish, &c.? Will he not publish your secret crimes on the house top? Even here in Boston, pride and prejudice have got to such a pitch, that in the very houses erected to the Lord, they have built little places for the reception of colored people, where they must sit during meeting, or keep away from the house of God; and the preachers say nothing about it—much less, go into the hedges and highways seeking the lost sheep of the house of Israel, and try to bring them in, to their Lord and Master. There are hardly a more wretched, ignorant, miserable, and abject set of beings in all the world, than the blacks in the Southern and Western sections of this country, under tyrants and devils. The preachers of America cannot see them, but they can send out missionaries to convert the heathens, notwithstanding. Americans! unless you speedily alter your course of proceeding, if God Almighty does not stop you, I say it in his name, that you may go on and do as you please for ever, both in time and eternity—never fear any evil at all!!!!!!!

3. Frederick Douglass
AUTOBIOGRAPHY (1845)

Frederick Douglass (1818–1895) was born a slave in Maryland, and in 1838, after enduring much cruelty, he escaped to the North, where he became perhaps the most celebrated abolitionist of the nineteenth century. His countless writings and public speeches on the hypocrisy of slavery helped bring the cause of abolitionism to a larger white audience than ever before. The reading below is an appendix to Douglass's first autobiography, in which he relates his early life as a slave and his eventual escape at the age of twenty. After repeatedly mocking the "piety" of slaveowners he had known, Douglass felt compelled to make a distinction between true Christianity, which he admired, and the hypocritical semblance of religion, which he abhorred. Douglass believed in the ethics of the gospel but argued that, until slavery was abolished, it was both foolish and sadistic for whites to expect enslaved African-Americans to respect either Christianity or the American ideal of freedom.

I find, since reading over the foregoing Narrative that I have, in several instances, spoken in such a tone and manner, respecting religion, as may possibly lead those unacquainted with my religious views to suppose me an opponent of all religion. To remove the liability of such misapprehension, I deem it proper to append the following brief explanation. What I have said respecting and against religion, I mean strictly to apply to the *slaveholding religion* of the land, and with no possible reference to Christianity proper; for, between the Christianity of this land, and the Christianity of Christ, I recognize the widest possible difference—so wide, that to receive the one as good, pure, and holy, is of necessity to reject the other as bad, corrupt, and wicked. To be the friend of one, is of necessity to be the enemy of the other. I love the pure, peaceable, and impartial Christianity of Christ: I therefore hate the corrupt, slaveholding, women-whipping, cradle-plundering, partial and hypocritical Christianity of this land. Indeed, I can see no reason, but the most deceitful one, for calling the religion of this land Christianity. I look upon it as the climax of all misnomers, the boldest of all frauds, and the grossest of all libels. Never was there a clearer case of "stealing the livery of the court of heaven to serve the devil in." I am filled with unutterable loathing when I contemplate the religious pomp and show, together with the horrible inconsistencies, which every where surround me. We have men-stealers for ministers, women-whippers for missionaries, and cradle-plunderers for church members. The man who wields the blood-clotted cowskin during the week fills the pulpit on Sunday, and claims to be a minister of the meek and lowly Jesus. The man who robs me of my earnings at the end of each week meets me as a class-leader on Sunday morning, to show me the way of life, and the path of salvation. He who sells my sister, for purposes of prostitution, stands forth as the pious advocate of purity. He who proclaims it a religious duty to read the Bible denies me the right of learning to read the name of the God who made me. He who is the religious advocate of marriage robs whole millions of its sacred influence, and leaves them to the ravages of wholesale pollution. The warm defender of the sacredness of the family relation is the same that scatters whole families,—sundering husbands and wives, parents and children, sisters and brothers,—leaving the hut vacant, and the hearth desolate. We see the thief preaching against theft, and the adulterer against adultery. We have men sold to build churches, women sold to support the gospel, and babes sold to purchase Bibles for the *poor heathen!*

All for the glory of God and the good of souls! The slave auctioneer's bell and the churchgoing bell chime in with each other, and the bitter cries of the heartbroken slave are drowned in the religious shouts of his pious master. Revivals of religion and revivals in the slave-trade go hand in hand together. The slave prison and the church stand near each other. The clanking of fetters and the rattling of chains in the prison, and the pious psalm and solemn prayer in the church, may be heard at the same time. The dealers in the bodies and souls of men erect their stand in the presence of the pulpit, and they mutually help each other. The dealer gives his blood-stained gold to support the pulpit, and the pulpit, in return, covers his infernal business with the garb of Christianity. Here we have religion and robbery the allies of each other—devils dressed in angels' robes, and hell presenting the semblance of paradise.

"Just God! and these are they,
    Who minister at thine altar, God of right!
Men who their hands, with prayer and bless-
        ing, lay
    On Israel's ark of light.
"What! preach, and kidnap men?
    Give thanks, and rob thy own afflicted poor?
Talk of thy glorious liberty, and then
    Bolt hard the captive's door?
"What! servants of thy own
    Merciful Son, who came to seek and save
The homeless and the outcast, fettering down
    The tasked and plundered slave!
"Pilate and Herod friends!
    Chief priests and rulers, as of old, combine!
Just God and holy! is that church which lends
    Strength to the spoiler thine?"

[Douglass then compares the Christianity of slaveholding America to the hypocritical piety of the ancient scribes and Pharisees, condemned by Jesus in Mt 6:23]

Dark and terrible as is this picture, I hold it to be strictly true of the overwhelming mass of professed Christians in America. They strain at a gnat, and swallow a camel. Could any thing be more true of our churches? They would be shocked at the proposition of fellowshipping a *sheep*-stealer; and at the same time they hug to their communion a *man*-stealer, and brand me with being an infidel, if I find fault with them for it. They attend with Pharisaical strictness to the outward forms of religion, and at the same time neglect the weightier matters of the law, judgment, mercy, and faith. They are always ready to sacrifice, but seldom to show mercy. They are they who are represented as professing to love God whom they have not seen, whilst they hate their brother whom they have seen. They love the heathen on the other side of the globe. They can pray for him, pay money to have the Bible put into his hand, and missionaries to instruct him; while they despise and totally neglect the heathen at their own doors.

Such is, very briefly, my view of the religion of the land; and to avoid any misunderstanding, growing out of the general use of general terms, I mean, by the religion of this land, that which is revealed in the words, deeds, and actions, of those bodies, north and south, calling themselves Christian churches, and yet in union with slave-holders. It is against religion, as presented by these bodies, that I have felt it my duty to testify.

BIBLIOGRAPHY

Primary Sources

Anthologies and Readers

Allitt, Patrick, ed., *Major Problems in American Religious History,* ed. Patrick Allitt (Boston: Houghton Mifflin, 2000).

Bowden, Henry, and P. C. Kemeny, eds., *American Church History: A Reader* (Nashville, Tenn.: Abingdon Press, 1998).

Bushman, Richard L., ed., *The Great Awakening: Documents on the Revival of Religion, 1740–45* (New York: Atheneum, 1970).

Butler, Jon, and Harry S. Stout, eds., *Religion in American History* (Oxford: Oxford University Press, 1997).

Hardman, Keith J., ed., *Issues in American Christianity: Primary Sources with Introductions* (Grand Rapids, Mich.: Baker, 1993).

Keller, Rosemary Skinner, and Rosemary Radford Ruether, eds., *In Our Own Voices: Four Centuries of American Women's Religious Writings* (San Francisco: HarperSanFrancisco, 1995).

Kenton, Edna, ed., *The Jesuit Relations and Allied Documents; Travels, Explorations of the Jesuit Missionaries in North America (1610–1791)* (New York: A & C Boni, 1925).

Miller, Perry, and Alan Heimert, eds., *The Great Awakening: Documents Illustrating the Crisis and Its Consequences* (Indianapolis, Ind.: Bobbs-Merrill, 1967).

Vaughn, Alden T., *The Puritan Tradition in America, 1620–1730* (New York: Harper & Row, 1972).

Selected Authors

Douglass, Frederick, *Life and Times of Frederick Douglass,* ed. Genevieve S. Gray (New York: Grosset & Dunlap, 1970).

———, *Frederick Douglass: The Narrative and Selected Writings,* ed. Michael Meyer (New York: Modern Library, 1984).

Eddy, Mary Baker, *Science and Health with Key to Scriptures* (Boston: Christian Science Board of Directors, 1994).

Edwards, Jonathan, *Letters and Personal Writings*, ed. George S. Claghorn (New Haven: Yale University Press, 1998).

————, *A Jonathan Edwards Reader*, ed. John E. Smith et al. (New Haven: Yale University Press, 1995).

Smith, Joseph, *Personal Writings of Joseph Smith*, ed. Dean Jesse (Salt Lake City: Deseret, 1984).

————, *Selected Sermons and Writings*, ed. Robert L. Millet (Mahwah, N.J.: Paulist Press, 1989).

————, *Book of Mormon*, trans. Joseph P. Smith Jr. (Salt Lake City: Church of Latter-Day Saints, 1977).

Walker, David, *One Continual Cry: David Walker's Appeal to the Colored Citizens of the World,* ed. Herbert Aptheker (Atlantic Highlands, N.J.: Humanities Press, 1965).

White, Ellen G., *The Great Controversy Between Christ and Satan; the Conflict of the Ages in the Christian Dispensation* (1888; reprinted by Pacific Press, 1911).

Whitefield, George, *Journal and Sermons* (Mahwah, N.J.: Paulist Press, 1985).

Secondary Works

Historical Overviews

Ahlstrom, Sydney E., *A Religious History of the American People*, 2 vols. (New Haven: Yale University Press, 1972).

Bonomi, Patricia, *Under the Cope of Heaven: Religion, Society and Politics in Colonial America* (New York: Oxford University Press, 1986).

Conkin, Paul K., *American Originals: Homemade Varieties of Christianity* (Chapel Hill, N.C.: University of North Carolina Press, 1997).

Dolan, Jay P., *The American Catholic Experience: A History from Colonial Times to the Present* (Garden City, N.Y.: 1985).

Handy, Robert T., *Christianity in the United States and Canada* (Oxford: Oxford University Press, 1977).

Matthews, Donald, *Religion in the Old South* (Chicago: University of Chicago Press, 1977).

New World Missions

Gagliano, Joseph A., and Charles E. Ronan, eds., *Jesuit Encounters in the New World: Jesuit Chroniclers, Geographers, Educators, and Missionaries in the Americas, 1549–1767* (Rome: Institutum Historicum S. I., 1997).

Hennesey, James J., *American Catholics: A History of the Roman Catholic Community in the United States* (Oxford: Oxford University Press, 1982).

Terrell, John Upton., *The Arrow and the Cross: A History of the American Indians and the Missionaries* (Santa Barbara, Calif.: Capra Press, 1979).

The Great Awakening and Revivalism

Gaustad, Edwin, *The Great Awakening in New England* (New York: Harper, 1957).

Hatch, Nathan, and Henry S. Stout, eds., *Jonathan Edwards and the American Experience* (Oxford: Oxford University Press, 1988).

Miller, Perry, *The New England Mind: From Colony to Province* (Cambridge, Mass.: Belknap Press of Harvard Unversity, 1953).

Stout, Harry, *The New England Soul: Preaching and Religious Culture in Colonial New England* (New York: Oxford University Press, 1986).

Millenarianism and Adventism

Knight, George R., *Millennial Fever and the End of the World: A Study of Millerite Adventism* (Boise, Idaho: Pacific Press, 1993).

Numbers, Ronald, *Prophetess of Health: A Study of Ellen G. White* (New York: Harper & Row, 1976).

Sandeen, Ernest R., *The Roots of Fundamentalism: British and American Millenarianism* (Chicago: University of Chicago Press, 1982).

Slavery and Abolitionism

Essig, James, *The Bonds of Wickedness: American Evangelicals Against Slavery, 1770–1808* (Philadelphia, Pa.: Temple University Press, 1982).

McKivigan, John, and Mitchell Snay, eds., *Religion and the Antebellum Debate over Slavery* (Athens, Ga.: University of Georgia Press, 1998).

Perry, Lewis, *Radical Abolitionism* (Ithaca, N.Y.: Cornell University Press, 1973).

Raboteau, Albert, *Slave Religion: The "Invisible Institution" in the Antebellum South* (New York: Oxford University Press, 1978).

Scherer, Lester B., *Slavery and the Churches in Early America, 1619–1819* (Grand Rapids, Mich.: Eerdmans, 1975).

CHAPTER 8
Nineteenth-Century Europe

A CHRISTIAN MISSIONARY IN TAGOLAND (GHANA). During the nineteenth century, thousands of European and North American missionaries traveled to every corner of Asia, Africa, and Latin America, ultimately winning millions of new converts to Christianity. The broader social legacy of their activity was mixed, including important victories against slavery and infectious disease but also the imposition of imperialist governments and European cultural norms. *(Culver Pictures)*

The "long nineteenth century"—the period that stretches roughly from the French Revolution of 1789 to the outbreak of World War I in 1914—has often been described by church historians as a period of crisis for Western Christianity. Certainly many of the faith's most fundamental doctrines were challenged by such modern developments as nationalism, socialism, secularism, and industrial capitalism. New discoveries in empirical science—particularly evolutionary biology—as well as in other areas of scholarship likewise demanded religious reconsideration and possibly accommodation. These challenges caused some Christians to turn away from their religion; others, by contrast, responded by defiantly resisting what they saw as the evils of modernity. To portray the nineteenth century as one long period of Christian decline or defiance, however, is to ignore the variety of creative responses with which many nineteenth-century Christians faced and often embraced the emerging culture of modernity. Thus despite the antagonistic language that sometimes flew between Christian leaders and critics of the church during this era, the nineteenth century is best viewed as a time of intensified self-scrutiny for Western Christianity, a period that ultimately gave rise to a rich variety of new movements and new interpretations of Christianity's mission in the modern world.

The sources of social modernization were many. First and foremost came the economic and demographic changes that resulted from the growth of market capitalism during the eighteenth century and its acceleration through the industrialization of the early nineteenth century. One immediate result was the emergence throughout Europe of a somewhat larger middle class, or bourgeoisie, characterized by higher levels of both affluence and education. Another consequence was the relatively rapid shift of a significant proportion of the labor force from agrarian to manufacturing or mining work. This change—in combination with a population boom of unprecedented scope—swelled the population of Europe's cities and resulted in a severe shortage of housing as well as a dramatic increase in urban poverty. In sharp contrast to these developments, industrialization also enabled a small number of factory owners and bankers to amass gigantic private fortunes. This new degree of social stratification touched on every aspect of public and private life throughout western Europe, including religion.

Meanwhile, the two great general political trends since the French Revolution were nationalism and democratization. Some nation-states of the nineteenth century, such as France and Britain, were the direct beneficiaries of unified kingdoms. Others, particularly Italy and Germany, had to be forged by alliance and warfare. Whatever their origin, all of the European nation-states shared the same notion of a political entity united by a common cultural heritage. This idealized homogeneity of the nation was in fact often at odds with the great cultural, linguistic, and especially religious diversity of their populations. Some of the tensions of forced assimilation were eased by the general political trend of democratization, allowing much greater personal liberty, including full toleration and civil parity for members of all religions. By the mid nineteenth century, the weakening of official state churches had even emboldened some reformers to demand complete separation of church and state at all levels, an unprecedented idea in European history. In Catholic countries such as France and Spain, public debate over the issue was especially fierce, pitting anticlerical "modernists" against conservative (and often royalist) defenders of the status quo. Patriotism, or more accurately nationalism, was often called into service by both groups, with each claiming to truly represent the spirit and interest of the nation. Although this essentially modern dilemma about the relationship between Christian and national loyalties has yet to be resolved, the conflict has indelibly shaped all Christian churches of the modern era.

Many anticlericalists and other political reformers were also members of intellectual circles that harbored an even more radical resentment of ecclesiastical authority. Among the moderate "progressive" thinkers of the day, Christianity was largely seen as a relic of another, less enlightened time, which could only maintain its relevance in the modern world by bringing its teachings into alignment with the discoveries of contemporary science and philosophy. Other thinkers and activists of the period went much further, declaring Christianity and all religions to be obstacles in the path of the righteous causes of the age, from the establishment of workers' rights to the elimination of human injustice. Some of these, most famously Karl Marx, advocated political revolution and the abolition of organized religion. Others, such as the philosopher Friedrich Nietzsche, merely denied the intellectual legitimacy of Christianity, claiming that it was a "slave religion" created by ruling classes and church leaders to prevent individuals from attaining their own self-realization. Aided by numerous scientific developments, such as Charles Darwin's theories of human evolution, a new breed of atheist philosophers and other thinkers took the "modern" case against Christianity to unprecedented lengths.

Christians of the nineteenth century tended to respond to the challenges of modern society in three general ways. The first was a conservative and even reactionary rejection of any religious accommodation of modernity, either in doctrine or practice. The sweeping denunciations of Pope Pius IX's 1864 "Syllabus of Errors" have come to symbolize this position, although it was by no means limited to the Catholic Church. For Pius and others of his opinion, all of the political and social upheavals of the day were the direct result of decades of Deist and atheist "propaganda" and populist agitation. The church's divine duty was to uphold Christ's message and ministry, which for conservatives meant resisting not just ecclesiastical change but also any attempt to alter the existing and "natural" social order. Some Christian conservatives, such as Pius, were in fact disillusioned liberals who saw the very notion of human progress as a dangerous self-deception. The loss of the pope's secular territory, the so-called Papal States, during the unification of Italy also did not endear nationalist and other modern ideologies to him. In any event, this fortress attitude, which was shared by many conservative nineteenth-century Christians, would continue to play a significant role in all European churches well into the twentieth century.

A second type of Christian response to the social transformations of the era was a greater emphasis on the experiential and even mystical aspects of religious life. In the early part of the century this tendency was most evident among the diverse thinkers and artists known as Romantics, who shared a common aversion to both Enlightenment rationalism and capitalist materialism. The Romantics felt that these two modern developments had left a spiritual void in the hearts of humankind, and they sought to fill this emptiness through emotional experiences of nature or of art. Interest in the supernatural, both Christian and pagan, was also a hallmark of this approach and led some Romantics to espouse a more transcendental, and yet also profoundly sensual, form of Christianity. Such eclecticism occasionally opened Romantics to accusations of pantheism. For the much larger number of orthodox Christians, however, fascination with the spiritual and miraculous took more traditional forms. Among Catholics these included an increase in the number of apparitions of the Virgin Mary and other miraculous occurrences and a subsequent rise in pilgrimages. Among Protestants, the religious enthusiasm and charismatic experience of Methodism and evangelism continued to thrive. While church attendance fluctuated considerably during the period, the enormous appeal of such fundamentally nonrationalist approaches to spiritual fulfillment remained constant.

A third type of reaction common among nineteenth-century Christians was to attempt some kind of constructive engagement with modern culture. Among Protestants and Catholics alike, traditional missionary work was universally expanded to include a wide spectrum of social work and political reform, both at home and abroad. Most of this work was charitable in nature, aiming to curb the inequities and suffering caused by industrial capitalism on an individual level. In addition to so-called inner missions established by national churches, new Christian organizations such as the Salvation Army, founded in 1878, undertook crusades to care for both the body and the soul of the poor and destitute. By the end of the century, "progressive" Christians in almost every European state had also formed political parties. Usually calling themselves Christian Democrats or Christian Socialists, these groups aimed at addressing modern problems in a more systematic yet still basically Christian way. Their willingness to combine Christian and Socialist goals sometimes earned them the wrath of both groups. Their political success, however, was undeniable, perhaps reflecting a broader interest in religious assimilation than some church leaders would have conceded. Some Christian intellectuals, meanwhile, attempted to bridge the gap between modernity and Christianity by applying the techniques of modern science and archaeology to the most sacred of Christian books. Although many church leaders were critical of these efforts, the popularized versions of such scholarship often met with widespread approval among ordinary Christians. For example, one scholar's somewhat radical biography of Jesus became a Europe-wide bestseller. Thus engagement with modernity, like confrontation, was never a simple or monolithic Christian response.

The oft-cited nineteenth-century "decline" of Western Christianity is thus better described as a transformation. While many individuals did abandon their respective churches and perhaps Christianity altogether, still more chose to find ways to make their faith fit in with the new conditions of modern life. In that sense, the "crisis" created by the monumental social changes of the modern era differed little from the challenges faced by Christian groups throughout the history of the religion. The availability of more non-Christian—or nonreligious—alternatives to the faith cannot be denied. But the centuries-old forces of Christian dynamism and adaptability remained as strong as ever.

CHAPTER 8 CHRONOLOGY

	Politics	Literature	Individuals	Other
18th cent.	1789 Beginning of French Revolution	1781 Kant, *Critique of Pure Reason* 1798 Wordsworth, *Lyrical Ballads*		1790 French Civil Constitution of Clergy 1795 London Missionary Society founded
19th cent.	1801 Concordat between Napoleon & Pope Pius VIII 1815 Congress of Vienna 1830 Revolutions in France, Belgium, Poland 1832 British Reform Bill 1848 Revolutions throughout Europe 1851–1870 Second Empire in France 1853–1856 Crimean War 1870 Italy annexes Papal States	1802 Chateaubriand, *Genius of Christianity* 1810 Blake, *Vision of the Last Judgment* 1825 St. Simon, *New Christianity* 1830 Stendhal, *Scarlet and Black* 1835 Strauss, *Life of Jesus* 1841 Feuerbach, *Essence of Christianity* 1848 Marx, *Communist Manifesto* 1859 Darwin, *Origin of Species* 1863 Renan, *Life of Jesus* 1880 Dostoevsky, *Brothers Karamazov*	1770–1831 G. W. F. Hegel 1768–1834 F. Schleiermacher 1798–1857 A. X. Comte 1792–1860 F. C. Baur 1813–1855 Kierkegaard 1801–1890 J. H. Newman 1844–1889 G. M. Hopkins 1844–1900 F. Nietzsche 1873–1897 St. Thérèse of Lisieux	1814 Jesuits reestablished 1817 Prussian Union of Lutheran & Reformed churches 1822 Formation of Catholic Society for the Propagation of the Faith 1829 R.C. emancipation in Britain 1833 Start of Oxford Movement 1834 Slavery abolished in all British dominions 1848–1853 Christian Socialist Movement 1854 Papal bull est. Immaculate Conception of Mary 1864 Pius IX, *Syllabus of Errors* 1869–1870 Vatican I 1873 May Laws of Bismarck's *Kulturkampf* 1878 Salvation Army founded 1891 Leo XIII, *Rerum Novarum*

A. Romanticism

Romanticism is a term used loosely to describe a variety of artistic, philosophical, and literary trends evident in Europe from the late eighteenth to mid nineteenth century. Although it would be difficult to summarize the many phases and forms of Romantic thought, it is possible to identify certain common themes. Most fundamentally, all self-described Romantics of this period stressed the primacy of experience, especially sensual experience, over rational thought. One of the earliest Romantics, Jean-Jacques Rousseau (1712–1778), proceeded from this elevation of human sensibility to describe a type of "natural religion," based solely on the nonrational (and therefore also nondogmatic) aspects of the divine. Reacting to what they saw as the overly rational approach of Enlightenment figures like Voltaire, Rousseau and later Romantics also violently rejected "mechanistic" descriptions of human existence in favor of a more organic model that emphasized the mystical union of body and soul. During the Napoleonic era of the early nineteenth century, this anti-Enlightenment reaction spread throughout western Europe, firmly pitting "scientific progressives" against a new generation of Romantic poets, artists, and composers. Among Germans the Romantic idea of a cultural *Volkgeist* (lit., "spirit of a people"), unique to each "nation," proved an especially popular counterweight to the pathetic state of German politics.

The direct implications of Romanticism for Christianity, on the other hand, remained as vaguely defined as Rousseau's first notion of a "natural religion." Some Romantics, such as the Viscount of Chateaubriand (1768–1848), attempted to define Christianity itself as a kind of *Volkgeist,* praising its inherent spiritual values and contributions to human civilization. Others, most notably William Wordsworth (1770–1850) and William Blake (1757–1827), moved towards an understanding of religion that transcended doctrine and ritual. Whatever form it took, however, the Romantic defense of Christianity was never more than partially acceptable to leaders of the established churches, despite their shared opposition to the secularizing influences of the Enlightenment and French Revolution. Traditional doctrines, their adherents argued, could not be minimized or rejected merely for the sake of popular approval or artistic sensibility. By the second half of the nineteenth century, most European Christians had apparently agreed, choosing either a specific denomination or abandoning the religion altogether.

1. Friedrich Schleiermacher
ON RELIGION: SPEECHES TO ITS CULTURED DESPISERS (1799)

Some historians have described Romanticism as a type of anti-intellectual intellectualism. No author better personified this paradoxical combination than the so-called father of modern theology, Friedrich Schleiermacher (1768–1834).

Educated in the traditions of both the sensualist Moravian Pietists and the rationalist Enlightenment, Schleiermacher found himself at first conflicted in his approach to religion. Eventually he was ordained as a Reformed (Calvinist) minister and undertook a personal campaign to win back much of the educated classes of Europe to religion. In speeches and publications, such as the one excerpted below, Schleiermacher showed traces of his formative intellectual influences, including Enlightenment philosophy. His message, however, is essentially a Romantic one: the divine is so utterly transcendent and "other" that all human attempts to capture it with words or philosophies merely demonstrate the feebleness and arrogance of human reason. Intuition, rather than science, is the better guide to developing a true understanding of reality, or what he called "God-consciousness." Religion, Schleiermacher wrote, was thus essentially a contemplative act, with the primary goal being the realization of "infinite humanity," a state he defined as a feeling of absolute dependence on God. Though this last assertion might seem predictable for a Calvinist minister, Schleiermacher's profoundly personal incorporation of Romantic sensibility into religious arguments was unprecedented.

DEFENSE

It may be an unexpected and even a marvelous undertaking, that any one should still venture to demand from the very class that have raised themselves above the vulgar, and are saturated with the wisdom of the centuries, attention for a subject so entirely neglected by them. And I confess that I am aware of nothing that promises any easy success, whether it be in winning for my efforts your approval, or in the more difficult and more desirable task of instilling into you my thought and inspiring you for my subject. From of old faith has not been every man's affair. At all times but few have discerned religion itself, while millions, in various ways, have been satisfied to juggle with its trappings. Now especially the life of cultivated people is far from anything that might have even resemblance to religion. Just as little, I know, do you worship the Deity in sacred retirement, as you visit the forsaken temples. In your ornamented dwellings, the only sacred things to be met with are the sage maxims of our wise men, and the splendid compositions of our poets. Suavity and sociability, art and science have so fully taken possession of your minds, that no room remains for the external and holy Being that lies beyond the world. I know how well you have succeeded in making your earthly life so rich and varied, that you no longer stand in need of an eternity. Having made a universe for yourselves, you are above the need of thinking of the Universe that made you. You are agreed, I know, that nothing new, nothing convincing can any more be said on this matter, which on every side by sages and seers, and I might add by scoffers and priests, has been abundantly discussed. To priests, least of all, are you inclined to listen. They have long been outcasts for you, and are declared unworthy of your trust, because they like best to lodge in the battered ruins of their sanctuary and cannot, even there, live without disfiguring and destroying it still more. All this I know, and yet, divinely swayed by an irresistible necessity within me, I feel myself compelled to speak, and cannot take back my invitation that you and none else should listen to me. . . .

THE NATURE OF RELIGION

In order to make quite clear to you what is the original and characteristic possession of religion, it resigns at once, all claims on anything that belongs either to science or morality. Whether it has been borrowed or bestowed it is now returned. What then does your science of being, your natural science, all your theoretical philosophy, in so far as it has to do with the actual world, have for its aim? To know things, I suppose, as they really are; to show the peculiar relations by which each is what it is; to determine for each its place in the Whole, and to distinguish it rightly from all else; to present the whole real world in its mutually conditioned necessity; and to exhibit the oneness of all phenomena with their eternal laws. This is truly beautiful and excellent, and I am not disposed to depreciate. Rather, if this description of mine, so slightly sketched, does not suffice, I will grant the highest and most exhaustive you are able to give. . . .

It is true that religion is essentially contemplative. You would never call anyone pious who went about in impervious stupidity, whose sense is not open for the life of the world. But this contemplation is not turned, as your knowledge of nature is, to the existence of a finite thing, combined with and opposed to another finite thing. It has not even, like your knowledge of God—if for once I might use an old expression—to do with the nature of the first cause, in itself and in its relation to every other cause and operation. The contemplation of the pious is the immediate consciousness of the universal existence of all finite things, in and through the Infinite, and of all temporal things in and through the Eternal. Religion is to seek this and find it in all that lives and moves, in all growth and change, in all doing and suffering. It is to have life and to know life in immediate feeling, only as such an existence in the Infinite and Eternal. Where this is found religion is satisfied, where it hides itself there is for her unrest and anguish, extremity and death. Wherefore it is a life in the infinite nature of the Whole, in the One and in the All, in God, having and possessing all things in God, and God in all. Yet religion is not knowledge and science, either of the world or of God. Without being knowledge, it recognizes knowledge and science. In itself it is an affection, a revelation of the Infinite in the finite, God being seen in it and it in God. . . .

What can man accomplish that is worth speaking of, either in life or in art, that does not arise in his own self from the influence of this sense for the Infinite? Without it, how can anyone wish to comprehend the world scientifically, or if, in some distinct talent, the knowledge is thrust upon him, how should he wish to exercise it? What is all science, if not the existence of things in you, in your reason? what is all art and culture if not your existence in the things to which you give measure, form and order? And how can both come to life in you except in so far as there lives immediately in you the eternal unity of Reason and Nature, the universal existence of all finite things in the Infinite?

Wherefore, you will find every truly learned man devout and pious. Where you see science without religion, be sure it is transferred, learned up from another. It is sickly, if indeed it is not that empty appearance which serves necessity and is no knowledge at all. And what else do you take this deduction and weaving together of ideas to be, which neither live nor correspond to any living thing? Or in ethics, what else is this wretched uniformity that thinks it can grasp the highest human life in a single dead formula? The former arises because there is no fundamental feeling of that living nature which everywhere presents variety and individuality, and the latter because the sense fails to give infinity to the finite by determining its nature and boundaries only from the Infinite. Hence the dominion of the mere notion; hence the mechanical erections of your systems instead of an organic structure, hence the vain juggling with analytical formulas, in which, whether categorical or hypothetical, life will not be fettered. Science is not your calling, if you despise religion and fear to surrender yourself to reverence and aspiration for the primordial. Either science must become as low as your life, or it must be separated and stand alone, a division that precludes success. If man is not one with the Eternal in the unity of intuition and feeling which is immediate, he remains, in the unity of consciousness which is derived, for ever apart. . . .

The sum total of religion is to feel that, in its highest unity, all that moves us in feeling is one; to feel that aught single and particular is only possible by means of this unity; to feel, that is to say, that our being and living is a being and living in and through God. But it is not necessary that the Deity should be presented as also one distinct object. To many this view is necessary, and to all it is welcome, yet it is always hazardous and fruitful in difficulties. It is not easy to avoid the appearance of making Him susceptible of suffering like other objects. It is only one way of characterizing God, and, from the difficulties of it, common speech will probably never rid itself. But to treat this objective conception of God just as if it were a perception, as if apart from His operation upon us through the world the existence of God before the world, and outside of the world, though for the world, were either by or in religion exhibited as science is, so far as religion is concerned, vain mythology. What is only a help for presentation is treated as a reality. It is a misunderstanding very easily made, but it is quite outside the peculiar territory of religion. . . .

The whole religious life consists of two elements, that man surrender himself to the Universe and allow himself to be influenced by the side of it that is turned towards him is one part, and that he transplant this contact which is one definite feeling, within, and take it up into the inner unity of his life and being, is the other. The religious life is nothing else than the constant renewal of this proceeding. When, therefore, anyone is stirred, in a definite way, by the World, is it his piety that straightway sets him to such working and acting as bear the traces of commotion and disturb the pure connection of the moral life? Impossible. On the contrary, his piety invites him to enjoy what he has won, to absorb it, to combine it, to strip it of what is temporal and individual, that it may no more dwell in him as commotion but be quiet, pure and eternal. From this inner unity, action springs of its own accord, as a natural branch of life. As we agreed, activity is a reaction of feeling, but the sum of activity should only be a reaction of the sum of feeling, and single actions

should depend on something quite different from momentary feeling. Only when each action is in its own connection and in its proper place, and not when, dependently and slavishly, it corresponds to one emotion, does it exhibit, in a free and characteristic way, the whole inner unity of the spirit. . . .

If then this, that I trust I have indicated clearly enough for you all, is really the nature of religion, I have already answered the questions, Whence do those dogmas and doctrines come that many consider the essence of religion? Where do they properly belong? And how do they stand related to what is essential in religion? They are all the result of that contemplation of feeling, of that reflection and comparison, of which we have already spoken. The conceptions that underlie these propositions are, like your conceptions from experience, nothing but general expressions for definite feelings. They are not necessary for religion itself, scarcely even for communicating religion, but reflection requires and creates them. Miracle, inspiration, revelation, supernatural intimations, much piety can be had without the need of any one of these conceptions. But when feeling is made the subject of reflection and comparison, they are absolutely unavoidable. In this sense all these conceptions do certainly belong to the sphere of religion, and indeed belong without condition or the smallest limit to their application.

The strife about what event is properly a miracle, and wherein its character properly consists, how much revelation there may be and how far and for what reasons man may properly believe in it, and the manifest endeavor to deny and set aside as much as can be done with decency and consideration, in the foolish notion that philosophy and reason are served thereby, is one of the childish operations of the metaphysicians and moralists in religion. They confuse all points of view and bring religion into discredit, as if it trespassed on the universal validity of scientific and physical conclusions. Pray do not be misled, to the detriment of religion, by their sophistical disputations, nor even by their hypocritical mystery about what they would only too willingly publish. Religion, however loudly it may demand back all those well abused conceptions, leaves your physics untouched, and please God, also your psychology.

What is a miracle? What we call miracle is everywhere else called sign, indication. Our name, which means a wonder, refers purely to the mental condition of the observer. It is only in so far appropriate that a sign, especially when it is nothing besides, must be fitted to call attention to itself and to the power in it that gives it significance. Every finite thing, however, is a sign of the Infinite, and so these various expressions declare the immediate relation of a phenomenon to the Infinite and the Whole. But does that involve that every event should not have quite as immediate a relation to the finite and to nature? Miracle is simply the religious name for event. Every event, even the most natural and usual, becomes a miracle, as soon as the religious view of it can be the dominant. To me all is miracle. In your sense the inexplicable and strange alone is miracle, in mine it is no miracle. The more religious you are, the more miracle would you see everywhere. All disputing about single events, as to whether or not they are to be called miraculous, gives me a painful impression of the poverty and wretchedness of the religious sense of the combatants. One party shows it by protesting everywhere against miracle, whereby they manifest their wish not to see anything of immediate relationship to the Infinite and to the Deity. The other party displays the same poverty by laying stress on this and that. A phenomenon for them must be marvelous before they will regard it as a miracle, whereby they simply announce that they are bad observers.

What is revelation? Every original and new communication of the Universe to man is a revelation, as, for example, every such moment of conscious insight as I have just referred to. Every intuition and every original feeling proceeds from revelation. As revelation lies beyond consciousness, demonstration is not possible, yet we are not merely to assume it generally, but each one knows best himself what is repeated and learned elsewhere, and what is original and new. If nothing original has yet been generated in you, when it does come it will be a revelation for you also, and I counsel you to weigh it well. . . .

You see that all these ideas, in so far as religion requires, or can adopt ideas, are the first and the most essential. They indicate in the most characteristic manner a man's consciousness of his religion, because they indicate just what necessarily and universally must be in it. The man who does not see miracles of his own from the standpoint from which he contemplates the world, the man in whose heart no revelation of his own arises, when his soul longs to draw in the beauty of the world, and to be permeated by its spirit; the man who does not, in supreme moments, feel, with the most lively assurance, that a divine spirit urges him, and that he speaks and acts from holy inspiration, has no religion. The religious man must, at least, be conscious of his feelings as the immediate product of the Universe; for less would mean nothing. He must recognize something individual in them, something that cannot be imitated, something that guarantees the purity of their origin from his own heart. To be assured of this possession is the true belief. . . .

I have tried, as best I could, therefore, to show you what religion really is. Have you found anything therein unworthy of you, nay, of the highest human culture? Must you not rather long all the more for that universal union with the world which is only possible through feeling, the more you are separated and isolated by definite culture and individuality? Have you not often felt this holy longing, as something unknown? Become conscious of the call of your deepest nature and follow it, I conjure you. Banish the false shame of a century which should not determine you but should be made and determined by you. Return to what lies so near to you, yes, even to you, the violent separation from which you cannot fail to destroy the most beautiful part of your nature. . . .

2. William Blake
POETRY

The life and work of William Blake (1757–1827) defies easy categorization. Entirely self-educated, he became one of the most popular poets and artists of the nineteenth century. Deeply mystical since childhood, he displayed a lifelong fascination with a variety of religious and occult themes in both his writings and drawings. In the two poems below, Blake reveals some of his most Romantic tendencies, openly disdaining the anti-Christian Enlightenment and at the same time reveling in the mystery of Creation. His precise religious beliefs were often obscure in his writings and perhaps made even more unintelligible by the heavily allegorical illustrations that often accompanied them. Clearly he opposed all dogmatic and ascetic approaches to Christianity or any religion, a conviction that led him into deep involvement with the theosophy movement, a syncretic and eclectic approach to the divine, which drew on various Asian mystical traditions.

a. "MOCK ON, MOCK ON, VOLTAIRE, ROUSSEAU" (c. 1800)

Mock on, Mock on, Voltaire, Rousseau;
Mock on, Mock on; 'tis all in vain!
You throw the sand against the wind,
And the wind blows it back again.

And every sand becomes a Gem
Reflected in the beams divine;
Blown back they blind the mocking eye,
But still in Israel's paths they shine.

The Atoms of Democritus
And Newton's Particles of light[1]
Are sands upon the Red sea shore,
Where Israel's tents do shine so bright.

---

[1]The tiniest, irreducible elements of matter, according to the Greek philosopher Democritus (c. 460–370 B.C.E.) and the English physicist Isaac Newton (1643–1727).

b. "THE TIGER" (1794)

Tiger! Tiger! burning bright
In the forests of the night,
What immortal hand or eye
Could frame thy fearful symmetry?

In what distant deeps or skies
Burnt the fire of thine eyes?
On what wings dare he aspire?
What the hand dare seize the fire?

And what shoulder, and what art,
Could twist the sinews of thy heart?
And when thy heart began to beat,
What dread hand forged thy dread feet?

What the hammer? what the chain?
In what furnace was thy brain?
What the anvil? what dread grasp
Dare its deadly terrors clasp?

When the stars threw down their spears,	Tiger! Tiger! burning bright
And watered heaven with their tears,	In the forests of the night,
Did he smile his work to see?	What immortal hand or eye,
Did he who made the Lamb make thee?	Dare frame they fearful symmetry?

B. Socialism

The European Industrial Revolution of the nineteenth century has been called one of the great watersheds in human history. Even before its eventual spread to the rest of the world by the next century, it transformed the very nature of global economics and politics and influenced every aspect of society and culture, including Christianity and religion in general. Thanks to improvements in mechanization and distribution, the boom in mass-produced goods created a new class of wealthy factory owners and other capitalist investors. At the same time, however, the material benefits of industrialization did not extend to the much larger majority of workers, most of whom had left dire rural circumstances for factories and mines that ironically proved even more hazardous and exploitative than the countryside had been. The growth of a resentful and perhaps dangerous "proletariat" provoked many different responses among the more affluent members of European society. While some conservative backers of capitalists' interests favored stronger police and other social controls, other individuals from all social classes put their faith in the political philosophy generally known as socialism.

The word socialism itself first appeared in England and France in 1825. Broadly speaking, its proponents favored a new, collective (or "social") response to the various problems wrought by industrialization. Rather than relying on private initiatives and the concentration of political power among a few individuals, socialists proposed a new organization of society and its resources, aimed largely at improving the economic and political lot of the proletariat. Their common inspiration of "the greatest happiness for the greatest number" owed something to a long utopian tradition reaching back to Plato as well as to the radical egalitarianism of the French Revolution of the 1790s. The place of Christianity in the progressive historical scheme of socialists was not always clear. One of the earliest socialists, the Count of Saint-Simon, for instance, argued that Christianity had served a vital function in furthering human civilization, though now the time had come for a new type of "scientific" religion. Others, such as Robert Owen (1771–1858), vehemently denounced all established religions for their common emphasis on moral guilt and human failings. Undoubtedly the best-known socialist of all was Karl Marx (1818–1883), who famously dismissed religion as "an opiate for the masses," preached by the ruling classes to prevent political revolt. Following the violent suppression of several socialist-inspired revolutions in 1848, however, a new political movement known as Christian Socialism gained momentum. While other socialist political parties increasingly adopted a Marxist stance towards religion and capitalism, Christian Socialists followed a more conciliatory approach, attacking only the excesses of capitalism and working to improve the education and living conditions of working people. Whatever their particular attitude towards Christianity, though, all of the socialist parties of the nineteenth and twentieth centuries (including the Communists) eventually agreed that they had vastly underestimated the religion's enduring strength in all of their societies.

1. Henri Saint-Simon
NEW CHRISTIANITY: FIRST DIALOGUE (1825)

The two great lifelong passions of the Frenchman Henri Count of Saint-Simon (1760–1825) were social justice and science. As a young man he had fought with Americans in their revolt against Great Britain and at the outbreak of his own country's revolution, he renounced his aristocratic title. While he continued to work on various reform projects, his equally deep commitment to scientific progress eventually led him to a socialist theory of history. In earlier stages of social development, he believed, human knowledge was necessarily formulated in theological and later metaphorical terms. In the dawning age of science, however, such theological language merely caused confusion and discord and should therefore be abandoned altogether. In the following "dialogue," written in the last year of Saint-Simon's life, the "Innovator" makes the author's argument for a "new Christianity," stripped of its clergy and dogma and focused only on its more essential creed of human equality and fraternity. Though the "Conservative" clings to the remnants of traditional "feudal" Christianity, Saint-Simon appears confident that "progressive" Protestants and Catholics alike will acknowledge that the greatest good of their religion is love for their fellow man—the same goal of socialist reform. Saint-Simon's influence on later politics and philosophy was considerable and is particularly evident in the work of the great positivist Auguste Comte (1798–1857) and the Christian Socialist Philippe Joseph Buchez (1796–1865).

Conservative. Do you believe in God?

Innovator. Yes, I believe in God.

Con. Do you believe that the Christian religion is of divine origin?

Inn. Yes, I believe that.

Con. If the Christian religion is of divine origin, it cannot possibly be improved. Yet in your writings you urge the artists, the industrials, and the scientists to improve this religion. You therefore contradict yourself, since your opinion and your belief are in opposition.

Inn. The opposition which you think you see between my opinion and my belief is only an apparent one. A distinction must be made between what God himself has said and what the clergy have said in his name.

What God has said certainly cannot be improved, but what the clergy have said in God's name forms a science which can be improved, just like all the other human sciences. There are times when the theory of theology must be brought up to date, just like the theory of physics, chemistry, and physiology. . . .

Con. The Christian religion is thus, according to you, in a very bad state?

Inn. On the contrary. There have never been so many good Christians; but today they nearly all belong to the laity. Since the fifteenth century the Christian religion has lost its unity of action, and there has no longer been a Christian clergy. All the clergies who are today trying to graft their opinions, their morals, their cults, and their dogmas onto the principle of morality given to man by God are heretics, because their opinions, their morals, their dogmas, and their cults are all more or less opposed to divine morality. The most powerful clergy is also the most heretical.

Con. What will become of the Christian religion if, as you think, those men responsible for teaching it have become heretics?

Inn. Christianity will become the universal and only religion. The Asians and Africans will be converted. The members of the European clergy will become good Christians; they will abandon the various heresies which they profess today. The true doctrine of Christianity, that is to say, the most general doctrine which can be deduced from the fundamental principle of divine morality, will be produced, and immediately the differences between religious opinions will come to an end.

The first Christian doctrine only provided society with a partial and very incomplete organization. The rights of Caesar remained independent of the rights attributed to the Church. *Render unto Caesar the things which are Caesar's* [Mt 22:21; Mk 12:17; Lk 20:25]: such is the famous saying which separated these two powers. The temporal power has continued to base its power on the law of the strongest, while the Church has taught that society should only recognize as legitimate those institutions which aim to improve the existence of the poorest class.

The new Christian organization will base both temporal and spiritual institutions on the principle that *all men should treat one another as brothers.* It will direct all institutions, whatever their nature, towards increasing the well-being of the poorest class. . . .

I have, then, a clear conception of the New Christian doctrine, and I shall produce it. I shall then review all the spiritual and temporal institutions in England, France, northern and southern Germany, Italy, Spain, Russia, and North and South America. I shall compare the doctrines of these different institutions with the doctrine deduced directly from the fundamental principle of divine morality, and I shall easily convince all men of good faith and good intentions that if all these institutions were directed towards the aim of improving the moral and physical well-being of the poorest class, they would bring prosperity to all classes of society and all nations with the greatest possible speed. . . .

I shall begin by examining the different religions which exist today. I shall compare their doctrines with the doctrine deduced directly from the fundamental principle of divine morality. . . .

I challenge the Pope, who calls himself Christian, who claims to be infallible, who assumes the title of Vicar of Jesus Christ, to reply clearly and without employing any mystical expressions to the four accusations of heresy which I shall bring against the Catholic Church.

I accuse the Pope and his Church of heresy on this first count: The teaching given by the Catholic clergy to their lay communicants is at fault, because it fails to guide their conduct along the path of Christianity.

The Christian religion teaches the faithful that their aim on earth should be to improve as quickly as possible the moral and physical condition of the poor. Jesus Christ promised eternal life to those who worked with the greatest zeal to increase the well-being of the most numerous class.

The mission of the Catholic clergy, as well as of all other clergies, should therefore be to direct the ardor of all members of society towards work of general utility.

Thus, all clergies should use all their intellectual resources and all their talents, in their sermons and more intimate conversations, to show laymen that an improvement in the existence of the lowest class will inevitably lead to an increase in the real and positive well-being of the higher classes: for God regards all men, even the rich, as his children.

Thus, in the teaching they give to children, in their sermons to the faithful, in the prayers they address to Heaven, as well as in every part of their cults and dogmas, the clergies should fix their audience's attention on this important fact: that the vast majority of the population could enjoy a much more satisfying moral and physical condition than the one they have enjoyed hitherto, and that the rich, by increasing the happiness of the poor, would improve their own condition. . . .

I accuse the Pope and the Cardinals of being heretics on this second count: of lacking the knowledge which fits them to guide the faithful towards their salvation.

I accuse them of giving a bad education to seminarists, of failing to insist that new members of the priesthood receive sufficient instruction to become worthy pastors, capable of looking after the flocks in their car. . . .

I accuse the Pope of heretical behavior on this third count: I accuse him of ruling in a way more opposed to the moral and physical interests of the temporal subjects belonging to the destitute class than the rule of any lay prince over his poor subjects. . . .

I accuse the Pope and all the present Cardinals, indeed all the Popes and all the Cardinals since the fifteenth century, of being and having been heretics on this fourth count: I accuse them first of having consented to the formation of two institutions diametrically opposed to the spirit of Christianity: the Inquisition and the Jesuits. Next, I accuse them of having protected these two institutions ever since, almost without interruption. . . .

THE PROTESTANT RELIGION

. . . The Protestant religion, as conceived by Luther, is still only a Christian heresy. It was certainly right of Luther to say that the Court of Rome had departed from the path selected by Jesus for his apostles, and to proclaim that the form of worship and the dogma established by the Popes were not suitable for fixing the attention of the faithful on Christian morality,

but could, on the contrary, only be considered as accessories to religion. But, on the basis of these two unquestionable truths, Luther did not have the right to conclude that morality should be taught to the faithful of his time in the same way that it had been taught by the Fathers of the Church to their contemporaries. Nor did he have the right to conclude that worship should be stripped of all the beauty with which the fine arts could enrich it.

The dogmatic part of Luther's reform was a failure. This reform was incomplete, and is itself in need of reform.

I accuse the Lutherans of being heretics on the first count: I accuse them of adopting a morality which is much inferior to the morality appropriate to Christians in their present state of civilization. . . .

The analysis of these four major questions will naturally lead to the conclusion that the Lutherans are heretics.

1. At the time when Jesus gave his apostles the sublime mission of organizing the human race in the interest of the poorest class, civilization was still in its infancy. . . .

2. By the time Luther introduced his reform, civilization had made great progress. Since the establishment of Christianity society had changed completely, and social organization was now based on new foundations.

Slavery was almost entirely abolished. The patricians no longer had exclusive control over law-making, and no longer occupied all the important posts. Temporal power, which was essentially unholy, no longer dominated spiritual power, and spiritual power was no longer under the control of the patricians. . . .

Christianity had become the basis of social organization, and had replaced the law of the strongest. The right of conquest was no longer considered the most legitimate right of all. . . .

3. If Luther's reform could have been completed, Luther would have produced and proclaimed the following doctrine, saying to the Pope and Cardinals:

"Your predecessors have sufficiently perfected and propagated the theory of Christianity. The Europeans are sufficiently imbued with it. You must now concentrate on the general application of this doctrine. The true Christianity should make men happy not only in heaven, but on earth.

"No longer should you keep the attention of the faithful fixed on abstract ideas. You will succeed in establishing Christianity as the general, universal, and sole religion only by making proper use of sensual ideas, and combining them so as to achieve the highest degree of felicity attainable by the human race during its earthly life.

"It is no longer enough to preach to the faithful of all classes that the poor are the cherished children of God. You must make bold and energetic use of all the powers and methods acquired by the militant Church in order quickly to improve the moral and physical condition of the most numerous class. The preliminary and preparatory work of Christianity is complete. You have a task to fulfill which is much more satisfying than the one accomplished by your predecessors. It consists in establishing the general and definitive Christianity, in organizing the whole human race according to the fundamental principle of morality.

"To fulfill this task you must make this principle the basis and aim of every social institution. . . ."

4. Luther was a very powerful and able critic; but it is only in this respect that he demonstrated any great ability. Thus, he proved in a most vigorous and thorough manner that the Court of Rome had left the path of Christianity; that on the one hand it was trying to establish itself as an arbitrary power, and that, on the other, it was striving to unite with the powerful against the poor, so that the faithful must compel it to reform.

But that part of his work relating to the reorganization of Christianity was much worse than it should have been. Instead of taking the necessary measures to increase the social importance of the Christian religion, he made this religion revert to its point of departure. He put it back again outside the social organization, thus recognizing the power of Caesar as the source of every other power. He reserved for his clergy only the right of humble petition to temporal power. Through these arrangements he delivered the peaceful capacities into a state of eternal dependence on the men of violence, the military. . . .

The accusation of heresy which I bring against the Protestants, on account of the morality which they have adopted, a morality which is very much behind the present level of our civilization, is thus well founded.

I accuse the Protestants of heresy on this second count: I accuse them of adopting a bad form of worship.

The more society improves morally and physically, the greater the division between intellectual and manual work. Thus, in the course of their daily lives, men find their attention fixed on an increasingly specialized interest, as the fine arts, sciences, and industry progress. . . .

I bring a third accusation of heresy against the Protestants: I accuse them of adopting a false dogma.

In the early days of religion, when the people were still steeped in ignorance, they had little inclination to study natural phenomena. Man's ambition had not risen to the point where he wanted to master his planet and transform it to his greatest advantage. At that time men had few needs of which they were clearly aware; but they were swayed by the most violent passions, reflecting their vague desires and whims, in particular the presentiment of the power they were destined to exercise over nature. Commerce, which has since civilized the world, still only existed in rudimentary form. Every small tribe was in a state of hostility towards the rest of the human race, and citizens had no moral links with any men who were not members of their city. Thus at this time philanthropy could still only exist as a speculative idea. At the same time all nations were divided into two great classes: masters and slaves. Religion could only have a powerful effect on the masters, since they alone were able to act according to their own free will. Morality was bound to be the least developed part of religion, since there was no reciprocity of common duties between the two great social classes. Worship and dogma were bound to appear much more important than morality. Religious practices, and reasoning on the utility of these practices and of the beliefs on which they were founded, were inevitably the parts of religion of chief concern to the priests and the mass of believers.

In short, the material part of religion originally played a much more important role; whereas the spiritual part has acquired increasing importance as man's intelligence has developed.

Today, worship should be regarded only as a means of drawing men's attention, on the day of rest, to philanthropic ideas and sentiments; and dogma should no longer be conceived as anything but a collection of commentaries aimed at the general application of those ideas and sentiments to major political events, and seeking to make it easy for the faithful to apply morality in their daily relationships. . . .

On the basis of these four major facts I conclude that my third accusation of heresy against Protestants, on account of the dogma they have adopted, is firmly established. . . .

Con. I have followed your speech with careful attention. While you were speaking my own ideas became clearer, my doubts disappeared, and I felt a growing love and admiration for the Christian religion. My devotion to the religious system which has civilized Europe has not prevented me from understanding that it can be improved, and on this point you have convinced me completely.

It is clear that the moral principle, *all men should treat one another as brothers,* given by God to his Church, embraces all the ideas which you include in the precept that *the whole of society should work to improve the moral and physical condition of the poorest class; society should be organized in the way most suitable for achieving this great aim.*

It is equally certain that when Christianity originated the first formula had to be used to express this principle, and that today the second formula should be used.

At the time of Christianity's foundation, you have said, society was divided into two great classes which were, politically, absolutely different: masters and slaves, forming, in one respect, two distinct human races, and yet closely interrelated. It was then absolutely impossible to establish complete reciprocity in the moral relations between the two races, so that the divine Founder of the Christian religion had to restrict his moral principle to an obligation on all the individuals belonging to each human race. He was not able to establish it as a link uniting the masters and the slaves.

We are now living at a time when slavery is completely abolished; when all men share the same political character; when classes are only separated by slight differences. You therefore conclude that the fundamental principle of Christianity should be formulated so that it becomes a mutual obligation for the people as a whole, without ceasing to be an obligation for men in their individual relations. I find your conclusion legitimate and of the greatest importance; and henceforth, New Christian, I shall join in the propagation of New Christianity. . . .

---

2. Karl Marx
"THE SOCIAL PRINCIPLES
OF CHRISTIANITY" (1847)

The most influential socialist thinker of all time was Karl Marx (1818–1883). Like Saint-Simon, Marx viewed human history in progressive terms, arguing that the time had come to transfer political and economic power to the "only truly productive class," the workers. For Marx, however, the role of organized religion, both in the past and in the present, was always that of lackey to the ruling classes, be they medieval aristocrats or modern capitalists. In the following newspaper editorial, published the year before his famous *Communist Manifesto,* he ridicules both the so-called social principles and the metaphysics of Christianity—all intended, in his view, to weaken and suppress the proletariat. Marx's socialist transformation would have no accommodation with such systematic delusion, he wrote, and would instead mean the abolition of all organized religion. Later Marxist disciples, especially the leaders of the Communist Soviet Union, attempted to carry out the philosopher's extreme vision but found Christianity and other religions to be more resilient than they had expected. Today almost all socialist parties have removed explicit opposition to religion from their official platform.

"What is the alpha and omega[2] of the Christian faith? The dogma of original sin and salvation. And therein lies the link of solidarity among humanity at its highest potential; one for all and all for one."

Happy people! The *cardinal question* is solved forever. The proletariat will find two inexhaustible life sources under the double wings of the Prussian eagle and the Holy Ghost: first, the income tax surplus over and above the ordinary and extraordinary needs of the state, which surplus is equal to null; and second, the revenues from the heavenly domains of original sin and salvation, which are likewise equal to null. Both of these nulls provide a splendid ground for the one-third of the nation that has no land for its subsistence, and a powerful support for another third which is in decline. In any case, imaginary surpluses, original sin, and salvation will satisfy the hunger of the people in quite a different way from the long speeches of the liberal deputies!

It is said further: "In the 'Our Father' we pray: *'Lead us not into temptation'* [Mt 6:13; Lk 11:4].' And what we ask for ourselves we must also practice toward our neighbors. But our social conditions do indeed tempt man, and excessive misery incites to crime."

And *we,* the gentlemen bureaucrats, judges, and consistorial councilors of the Prussian State,

exercise this respect [for our fellow men] by joyfully wracking people on the wheel, beheading, imprisoning, and flogging, and thereby "leading" the proletarians "into temptation," so that later they too can wrack, behead, imprison, and flog us. And that will not fail to happen.

"Such conditions," the consistorial councilor declares, "a Christian State *must not* tolerate; it must find a remedy for them."

Yes, with absurd babble about society's duties of solidarity, with imaginary surpluses and blank checks drawn on God the Father, Son, and Company.

"We can also be spared the already tedious talk about communism," our observant consistorial councilor remarks. "If those whose calling it is would only develop the social principles of Christianity, the communists would soon become silent."

The social principles of Christianity have now had eighteen hundred years to develop, and need no further development by the Prussian consistorial councilors.

The social principles of Christianity justified slavery in antiquity, glorified medieval serfdom, and, when necessary, also know how to defend the oppression of the proletariat, although they may do so with a piteous face.

The social principles of Christianity preach the necessity of a ruling and an oppressed class, and for the latter they have only the pious wish that the former will be benevolent.

---

[2]The first and last letters of the Greek alphabet—i.e., the beginning and the end.

The social principles of Christianity transfer the consistorial councilors' settlement of all infamies to heaven, and thereby justify the continuation of these infamies on earth.

The social principles of Christianity declare all vile acts of the oppressors against the oppressed to be either just punishment for original sin and other sins, or suffering that the Lord in his infinite wisdom has destined for those redeemed.

The social principles of Christianity preach cowardice, self-contempt, abasement, submission, humility—in brief, all the qualities of the *canaille*[3]; and the proletariat, not wishing to be treated as *canaille*, needs its courage, its self-respect, its pride, and its sense of independence even more than its bread.

The social principles of Christianity are hypocritical, but the proletariat is revolutionary.

So much for the social principles of Christianity.

_____

[3]I.e. the rabble.

---

3. Leo XIII
DE RERUM NOVARUM (1891)

The Christian churches varied greatly in their responses to socialism during the course of the nineteenth century. At one extreme was the wholesale condemnation of Pope Pius IX (r. 1846–1878) in his *Syllabus of Errors* encyclical of 1864. Like many other conservative Europeans, Pius saw socialism as just one of a host of modern evils unleashed by the Industrial Revolution, and believed that it was aimed at overthrowing every aspect of the existing religious and political order. Given the explicit anti-Christianity of socialists such as Marx, most Protestant church leaders shared the pope's antipathy. Less than half a century later, however, the less reactionary Pope Leo XIII (r.1878–1903) looked on those socialists not hostile to religion, notably the Christian Socialists, with some approval. In the encyclical excerpted below, *De Rerum Novarum,* Leo writes of the injuries to basic human dignity wrought by capitalists' elevation of profit over workers' rights. Though he opposes the socialist abolition of private property, the pope also rejects the selfish materialism of capitalism and business owners' indifference to the living and working conditions of their employees. Most significantly, Leo affirms that it is an inherent duty of the Catholic Church to further economic and political reform, albeit in a timely and moderate manner. Though subsequent Catholic and Protestant leaders continued to display ambivalent attitudes towards socialism, as the nineteenth century gave way to the twentieth, socialism's fundamental incompatibility with Christianity became less and less of an issue. This was especially true following the socialist-Communist schisms of the twentieth century, when the Communist party took a strongly Marxist stand against religion, while most socialist parties either embraced or at least tolerated the influence of the church.

Once the passion for revolutionary change was aroused—a passion long disturbing governments—it was bound to follow sooner or later that eagerness for change would pass from the political sphere over into the related field of economics. In fact, new developments in industry, new techniques striking out on new paths, changed relations of employer and employee, abounding wealth among a very small number and destitution among the masses, increased self-reliance on the part of the workers as well as a closer bond of union with one another, and, in addition to all this, a decline in morals, have caused conflict to break forth. . . .

The problem is difficult to resolve and is not free from dangers. It is hard indeed to fix the boundaries of the rights and duties within which the rich and the proletariat—those who furnish material things and those who furnish work—ought to be restricted in relation to each other. The controversy is truly dangerous, for in various places it is being twisted by turbulent and crafty men to pervert judgment as to truth and seditiously to incite the masses.

In any event, We see clearly, and all are agreed that the poor must be speedily and fittingly cared for, since the great majority of them live undeservedly in miserable and wretched conditions.

After the old trade guilds had been destroyed in the last century, and no protection was substituted in their place, and when public institutions and legislation had cast off traditional religious teaching, it gradually came about that the present age handed over the workers, each alone and defenseless, to the inhumanity of employers and the unbridled greed of competitors. A devouring usury, although often condemned by the Church, but practiced nevertheless under another form by avaricious and grasping men, has increased the evil; and in addition the whole process of production as well as trade in every kind of goods has been brought almost entirely under the power of a few, so that a very few rich and exceedingly rich men have laid a yoke almost of slavery on the unnumbered masses of non-owning workers.

To cure this evil, the Socialists, exciting the envy of the poor toward the rich, contend that it is necessary to do away with private possession of goods, and in its place to make the goods of individuals common to all, and that the men who preside over a municipality or who direct the entire State should act as admin-

istrators of these goods. They hold that, by such a transfer of private goods from private individuals to the community, they can cure the present evil through dividing wealth and benefits equally among the citizens.

But their program is so unsuited for terminating the conflict that it actually injures the workers themselves. Moreover, it is highly unjust, because it violates the rights of lawful owners, perverts the functions of the State, and throws governments into utter confusion.

Clearly the essential reason why those who engage in any gainful occupation undertake labor, and at the same time the end to which workers immediately look, is to procure property for themselves and to retain it by individual right as theirs and as their very own. When the worker places his energy and his labor at the disposal of another, he does so for the purpose of getting the means necessary for livelihood. He seeks in return for the work done, accordingly, a true and full right not only to demand his wage but to dispose of it as he sees fit. Therefore, if he saves something by restricting expenditures and invests his savings in a piece of land in order to keep the fruit of his thrift more safe, a holding of this kind is certainly nothing else than his wage under a different form; and on this account land which the worker thus buys is necessarily under his full control as much as the wage which he earned by his labor. But, as is obvious, it is clearly in this that the ownership of movable and immovable goods consists. Therefore, insomuch as the Socialists seek to transfer the goods of private persons to the community at large, they make the lot of all wage earners worse, because in abolishing the freedom to dispose of wages they take away from them by this very act the hope and the opportunity of increasing their property and of securing advantages for themselves.

But, what is of more vital concern, they propose a remedy openly in conflict with justice, inasmuch as nature confers on man the right to possess things privately as his own. . . .

The fact that God gave the whole human race the earth to use and enjoy cannot indeed in any manner serve as an objection against private possessions. For God is said to have given the earth mankind in common, not because He intended indiscriminate ownership of it by all, but because He assigned no part to anyone in ownership, leaving the limits of private possessions to be fixed by the industry of men and the institutions of peoples. Yet, however the earth may be apportioned among private owners, it does not cease to serve the common interest of all, inasmuch as no living being is sustained except by what the fields bring forth. Those who lack resources supply labor, so that it can be truly affirmed that the entire scheme of securing a livelihood consists in the labor which a person expends either on his own land or in some working occupation, the compensation for which is drawn ultimately from no other source than from the varied products of the earth and is exchanged for them.

For this reason it also follows that private possessions are clearly in accord with nature. The earth indeed produces in great abundance the things to preserve and, especially, to perfect life, but of itself it could not produce them without human cultivation and care. Moreover, since man expends his mental energy and his bodily strength in procuring the goods of nature, by this very act he appropriates that part of physical nature to himself which he has cultivated. On it he leaves impressed, as it were, a kind of image of his person, so that it must be altogether just that he should possess that part as his very own and that no one in any way should be permitted to violate his right. . . .

From all these considerations, it is perceived that the fundamental principle of Socialism which would make all possessions public property is to be utterly rejected because it injures the very ones whom it seeks to help, contravenes the natural rights of individual persons, and throws the functions of the State and public peace into confusion. Let it be regarded, therefore, as established that in seeking help for the masses this principle before all is to be considered as basic, namely that private ownership must be preserved inviolate.

It is a capital evil with respect to the question we are discussing to take for granted that the one class of society is of itself hostile to the other, as if nature had set rich and poor against each other to fight fiercely in implacable war. This is so abhorrent to reason and truth that the exact opposite is true; for just as in the human body the different members harmonize with one another, whence arises that disposition of parts and proportion in the human figure rightly called symmetry, so likewise nature has commanded in the case of the State that the two classes mentioned should agree harmoniously and should properly form equally balanced counterparts to each other. Each needs the other completely: neither capital can do without labor, nor labor without capital. Concord begets beauty and order in things. Conversely, from perpetual strife there must arise disorder accompanied by bestial cruelty. But for putting an end to conflict and for cutting away its very roots, there is wondrous and multiple power in Christian institutions.

And first and foremost, the entire body of religious teaching and practice, of which the Church is the interpreter and guardian, can pre-eminently bring together and unite the rich by recalling the two classes of society to their mutual duties, and in particular to those duties which derive from justice.

Among these duties the following concern the poor and the workers: To perform entirely and conscientiously whatever work has been voluntarily and equitably agreed upon; not in any way to injure the property or to harm the person of employers; in protecting their own interests, to refrain from violence and never to engage in rioting; not to associate with vicious men who craftily hold out exaggerated hopes and make huge promises, a course usually ending in vain regrets and in the destruction of wealth.

The following duties, on the other hand, concern rich men and employers: Workers are not to be treated as slaves; justice demands that the dignity of human personality be respected in them, ennobled as it has been through what we call the

Christian character. If we hearken to natural reason and to Christian philosophy, gainful occupations are not a mark of shame to man, but rather of respect, as they provide him with an honorable means of supporting life. It is shameful and inhuman, however, to use men as things for gain and to put no more value on them than what they are worth in muscle and energy. Likewise it is enjoined that the religious interests and the spiritual well-being of the workers receive proper consideration. Wherefore, it is the duty of employers to see that the worker is free for adequate periods to attend to his religious obligations; not to expose anyone to corrupting influences or the enticements of sin, and in no way to alienate him from care for his family and the practice of thrift. Likewise, more work is not to be imposed than strength can endure, nor that kind of work which is unsuited to a worker's age or sex.

Among the most important duties of employers the principal one is to give every worker what is justly due him. Assuredly, to establish a rule of pay in accord with justice, many factors must be taken into account. But, in general, the rich and employers should remember that no laws, either human or divine, permit them for their own profit to oppress the needy and the wretched or to seek gain from another's want. To defraud anyone of the wage due him is a great crime that calls down avenging wrath from Heaven. "Behold, the wages of the laborers . . . which have been kept back by you unjustly, cry out: and their cry has entered into the ears of the Lord of Hosts" [Jas 5:4]. Finally, the rich must religiously avoid harming in any way the savings of the workers either by coercion, or by fraud, or by the arts of usury; and the more for this reason, that the workers are not sufficiently protected against injustices and violence, and their property, being so meager, ought to be regarded as all the more sacred. Could not the observance alone of the foregoing laws remove the bitterness and the causes of conflict? . . .

Those who lack fortune's goods are taught by the Church that, before God as Judge, poverty is no disgrace, and that no one should be ashamed because he makes his living by toil. And Jesus Christ has confirmed this by fact and by deed, Who for the salvation of men, "being rich, became poor" [1 Cor 8:9]; and although He was the Son of God and God Himself, yet He willed to seem and to be thought the son of a carpenter; nay, He even did not disdain to spend a great part of his life at the work of a carpenter. "Is not this the carpenter, the Son of Mary?" [Mk 6:3] Those who contemplate this Divine example will more easily understand these truths: True dignity and excellence in men resides in moral living, that is, in virtue; virtue is the common inheritance of man, attainable equally by the humblest and the mightiest, by the rich and the poor; and the reward of eternal happiness will follow upon virtue and merit alone, regardless of the person in whom they may be found. Nay, rather the favor of God Himself seems to incline more toward the unfortunate as a class; for Jesus Christ calls the poor blessed [Mt 5:3], and He invites most lovingly all who are in labor or sorrow to come to Him for solace [Mt 11:28], embracing with special love the lowly and those harassed by injustice. At the realization of these things the proud spirit of the rich is easily brought down, and the downcast heart of the afflicted is lifted up; the former are moved toward kindness, the latter, toward reasonableness in their demands. Thus the distance between the classes which pride seeks is reduced, and it will easily be brought to pass that the two classes, with hands clasped in friendship, will be united in heart. . . .

It is vitally important to public as well as to private welfare that there be peace and good order; likewise, that the whole regime of family life be directed according to the ordinances of God and the principles of nature, that religion be observed and cultivated, that sound morals flourish in private and public life, that justice be kept sacred and that no one be wronged with impunity by another, and that strong citizens grow up, capable of supporting, and if necessary, of protecting the State. Wherefore, if at any time disorder should threaten because of strikes or concerted stoppages of work, if the natural bonds of family life should be relaxed among the poor, if religion among the workers should be outraged by failure to provide sufficient opportunity for performing religious duties, if in factories danger should assail the integrity of morals through the mixing of the sexes or other pernicious incitements to sin, or if the employer class should oppress the working class with unjust burdens or should degrade them with conditions inimical to human personality or to human dignity, if health should be injured by immoderate work and such as is not suited to sex or age—in all these cases, the power and authority of the law, but of course within certain limits, manifestly ought to be employed. And these limits are determined by the same reason which demands the aid of the law, that is, the law ought not undertake more, nor go farther, than the remedy of evils or the removal of danger requires.

Rights indeed, by whomsoever possessed, must be religiously protected; and public authority, in warding off injuries and punishing wrongs, ought to see to it that individuals may have and hold what belongs to them. In protecting the rights of private individuals, however, special consideration must be given to the weak and the poor. For the nation, as it were, of the rich, is guarded by its own defenses and is in less need of governmental protection, whereas the suffering multitude, without the means to protect itself, relies especially on the protection of the State. Wherefore, since wage workers are numbered among the great mass of the needy, the State must include them under its special care and foresight.

But it will be well to touch here expressly on certain matters of special importance. The capital point is this, that private property ought to be safeguarded by the sovereign power of the State and through the bulwark of its laws. And especially, in view of such a great flaming up of passion at the present time, the masses ought to be kept within the bounds of their moral obligations. For while justice does not oppose our striving for better things, on the other hand, it does forbid anyone to take from another what is his and, in the name of a certain absurd equality, to seize forcibly the property of others; nor does the interest of the common good itself permit this. Certainly, the great majority of working people prefer to secure better conditions by honest toil, without doing wrong to anyone. Nevertheless, not a few individuals are found who, imbued with evil ideas and eager for revolution, use every means to stir up disorder and incite to violence. The authority of the State, therefore, should intervene and, by putting restraint upon such disturbers, protect the morals of workers from their corrupting arts and lawful owners from the dangers of spoliation.

Labor which is too long and too hard and the belief that pay is inadequate not infrequently give workers cause to strike and become voluntarily idle. This evil, which is frequent and serious, ought to be remedied by public authority, because such interruption of work inflicts damage not only upon employers and upon the workers themselves, but also injures trade and commerce and the general interest of the State; and, since it is usually not far removed from violence and rioting, it very frequently jeopardizes public peace. In this matter it is more effective and salutary that the authority of the law anticipate and completely prevent the evil from breaking out by removing early the causes from which it would seem that conflict between employers and workers is bound to arise.

And in like manner, in the case of the worker, there are many things which the power of the State should protect; and, first of all, the good of his soul. For however good and desirable mortal life be, yet it is not the ultimate goal for which we are born, but a road only and a means for perfecting, through knowledge of truth and love of good, the life of the soul. . . .

C. Higher Criticism

Since the formation of the biblical canon in the third century, Christian scholars have continually debated the meaning, or hermeneutics, of Scripture as well as its exegesis, or how scriptural teachings should apply to everyday life. Beginning in the early nineteenth century, however, a number of German Protestant theology professors devoted themselves to a new type of historical-critical hermeneutics known as Higher Criticism. Using a combination of close textual analysis and broad historical research pioneered a century earlier by the French scholar Richard Simon (1638–1678), these scholars attempted to put aside all contemporary Christian questions and to interpret the various books of the Bible purely within their original historical context. The Old Testament, for example, could not be accurately understood unless one also considered what all of the archeological and other historical evidence revealed about the religious and political practices of ancient Israel. From this common presupposition, the proponents of Higher Criticism then proceeded to follow widely divergent paths in biblical study. The so-called Tübingen school, led by Ferdinand Christian Baur (1792–1860), developed a highly idealist theory of Christianity as a historical synthesis of Judaism and Greek philosophy, a view based on a historical-critical reading of the epistles of St. Paul. One of Baur's pupils, David Friedrich Strauss (1808–1874), took the methods of Higher Criticism even further, publishing a highly controversial biography of Jesus, supposedly based on authentic facts rather than later mythology. One of the most lasting products of the movement was the scholarship of Julius Wellhausen (1844–1918), who pioneered the "documentary hypothesis," which states that the Old Testament underwent at least four major (and detectable) revisions before reaching its final form around 200 B.C.E. Though most of these scholars disagreed widely about both hermeneutics and exegesis, they all concurred that the divergent styles and purposes of the Bible's various authors must be taken into consideration in any reading. In this respect, Higher Criticism undoubtedly contributed to a much greater consciousness of the historical development of Christianity among believers of all denominations

1. F. C. Baur
PAUL, THE APOSTLE OF JESUS CHRIST, LIFE, WORK, HIS EPISTLES, DOCTRINE: A CONTRIBUTION TO THE CRITICAL HISTORY OF PRIMITIVE CHRISTIANITY (1835)

Ferdinand Christian Baur studied and later taught theology at the University of Tübingen, in southwestern Germany. His admiration of both the theologian Friedrich Schleiermacher (see 8A1) and the philosopher Georg Wilhelm

Friedrich Hegel (1770–1831) is obvious in his highly abstract description of early Christian history. In the following excerpt, Baur summarizes his most famous conclusion, namely, that Christianity—especially as evident in its oldest documents by St. Paul—emerged out of a conflict between and eventual merger of Jewish religion (represented by Peter) and Greek philosophy (of which Paul had been a student). His application of the Hegelian notions of historical evolution and synthesis to the Judeo-Christian tradition often met with fierce resistance from his fellow theologians and biblical scholars who considered revealed truth an absolute and unchanging constant. Many other Christians were similarly offended by Baur's subsequent rejection of some Pauline epistles as inauthentic, as well as by his chronological ordering of the four gospels on the basis of their declining "Jewishness" (which thus declared Matthew to be the oldest and John the latest). In later years he applied the same principles to specific aspects of ancient Christian doctrine, such as the Incarnation of Jesus and the Trinity. Despite much initially negative reaction, Baur's overriding argument that many aspects of Christianity and the Bible were the products of historical processes was eventually accepted by most religious scholars.

. . . The criticism of the Gospel history, so far as it immediately concerns the life of the Founder of Christianity, with which so many weighty questions are allied, will long remain the most important object of the critical labors of our time. In view of the interests of the problem there next follows the historical and critical inquiry into the question how Christianity, so closely interwoven with Judaism, broke loose from it and entered on its sphere of world-wide historical importance. In regard to the life of Jesus, the conscious idea of Christianity and its principles, originated by him, and by him carried out through the devotion of his whole being, is what the Gospel history presents to us as the essence of the historical meaning of his life. But when we proceed from the Evangelical history to that of the time of the Apostles the practical realization of that idea becomes the proper object of historical research. This practical realization of the idea of Christianity was first dealt with when entering into the reality of its consciousness through the death and resurrection of Jesus, and becoming of itself a living power, the idea found in the bounds of the national Judaism, the chief obstacle to its universal historical realization.

How these bounds were broken through, how Christianity, instead of remaining a mere form of Judaism, although a progressive one, asserted itself as a separate, independent principle, broke loose from it, and took its stand as a new enfranchised form of religious thought and life, essentially differing from all the national peculiarities of Judaism is the ultimate, most important point of the primitive history of Christianity. Here also as in the Gospel history the individuality of a single life is the peculiar object of the historical and critical inquiry. That Christianity, in its universal historical acceptation, was the work of the Apostle Paul is undeniably an historical matter of fact, but in what manner he achieved this, in what light his relations with the elder Apostles must be viewed, whether it was in harmony with them or in contradiction and opposition to them, that he first authoritatively laid down principles and opinions, this it is that deserves a most thorough and accurate inquiry. As in the Gospel history, historical criticism has here two statements before it, differing from each other, which must be weighed and compared, in order to get from them their pure historical value. These are the accounts contained in the Acts of the Apostles and the historical data comprehended in the Apostle's own Epistles. . . .

The Acts of the Apostles are presented then as the chief source of the history of the apostolic life and labors of the Apostle Paul. But the historian cannot take his stand on it without first making himself acquainted with the position it holds with regard to its historical object. Between the Acts of the Apostles and the Pauline Epistles, as far as the historical contents of the latter can be compared with the Acts of the Apostles, there will be found in general the same relation as between the Gospel of John and the Synoptical Gospels.[4] The comparison of both these sources must lead to the conclusion that, considering the great difference between the two statements, historical truth can only belong to one of them. To which it does belong can only be decided by the undisputed historical rule that the statement which has the greatest claim to historical truth is that which appears most unprejudiced and nowhere betrays a desire to subordinate its historical material to any special subjective aim. For the history of the Apostolic Age the Pauline Epistles take precedence of all the other New Testament writings, as an authentic source. On this account the Acts must fill a secondary place; but there is also the further critical point that the same rule which defines the relation of the Synoptical Gospels to the Gospel of John, finds its application in the Acts of the Apostles; whilst in this place, and in order to indicate the standpoint of the following inquiry, I must express this opinion on the Acts of the Apostles, that I can find in it no purely objective statement, but only one which is arranged on subjective grounds; and I must also express a great wish to refer to a critical work which I venture to follow all the more, as it afforded me important results when I devoted myself to a quite different line of work some time ago. Schneckenburger[5] designated the aim of the Acts of the Apostles as apologetic. According to the results of his inquiry, we have to consider this work as a defense of the Apostle Paul in his apostolic dignity and his personal and apostolic conduct, especially in Gentile matters in the face of all Jewish opposition and censure. The idea that runs through the whole, that of a parallel between the two Apostles Peter and Paul, lies at the root of each of the principal parts into which the Acts of the Apostles is divided (Chapters 1 to 7 and 13 to the end). The unity of the work consists in this idea; its chief tendency is to represent the difference between Peter and Paul as unessential and trifling. To this end Paul is made in the second part to appear as much as possible like Peter, and Peter in the first part as much as possible like Paul. It is sought also to make both as nearly as possible of the same importance, so that one may sometimes be taken for the other, which, according to the undeniably Pauline author of the Acts of the Apostles, can only result in favor of Paul. But, as Schneckenburger points out, there is wanting in the second part any proof of Paul's righteousness according to the law, (such as zealous keeping of feasts, frequent journeys to the Temple, personal asceticism, and circumcision;) but on the other hand there is no trace of that side of Paul's piety which opposed itself to the law. The same Judaizing characteristics which meet us in the personal conduct of Paul, are evident in the account of his official labors. Paul observed the most fitting respect, not only towards the elder Apostles, who so completely agreed with him (Chapter 15), but also towards the Jewish people—especially in this, that he, as is here brought intentionally to our notice, first proclaimed the Gospel to the Jews, and then, when they rejected him and his Gospel, turned to the Gentiles. Schneckenburger with much ingenuity further endeavors to prove that all the important omissions in the Pauline history are to be accounted for by this apologetic tendency of the Acts. They refer to persons or facts whose mention or description would have given a completely different picture of Paul to that which is exhibited by the text as it stands, putting out of sight altogether as this does the Jewish prejudices and misrepresentations which we hear of in the Pauline Epistles. . . .

---

[4] I.e., Matthew, Mark, and Luke, all of which share the "same eye" (and sources) on the events of Jesus' life.
[5] Matthias Schneckenburger (1804–1848), Protestant theologian and theology professor at the University of Bern.

The two views which together make one Paul are, in fact, so divergent and heterogeneous that, although the author may be valuable as an historically faithful referee, the connection that is necessary to harmonize them is by no means self-evident, and must after all be sought for in the Apostle himself, that is to say, the historical character of the author can only be maintained at the cost of the moral character of the Apostle. When the whole bearing of the case, as set forth in accordance with Schneckenburger's investigation, is considered, it is impossible for us to remain within the limits which he sets to himself, where they appear to be only arbitrary; the results of his inquiries draw us on from the mere supposition of an apologetic aim to a much further point, which places the question as to the aim of the Acts of the Apostles and its author in a different position. If the idea of an undeniably existing apologetic interest be maintained then follows the unanswerable question—What can have decided the author to sacrifice historical truth to this bias? That this can only have been done on very weighty grounds is certainly a natural supposition, but these grounds do not concern the person of the Apostle, or any matters which touch him very nearly. Why then, if the Apostle needed an apology, could not the best apology have been found in an open historical detail of his apostolic life and labors? in the entire results of his whole conduct in his apostolic calling?

The reasons for the mode of treatment really pursued can only be sought for in circumstances which, in the interest of the community, made such concession necessary on the part of a disciple of Paul. These circumstances took place at a time when, in consequence of all those efforts which we see from the Epistles of the Apostle himself were made in the most strenuous manner by his Jewish-Christian opponents, the Pauline doctrine was so severely repressed that it could only maintain itself through a concession, which modified the hardness and bluffness of its opposition to the law and Judaism, and by this means put itself into a position as far as possible harmonizing the antagonistic views of the powerful Jewish-Christian party opposed to him. As far as we can follow the course of these circumstances we find it undeniable that they did exist, that they extended far into the second century, and that they were powerful enough during that period when a newly-established Church was rising out of the conflict of heterogeneous elements, to produce other literary results of a similar tendency. If we keep clearly in view these circumstances in their connection and in the meaning they took in their gradual development, we shall be carried on by them to a point when we can no longer maintain the authorship of Luke, as far as regards the Acts of the Apostles, in the form in which we possess them. Still it may not be impossible that preparations, collections, narratives, chronicles, especially those concerning the last journey of the Apostle, from the hand of Luke may be the foundation of the Acts. That the name of Luke has been prefixed to it presupposes only that as its whole purpose is preeminently devoted to the life and labors of the Apostle Paul, the work is evidently written in his interest, and can only have proceeded from the immediate circle of the Apostle. Was not this in the mind of the author, when in one place he allows himself, by the expression "We," to be brought forward as in existing and intimate relations with the person under consideration? Who is it that speaks of himself in this form? He calls himself by no name—the name of Luke nowhere occurs in the Acts of the Apostles—but as Luke (Col 4:14) is represented as standing in such close relations with Paul, why should not the author have put himself by the use of "We" in the place of Luke, and identified himself with him? Perhaps an existing account of the journey from the hand of Luke was the cause of this. In such passages the author is very willing to be considered as one person with Luke; but he does not dare as the writer of the Acts of the Apostles, to come forward openly in the character of Luke, for he was well aware of the difference in dates, and could not so completely forego his own identity.

The apologetic interest of his statement does not depend on its historical character, but limits and modifies it. Unhistorical as it appears in many points, on which we can bring to bear proofs from the Apostle's own declarations, it is on the other hand in agreement in many instances with other passages in the received history of that time. The Acts of the Apostles therefore, although it must be judged of in quite a different manner from that generally employed, with regard to its author, its aim, and the time of its production, remains a highly-important source of the History of the Apostolic Age. It is, however, a source which needs strict historical criticism before it can win a place as a trustworthy historical picture of the persons and circumstances of which it treats. . . .

2. Ernest Renan
THE LIFE OF JESUS (1863)[6]

In 1835, the same year that Baur's academic work on St. Paul appeared, another member of the Tübingen school, David Friedrich Strauss (1808–1874), published a book that introduced the techniques of Higher Criticism to a wide general audience and earned the movement immediate renown as well as infamy. In his otherwise cautious *Life of Jesus,* Strauss boldly dismissed all of the supernatural elements of the four gospels as creative myths, a stance that led to his own expulsion from academe. Almost thirty years later, another scholar, the Frenchman Ernest Renan (1823–1892), published an even more controversial biography of Jesus, bringing its author similar academic exclusion but also huge commercial success. Like Strauss, Renan portrays Jesus as an amiable Galilean preacher whose life was later given mythic dimensions by his followers. Drawing on extensive scriptural cross-referencing and historical evidence, however, Renan places even greater emphasis on the ordinariness of Jesus' background and early life, including in his book a speculative description of Jesus' village and the suggestion that he came from a typically large family. Embarrassed by the miraculous elements of the gospels, Renan concludes that Jesus would never have dreamt of passing himself off as divine, and that his healing and other so-called miracles were merely "performances" necessary to establish his preaching credibility alongside the other wonder-working rabbis of the day. Despite strong clerical opposition in his native France, Renan was eventually restored to his seat in the prestigious Collège de France in 1870 and continued to write popular books about St. Paul and other aspects of Christianity.

CHAPTER II
INFANCY AND YOUTH OF JESUS—HIS FIRST IMPRESSIONS

Jesus was born at Nazareth [Mt 13:54; Mk 6:1; Jn 1:45–46], a small town of Galilee, which before his time had no celebrity. All his life he was designated by the name of "the Nazarene" [Mk 1:24; Lk 18:37; Jn 19:19; Acts 2:22, 3:6], and it is only by a rather embarrassed and round-about way, that, in the legends respecting him, he is made to be born at Bethlehem. We shall see later the motive for this supposition, and how it was the necessary consequence of the Messianic character attributed to Jesus [Mt 13:54; Mk 6:1]. The precise date of his birth is unknown. It took place under the reign

[6]Most of the author's extensive footnotes have been omitted. All of Renan's scriptural citations, however, are included in the text.

of Augustus, about the Roman year 750, probably some years before the year 1 of that era which all civilized people date from the day on which he was born.

The name of *Jesus,* which was given him, is an alteration from *Joshua.* It was a very common name; but afterward mysteries, and an allusion to his character of Savior, were naturally sought for in it [Mt 1:21; Lk 1:31]. Perhaps he, like all mystics, exalted himself in this respect. It is thus that more than one great vocation in history has been caused by a name given to a child without premeditation. Ardent natures never bring themselves to see aught of chance in what concerns them. God has regulated everything for them, and they see a sign of the supreme will in the most insignificant circumstances. . . .

He proceeded from the ranks of the people. His father, Joseph, and his mother, Mary were people in humble circumstances, artisans living by their labor [Mt 13:55; Mk 6:3; Jn 6:42], in the state so common in the East, which is neither ease nor poverty. The extreme simplicity of life in such countries, by dispensing with the need of comfort, renders the privileges of wealth almost useless, and makes every one voluntarily poor. On the other hand, the total want of taste for art, and for that which contributes to the elegance of material life, gives a naked aspect to the house of him who otherwise wants for nothing. Apart from something sordid and repulsive which Islamism bears everywhere with it, the town of Nazareth, in the time of Jesus, did not perhaps much differ from what it is to-day. We see the streets where he played when a child, in the stony paths or little crossways which separate the dwellings. The house of Joseph doubtless much resembled those poor shops, lighted by the door, serving at once for shop, kitchen, and bedroom, having for furniture a mat, some cushions on the ground, one or two clay pots, and a painted chest.

The family, whether it proceeded from one or many marriages, was rather numerous. Jesus had brothers and sisters [Mt 12:46, 13:55; Mk 3:31, 6:3; Lk 8:19; Jn 2:12, 7:3, 5, 10; Acts 1:14], of whom he seems to have been the eldest [Mt 1:25]. All have remained obscure, for it appears that the four personages who were named as his brothers, and among whom one, at least—James—had acquired great importance in the earliest years of the development of Christianity, were his [first cousins]. Mary, in fact, had a sister also named Mary, who married a certain Alpheus or Cleophas (these two names appear to designate the same person), and was the mother of several sons who played a considerable part among the first disciples of Jesus. These [first cousins] who adhered to the young Master, while his own brothers opposed him [Jn 7:3], took the title of "brothers of the Lord." The real brothers of Jesus, like their mother, became important only after his death [Acts 1:14]. Even then they do not appear to have equaled in importance their cousins, whose conversion had been more spontaneous, and whose character seems to have had more originality. Their names were so little known, that when the evangelist put in the mouth of the men of Nazareth the enumeration of the brothers according to natural relationship, the names of the sons of Cleophas first presented themselves to him.

His sisters were married at Nazareth [Mk 6:3], and he spent the first years of his youth there. Nazareth was a small town in a hollow, opening broadly at the summit of the group of mountains which close the plain of Esdraelon on the north. The population is now from three to four thousand, and it can never have varied much. The cold there is sharp in winter, and the climate very healthy. The town, like all the small Jewish towns at this period, was a heap of huts built without style, and would exhibit that harsh and poor aspect which villages in Semitic countries now present. The houses, it seems, did not differ much from those cubes of stone, without exterior or interior elegance, which still cover the richest parts of the Lebanon, and which, surrounded with vines and fig-trees, are still very agreeable. The environs, moreover, are charming; and no place in the world was so well adapted for dreams of perfect happiness. Even in our times Nazareth is still a delightful abode, the only place, perhaps, in Palestine in which the mind feels itself relieved from the burden which oppresses it in this unequaled desolation. The people are amiable and cheerful; the gardens fresh and green. . . .

This name of *"kingdom of God,"* or *"kingdom of heaven,"* was the favorite term of Jesus to express the revolution which he brought into the world.[7] Like almost all the Messianic terms, it came from the book of Daniel. According to the author of this extraordinary book, the four profane empires, destined to fall, were to be succeeded by a fifth empire, that of the saints, which should last forever. [Dan 2:44, 7:13, 14, 22, 27] This reign of God upon earth naturally led to the most diverse interpretations. To Jewish theology, the "kingdom of God" is most frequently only Judaism itself—the true religion, the monotheistic worship, piety. In the later periods of his life, Jesus believed that this reign would be realized in a material form by a sudden renovation of the world. But doubtless this was not his first idea [Mt 6:33, 12:28, 19:12; Mk 12:34; Lk 12:31]. The admirable moral which he draws from the idea of God as Father, is not that of enthusiasts who believe the world is near its end, and who prepare themselves by asceticism for a chimerical catastrophe; it is that of men who have lived, and still would live. *"The kingdom of God is within you,"* said he to those who sought with subtlety for external signs [Lk 17:20, 21]. The realistic conception of the Divine advent was but a cloud, a transient error, which his death has made us forget. The Jesus who founded the true kingdom of God, the kingdom of the meek and the humble, was the Jesus of early life—of those chaste and pure days when the voice of

his Father re-echoed within him in clearer tones. It was then for some months, perhaps a year, that God truly dwelt upon the earth. The voice of the young carpenter suddenly acquired an extraordinary sweetness. An infinite charm was exhaled from his person, and those who had seen him up to that time no longer recognized him [Mt 13:54; Mk 6:2; Jn 5:43]. He had not yet any disciples, and the group which gathered around him was neither a sect nor a school; but a common spirit, a sweet and penetrating influence was felt. His amiable character, accompanied doubtless by one of those lovely faces which sometimes appear in the Jewish race, threw around him a fascination from which no one in the midst of these kindly and simple populations could escape. . . .

CHAPTER XV
COMMENCEMENT OF THE LEGENDS CONCERNING JESUS— HIS OWN IDEA OF HIS SUPERNATURAL CHARACTER

Jesus returned to Galilee, having completely lost his Jewish faith, and filled with revolutionary ardor. His ideas are now expressed with perfect clearness. The innocent aphorisms of the first part of his prophetic career, in part borrowed from the Jewish rabbis anterior to him, and the beautiful moral precepts of his second period, are exchanged for a decided policy. The Law would be abolished; and it was to be abolished by him. The Messiah had come, and he was the Messiah. The kingdom of God was about to be revealed; and it was he who would reveal it. He knew well that he would be the victim of his boldness; but the kingdom of God could not be conquered without violence; it was by crises and commotions that it was to be established [Mt 11:12; Lk 16:16]. The Son of man would reappear in glory, accompanied by legions of angels, and those who had rejected him would be confounded. . . .

One great difficulty presented itself—his birth at Nazareth, which was of public notori-

---

[7][Author's note:] The word "heaven" in the rabbinical language of that time is synonymous with the name of "God," which they avoided pronouncing. Compare Mt 21:25; Lk 15:18, 20:4. This expression occurs on each page of the synoptical Gospels, the Acts of the Apostles, and St. Paul. If it only appears once in John (3:3, 5), it is because the discourses related in the fourth Gospel are far from representing the true words of Jesus.

cty. We do not know whether Jesus strove against this objection. Perhaps it did not present itself in Galilee, where the idea that the son of David should be a Bethlehemite was less spread. To the Galilean idealist, moreover, the title of "son of David" was sufficiently justified, if he to whom it was given revived the glory of his race, and brought back the great days of Israel. Did Jesus authorize by his silence the fictitious genealogies which his partisans invented in order to prove his royal descent? [Mt 1:1; Lk 2:1] Did he know anything of the legends invented to prove that he was born at Bethlehem; and particularly of the attempt to connect his Bethlehemite origin with the census which had taken place by order of the imperial legate, Quirinus? [Mt 2:1; Lk 2:1] We know not. The inexactitude and the contradictions of the genealogies lead to the belief that they were the result of popular ideas operating at various points, and that none of them were sanctioned by Jesus. Never does he designate himself as son of David. His disciples, much less enlightened than he, frequently magnified that which he said of himself; but, as a rule, he had no knowledge of these exaggerations. Let us add, that during the first three centuries, considerable portions of Christendom[8] obstinately denied the royal descent of Jesus and the authenticity of the genealogies.

The legends about him were thus the fruit of a great and entirely spontaneous conspiracy, and were developed around him during his lifetime. No great event in history has happened without having given rise to a cycle of fables; and Jesus could not have put a stop to these popular creations, even if he had wished to do so. . . .

That Jesus never dreamt of making himself pass for an incarnation of God, is a matter about which there can be no doubt. Such an idea was entirely foreign to the Jewish mind; and there is no trace of it in the synoptical gospels [cf. Acts 2:22], we only find it indi-

cated in portions of the Gospel of John, which cannot be accepted as expressing the thoughts of Jesus. Sometimes Jesus even seems to take precautions to put down such a doctrine [Mt 19:17; Mk 10:18; Lk 18:19]. The accusation that he made himself God, or the equal of God, is presented, even in the Gospel of John, as a calumny of the Jews [Jn 5:18, 10:33]. In this last Gospel he declares himself less than his Father [Jn 14:28]. Elsewhere he avows that the Father has not revealed everything to him [Mk 13:35]. He believes himself to be more than an ordinary man, but separated from God by an infinite distance. He is Son of God, but all men are, or may become so, in diverse degrees [Mt 5:9, 45; Lk 3:38, 6:35, 20:36; Jn 1:12, 13, 10:34, 35. Cf. Acts 17:28, 29; Rom 8:14, 19, 21; 6: 26; 2 Cor 6:18; Gal 3:26; and in the Old Testament, Deut 14:1; and especially Wis 2:13, 18]. Every one ought daily to call God his father; all who are raised again will be sons of God [Lk 20:36]. The divine son-ship was attributed in the Old Testament to beings whom it was by no means pretended were equal with God [Gen 6:2; Job 1:6, 2:1, 28:7; Ps 2:7, 82:6; 2 Sam 7:14]. The word "son" has the widest meanings in the Semitic language, and in that of the New Testament.[9] . . .

CHAPTER XVI
MIRACLES

. . . As to miracles, they were regarded at this period as the indispensable mark of the divine, and as the sign of the prophetic vocation. The legends of Elijah and Elisha were full of them. It was commonly believed that the Messiah would perform many [Jn 7:34; IV. Esdr 13:50]. In Samaria, a few leagues from where Jesus was, a magician, named Simon, acquired an almost divine

---

[8][Author's note:] The Ebionites, the "Hebrews," the "Nazarenes," Tatian, Marcion.

[9][Author's note:] The child of the devil (Mt 13:38; Acts 13:10); the children of this world (Mk 3:17; Lk 16:8, 20:34); the children of light (Lk 16:8; Jn 12:36); the children of the resurrection (Lk 20:36); the children of the kingdom (Mt 8:12, 13:38); the children of peace (Lk 10:6), &c.

character by his illusions [Acts 8:9]. Afterward, when it was sought to establish the reputation of Apollonius of Tyana, and to prove that his life had been the sojourn of a god upon the earth, it was not thought possible to succeed therein except by inventing a vast cycle of miracles. The Alexandrian philosophers themselves, Plotinus and others, are reported to have performed several.[10] Jesus was, therefore, obliged to choose between these two alternatives—either to renounce his mission, or to become a thaumaturgus ["wonderworker"]. It must be remembered that all antiquity, with the exception of the great scientific schools of Greece and their Roman disciples, accepted miracles; and that Jesus not only believed therein, but had not the least idea of an order of Nature regulated by fixed laws. His knowledge on this point was in no way superior to that of his contemporaries. Nay, more, one of his most deeply rooted opinions was, that by faith and prayer man has entire power over Nature [Mt 17:19, 21:21, 22; Mk 11:23, 24]. The faculty of performing miracles was regarded as a privilege frequently conferred by God upon men [Mt 9:8], and it had nothing surprising in it. . . .

It is probable that the hearers of Jesus were more struck by his miracles than by his eminently divine discourses. Let us add, that doubtless popular rumor, both before and after the death of Jesus, exaggerated enormously the number of occurrences of this kind. The types of the gospel miracles, in fact, do not present much variety; they are repetitions of each other and seem fashioned from a very small number of models, accommodated to the taste of the country.

It is impossible, amongst the miraculous narratives so tediously enumerated in the Gospels, to distinguish the miracles attributed to Jesus by public opinion from those in which he consented to play an active part. It is especially impossible to ascertain whether the offensive circumstances attending them, the groanings, the strugglings, and other features savoring of jugglery [Lk 8:45, 46; Jn 11:33, 38], are really historical or whether they are the fruit of the belief of the compilers, strongly imbued with theurgy,[11] and living, in this respect, in a world analogous to that of the "spiritualists" of our times [Acts 2:2, 4:31, 8:15, 10:44]. . . .

We will admit, then, without hesitation, that acts which would now be considered as acts of illusion or folly, held a large place in the life of Jesus. Must we sacrifice to these uninviting features the sublimer aspect of such a life? God forbid. A mere sorcerer, after the manner of Simon the magician, would not have brought about a moral revolution like that effected by Jesus. If the thaumaturgus had effaced in Jesus the moralist and the religious reformer, there would have proceeded from him a school of theurgy, and not Christianity. . . .

In a general sense, it is therefore true to say that Jesus was only thaumaturgus and exorcist in spite of himself. Miracles are ordinarily the work of the public much more than of him to whom they are attributed. Jesus persistently shunned the performance of the wonders which the multitude would have created for him; the greatest miracle would have been his refusal to perform any; never would the laws of history and popular psychology have suffered so great a derogation. The miracles of Jesus were a violence done to him by his age, a concession forced from him by a passing necessity. The exorcist and the thaumaturgus have alike passed away; but the religious reformer will live eternally. . . .

---

[10]Renan here refers to the Neo-Platonist Plotinus (205–270 C.E.) as well as Proclus (410–485) and Isidore of Seville (560–636).

[11]I.e, miraculous powers.

D. Catholic Renewal

Given the variety of forces arrayed against the Catholic Church in the nineteenth century—from anticlerical nationalists and socialists to agnostic and atheist "progressives" to antipapist nativist movements—the siege mentality of many of its leaders was certainly understandable. The pontificate of Pope Pius IX (r. 1846–1878) was emblematic of this reactionary aspect of nineteenth-century Catholicism, as was the pope's scathing "Syllabus of Errors" (1864), a condemnation of practically every aspect of modern political and social life. The conservative council of Vatican I (1869–1870) likewise favored a position of defensive entrenchment, evident in its controversial decree of papal infallibility on issues of faith and morality. On the other hand, the century was also a time of startling religious renewal among Catholics in a variety of areas. Among the laity, special prayer practices such as recitation of the rosary experienced a dramatic resurgence, as did devotions to the Virgin Mary, the Sacred Heart of Jesus, and the consecrated Host. An unprecedented number of people were beatified or canonized by Pius IX, and there was a rise in pilgrimage to numerous shrines, including new sites of miracles such as Lourdes in southern France. Meanwhile many of the clergy shared the spirit of renewal, reforming old religious orders, founding new ones, and in general paying much greater attention to pastoral care. New seminaries for priests, with curriculums based on Thomas Aquinas and other scholastic theologians, played an especially important part in clerical reform. New standardizations of the liturgical calendar and church rites were also instituted, and the use of Gregorian Chant in mass was reintroduced. Most innovatively, the Catholic Church under Pope Leo XIII (r. 1878–1903) finally began a constructive engagement with many of its secularist and Protestant antagonists, thus ending the nineteenth century as a much more "modern" institution than it had been when the century began.

1. John Henry Newman
APOLOGIA PRO VITA SUA: BEING A HISTORY OF HIS RELIGIOUS OPINIONS (1865; 1886)

Religious converts have always been valued by all Christian denominations, but the Catholic Church's acquisition of the respected Anglican scholar John Henry Newman (1801–1890) was a particularly stunning coup in nineteenth-century England. Catholics had only attained full civil and political rights in the United Kingdom in 1829, and at the time of Newman's conversion they were still viewed with suspicion by most English Protestants. A church historian by training, Newman began his journey toward Catholicism in the 1830s, when he joined the Oxford movement. This group of Oxford University students and faculty members favored a more High Church orientation for the Church of

England, a position that moved them closer to Catholics on a number of religious issues. Initially Newman staunchly defended the Church of England as a "middle way" between Catholicism and other Protestant churches. But by 1841, as he describes in the excerpt below from his *Apologia Pro Vita Sua* or "defense of his life," he had begun to doubt his position. Four years later, he entered the Catholic Church and was ordained a priest. During his long and active life, Newman was one of the foremost champions of Catholicism in England, and his efforts won for the Church a new level of credibility among his fellow intellectuals. Newman was named a cardinal by Pope Leo XIII in 1879.

CHAPTER IV
HISTORY OF MY RELIGIOUS OPINIONS FROM 1841 TO 1845

From the end of 1841, I was on my death-bed, as regards my membership with the Anglican Church, though at the time I became aware of it only by degrees. I introduce what I have to say with this remark, by the way of accounting for the character of this remaining portion of my narrative. A death-bed has scarcely a history; it is a tedious decline, with seasons of rallying and seasons of falling back; and since the end is foreseen, or what is called a matter of time, it has little interest for the reader, especially if he has a kind heart. Moreover, it is a season when doors are closed and curtains drawn, and when the sick man neither cares nor is able to record the stages of his malady. I was in these circumstances, except so far as I was not allowed to die in peace, — except so far as friends, who had still a full right to come in upon me, and the public world which had not, have given a sort of history to those last four years. . . .

And first as to my position in the view of duty; it was this:—1. I had given up my place in the [Oxford] Movement in my letter to the Bishop of Oxford in the spring of 1841; but 2. I could not give up my duties towards the many and various minds who had more or less been brought into it by me; 3. I expected or intended gradually to fall back into Lay Communion [i.e., leave the priesthood]; 4. I never contemplated leaving the Church of England; 5. I could not hold office in its service, if I were not allowed to hold the Catholic sense of the Articles; 6. I could not go to Rome, while she

suffered honours to be paid to the Blessed Virgin and the Saints which I thought in my conscience to be incompatible with the Supreme, Incommunicable Glory of the One Infinite and Eternal; 7. I desired a union with Rome under conditions, Church with Church; 8. I called Littlemore my Torres Vedras,[12] and thought that some day we might advance again within the Anglican Church, as we had been forced to retire; 9. I kept back all persons who were disposed to go to Rome with all my might.

And I kept them back for three or four reasons; 1. because what I could not in conscience do myself, I could not suffer them to do; 2. because I thought that in various cases they were acting under excitement; 3. because I had duties to my Bishop and to the Anglican Church; and 4, in some cases, because I had received from their Anglican parents or superiors direct charge of them. . . .

[Three years later, Newman has changed his position decisively. He quotes from one of his letters to a friend:]

"The kind of considerations which weighs with me are such as the following:—1. I am far more certain (according to the Fathers) that we [i.e., the Church of England] *are* in a state of

---

[12]The village of Littlemore, located two miles southeast of Oxford, was the site of a parsonage which Newman increasingly frequented during his spiritual crisis. Torres Vedras refers to three lines of retreat constructed by Wellington during the Spanish campaign against Napoleon in 1810. By successfully staving off enemy armies for more than a month, Wellington was able to advance again and ultimately triumph.

culpable separation, *than* that developments do *not* exist under the Gospel, and that the Roman developments are not the true ones. 2. I am far more certain that *our* (modern) doctrines are wrong, *than* that the *Roman* (modern) doctrines are. 3. Granting that the Roman (special) doctrines are not found drawn out in the early Church, yet I think there is sufficient trace of them in it, to recommend and prove them, *on the hypothesis* of the Church having a divine guidance, though not sufficient to prove them by itself. So that the question simply turns on the nature of the promise of the Spirit, made to the Church. 4. The proof of the Roman (modern) doctrine is as strong (or stronger) in Antiquity, as that of certain doctrines which both we and Romans hold: e.g. there is more of evidence in Antiquity for the necessity of Unity, than for the Apostolical Succession; for the Supremacy of the See of Rome, than for the Presence in the Eucharist; for the practice of Invocation, than for certain books in the present Canon of Scripture, &c. &c. 5. The analogy of the Old Testament, and also of the New, leads to the acknowledgment of doctrinal developments."

4. And thus I was led on to a further consideration. I saw that the principle of development not only accounted for certain facts, but was in itself a remarkable philosophical phenomenon, giving a character to the whole course of Christian thought. It was discernible from the first years of the Catholic teaching up to the present day, and gave to that teaching a unity and individuality. It served as a sort of test which the Anglican could not exhibit, that modern Rome was in truth ancient Antioch, Alexandria, and Constantinople,[13] just as a mathematical curve has its own law and expression.

5. And thus again I was led on to examine more attentively what I doubt not was in my thoughts long before, viz. that concatenation of argument by which the mind ascends from its first to its final religious idea; and I came to the conclusion that there was no medium, in true philosophy, between Atheism and Catholicity,

and that a perfectly consistent mind, under those circumstances in which it finds itself here below, must embrace either the one or the other. And I hold this still: I am a Catholic by virtue of my believing in a God; and if I am asked why I believe in a God, I answer that it is because I believe in myself, for I feel it impossible to believe in my own existence (and of that fact I am quite sure) without believing also in the existence of Him, who lives as a Personal, All-seeing, All-judging Being in my conscience. Now, I dare say, I have not expressed myself with philosophical correctness, because I have not given myself to the study of what metaphysicians have said on the subject; but I think I have a strong true meaning in what I say which will stand examination.

6. Moreover, I found a corroboration of the fact of the logical connexion of Theism with Catholicism in a consideration parallel to that which I had adopted on the subject of development of doctrine. The fact of the operation from first to last of that principle of development in the truths of Revelation, is an argument in favour of the identity of Roman and Primitive Christianity; but as there is a law which acts upon the subject-matter of dogmatic theology, so is there a law in the matter of religious faith. In the first chapter of this Narrative I spoke of certitude as the consequence, divinely intended and enjoined upon us, of the accumulative force of certain given reasons which, taken one by one, were only probabilities. Let it be recollected that I am historically relating my state of mind, at the period of my life which I am surveying. I am not speaking theologically, nor have I any intention of going into controversy, or of defending myself; but speaking historically of what I held in 1843–4, I say, that I believed in a God on a ground of probability, that I believed in Christianity on a probability, and that I believed in Catholicism on a probability, and that these three grounds of probability, distinct from each other of course in subject matter, were still all of them one and the same in nature of proof, as being probabilities—probabilities of a special kind, a cumulative, a transcendent probability but still probability; inasmuch as He who made us has so willed, that in mathematics indeed we should arrive at certitude by rigid

---

[13]The sites of the most influential theological "schools" of ancient Christianity.

demonstration, but in religious inquiry we should arrive at certitude by accumulated probabilities;—He has willed, I say, that we should so act, and, as willing it, He co-operates with us in our acting, and thereby enables us to do that which He wills us to do, and carries us on, if our will does but co-operate with His, to a certitude which rises higher than the logical force of our conclusions. And thus I came to see clearly, and to have a satisfaction in seeing, that, in being led on into the Church of Rome, I was not proceeding on any secondary or isolated grounds of reason, or by controversial points in detail, but was protected and justified, even in the use of those secondary or particular arguments, by a great and broad principle. But, let it be observed, that I am stating a matter of fact, not defending it; and if any Catholic says in consequence that I have been converted in a wrong way, I cannot help that now. . . .

CHAPTER V
POSITION OF MY MIND SINCE 1845

From the time that I became a Catholic, of course I have no further history of my religious opinions to narrate. In saying this, I do not mean to say that my mind has been idle, or that I have given up thinking on theological subjects; but that I have had no variations to record, and have had no anxiety of heart whatever. I have been in perfect peace and contentment; I never have had one doubt. I was not conscious to myself, on my conversion, of any change, intellectual or moral, wrought in my mind. I was not conscious of firmer faith in the fundamental truths of Revelation, or of more self-command; I had not more fervour; but it was like coming into port after a rough sea; and my happiness on that score remains to this day without interruption.

Nor had I any trouble about receiving those additional articles, which are not found in the Anglican Creed. Some of them I believed already, but not any one of them was a trial to me. I made a profession of them upon my reception with the greatest ease, and I have the same ease in believing them now. I am far of course from denying that every article of the Christian Creed, whether as held by Catholics or by Protestants, is beset with intellectual difficulties; and it is a simple fact, that, for myself, I cannot answer those difficulties. Many persons are very sensitive of the difficulties of Religion; I am as sensitive of them as any one; but I have never been able to see a connexion between apprehending those difficulties, however keenly, and multiplying them to any extent, and on the other hand doubting the doctrines to which they are attached. Ten thousand difficulties do not make one doubt, as I understand the subject; difficulty and doubt are incommensurate. There of course may be difficulties in the evidence; but I am speaking of difficulties intrinsic to the doctrines themselves, or to their relations with each other. A man may be annoyed that he cannot work out a mathematical problem, of which the answer is or is not given to him, without doubting that it admits of an answer, or that a certain particular answer is the true one. Of all points of faith, the being of a God is, to my own apprehension, encompassed with most difficulty, and yet borne in upon our minds with most power. . . .

2. Gerard Manley Hopkins
POETRY

Gerard Manley Hopkins (1844–1889) was, like John Henry Newman, both a graduate of Oxford University and an adult convert to Catholicism. At the age of twenty-four he entered the Jesuit order, and he later became a professor of Greek at the Royal University in Dublin. His now famous poetry was almost completely unknown during his short lifetime, not appearing in a complete edition until 1918. Sometimes his poems deal with explicitly religious subjects; for example, in "The Habit of Perfection," Hopkins meditates on his own priestly vocation. Usually, though, the tension between sensuous wonder and ascetic withdrawal for which his poems are most celebrated is more implicit, provoking a great intensity of feeling while limiting or excluding overtly Christian references. This paradoxical tension between the world and the soul, between freedom and sacrifice, was at the core of Hopkins' Catholic vision. It also guided his inspired use of invented compound words ("lovely-dumb") as well as of images (silence singing). The freeflowing yet harmonious result has earned Hopkins countless admirers from all kinds of religious backgrounds.

a. "THE HABIT OF PERFECTION" (1866)

Elected Silence, sing to me
And beat upon my whorlèd ear,
Pipe me to pastures still and be
The music that I care to hear.

Shape nothing, lips; be lovely-dumb:
It is the shut, the curfew sent
From there where all surrenders come
Which only makes you eloquent.

Be shellèd, eyes, with double dark
And find the uncreated light:
This ruck and reel which you remark
Coils, keeps, and teases simple sight.

Palate, the hutch of tasty lust,
Desire not to be rinsed with wine:
The can must be so sweet, the crust
So fresh that come in fasts divine!

Nostrils, your careless breath that spend
Upon the stir and keep of pride,
What relish shall the censers[14] send
Along the sanctuary side!

O feel-of-primrose hands, O feet
That want the yield of plushy sward,
But you shall walk the golden street
And you unhouse and house the Lord.

And, Poverty, be thou the bride
And now the marriage feast begun,
And lily-colored clothes provide
Your spouse not labored-at nor spun.[15]

---

[14]Incense vessels.
[15]A reference to the lilies of the field, "who spin not neither do they toil" [Mt 6:28; Lk 12:27].

b. "GOD'S GRANDEUR" (1877)

The world is charged with the grandeur of God.

It will flame out, like shining from shook
    foil;
It gathers to a greatness, like the ooze of oil
Crushed. Why do men then now not reck his rod?
Generations have trod, have trod, have trod;
    And all is seared with trade; bleared,
        smeared with toil;
    And wears man's smudge and shares man's
    smell: the soil

Is bare now, nor can foot feel, being shod.
And for all this, nature is never spent;
    There lives the dearest freshness deep down
        things;
And though the last lights off the black West
    went
    Oh, morning, at the brown brink eastward,
        springs—

Because the Holy Ghost over the bent
    World broods with warm breast and with
        ah! bright wings.

c. "THE CAGED SKYLARK" (1877)

As a dare-gale skylark scanted in a dull cage
  Man's mounting spirit in his bone-house,
    mean house, dwells—
    That bird beyond the remembering his free
    fells;
This in drudgery, day-laboring-out life's age.

Though aloft on turf or perch or poor low
    stage,
    Both sing sometimes the sweetest, sweetest
    spells,
    Yet both droop deadly sometimes in their cells
Or wring their barriers in bursts of fear or rage.

Not that the sweet-fowl, song-fowl, needs no
  rest—
Why, hear him, hear him babble and drop
    down to his nest,
    But his own nest, wild nest, no prison.

Man's spirit will be flesh-bound when found at
    best,
But uncumbered: meadow-down is not dis-
    tressed
    For a rainbow footing it nor he for his bones
    risen.

3. Thérèse (Martin) of Lisieux
STORY OF A SOUL (1895)

Thérèse of Lisieux (1873–1897) was perhaps the most popular saint produced by nineteenth-century Catholicism. Though her life as a girl and young nun in and near the French town of Lisieux was outwardly unremarkable, the burning devotion described in her posthumously published autobiography, *Story of a Soul*, quickly made her into a cult figure, and she was canonized in 1925. In this excerpt, Thérèse conveys the intensity of the religious desires that had filled her since childhood. Joan of Arc, the medieval "maid of France" who also died at a young age, was a particular source of inspiration to her. At the age of fifteen, Thérèse joined three of her other sisters in the Carmelite convent at Lisieux, and she remained there until her premature death from tuberculosis nine years later. Her illness prevented her from participating in a mission to Viet Nam and also made her austere convent life even more uncomfortable. Her always pleasant and smiling demeanor generally concealed her suffering, though, as it did the passionate religious yearnings, which were only later revealed in her writing. Thérèse was not an innovative thinker nor was she prone to mystical experience. Her message, rather, was a simple one of total submission to the will of God. She is also known as the Little Flower or as Thérèse of the Child Jesus.

. . . One day, Léonie,[16] thinking she was too big to be playing any longer with dolls, came to us with a basket filled with dresses and pretty pieces for making others; her doll was resting on top. "Here, my little sisters, *choose;* I'm giving you all this." Céline[17] stretched out her hand and took a little ball of wool which pleased her. After a moment's reflection, I

---

[16]Older sister of Thérèse.

[17]Younger sister of Thérèse.

stretched out mine saying: "I choose all!" and I took the basket without further ceremony. Those who witnessed the scene saw nothing wrong and even Céline herself didn't dream of complaining (besides, she had all sorts of toys, her godfather gave her lots of presents, and Louise found ways of getting her everything she desired).

This little incident of my childhood is a summary of my whole life; later on when perfection was set before me, I understood that to become *a saint* one had to suffer much, seek out always the most perfect thing to do, and forget self. I understood, too, there were many degrees of perfection and each soul was free to respond to the advances of Our Lord, to do little or much for Him, in a word, to *choose* among the sacrifices He was asking. Then, as in the days of my childhood, I cried out: "My God *'I choose all!'* I don't want to be a *saint* by *halves*, I'm not afraid to suffer for You, I fear only one thing: to keep my *own will;* so take it, for *'I choose all'* that You will!" . . .

I forgot several details of my childhood before your[18] entrance into Carmel; for instance, I haven't spoken about my love for pictures and reading. And still, dear Mother, I owe to the beautiful pictures you gave me as rewards, one of the sweetest joys and strongest impressions which aided me in the practice of virtue. I was forgetting to say anything about the hours I spent looking at them. The *little flower* of the Divine Prisoner,[19] for example, said so many things to me that I became deeply recollected. Seeing that the name of *Pauline* was written under the little flower, I wanted Thérèse's name to be written there also and I offered myself to Jesus as His *little flower.*

I wasn't too good at playing games, but I did love reading very much and would have spent my life at it. I had human *angels,* fortunately for

me, to guide me in the choice of the books which, while being entertaining, nourished both my heart and my mind. And I was not to go beyond a certain time in my reading, which was the cause of great sacrifices to me as I had to interrupt my reading very often at the most enticing passage. This attraction for reading lasted until my entrance into Carmel. To state the number of books that passed through my hands would be impossible, but never did God permit me to read a single one of them which was capable of doing me any harm. It is true that in reading certain tales of chivalry, I didn't always understand the *realities* of *life;* but soon God made me feel that true glory is that which will last eternally, and to reach it, it isn't necessary to perform striking works but to hide oneself and practice virtue in such a way that the left hand knows not what the right is doing [Mt 6:3].

When reading the accounts of the patriotic deeds of French heroines, especially the *Venerable* JOAN OF ARC, I had a great desire to imitate them; and it seemed I felt within me the same burning zeal with which they were animated, the same heavenly inspiration. Then I received a grace which I have always looked upon as one of the greatest in my life because at that age I wasn't receiving the *lights* I'm now receiving when I am flooded with them. I considered that I was born for *glory* and when I searched out the means of attaining it, God inspired in me the sentiments I have just described. He made me understand my own *glory* would not be evident to the eyes of mortals, that it would consist in becoming a great *saint!* This desire could certainly appear daring if one were to consider how weak and imperfect I was, and how, after seven years in the religious life, I still am weak and imperfect. I always feel, however, the same bold confidence of becoming a great saint because I don't count on my merits since I have *none,* but I trust in Him who is Virtue and Holiness. God alone, content with my weak efforts, will raise me to Himself and make me a *saint,* clothing me in His infinite merits. I didn't think then that one had to suffer very

---

[18]Mother Agnes, her older sister and prioress of the convent at Carmel from 1893 to 1896

[19]A reference to Spanish mystic St. John of the Cross (1542–1591), a Discalced Carmelite imprisoned for nine months in a monastery by a displeased Visitor General. St. John was a special source of inspiration for Thérèse.

much to reach sanctity, but God was not long in showing me this was so and in sending me the trials I have already mentioned. . . .

One evening, not knowing how to tell Jesus that I loved Him and how much I desired that He be loved and glorified everywhere, I was thinking He would never receive a single act of love from hell; then I said to God that to please Him I would consent to see myself plunged into hell so that He would be loved eternally in that place of blasphemy. I realized this could not give Him glory since He desires only our happiness, but when we love, we experience the need of saying a thousand foolish things; if I talked in this way, it wasn't because heaven did not excite my desire, but because at this time my heaven was none other than Love, and I felt, as did St. Paul, that nothing could separate us from the Divine Being who so ravished me! [Rom 8:39]. . . .

I feel in me the *vocation of* the PRIEST. With what love, O Jesus, I would carry You in my hands when, at my voice, You would come down from heaven. And with what love would I give You to souls! But alas! while desiring to be a *Priest*, I admire and envy the humility of St. Francis of Assisi and I feel the *vocation* of imitating him in refusing the sublime dignity of the *Priesthood*.

O Jesus, my Love, my Life, how can I combine these contrasts? How can I realize the desires of my poor *little soul*?

Ah! in spite of my littleness, I would like to enlighten souls as did the *Prophets* and the *Doctors*. I have the *vocation of the Apostle*. I would like to travel over the whole earth to preach Your Name and to plant Your glorious Cross on infidel soil. But *O my Beloved,* one mission alone would not be sufficient for me. I would want to preach the Gospel on all the five continents simultaneously and even to the most remote isles. I would be a missionary, not for a few years only but from the beginning of creation until the consummation of the ages. But above all, O my Beloved Savior, I would shed my blood for You even to the very last drop.

Martyrdom was the dream of my youth and this dream has grown with me within Carmel's cloisters. But here again, I feel that my dream is a folly, for I cannot confine myself to desiring *one kind* of martyrdom. To satisfy me I need *all*. Like You, my Adorable Spouse, I would be scourged and crucified. I would die flayed like St. Bartholomew. I would be plunged into boiling oil like St. John; I would undergo all the tortures inflicted upon the martyrs. With St. Agnes and St. Cecelia, I would present my neck to the sword, and like Joan of Arc, my dear sister, I would whisper at the stake Your Name, O JESUS.[20] When thinking of the torments which will be the lot of Christians at the time of Anti-Christ, I feel my heart leap with joy and I would that these torments be reserved for me. Jesus, Jesus, if I wanted to write all my desires, I would have to borrow Your *Book of Life* [Rev 20:12], for in it are reported all the actions of all the saints, and I would accomplish all of them for You.

O my Jesus! what is your answer to all my follies? Is there a soul more *little*, more powerless than mine? Nevertheless even because of my weakness, it has pleased You, O Lord, to grant my *little childish desires* and You desire, today, to grant other desires that are *greater* than the universe.

During my meditation, my desires caused me a veritable martyrdom, and I opened the Epistles of St. Paul to find some kind of answer. Chapters 12 and 13 of the First Epistle to the Corinthians fell under my eyes. I read there, in the first of these chapters, that *all* cannot be apostles, prophets, doctors, etc., that the Church is composed of different members, and that the eye cannot be the hand *at one and the same time* [1 Cor 12: 29, 21]. The answer was clear, but it did not fulfill my desires and gave me no peace. But just as Mary Magdalene found what she was seeking by always stooping down and looking into the empty tomb, so I, abasing myself to the very depths of my nothing-

---

[20]All saints and martyrs of the faith; with the exception of Joan of Arc (d. 1329), all ancient figures.

ness, raised myself so high that I was able to attain my end. Without becoming discouraged, I continued my reading, and this sentence consoled me: "*Yet strive after THE BETTER GIFTS, and I point out to you a yet more excellent way*" [1 Cor 12:31, 13:1]. And the Apostle explains how all *the most PERFECT gifts* are nothing without LOVE. That *Charity is the EXCELLENT WAY* that leads most surely to God.

I finally had rest. Considering the mystical body of the Church, I had not recognized myself in any of the members described by St. Paul, or rather I desired to see myself in them *all*. *Charity* gave me the key to my *vocation*. I understood that if the Church had a body composed of different members, the most necessary and most noble of all could not be lacking to it, and so I understood that the Church *had a Heart and that this Heart was BURNING WITH LOVE. I understood it was Love alone* that made the Church's members act, that if *Love* ever became extinct, apostles would not preach the Gospel and martyrs would not shed their blood. I understood that LOVE COMPRISED ALL VOCATIONS, THAT LOVE WAS EVERYTHING, THAT IT EMBRACED ALL TIMES AND PLACES . . . IN A WORD, THAT IT WAS ETERNAL!

Then, in the excess of my delirious joy, I cried out: O Jesus, my Love . . . my *vocation*, at last I have found it. . . . MY VOCATION IS LOVE!

Yes, I have found my place in the Church and it is You, O my God, who have given me this place; in the heart of the Church, my Mother, I shall be *Love*. Thus I shall be everything, and thus my dream will be realized. . . .

You know, Mother, I have always wanted to be a saint. Alas! I have always noticed that when I compared myself to the saints, there is between them and me the same difference that exists between a mountain whose summit is lost in the clouds and the obscure grain of sand trampled underfoot by the passers-by. Instead of becoming discouraged, I said to myself: God cannot inspire unrealizable desires. I can, then, in spite of my littleness, aspire to holiness. It is impossible for me to grow up, and so I must bear with myself such as I am with all my imperfections. But I want to seek out a means of going to heaven by a little way, a way that is very straight, very short, and totally new.

We are living now in an age of inventions, and we no longer have to take the trouble of climbing stairs, for, in the homes of the rich, an elevator has replaced these very successfully. I wanted to find an elevator which would raise me to Jesus, for I am too small to climb the rough stairway of perfection. I searched, then, in the Scriptures for some sign of this elevator, the object of my desires, and I read these words coming from the mouth of Eternal Wisdom: "*Whoever is a LITTLE ONE, let him come to me*" [Prov 9:4]. And so I succeeded. I felt I had found what I was looking for. But wanting to know, O my God, what You would do to *the very little one* who answered Your call, I continued my search and this is what I discovered: "*As one whom a mother caresses, so will I comfort you; you shall be carried at the breasts, and upon the knees they shall caress you*" [Isa 66:13, 12]. Ah! never did words more tender and more melodious come to give joy to my soul. The elevator which must raise me to heaven is Your arms, O Jesus! And for this I had no need to grow up, but rather I had to remain *little* and become this more and more. . . .

E. Missionary Societies

The nineteenth century has been called "the Great Century" for Christian evangelization. From the founding of the British Methodist Missionary Society in 1786 until the beginning of the twentieth century, millions of people in Asia and

Africa were converted to Christianity through the work of European and American missionaries. Unlike earlier efforts by Jesuits and other Catholic missionaries, nineteenth-century Protestant missions were largely funded by private associations, known as missionary societies, which often drew on interdenominational support. By the middle of the century, many of these societies had begun to pool their efforts, holding missionary conferences from 1854 on and occasionally creating larger organizations such as the China Inland Mission, founded in 1865. In the United States, revivalist preachers such as Dwight L. Moody raised money for missions and recruited new missionaries, while in Britain, inspirational tales about the adventures of missionaries such as Dr. David Livingston (1813–1873) fired the imagination of supporters. Missionary work was sometimes dangerous and almost always tedious, but this did not deter tens of thousands from volunteering to spread Christianity to the "heathens" of Asia and Africa. Along with religion, these volunteers brought Western medicine, improved sanitation techniques, and education in European languages and culture. But they also imposed many Western ideas about behavior and social order as well as imperialist domination by their European governments. Although most Christian missionaries embarked with a desire to do good, many of their "civilizing" efforts, when viewed from today's perspective, appear insensitive at best and destructive at worst. Success for the missionaries was also frustratingly slow. For example, there were some twenty missionary societies in India alone by 1860, but during the next forty years they managed to convert only .2% of the population to Christianity. Still, many strong footholds were established, particularly in India and China, and by the beginning of the twentieth century, only the Himalayan region of Asia and the most remote jungles of Africa and South America remained closed to intrepid Christian missionaries. Because of their work, churches in countries outside of Europe and the Americas continued to grow throughout the twentieth century, and soon the Christians of Asia and Africa will outnumber those in the West.

1. Erastus Wentworth
JOURNAL (1856)

According to legend, the first Christian missionary in China was the apostle St. Thomas. The first historical evidence of Christians in the Middle Kingdom, though, is that of Syrian missionaries in the seventh century, with the first Western Christian missionaries arriving during the sixteenth century. Subsequent persecutions of Chinese converts, however, led to a decline of Christian groups until the great new missionary initiative of the mid nineteenth century. In 1842, the Treaty of Nanking opened up five Chinese port cities to foreigners, leading to a boom in Christian missionaries, from 80 in China at the time of the treaty to over 1,200 resident missionaries in the early 1860s. In 1855, the American Methodist Erastus Wentworth (1813–1886) joined the small community of fellow missionaries in Foochow, a large city of over 600,000, located midway along the coast between Hong Kong and Shanghai. Wentworth had left Connecticut with his family intent on converting as many "heathens" to the faith as possible. Within four months of their arrival in Foochow, however, his young wife had died, leaving him with a newborn daughter and a fifteen-year-old son from a previous marriage. Drowning in grief, Wentworth pushed on in his ministry, though with few tangible successes. The following excerpts from his journal convey his profound sense of isolation in Foochow as well as the slow progress of missionary work in general. His attempts at learning Chinese are comical as well as frustrating, and his attitude toward Chinese customs is condescending at best. Instead his time is spent largely with other missionaries or with correspondence. Still, by the end of his first year in Foochow, he has recovered somewhat from the loss of his wife and has made some initial progress with his Chinese and the construction of a small church. By the end of the century, the labors of Wentworth and his fellow missionaries had produced some fruit; there were at least 40,000 Protestant Chinese converts and over half a million Chinese Catholics.

FUH CHAU, JAN. 16TH 1856

Last evening arrived our long, long expected mail bringing down dates from home as late as Sept. 15th. They arrived in Hong Kong "Dec. 2nd" according to Post Mark & consequently were not long coming up the coast—Sixty-eight days from the U.S. by steam and forty-four here by ship. There were eight envelopes & between twenty & thirty sheets & pieces amounting perhaps to fifty or more pages of closely written letters. I trembled as it was handed me by the servant & still more violently as I tore off wrapper after wrapper & recognized one well-known hand after another & laid the coveted treasure in a pile. The servant looked on in mute astonishment at the mass of communication before me—

And now where begin! Take up one at hazard—"Dear Anna"—Cannot read that! Lamp too dim for suffused eyes! & the blood rushing from heart to brain blurs the sight with reeling shadows—To another & another & another "lie there! missions of love! lie there! ye are not for me." I have more than half wished in the selfishness of agony, they could quietly have found the depths of the ocean or the bottom of the Nile! Yet, the first excruciating thrust past, I have enjoyed line after line & page after page as if addressed solely to myself as I often do on

other occasions—"how Anna would have enjoyed this or that."

It was not until after her death—so closely did her condition confine my attention & care, that I paid my first visit to Fuh Chau—three miles from here & clambered to the summit of the rugged hill inside the city wall crowned with the monastery, inhabited by the English missionaries, & grounds beautified for the residence of the officers of the British Consulate. High up from the monastery itself rises an altar crowned peak—reach by flight after flight of granite steps & over topped by an urn for incense carved out of a gigantic boulder—As I stood for the first time on this lofty eminence panting for breath & surveying in awed silence its sublime & commanding prospects I almost cursed myself, if that is not too harsh an expression, that I had not brought Anna hither to see & enjoy it before she died. There was a month after our arrival in which she might have been brought hither by coolies & it seemed to me that one ought not to go to Heaven—even without witnessing so glorious a panorama when the view was to be obtained at so little expense— . . .

As usual I despatched those epistles that were furthest from the heart first. Those addressed to *me,* those that dealt in news &

indifferent matters & at length was dreamily aware of the contents of the whole pile & then went to bed to weep myself to sleep,—excited, restless, agitated & broken for the whole night. This morning I gave the dear pages a more careful perusal reading most of them aloud for Jimmy's[21] benefit who will scarcely allow a word of their contents to escape him so eager & covetous for home information do time & isolation make us.

How must it be with our neighbors the Spanish Jesuits immuned in the parsonage of the Roman Church near our new chapel, who when they left Spain for Fuh Chau dropped all correspondence with relatives & friends & became as literally dead to former associates as if the coffin lid & earth had closed upon their faces. . . .

Life has become a dull monotony. If it has any enjoyment it is intimately associated with the never ending feeling how Anna would enjoy this. When I have had two or three of the missionaries to dine with me, or have dined at Mr. Maclay's, as on Christmas, or Mr. Baldwin's[22] as on the week following New Years I have asked myself the same question. Above all I propose it day after day, as at the hour of twilight I drop in at the nursery to inquire of the bright & beautiful, radiant eyed "Anna Lewis"[23] if she will come to papa "for a little while." She was five months old on the 12th—yet strange to say, though she has seen me almost daily, she is shy of me yet. She loves to sit on my knees, between my arms while I play on the melodeon when she will alternately look & wonder, & chuckle & jump, at the manifest risk of pitching forward upon the instrument & bruising her chubby Lewis nose upon the keys. In a few days she is coming home to live with us. After a good deal of cogitation we have concluded to put her to house-keeping with her two nurses in our chambers. Her faithful Ling Choah is like a mother to her & the wet nurse E-yong Choah (in English "Mrs. Wood-House" & Mrs. "Sheep Fold"—or as Maclay bungles it,

"E-you Choah" "Mrs. Oil Jar!") is equally careful and attentive. I think we shall like the change prodigiously. . . .

JANUARY 27TH—

For two Sundays we have attended service with the Missionaries of the American Board. Our effort to invite the Ch. Of Eng. in an American enterprise has been a dead failure & has even resulted in our expulsion from the assemblies of the Church altogether. They can read prayers & that is all they desire—Preaching they do not value a brass farthing—And the devil cares as little for their prayers. We offered them the free use of our new chapel every other Sunday for English Service—Liturgy—Litany & all & bore ourselves to attend it—if they would give us an American service on the alternate days in which to pray that the Lord would grant Franklin Pierce[24] "in health & wealth long to live" & strengthen him that he might vanquish & overcome all his enemies" particularly the handy bottle & that the loving Lord would "abate the pride, assuage the malice & confound the devices" of all the enemies of Uncle Sam. The American Church Episcopal has had the good sense to leave out all this antiquated nonsense which Dr. Welton puts on his surplice to repeat Sunday after Sunday with as much pride & pomp of solemn diction as graced the age when Episcopalism was hatched from Popery—I do not regret the change—I only wish the Americans had as much national pride & spirit about their religion as have the attachés of the Establishment. Brother Hartnell read us a sermon from a book last Sunday. To-day brother Peet read us one of his own. A very good production. Next Sunday I am to preach at Bro. Maclay's.

JANUARY 28TH—

Paused, as I often do, in my evening's walk over Anna's grave. There has been no frost but the cold has deadened the grass as it does in the late

---

[21]His fifteen-year-old son by a previous marriage.
[22]Both fellow Christian missionaries in Foochow.
[23]His five-month-old daughter by his late wife, Anna.

[24]President of the United States from 1853 to 1857.

fall with us. Yet the turf on her grave is green. Only one sod is dead and out of that are keeping numerous leaves beautifully & brightly green & contrasting pleasingly with deadness & winter desolation all around there. The hard olives preserve the dark green lines of their heavy foliage & the pines like pines in all countries are darker still. . . .

MARCH 2ND—SUNDAY

Bro. Maclay preached at his own house to the assembled American Missionaries—Mrs. Jones wife of Amer. Consul, Mr. Williams merchant, Brit. Consul Medhurst—Vice Consul Hale & a student interpreter present. Afterward I administered the communion—It was a quiet & profitable time. At evening as Jimmy & I were strolling along one of the cemetery paths young Mr. Duus (pronounced deuce) overtook us & said our last chance for mail carriage by way of Amory had expired for the month.

MARCH 3RD—MONDAY

At 1 P.M. met the Missionaries at Bro. Gibson's for monthly concert at the conclusion of which I baptised their babe "William Franklin"—the latter name having been apprehended after he heard of the death of his brother Frank at the Wesleyan University. Both names are from departed brothers—The living wear the names of the dead and soon to hand them to a later posterity. Mrs. G. was out to church yesterday for the first time since her confinement. She is decidedly better. . . .

MARCH 5TH—WEDNESDAY

"Bang! bang! pop! pop!" by daylight—crackers firing in all directions like a 4th of July. It is the twenty-ninth day of the First month & sacred to some divinity. The Chinese number their months like Friends [i.e., Quakers] and have escaped the barbarism of disfiguring portions of God's time with the names of bad heathen princes & worse heathen divinities. They divide time like everything else—decimally, as far as possible—think the Sabbath a stupendous folly & observe no general abstinence from labor except New Years & its holidays which are most industriously improved by all classes in gambling. At 4 o'clock I attended missionary prayer meeting—Every afternoon we lock up the house & go out—Tonight when I returned I passed through the kitchen on my way to the dining room in the rear. The servants were at supper—Around a deal table on stools like carpenter's saw horses were huddled a swarthy group, just discernable in the twilight & grim & smoky dimness natural to the place—A stone bowl of chopped greens—boiled & seasoned with salt stood in the center of the table—leaves fried in lard & chopped fine—bowls of salted eels & other condiments surrounded it. Every sitter had his bowl of hot rice—boiled in little bamboo baskets poking it merrily into his mouth with chopsticks—& there sat, in the arms of her nurse, "baby"[i.e., his infant daughter] looking on most intently & illuminating the darkness—like a gem in a pile of charcoal—Poor little outcast—She is the only real missionary among us, for she is the only one that loves the heathens—I fear hers is not the wholly disinterested benevolence which some theologians account the height of christian perfection. I rather imagine it is to be mixed up with the memory of the good milk on which she is thriving. She jumped & sprung to come to me & I took her in my arms into the brightly lighted library—where, surrounded by the comforts of civilization she seemed more at home than in the murky vestibule of ladies in which I found her.

MARCH 6TH—THURSDAY

Studied as usual diligently till dinner time at 2 o'clock & then went out to make application—"Where are you going?" asked a Chinese savant. "Into the fire"—said I—by making an *e* instead of an *i* in the pronunciation of a word like the one I wanted to use to say "yonder." The bystanders stared but wondered at my meaning till some one happily guessed at the word & wanted to set me right—They are as grave as Frenchmen where an Englishman would split his sides with merriment. I was more successful with a knot of workmen among whom I paused, who began with "What is your coat made of?" "What did it cost" & actually dissected & inventoried my apparel from outside coat to undershirt—hat to boots—watch—pocket knife & pencil. The last they wanted to beg, I told them they could buy one at the foreign store for five cents that would last them a year or two. A foreign pencil or pen is an awkward thing in the hands of a Chinaman who sticks it straight up in the air & awkwardly produces faint impressions upon paper.

The foreign community have been commenting for some days upon a sacrilegious outrage committed by the Chinese out of revenge doubtlessly. Two bodies—one of a boy twelve years old—another of a child—were torn from their graves in the night & exposed to dogs & vultures till nothing but the bones remained before they were removed. They bury only two or three feet deep & there were some poor wretches that had been placed perhaps too near the cemetery of some nabob whose relatives took this method of signifying their displeasure. It is a high handed offence—considering the wonderful respect the celestials have for the dead. In widening the roads winding in every direction over our romantic cemetery hills the Brit. vice consul was obliged to respect every grave & stone & tomb however humble. The Chines will not scruple to sell a grave for a round price—but remove the remains carefully to some other locality—

In walking out tonight—I stumbled upon a child perfectly blotched with the scabs of recent small-pox—I gave it a wide berth you may be sure—The oriental do not understand & will not extensively practice vaccination—Inoculation is common—A mason with a terrible bruise on his leg asked of me, as they often do, a specific—I advised him to wash it & bathe it in oil—certainly harmless if not remedial—His limbs & water were certainly no intimate acquaintances. . . .

APRIL 6TH—SUNDAY

Church at the Hartwells. Always pleasant to meet the entire company of friends with their rosy cheeked little ones once a week. Returning from the American Consul, engaged in the very laudable business of beating the coolies off Wetmore's lot where they had persisted in working & making the Sabbath hideous by their vociferous garrulity notwithstanding order to the contrary.

Went to brother Maclay's Synagogue in the afternoon to listen to his instructions,—to me mainly unintelligible—to such of the street passengers as choose to drop in for community interest. Let open your door & the crowd flows in at once—hats on—if they are fortunate enough to own any—saunter up to the closed altar—lean over the rails—make remarks about the speaker, nod assent to his words—wonder that he speaks the dialect so well—interrupt him to inquire what his coat cost—whether the war is still going on between the English & Russians[25]—how far America is away—how long he has been in the country—

If the speaker declines answering these secular questions—They inquire if Jesus belongs to the tribe of idols. Some old fellow starts up with his load of market baskets—says it is getting late & he must go, & cries out "good night" to the preacher who says "here if you must go—take a 'Jesus book' along with you—" Others think they must go & beg to be served with books also & finally with a general rush for books & then for the door with many "Thank yous" & many "goodbyes" the house is emptied in the middle of the discourse—but as quickly replenished by new corners to whom the speaker may finish out, or begin again at pleasure—. . .

APRIL 10TH—THURSDAY

Engaged all day teaching two carpenters how to make the ornament work of the frieze and cornice of the church at Long T'an—Go to Long T'an in the afternoon—

---

[25]The Crimean War of 1853–1856.

APRIL 11TH—FRIDAY

Got a pretty flight of stone steps six in number laid up the first bank of the cemetery in the path leading to our own graveyard. . . .

APRIL 13TH—SUNDAY

At nine o'clock this morning witnessed the solemn ceremony of the baptism of the first native convert in Fuh Chau. A teacher of Rev. J. Doolittle—who has been soliciting instruction in Christianity as admission to the church for the last six months—Nearly all the missionaries were present with their teachers—& about a hundred Chinese, half of whom were adults & the rest youths of the schools—Several native women were present—Mr. Peet prayed & read the scriptures in Chinese—gave out a hymn which all joined in singing to Old Hundred—Mr. Baldwin preached on the nature of baptism & the sacrament—Mr. Doolittle administered the rite of baptism & Mr. Harwell the Sacrament all in Chinese. This is the first fruits—exactly eight years since brother Maclay landed in Fuh Chau. The laborers have had the language to learn—the Bible to translate & the prejudice of the people to overcome. Five years ago Msrs. Peet & Doolittle were *stoned off* the very spot where this seal of conversion to Christianity now took place. He is a man of education & intelligence—a public school teacher & of late a fluent expounder of the truths of the religion he has embraced. In the afternoon Mr. Maclay preached in his own parlor. . . .

JUNE 8TH—SUNDAY

A year ago today we were essaying to leave the harbor of Hong Kong—What an eventful year! It—added to the six months previous seem as long to me as any ten—of my previous life so rapidly did events of the utmost moment succeed each other—like the thickening incidents of a plot approaching a stirring close— . . .

Young Mr. Sargeant of Salem, Mass. has been staying with us for a day or two. He is a modest youth—well informed & agreeable company—It is refreshing to have a visit now & then from a white man.

JUNE 29TH—SUNDAY

Another contest with heathenism this morning. The workmen on Wetmore's lot next us commenced in full band to work this morning as usual—leaving our ears no rest from their din even upon the Sabbath. I sent for the head man told him it was Sunday & begged them to desist—He acquiesced—but many of his workmen demurred & raised such an outrageous din that Consul Jones threw open his blinds and discharged a pistol in that direction which quelled the noise & scattered the rioters—The Chinese have a wonderful fear of foreign arms. I was in the city one day when a crowd collected as usual curious to see my umbrella & asking if it contained a dagger like a sword cane. I took hold of the ivory head & made a motion to draw it out when the whole crowd stept back as instinctively as if I had flashed an actual sword in their faces. . . .

JULY 28TH—MONDAY

Cloudy & cool—It has been a remarkable summer. June was an uncomfortable month to me—July has had not more than a week of hot weather all told. August is yet in store. The Sam Russel {i.e., steamer} by which I intend to send this is reported ready for sea—My letters & Journals must go on board to-day. It is the first direct chance for America by ship for months—Several others will go shortly. She may sink & carry all our household experiences to the bottom of the sea. It will save "old eyes" if she does—I thought at first of retaining July for another opportunity—but a better way may not occur & my jottings may as well all sink or swim together—I am hourly sensible that the golden chain which bound my interests & affections to yours has been snapt asunder. That only a little silver link remains—so frail that the slightest touch of disease might part it &

leave as we were of yore—Our universe is one of motion. The probability is that no two particles in it occupy the same relation to it & each other for two successive instants together. How then can we expect permanency in our relations. From the changeable we pass to the changeless—Even here—memory immortalizes mortality & imparts durability to the passing &

transient. One of the brightest portions of my shifting panorama was that illuminated by the presence of our darling Anna. The brightness—like that of a painting by the old Masters—was enhanced by its solitariness & the darkness which surrounded it—It has dwindled to a star—Another guiding lamp to Heaven.

---

2. Rebecca J. Parker
"THE KEY OF THE HOME: A PICTURE OF WORK AMONG THE WOMEN OF INDIA" (1895)

The London Missionary Society (L.M.S.), founded in 1795, was one of the most influential of all interdenominational missionary groups working in the nineteenth century. By making the spread of the gospel the paramount issue and allowing converts to choose their own form of church government, the L.M.S. was able to overcome much of the crippling rivalry that previously characterized Protestant missionary work. The L.M.S. was also one of the first missionary societies to make extensive use of women both at home and abroad. In the following pamphlet, Rebecca J. Parker describes some of the Society's work in the Indian cities of Benares and Travancore. As in the ancient Roman Empire, Christian missionaries in India found their first and easiest success among the social outcasts, who apparently looked to the new religion for a higher social status. While not rejecting such "lower class" converts, Taylor and her "Bible-women" preferred to concentrate their efforts on the wives of prominent non-Christians—another similarity to the early church. Teaching, nursing, and gestures of friendship gained the Christian missionaries the needed entrée into the otherwise closed social circles of the Indian elites, where they then began to tell their new friends about Christ. The process was slow and the victories often small, but the English and Indian Bible-women remained determined, asking fellow Christians back in Britain only for the prayers and financial support that would allow them to expand their efforts.

In contemplating mission work in Benares and Travancore, which are 2,000 miles apart, we find two spheres so unlike that it is often almost impossible to believe that both places can belong to the same continent. Perhaps the one point of similarity is that the Gospel has made and is still making very little progress among the high castes in either place. This fact accounts for Benares, the home of caste, being the most unfruitful and difficult field of work in India; while on the other hand Travancore claims its thousands of Christians, chiefly because of a large and neglected low-caste population—unknown in Benares—from which the Christians are mainly gathered.

For any high-caste person in India, North or South, to become a Christian means complete ostracism and loss of social status; for wealth, friends, home, everything must be given up for Christ. Hence the conditions and results of work among those classes anywhere are much the same. But to the swarming out-castes and lower castes of Travancore Christianity offers something better than they can possess outside it, for it gives them a social position which Hinduism refuses; and though as a Hindu pariah a man may not even appear in the presence of his Máhar'ajá [i.e., king] in the common highway, that same man as a Christian can place a written petition in his own King's hand.

Hence we find great numbers of these poor, degraded people besieging our churches and eager to be counted among our people. The difficulty is to meet the needs of so many, who are so densely ignorant as to require a great amount of teaching even after they have entered the Christian fold. Hence not only is the class of people we have to deal with here in the main entirely different from those of the North, but the type of Christian is, as a rule, of a lower order.

IN THE ZENANAS[26]

As far as work amongst women is concerned, the North of India presents a unique opportunity such as can scarcely be met with elsewhere. The close observance of the Zenana system, by means of which high-caste Hindu and Mohammedan [i.e., Muslim] women are secluded in the homes of their husbands, afford great chances for the spread of the Gospel by women amongst women, because a growing number of these homes are now opening to the visits of Bible-women. Once inside the Zenana apartments of a high-caste house, you have your congregation before you from the grandmother to the latest-born infant of the household. Interest

them, show yourself to be their friend, help them in sickness or trouble, and you not only have their gratitude, but you may be sure of an attentive hearing for the good news you long to give.

In receiving the visits of Christians, the chief objects of the women thus immured are to learn to read, write, sew, and do fancy work, though to the Bible-woman these things are but the passport to the higher teaching she always gives in every house. A Bible-woman before whom such work lies should have had a good education, and if possible some special training for the work, for she will have to teach the wives and daughters of educated men, and will not infrequently meet with the men themselves. If she adds to her accomplishments the fact of having herself been converted from heathenism, and especially if she had been of good caste, she carries weight in her words, and her presence demands respect from her pupils. Thus a high type of worker is required, and is gradually being furnished by such institutions as the Bible-women's Training College in Allahabad,[27] under the care of Miss de Sélincourt.

The results of such work are almost impossible to tabulate. To teach women in Zenanas about Christ is to undermine Hinduism at its strongest point. The results do not lie on the surface for the few cases where Zenana women boldly leave all for Christ do not by any means represent the sway Christ has over the hearts of women thus taught. I have before me the reports of a number of Bible-women who worked with me for some years in Benares, and such remarks as the following are an index to the steady progress and coming results of their work:

"One of my city pupils keeps a copy of the New Testament in a hole in the wall, and she can only dare to read it when all the family are away, and even then she has to lock her door."

"One of my pupils died a few weeks ago. I went to see her, and at her request I sang some

---

[26]The Zenana is the part of the Indian household reserved for women.

[27]In north-central India, about 300 miles southwest of Delhi.

Christian hymns. She tried to join in, but was too weak. She was very happy in the thought that Jesus had died for her, and later on in the day she passed away believing in Jesus as her Saviour."

"In two of my Zenanas the women always ask us to pray and have learnt to pray themselves, which they do when I visit them."

"One of my pupils, now advanced in life, said one day to me: 'From my childhood until now I never heard such words as yours about Jesus, and from hearing them I feel my heart changed. What shall I do that I may go where He is?'"

"I was teaching a number of women in a certain house, when a woman, who seemed to have heard of Jesus before, said she had been a great sinner, and wondered if indeed He would forgive her, for if so He was the Saviour she wanted. Another woman said: 'I believe what you say is true, and if I believe in my heart will God accept me?'"

FROM NORTH TO SOUTH:
A CONTRAST

Thus it is seen that the work of a Bible-woman in North India is almost entirely among heathen people, and chiefly in Zenanas, though village work is also done by them.

In Travancore we find an entirely different state of things existing. There is practically no Zenana system, even among caste people. The Bible-woman visits the women in their homes, but the freedom of their life makes it uncertain whether she will see them, and the distractions of the outside world hinder the work.

A great part of the Bible-woman's work in Travancore is to visit among those who are called "Adherents" in the Christian churches. They are those who have begun to attend worship with baptized Christians in a Christian Church, but whose severance from the heathen world is often hardly perceptible.

There is still a greater work to be done in an "inner circle," namely, among those Adherents who have decided to cast off heathenism and embrace Christianity. Usually they are extremely ignorant, have no knowledge of reading or learning of any sort, and a most imperfect understanding of what is entailed in the step they have taken. To teach them the rudiments of the Christian Faith, the Lord's Prayer, Catechism, Commandments, and how to read the Bible for themselves, are preparatory steps to baptism, and this rite is administered here to all who put away heathenism and give satisfactory reasons for believing that they are in earnest following Christ. Admission to the Lord's Supper is the final step, and Bible-women find a great work in preparing candidates, conducting Prayer Meetings, and otherwise helping these women.

The work of a Deaconess is thus combined with that of a Bible-woman, for her time is divided between visiting the sick, instructing the would-be Christians, and preaching to the heathen. A few extracts from the reports of my Bible-women will illustrate these points:—

"Two families of fourteen persons have become Christians in houses I have visited. I conduct two weekly Prayer Meetings among Christian women in the congregation, and am teaching twenty-five women for admission to the Lord's Supper."

"My work is to teach a number of ignorant women to read the Bible, also to visit the sick in our village both among the heathen and Christians, to conduct Prayer Meetings, and to teach in the Sunday School. Many of those I visit are out-castes, and full of superstition, and work is slow among them, but they are coming into the light one by one."

"This year three families that had backslidden from Christianity have come back, and are trying to be sincere Christians. I have worked chiefly among the heathen low-castes, though I have also been able to help in the work of the congregation."

"My knowledge of sick-nursing has been very useful, and by means of it I have gained admission to many good houses, and I have had many opportunities of speaking of Christ to women who would not under ordinary circumstances allow me, as a Christian, to enter their homes."

WHO ARE THE BIBLE-WOMEN?

The class of women available for Bible work in Travancore is not of so high an order as that from which the Bible-women in North India are usually drawn. There our best women are set apart for this work, and the work is looked upon as a thing to be aspired to and earnestly desired. The most devout, intelligent and best educated women are engaged in this work, at salaries ranging from 10 [shillings] 6 [pence] to 20 [shillings] a month. Usually they are wives and mothers of families. As married women they can enter any home with safety, and as wives (not widows) they are received with respect.

But in Travancore it has been the custom to employ the widows of preachers and other indigent deserving Christians as Bible-women, at salaries of from 4 [shillings] to 8 [shillings] a month, until in many cases Bible-women's work has been looked upon as the sole right of such persons.

THE WORSHIP OF DEMONS

As in the old Bible days so in India today, demon possession is believed in, and women especially are supposed to be subject to it. Many distressing stories might be told of the sufferings of women said to be thus possessed, and deep down in her heart every woman has a dread of the all-powerful evil spirits, who, she thinks, at any time may bring upon her the punishments and pains of demon possession.

It is, therefore, not at all surprising that in Travancore, where a more degraded form of Hinduism holds sway than elsewhere in India, devil worship is prevalent.

The ignorant heathen knows only fear for beings who will oppress and injure him: he dreads them in the darkness, he beholds them in disease and in all his misfortunes, and to appease their wrath is the one object of his religious zeal. To such people the Gospel of Love comes as a marvellous revelation. But even after its acceptance they find it hard to cast off the works of darkness, and the terrible superstitions that have for so long enchained them, and not infrequently the old longing to once more behold a devil dance, or to aid at the exorcism of some demon in a heathen relative or friend, has broken through good resolutions and caused a weak brother to stumble and fall. To fight against these powerful evils and to show a better way to these poor people is one part of the work which falls to every Christian worker, man or woman, to perform.

WHERE ARE THE REAPERS?

From what has been said, it will be seen that there is a great work to be done for Christ. In our district alone there are 14,000 professing Christians, the majority of whom are of the kind described, and of these some 6,000 are women. We have six Bible-women and one Deaconess at work among this great number. How inadequate a force to accomplish so mighty a work! Does not the cry of these people enter the ears of the Lord of all, and will He not move the hearts of his more favoured children in Christian lands, that they may rise to their responsibilities and privileges and send out help to those who so sorely need it?

BIBLIOGRAPHY

Primary Sources

Anthologies and Readers

Fitzer, Joseph, ed., *Romance and the Rock: Nineteenth-Century Catholics on Faith and Reason* (Minneapolis: Fortress Press, 1989).

Goldstein, Jan, and John W. Boyer, eds., *Nineteenth-Century Europe: Liberalism and Its Critics* (Chicago: University of Chicago Press, 1988).

Park, Polly, ed., *To Save Their Heathen Souls: Voyage to and Life in Foochow, China, Based on Wentworth Diaries and Letters* (San Jose, Calif.: Pickwick, 1984).

Thompson, David M., ed., *Nonconformists in the Nineteenth Century* (New York: Routledge & K. Paul, 1972).

Selected Authors

Baur, F. C., *Paul: His Life and Works,* trans. A. Menzies, 2 vols. (London: Williams & Norgate, 1875).

Blake, William, *The Works of William Blake: Poetic, Symbolic, and Critical,* ed. Edwin John Ellis and William Butler Yeats (New York: AMS Press, 1979).

Hopkins, Gerard Manley, *Poems and Prose,* ed. W. H. Gardner (Melbourne: Penguin Classic, 1953).

Marx, Karl, *Karl Marx on Religion,* ed. Samuel K. Padover (New York: McGraw-Hill, 1974).

Newman, John Henry, *Apologia Pro Vita Sua,* ed. Ian Ker (New York: Penguin Classic, 1990).

————, *Selected Sermons,* ed. Ian Ker (Mahwah, N.J.: Paulist Press, 1994).

Renan, Ernest, *Life of Jesus* (New York: Modern Library, 1927).

Saint Simon, Henri, *Selected Writings on Science, Industry, and Social Organization,* ed. Keith Taylor (New York: Holmes & Meier, 1973).

Schleiermacher, Friedrich, *On Religion: Speeches to its Cultured Despisers,* ed. & trans. Richard Crouter (Cambridge: Cambridge University Press, 1988).

————, *On the Highest Good,* trans. H. Victor Froese (Lewiston, N.Y.: Edwin Mellen, 1992).

Stendhal, *Scarlet and Black: A Chronicle of the Nineteenth Century,* trans. Margaret Shaw (London: Penguin Classic,1953).

Strauss, David Friedrich, *In Defense of My Life of Jesus against the Hegelians,* trans. Marilyn Chapin Massey (Hamden, Conn.: Archon, 1983).

Thérèse of Lisieux, *The Autobiography of Saint Thérèse of Lisieux: The Story of a Soul* (New York: Image/Doubleday, 1987).

————, *Poems of St. Thérèse of Lisieux,* trans. Alan Bancroft (London: Fount, 1996).

Wordsworth, William, *Selected Prose,* ed. John O. Hayden (London: Penguin, 1988).

————, *William Wordsworth,* ed. Jonathan Wordsworth (Cambridge: Cambridge University Press, 1985).

Secondary Works

Historical Overviews

Helmstadter, Richard, ed., *Freedom and Religion in the Nineteenth Century* (Stanford, Calif.: Stanford University Press, 1997).

Jedin, Hubert, and John Dolan, *The Church in the Modern World: An Abridgement of the History of the Church,* vols. 7–10 (New York: Crossroad, 1993).

Latourette, Kenneth S., *Christianity in a Revolutionary Age,* 5 vols. (New York: Harper, 1958–62).

McLeod, Hugh, *Religion and the People of Western Europe, 1789–1990* (Oxford: Oxford University Press, 1997).

Pelikan, Jaroslav, *The Christian Tradition, Vol. 5: Christian Doctrine and Modern Culture Since 1700* (Chicago: University of Chicago Press, 1989).

Romanticism

Easterlin, Nancy, *Wordsworth and the Question of "Romantic Religion"* (Cranbury, N.J.: Bucknell University Press, 1996).

Gerrish, B. A., *A Prince of the Church: Schleiermacher and the Beginnings of Modern Theology* (Minneapolis: Fortress Press, 1984).

Jasper, David, ed., *The Interpretation of Belief: Coleridge, Schleiermacher and Romanticism* (New York: Macmillan, 1986).

Socialism and Industrialization

Cort, John, *Christian Socialism: An Informal History* (Maryknoll, N.Y.: Orbis, 1988).

Inglis, K. I., *The Churches and the Working Classes in Victorian England* (New York: Routledge, 1969).

Lichtheim, George, *The Origins of Socialism* (New York: Praeger, 1969).

Soloway, Richard, *Prelates and People: Ecclesiastical Social Thought in England, 1783–1852* (New York: Routledge, 1969).

Vidler, A. R., *A Century of Social Catholicism, 1820–1920* (London: S.P.C.K., 1964).

Anticlericalism

Chadwick, Owen, *The Secularization of the European Mind in the Nineteenth Century* (Cambridge: Cambridge University Press, 1975).

McManners, John, *Church and State in France, 1870–1914* (London: S.P.C.K., 1972).

Schapiro, J. Salwyn, *Anticlericalism: Conflict Between Church and State in France, Italy, and Spain* (Princeton, N.J.: Van Nostrand, 1967)

Higher Criticism and Biblical Scholarship

Nigel M. de S. Cameron, *Biblical Higher Criticism and the Defense of Infallibalism in Nineteenth-Century Britain* (Lewiston, N.Y.: Edwin Mellen, 1987).

Grant, Robert, *A Short History of the Interpretation of the Bible* (New York: Macmillan, 1963).

Harrisville, Roy A., and Walter Sundberg, *The Bible in Modern Culture: Theology and Historical-Critical Method from Spinoza to Käsemann* (Grand Rapids, Mich.: Eerdmans, 1995).

Lawler, Edwin G., *David Friedrich Strauss and His Critics: The Life of Jesus in Early Nineteenth-Century German Journals* (New York: Peter Lang, 1986).

Catholic Revival

Allitt, Patrick, *Catholic Converts: British and American Intellectuals Turn to Rome* (Ithaca, N.Y.: Cornell University Press, 1997).

Ker, I . T., *The Achievement of John Henry Newman* (Notre Dame, Ind.: University of Notre Dame, 1990).

Kselman, Thomas, *Miracles and Prophecies in Nineteenth-Century France* (Piscatawey, N.J.: Rutgers, 1983).

McCaffrey, Eugen, *Heart of Love: Saint Therèse of Lisieux* (Dublin: Veritas, 1998).

Norman, E. R., *The English Catholic Church in the Nineteenth Century* (Oxford: Oxford University Press, 1984).

Foreign Missions

Bebbington, David W., *Evangelicalism in Modern Britain* (Boston: Unwin Hyman, 1989).

Neill, Stephen, *A History of Christian Missions* (New York: McGraw Hill, 1966).

CHAPTER 9

The Twentieth Century

A Billy Graham Stadium Crusade at Earls Court, London. Long integral to the Christian tradition, impassioned preaching and spiritual revivals took on a special American character from the eighteenth-century Great Awakening onwards. The technological innovations of the twentieth century have allowed evangelists to reach even greater numbers of listeners, but the essential message of personal conversion and joyful gratitude to Christ have remained constant. *(Carlos Reyes-Manzo/Andes Press Agency)*

The last hundred years or so have witnessed many unprecedented events in human history. Stunning scientific and technological developments have led to revolutions in communication, transportation, manufacturing, and a number of other basic areas of the social infrastructure. Medical advances have similarly transformed both the quality of human life and its sustainability to a degree unknown in all the millennia of human existence. At the same time, violence and destructiveness have also reached new levels, both in armed conflicts such as the two world wars and in massive ethnic extermination campaigns against a variety of peoples. It is difficult to know which of these legacies will carry the most significance for future generations. Their immediate impact on Western Christianity is even more difficult to assess, yet some general observations can be made.

For example, one hallmark of the twentieth century has been the greatly expanded influence of the nation-state and its centralized form of government on all aspects of Western society, including Christianity. Modern centralized governments have taken many different forms, and the attitudes that these governments have held toward their respective Christian churches have varied according to each government's guiding ideology. For instance, in the Soviet Union and the states of Eastern Europe, the Communist governments in power for much of the century were controlled by zealous secularizers dedicated to removing all religious influences from society. Under these regimes, the price of actively expressing one's Christian faith could be as high as martyrdom. At the other end of the spectrum were dictatorships such as Nazi Germany, in which the state coerced the churches into functioning as a de facto arm of the government. Under such conditions some church leaders and individual Christians resisted and were harassed, imprisoned, or even executed for their beliefs. Many other Christian leaders, however, acquiesced to the ruling party's demands for cooperation, lending the stamp of religious approval to the policies of the dictator in power. Finally, in the liberal democracies of North America and western Europe, the relationship of Christianity and government has fallen somewhere between the extremes of Communist church-state enmity and Nazi church-state collaboration. Although the churches in most democracies are legally separated from—and protected from—the state, many churches nonetheless have demonstrated strong support for the policies of the government in power. For example, during the First World War (1914–1918), most Christian denominations accepted and even promoted nationalist ideologies and policies, leading to a violent polarization of Western Christians on the basis of national allegiance.

Even today, at the beginning of a new century, when liberty of conscience reigns in all Western countries, the conflicting demands of church and state continue to cause deep dilemmas for some Christians.

Some of these personal crises stem from large-scale social transformations in which the state merely serves as an arbiter for increasingly pluralist beliefs. During the first half of the twentieth century, for instance, when the governments of predominately Catholic countries tried to legalize divorce (and later contraception), they faced stiff resistance from the Catholic Church. While many Catholic citizens of these countries sided with the Church, many others found themselves torn between allegiance to the tenets of Catholicism and support for governmental policies that they believed were in the nation's best interest. Though the Church's teaching on marriage and procreation has not subsequently changed, both divorce and contraception are now legal in all majority Christian nations. Continuing disagreements over procreative issues, particularly abortion, similarly demonstrate a tension between many traditional Christian doctrines and the interests and demands of pluralist, democratic societies. Even more profoundly, the twentieth century witnessed a civil rights revolution among various previously disenfranchised segments of the population, from the descendants of African slaves in the United States to the once politically impotent majority of women in the Western world. Christianity, like all religions, has always had to address the changing needs of its followers, but never before has it had so many new issues thrust upon it in such a short period of time. On some issues—such as racism, which is now universally condemned—the many Christian denominations have long since reached a doctrinal consensus. Other issues—particularly certain feminist demands for church reform—continue to spawn controversy.

The other major twentieth-century challenge to Christianity's social preeminence in the West was atheism. From its nineteenth-century beginnings with such thinkers as Karl Marx and the nihilist Friedrich Nietzsche, this phosophically grounded alternative to religious belief spread throughout the West—and indeed throughout the world—during the twentieth century. Proceeding from a common denial of God and therefore Christianity, scientists and philosophers from a variety of scholarly disciplines proposed countless substitutes for the cosmology and ethics of Christianity. Until late in the century, Marx's own doctrine of class struggle and dialectical materialism was undoubtedly the most influential of these, at its peak supplying the official creed of half of the nations of Europe and much of the rest of the world. With the demise of the Soviet Union, however, Marxism has almost completely disappeared from the world stage, at least in terms of social and political influence. Other explanatory substitutes for Christianity, such as the psychological theories of Sigmund Freud or the sociological axioms of Max Weber have fared somewhat better through the century but have never enjoyed anything remotely near the political influence of Marxism. The same is true of the philosophical reflections of the Existentialists, which, while significant in artistic and academic circles, have never attracted a wide following among the population at large.

And while learned dismissals of Christianity continue to be common today, the most popular systematic alternatives to religion—such as psychotherapy—tend to focus more on individual self-fulfillment rather than on revolutionary reforms of politics or society. Like governmental suppression in Communist countries, in other words, intellectual attempts to supplant Christianity during the twentieth century have fallen far short of their proponents' ambitions.

Indeed, despite more organized hostility than at any time since the early days of Roman persecution, Western Christianity has thrived remarkably in the twentieth century. Part of this success is due to the ecumenical movement, which has broken down old barriers between the various Protestant denominations and the Catholic Church and has encouraged mutual understanding and cooperation. The most dramatic growth, however, has been among new denominations such as the various Holiness and Pentecostal churches, possibly bolstered by their elevation of firsthand religious experience over traditional theology and worship practices. Other small denominations such as the Mormons and other Adventist groups have likewise increased their numbers nearly tenfold during the second half of the century. Part of this membership boom has come at the expense of larger mainstream Protestant churches, but the majority of the new converts have come to Christianity through the extensive missionary work of these denominations throughout the globe. In this respect the smaller churches reflect a much more profound and universal trend within Western Christianity itself. For while the twentieth century began with over 95% of all Christians living in Western lands, it ended with the majority of all Christians living outside of Europe and North America. Just as the tiny Palestinian movement of the first century eventually spawned Western Christianity itself, Western Christianity has in this century given way to a truly global religion. While the number of nonbelievers or at least nonaffiliated individuals continues to rise in western Europe and North America, the number of Christians in Asia, Latin America, and especially Africa continues to rise. Africa alone now claims more believers than either Europe or North America and has given birth to over 7,000 new Christian denominations throughout the continent. Though this non-Western dynamism has yet to be fully reflected in the leadership of the major Christian churches, it is already shaping their future. At the dawn of the twenty-first century, the era of Western dominance over world Christianity thus appears to be finally drawing to a close.

Politics	Literature	Individuals	Other
1914–1918 World War I 1917 Russian Revolution 1922–1953 Stalin rules Soviet Union 1933–1945 Nazi rule in Germany 1933–1945 F. D. Roosevelt U.S. president 1939–1945 World War II 1941 U.S. enters war	1906 Troeltsch, *Protestantism and Progress* 1909 Scofield Reference Bible 1919 Barth, *Commentary on the Epistle to the Romans* 1927 Lewis, *Elmer Gantry* 1940 Greene, *The Power and the Glory* 1942 Camus, *The Stranger* 1949 Merton, *The Seven Storey Mountain* 1954 Beckett, *Waiting for Godot*	1827–1918 Ellen G. White 1865–1923 Ernst Troeltsch 1859–1939 Sigmund Freud 1862–1935 Billy Sunday 1890–1944 Aimee Semple McPherson 1906–1945 Dietrich Bonhoeffer 1866–1961 Charles Harrison Mason 1886–1965 Paul Tillich 1905–1980 J.-P. Sartre 1897–1980 Dorothy Day 1918– Billy Graham	1908 U.S. Federal Council of Churches founded 1910 Edinburgh mission meeting 1919 World's Christian Fundamentals Assoc. founded 1925 Scopes "Monkey" Trial 1929 Stock market crash 1932 German Christian platform 1934 Barmen Declaration in Germany 1940 Foundation of ecumenical order at Taizé 1948 World Council of Churches est. at Amsterdam
1960 Kennedy elected U.S. president		1929–1968 M. L. King, Jr.	1958–1964 Antireligious campaign in the U.S.S.R. 1962–1964 Vatican II council 1969 Apollo 11 lands on moon 1970 World Alliance of Reformed Churches 1979 Mother Teresa wins Nobel Peace Prize
1981–1989 Reagan U.S. president 1989 End of Cold War 1991 U.S.S.R. dissolved 1993–2001 Clinton U.S. president			

20th cent.

A. Fundamentalism

In the early twentieth century, a new kind of doctrinal controversy convulsed the dominant Protestant Christianity of the United States. As in previous denominational clashes, questions of biblical interpretation were prominent, but the much broader disagreement focused on the very essence of Christianity in the modern world. The most famous catalyst was the Darwinian theory of human evolution, which for some Christians challenged the entire authority of the Scriptures as well as the very notion of human dignity and uniqueness in Creation. Eventually known as "fundamentalists," such individuals considered many religious concessions to current secular "fads" to be profoundly dangerous to the fundamental revelations of Jesus and the Bible. Because of the diverse backgrounds and beliefs of Christians falling under this general rubric, it is often easier to define fundamentalism in terms of what it opposes than in terms of any distinctive doctrine. Contrary to "modernist" theologians, fundamentalist Christians affirm every detail of the scriptural accounts of Jesus' life and miracles (particularly his bodily resurrection) and embrace a traditional Protestant definition of both sin and salvation. Unlike evolutionists or many biblical historians, they believe in a specific rather than general or metaphorical interpretation of Holy Scriptures, thereby endorsing a more literal understanding of such biblical passages as the Creation narratives of the book of Genesis. Beginning with the 1895 Bible Conference of Conservative Christians, the central organization of this interdenominational movement steadily increased, reaching a climax during the 1920s, after the 1919 founding of the World's Christian Fundamentals Association (WFCA). As a result of much public ridicule among outsiders, the term "fundamentalist" has since become distasteful to most American Protestants who in fact share such convictions. Their common disdain for liberal theologians and "secular humanists," however, has continued to unite many Christians who embrace "that old-time religion" of revivalism, spiritual rebirth, and rigorous biblical study and usually call themselves simply evangelical Christians.

1. INTRODUCTION TO *THE SCOFIELD REFERENCE BIBLE* (1909)

The Scofield Reference Bible appeared in the same year as a series of twelve evangelical tracts entitled *The Fundamentals*. Together these works lent coherence to a rapidly growing fundamentalist movement in Protestant America. Cyrus I. Scofield (1843–1921) was a lawyer who converted to Christianity in his late thirties and became an ardent proponent and teacher of biblical studies. Unlike many contemporary scholars inspired by the German techniques of Higher Criticism (see 8C), Scofield believed that the varying historical circumstances in which different parts of the Bible were written did not affect the collection's overall status as one profoundly interconnected book. After years of intense work with this biblical "mosaic," Scofield developed a historical scheme of salvation, which he divided into seven "dispensations," or distinct eras. As he describes below, the culmination of the current, seventh dispensation will be the Second Coming of Christ. Though not necessarily embraced by all fundamentalists, Scofield's dispensationalist approach did systematically reaffirm a literalist interpretation of the Bible and many other beliefs at the heart of the movement. The second edition of the *Reference Bible,* issued in 1917, was a nationwide best-seller, attracting readers from a broad spectrum of Protestant America.

A PANORAMIC VIEW OF THE BIBLE

The Bible, incomparably the most widely circulated of books, at once provokes and baffles study. Even the non-believer in its authority rightly feels that it is unintelligent to remain in almost total ignorance of the most famous and ancient of books. And yet most, even of sincere believers, soon retire from any serious effort to master the content of the sacred writings. The reason is not far to seek. It is found in the fact that no particular portion of Scripture is to be intelligently comprehended apart from some conception of its place in the whole. For the Bible story and message is like a picture wrought out in mosaics: each book, chapter, verse, and even word forms a necessary part, and has its own appointed place. It is, therefore, indispensable to any interesting and fruitful study of the Bible that a general knowledge of it be gained.

First. The Bible is one book. Seven great marks attest this unity. (1) From Genesis the Bible bears witness to one *God.* Wherever he speaks or acts he is consistent with himself, and with the total revelation concerning him. (2) The Bible forms one *continuous story*—the story of humanity in relation to God. (3) The Bible hazards the most unlikely *predictions* concerning the future, and, when the centuries have brought round the appointed time, records their fulfilment. (4) The Bible is a *progressive* unfolding of truth. Nothing is told all at once, and once for all. The law is, "first the blade, then the ear, after that the full corn." Without the possibility of collusion, often with centuries

between, one writer of Scripture takes up an earlier revelation, adds to it, lays down the pen, and in due time another man moved by the Holy Spirit, and another, and another, add new details till the whole is complete. (5) From beginning to end the Bible testifies to *one redemption*. (6) From beginning to end the Bible has *one great theme*—the person and work of Christ. (7) And, finally, these writers, some forty-four in number, writing through twenty centuries, have produced a *perfect harmony* of doctrine in progressive unfolding. This is, to every candid mind, the unanswerable proof of the Divine inspiration of the Bible.

Second. The Bible is a book of books. Sixty-six books make up the one Book. Considered with reference to the unity of the one book the separate books may be regarded as chapters. But that is but one side of the truth, for each of the sixty-six books is complete in itself, and has its own theme and analysis. In the present edition of the Bible these are fully shown in the introductions and divisions. It is therefore of the utmost moment that the books be studied in the light of their distinctive themes. Genesis, for instance, is the book of beginnings—the seed-plot of the whole Bible. Matthew is the book of the King, &c.

Third. The books of the Bible fall into groups. Speaking broadly there are five great divisions in the Scriptures, and these may be conveniently fixed in the memory by five key-words, Christ being the one theme (Lk 24: 25–27):

PREPARATION	The Old Testament
MANIFESTATION	The Gospels
PROPAGATION	The Acts

EXPLANATION   The Epistles
CONSUMMATION   The Revelation.

In other words, the Old Testament is the *preparation* for Christ; in the Gospels he is *manifested* to the world; in the Acts he is preached and his Gospel is *propagated* in the world; in the Epistles his Gospel is *explained;* and in the Revelation all the purposes of God in and through Christ are *consummated.* And these groups of books in turn fall into groups. This is especially true of the Old Testament, which is in four well defined groups. Over these may be written, as memory aids:

REDEMPTION: Genesis, Exodus, Leviticus, Numbers, Deuteronomy

ORGANIZATION: Joshua, Judges, Ruth, I & II Samuel, I & II Kings, I & II Chronicles, Ezra, Nehemiah, Esther

POETRY: Job, Psalms, Proverbs, Ecclesiastes, Song of Solomon, Lamentations

SERMONS: Isaiah, Jeremiah, Ezekiel, Daniel, Hosea, Joel, Amos, Obadiah, Jonah, Micah, Nahum, Habakkuk, Zephaniah, Haggai, Zechariah, Malachi

Again care should be taken not to overlook, in these general groupings, the distinctive message of the several books composing them. Thus, while *redemption* is the *general* theme of the Pentateuch, telling as it does the story of the redemption of Israel out of bondage and into "a good land and large," each of the five books has its own distinctive part in the whole. Genesis is the book of beginnings, and explains the *origin* of Israel. Exodus tells the story of the *deliverance* of Israel; Leviticus of the *worship* of Israel as a delivered people, and Deuteronomy warns and instructs that people in view of their approaching entrance upon their inheritance.

The Poetical books record the spiritual experiences of the redeemed people in the varied scenes and events through which the providence of God led them. The prophets were inspired preachers, and the prophetical books consist of sermons with brief connecting and explanatory passages. Two prophetical books,

Ezekiel and Daniel, have a different character and are apocalyptic, largely.

Fourth. The Bible tells the Human Story. Beginning, logically, with the creation of the earth and of man, the story of the race sprung from the first human pair continues through the first eleven chapters of Genesis. With the twelfth chapter begins the history of Abraham and of the nation of which Abraham was the ancestor. It is that nation, Israel, with which the Bible narrative is thereafter chiefly concerned from the eleventh chapter of Genesis to the second chapter of the Acts of the Apostles. The Gentiles are mentioned, but only in connection with Israel. But it is made increasingly clear that Israel so fills the scene only because entrusted with the accomplishment of worldwide purposes (Deut 7:7).

The appointed mission of Israel was, (1) to be a witness to the unity of God in the midst of universal idolatry (Deut 6:4: Isa 43:10); (2) to illustrate to the nations the greater blessedness of serving the one true God (Deut 33:26–29; 1 Chr 17:20, 21; Ps 102:15); (3) to receive and preserve the Divine revelation (Rom 3:1, 2); and (4) to produce the Messiah, earth's Saviour and Lord (Rom 9:4). The prophets foretell a glorious future for Israel under the reign of Christ.

The biblical story of Israel, past, present, and future, falls into seven distinct periods: (1) From the call of Abram (Gen 12) to the Exodus (Ex 1–20); (2) From the Exodus to the death of Joshua (Ex 21 to Josh 24); (3) from the death of Joshua to the establishment of the Hebrew monarchy under Saul; (4) the period of the kings from Saul to the Captivities; (5) the period of the Captivities; (6) the restored commonwealth from the end of the Babylonian captivity of Judah, to the destruction of Jerusalem, A.D. 70; (7) the present dispersion.

The Gospels record the appearance in human history and within the Hebrew nation of the promised Messiah, Jesus Christ, and tell the wonderful story of his manifestation to Israel, his rejection by that people, his crucifixion, resurrection, and ascension.

The Acts of the Apostles record the descent of the Holy Spirit, and the beginning of a new thing in human history, the Church. The division of the race now becomes threefold—the Jew, the Gentile, and the Church of God. Just as Israel is in the foreground from the call of Abram to the resurrection of Christ, so now the Church fills the scene from the second chapter of the Acts to the fourth chapter of the Revelation. The remaining chapters of that book complete the story of humanity and the final triumph of Christ.

Fifth. The Central Theme of the Bible is Christ. It is this manifestation of Jesus Christ, his Person as *"God manifest in the flesh"* (1 Tim 3:16), his sacrificial death, and his resurrection, which constitute the Gospel. Unto this all preceding Scripture leads, from this all following Scripture proceeds. The Gospel is preached in the Acts and explained in the Epistles. Christ, Son of God, Son of man, Son of Abraham, Son of David, thus binds the many books into one Book. Seed of the woman (Gen 3:15) he is the ultimate destroyer of Satan and his works: Seed of Abraham he is the world blesser; Seed of David he is Israel's King, "Desire of all Nations." Exalted to the right hand of God he is *"head over all to the Church, which is his body,"* while to Israel and the nations the promise of his return forms the one and only rational expectation that humanity will yet fulfil itself. Meanwhile the Church looks momentarily for the fulfilment of his special promise: *"I will come again and receive you unto myself"* (Jn 14:1–3). To him the Holy Spirit throughout this Gospel age bears testimony. The last book of all, the Consummation book, is *"The Revelation of Jesus Christ"* (Rev 1:1).

2. THE SCOPES TRIAL TRANSCRIPTS (1925)

The spread of the fundamentalist movement during the 1920s led many states to pass laws specifically banning or restricting the teaching of evolution in public schools. In 1925, a Tennessee high-school teacher named John Scopes (1900–1970) was convinced by several like-minded evolutionists to test the legitimacy of his own state's prohibition of evolution in its classrooms. The result was one of the most celebrated trials of the century, the so-called Monkey Trial held in Dayton, Tennessee. In the following excerpts from the trial transcripts, the main antagonists attempt to frame the question in terms of monumental social and religious choices. For Scopes's defense attorney, Clarence Darrow (1857–1938), the case represented a showdown between the forces of progressive enlightenment and backward religious bigotry. As a famous criminal and labor attorney, Darrow reveled in courtroom confrontation and seized this opportunity to go after fundamentalist lawmakers in one of their strongholds. The state's case was prosecuted by perhaps the other most famous American lawyer of the day, three-time populist candidate for the presidency, William Jennings Bryan (1860–1925). In Bryan's opening speech he portrayed Darrow and other evolutionists as outside agitators, bent on overturning the will of the people of Tennessee. Though Bryan did not live to deliver the closing speech he composed, it is clear that he too saw the conflict in epic terms. The compatibility of science and religion proposed by the Modernist theologian Kirby Mather, whose testimony is excerpted in the third reading, did not seem to strike either the atheist Darrow or the fundamentalist Bryan as even a remote possibility, thereby indicating the depth of the antagonism the issue inspired. Scopes was found guilty and fined one hundred dollars, though the conviction was later overturned on a technicality by the Tennessee Supreme Court. The state's law against teaching evolution in public schools, however, was not revoked until the 1960s.

a. CLARENCE DARROW, OPENING SPEECH

"There is not a single line of any constitution that can withstand bigotry and ignorance when it seeks to destroy the rights of the individual; and bigotry and ignorance are ever active. Here we find today as brazen and as bold an attempt to destroy learning as was ever made in the Middle Ages, and the only difference is we have not provided that they shall be burned at the stake. But there is time for that, your Honor. We have to approach these things gradually.

"Now let us see what we claim with reference to this law. If this proceeding, both in form and substance, can prevail in this court, then, your Honor, any law, no matter how foolish, wicked, ambiguous, or ancient, can come back to Tennessee. All the guarantees go for nothing. All of the past has gone to waste, been forgotten, if this can succeed.

"I am going to begin with some of the simpler reasons why it is absolutely absurd to think that this statute, indictment, or any part of the proceedings in this case are legal; and I think the sooner we get rid of it in Tennessee the better for the people of Tennessee, and the better for the pursuit of knowledge in the world; so let me begin at the beginning.

"The first point we made in this suit is that it is unconstitutional on account of divergence and the difference between the statute and the caption and because it contains more than one subject.

"Every Constitution with which I am familiar has substantially this same proposition, that the caption and the law must correspond.

"Lots of things are put through the Legislature in the night time. Everybody does not read all of the statutes, even members of the Legislature—I have been a member of the Legislature myself, and I know how it is. They may vote for them without reading them, but the substance of the act is put in the caption, so it may be seen and read, and nothing may be in the act that is not contained in the caption. There is not any question about it, and only one subject shall be legislated on at once. Of course, the caption may be broader than the act. They may make a caption and the act may fall far short of it, but the substance of the act must be in the caption, and there can be no variance.

"Now let us see what they have done. There is not much dispute about the English language, I take it. Here is the caption:

'Public Act, Chapter 37, 1925, an act prohibiting the teaching of the evolution theory in all the universities, normals, and all the public schools of Tennessee which are supported in whole or in part by the public school funds of the State, and to prescribe penalties for the violation thereof.'

"Now what is it—an act to prohibit the teaching of the evolution theory in Tennessee? Is this the act? Is this statute to prevent the teaching of the evolution theory? There is not a word said in the statute about evolution. There is not a word said in the statute about preventing the teaching of the theory of evolution—not a word.

"This caption says what follows is an act forbidding the teaching of evolution, and the Catholic could have gone home without any thought that his faith was about to be attacked. The Protestant could have gone home without any thought that his religion could be attacked. The intelligent, scholarly Christians, who by the million in the United States find no inconsistency between evolution and religion, could have gone home without any fear that a narrow, ignorant, bigoted shrew of religion could have destroyed their religious freedom and their right to think and act and speak; and the nation and the state could have laid down peacefully to sleep that night without the slightest fear that religious hatred and bigotry were to be turned loose in a great State.

"Any question about that? Anything in this caption whatever about religion, or anything about measuring science and knowledge and learning by the Book of Genesis, written when everybody thought the world was flat? Nothing.

"They went to bed in peace, probably, and they woke up to find this, which has not the slightest reference to it; which does not refer to evolution in any way; which is, as claimed, a religious statute.

"That is what they found and here is what it is:

"'Be it enacted by the General Assembly of the State of Tennessee, that it shall be unlawful for any teacher in any of the universities, nor-mals, and all other public schools in the State, which are supported in whole or in part by the public school funds of the State, to teach'—what, teach evolution? Oh, no.—'To teach the theory that denies the story of the divine creation of man as taught in the Bible, and to teach instead that man has descended from a lower order of animals.'

"That is what was foisted on the people of this State, under a caption which never meant it, and could give no hint of it; that it should be a crime in the State of Tennessee to teach any theory,—not evolution, but any theory of the origin of man, except that contained in the divine account as recorded in the Bible.

"But the State of Tennessee, under an honest and fair interpretation of the Constitution, has no more right to teach the Bible as the Divine Book than that the Koran is one, or the Book of Mormon, or the Book of Confucius, or the Buddha, or the Essays of Emerson, or any one of the 10,000 books to which human souls have gone for consolation and aid in their troubles." . . .

b. WILLIAM JENNINGS BRYAN, OPENING SPEECH

"Our position is that the statute is sufficient. The statute defines exactly what the people of Tennessee decided and intended and did declare unlawful, and it needs no interpretation.

"The caption speaks of the evolutionary theory, and the statute specifically states that teachers are forbidden to teach in the schools supported by taxation in this State any theory of creation of man that denies the Divine record of man's creation as found in the Bible, and that there might be no difference of opinion—there might be no ambiguity—that there might be no such confusion of thought as our learned friends attempt to inject into it. The Legislature was careful to define what is meant by the first of the statute.

"It says 'to teach that man is a descendant of any lower form of life.' If that had not been there, if the first sentence had been the only sentence in the statute, then these gentlemen might come and ask to define what that meant or to explain whether the thing that was taught was contrary to the language of the statute in the first sentence. But the second sentence removes all doubt, as has been stated by my colleague.

"The second sentence points out specifically what is meant, and that is the teaching that man is the descendant of any lower form of life; and if the defendant taught that, as we have proved by the textbook that he used and as we have proved by the students that went to hear him, if he taught that man is a descendant of any lower form of life, he violated the statute, and more than that, we have his own confession that he knew he was violating the statute."

[After summarizing the evidence, Bryan continues:]

"We do not need any expert to tell us what the law means. An expert cannot be permitted to come in here and try to defeat the enforcement of a law testifying that it isn't a bad law, and it isn't—I mean a bad doctrine—no matter how these people phrase that doctrine, no matter how they eulogize it. This is not the place to try to prove that the law ought never to have been passed. The place to prove that was at the Legislature.

"If these people were so anxious to keep the State of Tennessee from disgracing itself, if they were so afraid that by this action taken by the Legislature, the State would put itself before the people of the nation as ignorant people and bigoted people—if they had half the affection for Tennessee that you would think they had as they come here to testify—they would have come at a time when their testimony would have been valuable, and not at this time to ask you to refuse to enforce a law because they did not think the law ought to have been passed.

"And if the people of Tennessee were to go into a state, into New York, the one from which this impulse comes to resist this law, or go into any state . . . and try to convince the people that a law they had passed ought not to be enforced (just because the people who went there didn't think it ought to have been passed), don't you think it would be resented as an impertinence? . . .

"The people of this State passed this law. The people of this State knew what they were doing when they passed the law, and they knew the dangers of the doctrine that they did not want it taught to their children. And, my friends, it isn't proper to bring experts in here to try to defeat the purpose of the people of this State by trying to show that this thing that they denounce and outlaw is a beautiful thing that everybody ought to believe in. . . .

"These people want to come here with experts to make your Honor believe that the law should never have been passed, and because in their opinion it ought not to have been passed, it ought not to be enforced. It isn't a place for expert testimony. We have sufficient proof in the book. Doesn't the book state the very thing that is objected to and outlawed in this State? Who has a copy of that book?"

JUDGE RAULSTON—Do you mean the Bible?

MR. BRYAN—No, sir, the biology. [*Laughter*]

A VOICE—Here it is, Hunter's Biology.

MR. BRYAN—No, not the Bible. You see, in this State they cannot teach the Bible. They can only teach things that declare it to be a lie, according to the learned counsel. These people in the State, Christian people, have tied their hands by their Constitution. They say we all believe in the Bible, for it is the overwhelming belief in the State, but we will not teach that Bible, which we believe—even to our children, through teachers that we pay with our money.

"No, no, it isn't the teaching of the Bible, and we are not asking it.

"The question is, Can a minority in this State come in and compel a teacher to teach that the Bible is not true and make the parents of these children pay the expenses of the teacher to tell their children what these people believe is false and dangerous?

"Has it come to a time when the minority can take charge of a state like Tennessee and compel the majority to pay their teachers while they take religion out of the heart of the children of the parents who pay the teachers?"

---

c. KIRTLEY F. MATHER, TESTIMONY

[Dr. Mather's statement was introduced as coming from a student of the Bible, lecturer to Bible students at the Boston University School of Religious Education, member of the Baptist Church at Newton Center, Mass., and teacher of the Mather Class in its Bible school. Professor Mather said that evolution was "not a power, not a force," but "a process, a method." God was "a power, a force"; He necessarily uses processes and methods in displaying His Power and exerting force.]

"... Not one of the facts of evolution contradicts any teaching of Jesus Christ known to me. None could, for His teachings deal with moral law and spiritual realities. Natural science deals with physical laws and material results. When men are offered their choice between science, with its confident and unanimous acceptance of the evolutionary principle on the one hand, and religion, with its necessary appeal to things unseen and unproven on the other, they are more likely to abandon religion than to abandon science.

"If such a choice is forced upon us the churches will lose many of their best educated young people, the very ones upon whom they must depend for leadership in the coming years.

"Fortunately such a choice is absolutely unnecessary. To say that one must choose between evolution and Christianity is exactly like telling the child as he starts for school that he must choose between spelling and arithmetic. Thorough knowledge of each is essential to success—both individual and racial—in life.

"Good religion is founded on facts, even as the evolutionary principle. A true religion faces the facts fearlessly, regardless of where or how the facts may be found. The theories of evolution commonly accepted in the scientific world do not deny any reasonable interpretations of the story of Divine creation as recorded in the Bible. Rather they affirm that story and give it larger and more profound meaning.

"This, of course, depends upon what the meaning and interpretation of the stories are to each individual. I have been a Bible student all of my life, and ever since my college days I have been intensely interested in the relations between science and the Bible.

"It is obvious to any careful and intelligent reader of the Book of Genesis that some interpretation of its account must be made by each individual. Very evidently, it is not intended to be a scientific statement of the order and method of creation.

"In the first chapter of Genesis we are told that man was made after the plants and the other animals had been formed, and that man and woman were both created on the same day.

"In the second chapter of Genesis we read that man was formed from the dust of the ground before plants and other animals were made; that trees grew until fruit was upon them; that all the animals passed in review before man to be named, and then, after these events, woman was made.

"There is obvious lack of harmony between these two Biblical accounts of creation so far as details of the process and order of events are concerned. They are, however, in perfect accord in presenting the spiritual truth that God is the author and the administrator of the universe, and that is the sort of truth we find in the Bible.

"It is a textbook of religion, not a textbook of biology or astronomy or geology. Moreover, it is just exactly the Biblical spiritual truth concerning God which rings clearly and unmistakably through every theory of theistic evolution. With it, modern science is in perfect accord.

"There are a number of reasons why sincere and honest Christians have recently come to distrust evolution. . . . Too many people who loudly proclaim their allegiance to the Book, know very little about what it really contains.

"The Bible does not state that the world was made about 6,000 years ago. The date 4004 B.C. set opposite Genesis 1:1 in many versions of the Bible, was placed there by Archbishop Usher[1] only a few centuries ago. It is a man's interpretation of the Bible; it is in the footnotes added recently; it is not a part of the book itself.

"Concerning the length of earth history and of human history, the Bible is absolutely silent. Science may conclude that the earth is 100,000,000 or 100,000,000,000 years old; the conclusion does not affect the Bible in the

---

[1]James Ussher (1581–1656), an Irish prelate whose close reading and calculations of biblical narratives established a long-accepted chronology of human history since the Creation.

slightest degree. Or, if one is worried over the progressive appearance of land, plants, animals, and man on the successive six days of a 'Creation Week,' there is a well-known Biblical support for the scientists' contention that eons rather than hours elapsed while these things were taking place.

"'*A day in the sight of the Lord is as a thousand years, and a thousand years as a day*" [2 Pet 3:8].

"Taking the Bible itself as an authority dissipates many of the difficulties which threaten to make a gulf between religion and science."

---

3. Jerry Falwell
LISTEN AMERICA! (1980)

The political influence of fundamentalist groups in the United States waned considerably after the 1920s, and by the early 1970s it was negligible. Then a new variety of social issues—feminism, the "sexual revolution," drug culture, etc.—prompted several evangelical Christians to mobilize and organize like-minded believers into a political force. By 1980, their informal network of political action groups such as the Moral Majority was well enough developed to play a pivotal role in the election of the conservative Republican Ronald Reagan as president that year. The Moral Majority was founded in 1974 by the popular Baptist preacher Jerry Falwell (1933–), a pioneer in televised evangelism with his "Old-Time Gospel Hour." In the excerpt below from his book *Listen America!,* Falwell explains his conviction that the political and social health of the nation is in decline and that this condition stems directly from a much deeper spiritual crisis. Fundamental "biblical values," he argues, are more important than ever in a society besieged by the "secular humanist" creed of self-indulgence above all else. More specifically, Falwell identifies new political developments—the women's rights movement, the gay rights movement, and misguided attempts to separate church and state—as dangerously exacerbating the problem. Only a return to the Christian family and nation that he envisions will reverse the moral decay and forestall certain divine wrath. The genius of Falwell and other modern fundamentalist leaders in picking up on a widespread sense of national malaise and proposing a "biblical" solution to the problem has allowed evangelical political activism to spread far beyond a small, concerned core of believers to permeate every aspect of local and national politics today.

Why do we have so few good leaders? Why is it that political and judicial decisions are made that horrify America? You will find that when society begins to fall apart spiritually, what we find missing is the mighty man, that man who is willing, with courage and confidence, to stand up for that which is right. We are hard-pressed to find today that man in a governmental position, that man of war, that judge, that prophet, that preacher who is willing to call sin by its right name. Vanishing from the scene is the prudent, the wise person, the ancient, the old, the honorable people, the grandparents who will stand up for righteousness year after year, generation after generation, and be an example to us. For the first time in history, we have few elderly honorable people on the national scene. We have few we can look to and say, "Here is an example of godliness in leadership." Instead we find confusion and selfishness, which is destroying the very basis of our society.

We must review our government and see where our leadership has taken us today and where our future leaders must take us tomorrow if we are to remain a free America. It is a sad fact today that Americans have made a god of government. They are looking to government rather than to God, who ordained government. The United States is a republic where laws rule. Although the people of the United States have a vote, America is not a democracy in the sense that the majority rules. Her citizens elect representatives who represent them and govern them by laws. I believe that God promoted America to a greatness no other nation has ever enjoyed because her heritage is one of a republic governed by laws predicated on the Bible.

America is facing a vacuum of leadership not only in regard to her elected officials, but also among her citizens who are not standing for what is right and decent. We need in America today powerful, dynamic, and godly leadership. Male leadership in our families is affecting male leadership in our churches, and it is affecting male leadership in our society. As we look across our nation today we find a tremendous vacuum of godly men who are willing to be the kind of spiritual leaders who are necessary not only to change a nation, but also to change the churches within our nation and the basic units of our entire society, our families.

If a man is not a student of the Word of God and does not know what the Bible says, I question his ability to be an effective leader. Whatever he leads, whether it be his family, his church, or his nation, will not be properly led without this priority. God alone has the wisdom to tell men and women where this world is going, where it needs to go, and how it can be redirected. Only by godly leadership can America be put back on a divine course. God

will give national healing if men and women will pray and meet God's conditions, but we must have leadership in America to deliver God's message.

We must reverse the trend America finds herself in today. Young people between the ages of twenty-five and forty have been born and reared in a different world than Americans of years past. The television set has been their primary baby-sitter. From the television set they have learned situation ethics and immorality—they have learned a loss of respect for human life. They have learned to disrespect the family as God has established it. They have been educated in a public-school system that is permeated with secular humanism. They have been taught that the Bible is just another book of literature. They have been taught that there are no absolutes in our world today. They have been introduced to the drug culture. They have been reared by the family and by the public school in a society that is greatly void of discipline and character-building. These same young people have been reared under the influence of a government that has taught them socialism and welfarism. They have been taught to believe that the world owes them a living whether they work or not.

I believe that America was built on integrity, on faith in God, and on hard work. I do not believe that anyone has ever been successful in life without being willing to add that last ingredient—diligence or hard work. We now have second- and third-generation welfare recipients. Welfare is not always wrong. There are those who do need welfare, but we have reared a generation that understands neither the dignity nor the importance of work. . . .

It is now time to take a stand on certain moral issues, and we can only stand if we have leaders. We must stand against the Equal Rights Amendment, the feminist revolution, and the homosexual revolution. We must have a revival in this country. It can come if we will realize the danger and heed the admonition of God found in 2 Chronicles 7:14, *"If my people, which are called by my name, shall humble them-*

selves, and pray, and seek my face, and turn from their wicked ways; then will I hear from heaven, and will forgive their sin, and will heal their land."

As a preacher of the Gospel, I not only believe in prayer and preaching, I also believe in good citizenship. If a labor union in America has the right to organize and improve its working conditions, then I believe that the churches and the pastors, the priests, and the rabbis of America have a responsibility, not just the right, to see to it that the moral climate and conscience of Americans is such that this nation can be healed inwardly. If it is healed inwardly, then it will heal itself outwardly.

It is not easy to go against the tide and do what is right. This nation can be brought back to God, but there must first be an awareness of sin. The Bible declares, *"Righteousness exalteth a nation: But sin is a reproach to any people"* [Prov 14:34]. It is right living that has made America the greatest nation on earth, and with all of her shortcomings and failures, America is without question the greatest nation on the face of God's earth. We as Americans must recommit ourselves to keeping her that way. . . .

I am positive in my belief regarding the Constitution that God led in the development of that document, and as a result, we here in America have enjoyed 204 years of unparalleled freedom. The most positive people in the world are people who believe the Bible to be the Word of God. The Bible contains a positive message. It is a message written by 40 men over a period of approximately 1,500 years under divine inspiration. It is God's message of love, redemption, and deliverance for a fallen race. What could be more positive than the message of redemption in the Bible? But God will force Himself upon no man. Each individual American must make His choice. . . .

Men and women today try to rationalize their sins by calling them shortcomings or errors. Many modern theologians evade the word "sin." It is time that we began calling sin by its right name and calling for what is America's only hope—a biblical and spiritual awakening in the lives of her people. The Bible declares,

"For the wages of sin is death; but the gift of God is eternal life through Jesus Christ our Lord" [Rom 6:23].

We live in a world under God's judgment. Until man realizes that his greatest problem is sin and that this is what has alienated him from God, his Creator, there can be little hope of curing the chaotic conditions in our nation and world. Countless people are searching desperately for something that will bring inner peace and stability to their lives. People are lonely and filled with fear about the future, about failure, about death.

Men and women cannot ignore God, live as they please, and expect to be happy and blessed. This is, however, precisely what has happened. Men and women have placed their priorities on acquiring tangible possessions and achieving tangible goals. Man, rather than God, has been placed at the center of all things. Humanism in some form has taken the place of the Bible. Secular humanism has become the religion of America. Through education and the media, man is constantly being told that he is nothing more than a machine.

According to Webster's New Collegiate Dictionary, humanism is "a doctrine, attitude, or way of life centered on human interests or values; a philosophy that asserts the dignity and worth of man and his capacity for self-realization through reason and that often rejects supernaturalism." Humanism is man's attempt to create a heaven on earth, exempting God and His Law. Humanists propose that man is in charge of his own destiny. Humanism exalts man's reason and intelligence. It advocates situation ethics, freedom from any restraint, and defines sin as man's maladjustment to man. It even advocates the right to commit suicide and recognizes evolution as a source of man's existence. Humanism promotes the socialization of all humanity into a world commune.

Christianity is ruled out of humanism and is said to be an obstacle to human progress and a threat to its existence. Mao Tse-tung once said, "Our God is none other than the masses of the people. Ye shall be as Gods." The first version of the *Humanist Manifesto* appeared in 1933. The second version appeared in 1973 and was printed in its entirety in the New York *Times*. *Humanist Manifesto I* and *Humanist Manifesto II* openly deny the existence of a Creator, urge abolition of national sovereignty in favor of world government, and embrace complete sexual freedom, abortion, homosexuality, and euthanasia. . . .

I believe that at the foundation of the women's liberation movement there is a minority core of women who were once bored with life, whose real problems are spiritual problems. Many women have never accepted their God-given roles. They live in disobedience to God's laws and have promoted their godless philosophy throughout our society. God Almighty created men and women biologically different and with differing needs and roles. He made men and women to complement each other and to love each other. Not all the women involved in the feminist movement are radicals. Some are misinformed, and some are lonely women who like being housewives and helpmeets and mothers, but whose husbands spend little time at home and who take no interest in their wives and children. Sometimes the full load of rearing a family becomes a great burden to a woman who is not supported by a man. Women who work should be respected and accorded dignity and equal rewards for equal work. But this is not what the present feminist movement and equal rights movement are all about.

The Equal Rights Amendment[2] is a delusion. I believe that women deserve more than equal rights. And, in families and in nations where the Bible is believed, Christian women are honored above men. Only in places where the Bible is believed and practiced do women receive more than equal rights. Men and women have differing strengths. The Equal Rights Amendment can never do for women what needs to be done for them. Women need to know Jesus Christ as their Lord and Savior and be under His Lordship. They need a man who knows Jesus Christ as his Lord and Savior, and they need to be part of a home where their husband is a godly leader and where there is a Christian family. . . .

Right living must be re-established as an American way of life. We as American citizens must recommit ourselves to the faith of our fathers and to the premises and moral foundations upon which this country was established. Now is the time to begin calling America back to God, back to the Bible, back to morality! We must be willing to live by the moral convictions that we claim to believe. There is no way that we will ever be willing to die for something for which we are not willing to live. The authority of Bible morality must once again be recognized as the legitimate guiding principle of our nation. Our love for our fellow man must ever be grounded in the truth and never be allowed to blind us from the truth that is the basis of our love for our fellow man.

As a pastor and as a parent I am calling my fellow American citizens to unite in a moral crusade for righteousness in our generation. It is time to call America back to her moral roots. It is time to call America back to God. We need a revival of righteous living based on a proper confession of sin and repentance of heart if we are to remain the land of the free and the home of the brave! I am convinced that God is calling millions of Americans in the so-often silent majority to join in the moral-majority crusade to turn America around in our lifetime. Won't you begin now to pray with us for revival in America? Let us unite our hearts and lives together for the cause of a new America . . . a moral America in which righteousness will exalt this nation. . . .

---

[2] The campaign for an Equal Rights Amendment to the U.S. Constitution, intended to guarantee equal rights for women, gained major momentum in 1972 when the proposed amendment received the support of President Nixon and two-thirds of both houses of Congress. Ten years later, however, after several extended deadlines, the amendment was still five states short of the minimum thirty-eight needed for ratification, and the reform proposal died.

B. Revivalism

Half a century after the Great Awakening of 1739–1742 (see 7B), the newly independent United States experienced another great surge of revivals, lasting from about 1795 to 1835. During this time, American revivals grew in both size and variety, encompassing camp meetings held under large tents on the frontier, congregational church gatherings, and small-town conventions. From that point on, revivalism became a staple of American religious life among Protestants, and revivals themselves evolved into more carefully orchestrated affairs that took place on a more regular basis. Later innovations in form included holding revivals not just in tents or churches but also in large lecture halls or stadiums; and, more recently, broadcasting them via radio and television. The greatest pioneers in these modern methods of "mass evangelization" were Dwight L. Moody (1837–1899), Billy Sunday (1862–1935), and Billy Graham (b. 1918). Early in the twentieth century, a series of revivals at the Azusa Street Mission in Los Angeles spawned a new style of worship known as Pentecostalism. Since then, dozens of new Pentecostal denominations—including the Church of God in Christ and the Assemblies of God—have spread throughout the country and the world, all of them emphasizing the spontaneous regeneration of the soul through the Holy Spirit and the many spiritual gifts and good works that result. Although modern revivals are normally open to members of any Christian denomination—as well as to non-Christians—the majority of the people drawn to these events have traditionally come from the Baptist, Methodist, Presbyterian, and Congregational churches as well as from Holiness and Pentecostal denominations.

1. Elsie W. Mason
THE MAN, CHARLES HARRISON MASON (1979)

The growth of Pentecostal and Holiness churches during the past century has been astonishing, producing at least two hundred distinct denominations, which together claim more than 10 million members. Like the Methodist movement from which they sprang, Pentecostal and Holiness churches profess the Wesleyan doctrine of sanctification after justification (see 6D). Citing the biblical event known as Pentecost—when Jesus' disciples were filled with the Holy Spirit and spoke in languages they had never learned (Acts 1:1–4)—Pentecostals also stress "spiritual baptism," an ecstatic experience of the ancient *charismata,* or gifts, of the Holy Spirit. These include "faith healing," prophecy, exorcism, and especially speaking in tongues, or glossolalia. The latter act consists of joyful exclamations in a "spiritual language," incomprehensible to all but a few who have the gift of interpretation. The pivotal moment in the modern Pentecostal movement came in 1906, when the Black Holiness preacher William J. Seymour (1870–1922) launched a series of revivals at his Azusa Street Mission in Los Angeles. One of the earliest and most enthusiastic participants was another

Holiness minister, Charles Harrison Mason (1866–1961), whose visit to Azusa Street is described below by his second wife, Elsie. After being dismissed from a Baptist church because of his teachings on sanctification, Mason had wandered the South as an itinerant preacher, eventually establishing his own church in an abandoned cotton-gin house in Lexington, Mississippi. Having heard about the dramatic success of the Azusa Street Mission, Mason traveled to Los Angeles in 1907. The Pentecostal revival he experienced there was remarkable in a number of ways, not least in that it attracted a crowd of both black and white enthusiasts who worshiped side by side. As Elsie Mason describes below, her husband returned from California "baptized with the Holy Ghost and fire" and proceeded to build his Church of God in Christ into the second largest black denomination in the country, today claiming over five million members.

Elder Mason began to thirst for a more complete relationship with God in 1907. He hoped to retreat to some secluded place to remain there until his soul was satisfied. Meanwhile, a very exciting report arrived from Los Angeles, California. The Azusa Street Revival was in progress, and large numbers of people were being saved, sanctified, filled with the Holy Ghost, healed, along with many other miracles and spiritual demonstrations.

Elder C. P. Jones, Mason's dearest friend, offered further information and insight concerning the baptism of the Holy Ghost (over which doctrine they were later destined to part company).[3] But as did Charles Mason, C. P. Jones contended that every saint [i.e., genuine Christian] should receive that spiritual baptism. This he believed would 'complete' the believer-in-Christ by a 'third work of grace' to empower him/her for effective service. However, Charles Mason and C. P. Jones were to finally dissolve their ministerial partnership and friendship because Jones did not agree that tongue-speaking was necessary and Mason felt that it was biblical and therefore necessary.

After studying the baptism of the Holy Ghost with C. P. Jones, Elder Charles H. Mason was directed by God to visit the Azusa Street Revival. Said Mason: "I was led by the Spirit to go to Los Angeles, California, where the great fire of the latter rain of the Holy Ghost had fallen on many" [cf. Jl 2:23]. Elder Mason travelled the great distance from Mississippi—accompanied by a few friends—with great anticipation of God's blessings. When he arrived on Azusa Street, the forty-year-old Elder Mason witnessed some very unique occurrences:

"The first day of the meeting I sat by myself, away from those who went with me. I saw and heard some things that did not seem scriptural to me, but at this I did not stumble. I began to thank God in my heart for all things for when I heard some speak in tongues I knew it was right, though I did not understand it. Nevertheless it was sweet to me."

Already Mason's heart was being prepared to receive 'the Gift.' And, the dynamic, Holy Ghost-filled preaching of Elder W. J. Seymour was the instrument that the Almighty had chosen to bring Elder Mason to the point of baptism:

"I also thank God for Elder Seymour who came and preached a wonderful sermon. His words were sweet and powerful and it seems that I can hear them now . . . When he closed his sermon, he said: All of those that want to be

---

[3]Mason's friend and assistant, Charles Parker Jones, went on to lead a splinter group that eventually became the Church of Christ (Holiness) U.S.A., a smaller rival to Mason's Church of God in Christ (COGIC). Seven years later, many white members of the COGIC broke away to form the all-white Assemblies of God.

sanctified or baptized with the Holy Ghost, go to the upper room, and all those that want to be healed, go to the prayer room, and all those that want to be justified, come to the altar. I said that (the altar) is the place for me, for it may be that I am not converted, and if not, God knows it and can convert me."

The great humility of the Church of God in Christ founder is portrayed strikingly herein as he is seen beginning again—at the very beginning—to assure himself of personal salvation and personal access to "the gift of the Holy Ghost." The sanctification of Elder Mason was never presented to 'the world' in a self-righteous manner, although he was firm and unwavering in personal commitment. Elder mason chose the 'low road' of personal piety and humility; and thereby, he was exalted by God. The founder continued to reflect on the Azusa Street Revival experiences:

"I stood on my feet while waiting at the altar, fearing someone would bother me. Just as I attempted to bow down someone called me and said, 'The pastor wants you three brethren in his room.' I obeyed and went up. He received us and seemed to be so glad to see us there. He said, 'Brethren, the Lord will do great things for us and bless us.' And he cautioned us not to be running around in the city seeking worldly pleasure, but to seek the pleasure of the Lord. The Word just suited me."

Because Elder Mason was obedient to the voice of the Lord which summoned him to Azusa Street, the adversary mounted a tremendous onslaught against him—desperately attempting to thwart what would be a tremendously successful personal ministry once he had received the spiritual baptism:

". . . a sister came into the room at the time we were bowing to pray, one that I had a thought about that might not have been right. I had not seen her in a number of years. I arose, took her into a room and confessed it to her. And we prayed."

And as if that were not enough in the way of temptation, Satan continued to present still others:

"I arose and returned to the pastor's room and began to pray again, and the enemy got into a minister, a brother, to tempt me. I said to him, 'go away, I do not want to be bothered.' And he tempted me the third time, but I refused to hear him. I told him that he did not know what he wanted, but I knew what I needed from God. I did not intend to be interfered with by anyone—so he gave up and ceased to annoy me further. . ."

Even among Elder Mason's associates, there were basic problems and misunderstandings:

"Elder J. A. Jeter of Little Rock, Arkansas, and Elder D. J. Young of Pine Bluff, Arkansas . . . we three, went together, boarded together, and prayed for the same blessing. The enemy had put into the ear of Brother Jeter to find fault with the work, but God kept me out of it."

It was tempting for Elder Mason to try his hand at correcting the situation, but he was warned of God not to interfere:

"That night the Lord spoke to me, that Jesus saw all of this world's wrongs but did not attempt to set it right until God overshadowed Him with the Holy Ghost. And I said, 'I am no better than my Lord, and if I want Him to baptize me I will have to let the people's rights and wrongs alone, and look to Him and not to the people. Then he will baptize me.' And I said 'yes' to God, for it was He who wanted to baptize me and not the people."

With this new insight, God began to literally 'unveil the heavens' and to speak directly to the mind and heart of Elder Mason every day:

"Glory! The second night of prayer I saw a vision. I saw myself standing alone and had a dry roll of paper in my hands. I had to chew it. When I had gotten it all in my mouth—trying to swallow it while looking up towards the heavens—a man appeared at my side. I turned my eyes at once, then I awoke and the interpretation came. God had me swallowing the whole book; and if I would not turn my eyes to anyone other than God and Him only, He would baptize me. I said 'yes' to Him, and at once, in the morning when I arose I could hear a voice in me saying, 'I see.'"

In spite of the clarity of those direct divine messages to Elder Mason—and despite his personal sincerity—Satan was yet present to tempt him to distraction from his purpose:

"I had joy but was not satisfied. A sister began to tell me about the faults that were among the saints, but stopped as she was not wanting to hinder me by telling me of them. I sat and looked at her and said, 'You may all stand on your heads, God has told me what to do. God is going to baptize me.'"

With this renewed resolve, Elder Mason was able to increase his spiritual momentum and to make the quest for the baptism somewhat easier:

"I got a place at the altar and began to thank God. After that I said, 'Lord, if I could only baptize myself I would do so.' For I wanted the baptism so badly that I did not know what to do. I said, 'Lord, you will have to do the work for me.' A brother came and prayed for me. I did not feel any better or any worse. One sister came and said, 'Satan will try to make you feel sad, but that is not the way to receive Him: you must be glad and praise the Lord.' I told her that I was letting the Lord search my heart, for I did not want to receive new wine in old bottles. But I said, 'My heart does not condemn me.' Then I quoted scripture to her which readeth thus: *'Beloved, if our hearts condemn us not, then have we confidence towards God, and whatsoever we ask we receive of him'* [1 Jn 3:21–22]. Then I realized in my heart that I had confidence in God and did not have to get it, for my heart was free from condemnation. Then I began to seek for the baptism of the Holy Ghost according to Acts 2:41, which readeth thus: *'Then they that gladly received His Word were baptized.'* Then I saw that I had a right to be glad and not sad. As the enemy was trying to make me believe the way to receive the Holy Ghost was to be sad, the light of the Word was putting his argument out. There came a reason in my mind which said, 'Were you sad when you were going to marry?' I said, 'No, I was glad.' The voice said that this baptism meant wedlock to Christ. Then I saw more in being glad than in being sad."

Satan was outraged at the progress that Charles Mason was making toward receiving 'the Gift.' He began to step up his attack on the mind of the Church of God in Christ founder. But his attempts were consistently vanquished by the Word of God.

"The enemy said to me, 'There may be something wrong with you.' Then a voice spoke to me and said: 'If there is anything wrong with you, Christ will find it and take away and will marry you, at any rate, and will not break the vow.' More light came and my heart rejoiced! Some said, 'Let us sing.' I arose and the first song that came to me was, 'He brought me out of the miry clay; He set my feet on the Rock to stay.' The Spirit came upon the saints and upon me! Afterwards I soon sat down and soon my hands went up and I resolved in my heart not to take them down until the Lord baptized me. The enemy tried to show me again how much pain it would cause me to endure not knowing how long it would be before the Lord would baptize me. The enemy said that I might not be able to hold out. The Spirit rebuked him and said that the Lord was able to make my stand and if not I would be a liar. And the Spirit gave me to know that I was looking to God and not to myself for anything."

The relentless attacks of Satan have not produced their intended result for Elder Mason has chosen to listen attentively to the voice of God. The Word of God, which Mason affirmed early in his ministry to be his singular guide for living, had sustained him and had brought him to the very point at which the Comforter was to come. And, Elder Charles Harrison Mason's heart quickened with anticipation:

"The sound of a mighty wind was in me and my soul cried, 'Jesus, only, one like you.' My soul cried and soon I began to die. It seemed that I heard the groaning of Christ on the cross dying for me. All of the work was in me until I died out of the old man. The sound stopped for a little while. My soul cried, 'Oh, God, finish your work in me.' Then the sound broke out in me again. Then I felt something raising me out of my seat without any effort of my own. I said, 'It may be imagination.' Then I looked down to see if it was really so. I say that I was rising. Then I gave up for the Lord to have His way within me. So there came a wave of glory into me, and all of my being was filled with the glory of the Lord. So when I had gotten myself straight on my feet there came a light which enveloped my entire being above the brightness of the sun. When I opened my mouth to say glory, a flame touched my tongue which ran down to me. My language changed and no word could I speak in my own tongue. Oh, I was filled with the glory of my Lord. My soul was then satisfied. I rejoiced in Jesus my Savior, whom I love so dearly. And from that day until now there has been an overflowing joy of the glory of the Lord in my heart."

The Holy Ghost had come! Finally, Elder Charles Harrison Mason had received "the promise" which he had so heartily sought. And, his personal baptism had been quite reminiscent of the first Day of Pentecost when the *"sound"* came from heaven *"like as a rushing mighty wind"* and *"cloven tongues like as of fire"* sat upon each of the 120 waiting disciples as they spake *"in other tongues as the Spirit gave them utterance"* [Acts 2:1–4]. He had experienced all three operations of divine grace: regeneration, sanctification, and spiritual baptism. And as a result, Elder Mason was fully equipped to lead God's people.

Remaining at the Azusa Street Revival for a total of five weeks, Elder Mason refined his knowledge of the operations of the Holy Spirit within the Body of Christ. And, just as the scriptures had stated, the Holy Ghost began to "teach" Elder Mason and to "lead" him. He noted dynamic differences in his ministry to the saints. And he was increasingly effective in his teaching and preaching ministry. When Elder Mason had returned home, he wrote:

"After five weeks I left Los Angeles, California for Memphis, Tennessee, my home. The fire had fallen before my arrival. Brother Glenn Cook, of Los Angeles, was there telling the story and the Lord was sending the rain. I was full of the power when I reached home. The Spirit had taken full control of me and everything was new to me and to all the saints. The way that He did things was all new. At the same time I soon found that He could and was teaching me all things and showing the things of the Lord. He taught me how and what to sing, and all His songs were new. The third day after reaching Memphis I asked Him to give me the interpretation of what was spoken in tongues, for I did not fully understand the operation of the Spirit. I wanted the church to understand what the Spirit was saying through me, so that they might be edified. My prayers were not in vain. The Lord stood me up and began to speak in tongues and interpret the same. He soon gave me the gift of interpretation—that is, He would interpret sounds, groans, and any kind of spiritual utterance."

Elder Charles Harrison Mason returned from California full of the Holy Ghost. Immediately, his ministry was launched into a more dynamic dimension. And the Church of God in Christ began to literally spread its 'branches' in all directions. No denomination in America has matched its rapid growth and development. And, it is all because of God's goodness and the personal dedication of one man who dared to believe wholly in the Word of God, Charles Harrison Mason.

---

2. Sinclair Lewis
ELMER GANTRY (1927)

Throughout its history, Christian revivalism was often the subject of criticism and even ridicule among outsiders. By the early twentieth century, the practice had become nearly synonymous for many in the United States with Protestant

"fundamentalism," or the rejection of "modernist" attempts to reconcile science and religion, philosophy and revelation (see 9C). One of the earliest and most influential sustained satires of the entire revivalist movement was the novel *Elmer Gantry,* by Sinclair Lewis (1885–1951). Though Lewis affects to convey some sympathy for the appeal of mass revivals and popular preaching, his novel as a whole represents a scathing indictment of both "mass hysteria" and corrupt and predatory evangelical leaders. In this excerpt, twenty-two-year-old Elmer, a hard-drinking college football player, experiences a type of personal conversion at a small-town revival. For Lewis, such allegedly religious experiences were in fact usually based, as in the case of Elmer, on the desire to belong to the group, the community, or—as the star athlete turned preacher in this excerpt puts it— "the team of Jesus." Though Elmer's cynical friend Jim warns him about the tricks of "the mob," Elmer succumbs to the frenzied pleas of his family and neighbors, publicly proclaiming his spiritual rebirth. Later in the book, whatever genuine religious inclinations Elmer possessed are gradually eroded during his transformation into a popular but corrupt and lecherous revivalist. Lewis's book is admittedly highly polemical, but his work does effectively convey something of the atmosphere of a 1920s revival in small-town America.

The climactic meeting of the Annual Prayer Week, to be addressed by President Quarles, four ministers, and a rich trustee who was in the pearl-button business, with Judson Roberts as star soloist, was not held at the Y. M. C. A. but at the largest auditorium in town, the Baptist Church, with hundreds of town-people joining the collegians.

The church was a welter of brownstone, with Moorish arches and an immense star-shaped window not yet filled with stained glass.

Elmer hoped to be late enough to creep in inconspicuously, but as his mother and he straggled up to the Romanesque portico, students were still outside, chattering. He was certain they were whispering, "There he is— Hell-cat Gantry. Say, is it really true he's under conviction of sin? I thought he cussed out the church more'n anybody in college."

Meek though Elmer had been under instruction by Jim and threats by Eddie and yearning by his mother, he was not normally given to humility, and he looked at his critics defiantly. "I'll show 'em! If they think I'm going to sneak in—"

He swaggered down almost to the front pews, to the joy of his mother, who had been afraid that as usual he would hide in the rear, handy to the door if the preacher should become personal.

There was a great deal of decoration in the church, which had been endowed by a zealous alumnus after making his strike in Alaskan boarding-houses during the gold-rush. There were Egyptian pillars with gilded capitals, on the ceiling were gilt stars and clouds more woolen than woolly, and the walls were painted cheerily in three strata—green, watery blue, and khaki. It was an echoing and gaping church, and presently it was packed, the aisles full. Professors with string mustaches and dog-eared Bibles, men students in sweaters or flannel shirts, earnest young women students in homemade muslin with modest ribbons, over-smiling old maids of the town, venerable saints from the back-country with beards which partly hid the fact that they wore collars without ties, old women with billowing shoulders, irritated young married couples with broods of babies who crawled, slid, bellowed, and stared with embarrassing wonder at bachelors.

Five minutes later Elmer would not have had a seat down front. Now he could not escape. He was packed in between his mother and a wheezing fat man, and in the aisle beside his pew stood evangelical tailors and ardent schoolteachers.

The congregation swung into "When the Roll Is Called Up Yonder" and Elmer gave up his frenzied but impractical plans for escape. His mother nestled happily beside him, her hand proudly touching his sleeve, and he was stirred by the march and battle of the hymn:

When the trumpet of the Lord shall sound, and
    time shall be no more,
And the morning breaks eternal, bright and
    fair. . . .

They stood for the singing of "Shall We Gather at the River?" Elmer inarticulately began to feel his community with these humble, aspiring people—his own prairie tribe: this gaunt carpenter, a good fellow, full of friendly greetings, this farm-wife, so courageous, channeled by pioneer labor; this classmate, an admirable basket-ball player, yet now chanting beatifically, his head back, his eyes closed, his voice ringing. Elmer's own people. Could he be a traitor to them, could he resist the current of their united belief and longing?

Yes, we'll gather at the river,
The beautiful, the beautiful river,
Gather with the saints at the river
That flows by the throne of God.

Could he endure it to be away from them, in the chill void of Jim Lefferts' rationalizing, on that day when they should be rejoicing in the warm morning sunshine by the river rolling to the imperishable Throne?

And his voice—he had merely muttered the words of the first hymn—boomed out ungrudgingly:

Soon our pilgrimage will cease;
Soon our happy hearts will quiver
With the melody of peace.

His mother stroked his sleeve. He remembered that she had maintained he was the best singer she had ever heard; that Jim Lefferts had

admitted, "You certainly can make that hymn dope sound as if it meant something." He noted that people near by looked about with pleasure when they heard his Big Ben dominate the cracked jangling.

The preliminaries merely warmed up the audience for Judson Roberts. Old Jud was in form. He laughed, he shouted, he knelt and wept with real tears, he loved everybody, he raced down into the audience and patted shoulders, and for the moment everybody felt that he was closer to them than their closest friends.

"Rejoiceth as a strong man to run a race," was his text.

Roberts was really a competent athlete, and he really had skill in evoking pictures. He described the Chicago-Michigan game, and Elmer was lost in him, with him lived the moments of the scrimmage, the long run with the ball, the bleachers rising to him.

Roberts' voice softened. He was pleading. He was not talking, he said, to weak men who needed coddling into the Kingdom, but to strong men, to rejoicing men, to men brave in armor. There was another sort of race more exhilarating than any game, and it led not merely to a score on a big board but to the making of a new world—it led not to newspaper paragraphs but to glory eternal. Dangerous—calling for strong men! Ecstatic—brimming with thrills! The team captained by Christ! No timid Jesus did he preach, but the adventurer who had joyed to associate with common men, with reckless fishermen, with captains and rulers, who had dared to face the soldiers in the garden, who had dared the myrmidons of Rome and death itself! Come! Who was gallant? Who had nerve? Who longed to live abundantly? Let them come!

They must confess their sins, they must repent, they must know their own weakness save as they were reborn in Christ. But they must confess not in heaven-pilfering weakness, but in training for the battle under the wind-torn banners of the Mighty Captain. Who would come? Who would come? Who was for vision and the great adventure?

He was among them, Judson Roberts, with his arms held out, his voice a bugle. Young men sobbed and knelt; a woman shrieked; people were elbowing the standers in the aisles and pushing forward to kneel in agonized happiness, and suddenly they were setting relentlessly on a bewildered Elmer Gantry, who had been betrayed into forgetting himself, into longing to be one with Judson Roberts.

His mother was wringing his hand, begging, "Oh, won't you come? Won't you make your old mother happy? Let yourself know the joy of surrender to Jesus!" She was weeping, old eyes puckered, and in her weeping was his every recollection of winter dawns when she had let him stay in bed and brought porridge to him across the icy floor; winter evenings when he had awakened to find her still stitching; and that confusing intimidating hour, in the abyss of his first memories, when he had seen her shaken beside a coffin that contained a cold monster in the shape of his father.

The basket-ball player was patting his other arm, begging, "Dear old Hell-cat, you've never let yourself be happy! You've been lonely! Let yourself be happy with us! You know I'm no mollycoddle. Won't you know the happiness of salvation with us?"

A thread-thin old man, very dignified, a man with secret eyes that had known battles and mountain-valleys, was holding out his hands to Elmer, imploring with a humility utterly disconcerting, "Oh, come, come with us—don't stand there making Jesus beg and beg—don't leave the Christ that died for us standing out in the cold, begging!"

And, somehow, flashing through the crowd, Judson Roberts was with Elmer, honoring him beyond all the multitude, appealing for his friendship—Judson Roberts the gorgeous, beseeching:

"Are you going to hurt me, Elmer? Are you going to let me go away miserable and beaten, old man? Are you going to betray me like Judas, when I've offered you my Jesus as the most precious gift I can bring you? Are you going to slap me and defile me and hurt me?

Come! Think of the joy of being rid of all those nasty little sins that you've felt so ashamed of! Won't you come kneel with me, won't you?"

His mother shrieked, "Won't you, Elmer? With him and me? Won't you make us happy? Won't you be big enough to not be afraid? See how we're all longing for you, praying for you!"

"Yes!" from around him, from strangers; and "Help *me* to follow you, Brother—I'll go if you will!" Voices woven, thick, dove-white and terrifying black of mourning and lightning-colored, flung around him, binding him— His mother's pleading, Judson Roberts' tribute—

An instant he saw Jim Lefferts, and heard him insist: "Why, sure, course they believe it. They hypnotize themselves. But don't let 'em hypnotize you!"

He saw Jim's eyes, that for him alone veiled their bright harshness and became lonely, asking for comradeship. He struggled; with all the blubbering confusion of a small boy set on by his elders, frightened and overwhelmed, he longed to be honest, to be true to Jim—to be true to himself and his own good honest sins and whatsoever penalties they might carry. Then the visions were driven away by voices that closed over him like surf above an exhausted swimmer. Volitionless, marveling at the sight of himself as a pinioned giant, he was being urged forward, forced forward, his mother on one arm and Judson on the other, a rhapsodic mob following.

Bewildered. Miserable. . . . False to Jim.

But as he came to the row kneeling in front of the first pew, he had a thought that made everything all right. Yes! He could have both! He could keep Judson and his mother, yet retain Jim's respect. He had only to bring Jim also to Jesus, then all of them would be together in beatitude!

Freed from misery by that revelation, he knelt, and suddenly his voice was noisy in confession, while the shouts of the audience, the ejaculations of Judson and his mother, exalted him to hot self-approval and made it seem splendidly right to yield to the mystic fervor.

He had but little to do with what he said. The willing was not his but the mob's; the phrases were not his but those of the emotional preachers and hysterical worshipers whom he had heard since babyhood:

"O God, oh, I have sinned! My sins are heavy on me! I am unworthy of compassion! O Jesus, intercede for me! Oh, let thy blood that was shed for me be my salvation! O God, I do truly repent of my great sinning and I do long for the everlasting peace of thy bosom!"

"Oh, praise God," from the multitude, and "Praise his holy name! Thank God, thank God, thank God! Oh, hallelujah, Brother, thank the dear loving God!"

He was certain that he would never again want to guzzle, to follow loose women, to blaspheme; he knew the rapture of salvation—yes, and of being the center of interest in the crowd.

Others about him were beating their foreheads, others were shrieking, "Lord, be merciful," and one woman—he remembered her as a strange, repressed, mad eyed special student who was not known to have any friends—was stretched out, oblivious of the crowd, jerking, her limbs twitching, her hands clenched, panting rhythmically.

But it was Elmer, tallest of the converts, tall as Judson Roberts, whom all the students and most of the townpeople found important, who found himself important.

His mother was crying, "Oh, this is the happiest hour of my life, dear! This makes up for everything!"

To be able to give her such delight!

Judson was clawing Elmer's hand, whooping, "Liked to had you on the team at Chicago, but I'm a lot gladder to have you with me on Christ's team! If you knew how proud I am!"

To be thus linked forever with Judson!

Elmer's embarrassment was gliding into a robust self-satisfaction.

Then the others were crowding on him, shaking his hand, congratulating him: the football center, the Latin professor, the town grocer. President Quarles, his chin whisker vibrant and his shaven upper lip wiggling from side to side, was insisting, "Come, Brother Elmer, stand up on the platform and say a few words to us—you must—we all need it—we're thrilled by your splendid example!"

Elmer was not quite sure how he got through the converts, up the steps to the platform. He suspected afterward that Judson Roberts had done a good deal of trained pushing.

He looked down, something of his panic returning. But they were sobbing with affection for him. The Elmer Gantry who had for years pretended that he relished defying the whole college had for those same years desired popularity. He had it now—popularity, almost love, almost reverence, and he felt overpoweringly his rôle as leading man.

He was stirred to more flamboyant confession:

"Oh, for the first time I know the peace of God! Nothing I have ever done has been right, because it didn't lead to the way and the truth! Here I thought I was a good church-member, but all the time I hadn't seen the real light. I'd never been willing to kneel down and confess myself a miserable sinner. But I'm kneeling now, and, oh, the blessedness of humility!"

He wasn't, to be quite accurate, kneeling at all; he was standing up, very tall and broad, waving his hands; and though what he was experiencing may have been the blessedness of humility, it sounded like his announcements of an ability to lick anybody in any given saloon. But he was greeted with flaming hallelujahs, and he shouted on till he was rapturous and very sweaty:

"Come! Come to him now! Oh, it's funny that I who've been so great a sinner could dare to give you his invitation, but he's almighty and shall prevail, and he giveth his sweet tidings through the mouths of babes and sucklings and the most unworthy, and, lo, the strong shall be confounded and the weak exalted in his sight!"

It was all, the Mithraic[4] phrasing, as familiar as "Good morning" or "How are you?" to the

---

[4] A reference to the ancient mystery cult of Mithras, with its extensive rituals of initiation and worship (see 1A).

audience, yet he must have put new violence into it, for instead of smiling at the recency of his ardor they looked at him gravely, and suddenly a miracle was beheld.

Ten minutes after his own experience, Elmer made his first conversion.

A pimply youth, long known as a pool-room tout, leaped up, his greasy face working, shrieked, "O God, forgive me!" butted in frenzy through the crowd, ran to the mourners' bench, lay with his mouth frothing in convulsion.

Then the hallelujahs rose till they drowned Elmer's accelerated pleading, then Judson Roberts stood with his arm about Elmer's shoulder, then Elmer's mother knelt with a light of paradise on her face, and they closed the meeting in a maniac pealing of

Draw me nearer, blessed Lord,
To thy precious bleeding side.

Elmer felt himself victorious over life and king of righteousness. . . .

C. Modernism

At the same time that many Christians considered their faith to be threatened by the evolutionary theories of Darwin and by modern biblical scholarship such as Higher Criticism (see 8C), other believers welcomed new views on nature and human history. Known among Protestants as modernists and among Catholics as liberals, these individuals believed that a greater understanding of science and of the historical context of early Christianity merely clarified which aspects of Scripture were essential to believers, and which were culturally specific to ancient Palestine and thus no longer relevant in the lives of Christians. The heart of Jesus' message, according to the modernists, was that the kingdom of God was a society of peace, joy, and love, and was within our grasp on earth. Many modernists consequently preached what they called "the social gospel," the idea that the power of Christ's spirit manifested itself primarily through large-scale social and political movements such as the spread of democracy throughout the world and the improvement of working conditions for the common man. Though the Baptist Walter Rauschenbusch (1861–1918) was the most prominent theologian of the social gospel, its most famous spokesman was probably the U.S. president and Presbyterian leader Woodrow Wilson (1856–1924), the idealistic architect of the postwar political order. By the 1930s, the terms "modernism" and "social gospel" had fallen out of usage, but many Christians in the years since—including proponents of "liberation theology"—have continued to be influenced by modernist ideas.

1. THE MODERNIST-PREMILLENARIAN DEBATE

During the first decades of the twentieth century, the conflict between fundamentalists and modernists threatened to tear American Protestantism apart. No issue better revealed the gulf between them than the subject of the Second Coming of Christ. For fundamentalist Christians, the Scriptures were quite explicit about the physical return of Jesus as well as the beginning of a golden millennium; to deny these teachings was to deny Christianity itself. For modernists such as Shailer Mathews (1864–1941), the people he called "premillenarians" (or premillennialists) were the ones who were endangering the true message of Christ. Mathews was a prominent advocate of historical criticism of the Bible, arguing that apocalypticism was a narrow and historically dated "Judaistic" belief. He also championed the "social gospel," arguing that premillenarians focused too narrowly on waiting for the apocalypse and ignored the Christian mandate to minister to the needs of their fellow humans in the here and now. From his post as dean of the University of Chicago Divinity School, the Baptist Mathews launched a pamphlet campaign against premillenarians in 1913. His 1917 essay, "Will Christ Come Again?, which is excerpted below, finally provoked the popular Congregationalist preacher Reuben A. Torrey (1856–1928) to respond in kind, and the 1918 pamphlet Torrey directed against Mathews is excerpted in the second reading. Though a fervent believer in premillennialism, Torrey hardly fit the stereotype of the ignorant premillenarian described in Mathews' tract. In fact, the Yale-educated Torrey readily applied all of his learning to demonstrate that it was Mathews who showed willful ignorance of the Bible in his arguments. Moreover, Torrey claimed, postmillennialist modernists like Mathews regularly substituted their own philosophical and political beliefs for the words of Jesus himself. The pivotal issue, as Torrey concluded, was not premillennialism but scriptural authority itself, and his assertion that his opponent failed to respect this authority was a common fundamentalist charge against modernists.

a. SHAILER MATHEWS, "WILL CHRIST COME AGAIN?" (1917)

Will Christ come again?

Some say yes, and immediately.

Others say, when did he ever go away? He is present spiritually. Has he not promised to be with us even to the end of the age?

These two answers are the outcome of two ways of using the Bible. *Which is correct?* . . .

Let us first look at the Scriptural material.

The early Christians believed that Jesus would return during the lifetime of their generation. This hope is on almost every page in the New Testament. And some of them, to judge from a sentence or two in the Revelation of John, believed that before he came there would be a time of great tribulation to be followed by the physical return of Jesus, the resurrection of the martyrs, and a thousand years when Satan would be bound and everything on earth would be prosperous and joyous. After the end of that

thousand years this group believed that there would be a mighty struggle between the Christ and Satan's forces, a general resurrection and a judgment, when spirits would be brought up from Sheol, a great cavern under the earth, and taken up into the sky, when they would meet living persons who had been "changed." The righteous would be given new bodies, and thereafter would live in eternal bliss while the wicked would be sent back to the abyss of fire prepared for the devil, his angels, and the giants, there to burn forever and ever. It should be remembered, however, that although all the early Christians believed in the speedy physical return of Jesus from heaven *there is no evidence that this fully elaborated program was held by Paul or the Church generally*. In its entirety it was apparently limited to a Jewish Christian group and its successors.

And this leads to a consideration of importance. *The entire messianic expectation in so far as it dealt with the future did not originate with the*

Christians. As Jews they inherited it from Judaism. To use only one example: the idea of the thousand years comes from the Jewish literature, such as the Book of Enoch,[5] written after the close of the Old Testament canon. It was reached by arguing that since the day of the Lord is as a thousand years, and there were six days in creation, there still remained a thousand years in which there would be the sabbath of joy. A study of the entire literature of the Jews from 175 B.C. will show where the other elements of premillenarianism originated.

It need hardly be emphasized that the immediateness of these events, the expectation of which was a part of the religious inheritance of the first Christians, was an essential element in their hope. *No fair interpretation of the words of the New Testament can lead us to think that the early Christians supposed that "immediateness" meant mere "unexpectedness."* It never entered the minds of the early church that this physical return of Jesus in the sky might occur after the lapse of thousands of years. The early church did not look forward to a historical period of any appreciable length. In whatever calling they were called they were to remain. The last days had come and each day they saw their salvation drawing nearer. The time was short.

It is simple honesty to admit that they were mistaken in this hope of a speedy winding up of earthly affairs. *Judaistic hopes were made no truer by being perpetuated by Christians.* The Christ did not come in the way the early Christians expected.

I.

How now is this scriptural material to be used? There are two possible answers.

1. The premillenarian says that these beliefs are to be used as infallible teaching. Whatever the New Testament records as having been the belief of early Christians he regards as the teaching of the Bible. This logically ought to include a belief in a flat earth, the perpetuation of slavery, the submission to rulers like Nero.

Premillenarians are inconsistent when they do not, as Christians not long ago did, insist on these elements of New Testament beliefs. They have to resort to all forms of ingenious and unwarranted interpretations of the texts to justify their misuse of scripture. Their method is more irresponsible than that which tries to prove that Bacon wrote the plays of Shakespeare.

Such a use of the scriptures involves its champions in three serious mistakes: First: *it makes a survival of pre-Christian Judaism the central truth of Christianity.*

Second: *It perpetuates a demonstrated mistake of early Christians* as to the time and character of the coming of Jesus.

Third: *It mistakes figures of speech for literal statements of facts.*

Misuse of the Bible as these three mistakes disclose, naturally requires corroboration by mis-statements regarding the fulfillment of prophecy. The limit to which current events are found prophesied in the Old Testament is measured only by the interpreter's ingenuity, lack of historical training and a saving sense of absurdity. Facts fight against his views as the stars fought against Sisera.[6] The world is not coming to an immediate end. We challenge any premillenarian to name the day, and then shall wait until that day, confident that he is mistaken. Indeed he is more seriously mistaken than the early Christians themselves, for he undertakes to explain away their original mistake.

Nor is his mistake unique. The history of Christianity is full of attempts to make Christianity center in this fashion about these Judaistic beliefs of the early Christians. In every great crisis in history and especially every period of new understanding of the scripture men have arisen who have insisted that those who have seen the profound scriptural meaning of Christianity are infidels; who have cried out against education and the proper use of scripture. They have repeatedly said that the world was coming to an immediate end. They have

---

[5]See 1B.

[6]Cf. Judg 20:5, on the Canaanite general Sisera, ultimately defeated by an Israelite army led by Barak and Deborah.

refused to assist in government or in social re-forms because they believed it was God's will that the world should grow worse and that Christ was soon to establish a miraculous king-dom on the earth. They have quoted the same texts that are used today by premillenarians. They have always been mistaken, just as the early Christians were mistaken. The world did not come to an end. Christ did not return in the way they expected. Whenever they named a day they have always had to revise their calcula-tions. They will always have to be making new calculations. The world is not coming to a speedy end. *History will continue to be made.*

2. The other way to use the Bible, sometimes called the historical, might better be called the common sense way. Those evangelicals who hold to it are not beyond making mistakes for this method is not without difficulties of detail, but they believe in the inspiration of prophets and apostles by the spirit of God. They know that this inspiration was progressive, accumula-tive, dependent upon and fitted to successive periods of human intelligence. Evidence com-pels them to believe that many of the beliefs of the early Christians can be understood only as they are studied in the light of the habits of thought prevalent in their times. *Historically-minded students of the Bible distinguish between fun-damental Christian truths and the method and language used by the early Christians in expressing these truths.* They believe that in order to realize these truths the conceptions of these ancient men of God have to be translated into modern conceptions exactly as the Hebrew or Greek language has to be translated into English.

Thus the issue is plain. It is not between those who believe the Bible and those who dis-believe it. It is between ways of using the Bible. The premillenarian propagandist claims to be true to the Bible. He is really true to an improper way of using the Bible. His loyalty to the Bible amounts to making outgrown or tem-porary words and conceptions equally true with what they attempt to express. He makes Ju-daistic hopes more important than the life and teaching of Christ. He treats figures of speech

as if they were literal statements of fact. The contrast is not between belief in revelation and disbelief in revelation. The contrast is between an incorrect method of using the scripture and a correct method. And in choosing his method it is the premillenarian who breaks with his-toric Christianity.

II.

This misuse of the Bible results in something much more dangerous....*The premillenarian's method of using the Jewish beliefs of the early Chris-tians recorded in scripture leads him to fundamental religious denials.* The evidence of this is to be found in the voluminous literature in which the immediate and literal coming of Jesus in the skies is set forth. Premillenarians miss the spirit in emphasizing the letter. In making a mistaken Judaistic belief central they distort Christianity.

This distortion is characterized by four chief elements.

First, the premillenarian interpretation of the gospel denies that God is capable of bringing about His victory by spiritual means. He is a spirit, but a spirit incapable of defeating evil spiritually. He cannot save the world by spiritual means. In order to succeed he has to revert to physical brutality. He abandons morality and uses miraculous militarism. He turns to fire and de-structive forces of impersonal nature. Certain persons will be rescued and taken up into the sky, but the earth is to be set on fire, the people left on it are to be killed, and after this the saints are to reign. Thus force is the final method by which God reigns.

Many premillenarians therefore thank God that the world is growing worse. What is this but joy in the spiritual defeat of God?

This sort of pessimism is unworthy of a Christian man. For what is it but a denial of the spiritual power of God in Jesus Christ? It is a putting of him again to an open shame. It makes the god of the Pharisees superior to the Father of our Lord Jesus Christ. It makes a mis-taken Jewish belief superior to the real message and revelation of Jesus.

Second, such a use of the scripture leads to the denial of the application of the gospel to social forces. Premillenarians vehemently attack all those who champion the "social gospel," asserting that they are mere humanitarians, believing simply in physical improvements and social reforms. In so doing, they not only grossly misrepresent those who urge the application of the gospel to society, but they belittle the gospel itself. True they attack vices, for they cannot be as consistent as the early Christians who refused to attempt the end of slavery or evil government, held marriage something to be avoided, and limited moral teachings to the church members. But they even say that Jesus did not engage in social service—Jesus, who taught men about marriage, wealth, and the treatment of enemies! We know so much today about the laws of life that every intelligent person is convinced that a gospel which cannot regenerate the institutions of humanity and the forces that are making history will be of little value in the world. For individuals embody these social forces, and the whole bearing of the teaching of the Bible is that there must be a social as well as individual morality.

Third, premillenarian writers are thus forced to deny that the moral ideals of Jesus Christ, while good for individuals, are applicable to social groups. They do not believe, for instance, that the ideas of righteousness contained in the Sermon on the Mount are really to operate among nations or industrial classes. They think the world is under the control of Satan and cannot be brought under the moral ideals which they themselves attempt to follow. The hope of the coming of the Christ is not for a moral renewal but for the triumph of physical force. Premillenarianism thus makes central a distrust of moral forces and a hope for violence, miraculous, it is true, but none the less violence. What then becomes of the teaching of Jesus as to the Father's love, the cross and the wickedness of revenge? Is the Father less moral and sacrificial than the Son?

It is clear to every thinking man that a morality that will not work in social groups sooner or later will fail among individuals. There are plenty of illustrations of this in history. Why have not Christians loved their fellows instead of persecuting them? Why has not Christianity put an end to war among nations? The answer is plain: they have expected God's triumph to be based on violence and imitated this falsely conceived king. The gospel is a message of salvation, not of mere rescue. The fact that the early Christians did not perceive the applicability of the moral principles of the gospel to slavery, war, politics, industry, argues that they missed the moral content of their faith. To perpetuate their mistake is to belittle the Christian religion. The seriousness of the matter is obvious. Any interpretation of the scripture which thus expects the triumph of Christ only after moral forces have been abandoned cannot be true to the spirit and purpose of our Lord and Savior, Jesus Christ. The military God of Judaism has replaced the Father of Jesus. A Christian who will not undertake to make the gospel universal is setting the gospel at naught.

Fourth, premillenarians deny that Christianity is consistent with the findings of modern science particularly as regards evolution. Many of these denials show that the writers know nothing about evolution or the world of science. In many cases their statements about science are untrue.

Such an attack upon modern science is demanded by the central principle of premillenarianism. No man can hold the premillenarian view whose mind has been really affected by the modern scientific methods and discoveries. One or the other has to be abandoned. Facts make it evident that we are in a constant process; that change leads to change; that society develops or degenerates. There are catastrophes in nature, but they are subject to the laws of nature and history. Religion must recognize these facts if it is to endure in our modern world.

The premillenarian views were shaped up by non-Christian Jews who knew nothing about the discoveries of modern science, who believed the earth was flat, who never dreamed of the circulation of the blood, who thought that the spirits of people when they died went into a cavern under the ground, who knew nothing about the law of gravitation or even the mariner's compass. Their followers who accepted Jesus were good people, and their faith in God saved them, but their way of thinking came from their own times. It can be introduced into our own times only as premillenarian writers attempt to introduce it; namely, by an attack upon modern science and an insistence that we accept the scientific conceptions of the Jewish writers.

The result is obvious. It makes a cleavage between what the premillenarian regards as the Christian religion and real culture. Men must choose between that Christianity and science. Similar demands have been made by premillenarians of every age. Their efforts have always failed but always after injuring religious faith. The separation of faith and knowledge is always attended with injury to religion. . . .

III.

What do those who use the Bible in the correct way think concerning the coming of Jesus?

Above all, *they undertake to interpret and use the Bible in accordance with the standards* of historical and literary study.

Believing that the revelation of God in Christ is the central, determining element in our religion they believe in bringing his teaching and spirit into human history. But they do not identify all recorded beliefs of those early Christians with their spiritual contribution to the spread of a true faith in God as revealed in Jesus. The gospel is more than early beliefs about the gospel. *They undertake therefore to discover the real hope and faith which the early Christians expressed in the forms of thought they had learned as Jews.* Fortunately this is not difficult. Pious Jews wrote a considerable number of apocalypses which appeared from about 175 B.C. and continued to be written until approximately 100 A.D. These apocalypses constitute a symbolical and allegorical literature. Their figures of speech are precisely those which the early Christians of the New Testament used. As time went on the tendency to literalize these figures of speech became very pronounced as they were used by men unaccustomed to the methods of such men as those who wrote the Book of Enoch, the Book of Jubilees, the Ascension of Isaiah, and other works of this class.[7] At last men came to take much of this symbolism literally. This was true of some of the early Christians.

The early Christians used these inherited Jewish opinions and expectations to express the great and precious facts born of their knowledge of Jesus and of their religious experience. A comparison of the gospels shows that they even read back some of these forms of expression into the sayings of Jesus himself. They thought as Jews, just as they talked as Jews. *The important matter is not what they said but what they meant by what they said.*

The properly historical interpreter of the scripture is not troubled by the fact that the early Christians were mistaken in details of these their expectations. He sees plainly that these details constitute a method of setting forth great evangelical truths. They are really figures of speech. It is the truth in the figures that count, not the figures themselves. . . .

V.

Will Christ come again? We answer in all reverence, not in the sense in which the early Christians in their perpetuation of their Jewish beliefs expected. Never in the sense that the premillenarians of today assert. The prophecies of the Old Testament are not highly ingenious puzzles to be worked out—always mistakenly, in charts, diagrams and "fulfillments." They are the discovery of God and his laws in social evolution. The pictures of the "last things" in the New Testament are not scientific statements but figures of speech expressing everlasting spiritual realities.

But will Jesus come again in the true sense of a spiritual presence, leading us through the

---

[7]Mathews refers to apocryphal works not accepted in the Jewish and Christian scriptural canon. See "Jewish sects" in 1B2.

Holy Spirit into all truth, regenerating men and institutions, giving us the fruit of the Spirit, the first element of which is love, and assuring the ultimate triumph of righteousness and joy? To doubt this is to lose confidence in the very heart of Christianity. . . .

That God is in the world, a saving God of love as well as a God of law; that humanity can find joy and peace in the conduct of its life according to the spirit and teaching of Christ; that lack of love expressed in individuals, social classes, and nations will bring suffering and social catastrophes; that God forgives those, who abandoning sin, are truly repentant and helps them to larger moral strength for their individual and social conflicts; that God is working in social evolution; that Jesus Christ is indeed a Savior; and that his gospel is the power of God unto salvation from sin and death; all this is the real gospel. Belief in these glorious facts is consistent with all the facts which science can disclose. Believing them we welcome all truth as new information as to the way of God's working and new direction for our own conduct.

Such a faith in the gospel of Jesus is a source of hope and positive Christian activity. It makes us surer of the immortal life after death. It leads to the widest social service; to faith in the power of God to bring in a reconstructed human society full of righteousness; to a conviction that if the world contains evil it can be—as it has been and is to be—made to grow better by the sacrificial giving of justice.

To bring Jesus thus into the control of human affairs is the real coming of the kingdom of God upon earth. This is the reality the Jewish pictures and apocalyptic symbols used by the early Christians really meant. *This is the real coming of Jesus Christ. . . .*

---

b. REUBEN A. TORREY, "'WILL CHRIST COME AGAIN?' AN EXPOSURE OF THE FOOLISHNESS, FALLACIES AND FALSEHOODS OF SHAILER MATHEWS" (1918)

One of the most dangerous and harmful pamphlets or books published in the last year or two is the leaflet of Shailer Mathews entitled, "Will Christ Come Again?" . . .

Let me say at the outset that the great fault of the pamphlet and the great danger that lies in it is not that it attacks the premillennial view of our Lord's return, but that it persistently and constantly seeks to discredit the teachings of our Lord Jesus Christ and the holy men of God whom God, by His Holy Spirit, inspired to write the New Testament Scriptures. If Shailer Mathews is right in his statements, then Jesus Christ, as we shall show later, was either an egregious fool or a consummate fraud. We shall see further on that there is no escaping this conclusion. To me the question of whether our Lord Jesus is coming before the millennium or after the millennium, or even the question whether He is coming again to this earth visibly and bodily at any time, is an entirely secondary question. The question of whether the inspired Apostles were infallible teachers or not, and above all the question whether our Lord Jesus Christ was an infallible teacher or not, is of the very first importance. That Jesus Christ claimed to be a teacher sent from God, who spoke the very words of God, admits of no honest question (see Jn 12:48, 49; 14:24; Jn 7:16). If our Lord Jesus was not a teacher sent from God, who spoke the very words of God, a Divinely inspired and absolutely infallible teacher, then He was either a sadly deluded fanatic or a deliberate liar. If He were either one or the other I must refuse to believe on Him, and become an infidel. There is no middle ground for any logical thinker to take. There is not enough of the intellectual trickster about me, even if there is about Shailer Mathews and his school, to believe that Jesus was either a sadly deluded fanatic or a deliberate liar and still claim to believe in Him as my Saviour and Lord. But our Lord Jesus was neither a sadly deluded fanatic nor a deliberate liar, He was what he claimed to be, a teacher sent from God, who spoke the very words of God, a Divinely inspired and absolutely infallible teacher. Yes, He was more than that; He was so entirely, even during His earthly life, *God manifest in the flesh*, that He could say truly: *"He that hath seen me hath seen the Father"* (Jn 14:9), *and could say again concerning Himself: "All men should honor the Son, even as they honor the Father"* (Jn 5:23). God Almighty has set His seal to these stupendous claims of our Lord Jesus by raising Him from the dead; and by the resurrection of Jesus Christ from the dead, which can be easily shown to be one of the best proven facts of history, Shailer Mathews, in seeking, even though it be in underhanded ways and with much subtlety, to discredit our Lord Jesus Christ, is proven to be a blasphemer. So much by way of introduction.

Now we are ready for a direct examination of some of the childish follies and absurd fallacies and gross falsehoods and insidious blasphemies of Shailer Mathews' pamphlet.

Dr. Mathews begins his pamphlet with these words: "Will Christ come again? Some say yes, and immediately. Others say, when did he ever go away? He is present spiritually. Has he not promised to be with us even to the end of the age? These two answers are the outcome of two ways of using the Bible. *Which is correct?"*

In what immediately follows and in his whole booklet Shailer Mathews makes it plain that he believes that the latter "way of using the Bible" is correct. So the primary question that Shailer Mathews puts in his pamphlet, and which he implies cannot be answered, is, "When did He (i.e., our Lord Jesus) ever go away?" How any student of the Bible, even of ordinary intelligence and honesty, could ask such a question it is difficult to understand. Our Lord Jesus Himself answered the question; He answered it, for example, in John 14:28 where He says: "Ye heard how I said to you, I GO AWAY, and I come unto you. If ye loved me, ye would have rejoiced, because *I go unto the Father: for the Father is greater than I."* Now if our Lord Jesus Christ meant anything by these words, and He certainly meant something for He was not a fool, He meant to say that He was GOING AWAY to the Father in Heaven. So Jesus Christ Himself tells us when He went away. . . . Of course, we all know that there is a sense in which Jesus is here today, that "He is here spiritually," that He has promised to be with us by His Holy Spirit to the end of the age, if we go forth according to His commandment, and make disciples of all the nations (Mt 28:18–20; cf. Jn 14:15–23). Premillenarians insist upon this as much as postmillenarians, or rather more than postmillenarians; but the Bible makes it just as plain, that He is not here in the way that He was here during His bodily presence on earth before His bodily ascension from Olivet, *and in the way that He is to be here again when He comes the second time.* The Bible makes it as plain as day that Jesus went away from this world from Mount Olivet, that He went into Heaven, and that He is to stay in Heaven until the appointed time comes for Him to come back again. . . . What Shailer Mathews here calls "the historical method of interpretation," in plain English is the infidel method, not a manly and courageous infidel method, but a sneaking and cowardly infidel method. By any such method of interpretation you can make the Koran, or all the morally rotten literature of India, reeking with the most unmentionable and indescribably vileness, as valuable as the Bible. If Shailer Mathews wishes to get rid of the plain and crystal clear teaching of the Bible, as he undoubtedly does, why is he not honest enough to come right out and say so? Why does he not come right out and say that the Bible is a jumble of errors and falsehoods? The fundamental lack with Shailer Mathews and his whole school of thought is a lack of common intellectual honesty, and of a decent amount of courage. When he refers, as he unmistakably does from what he says in the connection, to the teachings of the inspired Apostles and of the Lord Jesus Christ Himself, he never speaks of them as the teachings of the Apostles and of the Lord Jesus, but speaks of them over and over again as *"the beliefs of the early Christians."* He knew perfectly well that any man or woman who had even a measurably decent amount of faith in Jesus Christ and the Bible, would resent it if he spoke so contemptuously of what were clearly set forth as the teachings of Jesus Christ Himself and of the inspired Apostles, so he does not call these teachings the teachings of the Apostles and of Jesus Christ, but "the beliefs of the early Christians." This he does over and over again, and then goes on immediately, time and time again, to refer to things that either the Apostles or Jesus Christ Himself taught, and oftentimes he refers to what they both taught, in ridicule and contempt. His whole method of argument would be unworthy of a pettifogging police court lawyer.

On page 4 Shailer Mathews says: "Let us first look at the Scriptural material." This sounds encouraging, but in what follows not for one moment does he look at the Scriptural material in any specific and honest way, or with any intention of accepting the teaching of the Scriptures. *There is not one explicit quotation from the Scriptures in the entire book.* The whole attempt of the booklet is to turn the reader's attention away from the things that the Bible explicitly says. There are undoubted allusions to the Scriptures, but Dr. Mathews scrupulously avoids quoting the Scriptures, and some of his allusions are gross caricatures. In one of his allusions given in direct connection with his words: "Let us first look at the Scripture material," in fact the words immediately following, he says, "The early Christians believed that Jesus would return during the lifetime of their generation. *This hope is on almost every page in the New Testament."* Any one who is at all familiar with the New Testament knows that this statement is one of the wildest and most reckless assertions ever written by a supposedly serious minded man. How any man who hoped to retain the confidence of his readers could have allowed himself to be betrayed into such a wild and reckless statement it is difficult to under-

stand. There are 285 pages in the copy of the New Testament which I now hold in my hand. Does any one believe for a moment that there are 285 places that indicate, or suggest, or hint that "the early Christians believed that Jesus would return during the lifetime of their generation?" Such a hope so far from being found 285 times in the New Testament is not found one hundred times, nor ten times, *nor is there even one single instance in which it is asserted that the Lord Jesus would return during the lifetime of the generation then living.* It is true that there are a few passages in the New Testament which some commentators have held taught that Jesus Christ would return during the lifetime of that generation, the most notable instances, those most frequently appealed to, being Mt 24:34 and 1 Thes 4:16. In Mt 24:34 we are told that our Lord said: *"Verily I say unto you, This generation shall not pass away, till all these things be accomplished."* This is taken as showing that the Lord Jesus Christ taught that the generation *living when He spoke* would not pass away until His coming again was accomplished. But if any one will study this passage in the context, the only way to study any passage in the Bible, he will discover that by "this generation" our Lord did not mean the generation living upon the earth when He was here, but the generation living when the signs of which He had just spoken came to pass. . . . *It may be* that at this period of his life Paul hoped to be alive when the Lord came, but we are not concerned with what Paul hoped, or even thought, *but what Paul actually taught*, and he certainly does not teach here nor anywhere else that Jesus would return during his lifetime. Neither does the Lord Jesus teach it in any place, nor does any other New Testament writer so teach. The whole purpose of this argument on Shailer Mathews' part is, of course, to discredit the testimony of the Lord Jesus and the Apostle Paul by attempting to show *that they were mistaken on this point of the time of His return,* and therefore might be mistaken on the whole question; but the attempt results in utter failure. The premillenarians *do not base their view upon what "the early Christians believed," but upon what our Lord Jesus taught and what "the holy men of God" who were "moved by the Holy Spirit" taught. . . .*

Shailer Mathews continues: "This logically ought to include belief in a flat earth, the perpetuation of slavery, the submission to rulers like Nero. Premillenarians are inconsistent when they do not, as Christians not long ago did, insist on these *elements of New Testament beliefs.*" May we ask where in the New Testament we are taught to "believe in a flat earth?" Where does the Lord Jesus Christ, or Peter, or Paul, or John, or any New Testament writer teach that the earth is flat? We might ask, where do they even record that early Christians taught that the earth was flat? Where does Jesus Christ, or Peter, Paul, or John, or any New Testament writer teach "the perpetuation of slavery?" The Apostles Paul did teach that the Christian should "be in subjection to the higher powers," and premillenarians teach that too, and why shouldn't they? Would Shailer Mathews have Christians teach Bolshevism? Why should premillenarians, in order to be consistent, "insist" on these (as Shailer Mathews characterizes them) "elements of New Testament beliefs?" He goes on to say: "They (i.e., premillenarians) have to resort to all sorts of ingenious and unwarranted interpretations of the texts to justify this misuse of scripture." This also is beyond a question a falsehood. If there is any one who "resorts to ingenious and unwarranted interpretations of the texts to justify their misuse of Scripture" it is not the premillenarians, but the postmillenarians. Of this fact Shailer Mathews himself is a striking illustration in this very pamphlet in which, as we have already seen, he is so convinced that his views cannot be maintained by taking the Scriptures at their face value and in their evident meaning, that he says in so many words that "The conceptions of these ancient men of God have to be translated into modern conceptions." That is to say, that for what the Lord Jesus Christ and the Apostles say, something else must be substituted which is just the opposite of what they say. Can "ingenious and unwar-

ranted interpretation of texts" go beyond that? . . .

On Page 7, Shailer Mathews throws out this challenge, which is another startling illustration of his ignorance of premillenarian literature: he says: "We challenge any premillenarian to name the day (i.e., the day of our Lord's return), and then shall wait until that day, confident that he is mistaken." Of course, no intelligent premillenarian will attempt "to name the day;" for premillenarians stoutly, as stoutly as any postmillenarian, affirm that the Lord Jesus Christ has in the strictest and sternest terms forbidden us to even try to discover the exact date of His return, that the Lord Jesus Christ has said: *"It is not for you to know times or seasons, which the Father hath set within His own authority"* [Acts 1:7]. No one contends more earnestly against this whole folly of date setting than the leading premillenarians. The writer of the present tract has said repeatedly in public address and on printed page that any attempt to set a date for the return of our Lord, or any event connected therewith is most daring presumption and an act of gross disobedience to the revealed will of God. In his book, "What the Bible Teaches," published in 1898 he says: "The exact time of the Coming Again of Jesus Christ is not revealed to us." "Calculations from the data given in Daniel by which some try to fix the exact date of Christ's return are utterly unreliable. They attempt the impossible. The statements were not intended to give us a clue to the exact date of Christ's return. It is part of God's purpose and method in dealing with men to keep them in uncertainty on this point." "Any teacher who attempts to fix the date of Christ's return is at once discredited, and it is entirely unnecessary to wade through his calculations. God does not desire us to know just when His Son shall return.". . . This attempt on Shailer Mathews' part to identify premillenarianism with date setting is another illustration of the gross, egregious, deliberate and outrageous unfairness of Shailer Mathews in his discussion of the whole subject.

On page 10 Shailer Mathews says: "Premillenarians miss the spirit in emphasizing the letter. In making a mistaken Judaistic belief central they distort Christianity. This distortion is characterized by four chief elements. *First, the premillenarian interpretation of the gospel denies that God is capable of bringing about His victory by spiritual means.*" This is one of the main points, if not the main point in Shailer Mathews' whole attack upon premillenarianism. At the first glance, to the superficial thinker, there may seem to be something in this argument of Shailer Mathews, but if any one of average intelligence and ability and historical knowledge will stop to reflect upon it he will see that it is arrant nonsense. We know from history and experience as well as from the Bible, that God has always used material means, "force" if you please, "to bring about His victory," the victory of righteousness. How is God teaching the Kaiser and the Germans (and through them all who would cultivate a spirit of damnable and murderous self-aggrandizement), a sorely needed lesson? Is it "by (purely) spiritual means?" Is it not by "force," the military forces of America and our allies? And by so doing it is God "reverting to physical brutality?" Shailer Mathews or any one else who asserts it, or implies it, is a blasphemer. That is plain and severe speech, but it is an inescapable fact. To be consistent Shailer Mathews should be an extreme pacifist and demand that America should recall her soldiers, destroy her guns and ammunition and bring the Germans to repentance and to a just and humane treatment of weaker nations and outraged women and children "by spiritual means." Why has Shailer Mathews, if he believes what he here implies, accepted for 1917–1918 the position of "State Secretary for War Savings for Illinois?" Why has he left the purely "spiritual means" of teaching for collecting money to arm, equip and sustain our "brutal" forces in the field to bring the Kaiser and Germany to their senses. Fortunately Shailer Mathews does not himself believe a word of the nonsense which he writes, and makes the very central argument of his pamphlet in order to bolster up a bad cause. As a matter of historical fact is not God carrying out the purposes of His love, and has He not carried them out through all the history of mankind, by the intelligent and loving use of "force?" If Shailer Mathews' words were carried out to their logical conclusion they would mean that we must dispense with all use of force to punish offenders against righteousness. . . .

On page 11 Shailer Mathews says: "Many premillenarians therefore thank God that the world is growing worse." This statement is an evident falsehood and a gross slander. It is true that intelligent premillenarians, when they see the triumph of iniquity that has been so apparent in the past four years, are not thrown into the abyss of utter despair and pessimism that many postmillenarians were thrown into. It is true that in these things they saw the things predicted as preceding the return of our Lord Jesus Christ, and therefore, instead of being disheartened when they saw, "upon the earth distress of nations," in perplexity for the roaring of the sea and the billows; men fainting for fear, and for expectation of the things that are coming on the world," they do just what the Lord Jesus Christ bade us do under such circumstances, viz., "Lift up our heads; because our redemption draweth nigh." *They do not rejoice in these things;* they see and feel the horror of them; they do what they can to alleviate them, but they are not discouraged by them, because the Lord Jesus Christ Himself predicted these things, and their coming to pass is simply an additional guarantee of the absolute truthfulness of the Word of God. Furthermore, in the increasing darkness of the night they see the indication that the glorious day is at hand. . . .

Shailer Mathews' second argument against premillenarianism is:

2. *"Such a use of the Scripture* (the premillenarians' use of Scripture) *leads to the denial of the application of the gospel to social forces."* This statement is another false accusation. We would like to know whether Shailer Mathews or any other postmillenarian has done more in modern times to apply the gospel to social forces than for example, D. L.

Moody, who was an avowed and consistent premillenarian, or Billy Sunday,[8] who in all his meetings in recent years has preached at least one sermon of the most ultra-premillennial type. It would be easy to mention many other prominent premillenarians who have accomplished great things in the "application of the gospel to social forces." It is true that premillenarians do not indulge in the vain hope of gospelizing social organizations without regenerating the individual. It is true that the premillenarian as a rule seeks to reach social forces through reaching individuals with the saving truth of the gospel which our Lord Jesus Christ taught, but to assert that the premillenarian denies the application of the gospel to social forces is to shut one's eyes to what premillenarians in this and all other lands are doing for true and permanent social uplift. But premillenarians are not guilty of the folly of attempting to "regenerate the institutions of humanity and the forces that are making history" in any other way than by the regeneration of the individuals who "embody these social forces." . . .

There is no need to pursue this criticism of Shailer Mathews' widely circulated pamphlet any further. We see it is a continuous mass of illogical arguments, gross misrepresentations, demonstrable falsehoods, and rank blasphemies. The pamphlet itself is a fulfillment of the very Scriptures which it seeks to discredit. The Apostle Peter, inspired of God, foresaw the work of Shailer Mathews and his class, and has plainly described him when he says: "This is now, beloved, the second epistle that I write unto you; and in both of them I stir up your sincere minds by putting you in remembrance; that ye should *remember the words which were spoken before by the holy prophets, and the commandment of the Lord and Saviour through your Apostles*: knowing this first, that in the last days *mockers shall come* with mockery, walking after their own lust, and *saying, Where is the promise of His coming?* for from the day that the fathers fell asleep, all things continue as they were from the beginning of creation" (2 Pet 3:1–4).

---

[8]Dwight L. Moody (1837–1899) and Billy Sunday (1862–1935) were the most popular revivalists of the late nineteenth and early twentieth centuries.

D. Nazism

The totalitarian regimes of the twentieth century represented a new challenge for Western Christianity, which was still reeling from the anticlericalism and aggressive secularization of the nineteenth century. In some countries—such as fascist Italy and Spain—church leaders responded to the rise of totalitarianism by reaching terms of coexistence and sometimes even collaboration with dictators. In other countries—most notably the Communist nations of Eastern Europe, where churches were openly persecuted—some clergy and other Christians responded by forming and leading organized resistance movements. However, at least one totalitarian government, that of Nazi Germany (1933–1945), inspired dramatic examples of both responses—collaboration as well as resistance—from the churches that fell under its regime. Even before Adolf Hitler's 1933 inauguration as chancellor, his National Socialist followers had entered into negotiations with Protestant and Catholic church leaders, seeking to allay any fears raised by the Nazis' frequent use of neo-pagan symbolism. Once in power, Hitler rapidly pursued a twofold offensive against the churches, on the one hand promising them continuing autonomy under his regime and on the other systematically dismantling or assimilating all organizational apparatuses in their possession. Thus, despite a 1933 concordat with the Vatican, the German government dissolved the Catholic Center Party, gradually closed down almost all Catholic newspapers, and placed increasing restrictions on the activity of Catholic priests and nuns. The growth of the pro-Nazi German Christian movement among Protestants merely delayed the imposition of similar restrictions on Protestant clerics and associations. The clergy and laypeople who dared to openly oppose the government's domination of the churches—as well as its cruel campaign against Jews and other minorities—first met with harassment and later imprisonment or even execution. By the outbreak of the Second World War in 1939, all church-organized resistance to the dictatorship had been quashed, leaving the banner of Christian protest against the Nazis to be carried forward by a small number of remarkable individuals.

1. THE PLATFORM OF THE GERMAN CHRISTIANS (1932)

The German Christian movement represented the greatest degree of Christian accommodation to Nazi ideology. Its Protestant adherents despised both the atheist Communists and the "foreign-spirited" (i.e., Catholic) Center Party and considered the National Socialists the only true advocates of the German "race." Naturally Jews, as well as Jewish aspects of Christianity (particularly the Old Testament and the "rabbi" St. Paul), were also considered polluters of "pure" Christianity. The platform reproduced below propelled the German Christians to a majority in the German Evangelical church elections in 1932, foreshadowing the nationwide electoral victory of the Nazis later that year and the consolidation of 28 regional Protestant churches into one "imperial" church. The church's new *Reichsbischof* ("imperial bishop"), Ludwig Müller (1883–1946) quickly earned the wrath of many of his clergy, as well as the approval of National Socialists, by enacting several new pro-Nazi policies—for example, the absorption of the Evangelical Youth movement into the Hitler Youth. Still, despite several conflicts, the German Christians maintained their domination of the country's Protestant churches until the end of the war in 1945.

1. These directives are to point out to all believing Germans the ways and the goals by which they can attain a new order in the church. These directives are not intended to constitute a creed nor to replace one; neither are they intended to disturb the confessional foundations of the Evangelical Church. They state a way of life.

2. We are fighting for the union of the 29 churches embraced by the "German Evangelical Church Federation" in one evangelical National Church, and we march to the call and goal:

Outwards one and mighty in spirit,
Gathered around Christ and His Word,
Inwards rich and multifarious,
Every Christian according to his calling and
    way.[9]

3. The voting list "German Christians" will be no ecclesiastical party in the usual sense. It ap-

---

[9]From a song text of Emmanuel Geibel (1815–1884), German poet and lyricist. (Translation by Joel F. Harrington.)

peals to all Christians of German type. The age of parliamentarianism is past, also in the church. Ecclesiastical parties have no spiritual claim to represent the church folk, and they obstruct the high purpose to become *one* church. We want a living People's Church [*Volkskirche*] which is the expression of all the religious powers of our nation [*Volk*].

4. We take our stand on the platform of positive Christianity. We affirm an affirmative style of Christian faith, as appropriate to the German spirit of Luther and heroic piety.

5. We want to bring to the fore in our church the reawakened German feeling for life and to make our church life of positive value for life. In the fateful battle for German freedom and future, the church has shown itself too weak in its leadership. The church has not yet marshaled for decisive battle against the God-hating Marxism and the foreign-spirited Center Party[10] but instead reached an agreement with the political parties which represent these forces. We want our church to fight in the forefront in the decisive struggle for the existence or extinction of our nation. She dare not stand aside or indeed shy away from the fighters for freedom.

6. We demand a change in the legal constitution [political paragraph] and open battle against Marxism, hostile to religion and to the nation, and against its socialist-Christian fellow-travelers of all degrees. We miss in this legal constitution the trusting dependence upon God and the mission of the church. The way into the Kingdom of God leads through battle, cross and sacrifice, not through false peace.

7. We see in race, national character and nation orders of life given and entrusted to us by God, to maintain which is a law of God for us. Therefore racial mixing is to be opposed. On the basis of experience, the German *foreign mis-*

sions have for a long time called to the German nation: "Keep yourself racially pure," and tell us that faith in Christ doesn't disturb race but rather deepens and sanctifies it.

8. We see in home missions,[11] properly understood, a living Christianity of action which, according to our understanding, roots not in mere pity but in obedience to God's will and in gratitude for Christ's death on the cross. Mere pity is "charity" and becomes arrogance, coupled with bad conscience, and weakens a nation. We know something of Christian duty and love toward the helpless, but we demand also the protection of the nation from the incapable and inferior. [The Inner Mission] . . . must moreover keep its distance from economic adventures and must not become a mere shopkeeper.

9. In the mission to [convert] the Jews we see a grave danger to our national character. It is the entryway for foreign blood into our national body. It has no traditional justification side by side with foreign missions. We deny the validity of the mission to the Jews in Germany, as long as the Jews have the rights of citizenship and thereby there exists the danger of racial deterioration and bastardization. The Holy Scriptures also say something about the divine wrath and self-betraying love. Marriage between Germans and Jews is especially to be forbidden.

10. We want an Evangelical Church which roots in the national character, and we repudiate the spirit of a Christian cosmopolitanism. We want to overcome the corrupt developments which have sprung from the spirit—such as pacifism, internationalism, Freemasonry,[12] etc.—through faith in the national mission given us by God. Membership

---

[10]Political party founded by Prussian Catholics in 1871 as a reaction against the anti-Catholic measures of Bismarck's *Kulturkampf*. This "foreign-spirited" and "papist" party was suppressed by the Nazis in 1933.

[11]Literally, "the inner mission," a term used since the mid nineteenth century to describe all charitable and social work of German Lutheran churches apart from actual parish obligations.

[12]A pan-European voluntary association dating back at least to the twelfth century. Since the Enlightenment, Freemasons had been openly critical of both Protestant and Catholic churches.

of an Evangelical minister in a lodge of Free Masons is not to be allowed.

These ten points of the "German Christians" are a call to rally, and they constitute in great outline the direction of the future Evangelical National Church [*Reichskirche*], which by the maintaining of confessional peace will develop

the powers of our Reformation faith into the finest of the German nation.

(signed) Hossenfelder,[13] clergyman

---

[13]Joachim Hossenfelder (1899–?), Lutheran minister and leader of the German Christian movement in 1932. He was also bishop of Brandenburg during the Third Reich, from 1933 to 1945.

2. THE BARMEN DECLARATION (1934)

In November 1933, after almost a year of Nazi rule, several alarmed Protestant ministers founded the Pastors' Emergency League to oppose the German Christians and their Nazi-inspired interpretation of Christianity. Six months later, their leader, Martin Niemöller (1892–1984), organized a larger conference in the Ruhr village of Barmen with over 140 delegates from Protestant churches throughout Germany in attendance. The resulting statement, excerpted below, presents in succinct form the delegates' belief that there existed a stark contrast between the message of the gospel and that of the National Socialist party. The church of Christ, wrote the pastors, was not an extension of any secular authority nor of any political ideology. Its primary mission was one of charity and unity rather than of the hate and divisiveness preached by the German Christians. Unfortunately the signatories of the Barmen Declaration, as well as their allies throughout the country, were systematically harassed and persecuted by the Nazi government. Finally, in 1939, the Confessing Church, as the group of dissenters had come to be known, was definitively dissolved, and the majority of its pastors were drafted into the army or imprisoned. Though some of its members continued their active opposition in exile, the movement's influence within Germany was effectively ended.

According to the introductory words of its constitution of 11 July 1933, the German Evangelical Church is a federal union of confessional churches which grew out of the Reformation, of equal rights and parallel existence. The theological premise of the association of these churches is given in Article 1 and Article 2, paragraph 1 of the constitution of the German Evangelical Church, recognized by the national government on 14 July 1933:

ARTICLE 1 The impregnable foundation of the German Evangelical Church is the Gospel of Jesus Christ, as it is revealed in Holy Scripture and came again to the light in the creeds of the Reformation. In this way the authorities,

which the church needs for her mission, are defined and limited.

ARTICLE 2, PARAGRAPH 1 The German Evangelical Church consists of churches (territorial churches).

We, assembled representatives of Lutheran, Reformed and United churches, independent synods [conferences], and local church groups, hereby declare that we stand together on the foundation of the German Evangelical Church as a federal union of German confessional churches. We are held together by confession of the one Lord of the one, holy, universal and apostolic church.

We declare, before the public view of all the Evangelical Churches of Germany, that the unity of this confession and thereby also the unity of the German Evangelical Church is severely threatened. In this year of the existence of the German Evangelical Church it is endangered by the more and more clearly evident style of teaching and action of the ruling ecclesiastical party of the German Christians and the church government which they run. This threat comes from the fact that the theological premise in which the German Evangelical Church is united is constantly and basically contradicted and rendered invalid, both by the leaders and spokesmen of the German Christians and also by the church government, by means of strange propositions. If they obtain, the church—according to all the creeds which are authoritative among us—ceases to be the church. If they obtain, moreover, the German Evangelical Church will become impossible as a federal union of confessional churches.

Together we may and must, as members of Lutheran, Reformed and United churches, speak today to this situation. Precisely because we want to be and remain true to our various confessions of faith, we may not keep silent, for we believe that in a time of common need and trial a common word has been placed in our mouth. We commit to God what this may mean for the relationship of the confessional churches with each other.

In view of the destructive errors of the German Christians and the present national church government, we pledge ourselves to the following evangelical truths:

1. *"I am the way and the truth and the life: no man cometh unto the Father, but by me"* (Jn 14:6).

"Verily, verily I say unto you, He that entereth not by the door into the sheepfold, but climbeth up some other way, the same is a thief and a robber. . . . I am the door; by me if any man enter in, he shall be saved" (Jn 10:1, 9).

Jesus Christ, as he is testified to us in the Holy Scripture, is the one Word of God, whom we are to hear, whom we are to trust and obey in life and in death.

We repudiate the false teaching that the church can and must recognize yet other happenings and powers, images and truths as divine revelation alongside this one Word of God, as a source of her preaching.

2. *"But of him are ye in Christ Jesus, who of God is made unto us wisdom, and righteousness, and sanctification, and redemption"* (1 Cor 1:30).

Just as Jesus Christ is the pledge of the forgiveness of all our sins, just so—and with the same earnestness—is he also God's mighty claim on our whole life; in him we encounter a joyous liberation from the godless claims of this world to free and thankful service to his creatures.

We repudiate the false teaching that there are areas of our life in which we belong not to Jesus Christ but another lord, areas in which we do not need justification and sanctification through him.

3. *"But speaking the truth in love, may grow up into him in all things, which is the head, even Christ: from whom the whole body {is} fitly joined together and compacted"* (Eph 4:15–16).

The Christian church is the community of brethren, in which Jesus Christ presently works in the word and sacraments through the Holy Spirit. With her faith as well as her obedience, with her message as well as her ordinances, she has to witness in the midst of the world of sin as the church of forgiven sinners that she is his alone, that she lives and wishes to live only by his comfort and his counsel in expectation of his appearance.

We repudiate the false teaching that the church can turn over the form of her message and ordinances at will or according to some dominant ideological and political convictions.

4. *"Ye know that the princes of the Gentiles exercise domination over them, and they that are great exercise authority upon them. But it shall not be so among you: but whosoever will be great among you, let him be your minister"* (Mt 20:25–26).

The various offices in the church establish no rule of one over the other but the exercise of the service entrusted and commanded to the whole congregation.

We repudiate the false teaching that the church can and may, apart from this ministry, set up special leaders [*Führer*] equipped with powers to rule.

5. *"Fear God, honor the king!"* (1 Pet 2:17)

The Bible tells us that according to divine arrangement the state has the responsibility to provide for justice and peace in the yet unredeemed world, in which the church also stands, according to the measure of human insight and human possibility, by the threat and use of force.

The church recognizes with thanks and reverence toward God the benevolence of this, his provision. She reminds men of God's Kingdom, God's commandment and righteousness, and thereby the responsibility of rulers and ruled. She trusts and obeys the power of the word, through which God maintains all things.

We repudiate the false teaching that the state can and should expand beyond its special responsibility to become the single and total order of human life, and also thereby fulfill the commission of the church.

We repudiate the false teaching that the church can and should expand beyond its special responsibility to take on the characteristics, functions and dignities of the state, and thereby become itself an organ of the state.

6. *"Lo, I am with you alway, even unto the end of the world"* (Mt 28:20). "The word of God is not bound" (2 Tim 2:9).

The commission of the church, in which her freedom is founded, consists in this: in place of Christ and thus in the service of his own word and work, to extend through word and sacrament the message of the free grace of God to all people.

We repudiate the false teaching that the church, in human self-esteem, can put the word and work of the Lord in the service of some wishes, purposes and plans or other, chosen according to desire.

The confessing synod of the German Evangelical Church declares that she sees in the acknowledgment of these truths and in the repudiation of these errors the not-to-be-circumvented theological foundation of the German Evangelical Church as a federal union of confessional churches. [The synod] calls upon all who can join in its declaration to be aware of these theological lessons in their ecclesiastical decisions. It begs all concerned to turn again in the unity of faith, of love, and of hope. *Verbum Dei manet in aeternum.*[14]

---

[14]"The Word of God endures forever."

3. Franz Jägerstätter
LETTERS FROM PRISON (1943)

Franz Jägerstätter (1907–1943) was an unlikely hero in the Christian opposition to Nazism. As a youth in the Austrian village of St. Radegund he was widely known as a ruffian, most famous for owning the first motorcycle in town. Shortly before his thirtieth birthday, however, Jägerstätter married and underwent a religious conversion. As a result of his rediscovered Catholic faith, he embarked on an unwavering path of passive resistance to the Nazi cause. In 1938 he was the only person in his village to vote against the German annexation, or *Anschluss,* of Austria, and in 1943 he refused to serve in the German army. While in prison he wrote several letters and commentaries on his understanding of Christian duty. His response to the evil of Nazism, he explained, was simply the only choice possible for someone who took God's commands seriously. After Jägerstätter's execution for treason, his notebook and farewell letter to his family were returned to his wife, though they were not published until two decades later.

a. "COMMENTARIES" (JULY 1943)

Is There Anything the Individual Can Still Do?

Today one can hear it said repeatedly that there is nothing any more that an individual can do. If someone were to speak out, it would mean only imprisonment and death. True, there is not much that can be done any more to change the course of world events. I believe that should have begun a hundred or even more years ago. But as long as we live in this world, I believe it is never too late to save ourselves and perhaps some other soul for Christ. One really has no cause to be astonished that there are those who can no longer find their way in the great confusion of our day. People we think we can trust, who ought to be leading the way and setting a good example, are running along with the crowd. No one gives enlightenment, whether in word or in writing. Or, to be more exact, it may not be given. And the thoughtless race goes on, always closer to eternity. As long as conditions are still half good, we don't see things quite right, or that we could or do otherwise.

But, alas, once hardship and misery break over us, then it will come to us as with the light of day whether everything the crowd does is so right and good, and then for many the end will pass over into despair.

I realize, too, that today many words would accomplish little more than make one highly eligible for prison. Yet, in spite of this, it is not good if our spiritual leaders remain silent year after year. By "words" I mean, of course, instruction; but example gives direction. Do we no longer want to see Christians who are able to take a stand in the darkness around us in deliberate clarity, calmness, and confidence—who, in the midst of tension, gloom, selfishness, and hate, stand fast in perfect peace and cheerfulness—who are not like the floating reed which is driven here and there by every breeze—who do not merely watch to see what their friends will do but, instead, ask themselves, "What does our faith teach us about this," or "can my conscience bear this so easily that I will never have to repent?"

If road signs were ever stuck so loosely in the earth that every wind could break them off or blow them about, would anyone who did not know the road be able to find his way? And how much worse it is if those to whom one turns for information refuse to give him an answer or, at most, give him the wrong direction just to be rid of him as quickly as possible!

---

b. FAREWELL TO HIS FAMILY (AUGUST 1943)

All my dear ones, the hour comes ever closer when I will be giving my soul back to God, the Master. I would have liked to say so many things to you in farewell so that it is hard not to be able to take leave of you any more. I would have liked, too, to spare you the pain and sorrow that you must bear because of me. But you know we must love God even more than family, and we must lose everything dear and worthwhile on earth rather than commit even the slightest offense against God. And if, for your sake, I had not shrunk back from offending God, how can we know what sufferings God might have sent us on my account? It must surely have been hard for our dear Savior to bring such pain upon His dear Mother through His death: what, then, are our sorrows compared with what these two innocent hearts had to suffer—and all on account of us sinners?

And what kind of a leave-taking must it be for those who only halfway believe in an eternal life and, consequently, no longer have much hope of a reunion? If I did not have faith in God's mercy, that He would forgive me all my sins, I could scarcely have endured life in a lonely prison with such calm. Moreover, though people charge me with a crime and have condemned me to death as a criminal, I take comfort in the knowledge that not everything which this world considers a crime is a crime in the eyes of God. And I have hope that I need not fear the eternal Judge because of this crime.

Still this sentence of death should serve as a warning. For the Lord God will not deal much differently with us if we think we do not have to obey everything He commands us through His Church to believe and to do. Except that the eternal Judge will not only condemn us to mortal death but to everlasting death as well. For this reason, I have nothing pressing upon my heart more urgently than to make the firm decision to keep all the commandments and to avoid every sin. You must love God, your Lord, and your neighbor as yourself. On these two commandments rests the whole law. Keep these and we can look forward to an early reunion in heaven. For this reason, too, we must not think evil of others who act differently than I. It is much better to pray for everyone than to pass judgment upon them, for God desires that all become blessed.

Many actually believe quite simply that things have to be the way they are. If this should happen to mean that they are obliged to commit injustice, then they believe that others are responsible. The [military] oath would not be a lie for someone who believes he can go along and is willing to do so. But if I know in advance that I cannot accept and obey everything I would promise under that oath, then I would be guilty of a lie. For this reason I am convinced that it is still best that I speak the truth, even if it costs me my life. For you will not find it written in any of the commandments of God or of the Church that a man is obliged under pain of sin to take an oath committing him to obey whatever might be commanded of him by his secular ruler. Therefore, you should not be heavy of heart if others see my decision as a sin, as some already have.

In the same way, if someone argues from the standpoint of the family, do not be troubled, for it is not permitted to lie even for the sake of the family. If I had ten children, the greatest demand upon me would still be the one I must make of myself.

Educate the children to be pious Catholics as long as it is possible. (Now, of course, one cannot expect them to understand much.) I can say from my own experience how painful life is when we live like halfway Christians, that is more like vegetating than living.

If a man were to possess all the wisdom of the world and call half the earth his own, he still could not and would not be as happy as one of those men who can still call virtually nothing in this world their own except their Catholic faith. I would not exchange my lonely cell—which is not at all bad [next word illegible]—for the most magnificent royal palace. No matter how great and how beautiful it might be, it will pass away, but God's word remains for all eternity. I can assure you that if you pray a single sincere "Our Father" for our children, you will have given them a greater gift than if you had provided them with the most lavish dowry a landholder ever dreamed of giving his daughter. Many people would laugh at these words, but they are true just the same.

Now, my dear children, when Mother reads this letter to you, your father will already be dead. He would have loved to come to you again, but the Heavenly Father willed it otherwise. Be good and obedient children and pray for me so that we may soon be reunited in heaven.

Dear wife, forgive me everything by which I have grieved or offended you. For my part, I have forgiven everything. Ask all those in Radegund whom I have ever injured or offended to forgive me too.

4. Dietrich Bonhoeffer
LETTERS FROM PRISON

Dietrich Bonhoeffer (1906–1945) was a highly promising young theologian and pastor when he decided to sign the Barmen Declaration of the Confessing Church and thus jeopardize his entire career. In the years that followed, he was frequently invited to lecture in England and the United States and so had many opportunities to escape Nazi persecution. Instead, motivated by a deep sense of patriotism and Christian duty, he returned to Germany at the end of each foreign lecture tour. His subsequent attempts to smuggle several German Jews to safety in Switzerland, however, led to his arrest in 1943 and eventually to his execution on the eve of the war's end in April 1945. During the intervening two years of imprisonment, Bonhoeffer meditated on a variety of subjects, including the meaning of Christianity in the modern secular world. His letters, excerpted below, reflect his attempts to find true faith through a complete immersion in the suffering of the world. True Christian faith, he muses, is not a rejection of the world but an embrace of it, in all its imperfections. Certainly there was no better illustration of this belief than Bonhoeffer's own choice to actively resist Nazism and his acceptance of the ultimate personal sacrifice his decision entailed.

a. TO HIS PARENTS (MAY 25, 1943)

Dear parents,

By the time you get this letter, all the final preparations and the wedding itself will be over, as will my own bit of longing to be there myself. . . . I'm looking back today in gratitude for the happy times that we have had, and am happy about them all. I'm anxious to hear what the text of the sermon was; the best I can think of Romans 15:7; I've often used it myself. What splendid summer weather they're having; I expect this morning's hymn was Paul Gerhardt's[15] "The Golden Sun." After a lengthy interval, I received your letter of the 9th very quickly, on May 11. Many thanks for it. Anyone for whom the parental home has become so much a part of himself as it has for me feels specially grateful for any message from home. If

only we could see each other or talk together for a short time, what a great relief it would be.

Of course, people outside find it difficult to imagine what prison life is like. The situation in itself—that is each single moment—is perhaps not so very different here from anywhere else; I read, meditate, write, pace up and down my cell—without rubbing myself sore against the walls like a polar bear. The great thing is to stick to what one still has and can do—there is still plenty left—and not to be dominated by the thought of what one cannot do, and by feelings of resentment and discontent. I'm sure I never realized as clearly as I do here what the Bible and Luther mean by "temptation." Quite suddenly, and for no apparent physical or psychological reason, the peace and composure that were supporting one are jarred, and the heart becomes, in Jeremiah's expressive phrase, "deceitful above all things, and desperately corrupt; who can understand it?" [19:9] It feels

[15]Lutheran hymn-writer (c. 1607–1676).

like an invasion from outside, as if by evil powers trying to rob one of what is most vital. But no doubt these experiences are good and necessary, as they teach one to understand human life better.

I'm now trying my hand at a little study on "The feeling of time," a thing that is specially relevant to anyone who is being held for examination. One of my predecessors here has scribbled over the cell door, "In 100 years it will all be over." That was his way of trying to counter the feeling that life spent here is a blank; but there is a great deal that might be said about that, and I should like to talk it over with father. "My time is in your hands" (Ps 31) is the Bible's answer. But in the Bible there is also the question that threatens to dominate everything here: "How long, O Lord?" (Ps 13).

Things continue to go well with me, and I must be grateful for the past six weeks. I'm particularly pleased that Maria's[16] mother has been with you. Is there any news yet of Konstantin in Tunisia? That's going through my head a great deal as I think of Maria and the family. If only it isn't too long before I see Maria again and we can get married! We need a cease-fire really soon; there are all sorts of other earthly wishes that one has.

The parcel of laundry has just been brought again. You've no idea what a joy and strength even this indirect link is. Many thanks and please thank Susi[17] very specially for all the help that she is giving you now. I'm also very pleased that you have got the asthma sweets again; they are most acceptable. I've already made myself a mirror here. I would be grateful for some ink, stain remover, laxative, two pairs of short underpants, a cellular shirt and the repaired shoes, collar studs. Once the sun has burnt itself into the thick walls it certainly becomes very hot, but so far it is still very pleasant. I hope that father has not given up

smoking altogether by now in my favor! Also, many thanks for the Jeremias Gotthelf.[18] In a fortnight I would very much like his *Uli der Knecht*. Renate[19] has it. By the way, you really ought to read his *Berner Geist,* and if not the whole of it, at least the first part; it is something out of the ordinary, and it will certainly interest you. I remember how old Schöne always had a special word of praise for Gotthelf, and I should like to suggest to the Diederich Press that they bring out a Gotthelf day-book. Stifter's background, too, is mainly Christian; his woodland scenes often make me long to be back again in the quiet glades of Friedrichsbrunn.[20] He is not so forceful as Gotthelf, but he is wonderfully clear and simple, and that gives me a great deal of pleasure. If only we could talk to each other about these things. For all my sympathy with the contemplative life, I am not a born Trappist.[21] Nevertheless, a period of enforced silence may be a good thing, and the Roman Catholics say that the most effective expositions of scripture come from the purely contemplative orders. I am reading the Bible straight through from cover to cover, and have just got as far as Job, which I am particularly fond of. I read the Psalms every day, as I have done for years; I know them and love them more than any other book. I cannot now read Psalms 3, 47, 70, and others without hearing them in the settings by Heinrich Schütz.[22] It was Renate who introduced me to his music, and I count it one of the greatest enrichments of my life.

---

[16]Maria von Wedemeyer, Bonhoeffer's fiancée; they were never married. Konstantin is her brother.

[17]Bohoeffer's youngest sister, Susanne (b. 1909).

[18]Pseudonym of Albert Bitzius (1797–1854), a Swiss Romantic author whose works celebrated pre-capitalist village life.

[19]Bonhoeffer's niece, who married Eberhard Berthge, a frequent correspondent (see 9D4b) and the editor of Bonhoeffer's surviving letters.

[20]Austrian author Adalbert Stifter (1805–1868), who saw art as a way to restore the harmony between humans and nature. Friedreichsbrunn is a spa town in the Harz mountains of north-central Germany.

[21]A branch of the Catholic Cistercian order of monks whose vows include long periods of silence.

[22]German composer (1585–1672), especially known for his Passion music and his influence on J. S. Bach.

Many congratulations to Ursel[23] on her birthday; I think of her a lot. Greetings to all the family and friends and especially to the young couple. I hope Maria will come to you soon. I feel myself so much a part of you all that I know that we live and bear everything in common, acting and thinking for one another, even though we have to be separated. Thank you for all your love and concern and loyalty day by day and hour by hour.

Your Dietrich

---

[23]Ursula, another sister (b. 1902), the mother of Renate. Ursula's husband, Rüdiger Schleicher, was also imprisoned for resistance, and, together with Dieterich's brother Klaus he was finally executed by the Nazi government on April 23, 1945.

b. TO EBERHARD BETHGE (JULY 21, 1944)[24]

Dear Eberhard,

All I want to do today is to send you a short greeting. I expect you are often with us here in your thoughts and are always glad of any sign of life, even if the theological discussion stops for a moment. These theological thoughts are, in fact, always occupying my mind; but there are times when I am just content to live the life of faith without worrying about its problems. At those times I simply take pleasure in the days' readings—in particular those of yesterday and today; and I'm always glad to go back to Paul Gerhardt's beautiful hymns.[25]

During the last year or so I've come to know and understand more and more the profound this-worldliness of Christianity. The Christian is not a *homo religiosus*,[26] but simply a man, as Jesus was a man—in contrast, shall we say, to John the Baptist. I don't mean the shallow and banal this-worldliness of the enlightened, the busy, the comfortable, or the lascivious, but the profound this-worldliness, characterized by discipline and the constant knowledge of death and resurrection. I think Luther lived a this-worldly life in this sense.

I remember a conversation that I had in America thirteen years ago with a young French pastor.[27] We were asking ourselves quite simply what we wanted to do with our lives. He said that he would like to become a saint (and I think it's quite likely that he did become one). At the time I was very impressed, but I disagreed with him, and said, in effect, that I should like to learn to have faith. For a long time I didn't realize the depth of the contrast. I thought I could acquire faith by trying to live a holy life, or something like it. I suppose I wrote *The Cost of Discipleship*[28] as the end of that path. Today I can see the dangers of that book, though I still stand by what I wrote.

I discovered later, and I'm still discovering right up to this moment, that it is only by living completely in this world that one learns to have faith. One must completely abandon any attempt to make something of oneself, whether it be a saint, or a converted sinner, or a churchman (a so-called priestly type!), a righteous man or an unrighteous one, a sick man or a healthy one. By this-worldliness I mean living unreservedly in life's duties, problems, successes and failures, experiences and perplexities. In so doing we throw ourselves completely into the arms of God, taking seriously, not our own sufferings, but those of God in the world—watching with Christ in Gethsemane. That, I

---

[24]The husband of Dietrich's niece, Renate, who was also a frequent correspondent of Bonhoeffer and later the editor of his published letters.
[25]See note 15.
[26]Literally, "religious human" intended as an anthropological classification such as *homo sapiens* ("wise human") or *homo habilis* ("tool-using human").

[27]Jean Lassere, French pacifist and activist in the ecumenical movement, whom Bonhoeffer met during his trip to the United States.
[28]First published in 1937.

think, is faith; that is *metanoia*;[29] and that is how one becomes a man and a Christian (cf. Jer 45!). How can success make us arrogant, or failure lead us astray, when we share in God's sufferings through a life of this kind?

I think you see what I mean, even though I put it so briefly. I'm glad to have been able to learn this, and I know I've been able to do so only along the road that I've traveled. So I'm grateful for the past and present, and content with them.

You may be surprised at such a personal letter; but if for once I want to say this kind of thing, to whom should I say it? Perhaps the time will come one day when I can talk to Maria like this; I very much hope so. But I can't expect it of her yet.

May God in his mercy lead us through these times; but above all, may he lead us to himself.

I was delighted to hear from you, and am glad you're not finding it too hot. There must be a good many letters from me on the way. Didn't we go more or less along that way in 1936?

Good-bye. Keep well, and don't lose hope that we shall all meet again soon. I always think of you in faithfulness and gratitude.

Your Dietrich

---

[29]A key Greek word in both Testaments of the Bible, translated by Erasmus and Luther as "repentance," sometimes also as "conversion."

E. Ecumenism

By the middle of the nineteenth century, there existed dozens of very different dominations that all called themselves Christian. This diversity was the result of centuries of disagreement among Christians over various aspects of belief and practice. The church's first major schism had occurred following the Council of Chalcedon in 451, when several "Monophysite" churches broke away from the Catholic Church (see 2B). Later, in 1054, came the definitive break between Eastern Orthodox churches and the West. Then, in the sixteenth century, the Protestant Reformation shattered Western Christianity from within, producing an ever-widening variety of Protestant churches across Europe and later the Americas. Faced with this staggering diversity—and the discord it often caused among the faithful—some nineteenth-century Christians began to espouse ecumenism (from Greek *Oikomenos,* "whole inhabited world"), the idea that all Christians would benefit if at least a few of the many different denominations could be brought together. The first major attempt to restore some unity, at least among Protestant churches, occurred with the establishment of the Prussian Union of Lutheran and Reformed (Calvinist) churches in 1817. By the beginning of the twentieth century, the ecumenical movement had gathered considerable momentum, with many Protestant and Eastern Orthodox denominations establishing closer ties. More recently, some of them have even made overtures toward the Roman Catholic Church. Though still divided by a number of serious doctrinal disagreements, the Christian churches of today are more inspired than ever before by the ecumenical spirit, rigorously studying the obstacles to unity and discussing ways to overcome them.

1. Encyclical of the Ecumenical Patriarchate "UNTO THE CHURCHES OF CHRIST EVERYWHERE" (1920)

The single greatest factor responsible for the emergence of modern ecumenism was undoubtedly the Christian missionary movement of the nineteenth century. As more European and American churches sent missionaries to convert peoples living in Africa and Asia, missionaries of different denominations—and their sponsoring churches and organizations—found themselves working together toward the same goal of world evangelization. In 1910 this convergence of interests culminated in the Missionary Conference of Edinburgh, which brought together more than four hundred delegates from a variety of Christian churches and led to the establishment of the International Missionary Council. Soon after, however, came the nationalist divisions of World War I, which, along with deep historical traditions of mistrust and bitterness among denominations, threatened to halt the ecumenical movement in its tracks. In 1920, the Eastern Orthodox Patriarchate of Constantinople attempted to revive the spirit of Christian unity by issuing the encyclical, or circular letter, excerpted below. Perhaps the most noteworthy proposal in this document was for the eventual establishment of a permanent institution to promote fellowship and cooperation among all Christian churches, to be modeled on the new League of Nations for world states. Two such groups were indeed soon organized: the Universal Christian Conference on Life and Work, begun in 1925, and the World Conference on Faith and Order, created in 1927. In 1937 these two groups decided to merge into a single organization to be known as the World Council of Churches, but they were unable to carry through their plan because of the outbreak of the Second World War. Finally, in 1948, the World Council of Churches was established in Amsterdam with 147 member churches.

Our own church holds that rapprochement between the various Christian Churches and fellowship between them is not excluded by the doctrinal differences which exist between them. In our opinion such a rapprochement is highly desirable and necessary. It would be useful in many ways for the real interest of each particular church and of the whole Christian body, and also for the preparation and advancement of that blessed union which will be completed in the future in accordance with the will of God. We therefore consider that the present time is most favorable for bringing forward this important question and studying it together.

Even if in this case, owing to antiquated prejudices, practices or pretensions, the difficulties which have so often jeopardized attempts at reunion in the past may arise or be brought up, nevertheless, in our view, since we are concerned at this initial stage only with contacts and rapprochement, these difficulties are of less importance. If there is good will and intention, they cannot and should not create an invincible and insuperable obstacle.

Wherefore, considering such an endeavor to be not possible and timely, especially in view of the hopeful establishment of the League of Nations, we venture to express below in brief our thoughts and our opinion regarding the way in which we understand this rapprochement and contact and how we consider it to be realizable; we earnestly ask and invite the judgement and the opinion of the other sister churches in the East and of the venerable Christian churches in the West and everywhere in the world.

We believe that the two following measures would greatly contribute to the rapprochement which is so much to be desired and which would be so useful, and we believe that they would be both successful and fruitful:

First, we consider as necessary and indispensable the removal and abolition of all the mutual mistrust and bitterness between the different churches which arise from the tendency of some of them to entice and proselytize adherents of other confessions. For nobody ignores what is unfortunately happening today in many places, disturbing the internal peace of the churches, especially in the East. So many troubles and sufferings are caused by other Christians and great hatred and enmity are aroused, with such insignificant results, by this tendency of some to proselytize and entice the followers of other Christian confessions.

After this essential re-establishment of sincerity and confidence between the churches, we consider,

Secondly, that above all, love should be rekindled and strengthened among the churches, so that they should no more consider one another as strangers and foreigners, but as relatives, and as being a part of the household of Christ and *"fellow heirs, members of the same body and partakers of the promise of God in Christ"* [Eph 3:6].

For if the different churches are inspired by love, and place it before everything else in their judgment of others and their relationships with them, instead of increasing and widening the existing dissensions, they should be enabled to reduce and diminish them. By stirring up a right brotherly interest in the condition, the well-being and stability of the other churches; by readiness to take an interest in what is happening in those churches and to obtain a better knowledge of them, and by willingness to offer

mutual aid and help, many good things will be achieved for the glory and the benefit both of themselves and of the Christian body. In our opinion, such a friendship and kindly disposition towards each other can be shown and demonstrated particularly in the following ways:

a) By the acceptance of a uniform calendar for the celebration of the great Christian feasts at the same time by all the churches.

b) By the exchange of brotherly letters on the occasion of the great feasts of the churches' year as is customary, and on other exceptional occasions.

c) By close relationships between the representatives of all churches wherever they may be.

d) By relationships between the theological schools and the professors of theology; by the exchange of theological and ecclesiastic reviews, and of other works published by each church.

e) By exchanging students for further training between the seminaries of the different churches.

f) By convoking pan-Christian[30] conferences in order to examine questions of common interest to all the churches.

g) By impartial and deeper historical study of doctrinal differences both by seminaries and in books.

h) By mutual respect for the customs and practices in different churches.

i) By allowing each other the use of chapels and cemeteries for the funerals and burials of believers of other confessions dying in foreign lands.

j) By the settlement of the question of mixed marriages between the confessions.

k) Lastly, by whole-hearted mutual assistance for the churches in their endeavors for religious advancement, charity, and so on.

Such a sincere and close contact between the churches will be all the more useful and

---

[30]Literally, "embracing all Christians."

profitable for the whole body of the Church, because manifold dangers threaten not only particular churches, but all of them. These dangers attack the very foundations of the Christian faith and the essence of Christian life and society. For the terrible world war which has just finished brought to light many unhealthy symptoms in the life of the Christian peoples, and often revealed great lack of respect even for the elementary principles of justice and charity. Thus it worsened already existing wounds and opened other new ones of a more material kind, which demand the attention and care of all the churches. Alcoholism, which is increasing daily; the increase of unnecessary luxury under the pretext of bettering life and enjoying it; the voluptuousness and lust hardly covered by the cloak of freedom and emancipation of the flesh; the prevailing unchecked licentiousness and indecency in literature, painting, the theater, and in music, under the respectable name of the development of good taste and the cultivation of fine art; the deification of wealth and the contempt of higher ideals; all these and the like, as they threaten the very essence of Christian societies are also timely topics requiring and indeed necessitating common study and cooperation by the Christian churches.

Finally, it is the duty of the churches which bear the sacred name of Christ not to forget or neglect any longer his new and great commandment of love. Nor should they continue to fall piteously behind the political authorities, who, truly applying the spirit of the Gospel and of the teaching of Christ, have under happy auspices already set up the so-called League of Nations in order to defend justice and cultivate charity and agreement between the nations.

For all these reasons, being ourselves convinced of the necessity for establishing a contact and league (fellowship) between the churches and believing that the other churches share our conviction as stated above, at least as beginning we request each one of them to send us in reply a statement of its own judgement and opinion on this matter so that common agreement or resolution having been reached, we may proceed together to its realization, and thus *"speaking the truth in love, may grow up into Him in all things, which is the head, even Christ; from whom the whole body fitly joined together and compacted by that which every joint supplieth, according to the effectual working in the measure of every part, maketh increase of the body unto the edifying of itself in love"* [Eph 4:15,16].

2. Second Vatican Council
"THE CONSTITUTION OF THE CHURCH" (1965)

Following the breakdown of ecumenical talks between Protestants and Catholics at Regensburg, Germany, in 1541, any reconciliation between the two groups was thereafter regarded by both sides as impossible. Even as late as the mid twentieth century, the popes Pius XI (r. 1922–1939) and Pius XII (r. 1939–1958) consistently resisted joining the ecumenical movement that was drawing many long-divided Protestant churches closer together. In this respect, as in many others, the pontificate of Pope John XXIII (r. 1958–1963) marked a crucial turning point in the history of the Catholic Church. Within one year of his ascension to the papacy, John announced his plans to convene an ecumenical council, which would focus primarily on reforms within the Catholic Church but would also begin talks with fellow Christians of other denominations. In 1960 the Vatican established a permanent Secretariat for the Promotion of

Christian Unity, as well as offices for similar relations with non-Christian religions and with nonbelievers. During the monumental Vatican II council that first convened in 1962, eighteen observers from non-Catholic churches were invited to attend, and they eventually contributed to the council's "Decree on Ecumenism" (1964) and "Constitution of the Church," excerpted below. Pope John's successor, Paul VI (r. 1963–1978), continued the policy of ecumenical outreach, meeting with the leaders of all major churches and with the heads of some non-Christian religions as well. Although the initial excitement of Catholic ecumenism has cooled somewhat in the intervening years, continuing cooperation and dialogue between Protestants and Catholics have produced several important joint statements of doctrinal agreement.

. . . All men are called to belong to the new people of God. Wherefore this people, while remaining one and only one, is to be spread throughout the whole world and must exist in all ages, so that the decree of God's will may be fulfilled. In the beginning God made human nature one and decreed that all His children, scattered as they were, would finally be gathered together as one [cf. Jn 11:52]. It was for this purpose that God sent His Son, whom He appointed heir of all things [cf. Heb 1:2], that He might be teacher, king and priest of all, the head of the new and universal people of the sons of God. For this, too, God sent the Spirit of his Son as Lord and Lifegiver. He it is who for the whole Church and each and every believer is the wellspring of their assembly unity in the teaching of the apostles and in fellowship, in the breaking of bread and prayers [cf. Acts 2:42].

So among all the nations there is but one people of God, which takes its citizens from every nation, making them citizens of a kingdom that is of a heavenly rather than of an earthly nature. All the faithful, scattered though they be throughout the world, are in communion with each other in the Holy Spirit, so that "he who occupies the see of Rome knows those afar as his members." Since the kingdom of Christ is not of this world [cf. Jn 18:36] the Church or people of God in establishing that kingdom takes nothing away from the temporal welfare of any people. Rather does it foster and adopt, insofar as they are good, the

ability, riches and customs of each people. Taking them to itself it purifies, strengthens, elevates and consecrates them. In this the Church is mindful that she must work with and for that King to whom the nations were given for an inheritance [Ps 71:10; Isa 9:4–7; Rev 21:24]. This characteristic of universality that adorns the people of God is a gift from the Lord himself. By reason of it, the Catholic Church strives constantly and with due effect to gather all humanity and all its possessions under Christ, its head in the unity of His Spirit.

In virtue of this catholicity each individual part contributes through its special gifts to the good of the other parts and of the whole Church. Through the common sharing of gifts and through the common effort to attain fullness in unity, the whole and each of the parts receive increase. Not only, then, is the people of God made up of different peoples, but in its inner structure also it is composed of various ranks. This diversity among its members arises either by reason of their duties, as is the case with those who exercise the sacred ministry for the good of their brethren, or by reason of their condition and state of life, as is the case with those many who enter the religious state and, tending toward holiness by a narrower path, stimulate their brethren by their example. Moreover, within the Church, particular Churches hold a rightful place; these Churches retain their own traditions without lessening the primacy of the Chair of Peter, which presides over the whole assembly of charity and protects legitimate differences, while at the same time assuring that such differences do not hinder unity but rather contribute toward it. Between all the parts of the Church there remains a bond of close communion whereby they share spiritual riches, apostolic workers and temporal resources. For the members of the people of God are called to share these goods in common, and concerning each of the Churches the words of the apostle hold good: *"According to the gift that each has received, administer it to one another as good stewards of the manifold grace of God"* [1 Pet 4:10].

All men are called to be part of this catholic unity of the people of God which forecasts and promotes universal peace. And the Catholic faithful, all who believe in Christ, and indeed the whole of mankind belong to or are related to it in various ways. For all men are called by the grace of God to salvation.

This Sacred Council wishes to turn its attention firstly to the Catholic faithful. Basing itself upon Sacred Scripture and Tradition, it teaches that the Church, now sojourning on earth as an exile, is necessary for salvation. Christ, present to us in His Body, which is the Church, is the one Mediator and the unique way of salvation. In explicit terms He Himself affirmed the necessity of faith and baptism [cf. Mk 16:16; Jn 3:5] and thereby affirmed also the necessity of the Church, for through baptism as through a door men enter the Church. Whosoever, therefore, knowing that the Catholic Church was made necessary by Christ, would refuse to enter it or to remain in it, could not be saved.

They are fully incorporated in the society of the Church who, having the Spirit of Christ, accept her entire system and all the means of salvation given to her, and are united with her as part of her visible bodily structure and through her with Christ, who rules her through the Supreme Pontiff and the bishops. The bonds that bind men to the Church in a visible way are profession of faith, the sacraments and ecclesiastical government and communion. He is not saved, however, who, though part of the body of the Church, does not persevere in charity. He remains indeed in the bosom of the Church, but, as it were, only in a "bodily" manner and not "in his heart." All the Church's children should remember that their exalted status is to be attributed not to their own merits but to the special grace of Christ. If they fail moreover to respond to the grace in thought, word and deed, not only shall they not be saved but they will be the more severely judged.

Catechumens[31] who, moved by the Holy Spirit, seek with explicit intention to be incorporated into the Church are by that very intention joined with her. With love and solicitude Mother Church already embraces them as her own.

The Church recognizes that in many ways she is linked with those who, being baptized, are honored with the name of Christian, though they do not profess the faith in its entirety or do not preserve unity of communion with the successor of Peter. For there are many who honor Sacred Scripture taking it as a norm of belief and a pattern of life, and who show a true apostolic zeal. They lovingly believe in God the Father Almighty and in Christ, the son of God and Savior. They are consecrated by baptism, in which they are united with Christ. They also recognize and accept other sacraments within their own Churches or ecclesiastical communities. Many of them rejoice in an episcopate, celebrate the Holy Eucharist and cultivate devotion toward the Virgin Mother of God. They also share with us in prayer and other spiritual benefits, even in some true union, in the Holy Spirit, for to them, too, He gives His gifts and graces whereby He is operative among them with His sanctifying power. Some indeed He has strengthened to the extent of the shedding of their blood. In all of Christ's disciples the Spirit arouses the desire to be peacefully united, in the manner determined by Christ, as one flock under one shepherd. Mother Church never ceases to pray, hope and work that this

---

[31]Aspiring Catholics in a probationary period of preparation for baptism.

may come about. She exhorts her children to purification and renewal so that the sign of Christ may shine more brightly over the face of the earth.

Finally, those who have not yet received the Gospel are related in various ways to the people of God. In the first place we must recall the people to whom the testament and the promises were given and from whom Christ was born according to the flesh [i.e., the Jews]. On account of their fathers this people of election remains most dear to God, for God does not repent of the gifts He makes nor of the calls He issues [cf. Rom 11:28–29]. But the plan of salvation also includes those who acknowledge the Creator. Among whom, in the first place are the Moslems, who, professing to hold the faith of Abraham, along with us adore the one and merciful God, who on the last day will judge mankind. Nor is God far distant from those who in shadows and images seek the unknown God, for it is He who gives to all men life and breath and all things [cf. Acts 17:25–28], and as Savior wills that all men be saved [cf. 1 Tim 2:4]. Those also can attain to salvation who through no fault of their own do not know the Gospel of Christ of His Church, yet sincerely seek God and moved by grace strive by their deeds to do His will as it is known to them through the dictates of conscience. Nor does Divine Providence deny the helps necessary for salvation to those who, without blame on their part, have not yet arrived at an explicit knowledge of God and with His grace strive to live a good life. Whatever good or truth is found among them is looked upon by the Church as a preparation for the Gospel. She knows that it is given by Him who enlightens all men so that they may finally have life. But often men, deceived by the Evil One, have become vain in their reasonings and have exchanged the truth of God for a lie, serving the creature rather than the Creator. Or some there are who, living and dying in this world without God, are left finally in a state of hopelessness. Wherefore to promote the glory of God and procure the salvation of all the aforementioned, and mindful of the command of the Lord, *"Preach the Gospel to every creature"* [Mk 16:16], the Church fosters the mission with care and attention.

As the Son was sent by the Father [cf. Jn 20:21], so He too sent the Apostles, saying: *"Go, therefore, make disciples of all nations, baptizing them in the name of the Father and of the Son and of the Holy Spirit, teaching them to observe all things whatsoever I have commanded you. And behold I am with you all days even to the consummation of the world"* [Mt 21:18–20]. The Church has received this solemn mandate of Christ to proclaim the saving truth from the apostles and must carry it out to the very ends of the earth [cf. Acts 1:8]. Wherefore she makes the words of the Apostle her own: *"Woe to me, if I do not preach the Gospel"* [1 Cor 9:16], and continues unceasingly to send heralds of the Gospel until such time as the infant churches are fully established and can themselves continue the work of evangelizing. For the Church is compelled by the Holy Spirit to do her part that God's plan may be fully realized, whereby He has constituted Christ as the source of salvation for the whole world. By the proclamation of the Gospel she prepares her hearers to receive and profess the faith, prepares them for baptism, snatches them from the slavery of error and of idols and incorporates them in Christ so that through charity they may grow up into full maturity in Christ. Through her work, whatever good is in the minds and hearts of men, whatever good lies latent in the religious practices and cultures of diverse peoples, is not only saved from destruction but is also cleansed, raised up and perfected unto the glory of God, the confusion of the devil and the happiness of man. The obligation of spreading the faith is imposed on every disciple of Christ, according to his state. Although, however, all the faithful can baptize, the priest alone can complete the building up of the Body in the eucharistic sacrifice. Thus are fulfilled the words of God, spoken through His prophet: *"From the rising of the sun until the going down thereof my name is great among the gentiles, and in every place a clean obla- tion is sacrificed and offered up in my name"* [Mal 1:11]. In this way the Church both prays and labors in order that the entire world may be- come the People of God, the Body of the Lord and the Temple of the Holy Spirit, and that in Christ, the Head of all, all honor and glory may be rendered to the Creator and Father of the Universe.

---

3. Joseph A. Harriss
"WHICH MASTER IS THE WORLD COUNCIL OF CHURCHES SERVING . . . KARL MARX OR JESUS CHRIST?" (1982)

Since its founding in 1948, the World Council of Churches (WCC) has steadily expanded to incorporate more than three hundred Christian denominations, in- cluding all major groups except the Roman Catholic Church and Unitarian churches. Headquartered in Geneva, Switzerland, the WCC is run by a central committee, which meets annually, and a representative assembly made up of delegates from all member denominations, which gathers every six or seven years. The Council's work is mainly advisory and philanthropic and includes projects such as campaigns against world hunger and poverty. Many of these programs involve sensitive social and political issues, leading some critics to be- moan the Council's mixing of secular and religious agendas. In an article that appeared in the popular secular magazine, *Reader's Digest,* journalist Joseph A. Harriss (b. 1936) went even further, accusing the WCC of supporting "leftist" Third World governments and funding their anticapitalist propaganda. Writing in the last decade of the Cold War, Harriss was especially irritated by the double standard he perceived at work among WCC members, who seemed to aim their criticism only at oppressive Western regimes while ignoring the injustices of the Soviet Union and other Marxist countries. Although Harriss' concerns about pro-Marxist sentiment in the WCC have largely gone by the wayside with the demise of the Soviet Union, many Christians remain critical of the Council's con- tinued political involvement in the name of religion.

Bible-toting Masai tribeswomen, necks ringed with ceremonial beads, bearded Russian Ortho- dox bishops and sari-gowned women from Sri Lanka were among the colorful throng of dele- gates attending the last Assembly of the World Council of Churches (WCC) in Nairobi, Kenya, in 1975. Almost half of the delegates who gathered were from Third World countries, and the speeches reflected a militant anti-Western mood. Michael Manley, then prime minister of Jamaica, was applauded when he called for peoples' democracies to replace capitalist states.

The 18-day conference heartily endorsed the WCC's Program to Combat Racism, which gives money to a variety of political organiza- tions, including revolutionary guerrilla move- ments. It urged the creation of a program to challenge corporations accused of exploiting the Third World. And it denounced South Africa's intervention in Angola, overlooking the fact that the Soviet Union was engineering the arrival of thousands of Cuban troops in Angola.

All in all, the Geneva-based ecumenical organization made clear its preference of social concerns over purely religious ones. It showed that its approach to solving the world's ills owes almost as much to Marxism as to Christianity.

Still, countless World Council supporters were shocked in August 1978 when the WCC announced that its Program to Combat Racism had give $85,000 to the Patriotic Front, a Marxist guerrilla organization then fighting the white-dominated regime in Rhodesia. At the time of the grant, the Patriotic Front had murdered 207 white civilians and 1712 blacks, and only weeks before had slaughtered nine white missionaries and their children. London's *Daily Express* headlined: "Blood Money—Rhodesian mission killers get cash aid—courtesy of world's churches." The Salvation Army, a founding member of the WCC, suspended its membership in protest, as did the Irish Presbyterian Church, which called the grant "racism in reverse."

The World Council of Churches, today representing 400 million believers, was founded in 1948 in the hope of uniting the world's fragmented Christian churches. But its increasingly aggressive involvement in politics and in financial support of violence have made it a factor of division rather than unity.

The irony is tragic, for the organization is capable of much good. The World Council has helped millions of victims of wars and natural disasters. More than two million refugees have been resettled thanks to WCC funds.

But the council has been focusing its attention more and more on political matters. This change can be attributed to two main causes: First, its initial goal of Christian unity withered over the years, as the doctrinal differences among the various churches proved to be unyielding, and the largest Christian church of all, the Roman Catholic, refused to join. The organization then shifted to "secular ecu-

menism." Church unity, the World Council's leaders argued, would be furthered by overcoming mankind's economic, racial, educational and other social ills and problems.

The second reason for the change is the WCC's altered composition. At the council's founding assembly in Amsterdam, churchmen from the Third World made up only a small percentage of the voting delegates; at Nairobi, they amounted to almost half. Of the 301 member churches, only 28 are American.

The Third World viewpoint is incarnate in General Secretary Philip Potter, a 61-year-old West Indian Methodist clergyman. Potter, who presides over a staff of nearly 300 from some 40 countries, makes no bones about his anti-Western, anti-capitalist attitude in his writings and speeches. He is fond of citing Marxist writers. He also admires black-power advocates like Stokeley Carmichael and Malcolm X.

Predictably, many WCC senior staff officers share Potter's views. Says Uruguayan Emilio Castro, head of the council's Commission on World Missions and Evangelism, "The philosophical basis of capitalism is evil, totally contrary to the Gospel."

[Harriss then cites several specific examples of WCC funding for "leftist" and "Soviet-front" regimes and organizations.]

Incredibly, not a cent of PCR [Program to Combat Racism] money goes to dissident groups in the Soviet Union, where the government practices overt repression of ethnic and religious minorities such as Lithuanians, Ukrainians, Moslems, and evangelical Christians. Marxist governments in general—and the Soviet Union in particular—get kid-glove treatment by the WCC.

Usually so articulate on human rights, the WCC turns a blind eye to the plight of Ethiopia, where the Marxist government has summarily executed over 10,000 persons for political reasons and closed more than 200 churches. When the WCC Executive Committee got around to mentioning the Soviet invasion of Afghanistan, two months after the fact, it said merely that the move had "heightened tension"; in the same communiqué, it went out of its way to express "serious concern" over the NATO decision to deploy new missiles in Europe.

WCC officials justify the lack of public criticism of Soviet human-rights violations by arguing that, with the Kremlin, private approaches are best. In fact, the few polite inquiries the WCC has sent to Moscow—about trials of Russian religious dissidents, for example—have had no visible effect.

The council also contends that not criticizing the Russians ensures that the Russian Orthodox Church will not resign from the WCC in protest. But being gentle with the Kremlin is a high price to pay for the continuing membership of the Russian Orthodox delegation. As Bernard Smith, head of Britain's Christian Affirmation Campaign, asks, "Is this an admission that the WCC is being blackmailed into silence by the Russians? Or does it mean that the WCC is a willing partner to a private arrangement by which the Russian delegates agree to retain their seats provided there is no criticism of the Soviet Union?" Either way, Russian membership effectively neutralizes WCC criticism of socialist countries.

Even before the Russians were admitted to the WCC in 1961, Martin Niemöller, a leading West German theologian who was involved in the long negotiations, asked, "Is there really a church here or only a propaganda instrument? Is the Russian church a servant of Stalin first or of Christ first?"

After years of delay the Kremlin authorized the admission of the Russian church to the WCC at the height of Krushchev's determined persecution of Russian Christians, one of the worst in the history of the Soviet Union, where over 10,000 Orthodox churches were forcibly closed. Allowing the Russian church to join the WCC tended to camouflage that action and forestall outside protests. Judging by the results, it was a shrewd move.

The WCC today faces a growing backlash. It began with Protestant laity, who have been voting with their feet and their pocketbooks. The United Presbyterian Church, which gives more per capita than any other American WCC affiliate, has lost nearly one million members in the last decade. As one Presbyterian lay representative has observed, " We hear deep resentment about the World Council from many church members. They simply feel that the WCC is dominated by people with a leftist ideology." Financial support by U.S. congregations for activities like the WCC has dropped drastically, to less than half of what these activities received in the past.

The grass-roots backlash is now gaining the support of theologians and professional churchmen. Lutheran theologian Richard John Neuhaus, for instance, says, "The WCC has almost become an anti-ecumenical organization by using social and political criteria to distinguish good guys from bad guys. This creates much sharper divisions in the church than any of the old denominational and doctrinal problems did." Says West Germany's Peter Beyerhaus, head of the International Christian Network, "If we don't succeed in bringing the WCC back onto a course that represents its true calling, it would be far better to simply dissolve it."

Plans are now being made for the WCC's Sixth General Assembly, scheduled for July 1983, in Vancouver. This, say many church authorities, is the time for the council to search its soul and rediscover its ecumenical purpose. This time, instead of leaving the entrenched WCC bureaucracy free to determine the assembly's results beforehand, member churches need to take the initiative.

The world's Christians today generally agree that the church must be present with its unique witness on the troubled international scene. For the best example of how to do that, however, WCC officials need turn not to Karl Marx but to Jesus Christ.

BIBLIOGRAPHY

Primary Sources

Anthologies and Readers

Allen, Leslie, ed., *Bryan and Darrow at Dayton* (New York: Russell & Russell, 1967).

Allitt, Patrick, ed., *Major Problems in American Religious History* (Boston: Houghton Mifflin, 2000).

Butler, Jon, and Harry S. Stout, eds., *Religion in American History* (Oxford: Oxford University Press, 1997).

Carpenter, Joel A., ed., *The Fundamentalist-Modernist Conflict: Opposing Views of Three Major Issues* (New York: Garland, 1988).

Ellis, John Tracy, ed., *Documents of American Catholic History,* 2nd ed. (Chicago: Henry Regnery, 1967).

Gaustad, Edwin S., ed., *A Documentary History of Religion in America,* 2 vols. (Grand Rapids, Mich.: Eerdmans, 1982, 1983).

Guignon, Charles, and Derk Pereboom, eds., *Existentialism: Basic Writings* (Indianapolis: Hackett, 1995).

Limouris, Gennadios, ed., *Orthodox Visions of Ecumenism* (Geneva: World Council of Churches, 1994).

Littell, Franklin Hamlin, ed., *The German Phoenix* (New York: Doubleday, 1960).

McBride, William L., ed., *Existentialist Background: Kierkegaard, Dostoevsky, Nietzsche, Jaspers, Heidegger* (New York: Garland, 1997).

O'Brien, David J., and Thomas A. Shannon, eds., *Catholic Social Thought: The Documentary Heritage* (Maryknoll, N.Y.: Orbis, 1992).

Selected Authors

Barth, Karl, *Against the Stream* (New York: Philosophical Library, 1954)

Beckett, Samuel, *Waiting for Godot* (New York: Grove Press, 1954).

Bonhoeffer, Dietrich, *The Cost of Discipleship* (New York: Simon & Schuster, 1995).

————, *Letters and Papers from Prison,* ed. Eberhard Bethge (New York: Macmillan, 1971).

Falwell, Jerry, *Listen America!* (New York: Doubleday, 1980).

Lewis, Sinclair, *Elmer Gantry* (Orlando, Fla.: Harcourt Brace & Co., 1927).

Machen, J. Gresham, *The Christian Faith in the Modern World* (New York: Macmillan, 1936).

The New Scofield Reference Bible, ed. C. I. Scofield (Oxford: Oxford University Press, 1967).

Niebuhr, Reinhold, *The Nature and Destiny of Man,* 2 vols., (New York: C. Scribner's Sons, 1949).

Sartre, Jean Paul, *Existentialism and Human Emotions* (New York: Philosophical Library, 1957).

Secondary Works

Historical Overviews

Gilbert, Felix, *The End of the European Era, 1890 to the Present,* 3rd ed. (New York: Norton, 1984).

Lincoln, Eric, and Lawrence H. Mnamiya, *The Black Church in the African-American Experience* (Durham, N.C.: Duke University Press, 1990).

Marty, Martin E., *Modern American Religion, Vol. I: The Irony of It All, 1893–1919* (Chicago: University of Chicago Press, 1986); *Vol. II: The Noise of Conflict, 1919–1941* (1991); *Vol. III: Under God, Indivisible, 1941–1960* (1996).

Miller, L., and Stanley Grenz, eds., *Fortress Introduction to Contemporary Theologies* (Minneapolis: Fortress Press, 1998).

Wuthnow, Robert, *After Heaven: Spirituality in America Since the 1950s* (Berkeley, Calif.: University of California Press, 1998).

Revivalism and Pentecostalism

Anderson, Robert, *Vision of the Disinherited: The Making of American Pentecostalism* (New York: Oxford University Press, 1979).

Blumhofer, Edith, *Restoring the Faith: The Assemblies of God, Pentecostalism, and American Culture* (Urbana, Ill.: University of Illinois Press, 1993).

McLoughlin, William G., *Revivals, Awakenings, and Reform: An Essay on Religion and Social Change in America, 1607–1977* (Chicago: University of Chicago Press, 1978).

———, *Revivals, Awakenings, and Reforms* (Chicago: University of Chicago Press, 1978).

Washington, Joseph P., *Black Sects and Holiness* (New York: Anchor/Doubleday, 1972).

Fundamentalism

Larson, Edward J., *Summer for the Gods: The Scopes Trial and America's Continuing Debate over Science and Religion* (Cambridge: Harvard University Press, 1998).

Marsden, George M., *Understanding Fundamentalism and Evangelicalism* (Grand Rapids, Mich.: Eerdmans, 1991).

Martin, William, *With God on Our Side: The Rise of the Religious Right in America* (New York: Broadway/Doubleday, 1996).

Noll, Mark A., *One Nation Under God? Christian Faith and Political Action in America* (New York: Harper & Row, 1988).

Numbers, Ronald, *The Creationists* (New York: Knopf, 1992).

Modernism and Social Gospel

Hutchinson, William R., *The Modernist Impulse in American Protestantism* (Cambridge: Harvard University Press, 1976).

White, Ronald C., Jr., *Liberty and Justice for All: Racial Reform and the Social Gospel (1877–1925)* (San Francisco: Harper & Row, 1990).

White, Ronald, Jr., and C. Howard Hopkins, *The Social Gospel: Religion and Reform in Changing America* (Philadelphia, Pa.: Temple University Press, 1976).

Totalitarianism

Berger, Doris, *The Twisted Cross: The German Christian Movement in the Third Reich* (Chapel Hill, N.C.: University of North Carolina Press, 1996).

Chadwick, Owen, *The Christian Church in the Cold War* (London: Penguin, 1993).

Conway, J. S., *The Nazi Persecution of the Churches, 1933–45* (London: Weidenfeld & Nicolson, 1968).

Forstman, Jack, *Christian Faith in Dark Times: Theological Conflicts in the Shadow of Hitler* (Louisville, Ky.: Westminster/John Knox, 1992).

Marsh, Charles, *Reclaiming Dietrich Bonhoeffer: The Promise of His Theology* (Oxford: Oxford University Press, 1996).

Atheism and Existentialism

Bociurkiw, R. R., and J. W. Strong, eds., *Religion and Atheism in the USSR and Eastern Europe* (Toronto: University of Toronto Press, 1975).

Buckley, Michael J., *At the Origins of Modern Atheism* (New Haven: Yale University Press, 1987).

McBride, William L., *The Development and Meaning of Twentieth-Century Existentialism* (New York: Garland, 1997).

Pattison, George, *Anxious Angels: A Retrospective View of Religious Existentialism* (Boston: St. Martin's, 1999).

Ecumenism

Goodall, N., *The Ecumenical Movement,* 2nd ed. (Oxford: Oxford University Press, 1964).

Rouse, Ruth, and Stephen Charles Neill, eds., *A History of the Ecumenical Movement, 1517–1968,* 2 vols., 3rd ed. (Geneva: World Council of Churches, 1986).

Western Christianity and Contemporary Society

ABORTION RALLY IN FRONT OF THE U.S. SUPREME COURT BUILDING. No other social issue has divided modern American Christians more than legalized abortion, a controversy fueled by profound disagreements over personal liberty, moral imperatives, and the definition of life itself. *(Agence France Press/Corbis-Bettmann)*

As the twenty-first century begins, Christianity faces challenges that the religion's first-century founders could never have imagined. The many social and technological changes of the twentieth century have occurred at such an accelerated rate that Christians, like members of other traditional world religions, are only now beginning to assimilate them more fully into their beliefs and practices. Meanwhile, the current trend toward economic—and to a lesser degree, political—globalization has made Western Christians much more aware of other world religions and of Christianity's minority status among them. In light of these sweeping changes, many twenty-first-century Christians find themselves reexamining and in some cases reinterpreting fundamental aspects of their religious identity and faith.

Since the mid twentieth century, for instance, many of Western society's oldest and most entrenched practices have been revised and even rejected. Legalized racial segregation and discrimination, most notably in the United States, have been gradually dismantled since the 1950s. Systemic double standards for women and men, particularly in the workplace, have been repeatedly challenged and often corrected. More recently, the concept of legal rights for homosexual couples, a radically new notion in Western society, has also begun to gain ground. Of course, legal revisions do not always reflect widespread changes in attitudes or practices, and all of these issues continue to provoke debate in the halls of government as well as the living rooms of ordinary citizens. Similarly, Christians of various denominations continue to disagree about whether the church should promote or resist such social transformations. Some individuals believe that the quest for justice lies at the very core of Christian identity and that loving one's neighbor by definition requires "liberation" of all those who suffer oppression and physical need. Political or other activism on behalf of racial minorities, women, or the poor is thus considered as an essentially religious act, expressing the love of Christ in the world. The majority of Christian churches, however, have been somewhat cautious and reactive on such issues of social change. Thirty years after the beginning of the women's movement, for example, most church leadership positions are still held by men, and the "feminization" of Christian theology proceeds at a snail's pace. Some Christians are even more resistant to any fundamental structural changes in society and in fact consider the church to be a unique sanctuary of God-given traditions, which dictate not only the road to salvation but also the way to live a godly life. For these Christians, traditions such as the nuclear family have religious as well as social significance, and deviations from these divinely ordained norms carry serious theological implications. To complicate matters still further, occasionally in recent years the leadership of a denomination has taken a position on a controversial social issue that differs significantly from the views of the majority of its membership. For example, although more than two-thirds of American Catholics support lifting the ban on the ordination of women and married people as priests, the church's leadership remains opposed to such revisions.

Individual Christians and churches remain similarly divided over new questions stemming from technological innovations. From organ transplants to the manipulation of genetic codes, medical breakthroughs in particular continue to challenge the applicability of many traditional Christian teachings. Since its emergence in the 1960s, the new field of bioethics has attempted to address this challenge by combining the learning and deliberations of theologians with those of philosophers, lawyers, and physicians. Much of the work of bioethicists, however, has yet to make the successful transition from the hypothetical "worst-case scenarios" of the seminar room to the real and immediate needs of individual Christians trapped in confusing moral dilemmas. Most of the churches have also been slow to appreciate and respond to the profound implications of many contemporary scientific innovations, thus leaving troubling questions to be resolved by the individual and possibly his or her pastor. If Christianity is to remain morally relevant in a time when genetic engineering and perhaps human cloning are not far off, the churches must soon respond to bioethical issues in a more systematic and organized manner.

The greatest challenge to the identity and mission of contemporary Christianity, however, probably comes from the current social transformation known as "globalization." As the diverse peoples of the world become more economically and thus politically interdependent, we are also witnessing an unprecedented mixing—and often clashing—of cultures. For some Christians, this merely represents the last and greatest opportunity to engage in the ancient Christian tradition of evangelization, the spreading of the gospel throughout the entire world. Taking advantage of modern transportation and communication technologies, these contemporary missionaries reject accusations of "cultural imperialism" when it comes to bringing the light of Truth to those in darkness. Other Christians are less comfortable with the idea of Western superiority, especially in matters of faith, and refrain from aggressive attempts at conversion, instead proclaiming that peaceful coexistence with non-Christians is God's will. Still others favor an even more fundamental transformation of all human attitudes toward religion. Known as religious pluralists, they call for Christians and those of other faiths to abandon exclusivist claims to "the Truth" and permit individuals to subscribe to syncretic combinations of various religious and philosophical traditions. Although they admit that this would mean the end of Western Christianity as we have known it, religious pluralists claim that their approach would still preserve the essence of Jesus' teachings.

Like all other ancient religious traditions, Christianity has grown and thrived by constantly adapting to suit new social and cultural climates. Those today who proclaim the secularization of the West and the demise of Christianity obviously have little appreciation of this long history of success. The pace of social change has clearly increased during the past century, but, if the past is any indication, Christians will once again prove themselves capable of grappling with those changes in a way that both preserves and enriches their religious tradition. That is, after all, the same challenge that has faced every Christian since Jesus himself. The more meaningful question then is not *whether* Western Christianity will survive the twenty-first century but *how*.

CHAPTER 10 CHRONOLOGY

	Politics	Literature	Individuals	Other
20th cent.	1914–1918 World War I 1917 Russian Revolution 1922–1953 Stalin rules Soviet Union 1933–1945 Nazi rule in Germany 1939–1945 World War II 1941 U.S. enters war 1964–1973 U.S. military engagement in Vietnam 1964 Civil Rights Act passed in U.S. 1974 President Nixon resigns 1981–1989 Reagan U.S. president 1989 End of Cold War 1991 U.S.S.R. dissolved 1993–2001 Clinton U.S president	1906 Troeltsch, *Protestantism & Progress* 1919 Barth, *Commentary on the Epistle to the Romans* 1940 Greene, *The Power and the Glory* 1942 Camus, *The Stranger* 1954 Beckett, *Waiting for Godot*	1865–1923 Ernst Troeltsch 1859–1939 Sigmund Freud 1906–1945 Dietrich Bonhoeffer 1886–1965 Paul Tillich 1905–1980 J.-P. Sartre 1892–1971 Reinhold Niebuhr 1897–1980 Dorothy Day 1929–1968 M. L. King, Jr. 1922– John Hick 1936– Rosemary R. Ruether	1910 Edinburgh mission meeting 1940 Foundation of ecumenical order at Taizé 1948 World Council of Churches est. at Amsterdam 1958–1964 Antireligious campaign in the U.S.S.R. 1962–1964 Vatican II council 1968 Paul VI, *Humanae Vitae* 1968 Meeting of Latin American bishops at Medellín 1970 World Alliance of Reformed Churches 1973 Abortion legalized in U.S. 1978 First "test tube" baby 1979 Mother Teresa wins Nobel Peace Prize

A. Social Justice

Christianity has always held the poor, excluded, and persecuted in special regard. It was no coincidence that a new religion preaching otherworldly rewards and spiritual equality among all true believers gained marked popularity among the lower classes and social outcasts of the ancient Roman Empire. In later eras, as Christianity became the religion of all of society, Jesus' words about "the least of my brethren" [Mt 25:40] and his plea to "feed my sheep" [Jn 21:17] continued to inspire many better-off Christians to help the poor and the marginalized. Although many individual Christians throughout the ages have been active advocates of a fairer distribution of worldly goods and privileges, the institutional church has traditionally limited itself to providing temporary relief—such as food, alms, and shelter—while reassuring the poor of the better life that awaits them after death. Much less often were churches or their leaders willing to challenge politically powerful secular authorities in an effort to establish some of that better life for the poor here on earth. Starting with the Christian Socialist movement of the late nineteenth century, however, many Christians began to view social reform as a legitimate religious goal. During the twentieth century, such groups as the Protestant Progressives and the Catholic Action movement succeeded in bringing a variety of social and political issues into the mainstream of Christian discussion and involvement. The modern Christian advocate of social justice knows no boundaries in responding to the gospel question of *"Who is my neighbor?"* [Lk 10:29]. Exploited migrant workers, victims of racial bigotry, abused women and children, and all others who suffer injustice are the beneficiaries of determined Christian activism, aimed not just at short-term relief but also at long-term legal and other institutional reforms. Though the trend of growing political involvement among Protestant and Catholic clerics in particular has made some fellow Christians uncomfortable, the movement shows no sign of retreat.

1. Dorothy Day
THE LONG LONELINESS (1952)

Dorothy Day (1897–1980) was a lifelong advocate of the poor and dispossessed of twentieth-century American society. Her 1927 conversion to Catholicism did not diminish her socialist fervor but rather intensified it. In 1933 she founded *The Catholic Worker,* a monthly newspaper publicizing various instances of social injustice towards the country's working poor. Together with Peter Maurin (1877–1949), a self-described peasant-priest and Christian radical, Day established "hospitality houses" in many U.S. cities that served as refuges for the multitudes of people rendered destitute by the Great Depression. Day's Catholic Worker movement garnered numerous admirers among social reformers of the day, but because of its simultaneous activism on the behalf of workers it also attracted its share of enemies, particularly among businessmen and politicians who opposed the organization of labor unions. By the end of World War II, all of the hospitality houses had closed down, but the newspaper and Day herself continued to act as outspoken defenders of workers' rights and absolute pacifism. In the following excerpt from her autobiography, *The Long Loneliness,* Day describes some of the movement's work during the 1930s and stresses her oft-repeated personal creed: that while economic and legal justice were important, more important still was the fundamental Christian duty to restore human dignity to one's suffering neighbors.

The Catholic Worker, as the name implied, was directed to the worker, but we used the word in its broadest sense, meaning those who worked with hand or brain, those who did physical, mental or spiritual work. But we thought primarily of the poor, the dispossessed, the exploited.

Every one of us who was attracted to the poor had a sense of guilt, of responsibility, a feeling that in some way we were living on the labor of others. The fact that we were born in a certain environment, were enabled to go to school, were endowed with the ability to compete with others and hold our own, that we had few physical disabilities all these things marked us as the privileged in a way. We felt a respect for the poor and destitute as those nearest to God, as those chosen by Christ for His compassion. Christ lived among men. The great mystery of the Incarnation, which meant that God became man that man might become God, was a joy that made us want to kiss the earth in worship, because His feet once trod that same earth. It was a mystery that we as Catholics accepted, but there were also the facts of Christ's life, that He was born in a stable, that He did not come to be a temporal King, that He worked with His hands, spent the first years of His life in exile, and the rest of His early manhood in a crude carpenter shop in Nazareth. He fulfilled His religious duties in the synagogue and the temple. He trod the roads in His public life and the first men He called were fishermen, small owners of boats and nets. He was familiar with the migrant worker and the proletariat, and some of His parables dealt with them. He spoke of the living wage, not equal pay for equal work, in the parable of those who came at the first and the eleventh hour.

He died between two thieves because He would not be made an earthly King. He lived in an occupied country for thirty years without starting an underground movement or trying to get out from under a foreign power. His teaching transcended all the wisdom of the scribes and Pharisees, and taught us the most effective means of living in this world while preparing for the next. And He directed His sublime words to the poorest of the poor, to the people who thronged the towns and followed after John the Baptist, who hung around, sick and poverty-stricken at the doors of rich men.

He had set us an example and the poor and destitute were the ones we wished to reach. The poor were the ones who had jobs of a sort, organized or unorganized, and those who were unemployed or on work-relief projects. The destitute were the men and women who came to us in the breadlines and we could do little with them but give what we had of food and clothing. Sin, sickness and death accounted for much of human misery. But aside from this, we did not feel that Christ meant we should remain silent in the face of injustice and accept it even though He said, *"The poor ye shall always have with you."* [Mt 21:11; Mk 14:7; Jn 12:8]

In the first issue of the paper we dealt with Negro labor on the levees in the South, exploited as cheap labor by the War Department. We wrote of women and children in industry and the spread of unemployment. The second issue carried a story of a farmers' strike in the Midwest and the condition of restaurant workers in cities. In the third issue there were stories of textile strikes and child labor in that industry; the next month coal and milk strikes. In the sixth issue of the paper we were already combating anti-Semitism. From then on, although we wanted to make our small eight-page tabloid a local paper, that is, covering the American scene, we could not ignore the issues abroad. They had their repercussions at home. We could not write about these issues without being drawn out on the streets on picket lines, and we found ourselves in 1935 with the Communists picketing the German consulate at the Battery.

It was not the first time we seemed to be collaborators. During the Ohrbach Department Store strike the year before I ran into old friends from the Communist group, but I felt then, and do now, that the fact that Communists made issue of Negro exploitation and labor trouble was no reason why we should stay out of the situation. "The truth is the truth," writes St. Thomas,[1] "and proceeds from the Holy Ghost, no matter from whose lips it comes.". . .

One winter I had a speaking engagement in Kansas and my expenses were paid, which fact enabled me to go to Memphis and Arkansas to visit the Tenant Farmers' Union,[2] which was then and is still headed by a Christian Socialist group. The headquarters were a few rooms in Memphis, where the organizers often slept on the floor because there was no money for rent other than that of the offices. Those days I spent with them I lived on sandwiches and coffee because there was no money to spend on regular meals either. We needed to save money for gas to take us around to the centers where dispossessed sharecroppers and tenant farmers were also camping out, home-

less, in railroad stations, schools and churches. They were being evicted wholesale because of the purchase of huge tracts of land by northern insurance agencies. The picture has been shown in *Tobacco Road, In Dubious Battle,* and *Grapes of Wrath*[3]—pictures of such desolation and poverty and in the latter case of such courage that my heart was lifted again to hope and love and admiration that human beings could endure so much and yet have courage to go on and keep their vision of a more human life.

During that trip I saw men, women and children herded into little churches and wayside stations, camped out in tents, their household goods heaped about them, not one settlement but many—farmers with no land to farm, housewives with no homes. They tried with desperate hope to hold onto a pig or some chickens, bags of seed, some little beginnings of a new hold on life. It was a bitter winter and frame houses there are not built to withstand the cold as they are in the north. The people just endure it because the winter is short—accept it as part of the suffering of life.

I saw children ill, one old man dead in bed and not yet buried, mothers weeping with hunger and cold. I saw bullet holes in the frame churches, and their benches and pulpit smashed up and windows broken. Men had been kidnapped and beaten; men had been shot and wounded. The month after I left, one of the organizers was killed by a member of a masked band of vigilantes who were fighting the Tenant Farmers' Union.

There was so little one could do—empty one's pockets, give what one had, live on sandwiches with the organizers, and write, write to arouse the public conscience. I telegraphed Eleanor Roosevelt[4] and she responded at once

---

[1] The medieval theologian Thomas Aquinas (1225–1274).
[2] The Southern Tenant Farmers' Union, founded in northeastern Arkansas in 1934, was an organization of poor white and black rural laborers who banded together to reform their own living and working conditions.

[3] *Tobacco Road* by Erskine Caldwell (1903–1987) and the other two novels by John Steinbeck (1902–1968) describe the harsh reality of American poverty during the Great Depression of the 1930s.
[4] Eleanor Roosevelt (1884–1962) was First Lady of the United States from 1933 to 1945, and she later served as U.S. ambassador to the United Nations. She was a consistent supporter of civil rights and other social reforms.

with an appeal to the governor for an investigation. The papers were full of the effrontery of a northern Catholic social worker, as they called me, who dared to pay a four-day visit and pass judgment on the economic situation of the state. The governor visited some of the encampments, and sarcastic remarks were made in some of the newspaper accounts about the pigs and chicken. "If they are starving, let them eat their stock," they wrote. . . .

Yes, we have lived with the poor, with the workers, and we know them not just from the streets, or in mass meetings, but from years of living in the slums, in tenements, in our hospices in Washington, Baltimore, Philadelphia, Harrisburg, Pittsburgh, New York, Rochester, Boston, Worcester, Buffalo, Troy, Detroit, Cleveland, Toledo, Akron, St. Louis, Chicago, Milwaukee, Minneapolis, Seattle, San Francisco, Los Angeles, Oakland, even down into Houma, Louisiana where Father Jerome Drolet worked with Negroes and whites, with shrimp shellers, fishermen, longshoremen and seamen.

Just as the Church has gone out through its missionaries into the most obscure towns and villages, we have gone too. Sometimes our contacts have been through the Church and sometimes through readers of our paper, through union organizers or those who needed to be organized.

We have lived with the unemployed, the sick, the unemployables. The contrast between the worker who is organized and has his union, the fellowship of his own trade to give him strength, and those who have no organization and come in to us on a breadline is pitiable.

They are stripped then, not only of all earthly goods, but of spiritual goods, their sense of human dignity. When they are forced into line at municipal lodging houses, in clinics, in our houses of hospitality, they are then the truly destitute. Over and over again in our work, many young men and women who came as volunteers have not been able to endure it and have gone away. To think that we are forced by our own lack of room, our lack of funds, to perpetuate this shame, is heartbreaking. . . .

We published many heavy articles on capital and labor, on strikes and labor conditions, on the assembly line and all the other evils of industrialism. But it was a whole picture we were presenting of man and his destiny and so we emphasized less, as the years went by, the organized-labor aspect of the paper.

It has been said that it was *The Catholic Worker* and its stories of poverty and exploitation that aroused the priests to start labor schools, go out on picket lines, take sides in strikes with the worker, and that brought about an emphasis on the need to study sociology in the seminaries.

And many a priest who afterward became famous for his interest in labor felt that we had in a way deserted the field, had left the cause of the union man. Bishops and priests appearing on the platform of the A. F. of L. and C. I. O.[5] conventions felt that we had departed from our original intention and undertaken work in the philosophical and theological fields that might better have been left to the clergy. The discussion of the morality of modern war, for instance, and application of moral principle in specific conflicts. Labor leaders themselves felt that in our judgment of war, we judged them also for working in the gigantic armaments race, as indeed we did. Ours is indeed an unpopular front.

---

[5]The American Federation of Labor and the Congress of Industrial Organizations, two labor unions that later merged in 1955.

2. Martin Luther King, Jr.
"LETTER FROM BIRMINGHAM JAIL"
(April 16, 1963)

No issue of social justice has more deeply divided modern Christians than that of racial prejudice and intolerance. By the mid twentieth century—nearly one hundred years after Abraham Lincoln's emancipation of African-American slaves—black Americans were still regularly harassed and treated as second-class citizens. As outrage over this situation began to mount, the leaders of many African-American churches stepped forward as passionate advocates for civil rights, and their churches became rallying points for a growing movement of nonviolent protest against racial injustice. Meanwhile, although some white Christians supported and even joined in the civil rights movement, many others remained resolutely opposed to full equality for black Americans, and some were even willing to use violence to maintain the status quo. After almost ten years of boycotts and other nonviolent protests against racial segregation, a confrontation in Birmingham, Alabama, marked by especially brutal police behavior resulted in the arrest and brief imprisonment of the most famous leader of the civil rights movement, Martin Luther King, Jr. (1929–1968). King was a Baptist minister from Atlanta, long accustomed to accusations of "outside agitation" for his organizational work in civil rights protests across the country. But when eight fellow clergymen from Alabama published a virulent condemnation of the civil rights work for which he had been jailed, it provoked King to write his "Letter from Birmingham Jail," an eloquent justification of his activism on the grounds of basic Christian charity. Comparing his situation to that of the oft-imprisoned St. Paul, King proclaimed that he was proud to be an extremist for Christian love and justice and that his critics' pleas for more patience would have required him to blind himself to the suffering of his brothers and sisters. Nonviolent pacifism does not mean inaction, he argued, and radical action was needed to reverse the many social injustices caused by racism in America. Unfortunately, King's own Christian activism was cut short five years later by an assassin's bullet in Memphis, Tennessee. The movement he helped to lead, however, went on to score many victories in the fight for full civil rights for Americans of every race.

MY DEAR FELLOW CLERGYMEN:

While confined here in the Birmingham city jail, I came across your recent statement calling my present activities "unwise and untimely." Seldom do I pause to answer criticism of my work and ideas. If I sought to answer all the criticisms that cross my desk, my secretaries would have little time for anything other than such correspondence in the course of the day, and I would have no time for constructive work. But since I feel that you are men of genuine good will and that your criticisms are sincerely set forth, I want to try to answer your statement in what I hope will be patient and reasonable terms.

I think I should indicate why I am here in Birmingham, since you have been influenced by the view which argues against "outsiders coming in." I have the honor of serving as president of the Southern Christian Leadership Conference,[6] an organization operating in every southern state, with headquarters in Atlanta, Georgia. We have some eighty-five affiliated organizations across the South, and one of them is the Alabama Christian Movement for Human Rights. Frequently we share staff, educational and financial resources with our affiliates. Several months ago the affiliate here in Birmingham asked us to be on call to engage in a nonviolent direct-action program if such were deemed necessary. We readily consented, and when the hour came we lived up to our promise. So I, along with several members of my staff, am here because I was invited here. I am here because I have organizational ties here.

But more basically, I am in Birmingham because injustice is here. Just as the prophets of the eighth century B.C. left their villages and carried their "thus saith the Lord" far beyond the boundaries of their home towns, and just as the Apostle Paul left his village of Tarsus and carried the gospel of Jesus Christ to the far corners of the Greco-Roman world, so am I compelled to carry the gospel of freedom beyond my own home town. Like Paul, I must constantly respond to the Macedonian call for aid.

Moreover, I am cognizant of the interrelatedness of all communities and states. I cannot sit idly by in Atlanta and not be concerned about what happens in Birmingham. Injustice anywhere is a threat to justice everywhere. We are caught in an inescapable network of mutuality, tied in a single garment of destiny. Whatever affects one directly, affects all indirectly. Never again can we afford to live with the narrow, provincial "outside agitator" idea. Anyone who lives inside the United States can never be considered an outsider anywhere within its bounds.

You deplore the demonstrations taking place in Birmingham. But your statement, I am sorry to say, fails to express a similar concern for the conditions that brought about the demonstrations. I am sure that none of you would want to rest content with the superficial kind of social analysis that deals merely with effects and does not grapple with underlying causes. It is unfortunate that demonstrations are taking place in Birmingham, but it is even more unfortunate that the city's white power structure left the Negro community with no alternative.

In any nonviolent campaign there are four basic steps: collection of the facts to determine whether injustices exist; negotiation; self-purification; and direct action. We have gone through all these steps in Birmingham. There can be no gainsaying the fact that racial injustice engulfs this community. Birmingham is probably the most thoroughly segregated city in the United States. Its ugly record of brutality is widely known. Negroes have experienced grossly unjust treatment in the courts. There have been more unsolved bombings of Negro homes and churches in Birmingham than in any other city in the nation. These are the hard, brutal facts of the case. On the basis of these conditions, Negro leaders sought to negotiate with the city fathers. But the latter consistently refused to engage in good-faith negotiation. . . .

You may well ask: "Why direct action? Why sit-ins, marches and so forth? Isn't negotiation a better path?" You are quite right in calling for negotiation. Indeed, this is the very purpose of direct action. Nonviolent direct action seeks to create such a crisis and foster such a tension that a community which has constantly refused to negotiate is forced to confront the issue. It seeks so to dramatize the issue that it can no longer be ignored. My citing the creation of tension as part of the work of the nonviolent-resister may sound rather shocking. But I must confess that I am not afraid of the word "tension." I have earnestly opposed violent tension, but there is a type of constructive, nonviolent tension which is necessary for growth. . . .

---

[6]Founded by King and other civil rights proponents in 1957. The SCLC played a key role in the March on Washington in 1963 and various voter-registration drives in southern states.

We know through painful experience that freedom is never voluntarily given by the oppressor; it must be demanded by the oppressed. Frankly, I have yet to engage in a direct-action campaign that was "well timed" in the view of those who have not suffered unduly from the disease of segregation. For years now I have heard the word "Wait!" It rings in the ear of every Negro with piercing familiarity. This "Wait!" has almost always meant "Never." We must come to see, with one of our distinguished jurists, that "justice too long delayed is justice denied."

We have waited for more than 340 years for our constitutional and God-given rights. The nations of Asia and Africa are moving with jet-like speed toward gaining political independence, but we still creep at horse-and-buggy pace toward gaining a cup of coffee at a lunch counter. Perhaps it is easy for those who have never felt the stinging darts of segregation to say, "Wait." But when you have seen vicious mobs lynch your mothers and fathers at will and drown your sisters and brothers at whim; when you have seen hate-filled policemen curse, kick and even kill your black brothers and sisters; when you see the vast majority of your twenty-million Negro brothers smothering in an airtight cage of poverty in the midst of an affluent society; when you suddenly find your tongue twisted and your speech stammering as you seek to explain to your six-year-old daughter why she can't go to the public amusement park that has just been advertised on television, and see tears welling up in her eyes when she is told that Funtown is closed to colored children, and see ominous clouds of inferiority beginning to form in her little mental sky, and see her beginning to distort her personality by developing an unconscious bitterness toward white people; when you have to concoct an answer for a five-year-old son who is asking: "Daddy, why do white people treat colored people so mean?"; when you take a cross-country drive and find it necessary to sleep night after night in the uncomfortable corners of your automobile because no motel will accept you; when you are humili-

ated day in and day out by nagging signs reading "white" and "colored"; when your first name becomes "nigger" your middle name becomes "boy" (however old you are) and your last name becomes "John," and your wife and mother are never given the respected title "Mrs."; when you are harried by day and haunted by night by the fact that you are a Negro, living constantly at tiptoe stance, never quite knowing what to expect next, and are plagued with inner fears and outer resentments; when you are forever fighting a degenerating disease of "nobodiness"—then you will understand why we find it difficult to wait. There comes a time when the cup of endurance runs over, and men are no longer willing to be plunged into the abyss of despair. I hope, sirs, you can understand our legitimate and unavoidable impatience.

You express a great deal of anxiety over our willingness to break laws. This is certainly a legitimate concern. Since we so diligently urge people to obey the Supreme Court's decision of 1954 outlawing segregation in the public schools,[7] at first glance it may seem rather paradoxical for us consciously to break laws. One may well ask: "How can you advocate breaking some laws and obeying others?" The answer lies in the fact that there are two types of laws: just and unjust. I would be the first to advocate obeying just laws. One has not only a legal but a moral responsibility to obey just laws. Conversely, one has a moral responsibility to disobey unjust laws. I would agree with St. Augustine that "an unjust law is no law at all.". . .

In your statement you assert that our actions, even though peaceful, must be condemned because they precipitate violence. But is this a logical assertion? Isn't this like condemning a robbed man because his possession of money precipitated the evil act of robbery? Isn't this like condemning Socrates because his unswerv-

---

[7]The landmark case of *Brown* v. *Board of Education of Topeka,* which determined that segregation in the public schools was a violation of the equal protection clause of the Fourteenth Amendment to the U.S. Constitution.

ing commitment to truth and his philosophical inquiries precipitated the act by the misguided populace in which they made him drink hemlock? Isn't this like condemning Jesus because his unique God-consciousness and never-ceasing devotion to God's will precipitated the evil act of crucifixion? We must come to see that, as the federal courts have consistently affirmed, it is wrong to urge an individual to cease his efforts to gain his basic constitutional rights because the quest may precipitate violence. Society must protect the robbed and punish the robbery. . . .

You speak of our activity in Birmingham as extreme. At first I was rather disappointed that fellow clergymen would see my nonviolent efforts as those of an extremist. I began thinking about the fact that I stand in the middle of two opposing forces in the Negro community. One is a force of complacency, made up in part of Negroes who, as a result of long years of oppression, are so drained of self-respect and a sense of "somebodiness" that they have adjusted to segregation; and in part of a few middle-class Negroes who, because of a degree of academic and economic security and because in some ways they profit by segregation, have become insensitive to the problems of the masses. The other force is one of bitterness and hatred, and it comes perilously close to advocating violence. It is expressed in the various black nationalist groups that are springing up across the nation, the largest and best-known being Elijah Muhammad's Muslim movement.[8] Nourished by the Negro's frustration over the continued existence of racial discrimination, this movement is made up of people who have lost faith in America, who have absolutely repudiated Christianity, and who have concluded that the white man is an incorrigible "devil."

I have tried to stand between these two forces, saying that we need emulate neither the "do-nothingism" of the complacent nor the hatred and despair of the black nationalist. For there is the more excellent way of love and nonviolent protest. I am grateful to God that, through the influence of the Negro church, the way of nonviolence became an integral part of our struggle. . . .

But though I was initially disappointed at being categorized as an extremist, as I continued to think about the matter I gradually gained a measure of satisfaction from the label. Was not Jesus an extremist for love: *"Love your enemies, bless them that curse you, do good to them that hate you, and pray for them which despitefully use you, and persecute you"* [Mt 5:11]. Was not Amos an extremist for justice: *"Let justice roll down like waters and righteousness like an ever-flowing stream"* [Amos 5:24]. Was not Paul an extremist for the Christian gospel: *"I bear in my body the marks of the Lord Jesus"* [Gal 6:17]. Was not Martin Luther an extremist: "Here I stand; I cannot do otherwise, so help me God." And John Bunyan: "I will stay in jail to the end of my days before I make a butchery of my conscience."[9] And Abraham Lincoln: "This nation cannot survive half slave and half free." And Thomas Jefferson: "We hold these truths to be self-evident, that all men are created equal. . . ." So the question is not whether we will be extremists, but what kind of extremists we will be. Will we be extremists for hate or for love? Will we be extremists for the preservation of injustice or for the extension of justice? In that dramatic scene on Calvary's hill three men were crucified. We must never forget that all three were crucified for the same crime—the crime of extremism. Two were extremists for immorality, and thus fell below their environment. The other, Jesus Christ, was an extremist for love, truth and goodness, and thereby rose above his environment. Perhaps the South, the nation and the world are in dire need of creative extremists. . . .

---

[8]The Nation of Islam, a black separatist religious movement founded by Elijah Muhammad (1897–1975) and promoted with the help of his disciples Malcolm X (1925–1964) and Louis Farrakhan (b. 1932).

[9]English author (1628–1688) of *Pilgrim's Progress,* a popular allegorical account of Christian salvation. Bunyan was imprisoned for his Nonconformist views during the Jacobean Restoration.

Before closing I feel impelled to mention one other point in your statement that has troubled me profoundly. You warmly commended the Birmingham police force for keeping "order" and "preventing violence." I doubt that you would have so warmly commended the police force if you had seen its dogs sinking their teeth into unarmed, nonviolent Negroes. I doubt that you would so quickly commend the policemen if you were to observe their ugly and inhumane treatment of Negroes here in the city jail; if you were to watch them push and curse old Negro women and young Negro girls; if you were to see them slap and kick old Negro men and young boys; if you were to observe them, as they did on two occasions, refuse to give us food because we wanted to sing our grace together. I cannot join you in your praise of the Birmingham police department. . . .

Never before have I written so long a letter. I'm afraid it is much too long to take your precious time. I can assure you that it would have been much shorter if I had been writing from a comfortable desk, but what else can one do when he is alone in a narrow jail cell, other than write long letters, think long thoughts and pray long prayers?

If I have said anything in this letter that overstates the truth and indicates an unreasonable impatience, I beg you to forgive me. If I have said anything that understates the truth and indicates my having a patience that allows me to settle for anything less than brotherhood, I beg God to forgive me.

I hope this letter finds you strong in the faith. I also hope that circumstances will soon make it possible for me to meet each of you, not as an integrationist or a civil-rights leader but as a fellow clergyman and a Christian brother. Let us all hope that the dark clouds of racial prejudice will soon pass away and the deep fog of misunderstanding will be lifted from our fear-drenched communities, and in some not too distant tomorrow the radiant stars of love and brotherhood will shine over our great nation with all their scintillating beauty.

Yours for the cause of Peace and Brotherhood,

MARTIN LUTHER KING, JR.

---

3. Leonardo Boff and Clodovis Boff
LIBERATION THEOLOGY: FROM CONFRONTATION TO DIALOGUE (1985)

Since the earliest Spanish and Portuguese conquests in the New World, the Catholic Church's relationship with ruling secular authorities in Latin America has been marked by extreme contrasts. On the one hand, many bishops and other powerful clerics have supported various authoritarian regimes and rigid social hierarchies, seeing them as part of the divine order. On the other hand, numerous individual priests, brothers, and nuns have attempted to correct, sometimes by revolutionary means, the profound economic and political inequity that still characterizes many nations of Central and South America. In the wake of the reform council Vatican II (1962–1965), the forces of social change were given an enormous boost when the Latin American Bishops' Conference (CELAM) issued a scathing indictment of "institutional violence" at its 1968 meeting in Medellín, Colombia. This document, sometimes referred to as the Magna Carta of the liberation theology movement, inspired several activist clerics to use ever more radical interpretations of church doctrine to justify their own involvement in political reform. The most famous of these have been the Peruvian theologian Gustavo Gutierrez (b. 1928) and the Brazilian Franciscan and theologian Leonardo Boff (b. 1938). In the following defense of liberation theology, written with his brother and fellow theologian Clodovis, Boff rejects assertions that Christianity must remain apolitical or neutral in the face of mass social injustice. His theologically based demands for a fundamental restructuring of Latin American societies, combined with his frequent reliance on Marxist terminology, resulted in his suspension from teaching by Pope John Paul II in 1984. By the time this work was published a year later, the ban on Boff was lifted, but he eventually left the priesthood in 1992. The term "liberation theology" has since come to be applied to other oppressed groups as well, particularly women and African-Americans.

. . . Before the emergence of a theology of liberation at the close of the 1960s, a full-fledged liberation praxis was already under way in Latin America. Before liberation theology there were the prophetic bishop, the committed lay person, and liberation communities. A life *practice* was well under way even in the early 1960s. The *theology* of liberation, then, came in a "second moment." It came as the *expression* of this liberation praxis on the part of the Church. Liberation theology is the *theology of a liberation Church*—a Church with a preferential option for solidarity with the poor.

Of course, the theology of liberation is not the mere *reflex* of a liberation faith. It is also a *reflection* on that faith—an in-depth explanation, a purification, a systematization of that faith. In other words: liberation theology enlightens and stimulates the life and practice of the actual, concrete Church.

To be sure, a *reciprocal relation* obtains between action and reflection—faith action and theological reflection in the Church maintain a two-way relationship. Still, theology is more an effect than a cause of the practice of faith, and it is a cause only because it is an effect.

Removed from its *Sitz im Leben* [lit., "seat in life"] withdrawn from the vital context of its origin and development, the theology of liberation becomes altogether incomprehensible. Liberation theology cannot be understood merely by reading books and articles. The books and articles absolutely must be connected with the soil of the Church and of society, from which these writings have sprung, inasmuch as they seek to interpret and illuminate that Church and that society.

It is *only within a process,* then, a fabric whose warp and woof are suffering and hope, that liberation theology is born, and therefore understood. From above, or from without, there is no understanding it at all. We might even go so far as to say that the theology of liberation can be understood only by two groupings of persons: the poor, and those who struggle for justice at their side—only by those who hunger for bread, and by those who hunger for justice in solidarity with those hungering for bread. Conversely, liberation theology is not understood, nor can it be understood, by the satiated and satisfied—by those comfortable with the status quo.

The implication here is that, down at the "base," antecedent to all theologizing, is an option for life, a particular, determinate faith experience, the taking of a position vis-à-vis the concrete world in which we live. It is from a pre-theological element as one's starting point, then, that one is totally "for," or totally "against," the theology of liberation.

In other words, it is crucial to grasp liberation theology in its locus. Theologians of liberation must be read not in the ivory towers of certain departments of theology (to borrow an image from Pope John Paul II), but in the slums, in the miserable neighborhoods of the destitute, in the factories, on the plantations—wherever an oppressed people live, suffer, struggle, and die.

To pretend to "discuss liberation theology" *without seeing the poor* is to miss the whole point, for one fails to see the central problem of the theology being discussed. For the kernel and core of liberation theology is not theology but liberation. It is not the theologian but the poor who count in this theology. Were the theology of liberation somehow to pass into oblivion, would the problem it has raised thereby be solved? To fail to see this is to fit the Brazilian proverb to a tee: "You heard the rooster crow, but you don't know where."

We must face the fact. For many persons, a living, direct experience of poverty and of the people's struggle with poverty will be required of them before they will be able to understand this theology. Cardinal Daneels, Archbishop of Brussels, on his return from a visit to Brazil, grasped this very clearly:

> There is something tragic in what is going on in and around the theology of liberation today. Liberation theology begins with a very acute, very profound sensitivity to poverty. We see this poverty every day on television. It is another matter, however, to see it on the spot—to allow it to penetrate all five senses, to let ourselves be touched by the suffering of the poor, to feel their anguish, to experience the filth of the slums sticking to our skin. . . .This is problem number one: the plight of the poor. . . .We cannot let these people down! We must support their theologians. [*Entraide et fraternité* newswire, September 20, 1984]

The theology of liberation is the thinking of the faith under the formality of a leaven of historical transformation—as the *"salt of the earth"* and the *"light of the world"* [Mt 5:13–14], as the theological virtue of charity exercised in the area of the social.

More simply, the theology of liberation is reflection on the life of the Christian community from a standpoint of its contribution to liberation. "Life" here is a richer and more flexible concept than that of "praxis," which is an external activity of historical transformation. We might be tempted to represent the theology of liberation as a kind of "chemical reaction":

Faith + Oppression → Liberation Theology

The social or political dimension of faith is the new aspect (not the only aspect) of the faith that is emphasized by the theology of liberation. We explore a specific "integral" or "constitutive part" of the "evangelization or mission" of the Church: "action on behalf of justice, and participation in the transformation of the world."

The theology of liberation seeks to demonstrate that the kingdom of God is to be established not only in the *soul*—this is the individual personal dimension of the kingdom—and not only in *heaven*—this is its transhistorical dimension—but in relationships among human beings, as well. In other words, the kingdom of God is to be established in social projects, and this is its historical dimension. In sum, liberation theology is a theology that seeks to take history, and Christians' historical responsibility, seriously.

Christians today are faced with an enormous, unprecedented challenge. Today, as we read in the documents of Vatican II, the Church faces a "new age in human history." Medellín[10] translates this novelty as follows, where Latin America is concerned:

> We stand on the threshold of a new age in the history of our continent—an age

---

[10]The central document of liberation theology, issued by the 1968 meeting of Latin American bishops in Medellín, Colombia; it denounces institutional violence and other forms of social oppression.

bursting with a desire for total emancipation, for liberation from all manner of servitude. . . .

For perhaps the first time in history, the faith of the Christian community faces this challenge: to make a determined contribution—and may it be decisive!—to the building of a new society, in which the great "social dominations" will be no more.

In the first Christian centuries, the faith discharged a function, generally speaking, of *protest against the social order*. Then, during the long Constantinian era, the faith developed a function, predominantly, of the *conservation of the status quo*. Today the moment in history has arrived for the faith to perform a function of *social construction*. The end and aim of the theology of liberation is to serve as an echo of and a response to this immense challenge facing the Church, especially since the time of *Rerum Novarum*.[11] . . .

Commitment to liberation implies a denunciation of situations in society and the Church that are displeasing to God, such as hunger, the premature death of thousands of children, subhuman working conditions, economic exploitation, military repression, and the manipulation of Christianity for the maintenance of these conditions, with the connivance of Church authorities who limit the concept of evangelization to the strictly intra-ecclesial, "religious" sphere, as if there were no sin, no love, no conversion, and no forgiveness in the social and political areas of society. In order to grasp the proportions of prevailing social inequities, theology needs an *ancilla*[12] in the form of a theoretical lucidity that can be the product only of the social and human sciences, as it is these that demonstrate the functioning of the mechanisms of poverty and thus enable theology to decide what to label as social sin. It is not a matter of whether to accept contributions of Marxism, as we shall see below, but of understanding where we can obtain the wherewithal to demonstrate that the poverty of the masses "is in many cases the result of a violation of the dignity of labor."

Christians seek liberation, but they seek a liberation deriving from their very faith, for it is this faith that leads them and stirs them to their liberation commitment. Indeed, otherwise their faith is the dead faith of the demons, who "believe . . . and shudder" in hell itself (Jas 2:19, 26).

The theology of liberation, before being a "movement of ideas" or the "generator of a commitment to justice," as the *Instruction*[13] would have it (chap. 3, no. 3), is itself generated by an antecedent concrete commitment to the exalted struggle for justice. Liberation theology is "second word" that grows out of a first, primary, basic "word" of practice. It is not a theology primarily of "conclusions"—one concluding merely to the *will* to act—but is a theology fundamentally involving action itself: an action always driven and guided by faith and by the Gospel present in the life of a people at once oppressed and Christian. The concrete practice of liberation calls for something besides evangelical inspiration and theological reflection. . . .

_____

[11]A papal encyclical of Pope Leo XIII (r. 1878–1903); see 8B3.

[12]Supplement, or "helper."

[13]The Vatican's response to Latin American liberation theology, issued by the head of the Society for the Propagation of the Faith, Cardinal Ratzinger (b. 1927).

B. Feminism

Women have always played significant roles in the Christian church. Throughout most of the past two millennia, however, their involvement in worship, theology, and church administration has been generally constrained by the systematic social and political domination of men, a tradition known as "patriarchy." Beginning in the 1960s, however, the women's movement that was challenging male dominance in Western society at large started to make inroads in the church as well. Feminist theologians and other reformers demanded that the language, rituals, and authority structure of Christianity change to reflect the widely acknowledged equality of the sexes. Their proposals, as well as the consequences, have varied considerably in scope, from modest to quite radical. Some churches, for instance, have implemented linguistic changes in their readings, prayers, and hymns, substituting more inclusive terms for traditional, patriarchal ones. For example, the term "sovereign" might replace "lord," and "God the Father" might give way to "Our Father and Mother" or, more controversially, "Mother Goddess." Some denominations have allowed women to move into leadership positions formerly held only by men, including the Episcopal Church, which began ordaining women as priests in the mid-1970s. Like other major societal shifts, the changing role of women has sparked disagreement among Christian denominations as well as individual believers. Some conservative churches have refused to revise their theology or practice at all, choosing instead to mount a vigorous defense of traditional female roles, which they consider to be ordained by God. At the other end of the spectrum, some of the more revolutionary feminists have argued that Christianity itself is hopelessly patriarchal and must therefore be abandoned. Even those feminists who have chosen to remain within the church, however, agree that the task of reshaping both the ideas and practices of Christianity remains a daunting one: the deeply embedded patriarchal structures of an ancient religious tradition will not give way quickly or without great resistance.

1. Rosemary Radford Ruether
SEXISM AND GOD-TALK: TOWARD A FEMINIST THEOLOGY (1983)

Rosemary Radford Ruether (b. 1936) is one of the most influential voices in feminist theology. Her upbringing in an ecumenical Catholic family and early exposure to the writings of Protestant theologian Paul Tillich (1886–1965) helped convince her that each human society fashions its own understanding of divine revelation. This means that Christianity—like other religions—does not consist of one universal, objective theology, but rather is always interpreted through the symbols and images of a given historical culture. Unfortunately, Ruether writes, the Judeo-Christian tradition that shapes the church today remains deeply embedded in the language and thinking of several past patriarchal societies. In order to remove centuries of accumulated misogyny, or hatred of women, modern Christians must work hard to replace such images with positive representations of women and their relationship to the divine. Her proposed method is to search the nooks and crannies of Christianity and other religious traditions for any neglected material that will promote "the full humanity of women." Only then, she believes, can women find a "God-image" that includes them and construct a nonhierarchical and "earth friendly" society that reflects that image.

The critical principle of feminist theology is the promotion of the full humanity of women. Whatever denies, diminishes, or distorts the full humanity of women is, therefore, appraised as not redemptive. Theologically speaking, whatever diminishes or denies the full humanity of women must be presumed not to reflect the divine or an authentic relation to the divine, or to reflect the authentic nature of things, or to be the message or work of an authentic redeemer or a community of redemption.

This negative principle also implies the positive principle: what does promote the full humanity of women is of the Holy, it does reflect true relation to the divine, it is the true nature of things, the authentic message of redemption and the mission of redemptive community. But the meaning of this positive principle—namely, the full humanity of women—is not fully known. It has not existed in history. What we have known is the negative principle of the denigration and marginalization of women's humanity. Still, the humanity of women, although diminished, has not been destroyed. It has constantly affirmed itself, often in only limited and subversive ways, and it has been touchstone against which we test and criticize all that diminishes us. In the process we experience our larger potential that allows us to begin to imagine a world without sexism.

This principle is hardly new. In fact, the correlation of original, authentic human nature (*imago dei*[14] Christ) and diminished, fallen humanity provided the basic structure of classical Christian theology. The uniqueness of feminist theology is not the critical principle, full humanity, but the fact that women claim this principle for themselves. Women name themselves as subjects of authentic and full humanity.

The use of this principle in male theology is perceived to have been corrupted by sexism. The naming of males as norms of authentic humanity has caused women to be scapegoated for sin and marginalized in both original and redeemed hu-

manity. This distorts and contradicts the theological paradigm of *imago dei*/Christ. Defined as male humanity against or above women, as ruling-class humanity above servant classes, the *imago dei*/Christ paradigm becomes an instrument of sin rather than a disclosure of the divine and an instrument of grace.

This also implies that women cannot simply reverse the sin of sexism. Women cannot simply scapegoat males for historical evil in a way that makes themselves only innocent victims. Women cannot affirm themselves as *imago dei* and subjects of full human potential in a way that diminishes male humanity. Women, as the denigrated half of the human species, must reach for a continually expanding definition of inclusive humanity—inclusive of both genders, inclusive of all social groups and races. Any principle of religion or society that marginalizes one group of persons as less than fully human diminishes us all. In rejecting androcentrism (males as norms of humanity), women must also criticize all other forms of chauvinism: making white Westerners the norm of humanity, making Christians the norm of humanity, making privileged classes the norm of humanity. Women must also criticize humanocentrism, that is, making humans the norm and crown of creation in a way that diminishes the other beings in the community of creation. This is not a question of sameness but of recognition of value, which at the same time affirms genuine variety and particularity. It reaches for a new mode of relationship, neither a hierarchical model that diminishes the potential of the "other" nor an "equality" defined by a ruling norm drawn from the dominant group; rather a mutuality that allows us to affirm different ways of being.

IS THERE A HISTORICAL TRADITION FOR FEMINIST THEOLOGY?

First we must say that there is no final and definitive feminist theology, no final synthesis that encompasses all human experience,

---

[14]"In the image of God."

criticizes what is sexist, and appropriates what is usable in all historical traditions. This book, therefore, represents not *the* feminist theology but *a* feminist theology. However wide its historical sweep, back to Biblical traditions, forward toward a post-Christian world, encompassing minority as well as majority tradition, it is nevertheless an exercise in feminist theology with a particular selection of human experience. This selection is and can only be from the historical tradition, in its broadest sense, that has defined my identity. If I seek out the minority as well as the majority traditions of that community, its repressed pre-Christian side as well as its dominant tradition, I still operate within a particular historical tradition. . . .

While particularity is affirmed, exclusivism is rejected. God is not a Christian or a Jew rather than a pagan, not white rather than Asian or African. Theological reflections drawn from Judeo-Christian or even the Near-Eastern-Mediterranean-European traditions do not have a privileged relation to God, to truth, to authentic humanity over those that arise from Judaism, Islam, and Buddhism. Nor are they presumed to be the same. Exactly how a feminist theology drawn from other cultural syntheses would differ is not yet known. But we affirm at the outset the possibility of equivalence, or equal value, of different feminist theologies drawn from different cultural syntheses. . . .

[After several chapters describing the theological and cultural material available for a feminist theology, Ruether concludes her book with her own vision of an alternate, feminist Christianity.]

Those who rule pay their professors to proliferate lies, to generate a mental universe that turns everything upside down. The Big Lie makes those who toil appear to be idle, while those who speak into dictaphones appear to be the hard workers. It makes women appear the offspring of males, and males the primary creators of babies. It makes matter the final devo-

lution of the mind, and mind the original source of all being. It regards the body as an alien tomb of the soul, and the soul as growing stronger the more it weakens the body. It abstracts the human from the earth and God from the cosmos, and says that that which is abstracted is the original, and the first, and can exist alone and independent.

The Big Lie tells us that we are strangers and sojourners on this planet, that our flesh, our blood, our instincts for survival are our enemies. Originally we lived as disincarnate orbs of light in the heavenly heights. We have fallen to this earth and into this clay through accident or sin. We must spend our lives suppressing our hungers and thirsts and shunning our fellow beings, so that we can dematerialize and fly away again to our stars.

It is said that mothers particularly are the enemy, responsible for our mortal flesh. To become eternal and everlasting we must flee the body, the woman, and the world. She is the icon of the corruptible nature, seduced by the serpent in the beginning. Through her, death entered the world. Even now she collaborates with devils to hold men in fast fetters to the ground. A million women twisted on the rack, smoldered in burning fagots to pay homage to this Lie.

It is said that enlightened man must drive the devils and witches from the world, restore order, put himself in charge, reduce nature to his control. With numbers and formulas he can search out her innermost secrets, learn all the laws of her ways, become her lord and master. The cosmos is reduced to elements, molecules, atoms, positive and negative charges, infinitely manipulatable, having no nature of her own, given to him to do with what he will. He will mount upon her with wings, fly away to the moon, blow her up in the flash of atomic energy, live forever in a space capsule, entombed in plastic, dining on chemicals.

The façade starts to crumble. We discover buried histories. "We Shall Overcome." "Sisterhood Is Powerful." "Viva la Huelga." "Bury My Heart at Wounded Knee." We begin to understand the hidden costs. "Hello, carbon dioxide; the air, the air is everywhere." Carcinogens in our health food, strontium 90 in mother's milk. Atomic fallout in our swimming pool. Threats to generations yet unborn. We are held hostage by the colonized, blackmailed by the poor rich in raw materials. The Petroleum Age starts to run out of gas.

Through the fissures of the system we glimpse the forgotten world of our homeland. We learn to walk again; to watch sunsets; to examine leaves; to plant seeds in soil. Turn off the TV; talk to each other to ease the frenetic pace; get in touch with our circulatory system, with the rhythms of our menstrual cycle that links us to the pull of the moon and tides of the sea.

The scales begin to fall from our eyes, and all around us we see miracles. Babies grow in wombs without help from computers. The sun rises every day. ConEd sends no bill for sunshine. The harmony is still there, persisting, supporting, forgiving, preserving us in spite of ourselves. Divine Grace keeps faith with us when we have broken faith with her. Through the years of alien madness, she did not abandon us; she kept the planets turning, the seasons recurring, even struggled to put the upside down right side up, to cleanse the channels of the garbage, to blow the smog out to sea.

To return Home: to learn the harmony, the peace, the justice of body, bodies in right relation to each other. The whence we have come and whither we go, not from alien skies but here, in the community of earth. Holy One, Thy Kingdom come, Thy will be done on earth [Mt 6:19; Lk 11:2]. All shall sit under their own vines and fig trees and none shall be afraid [3 Kng 4:25]. The lion will lay down with the lamb and the little child will lead them [Isa 11:6]. A new thing is revealed; the woman will encompass the warrior. Thou shalt not hurt, thou shalt not kill in all my holy mountain.

The Shalom of the Holy; the disclosure of the gracious *Shekinah,*[15] Divine Wisdom; the empowering Matrix; She, in whom we live and move and have our being—She comes; She is here.

---

[15]A visible (and often feminine) manifestation of the divine presence as described in Jewish theological tradition.

---

2. Joanmarie Smith
"THE NUN'S STORY" (1982)

Religious orders for women have been an integral part of the Catholic Church since ancient times. By the mid twentieth century, hundreds of thousands of nuns of various orders, or congregations, had become indispensable to the operation of Roman Catholic schools, hospitals, and other service institutions throughout the world. Then came the 1960s and Vatican II (1962–1965), the church council that modernized and liberalized much of Catholic tradition. Its influence—along with that of the women's movement—sent the sisterhood into a vocational crisis from which it has yet to recover. According to Joanmarie Smith, a Sister of Saint Joseph, the key reason that so many women left her own order and that so many young women have decided not to become nuns in the first place is the question of identity. The pillars of a nun's identity since the early days of the church—vows of poverty, celibacy, and obedience—no longer seem as sturdy or even commendable in a modern society where personal independence and initiative are much more valued by the mainstream. Conformity in dress (e.g., the nun's habit) as well as communal living have accordingly given way in most religious orders for women, succeeded by a "new framework" of individual choice in practically every aspect of life. Celibacy remains the only common bond among modern nuns, and Smith even questions its virtue or necessity in a modern Christian's life. Clearly Smith believes that being a nun is still a valid feminist way to realize the "full humanity of women," but her definition of what it means to be a nun remains purposely open-ended.

God's plan was that I become a Sister of St. Joseph. He called me, held out a vocation to me. And I answered that call. In the novitiate I was educated to what being a nun involved. One became a bride of Christ. The rule provided such a detailed blueprint for living out that title that lay persons could only envy us. "You keep the holy rule and the holy rule will keep you" was a frequently heard adage that made eminent sense to me then—in that framework; in fact, it still does—in that framework.

It is my impression that priests who entered the seminary at this same time were similarly educated—that they saw themselves in analogous terms and that their framework was characterized (as was ours) by stability, simplicity, and certitude. The framework was God-given and, therefore, changeless. They would be "priests forever." And there was no complexity about what that involved. Moreover, one could be certain that in obeying one's pastor or bishop one could do no wrong—even if the pastor's or bishop's orders were wrong (Shades of "You keep the rule and the rule will keep you"). Then a funny thing happened on the way from Vatican Council II.

Vatican II, of course, did not usher in the shift in framework; it simply crystallized the shift as a possibility. The question could now at least be posed: After the Galileo case,[16] we no longer think that our act of faith commits us to a particular physics; must we still think that

our faith commits us to a particular metaphysics? Theoretically, the jury is still out on that one. But, more and more, nuns have consciously or unconsciously changed their framework. For priests, the change has not been so easy or so widespread. It is my contention that the clash in frameworks has been the source of much of any conflict which exists between nuns and priests who must work together. . . .

The nuns' story began to change to a myriad of stories in the late 1960s. From 1965 to 1970, I taught in a sister formation college. Setting up these intercongregational institutions had the effect, first of all, of fostering relationships across congregational lines. It was simultaneously discovered that the differences among congregations were minuscule. In fact, any differences stemmed more from the different personalities at the helm of the order than from differing philosophies or theologies informing them. An even more important effect was the focused inquiry that was promoted among these young women. During a council when the Church was questioning its own identity, no area was beyond the pale of investigation. In the fall-out from that period, nuns' stories changed radically. Among those who entered the convent from 1960 to 1975, approximately two-thirds have left. The median age of my own congregation is, at this time fifty-six and rising! Those who stayed began to live a different story-framework—a story now characterized by uncertainty, complexity, and instability. . . .

One of the most prominent features of this new story-framework is that it lacks a neat theology of what it is to be a nun. The bride of Christ theology, except in the most conservative congregations, disappeared somewhat in

---

[16]The inquisitional trial and subsequent condemnation of astronomer Galileo Galilei (1564–1642) for his defiant teaching of Copernicus' heliocentric model of the solar system. Over 350 years later, the Vatican issued a statement regretting this error on the part of the Church.

the way the ideology of indulgences[17] did. People just stopped using the term and the trappings that reinforced it. There were no more wedding gowns at the reception of postulants into the novitiate, no more books or hymns about "sponsae Christi."[18] The vows themselves became more problematic.

Poverty is an evil. The dilemma is obvious. To embrace what is universally seen to be an evil smacks of masochism. On the other hand, to call the relatively middle-class security that most congregations enjoy "poverty" smacks of obscenity. In the old context, fidelity to the vow had hinged on permission. Poverty was equated with dependence. The ideal of dependence was subverted by studies into the psychology of maturity. Independence and interdependence are the values pursued by actualizing adults. Simultaneously, the incongruity of a situation where one thinks oneself poor yet could study abroad, take trips, have a car for personal use, etc., as long as one had permission, became apparent. The new interpretation of poverty is simplicity. Members of congregations are enjoined to simplify their lives as much as possible—an ideal, it must be noted, enjoined not only on all Christians but upon everyone as the world's population increases and its resources decrease. That left obedience and chastity as the defining notes of women in religious orders.

I sometimes mark the unraveling of the theology of sisterhood in my religious congregation with a letter from the motherhouse saying that a sister could take a walk around the block without asking the superior. We had been taught that obedience was the linchpin of our religious vocation. Obviously the other two vows could be absorbed by it. We heard that, in fact, there were some congregations who "took" only the vow of obedience. If the bell calling us to prayer or work or recreation was considered "the voice of God," how much more so were the superior's words. God spoke through her so that anything she enjoined was God's will for us. Moreover, anything we asked to do and were permitted to do then became blessed by the assurance that it, too, was God's will. In that context, then, it was not at all absurd that in my congregation, once a month, the sisters would gather in their convents to ask permission "to pass from one part of the house to another, to wash and mend our clothes. . . ." Such an exercise ever more closely allied our lives with our "calling." But if one could walk around the block without permission, why couldn't one go home to visit the family without permission? Or, for that matter, why couldn't one go to Europe? With that letter from the motherhouse, therefore, the toothpaste started coming out of the tube, as it were. And it became impossible to put back—at least it would not go back into the same tube.

The period from the change that this letter presaged to its verbalization in the documents of the congregation seemed endless at the time. In retrospect, however, the shift occurred with marvelous speed. Our temporary "rule" (an interesting juxtaposition of terms) still speaks of discerning God's will (there's still a blueprint somewhere), but now describes this will being made known "in a multiplicity of ways—in prayer, Scripture, personal events, the needs of our time, dialogue with the sisters with whom we live, with those in authority and the people to whom we minister." In addition, in the section where the rule treats of obedience, the emphasis is on personal decisions, responsibility and dialogue. The rule no longer "keeps us." The certitude is gone. What is left, then to mark off the vocation? Chastity?

[17]The papacy's practice of granting remission for the punishment of sins in purgatory, based on St. Peter's "power of the keys" [Mt 16:19] and passed down to his successors as bishop of Rome. The sale of indulgences during the early sixteenth century spurred Martin Luther to write his famous 95 Theses in 1517, eventually triggering the Protestant Reformation. The Council of Trent (1545–1563) later condemned the merchandizing of these spiritual benefits but reaffirmed the popes' power to grant indulgences in general.

[18]Before taking their final vows, aspiring nuns, or postulants, are trained in the novitiate. With their vows, they become "Brides of Christ."

But chastity is also a human value. To be respectful and modest—in the richest sense of those terms—toward oneself and others is, again, a value of personhood, not specifically of persons in religious orders. Not so celibacy. The Jews remind us that the *very* first commandment is to increase and multiply [Gen 1:28]—a commandment most people are happy to obey. To forgo fulfilling this commandment is unique in the universe. Such a stance remarkably specifies a group who embraces it. It is not surprising, then, that "chastity" like "bride of Christ" has disappeared from our vocabulary. Celibacy has replaced it. At this critical point our lives overlap those of priests. There is a crucial difference, however. Celibacy is not an essential note of priesthood. It is grounded in an historical necessity. As such, it is recognized as purely disciplinary, and most theologians agree that the celibacy requirement of the Roman rite will, in the future, become as optional as it has always been in the Eastern rite. With nuns, however, a paradox has arisen. More and more, celibacy has become the specifying note of their vocation. This has the effect of having one's identity based on a sexual anomaly. Of course, there is nothing wrong with that if you can ground the value of the situation in a compelling framework. My constitutions speak of celibacy freeing the sister "to respond to God and his people with her entire sensitivity and affectivity." At first reading this seems obvious enough. Yet, it seems to me, there is an unfortunate implication embedded in such thinking. It overlooks the fact that most of the most dramatic service to humanity is rendered by married persons—doctors, statesmen, religious missionaries of other communions, among them. Such oversight neglects the common wisdom that their service is energized and enhanced in and by their marriage. Another form of the implication might go: If celibacy is freeing, sex must be a drag—literally and figuratively.

Not all the theory of celibacy is in that bag, however. There is also the thesis that celibacy acts as a sign in this world of the eschaton.[19]

"By the consecration of her entire humanity, with all that this implies for her as a woman, she is a sign of the transcendence of God calling her and all people to the fullness of life—total union with him." This may, of course, be the case, but it does not seem that a radical commitment to justice could serve similarly, if not so uniquely, as that sign. But if celibacy were no longer held as a specifying note of what it means to be a nun, what would be left? That question anguishes many of us today. But some have learned not simply to live with the ambiguity of our situation, but to embrace it as the human condition because they have completely abandoned the old framework or paradigm against which they previously lived out their stories. Ambiguity has replaced certitude as the primary color of their lives. However, an even more fascinating characteristic of life in religious orders today is that sisters with different contexts can live in the same congregation and even, at times, side by side. . . .

Such diversity dramatically reflects the multiplicity of stories being lived simultaneously. Most of the communities in my congregation operate without a superior. The buck of responsibility for these communities stops at each sister. The style and content of our prayer life is also the responsibility of the local community, and each sister shapes her spirituality in the light of the local decision. We group and determine how the money which comes into the house will be dispersed after we pay our tax to the larger congregation. We also choose our work, our living situation. The complexity that such variety introduces into the congregation as a whole and into each local community, potentially at least, enriches the texture of our lives or, to use Whitehead's term, the intensity. Harmony in music provides a fruitful analogy. The texture and richness of a harmony depends upon the quality and spread of the notes. Any single note that becomes another or is not "true" to its identity diminishes the entire harmony.

But nuns must now face the dawning realization that with such ambiguity in defining our-

---

[19] I.e., last days before the Final Judgment.

selves and with such an assortment of lifestyles (with the exception of celibacy) we may not really be a unique entity after all. The question is endemic to nuns' meetings: "What is the essence of religious life?" The anguish of the question is exacerbated by those persons (especially those women who have left religious orders) who justifiably take umbrage at our equating *religious* life with life in a religious order. It seems that whatever we are doing as nuns we could readily do as "women in the world." We know this to be so because, more often than not, we are already doing whatever we are doing with "women in the world." In the light of these realities, and faced with the statistics of decreasing numbers and an increasing median age, members of religious orders are having to learn to live with an instability more profound than economic anxiety. It is the instability introduced in the face of ultimately losing one's identity—of dying. . . .

People die, and institutions die, of course, but they are other people, other institutions. In the past ten years, nuns have had to confront, with varying degrees of consciousness and with varying degrees of success, the possible (some would say the "imminent") death of nunhood as an institution. It a way, it's easier to accept the inevitability that one's own life will end than the inevitability that the institution in which one has lived this life will end. A frequently heard comment on this situation goes: "Well, religious life as we know it may change, but it will survive in some form." This may, in fact, be the case, or it may be an advanced form of denial, the first stage of the response to dying.

Then there is the danger of self-fulfilling prophecy. We may not be dying, but sounding the death knell will certainly discourage any vibrant young women from joining us. It is an especially acute sorrow to think of the possible death of an institution which can now, more than ever, offer both its members and those it serves such a maturing and rich existence. And so it goes.

C. Bioethics

The modern Christian concern with bioethics, or the morality of various biological decisions, represents a fundamental reassessment of humankind's relation to the natural world. Since the mid twentieth century, breakthroughs in medical technology have regularly altered the human experience of life and death in dramatic ways. For example, new procedures to aid in or inhibit conception have given modern individuals an awesome new power over procreation, spawning a number of profound ethical controversies among Christians. Surrogate motherhood and artificial insemination by a donor both call into question the very definition of "parenthood" and "family," completely separating the biological process of procreation from the ideal of marital union traditionally upheld by most Christian churches. More controversial still is the issue of abortion. While many Christians condemn it as the taking of a human life, others argue that any discussion of the ethics of abortion must take into account the historical oppression of women as well as recent medical discoveries about the process by which a fertilized human egg develops into a fetus. Meanwhile, new medicines and technologies that have dramatically improved the sustainability—but not necessarily the quality—of life for the aged and critically ill have spurred many to call for the legalization of euthanasia, an act long prohibited by the majority of churches. Most recently, startling new developments in the field of genetic engineering have begun to allow scientists to create and alter human tissue in the laboratory, sparking heated debate over how such technology should be used—and how it might be misused. Some Christians believe that although the technological advances of the last century place a heavy burden of choice on the individual, it is possible to construct a modern approach to bioethics that is in accord with traditional Christian beliefs. For others, however, the temptation to "play God" must be resisted at all costs. Meanwhile, the ever-increasing pace of technological change has left theologians and moralists scrambling to develop new doctrinal traditions that might adequately address the complex social and ethical questions being raised.

1. Beverly Wildung Harrison
"THEOLOGY OF PRO-CHOICE: A FEMINIST PERSPECTIVE" (1982)

The intentional termination of a fetus after the "quickening" (first detectable motion) of the fifth month of pregnancy has been consistently condemned by Christian moralists from the Council of Elvira (306) until the present century. The recent improvement of medical technology and the revision of several legal standards on abortion, however, have prompted many contemporary theologians and Christian thinkers to reconsider traditional teachings on the subject. Within the United States, the Supreme Court's landmark 1973 *Roe* v. *Wade* decision, which legalized abortion for any reason within the first trimester, has had a particularly divisive effect on Christians. Many, especially the majority of Roman Catholics and evangelicals, continue to condemn the practice as immoral under any circumstances. Others, such as Protestant theologian Beverly Wildung Harrison (b. 1932), see the longstanding Christian prohibition against abortion as part of an ancient tradition of misogyny among male church leaders. Like other prominent feminists (see 10B), Harrison views the issue primarily as one of female power and freedom—in this instance a woman's freedom to decide how she will use her body—versus male oppression. Men, she argues, routinely decide matters of creation and destruction, of life and death—why should the same right not be accorded women? Harrison asserts that the patriarchal bias in Christian doctrinal tradition, as well as a certain vagueness on the overall status of the fetus, make it necessary for Christian thinkers to reconsider the theological context and implications of abortion.

Much discussion of abortion betrays the heavy hand of misogyny or the hatred of women. We all have a responsibility to recognize this bias—sometimes subtle—when ancient negative attitudes toward women intrude into the abortion debate. It is morally incumbent on us to convert the Christian position to a teaching more respectful of women's concrete history and experience.

My professional peers who are my opponents on this question feel they own the Christian tradition in this matter and recognize no need to rethink their positions in the light of this claim. As a feminist, I cannot sit in silence when women's right to shape the use of our own procreative power is denied. Women's competence as moral decision-makers is once again challenged by the State, even before the moral basis of women's right to procreative choice has been fully elaborated and recognized. Those who deny women control of procreative power claim that they do so in defense of moral sensibility, in the name of the sanctity of human life. We have a long way to go before the sanctity of human life will include genuine regard and concern for every female already born, and no social policy discussion that obscures this fact deserves to be called moral.

Although some Protestants wrongly claim scriptural warrant for antiabortion teaching, it is, in fact, the assumptions about women and sexuality imbedded in ancient natural-law reasoning that have shaped abortion teaching in Christianity. Unfortunately, all major strands of natural-law reflection have been every bit as awful as Protestant Biblicism on any matter involving human sexuality, including discussion of women's nature and women's divine vocation in relation to procreative power.

As a result, Protestants who oppose procreative choice either tend to follow official Catholic moral theology on these matters or ground their positions in Biblicist anti-intellectualism, claiming that God's word requires no justification other than their claim that it (God's word) says what it says. Against such irrationalism, no rational objections have a chance. But when Protestant fundamentalists give clear reasons why they believe abortion is evil, they, too, invariably revert to traditional natural-law assumptions about women, sex, and procreation. Therefore, it is from the claims of traditional Catholic natural-law thinking on the subject of sexuality, procreation, and women's power of rational choice that misogyny stems and to which direct objection must be registered. . . .

MISOGYNY IN THEOLOGICAL ARGUMENT

In the history of Christian theology, a central metaphor for understanding life, including human life, is as a gift of God. Creation itself has always been seen primarily under this metaphor. It follows that in this creational context procreation itself took on special significance as the central image for divine blessing, the more so within patriarchal societies where it is the male's power that is enhanced by this divine gift. To this day males tend to romanticize procreation as *the* central metaphor for divine blessing.

Throughout history, however, women's power of procreation stands in definite tension with male social control. In fact, what we feminists call patriarchy, i.e., patterned or institutionalized legitimations of male superiority, derives from the need of men, through male-dominated political institutions, such as tribes, states, and religious systems, to control women's power to procreate the species. One with critical consciousness should begin by assuming, then, that many of these efforts at social control of procreation—including some church teaching on contraception and abortion—were part of this institutional system. The perpetuation of patriarchal control itself depended on wresting the power of procreation from women and shaping women's lives accordingly. Natural-law teaching about women's nature is itself part of this system of control.

In the past four centuries the entire Christian story has had to undergo dramatic accommodation to new and emergent world conditions and to the scientific revolution. As the older theological metaphors for creation encountered the rising power of science, a new self-understanding including our human capacity to affect nature had to be incorporated into Christian theology or its central theological story would have become obscurantist. Human agency had to be introjected into a dialectical understanding of creation.

The range of human freedom to shape and enhance creation is now celebrated theologically, but only up to the point of changes in our understanding of what is natural for women. Here a barrier has been drawn that declares, No Radical Freedom! The only difference between mainline Protestant and Roman Catholic theologians on these matters is on the point of contraception, which Protestants more readily accept. However, Protestants like Karl Barth and Helmut Thielicke[20] exhibit a whole shift of mood when they turn to discussing issues regarding women. They exhibit the typical Protestant pattern; they have accepted contraception or family planning as part of the new freedom, granted by God, but both draw back from the idea that abortion could be morally acceptable. In the *Ethics of Sex,* Thielicke offers a romantic, ecstatic celebration of family planning on one page and a total denunciation of abortion as unthinkable on the next. Most Christian *theological* opinion draws the line between contraception and abortion, whereas the *official* Catholic teaching still anathematizes contraception.

The problem, then, is that Christian theology celebrates the power of human freedom to shape and determine the quality of human life except when the issue of procreative choice arises. Abortion is anathema, and widespread sterilization abuse is hardly mentioned! The power of *man* to shape creation radically is never rejected. When one stops to consider the awesome power over nature that males take for granted and celebrate, including the power to alter the conditions of human life in myriad ways, the suspicion dawns that the near hysteria that prevails about the immorality of women's right to choose abortion derives its forces from misogyny rather than from any passion for the sacredness of human life. The refusal of male theologians to incorporate the full

range of human power to shape creation into their theological world view when this power relates to the quality of women's lives and women's freedom and women's role as full moral agents, is an index of the continuing misogyny in Christian tradition.

By contrast, a feminist theological approach recognizes that *nothing* is more urgent, in light of the changing circumstances of human beings on planet Earth, than to recognize that the entire natural-historical context of human procreative power has shifted. We desperately need a desacralization of our *biological* power to reproduce, and at the same time a real concern for human dignity and the social conditions for personhood and the values of human relationship. And note that desacralization does not mean complete devaluation of the worth of procreation. It means we must shift away from the notion that the central metaphors for divine blessing are expressed at the biological level to the recognition that our social relations bear the image of what is most holy. The best statement I know on this point comes from Marie Augusta Neal, a Roman Catholic feminist who is also a distinguished sociologist of religion:

As long as the central human need called for was continued motivation to propagate the race, it was essential that religious symbols idealize that process above all others. Given the vicissitudes of life in a hostile environment, women had to be encouraged to bear children and men to support them; childbearing was central to the struggle for existence. Today, however, the size of the base population, together with knowledge already accumulated about artificial insemination, sperm banking, cloning, make more certain a peopled world.

The more serious human problems now are who will live, who will die and who will decide.

MISOGYNIST MORAL FACTORS IN THE DEBATE

The greatest *strategic* problem of pro-choice advocates is the wide-spread assumption that pro-lifers have a monopoly on the moral factors that

---

[20]The Swiss theologian Karl Barth (1886–1968) and the German theologian Helmut Thielicke (1908–1986), best known for their resistance to Nazism and their influential revival of traditional Lutheran teachings.

ought to enter into decisions about abortion. Moral legitimacy seems to adhere to *their* position in part because traditionalists have an array of religiomoral terminology at their command that the sometimes more secular proponents of choice lack. But those who would displace women's power of choice by the power of the State and/or the medical profession do not deserve the aura of moral sanctity. We must do our homework if we are to dispel this myth of moral superiority. A major way in which Christian moral theologians and moral philosophers contribute to this monopoly of moral sanctity is by equating fetal or prenatal life with human personhood in a simplistic way, and by failing to acknowledge changes regarding this issue in the history of Christianity.

We need to remember that even in Roman Catholic teaching the definition of the status of fetal life has shifted over time and that the status of prenatal life involves a moral judgment, not a scientific one. The question is properly posed this way: What status are we morally wise to predicate to prenatal human life, given that the fetus is not yet a fully existent human being? Those constrained under Catholic teaching have been required for the past ninety years to believe a human being exists from conception, when the ovum and sperm merge. This answer from *one* tradition has had far wider impact on our culture than most people recognize. Other Christians come from traditions that do not offer (and could not offer, given their conception of the structure of the church as moral community) a definitive answer to this question. . . .

Two other concerns related to our efforts to make a strong moral case for women's right to procreative choice need to be touched on.

The first has to do with the problems our Christian tradition creates for any attempt to make clear why women's right to control our bodies is an urgent and substantive moral claim. One of Christianity's greatest weaknesses is its spiritualizing neglect of respect for the physical body and physical well-being. Tragically, women, more than men, are expected in Christian teaching never to take their own well-being as a moral consideration. I want to stress, then, that we have no moral tradition in Christianity which starts with body-space, or body-right, as a basic condition of moral relations. Hence, many Christian ethicists simply do not get the point when we speak of women's right to bodily integrity. They seem to think such talk is a disguise for women to plead self-indulgence.

We must articulate our view that body-right is a basic moral claim and also remind our hearers that there is no analogy among other human activities to women's procreative power. Pregnancy is a unique human experience. In any social relation, body-space must be respected or nothing deeply human or moral can be created. The social institutions most similar to compulsory pregnancy in their moral violations of body-space are chattel slavery or peonage. These institutions distort the moral relations of the community and deform this community over time. (Witness racism in the United States.) Coercion of women, through enforced sterilization or enforced pregnancy legitimates unjust power in the intimate human relationships, and cuts to the heart of our capacity for moral social relations. As we should recognize, given our violence-prone society, people learn violence at home and at an early age when women's lives are violated! . . .

A final point that needs to be mentioned is the need, as we work politically for a pro-choice social policy, to avoid the use of morally objectionable arguments to mobilize support for our side of the issue. One can get a lot of political mileage in U.S. society by using covert racist and classist appeals ("abortion lowers the cost of welfare rolls or reduces illegitimacy," or "paying for abortions saves the taxpayers money in the long run"). Sometimes it is argued that good politics is more important than good morality and that one should use whatever arguments work to gain political support. I do not believe these crassly utilitarian arguments turn out, in the long run, to be good politics— for they are costly to our sense of polis and of community. But even if they were effective in the short run, I am doubly sure that on the issue of the right to choose abortion, good morality doth a good political struggle make. I believe, deeply, that moral right is on the side of the struggle for the freedom and self-respect of women, especially poor and nonwhite women, and on the side of developing social policy which assures that every child born can be certain to be a wanted child. Issues of justice are those that deserve the deepest moral caretaking as we develop a political strategy.

2. Edmund D. Pellegrino
"EUTHANASIA AND ASSISTED SUICIDE" (1996)

The intentional termination of life on humanitarian grounds, known since the late nineteenth century as euthanasia (Greek, "good death"), is another ethical issue that has taken on increased significance with the improvement of medical technology during the twentieth century. Like abortion, the practice has deeply divided Christians of all denominations. In the following excerpt, the Catholic physician Edmund Pellegrino (b. 1920) makes the case against so-called mercy killings, regardless of the wishes of the sufferer or the gentleness of the methods employed. Pellegrino follows the approved Catholic teaching that, while a suffering person's life need not be extended against his or her wishes, both assisted suicide and euthanasia usurp God's prerogative over life and death and are thus morally wrong. Like many Christian opponents to abortion, Pellegrino believes that human freedom is never absolute nor can any human presume to define what is or isn't a "meaningful" life. Human dignity, he argues, is in fact diminished, not enhanced, by the euthanasiast's rejection of God's plan, which often includes suffering whose purpose is not immediately clear. Heartfelt compassion must always be balanced with obedience to God's laws, for only then can genuine Christian faith, hope, and especially charity blossom.

Everyone wishes for a good death—a peaceful and expeditious closing to life. Indeed, this is what the word "euthanasia" means in its etymology. What is at issue today is not the desire for a good death but what form that ideal should take. For an increasing number of people, a good death must include the possibility—even, perhaps, the obligation—of euthanasia and assisted suicide.[21] For most Christians, and most followers of the monotheistic religions, deliberate and intentional hastening of death for any reason is a distortion of the ideal of good death. It is an insult to the sovereignty of God and failure of human stewardship over God's gift of life.

Nothing illustrates more vividly how different are the world-views of Christians and secularists than their diametrically opposed views on how to approach human suffering. For the secularist, extinction of the suffering person is a rational act of compassion. For the Christian believer, suffering is to be relieved to the extent possible within the constraints imposed by biblical teachings and Christian ethics. Between these two construals of a good death, there is a growing and increasingly divisive gap.

---

[21][Author's note:] Throughout this essay, I will use the term "euthanasia" in its loose contemporary sense in the active, direct, deliberate, and intentional killing of a human being for generally commendable ends such as the relief of pain and suffering. Assisted suicide will mean providing the means whereby a suffering person may kill himself or herself.

While secular and Christian advocates are on opposite sides of this gap, both are typically sincere and conscientious in their desire to be compassionate, beneficent, and respectful of the dignity of suffering persons. Christians must appreciate this sincerity for it imposes upon them the obligation of a response that goes beyond condemnation. . . .

To fulfill these obligations, Christians must be able to respond to the genuine concerns for suffering and dying well that motivate those who sincerely believe that euthanasia and assisted suicide are morally sound solutions. At a minimum, Christians are obliged to respond in four ways: (1) to the persons who hold such views, (2) to the reasons they advance for holding them, (3) to the persons actually confronting the facts of suffering and death, and (4) to the debate about public policy and legalization of euthanasia and assisted suicide.

I shall examine these four responses in turn, but before doing so, at the outset, it is important to make clear the perspective from which I shall conduct my inquiry: First of all, I do not presume to provide "the" Christian response, even though I believe the one I will espouse to be authentically Christian. I appreciate that other, equally committed Christians may place their emphases elsewhere. However, I do not believe, as some Christians do, that one can ever reconcile authentic Christian belief with an acceptance of euthanasia and assisted suicide, compassionate though we may wish to be to those who are suffering. I wish to appeal to all who have a Christian faith commitment, but also to those outside that tradition. I speak as someone engaged in the heart-rending and mind-challenging realities of death, dying, and suffering as a Christian physician for the last fifty years. . . .

FREEDOM AND AUTONOMY AS JUSTIFICATION

In the last twenty-five years, in ethics generally, and medical ethics in particular, autonomy, freedom, and the supremacy of private judgement have become moral absolutes. On this view, human freedom extends to absolute mastery over one's own life, a mastery which extends to being killed or assisted in suicide so long as these are voluntary acts. This is a right, it is argued, that should be protected by law and physicians should be authorized to satisfy such requests.

For the Christian, this is a distorted sense of freedom that denies life as a gift of God over which we have been given stewardship as with other good things. This kind of freedom violates the truth of God's creative act and providential purposes for each individual's life. It also assumes that the only purpose of human life is freedom from all discomfort and pursuit of each individual's notion of "quality" of life. It denies any idea of solidarity or community in which each person's life has its special meaning regardless of how demeaned it may seem to the beholder. It accords rights only to those who are fully autonomous, putting the demented, the retarded, or the permanently comatose at serious risk.

Most of all, the secularized notion of freedom fosters a radical moral solipsism, a supreme act of pride, that denies that our lives, however difficult, may be instruments in God's hands to shape the lives of those among whom we reside. Much of our freedom resides in the extent to which we give of ourselves freely to others. The way we live and die may be the gift we are asked to give to others in ways we cannot understand. Christian freedom is not absolute. We are free to accept or reject God's purposes but not to define them in our own terms.

The supreme act of freedom is the act of sacrifice of self for another, or to yield up our freedom to God's purposes. Jesus' words, "Father, into thy hands I commend my spirit" [Lk 24: 48–49], is Jesus' act of abandonment to the will of the Father, a paradigm of the yielding of freedom to fulfill a will larger than one's own. This is freedom firmly attached to the source of freedom and the ultimate act of freedom of which humans are capable.

THE JUSTIFICATION
OF COMPASSION

. . . Christians and secular humanists share a concern for the sufferings of people. Both start with what is a universal human experience—feeling and suffering something of the suffering of another person and being impelled, in consequence, to help to relieve it. Christian and secular humanists differ, however, in the moral status they assign to compassion. For the humanists, the emotion of compassion becomes a principle of justification. Simply feeling compassion warrants taking whatever measures will end suffering or satisfy the desires of the sufferer. Not to act from compassion alone is thought to be cruel and even sadistic.

For Christians, compassion has a different meaning. It is a laudable emotion and motivation, but, by itself, it is not a moral principle, a justification for whatever action appeals to a moral agent as compassionate. Compassion should accompany moral acts but it does not justify them. Compassion cannot justify intrinsically immoral acts like usurping God's sovereignty over human life. Like other emotions, compassion must always be expressed within ethical constraint.

Compassion is a virtue only if its end is a good end. We must never forget what atrocities were committed in the name of "compassion" in Holocaust and pre-Holocaust Germany when the medical profession practiced euthanasia of those whose lives were not "worth living," who were "useless eaters." It is compassion to which the Dutch medical profession and public turn to sanction euthanasia as social policy. I cite these examples not to suggest that the advocates of euthanasia and assisted suicide are driven by malicious intent, but to point to the consequences of compassion wrested from its moral and spiritual roots. Christian compassion is grounded in God's love for humans, in Christ's passion and compassion for us. Christian compassion finds its legitimate expression only in terms of that supreme example of love. Without that example to guide it, compassion may end in terror.

THE MEANING OF SUFFERING

. . . Suffering is a difficult conundrum even for believers. Indeed, the problem of evil is perhaps more responsible than any other consideration for defections from faith and prevented conversions. There is no sign or assurance that all suffering is redemptive. Even those who feel steadfast in their faith may utter understandable but peculiar judgements when suffering strikes the "innocent"—such things as, "The God to whom I pray would not let this happen." This is to say that God must fit our definition of goodness or we will disavow him. It is also to fashion God in a way to make him acceptable to us, rather than admitting that we can never know *His* ways, which are not *our* ways. God does not act within the confines of our reason, but mysteriously. It is the nature of mystery to surpass our reason.

None of this is to imply that Christians are compelled to suffer, to seek it out, or to prolong it. We have Christ's many examples of healing to show us that suffering can and should be relieved. We must take advantage of the knowledge of optimum pain management. We must also address the more complex task of suffering and its relief. This is a topic to which I shall return in Section III of this essay. Like their secular counterparts, Christians are called upon to relieve pain and suffering. But, because suffering has meaning, even though a mysterious one, Christians can offer something more than extinction to the suffering person.

LOSS OF HUMAN DIGNITY

Prominent among the justifications for tolerating or legalizing euthanasia and assisted suicide is the desire to provide a "death with dignity." Who would not want a dignified death for oneself and one's friends and family? The difficulty arises when we fill in the content of the notion of dignity. It is here that the Christian and secular outlooks diverge.

For the advocates of euthanasia and assisted suicide, dignity consists in retaining absolute control over one's own dying process. It means choosing death rather than a life marked by dependence on others, pain, wasting, or loss of physical powers. By choosing when, where, and how to die, a person can forestall the ravages of disease which reduce a person to a semblance of his or her former self. Thus, it is alleged that one acts independently, and even nobly, by refusing to burden others financially, emotionally, or physically by one's continued living.

There is no doubt that the realities of serious illness are humiliating and that, in the eyes of observers and in the suffering person's own eyes, he or she seems to have lost dignity. But this is *imputed,* not *true,* dignity. This kind of loss of dignity exists in the eyes of the beholders of pain, depression, wasting, anxiety, and physical dissolution perceived in a person's appearance and psychic responses. But, on the Christian view of dignity, imputed dignity is not true dignity. The true dignity of a human being resides neither in one's own estimation of oneself nor in the way in which others perceive one.

For Christians, human dignity resides in the fact that a person is a creature of God who has value simply because one is a person, and not because others attribute dignity to him or her. Human dignity, therefore, can never be lost, even when one is diminished in one's own eyes or the eyes of others, even when one is shunned because of one's appearance, incontinence, or pain. A human person is a creature for whom God chose to die. How can such a creature lose his or her God-given dignity? Human dignity, therefore is not lost by the retarded, the demented, those in permanent vegetative states. The very term "vegetative," though it has physiological accuracy of a kind, is, itself, part of the demeaning process. To deny dignity to those whose sensorial states are impaired is to deny the respect owed them as persons. That road leads to the "merciful" extirpation of all to whom we no longer impute dignity.

On the Christian view, a dignified death is one in which the suffering person takes advantage of all the measures available to relieve pain and ameliorate the things that cause a loss of imputed dignity but also recognizes that his or her innate dignity remains. A dignified and humane death is one in which we participate in the mystery which is at the root of our existence as creatures. In a dignified death, we affirm ourselves as persons by giving ourselves over to God's presence even in our most despairing moments, just as Jesus did in the awful hours of Gethsemane and Golgotha. Paradoxically, the death by crucifixion was, for the Romans who crucified Jesus, the most undignified of deaths. Yet, in the way Jesus confronted crucifixion, it became the most dignified death the world has ever experienced. . . .

RESPONSES TO PERSONS SUFFERING HERE AND NOW

What is the affirmative, practical content of Christian teaching with respect to dying in a world in which medical technology has vastly complicated the traditional obligations of Christians to suffering and dying persons? What is required of those of us who claim to be moved by solicitude for those who are dying and reject euthanasia and assisted suicide as morally legitimate answers? How do we respond effectively, genuinely, and compassionately to persons suffering here and now? What, in effect, are the elements of a Christian, comprehensive, palliative approach for those who aim to support the sufferer, his or her family and friends, and the other health professionals attending to the sufferer?

The first component is to acknowledge the genuine human dimensions of the problem of dying today. This means recognizing the power of medical technology to prolong life as well as the resulting fears of loss of control, of overuse of treatment, and of inadequate pain control that can drive even conscientious Christians to the desperate request for extinction as the only release from technology's grasp.

There is nothing in the Christian tradition that binds patients or physicians to pursue futile and excessively burdensome treatment, *i.e.,* treatment whose benefits are disproportionate to the burdens it imposes—physical, emotional, or fiscal. Patients may reach a point, therefore, in the natural history of their illnesses at which further treatment serves no beneficial purpose. The Christian view of autonomy permits refusing such disproportionate treatments directly or through a living will, durable power of attorney, or a "do not resuscitate" order.

There is also an obligation to refrain from demanding treatment judged futile by competent medical advice. This is to accept mortality as a fact of the human condition. Preparing for death is most consistent with the Christian tradition. Indeed, we have an obligation to be prepared when the summons comes. Of course, care, pain relief, and addressing suffering are always required. Refusal or discontinuance of treatment with little or no effectiveness or benefit, therefore, does not mean abandonment. On the contrary it enjoins and entails an obligation for more vigorous efforts at palliative care, hospice, or home support. . . .

CHRISTIANS IN THE PUBLIC DEBATE

Perhaps no aspect of the public debate about the social and legal status of euthanasia and assisted suicide is more intense or acrimonious than the extent to which Christian perspectives may be legislated. Advocates of euthanasia and assisted suicide, and some libertarian-minded Christians, object to the introduction of any religious beliefs in public or private debate. They invoke the so-called right of privacy, the right of citizens to do what they wish in their private lives provided no one is injured by their choices.

There are three errors in this argument. For one, there is no constitutional right of privacy. For another, euthanasia and assisted suicide are not private acts. And, finally, euthanasia and assisted suicide are maleficent, rather than beneficent, acts. However, there is a constitutional right of liberty of speech, freedom of religious expression, and the right of access to the mechanisms a democratic society affords all its members to share in fashioning the society in which they live.

Christians, therefore, cannot justly be disenfranchised because their positions on public issues may be inspired by their religious faith. They enjoy as much right as any other group of citizens in a democracy to use the democratic process to shape public opinion and policy. For many of us, a good society would not countenance euthanasia or assisted suicide, for example. These are violations of the sanctity of life imposed on the most vulnerable members of our society, those most in need of the greatest protection from the exigencies of economics or other purely utilitarian purposes.

The argument that restricting access to euthanasia and assisted suicide is an imposition of religious values on those who do not accept them is specious. Most legislation limits our freedom in some way in the interest of the common good. Furthermore, it is just as much an imposition on those who oppose liberalized killing of the terminally ill to impose the values of secularism, which is, in many ways, a substitute religion. . . .

CONCLUSION

. . . The Christian "response" is not just a negative denial of the reality of suffering. Traditional Christian ethics and teachings have something affirmative and invaluable to offer. With the proponents of euthanasia and assisted suicide, we share a common dedication to a good death, to ending life well. We differ in what we believe constitutes a good death. In making clear to the whole of society what Christian teaching offers in an affirmative way, we may be able to slow or reverse our society's current descent into the moral maelstrom that Pope John Paul II has recently called the "culture of death."

D. RELIGIOUS PLURALISM

Just as the twentieth century witnessed a new rapprochement among the various denominations of Christianity, the twenty-first century—with its improved technology and trend toward globalization—appears likely to be a time of ever greater contacts and perhaps better understanding between Christianity and the other religions of the world. Faced with this opportunity, Christians are responding in many different ways. Perhaps the most radical approach comes from a group of Christian theologians who espouse what they call religious pluralism. They emphasize the common and syncretic aspects that Christianity shares with all other religions and reject the long-held Christian position that "there is no salvation outside the church." Similar claims by other world religions are equally chauvinistic, they argue, and are based on centuries of ethnocentric arrogance rather than on possession of the one "Truth." Other Christians are less comfortable with this demotion of Jesus and what they consider to be his unique message and act of reconciliation with God the Father. Some of this latter group support closer ties with other religions in the interest of peace and mutual understanding and would even go so far as to argue that certain non-Christians, by virtue of their holy lives, might be saved by Christ without knowing it. Other, more traditional Christians, however, reject both of these approaches, seeing in them a dereliction of the Christian's duty to spread the Word and baptize in Christ's name. Truth is not a relativist matter of preference, they object, nor is Hinduism, Islam, or any other religion the equivalent of Christianity. The debate between these exclusivists and the religious pluralists is far from over and will likely determine the very future of Western Christianity in the new century.

1. John Hick
PROBLEMS OF RELIGIOUS PLURALISM (1985)

The English philosopher John Hick (b. 1922) is a towering figure among religious pluralists. After experiencing a youthful conversion, which he later described as "fundamentalist," Hick trained as a Presbyterian minister and lectured on the philosophy of religion at various institutions in Great Britain and the United States. While teaching at the English University of Birmingham in the 1960s, he was struck by the city's remarkable ethnic and religious diversity and became increasingly uncomfortable with the exclusivist claims of Christianity. This experience prompted him to develop a new theory of religious pluralism. He decided that there are many different paths to the Ultimate, or God, and that only "tribal loyalties" and pride prevent humans of different backgrounds from seeing this. In the following excerpt from one of his many books on the subject, Hick describes the change in perspective required to embrace religious pluralism. He compares it to the spiritual and ideological shift that occurred when sixteenth- and seventeenth-century Europeans began to discard the notion that the heavenly bodies revolved around the Earth and instead embraced Copernicus' heliocentric model of the solar system. Once Christians abandon their own ethnocentric religious views, he writes, they will come to a new understanding of Jesus' identity, one that is free of "mythic" and dogmatic aspects, and focused only on the connection he provides with the Ultimate. Until then, however, they will continue to have a distorted and confrontational understanding of other religions—not unlike their close-minded ancestors, who clung to their vision of a universe with themselves at its center.

In one sense the absoluteness of, say Christianity, means the salvific sufficiency of its gospel and its way for Christians—that is, for those whose religious life is determined by that gospel and way. In this sense the absoluteness of Christianity is compatible with the absoluteness of Islam, or again of Hinduism, or Buddhism or Judaism, salvifically sufficient as these different messages and ways are for those who have been spiritually formed by them. But, since "absolute" so strongly suggests uniqueness, and the impossibility of being surpassed or even equaled, it seems inappropriate to apply it to this pluralistic conception. And in fact this plural sense is the polar opposite of the religious absolutism that I want to discuss here. Let me approach it, however, through the opposite, namely religious pluralism.

By this I mean the view that the great world faiths embody different perceptions and conceptions of, and correspondingly different responses to, the Real or the Ultimate from within the major variant cultural ways of being human; and that within each of them the transformation of human existence from self-centeredness to Reality-centeredness is manifestly taking place—and taking place, so far as human observation can tell, to much the same extent. Thus the great religious traditions are to be regarded as alternative soteriological[22] "spaces" within which, or "ways" along which, men and women find salvation/liberation/fulfillment.

From this point of view, the proper understanding of one's own religious faith and commitment in comparison with others' can be well expressed by adapting a phrase of Rosemary Ruether's.[23] She speaks of her own commitment as a Roman Catholic, rather than as some other kind of Christian, as a matter of "ecclesial ethnicity" rather than as involving a judgement that her church is superior to others. Extending the idea, we may say that one's being a Muslim, or a Christian, or a Hindu, or whatever is normally a matter of "religious ethnicity." That is to say, Christianity, or Buddhism, or Islam, or whatever, is the religious community into which one was born, into whose norms and insights one has been inducted, and within which (usually at least) one can therefore most satisfactorily live and grow. There are of course spiritual immigrants; but they are very few in comparison with the vast populations through which each religious tradition is transmitted from generation to generation. And having been born into, say, the Christian religious world one does not have to be able to prove (even to one's own satisfaction) that it is superior to the other religious worlds in order for it to be right and proper for one to be wholeheartedly a Christian. Realistically viewed, one's religious commitment is usually a matter of "religious ethnicity" rather than of deliberate comparative judgement and choice.

But nevertheless each of the great traditions has long since developed a self-understanding which at some point jars, or even positively clashes, with this conception of religious pluralism.

---

[22] I.e., concerned with the subject and process of personal salvation.

[23] An influential feminist theologian; see 10B1.

Thus in the Hindu tradition one believes that one has access to the *sanatana Dharma,* the eternal truth, incarnated in human language in the Vedas. There is a general tolerance of other ways, often however combined with the assumption that sooner or later everyone in his or her own time—and if not in the present life then in another—will come to the fullness of the Vedic understanding. . . . In the Hebrew tradition it is held that the Jews are God's "chosen people," partners in a special covenant, so that they may be God's means of revelation to all mankind. Thus, whilst to be a Jew has often involved special burdens and sufferings, sometimes of the most extreme and appalling kind, yet to be a Jew is also, from the Jewish point of view, to stand in a unique relationship to God. . . . In the Buddhist tradition it is held that the true appreciation of our human situation occurs most clearly and effectively in the teachings of Gautama Buddha; and that any doctrine which denies the ceaselessly changing and insubstantial character of human life, or the possibility of attaining to the "further shore" of *nirvana,* is not conducive to liberation from the pervasive unsatisfactoriness of ordinary human existence. . . . In Islam there is the firm belief that Muhammad was "the seal of the prophets" and that through the Qur'an God has revealed to mankind the true religion, taking up into itself and fulfilling all previous revelations. . . . And in the Christian tradition there is a powerful inbuilt basis for the sense of the unique superiority of the Christian faith in the doctrine that Jesus Christ, the founder and focus of the religion, was God himself—or more precisely, the Second Person of the divine Trinity—in human form. . . .

Psychologically, then, the sense of the unique superiority of one's own religious tradition may be simply a natural form of pride in and ingrained preference for one's own familiar group and its ways. And thus far it is to be accepted and taken into account as an inevitable feature of human life; though it must not be allowed to inhibit the spiritual travel which has been called the imaginative "passing-over" into another religious world and then coming back with new insight to one's own.

But natural pride, despite its positive contribution to human life, becomes harmful when it is elevated to the level of absolute truth and built into the belief system of a religious community. This happens when its sense of its own validity and worth is expressed in doctrines implying an exclusive or a decisively superior access to the truth or the power to save. A natural human tribal preference thereby receives the stamp of divine approval or the aura of a privileged relationship to the Divine. The resulting sense of a special status has in turn, in some cases, either spontaneously motivated or been manipulated to motivate policies of persecution, coercion, repression, conquest and exploitation, or a sense that others cannot be left to follow their own faith or insight but must be converted to one's own gospel. It is at this point, at which the sense of the superiority of one's own tradition is enshrined in formal doctrines, as an essential article of faith, that the idea of a religious pluralism is felt as a challenge and may be resisted as a threat. It is also at this point however that the acceptance of religious pluralism can lead to creative doctrinal development.

It is for the adherents of each of the great traditions to look critically at their own dogmas in the light of their new experience within a religiously plural world. . . . The clear trend of mainline Catholic and Protestant attitudes is away from the absolutism of the past. But it is easier for this to happen at the level of practice than at the level of theological theory. For there can be no doubt that traditional Christian belief, as expressed in the scriptures, the ecumenical creeds, and the major dogmatic pronouncements and confessions, has been understood as embodying an absolute claim for the Christian Gospel and the Christian way of salvation. According to this system of belief, the historical Jesus was God the Son, the Second Person of the divine Trinity, living a human life; and by his death on the cross he has atoned for human sin, so that by responding to him in genuine repentance and faith, and gratefully accepting the benefits of his sacrifice, we may be reconciled to God and so become part of Christ's Church and heirs of eternal life.

Probably the majority of Christian theologians today want to remain loyal to the heart, at least, of this traditional teaching, centering upon the unique significance of Christ as God incarnate and as the source of human salvation, whilst however at the same time renouncing the old Christian absolutism. And so it has become common to give the old doctrines a universal rather than a restrictive meaning. It is taught that the salvation won by Christ is available to all mankind; though whenever and wherever it occurs it has been made possible only by his atoning death. His sacrifice on the cross is thus the necessary condition of human salvation; but its benefits may nevertheless be enjoyed by people who know nothing of him, or even who consciously reject the Christian interpretation of his life and death. Again, the divine Logos which became personally incarnate within the Jewish stream of religious life as Jesus of Nazareth has also been at work within other streams of religious life, inspiring spiritual leaders and thus being actively present (though no doubt in varying degrees) in Hinduism, Buddhism, Islam, and so on. Consequently there may well be significant religious lessons which Christians can learn from the people of these other traditions.

But I want to suggest that these moves, whilst admirably ecumenical in intent, only amount to epicycles added to a fundamentally absolutist structure of theory in order to obscure its incompatibility with the observed facts. In analogy with the old Ptolemaic picture of the universe, with our earth at its center, traditional Christian theology sees the religious universe as centered in the person of Christ and his Gospel. In the history of astronomy, when new observations of the movements of the planets seemed to conflict with the Ptolemaic scheme smaller circles were added to the theory, centering on the original circles, to complicate the projected planetary paths and bring them nearer to what was observed; and these epicycles enabled the old picture to be retained for a while longer. Analogously, the Ptolemaic theology, with Christianity at the center, is now being complicated by epicycles of theory to make it more compatible with our observations of the other great world faiths.

Purely theoretically, these moves can succeed. Further epicycles can be added indefinitely, as required, and the abandonment of the old scheme thereby indefinitely postponed. The problem is one not of logical possibility but of psychological plausibility. Natural human candidness sooner or later finds it unprofitable, and even perhaps undignified, to go on investing intellectual energy in defence of a dogma which seems to clash with the facts. And so when a simpler and more realistic model emerges there is liable to be a paradigm-shift such as took place in the Copernican revolution from the earth-centered to the helio-centric conception of the universe. In the theology of religions a comparably simpler and more realistic model is today available in the theocentric or, better, Reality-centered, conception with its pluralistic implications. Here the religious universe centers upon the divine Reality; and Christianity is seen as one of a number of worlds of faith which circle around and reflect that Reality.

A wholehearted shift to religious pluralism would mean abandoning not only the older and cruder Ptolemaic theology but also the more sophisticated versions with their new epicycles. For to hold that divine grace reaches the other worlds of faith via our own (i.e., via the person and cross of Christ) would be like holding that the light of the sun can only fall upon the other planets by being first reflected from the earth. To take a different analogy, it is as though there were a life-saving medicine the true chemical name of which is Christ. This medicine is available in its pure form only under the brand name of Christianity. But there are other products which, unknown to their purveyors, also contain Christ, though diluted with other elements and marketed under other names. In these circumstances a knowledgeable pharmacist would always recommend Christianity if it is available. However, there may be places where it is not available; and there, for the time being at least, another product will serve as an adequate second-best. This, I would suggest, is essentially the theology of religions created by the currently favoured theological epicycles.

But, once these epicycles are seen for what they are, it is I think clear that a Christian acceptance of religious pluralism must involve the kind of rethinking of the doctrine of the Incarnation that has in fact been taking place during the last fifty years or so. . . .

---

2. James A. Borland
"A THEOLOGIAN LOOKS AT THE GOSPEL AND WORLD RELIGIONS" (1989)

James A. Borland (b. 1927), a Baptist professor of theology and the Bible, represents the repudiation of religious pluralism sometimes known as "hard exclusivism." In this excerpt from his 1989 presidential address to the annual meeting of the Evangelical Theological Society, Borland briefly ponders some of the claims of religious pluralists before adamantly rejecting them as counter to the express wishes of Jesus and the apostles as recorded in the Bible. It is wrong and deceitful, he argues, to claim that any other religion can offer the salvation that Christianity alone can promise. No matter how harsh and "politically incorrect" it may seem, the New Testament is quite explicit in proclaiming that the way to salvation is through faith in Christ alone. Moreover, Borland says, the imperative to convert non-Christians by spreading the gospel is as valid today as it was two thousand years ago. God has given no indication of changing his "method" of salvation, Borland concludes, and until he does, all Christians are bound to honor his Word.

Is it possible to be saved apart from believing the gospel of Christ? Can Christ save a good Hindu through his Hinduism? Are there "ascended masters" from all religions in heaven today? Can other religions be termed "saving structures" because they in some way direct people to the "cosmic Christ," as Raymond Panikkar teaches? Is Cantwell Smith wrong to claim that non-Christian religions are "channels through which God Himself comes into touch with these His children" and that "both within and without the Church, so far as we can see, God does somehow enter into men's hearts?"

Norman Anderson states: "I have no doubt whatever that the presentation of the gospel, by voice or writing, is the normal way by which people are reached and won." But is he correct when he continues by saying that "I do not believe that we have any biblical warrant to assert that this is the *only* way"? He further claims: "On the contrary, I believe there is much, in the Bible and experience, to point to the fact that God *can*, and sometimes does, work directly in men's hearts to convict them of sin, and prompt them to throw themselves on his mercy." . . .

At this juncture I must register my dissent from Anderson's viewpoint. I find nothing in the Bible to support his contentions. In fact, God's Word continuously presents many disclaimers. Jesus was fairly emphatic about the absolute impossibility of reaching heaven apart from himself. The English translation of John 14:6 preserves the precise original word order with its usual emphases: *"I am the way, the truth, and the life. No one comes to the Father except through me."*

The apostles of Christ are not evasive in this regard either. The apostle Peter, said to be filled with the Holy Spirit, boldly stated: *"There is no salvation by anyone else, for no one else in all the wide world has been appointed among men as our only medium by which to be saved"* (Acts 4:12).

The apostle Paul declared: *"For no other foundation can anyone lay than that which is laid, which is Jesus Christ"* (1 Cor 3:11). Again he stated: *"For there is one God and one Mediator between God and men, the Man Christ Jesus"* (1 Tim 2:5).

The apostle John plainly said, *"This life is in his Son. He who has the Son has life; he who does not have the Son of God does not have life"* (1 Jn 5:11b–12). John's Gospel contains equally plain and strong statements as seen below.

Christ and the apostles taught that in order for one to appropriate the provision of Christ personal faith or belief was a necessity. Furthermore faith cannot be nebulous but must have an object—a correct object if one aspires to a certain goal. The ultimate provision for salvation has always been the death of Jesus Christ. The means of securing salvation has always been faith. But the actual content of faith— that is, what must be believed—has changed with the progressive nature of God's revelation.

Abel's faith, for example, was exhibited in that he "offered *the God-appointed sacrifice.*" The content of Abraham's justifying faith, as stated in Genesis 15:6, was that God would fulfill his promise of many descendants.

Since Calvary, the unchanging required content of one's faith is the gospel. Nothing else saves, while all else damns. No substitutions, additions or imitations are permitted. Any other gospel is not another that can save. It only brings with it an anathema [i.e., curse] (Gal 1:6–9).

I take issue with Anderson's idea that it is "through the basic fact of God's general revela-

tion, vouchsafed in nature and in all that is true (including, of course, the truth there is in other religions), and the equally fundamental facts of our common humanity, that the Spirit of God, or the 'cosmic Christ,' brings home to men and women something of their need." Anderson's suggestions is that this conviction may be enough enlightenment to result in salvation apart from ever naming the name of Christ.

Is this possible? If it were, then it seems strange for Paul, who understood so much about general revelation in Romans 1–2, to insist several chapters later that men cannot *"call on him in whom they have not believed. . . . And how shall they believe in him of whom they have not heard? And how shall they hear without a preacher? And how shall they preach unless they are sent?"* (10:14–15a). Indeed, Paul declared: *"So then, faith comes by hearing, and hearing by the word of God"* (10:17).

Christianity's founder and writing apostles unanimously state the absolute dictum that faith during this dispensation must be placed in none other than Jesus Christ and his finished work on Calvary.

Several examples of cross-cultural conversion in our dispensation are recorded in the New Testament.. Each demonstrates hearing this special revelation of the gospel and placing faith in Christ, not a nebulous repentance and faith based on general revelation. . . .

Every heathen who has ever gotten saved has had to believe that same gospel. The eunuch was saved that way [Acts 8:5 ff.]. Cornelius was saved that way [Acts 10–11]. The jailer at Philippi was saved that way [Acts 16:23 ff.]. I was saved that way, and so were you if you name the name of Christ. And I do not believe we have any warrant to claim that God is doing things differently today, no matter how frequently it may be surmised.

The New Testament makes it abundantly clear that saving faith must be focused on the person and work of Jesus Christ. Ponder some of Jesus' own words in John's Gospel: *"Whoever believes in him should not perish but have eternal life"* (3:15). *"Whoever drinks the water that I shall* give *him will never thirst*" (4:14). "*You are not willing to come to me that you may have life*" (5:40). "*This is the work of God, that you believe in him whom he sent*" (6:29). "*I am the bread of life. He who comes to me shall never hunger, and he who believes in me shall never thirst*" (6:35). "*Everyone who sees the Son and believes in him may have everlasting life*" (6:40). "*He who believes in me has everlasting life*" (6:47). "*Unless you eat the flesh of the Son of Man and drink his blood, you have no life in you*" (6:53). . . .

Were the apostles a bit too idealistic to hold that all are condemned who do not personally name Jesus on their lips and believe his gospel? Not at all. They were simply following orders, Jesus' marching orders for the Church as found in the great commission. It was Jesus who said, "*Make disciples of all the nations*" (Mt 28:19). It was Jesus who said, "*Go into all the world and preach the gospel to every creature. He who believes and is baptized will be saved; but he who does not believe will be condemned*" (Mk 16:15–16). It was Jesus who said, "*It was necessary for the Christ to suffer and rise from the dead the third day, and that repentance and remission of sins should be preached in his name to all nations, beginning at Jerusalem*" (Lk 24:46–47).

If it was necessary to go then, why not now? If preaching the gospel is required to reach those who are near at hand, why should it not be required to reach those in far-flung lands? Let me pose the question in reverse. If God can save people in faraway places without their hearing and believing the gospel, why can he not accomplish the same everywhere? If taking the gospel to every creature was a concern of Christ's two thousand years ago, why should his *modus operandi*[24] be abandoned now, especially without a word from him to that effect?

Are we more enlightened than our Master? Do we know something that Jesus failed to understand? Our methods can be improved, but our message never. Our methods can change, but our mission is unchanging. To hold out the possibility of any other way of salvation does not add to God's greatness but depreciates his Word and the work of the Church through the ages. To teach any other way of salvation for the heathen diminishes missionary zeal and leaves the helpless hopeless.

[24]"Method of operation."

BIBLIOGRAPHY

Primary Sources

Anthologies and Readers

Baird, Robert M., and Stuart E. Rosenbaum, eds., *The Ethics of Abortion: Pro-Life vs. Pro-Choice* (Amherst, N.Y.: Prometheus Books, 1993).

Carson, Clayborne, et al., eds., *The Eyes on the Prize Civil Rights Reader: Documents, Speeches, and Firsthand Accounts from the Black Freedom Struggle, 1954–90* (New York: Penguin, 1991).

Hastings, Adrian, ed., *Modern Catholicism: Vatican II and Afterwards* (London: S.P.C.K., 1991).

Keller, Rosemary Skinner, and Rosemary Radford Ruether, eds., *In Our Own Voices: Four Centuries of American Women's Religious Writings* (San Francisco: HarperSanFrancisco, 1995).

Loades, Ann, ed., *Feminist Theology: A Reader* (London: S.P.C.K., 1990).

MacHaffie, Barbara J., ed., *Readings in Her Story: Women in Christian Tradition* (Minneapolis: Fortress Press, 1992).

Mulla, David G., ed., *Religious Pluralism in the West: An Anthology* (Malden, Mass.: Blackwell, 1998).

Pittman, Don A., et al., eds., *Ministry and Theology in Global Perspective: Contemporary Challenges for the Church* (Grand Rapids, Mich.: Eerdmans, 1996).

Pojman, Louis J., and Francis J. Beckwith, eds., *The Abortion Controversy: A Reader* (Sudbury, Mass.: Jones and Bartlett, 1994).

Reich, Warren Thomas, ed., *Encyclopedia of Bioethics* (New York: Simon & Schuster/Macmillan, 1995).

Tickle, Phyllis, ed., *Confessing Conscience: Church Women on Abortion* (Nashville, Tenn.: Abingdon Press, 1990).

Walton, Heather, and Susan Durber, eds., *Silence in Heaven: A Book of Women's Preaching* (London: SCM Press, 1994).

Weidman, Judith, ed., *Christian Feminism: Visions of a New Humanity* (New York: Harper & Row, 1989).

Selected Authors

Boff, Leonardo, and Clodovis Boff, *Liberation Theology: From Confrontation to Dialogue* (New York: Harper & Row, 1986).

Day, Dorothy, *The Long Loneliness* (New York: Harper & Row, 1952).

————, *Selected Writings*, ed. Robert Ellsberg (Maryknoll, N.Y.: Orbis, 1992).

Gutierrez, Gustavo, *Essential Writings,* ed. James E. Nickloff (Maryknoll, N.Y.: Orbis, 1996).

Hick, John, *A John Hick Reader,* ed. Paul Badham (Harrisburg, Pa.: Trinity Press International, 1990).

————, *Problems of Religious Pluralism* (New York: Macmillan, 1988).

King, Martin Luther, Jr., *The Autobiography of Dr. Martin Luther King,* ed. Clayborne Carson (New York: Warner Books, 1998).

————, *The Wisdom of Martin Luther King, Jr.,* ed. Alex Ayers (New York: Meridian, 1993).

Ruether, Rosemary Radford, *Sexism and God-Talk: Toward a Feminist Theology* (London: SCM Press, 1992).

————, *Introducing Redemption in Christian Feminism* (Sheffield, England: Sheffield Academic Press, 1998).

Williams, Dolores S., *Sisters in the Wilderness: The Challenge of Womanist God Talk* (Maryknoll, N.Y.: Orbis, 1993).

Historical Overviews

Baer, Hans A., and Merrill Singer, *African American Religion in the Twentieth Century; Varieties of Protest and Accommodation* (Knoxville, Tenn.: University of Tennessee Press, 1992).

Barrett, David B., *The World Christian Encyclopedia* (Oxford: Oxford University Press, 1982).

Gilbert, Felix, *The End of the European Era, 1890 to the Present,* 3rd ed. (New York: Norton, 1984).

Hastings, Adrian, *A World History of Christianity* (New York: Eerdmans, 1999).

Machin, G. I. T., *Churches and Social Issues in Twentieth-Century Britain* (Oxford: Oxford University Press, 1998).

Scarfe, Alan, and Patrick Sookhdeo, eds., *Christianity and Marxism* (Exeter, England: Paternoster, 1982).

Social Justice Movements

Berryman, Phillip, *Liberation Theology: The Essential Facts About the Revolutionary Movement in Latin America and Beyond* (Philadelphia, Pa.: Temple University Press, 1987).

Findlay, James F., Jr., *Church People in the Struggle: The National Council of Churches and the Black Freedom Movement, 1950–70* (Oxford: Oxford University Press, 1997).

Lischer, Richard, *The Preacher King: Martin Luther King, Jr. and the Word that Moved America* (Oxford: Oxford University Press, 1997).

Miller, William D., *Dorothy Day: A Biography* (San Francisco: Harper & Row, 1982).

Feminism

Edwards, Ruth, *The Case for Women's Ministry* (London: S.P.C.K., 1991).

Parsons, Susan Frank, *Feminism and Christian Ethics* (Cambridge: Cambridge University Press, 1996).

Townes, Emile M., ed., *A Troubling in My Soul: Womenist Perspectives on Evil and Suffering* (Maryknoll, N.Y.: Orbis, 1993).

Bioethics

Demy, Timothy, and Gary P. Stewart, *Genetic Engineering: A Christian Response* (Grand Rapids, Mich.: Kregel, 1999).

Nelson, J. Robert, *On the New Frontiers of Genetics and Religion* (Grand Rapids, Mich.: Eerdmans, 1994).

Rachels, James, *The End of Life: Euthanasia and Morality* (Oxford: Oxford University Press, 1986).

Rea, Scott B., *Brave New Families: Biblical Ethics and Reproductive Technologies* (Grand Rapids, Mich.: Baker Books, 1996).

Risen, James, and Judy L. Thomas, *The Wrath of Angels: The American Abortion War* (New York: Basic Books, 1998).

Religious Pluralism

Hick, John, and Paul F. Knitter, eds., *The Myth of Christian Uniqueness: Toward a Pluralistic Theology of Religions* (Maryknoll, N.Y.: Orbis, 1987).

Appendix A
Alphabetical List of Key Terms
—⁓—

Abolitionism (7D)

Anabaptists (5C)

Arianism (2B)

Asceticism (2A)

Barbarian Conversion (2E)

Bioethics (10C)

Bishop (1E)

Catholic Renewal (8D)

Charisma (1B)

Contémptus Mundi (4B)

Crusade (3B)

Cult Worship (1A)

Deism (6C)

Ecumenism (9E)

Evangelicalism (5A)

Feminism (10B)

Fundamentalism (9A)

Great Awakening (7B)

Higher Criticism (8C)

Humanism (4E)

Indoctrination (5D)

Investiture Crisis (3A)

Inquisition (4C)

Justification (5B)

Mendicants (3E)

Methodism (6D)

Missionary Societies (8E)

Modernism (9C)

Mysticism (4D)

Nazism (9D)

New World Missions (7A)

Noncomformists (6A)

Original Sin (2C)

Philosophy (1D)

Pilgrimage (4A)

Premillennialism (7C)

Relic Veneration (2D)

Religious Pluralism (10D)

Religious Toleration (5E)

Revivalism (9B)

Romanticism (8A)

Sacrament (3D)

Scholasticism (3C)

Social Justice (10A)

Socialism (8B)

Witch-Hunt (6B)

Appendix B
Ecumenical Councils

—⌇∿⌇—

The Council of Jerusalem (c. 49 C.E.; Acts 15)—not counted among the twenty-one ecumenical councils

"The Four Rivers of Paradise" (Trinity and Christology)

1. **Nicaea (325)**: creed with *homoousios* drafted; Arius condemned
2. Constantinople I (381): Nicaea reaffirmed; Apollinarianism condemned
3. Ephesus (431): Nestorianism and Pelagianism condemned
4. **Chalcedon (451)**: Christ's two natures declared indivisible; Monophysite schism

Four More Eastern Councils (Close of the First Phase)

5. Constantinople II (553): conciliatory gestures towards Monophysites; "three chapters" condemned
6. Constantinople III (680): Monothelitism and Monergism rejected
7. Nicaea II (787): veneration of images declared legitimate
8. Constantinople IV (869–870): Photius condemned and Photian schism ended

The Great Medieval Reforming Councils

9. Lateran I (1123): confirmation of Concordat of Worms
10. Lateran II (1139): antipope Anacletus condemned; clerical discipline
11. Lateran III (1179): two-thirds rule on papal elections; measures against heretical Waldensians and Albigensians
12. **Lateran IV (1215)**: major doctrinal statements of Middle Ages
13. Lyons I (1245): moral reform and deposition of Emperor Frederick II
14. Lyons II (1274): attempted (and failed) reunion with Greek church

Four Later Medieval and Renaissance Councils

15. Vienne (1311–1312): decrees on Templars and Franciscan poverty
16. **Constance (1414–1418)**: Hus condemned and executed; Great Schism of papacy resolved
17. Basel (1431–1449) OR Florence-Ferrara (1438–1445): conciliar reform; another attempted union with Greek church
18. Lateran V (1512–1517): reversal of conciliarism; minor clerical reforms

Post-Reformation Councils

19. **Trent (1545–1563)**: reaffirmation of Catholic dogma; reforms of clergy and laity; strengthening of hierarchical (esp. episcopal) administration
20. **Vatican I (1869–1870)**: papal primacy and infallibility
21. **Vatican II (1962–1965)**: ecumenical decrees; wide-ranging structural and liturgical reforms

Note: Decrees and reforms listed with each council are the most significant but by no means the only results of the gathering. Councils with especially wide-ranging repercussions appear in boldface.

Appendix C

General Schematic History of Christian Churches

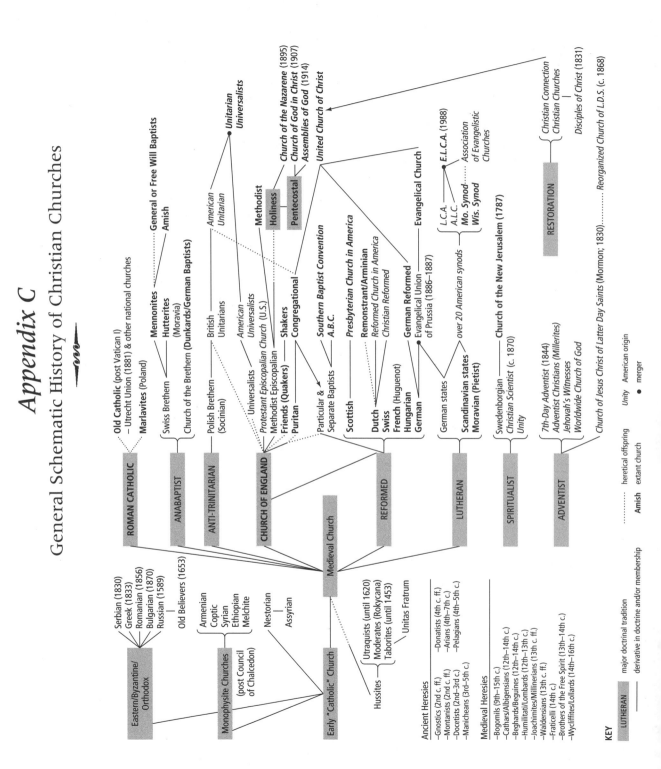

Credits

Chapter 1

Section A P. 7: "Letter of Emperor Tiberius." Reprinted by permission from *Paganism and Christianity, 100–425 C.E.*, edited by Ramsay Macmullen and Eugene Lang, copyright © 1992 Augsburg Fortress. P. 9: Apuleius, "Metamorphoses," anonymous translation (London, 1853), in Ramsay MacMullen and E. N. Lane, ed. *Paganism and Christianity, 100–425 C.E.: A Sourcebook* (Fortress Press, 1992). P. 15: "Yoma," in C. K. Barrett, ed., *The New Testament Background: Selected Documents* (Macmillan, 1957). Reprinted by permission of the Society for Promoting Christian Knowledge. P. 17: Didache, in *The Didache, the Epistle of Barnabas. The Epistle and the Martyrdom of St. Polycarp. The Fragments of Papias. The Epistle of Diogenes,* trans. James A. Kleist, S. J. (Newman Press, 1948), 6:15–25 (excerpted). P. 20: Justin Martyr, *Apologia,* Joseph Cullen Ayer, *A Sourcebook for Ancient Church History* (C. Scribner's Sons, 1913). *Section B* P. 22: Reprinted by permission from Artemidorus, *Oneirocritica,* translator Prof. Robert J. White, copyright © 1990 ORIGINAL BOOKS, Inc. Torrance, CA, USA. P. 24: From *The Book of Enoch* by R. H. Charles (Society for Promoting Christian Knowledge: London, reprinted by Macmillan: NY, 1935). P. 28: Gregory of Nyssa, "Letter of Emperor Tiberius." Reprinted by permission from *Paganism and Christianity, 100–425 C.E.,* edited by Ramsay Macmullen and Eugene Lang, copyright © 1992 Augsburg Fortress. P. 32: Hermas, *The Shepherd,* in B. J. Kidd, ed. & trans., *Documents Illustrative of the History of the Church* (Society for the Propagation of Christian Knowledge, 1923). P. 34: Tertullian, *De Anima* in B. J. Kidd, ed. & trans., Documents Illustrative of the History of the Church (Society for the Propagation of Christian Knowledge, 1923). *Section C* P. 35: Copyright © Oxford University Press 1972. Reprinted from *Acts of the Christian Martyrs.* Introduction, texts, and translations by Herbert Musurillo (1972) by permission of Oxford University Press. P. 40: Reprinted by permission of the publishers and the Loeb Classical Library from *Eusebius: The Ecclesiastical History, Books VI–X, Volume II,* translated by J. E. L. Oulton (Cambridge, Mass.: Harvard University Press, 1932). *Section D* P. 42: Marcus Aurelius, *Meditations,* trans. George Long (Promotheus, 1909). P. 46: From *Philo of Alexandria,* translation and introduction by David Winston. Copyright © 1981 by David Winston. Used by permission of Paulist Press. P. 49: Specified excerpts from *The Nag Hammadi Library in English,* third edition, completely revised ed. by James M. Robinson, General Editor. Copyright © 1978, 1988 by E. J. Brill, Leiden, the Netherlands. Reprinted by permission of HarperCollins Publishers, Inc., pp. 126–128, 130, 132, 134–138. P. 53: Clement of Alexandria, *Stromata* in Joseph Cullen Ayer, *A Sourcebook for Ancient Church History* (C. Scribner's Sons, 1913). P. 55: Tertullian, *De Prescriptione Haer,* in J. A. Stevenson, ed., *A New Eusebius* (Society for the Propagation of Christian Knowledge, 1957). Reprinted by permission of the publisher. *Section E* P. 57: Ignatius of Antioch, *Letter to the Ephesians* in *The Epistles of St. Clement of Rome and St. Ignatius of Antioch,* trans. James A. Kleist , S. J. (Newman Press, 1946), I:60–68. P. 59: Irenaeus, *Adv. Haer,* in Joseph Cullen Ayer, *A Sourcebook for Ancient Church History* (C. Scribner's Sons, 1913).

Chapter 2

Section A P. 70: *St. Athanasius: The Life of Saint Anthony,* trans. Robert T. Meyer (Westminster, MD: Newman Press, 1950). P. 76: St. Ephraem of Edessa, "The Life of St. Mary the Harlot," in *The Desert Fathers,* trans. Helen Waddell (Constable & Co. Ltd., 1936). Reprinted by permission of University of Michigan Press. P. 80: *The Rule of St. Benedict: Translated with an Introduction by Abbot Gasquet* (London: Chatto and Windus, 1909), 9–16, 26–35, 54–60, 84–87, 123–124. *Section B* P. 87: Letter of Arius to Eusebius of Nicodemia, in J. A. Stevenson, ed., *A New Eusebius* (Society for the Propagation of Christian Knowledge, 1957). Reprinted by permission of the publisher. P. 89: Circular Letter of Alexander of Alexandria, in J. A. Stevenson, ed., *A New Eusebius* (Society for the Propagation of Christian Knowledge, 1957). Reprinted by permission of the publisher. P. 90: Athanasius [Ad Africanos] in B. J. Kidd, ed. & trans., *Documents Illustrative of the History of the Church* (Society for the Propagation of Christian Knowledge, 1923). P. 91: Nicene Creed, in *Creeds of the Churches,* ed. John H. Leith (John Knox Press, 1963). English translation prepared by the English Language Liturgical Consultation (ELLC), 1988. *Section C* P. 92: From *Confessions of St. Augustine,* by St. Augustine, translated by Rex Warner, copyright © 1963 by Rex Warner, copyright renewed © 1991 by S. C. Warner. Used by permission of Dutton Signet, a division of Penguin Putnam Inc. P. 99: Pelagius, *Letter to Demetrias,* in B. J. Kidd, ed. & trans., *Documents Illus-*

trative of the History of the Church (Society for the Propagation of Christian Knowledge, 1923). **Section D** P. 102: Jerome, *Against Vigilantius*, in J. A. Stevenson, ed., *Creeds, Councils, and Controversies* (London, 1966). Reprinted by permission of the publisher. P. 105: Reproduced with permission from *Gregory of Tours, The Glory of the Martyrs,* trans. Raymond Van Dam (Liverpool University, 1988), pp. 22–25, 106–109. **Section E** P. 110: Willibald, *Life of Boniface,* in C. H. Talbot, ed., *Anglo-Saxon Missionaries in Germany* (Sheed & Ward, 1954), pp. 45–47, 55–59. P. 113–115: Correspondence of Boniface and Bishop Daniel, in C. H. Talbot, ed., *Anglo-Saxon Missionaries in Germany* (Sheed & Ward, 1954), pp. 75–78, 116–119. P. 116: Rudolf of Fulda, *Life of Leoba,* in C. H. Talbot, ed., *Anglo-Saxon Missionaries in Germany* (Sheed & Ward, 1954), pp. 210–213, 214–218, 222–224.

Chapter 3

Section A P. 132: From *Correspondence of Pope Gregory VII* ed. E. Emerton. Copyright © 1932 Columbia University Press. Reprinted by permission of the publisher. **Section B** P. 138: From *The First Crusade: The Chronicle of Fulcher of Chartres and Other Source Materials*. Edited with an Introduction by Edward Peters. Copyright © 1971 University of Pennsylvania Press. Reprinted by permission of the publisher. All rights reserved. **Section C** P. 145: Peter Abelard, *Historia Calamitanum,* trans. Henry Adams Bellow (St. Paul: T. A. Boyd, 1922, pp. 83–87 as cited in Edward Peters, ed., *Heresy and Authority in Medieval Europe* (Philadelphia: University of Pennsylvania Press, 1980). P. 148: Thomas Aquinas, *Summa Theologica,* trans. Laurence Shapcote, *Great Books of the Western World* (Encyclopedia Britannica, 1952), pp. 3–10 (Abridge). Reprinted by permission of Glencoe, McGraw Hill Publishing. **Section D** P. 155: Peter Lombard, *Four Sentences,* in *Peter Lombard and the Sacramental System,* trans. Elizabeth F. Rogers (New York, 1917), pp. 79–82 in Marshall W. Baldwin, ed., *Christianity Through the Thirteenth Century* (Harper and Row, 1970). P. 157: "Statutes of Robert Grosseteste," from *Christianity Through the Thirteenth Century,* edited by Marshall W. Baldwin. Copyright © 1970 by Marshall W. Baldwin. Reprinted by permission of HarperCollins Publishers, Inc. **Section E** P. 161: Franciscan Press, Quincy University, Quincy, IL, for passages from Thomas of Celano Life of St. Francis, in *Francis of Assisi: Writings and Early Biographies, English Omnibus of the Sources for the Life of St. Francis,* ed. Marion Habig copyright © 1963, 1973 by the Franciscan Herald Press. P. 167: From *Francis and Clare,* translation and introduction by Regis J. Armstrong, O. F. M. CAP and Ignatius C. Brady, O.F. M. Copyright © 1982 by Paulist Press. Used by permission of Paulist Press.

Chapter 4

Section A P. 176: From William Melczer, *The Pilgrim's Guide to Santiago de Compostela* (New York: Italica Press, 1993). Copyright © 1993 by William Melczer. By permission of Italica Press, Inc. P. 181: Desiderius Erasmus, "A Pilgrimage for Religion's Sake," in *Ten Colloquies,* by Craig R. Thompson copyright © 1957. Reprinted by permission of Prentice-Hall, Inc., Upper Saddle River, NJ. **Section B** P. 188: From *The Imitation of Christ,* by Thomas à Kempis, trans. & ed. Leo Sherley-Price (Penguin, 1952), pp. 27–29, 33–35, 36–39, 42–43, 50–51, 57–60. Copyright © 1952 by Leo Sherley-Price. Reproduced by permission of Penguin Books Ltd. P. 194: San Bernadino da Siena, "On the Vanity of the World and Especially of Women," in *Readings in Western Civilization,* Vol. V: *The Renaissance,* eds. Eric Cochrane & Julius Kirschner (University of Chicago, 1986). **Section C** P. 200: Bernard Gui, *Manual of the Inquisitor* in *Readings in Western Civilization,* Vol. IV: *Medieval Europe,* eds. Julius Kirschner and Karl Morrison (University of Chicago, 1986). **Section D** P. 205: Meister Eckhart, "Sermon I," in *Meister Eckhart,* ed., Franz Pfeiffer, trans. C. de B. Evans (London: John M. Watkins, 1924), pp. 3–9. P. 210: *Catherine of Genoa, Purgation and Purgatory,* translation and notes by Serge Hughes. Copyright © 1979 by Paulist Press, Inc., Mahwah, NJ. Used by permission of Paulist Press. **Section E** P. 215: Giannozzo Manetti "On the Dignity of Man," in *Two Views of Man: Pope Innocent II and Giannozzo Manetti, On the Dignity of Man,* trans. & ed. Bernard Murchland (New York: Frederick Ungar Publishing, 1966), pp. 63, 89–98. P. 220: "Pope Nicholas V" in Florentino Vespasiano da Bisticci, *Renaissance Princes, Popes, & Prelates,* trans. William George and Emily Waters (Harper & Row, 1963). Used by permission of Taylor & Francis, ITPS Ltd.

Chapter 5

Section A P. 232: From *The Praise of Folly and Other Writings: A Norton Critical Edition* by Desiderius Erasmus, translated by Robert M. Adams. Copyright © 1989 by W. W. Norton & Company, Inc. Used by permission of W. W. Norton & Company, Inc. P. 236: Reprinted from *The Works of Martin Luther—The Philadelphia Edition.* Copyright © 1932 by Muhlenberg Press. Used by permission of Augsburg Fortress. P. 239: William Tyndale, "The Preface to the Pentateuch," in *Doctrinal Treatises and Introductions to Different Portions of the Holy Scriptures by William Tyndale, Martyr, 1536,* ed. H. Walter (The Parker Society; Cambridge University Press, 1848). **Section B** P. 241: Reprinted from *The Works of Martin Luther—The Philadelphia Edition,* Volume 6, copyright © 1932 by Muhlenberg Press. Used by permission of Augsburg Fortress.

P. 249: Reproduced from *Calvin: Theological Treatises* (Library of Christian Classics) edited by J.K.S. Reid. Used by permission of Westminster John Knox Press. P. 254: From *The Life of Saint Teresa of Avila by Herself,* translated by J. M. Cohn (Penguin Classics, 1957). Copyright © JM Cohen, 1957. **Section C** P. 258: Reprinted by permission of Herald Press, Scottsdale, PA 15683 from *Sources of Swiss Anabaptism,* by Leland Harder. All rights reserved. P. 261: 13 Statements of Munster Anabaptists in *Christianity and Revolution: Radical Christian Testimonies, 1520–1650,* ed. Lowell Zuck (Temple University Press, 1975). Reprinted by permission of the author. P. 262: Reprinted by permission of Herald Press, Scottsdale, PA 15683 from *Martyrs Mirror: The Story of Seventeen Centuries of Christian Martyrdom, From the Time of Christ to A.D. 1660,* by Thieleman J. van Braght. All rights reserved. **Section D** P. 269: Text copyright © 1978 *Lutheran Book of Worship.* Reprinted by permission of Augsburg Fortress. P. 270: Text copyright © 1978 *Lutheran Book of Worship.* Reprinted by permission of Augsburg Fortress. P. 270: From *Calvin: Theological Treatises* (Library of Christian Classics) edited by J. K. S. Reid. Used by permission of Westminster John Knox Press. P. 272: "Dilemma of a Calvinist Minister with a Rural Charge (1602)" in *Calvinism in Europe,* ed. Alastair Duke et al. (Manchester University Press, 1992). P. 273: Reproduced with permission from *The Spiritual Exercises of St. Ignatius of Loyola.* Copyright © 1949 Catholic Book Publishing Co., New York, NY. All rights reserved. **Section E** P. 279: Théodore Beza, letter, in *Calvinism in Europe,* ed. Alastair Duke et al. (Manchester University Press, 1992). Reprinted by permission. P. 281: Letter of Fr. Joachim Opser in *The Western Tradition,* ed. Eugen Weber, 4th ed. (D. C. Heath, 1990), Vol I: 356–357. Copyright © 1990 by D. C. Heath and Company. P. 282: From *Sebastio Castellio, Concerning Heretics,* trans. & ed. Roland Bainton. Copyright © 1935 Columbia University Press. Reprinted by permission of the publisher.

Chapter 6

Section A P. 296: *Lucy Hutchinson, Memoirs of Colonel Hutchinson* (London: Dent & Sons, 1908). P. 301: John Milton, "Sonnet to the Lord General Cromwell" (1652), in *The Sonnets of Milton,* ed. John S. Smart (Glascow: Machlehose, Jackson & Co., 1922). P. 301: John Milton, "On His Blindness" (1655) as quoted in *Sound and Sense: An Introduction to Poetry,* ed. Laurence Perrine, 4th ed. (Harcourt Brace Jovanovich, 1973). P. 302: From *The Journal of George Fox.* Used by permission of the Library Committee of the Religious Society of Friends in Britain. **Section B** P. 308: "The Apprehension and Confession of Three Notorious Witches . . ." (London, 1589). P. 312: Cornelius Loos, "Recantation," in George L. Burr, *The Witchcraft Persecutions* (University of Pennsylvania, 1897). P. 314: Cotton Mather, "A Discourse on Witchcraft," in George L. Burr, *The Witchcraft Persecutions* (University of Pennsylvania, 1897). **Section C** P. 317: Isaac Newton, *The Mathematical Principles of Natural Philosophy,* ed. by Florian Cajori; translated and edited by Motte Andrew. Copyright © 1934 and 1962 Regents of the University of California. Used by permission of the publisher. P. 319: Voltaire, "Miracle" and "Sect" in *Voltaire's Philosophical Dictionary,* trans. & ed. Peter Gay (New York: Basic Books, 1962). Reprinted by permission of Peter Gay, Sterling Professor of History Emeritus, Yale University. **Section D** P. 325: *The Works of Rev. John Wesley, A. M.,* Third American Complete and Standard Edition from the latest London ed. (New York: Carlton & Porter, 1831). P. 330: "Preface," "Come Sinners, to the Gospel Feast," "O God, Our Help in Ages Past," "Alas! Did My Saviours Bleed?" all in *A Collection of Hymns for the Use of the People Called Methodists by the Rev. John Wesley, M. A.* (London, 1876). P. 331: "Preface," "Come Sinners, to the Gospel Feast," "O God, Our Help in Ages Past," "Alas! Did My Saviours Bleed?" all in *A Collection of Hymns for the Use of the People Called Methodists by the Rev. John Wesley, M. A.* (London, 1876). P. 332: "O for a Thousand Tongues to Sing," in *The Hymnal 1982 of the Episcopal Church* (The Church Hymnal Corporation, 1985, #493).

Chapter 7

Section A P. 340: Jean de Brébeuf, "Instructions" (1637), in R. G. Thwaites, ed. *Jesuit Relations in Allied Documents* (Cleveland: Burrows Bros., 1896–1901). P. 344: Jacques de Lamberville, S. J., "Conversions and Holy Death of Catherine Tegahkouika," in Pierre François Xavier Charlevoix, S. J. ed., *History and General Description of New France* (New York: John Gilmary Shea, 1870). P. 348: Junípero Serra, "Final Report on Mission of San Carlos de Montery," Manuscript at Academy of American Franciscan History, in J. T. Ellis, *Documents of American Catholic History* (Chicago: Henry Regnety, 1967). Reprinted by permission of the publisher. **Section B** P. 354: Jonathan Edwards, "Letter to George Whitefield," as quoted in *A Jonathan Edwards Reader,* eds. John E. Smith, Harry S. Stout, and Kenneth Minkema (Yale University Press, 1995). P. 355: George Whitefield, *George Whitefield's Journals* (London: The Banner of Truth Trust, 3 Murrayfield Road, Edinburgh EH12 6EL, 1960). P. 357: Benjamin Franklin, *Autobiography of B. Franklin,* eds. L. W. Labaree et al. (Yale University Press, 1964) pp. 176–180. P. 359: Nathan Cole's diary (Manuscript) in G. C. Walker,

Some Aspects of the Religious Life of New England (New York, 1897). P. 360: W. S. Perry, ed., *Historical Collections Relating to the American Colonial Church* (New York: AMS Press, 1969; reprint of 1873 edition). **Section C** P. 362: Ellen G. White, *The Great Controversy* (Mountain View, CA: Pacific Press Publishing Assoc., 1888, 1907, 1911). **Section D** P. 366: From Samuel Sewall, "The Selling of Joseph in Memorial," in Roger Bruns, ed., *Am I Not a Man and a Brother . . .* (Chelsea House, 1977). Reprinted by permission of Chelsea House Publishers, LLC. P. 368: David Walker, *Four Articles, in Walker's Appeal, in Four Articles; Together with a Preamble, to the Coloured Citizens of the World, But in Particular, and Vary Expressively, to Those in the United States of America. Written in Boston, State of Massachusetts, September 28, 1829.* Third Edition (D. Walker, 1830). P. 371: Frederick Douglass, *Narrative of the Life of Frederick Douglass, An American Slave* (Boston: Anti-Slavery Office, 1845).

Chapter 8

Section A P. 382: Friedrich Schleiermacher, *On Religion: Speeches to Its Cultural Despisers,* ed. & trans. John Oman (London: Routledge & Kegan Paul, Ltd., 1893). PP. 387–388: William Blake, a: "Mock on, Mock on, Voltaire, Rousseau": b: "The Tiger," in *The Poetical Works of William Blake,* John Sampson, ed. (Oxford University Press, 1925). **Section B** P. 389: From *Henri Saint-Simon: Selected Writing on Science, Industry, and Social Organization,* translated and edited by Keith Taylor. (Holmes & Meier, 1975.) Copyright © 1975 by Keith Taylor. Reproduced with permission of the publisher. P. 393: Karl Marx, "The Social Principles of Christianity," in *Karl Marx on Religion,* ed. Samuel K. Padover (McGraw Hill, 1974). Reproduced by permission of The McGraw-Hill Companies. P. 395: Leo XIII, "De Rerum Novarum," in *The Great Encyclical Letters of Pope Leo XIII,* John J. Wynne (New York: Benziger Brothers, 1903). **Section C** P. 400: F. C. Baur, *Paul—His Life and Works,* trans. A. Menzies (London: William & Norgate, 1875). P. 404: From Ernest Renan, *The Life of Jesus* (New York: The Modern Library, 1927). **Section D** P. 409: John Henry Newman, *Apologia Pro Vita Sua,* ed. Martin J. Svaglic (Oxford: Clarendon Press, 1967). Copyright © 1967 by Oxford University Press. Used by permission of Oxford University Press. PP. 412–414: Gerard Manley Hopkins, a: "The Habit of Perfection": b: "God's Grandeur": c: "The Caged Skylark," in *Poems of Gerard Manley Hopkins* ed. Robert Bridges (Oxford University Press, 1918). P. 414: From *Story of a Soul,* translated by John Clarke, O.C.D. Copyright © 1975, 1976 by Washington Province of Discalced Carmelite Friars ICS Publications, 2131 Lincoln Road N.E. Washington, D.C. 20002, U.S.A. **Section E** P. 418: "To Save Their Heathen Souls: Voyage to and Life in Foiochow, China," Based on *Wentworth Diaries*

and Letters, 1854–1858, ed. Polly Park (Pickwick Publications: Allsion Park, PA, 1984). Reprinted by permission of the publisher. P. 424: Rebecca Parker, "The Key of the Home: A Picture of Work among the Women of India" (London Missionary Society, 1895).

Chapter 9

Section A P. 435: *The Scofield Reference Bible,* ed. C. I. Scofield (New York: Oxford University Press, 1909, 1917). P. 438: Excerpts from Leslie Allen, ed., *Bryan and Darrow at Dayton* (New York: Lee & Co., 1925) as quoted in *A Documentary History of Religion in America,* second edition, ed. Edwin S, Gaustad (Grand Rapids, MI: Eerdmans, 1993). P. 443: From *Listen America!* by Jerry Falwell, copyright © 1980 by Jerry Falwell. Used by permission of Doubleday, a division of Random House, Inc. **Section B** P. 447: Elsie W. Mason, *The Man, Charles Harrison Mason* (Church of God in Christ, 1979), pp. 14–20. P. 451: Excerpt from *Elmer Gantry* by Sinclair Lewis, copyright 1927 by Harcourt, Inc. and renewed 1955 by Michael Lewis, reprinted by permission of the publisher. P. 457: Shailer Mathews, "Will Christ Come Again?" (Chicago: American Institute of Sacred Literature, 1917). P. 462: Reuben Torrey, "'Will Christ Come Again?' An Exposure of the Foolishness, Fallacies, and Falsehoods of Shailer Mathews" (Los Angeles: Biola Book Room, 1919). **Section D** PP. 468, 470: 1: "The Platform of the German Christians," 2: "The Barmen Declaration," both in *The German Phoenix,* ed. Franklin Hamlin Littell (Doubleday, 1960). Reprinted by permission of the editor. P. 472: Franz Jaëgerstaëtter, Letter in *In Solitary Witness: The Life and Death of Franz Jaëgerstaëtter,* ed. Gordon Zahn (Holt Rinehart & Winston, 1964). P. 475: Reprinted by permission of Scribner, a Division of Simon & Schuster from *Letters and Papers from Prison,* Revised, Enlarged Edition by Dietrich Bonhoeffer, translated by Reginald Fuller, Frank Clark et al. Copyright © 1953, 1967, 1971 by SCM Press, Ltd. **Section E** P. 479: "Encyclical of the Ecumenical Patriarchate: Unto the Churches of Christ Everywhere" in *Orthodox Visions of Ecumenism,* ed. Gennadios Limouris (World Council of Churches, 1994). Reprinted by permission of the publisher. P. 481: *De Ecclesia: The Constitutions of the Church of Vatican Council II* (New York: Paulist Press, 1965). P. 485: Joseph A. Harriss, "Which Master is the World Council of Churches serving . . . Karl Marx of Jesus Christ?" Reprinted with permission from the August 1982 *Reader's Digest.* Copyright © 1982 by The Reader's Digest Assn., Inc.

Chapter 10

Section A P. 496: Specified excerpts from *The Long Loneliness* by Dorothy Day. Copyright © 1952 by Harper & Row, Publishers, Inc. Copyright renewed © 1980 by Tamar Teresa Hennessy. Reprinted by permis-